Critical theory and legal autopoiesis

Manchester University Press

Critical theory and contemporary society

Series editors:
David M. Berry, Professor of Digital Humanities, University of Sussex

Darrow Schecter, Professor of Critical Theory and Modern European History, University of Sussex

The *Critical Theory and Contemporary Society* series aims to demonstrate the ongoing relevance of multi-disciplinary research in explaining the causes of pressing social problems today and in indicating the possible paths towards a libertarian transformation of twenty-first century society. It builds upon some of the main ideas of first generation critical theorists, including Horkheimer, Adorno, Benjamin, Marcuse and Fromm, but it does not aim to provide systematic guides to the work of those thinkers. Rather, each volume focuses on ways of thinking about the political dimensions of a particular topic, which include political economy, law, popular culture, globalization, feminism, theology and terrorism. Authors are encouraged to build on the legacy of first generation Frankfurt School theorists and their influences (Kant, Hegel, Kierkegaard, Marx, Nietzsche, Weber and Freud) in a manner that is distinct from, though not necessarily hostile to, the broad lines of second-generation critical theory. The series sets ambitious theoretical standards, aiming to engage and challenge an interdisciplinary readership of students and scholars across political theory, philosophy, sociology, history, media studies and literary studies.

Previously published by Bloomsbury

Critical theory in the twenty-first century   Darrow Schecter
Critical theory and the critique of political economy   Werner Bonefeld
Critical theory and contemporary Europe   William Outhwaite
Critical theory of legal revolutions   Hauke Brunkhorst
Critical theory of libertarian socialism   Charles Masquelier
Critical theory and film   Fabio Vighi
Critical theory and the digital   David Berry
Critical theory and disability   Teodor Mladenov
Critical theory and the crisis of contemporary capitalism   Heiko Feldner and Fabio Vighi

Previously published by Manchester University Press

Critical theory and epistemology   Anastasia Marinopoulou
Critical theory and feeling   Simon Mussell

Forthcoming from Manchester University Press

Critical theory and contemporary technology   Ben Roberts
Critical theory and sociological theory   Darrow Schecter
Critical theory and demagogic populism   Paul K. Jones

Critical theory and legal autopoiesis

The case for societal constitutionalism

GUNTHER TEUBNER

Edited by DIANA GÖBEL

Manchester University Press

Copyright © Gunther Teubner 2019

except for

chapter 1 © John Wiley and Sons 2009
chapter 2 © Sage Publications 2001
chapter 4 © German Law Journal GbR 2013
chapter 5 © The Modern Law Review Limited 2006
chapter 6 © Oxford University Press 1998
chapter 7 © Walter de Gruyter GmbH & Co. KG, Berlin/Boston 2011
chapter 10 © Andreas Fischer-Lescano and Gunther Teubner 2004
chapter 11 © Cambridge University Press 2016

The right of Gunther Teubner to be identified as the author of this work has been asserted by him in accordance with the Copyright, Designs and Patents Act 1988.

Published by Manchester University Press
Oxford Road, Manchester M13 9PL
www.manchesteruniversitypress.co.uk

British Library Cataloguing-in-Publication Data
A catalogue record for this book is available from the British Library

ISBN 978 1 5261 0722 0   hardback
ISBN 978 1 5261 0723 7   paperback

First published 2019
Paperback published 2023

The publisher has no responsibility for the persistence or accuracy of URLs for any external or third-party internet websites referred to in this book, and does not guarantee that any content on such websites is, or will remain, accurate or appropriate.

Typeset by
Toppan Best-set Premedia Limited

Contents

Acknowledgements vii
List of abbreviations viii

Introduction: Gunther Teubner's foundational paradox 1
Andreas Philippopoulos-Mihalopoulos

Part I: Law, literature and deconstruction
1. Self-subversive justice: contingency or transcendence formula of law? 13
2. The economics of the gift – the positivity of justice: the mutual paranoia of Jacques Derrida and Niklas Luhmann 40
3. Dealing with paradoxes of law: Derrida, Luhmann, Wiethölter 59
4. The Law before its law: Franz Kafka on the (im)possibility of Law's self-reflection 84

Part II: Juridical epistemology: reconstructing the horizontal effects of human rights, the private–public dichotomy and contracting
5. The anonymous matrix: human rights violations by 'private' transnational actors 105
6. After privatisation? The many autonomies of private law 128
7. In the blind spot: the hybridisation of contracting 154

Part III: The dark side of functional differentiation: the normative response of societal constitutionalism

8 A constitutional moment? The logics of 'hitting the bottom' 175
9 Global Bukowina: legal pluralism in the world society 213
10 Regime-collisions: the vain search for legal unity in the fragmentation of global law 237
   Andreas Fischer-Lescano and Gunther Teubner
11 Horizontal constitutional rights as conflict-of-laws rules: how transnational pharmaceutical groups manipulate scientific publications 278
   Isabell Hensel and Gunther Teubner
12 The project of constitutional sociology: irritating nation-state constitutionalism 302
13 Exogenous self-binding: how social subsystems externalise their foundational paradoxes in the process of constitutionalisation 317

Afterword: the milestones of Teubner's neo-pluralism 339
Alberto Febbrajo

Bibliography 349
Index 387

Acknowledgements

I would like to thank Darrow Schecter for the encouragement and support he gave me throughout the production of this book. In my view, his series on Critical Theory has successfully contributed to the exchange of ideas between British and continental social theorists. I am happy that this collection of my most important articles is being published in this series. My thanks go as well to Diana Göbel and Fiona Little for carefully editing the book. I received perfect professional support from Manchester University Press, especially from David Appleyard. Finally, I would like to thank Iain Fraser, Alison Lewis and Cornelia Moser for their careful translation of some of the articles in this book.

The quotations in the text are taken from English translations where they exist. All other translations are my (or our) own.

Abbreviations

BVerfG	Bundesverfassungsgericht (German Federal Constitutional Court)
BVerfGE	Bundesverfassungsgericht, Entscheidungssammlung (German FederalConstitutional Court, collection of decisions)
DSB	Dispute Settlement Body (World Trade Organization)
DSU	Dispute Settlement Understanding (World Trade Organization)
EAS	East African Standards
EFTA	European Free Trade Association
ENAA	Engineering Advancement Association of Japan
GATT	General Agreement on Tariffs and Trade
ICANN	Internet Corporation for Assigned Names and Numbers
ICC	International Chamber of Commerce
ICJ	International Court of Justice
ICTR	International Clinical Trials Registry
ICTRP	International Clinical Trials Registry Platform
ICTY	International Criminal Tribunal for the Former Yugoslavia
ILC	International Law Commission
IMF	International Monetary Fund
IQWiG	Institut für Qualität und Wirtschaftlichkeit im Gesundheitswesen (Institute for Quality and Efficiency in Healthcare)
OECD	Organization for Economic Cooperation and Development
PICT	Project on International Courts and Tribunals
TRIPS	Agreement on Trade Related Aspects of International Property Rights
UNCITRAL	United Nations Commission on International Trade Law
UNECE	United Nations Economic Commission for Europe
UNIDROIT	International Institute for the Unification of Private Law
WHO	World Health Organization
WIPO	World Intellectual Property Organization
WTO	World Trade Organization

Introduction: Gunther Teubner's foundational paradox

Andreas Philippopoulos-Mihalopoulos

Professor of Law and Theory, University of Westminster, London

At the heart of Gunther Teubner's work, there is a foundational paradox. The work, as attested in this long-awaited collection of Teubner's texts that span several decades, is erudite, expansive, involved with the world and of high theoretical merit. It is populated with references as varied as von Kleist, Derrida, Latour, Kafka and of course Luhmann but also global financial markets, Africa and HIV pharmaceuticals, private law and contract, politics, media, protest movements: a kaleidoscope of issues and references that attempt to capture the world, to describe and indeed to change it for the better. Yet at the same time, the work refuses to be captured by the world. It never allows itself to become a simple blueprint, an incontestable theoretical suggestion with pretences of universality, or even a text devoid of deliberate ambiguity, closed to the contingent and the differently interpreted. The work hardly ever surrenders itself to the world. Rather, it superimposes a layer onto the world, an exegetic membrane that offers both distance and a reassurance that this is how things 'really' are: complex, multiple, closed, engaged in cumbersome internalisations and externalisations, fighting with absences, compulsions and addictions, extreme pressures and deft steerings, riddled with anxiety about identity, limits, otherness. Teubner's world is an apparatus of capture, seductive and indeed optimistic; yet it offers no space of rest, no finite certainty of how things should or even can possibly carry on.

It is often the case that, just when the reader thinks, 'aha, this is what Teubner is getting at', a reversal takes place that unsettles the previous balance, throwing one into yet another perspective, another way of understanding the world – in this way making sure that neither the world nor we as readers would ever freeze in any one permanent position. This does not mean that we are faced with a form of relativist thinking. Quite the opposite: Teubner is a pragmatist through and through, and he understands well the need for realistic descriptions of society. But in the same vein, he understands too the uselessness of any universal position, the overarching necessity of not succumbing to 'pure' critique without the possibility of simultaneous action, and the supreme reign of paradoxes over conflicts (which is supreme also by necessity, hence the normative indictment, in Niklas Luhmann's footsteps, of never, whatever happens, questioning the foundational paradox). The intense flirtation with the paradox, and especially with the observation of de-paradoxification, that permeates Teubner's oeuvre finds full expression in the way the ideas are put forth in the texts included in this collection: in a performatively paradoxical way, the texts often arrive at what could be seen as abrupt conclusions, where matters are left unresolved, in progress, hanging there. All this, despite frequent bullet-pointed directions, suggestions for future solutions, practical recommendations: undoubtedly strong and sound normative directions, which, however, rely on such fine and complex manoeuvring that may never be followed to the letter. Rather than detracting from it, this adds to the conviction that Teubner's work remains that rare combination of scholarship that is both solid and fleeting, both actionable and highly critical, both practical and evanescent.

Beyond and below all this, if one cares to look, one might come upon the crux of Teubner's foundational paradox in all its improbability, if not outright impossibility: on the one hand, the desire to be connected, involved in and engaged with the world; and on the other, an equally strong desire to take leave from the shackles of such connection, and to carry on building upward spires of theoretical inventiveness that continue to spread layers of different perspectives on top of existing ones. The paradox, to put it in a slightly more author-focused way, is the delicate co-existence of the craftsman and the visionary, the scholar dedicated to *techne* and solution-finding on the one hand, and the thinker who wants to immerse himself in the intricacies of a beautiful theory.

Because this paradox is never resolved, the oscillation and perpetual re-entry between the two sides remain the source of creativity and originality. The two sides, let's call them the empirical and the theoretical, constantly cross-fertilise each other by gently steering towards a more plausibly actionable or more theoretically solid direction. In most cases, as if it were an exemplary moment of Spinozan parallelism, the two sides end up in the same locus of hopeful despair: the world is deeply problematic, but fear not! we have a good theory in hand that may and should make a difference. Teubner's writing pulsates with socially responsible and responsive admonitions, constantly in the toil of building bridges between theories, social systems, layers of constitutions and aspects of international law. The fact that, often, these differences are shown by Teubner himself to be unbridgeable does not deter him from the effort. It is in the act of engaging with other perspectives, of revealing their 'reciprocal paranoia', that one of Teubner's greatest ambitions lies: to think, ultimately and unapologetically, as the goal of all efforts and in relation to every topic, of the one thing for which law is deemed not just necessary but unavoidable: to think of justice.

Justice

Justice is not only an overarching theme in Teubner's work, and this collection in particular, but indeed the grand formula at the core of Teubner's scriptural pathos, which, in its turn, is often dissimulated as cool detachment. In a caustic remark that still holds true, Teubner positions himself: 'legal sociology has no idea of justice.' And it is not just legal sociology that is found lacking. The actual idea and practice of justice in law are inadequate: 'Does the law, in the way it tests the equality or inequality of cases, do justice to contemporary polycontextural society? Does it do justice to the natural environment? Does it do justice to individual minds and bodies?' And he carries on: 'the search for a just society cannot follow one ideal path. From the beginning it is split into multiple and different avenues.' This is the only way to address the needs of a polycontextural society, namely the social multiplicity of contexts that takes form in the emergence of highly fragmented intermediary social structures: context and textures, social systems and humans, abstractions and matter, bodies and antibodies, system and environment. A plurality of mutually exclusive perspectives that suggest something more than just 'a perspective': these are neither subjective nor relativist pieces of the social pie. They are not ways of seeing but ways in which reality is textured, formed ontologically in perennial fragmentation and mutual exclusion. These textures are ushered in, angularly and exigently, in the form of justice.

Justice is the re-entry of the environment, of what-is-not, into the system, into what-is. Justice is the re-entry of the non-legal into the legal system, a wind (breeze or gale) that plants in the heart of the system a detonating *memento mori*: a reminder of one's limits and limitations. But it is also a reminder of the system's very own end, its *telos* as ultimate mission.

Teubner is all too aware of the need for limits and limitations (if not of ultimate teleologies, despite frequent nods to theology and what is hidden behind it): 'there are positive aspects to the disciplining constraints. They put the law under enormous pressure to innovate.' Limits are (or ought to be) in place for another important reason: it is only within those limits, of the system, of the context and of its texture, that justice can be materialised. It is only the law that can deliver the justice that is expected of it (and which the law expects of itself). But it is only by law's self-transcending, its becoming-other, like some sort of Deleuzian flurry in a mad effort of self-preservation, that the law delivers justice. By ingesting its environment, what-is-not, the law becomes it. Co-extensive with a vast, polycontextual environment, the law begins its fiery crusade for justice (or its conception of it), and in the process, it forgets its limits: 'The darkest side of juridical justice, however, is its relentless drive towards universalisation.' But this tendency seems to be inevitable and not confined to law only. It is an ontological trait of systems. But it is our responsibility to deal with it. How to do this is a big question for Teubner. As in several cases, so in this one, he takes recourse to a parallel reading of Derrida's deconstruction and Luhmann's social systems. In Teubner's reading, Derrida 'drives the law into an obscure world where Luhmann would anticipate only paralysis and horror'. Teubner, true to his paradox, remains in magisterial buoyancy, floating in between, facing the horror but gently, opening his and our ears to 'the disquieting awareness of transcendence'.

Paradox

Teubner diagnoses a modern fascination with paradoxes. Paradoxes have often replaced conflicts, and not always to good effect: 'conflicts require criteria, venues, procedures in order for a decision to be possible. Paradoxes cannot be overcome that way. There is no *via regis* towards a "solution" for them, at most a *via indirecta*. It is not the decision of the conflict that they call into question, but the very conflict itself.' Paradoxes might be thought of as the diplomatic route that supplants the conflict: the sides of the paradox that bleed into each other without ever bleeding to death. Does this fascination, however, still hold true? Have we not moved well into an era of immediate, gratifying de-paradoxification? Fake news, complex finance, the spectral threat of a nuclear war: what is the relevance of an arcane theory of paradoxes in an era where action (even if misplaced), and resistance to such action, are so prominent?

Teubner's answer is resolutely affirmative. Paradoxes remain the core of legal, political, financial and other system operations. It is just that, now, everyone externalises their paradoxes. What used to be a ping-pong match between law and politics has now spread across social systems. Take, for example, protest movements that react to the way law has changed its externalisation of paradoxes – no longer state law but a transnational form of public order that turns to contract, organisations and standardisation in order to alleviate itself from the paradoxical burden: 'this explains why within protest movements, there is a growing potential for a repoliticisation, a re-regionalisation and a re-individualisation of processes of lawmaking that are no longer concentrated in the political system, but can be found in various different social subsectors'. Once again, this becomes a question of limits, or more precisely lack of limits. The law has become so omnipresent that it has colonised the world in the form of excessive juridification, in its turn a form of universalised irrelevance. Teubner laments the loss of positive law criteria, and the consequent paucity of law's meaningful bearing on the world: 'Modern Law only has its constricted, inadequate (for the purposes of describing the world), context-free, ultimately meaningless legal/illegal binary code – this "cant" of modern legality – at its disposal.' This does not mean that the well-known Luhmannian binary code of the legal system is obsolete. But Teubner throws another layer on top of it, the meta-code constitutional-non-constitutional (which splits into a multitude of system-specific meta-codes) to which all social systems, in a roundabout way and through the legal system, currently conform.

This expansion of constitutional theory is Teubner's most recent development, but once again, it unfolds in surprising ways. While taking inspiration from traditional state constitutional theory, he moves on to what I would describe as an ontology of constitutional structures and a diagnostics of the present on the basis of such constitutions, which are both present in every social system and shared in by all of them in the form of a multitude of constitutional meta-codes. This is Teubner's global constitutionalism, another iteration of the foundational paradox: Teubner seems to have a certain amount of confidence in these global institutions, provided, however, that the sociological preconditions are in place in order for more normative perspectives in law and politics to emerge. The lack of social substratum, in the sense of the demos of the traditional state-focused constitutional theory, is not an issue for Teubner. We have moved irreversibly away from the era of human-centred politics.

Hybrid

So far, only a few instances can be discerned in which Teubner has moved beyond Niklas Luhmann's theoretical credos. This does not mean that he has not developed Luhmann's theory in new directions, or read the theory in ways that departed from what one would consider a strict reading of Luhmann.

With the concept of hybrids, however, Teubner leaves Luhmann well behind, and specifically one of Luhmann's most basic operations, that of structural couplings between social systems. Hybridisation in Teubner's work begins with issues of private-public emergences, moves on to global constitutionalism, and returns to issues of the contract as hybrid. Hybridisation is often the one side of the form, the other being fragmentation. Although hybridisation relies on differentiation (one of Luhmann's main conceptual tools, usually accompanied by the great normative anathema of 'do not de-differentiate!'), it aims at the same time explicitly to bridge the differences of differentiation while resisting full dissolution of the two sides: 'It is only the combination of both sides of the difference that brings out the special nature of the hybrid: neither mediation nor synthesis, but extremely ambivalent (or polyvalent) unity.' A hybrid, therefore, is not simple structural coupling. Rather than relying on the rather more reassuring understanding of structural coupling as coupling of known structures, a hybid relies on the ambivalence that comes from the unknowability of otherness.

Once again, Teubner is bringing in a third position, the floating possibility of having one's cake and eating it. Instead of cake being the centrepiece, however, Teubner suggests that it is the blind spot. Blind spots are the loci of focus when three (social systems, aspects of contract, theories – the method applies diagonally to all of them) come together in a unity of not so much difference as ambivalence. Blind spots become visible in the process, while naturally new blind spots emerge. This process, however, generates an absence within (in this case, the contract as hybrid) which allows a most lyrical Teubner to emerge: 'At the centre of the contractual phenomenon, there is thus a void, the central absence in the modern contract. Altogether, the contract 'as such' remains a mere configuration with no operative substrate of its own, an invisible dance of mutual adaptation, a secret coordination of consent, a grandiose relation consisting in the structural coupling of a multiplicity of meaning-processing systems.' This choreography of multiple structural couplings spirals up in the emergent quality of a hybrid, and with it a new awareness: that in the core of this choreography, there is a void, a central absence, which remains untameable. Teubner dips his toe into chaos, while keeping his other foot on systemic order. But unlike Luhmann, he dithers for longer. And what he brings along is often even more chilling than Luhmann's cool and orderly outlook.

Posthuman

Teubner continues Luhmann's (albeit never explicit) posthuman thinking with conviction. Humans are no longer central to the way society operates and decisions are taken. Social systems are the great progenies of humans, having already taken over the planet while humans still worry about robots. But in some ways, social systems are becoming the new humans, merging their operations with human traits – this is the nature of polytheism, where gods are no longer immune to human affects, and, unable to hide behind the imperturbable unity of difference of monotheism, they end up becoming even more human than humans. In Teubner's polycontextural society, social systems are affected by addictions, delusions of universal grandeur, extreme territoriality, greed. This is not anthropomorphisation: it is finally a realisation that systems are both less and more intelligent that we have thought. Systems fall in a habit of compulsion, just like any body, human or non-human, that thinks of the outer layer of its skin as the end of the universe. Systems are Leibnizian monads, without doors or windows, blind units of isolation fed on illusions about how there is nothing outside. So everything is for the taking.

Teubner's diagnosis of systems' 'underlying self-destructive growth compulsions' initially seems to be a step beyond autopoietic self-preservation: 'The theory of autopoietic systems has already broken with the axiom of classical structuralist-functionalist theory, that is, with the imperative of self-preservation. Connectivity (*Anschlussfähigkeit*) of recursive operations is the new imperative – autopoiesis proceeds or not, as the case may be.' But is this really the case? Rightly, Teubner is not convinced: 'the disquieting question remains of whether autopoiesis is not secretly dependent on the logic of growth.' He goes on to note instances of excessive growth, pathological forms, addiction phenomena in nearly every system: 'politicisation, economisation, juridification, medialisation or medicalisation of the world'. The world is at the mercy of amoeba-like amorphous formations that blindly self-reproduce, indiscriminately extending their boundaries, like gases released in space and taking up all available room.

The solution, once again, might come immanently, from within the very amoebas. Teubner's ambition is to point out the constitutional self-limitation of social systems and its fine relation with external steering (which is itself very limited). We are, once again, on familiar ground: only the addict can save themselves; only from within law can justice emerge; only from within the system can the limits of the system materialise. In a way, this is the ultimate posthuman gesture: in a planet fully colonised by humans to the point of alteration of the planetary geological footprint, and where humans can no longer be thought of as rational, enlightened human beings but as a chain of continuous mediations, there is nothing outside that can save humans from their compulsions. Whatever limitation can be set can only come from within.

Ontology

Teubner, at least in the ambits of this collection, does not worry about whether his work is constructivist, epistemological or ontological. Orthodox Luhmann readers will take the former two for granted, but Teubner (just like Luhmann) allows us to think differently. While he never stops talking about perspectives, theoretical vantage points and blind spots, all of which point to a solid epistemological tradition, he hardly talks about observation in the same way that Luhmann does. It would seem that Luhmann's favourite level of conflict resolution, that of second-order observation, is of a much lesser importance to Teubner. What we have here instead is a thinking process that could be profitably compared to speculative realism: resolutely posthuman, material and emplaced, but also comfortable with abstraction. Teubner's geographical credentials, starting with his use of Global Bukowina and moving on to global constitutionalism, have a distinct localisable quality that was never present in Luhmann's work. His use of polycontexturality opens up planes of textures that are a short step away from explicit materiality. Finally, his understanding of corporeality in the context of HIV medication in Africa follows the steps that Luhmann famously took in the Brazilian favelas.

All the above attest to the fact that the world Teubner has formed is not just a perspective. It is an ontological happenstance – a happenstance because nothing could not have been otherwise. But the point is that this is how it is. It is of course a perspective and often a vision – Teubner's own – but this only superficially hides the fact that the world about which Teubner writes is material through and through, and what we are offered is an ontological shot at this materiality. Perhaps the most clearly ontological gesture is where he situates existence, and how closely connected it is to an ontological becoming towards justice: 'The decisive thing is the "moment": the simultaneity of consciousness and communication, the cry that expresses pain: hence the closeness of justice to spontaneous indignation, unrest and protest, and its remoteness from philosophical, political and legal discourses.'

Like many scholars in the Anglophone academic world, I too discovered Luhmann via Teubner's work. Like many readers, I too had this floating feeling when I first read Teubner's work, acknowledging both the depths of the text and my own shallowness in attempting to understand it. I have always followed Teubner's work, while carving out my own irreverent Luhmann niche all along. Teubner and I have different spires to climb, different vistas to behold. But I am indebted to him for opening the way towards a different reading of Luhmann, irreverent yet loyal, inventive yet always re-entering. But let us make this clear: what you have in your hands is not just another reading of Luhmann. It is a different, bolder world, at the same time more grounded in empirical reality and yet more melancholy, with a greater confidence in institutions yet with an indefatigable insistence on guarantees, whether these are respect for human rights or public registers preventing publication bias. Teubner's work impresses upon us the possibility of a better place, a better world, for which we can work and towards which he generously offers directions and methodological suggestions. Just as this world is not something transcendent, outside the world we inhabit, in the same way the work for it can take place only immanently, from within. Yet whatever direction this world takes, it can be truly better only if justice remains as its corollary. And in this way, Teubner leaves a window ajar.

Part I

Law, literature and deconstruction

1

Self-subversive justice: contingency or transcendence formula of law?

Law and society without justice

'Towards the middle of the sixteenth century, there lived on the banks of the Havel a horse dealer by the name of Michael Kohlhaas, the son of a schoolmaster, one of the most upright and at the same time one of the most terrible men of his day ... the world ... would have every reason to bless his memory, if he had not carried one virtue to excess. But his sense of justice turned him into a brigand and a murderer.' This is how Heinrich von Kleist begins his novella about Michael Kohlhaas, one of the most stirring tales of the quest for justice ever written.[1] 'He rode abroad one day with a string of young horses, all fat and glossy-coated.' At one of the many tollgates in old Germany he was told to stop and requested to pay a toll fee and to present a permit in order to pass, supposedly in accordance with the seigniorial privilege bestowed on the Junker Wenzel von Tronka. The whole story of a permit was a fabrication. Under the pretext that he had to leave a pledge behind as security before he could go and get the permit, Kohlhaas was forced to hand over two of his horses to the Junker. They were subsequently used for heavy labour in the fields and treated so badly that when Kohlhaas returned after some weeks, 'instead of his two sleek, well-fed blacks he saw a pair of scrawny, worn-out nags'. Kohlhaas tried to seek justice in the courts – in vain.

The Junker had so many kinship relations in the bureaucracy that he was always in a privileged position vis-à-vis the horse dealer.

Deeply hurt in his sense of justice, Kohlhaas sold his house, gathered a group of armed men around him and began a private vendetta. He relentlessly pursued the Junker, who had escaped from his castle. When he hid in Wittenberg, Kohlhaas set fire to the town. Led to believe that the Junker had fled to Leipzig, Kohlhaas burnt that city down to the ground. Finally, the authorities were so terrified that they promised Kohlhaas a fair trial and he surrendered. He won his civil law suit against the Junker. However, in a criminal trial, he was sentenced to death for breach of the peace.

But then a mysterious gipsy woman, endowed with powers of witchcraft and fortune telling, takes a hand in events. At an earlier meeting, she had given Kohlhaas an amulet, saying it would one day save his life. In the capsule there was a piece of paper which contained the date on which the Elector of Saxony would fall from power. The Elector was ready to do anything to learn the contents of the amulet – he was even prepared to save Kohlhaas from the scaffold. On the day of the execution, Kohlhaas, before the eyes of the Elector and the people, drew out the capsule, removed the paper, unsealed it, read it through, looked at the Elector – and put the paper in his mouth and swallowed it. Kohlhaas was decapitated. His children were dubbed knights. The Elector lost his crown.

Has legal sociology anything to say about the case of Michael Kohlhaas? Apparently not: legal sociology has no idea of justice. There is plenty of empirical research on local justice, collecting people's opinions on what they think is just and fair in different contexts, and there is much theorising about legal norms and sanctions, about the legal profession and the courts. But there is no socio-legal theory of justice.[2] While critical and cultural studies of law have produced alarming reports of the injustice of the law in relation to gender, race, poverty and culture, they refuse to associate a positive idea of justice with the law itself. Instead, the normativity of justice appears, if at all, as a political, not as a legal project. So is justice itself, the most profound expectation that people have of the law, the blind spot in the distinction between law and society?

Two external observers of law and society, Jacques Derrida and Niklas Luhmann, shed light on this blind spot and ask whether there is something specific that the sociology of law – as compared to moral, political or legal philosophy – can contribute to a viable concept of justice today. Autopoiesis and deconstruction, in my view the most important theoretical irritations of law and society in the last decades, contribute two lines of thought, namely that of reconstructing the genealogy of justice on the one hand and that of observing the decisional paradoxes of modern law on the other.[3] Derrida says of these two styles: 'One takes on the demonstrative and apparently ahistorical allure of logic-formal paradoxes. The other, more historical or more anamnesic, seems to proceed through reading of texts, meticulous interpretations and genealogies.'[4]

Within a genealogical agenda, justice is no longer only a construct of philosophical discourse, but is to be reconstructed from concrete social practices, such as litigation, contracting, standard setting and legislation, and the incessantly changing self-images of the practice of law. This opens up a perspective for detailed socio-historical analyses that search for varieties of justice and their affinities with changing fundamental distinctions in social structures.[5] Historicising justice in this sense does abandon legal-philosophical claims for a temporally and spatially universal justice. But it does not indulge in a relativism where anything goes. Instead, it traces hidden connections between legal epistemes and social distinctions and highlights co-variations of justice and social structure. This may ultimately result in the reformulation of a concept of justice that is viable for present conditions.

Social theory has demonstrated that the structures of segmentary and stratified societies possessed an affinity with the semantics of distributive and commutative justice, orienting them towards the equality of segments and to the ranking of social hierarchies. But what is the relation between social structures and the semantics of justice today?[6] Not only does this question serve to guide theoretical and empirical research, it also produces normative impulses for a different understanding of justice in contemporary legal theory and practice. The re-entry of sociological theory into legal practice could create an imaginary space for the normativity of justice today, a space which is located beyond natural law and positivism.[7] Here, the problematic hiatus between legal norms and legal decisions and the decisional paradoxes of law it produces may lead to a deeper understanding of justice.[8] My main thesis is that justice thus needs to be understood in terms of the subversive practices of the self-transcendence of law which are neglected in official legal theory and doctrine. In the last instance, justice would then be seen as a self-description of law which undermines its own efforts because in its realisation it creates new injustice. In Michael Kohlhaas, Heinrich von Kleist anticipated this experience of self-subversive justice.

Against reciprocity: the asymmetry of juridical justice

A sociological theory of law criticises the most prominent current philosophical theories of justice for being neither sufficiently historical nor sufficiently sociological. John Rawls and Jürgen Habermas conceive of justice without history, justice without society. Although they claim to reformulate the Kantian concept of justice under contemporary historical conditions – Rawls adapts modern economic theory, Habermas introduces intersubjectivity and the evolution of normative structures – their ideas still reflect the old European relation between structure and semantics when they define the basic components of justice as universal reciprocity, consensus and rationality.[9] After Derrida and Luhmann, each of these needs to be replaced by different key concepts: particularistic asymmetry, ecological orientation and the non-rational other of justice.

Rawls and Habermas build on the moral principle of reciprocity between human beings and on its universalisation into general, abstract norms that form the basis of a just society. The 'veil of ignorance' means that norms are projected by individual rational actors in abstraction from their particular circumstances, and this induces them to design fair political institutions. In Habermas's 'ideal speech situation', formal procedures are supposed to guarantee the undistorted reciprocal expression of individual interests as well as their universalisation into morally just norms. However, polycontexturality, one of the most disturbing experiences of our times, thoroughly discredits these recent variations of a Kantian concept of justice.[10] With polycontexturality understood as the emergence of highly fragmented intermediary social structures based on binary distinctions, society can no longer be thought of as directly resulting from individual interactions, and justice can no longer be plausibly based on universalising the principle of reciprocity between individuals.[11]

A variety of social theories have identified the problematic relation between polycontexturality and justice. A fundamental analysis of the fragmentation of society does not originate with contemporary theoreticians of discourse plurality. Rather, it arises with Emile Durkheim's organic solidarity, Max Weber's polytheism of modern formal rationalities, Wittgenstein's plurality of language games and Theodor Adorno's sociological critique of Kantian morality.[12] Max Weber in particular analysed modernity as the 'rationalisation' of different value spheres, which led to insoluble conflicts between depersonalised beliefs and authority claims. In such a situation, justice cannot be achieved via reference to the one, single, unified rationality of reciprocity and universalisation. In Wittgenstein's plurality of 'language games' the idiosyncratic rules of each language game can be justified neither by principles of reason nor by abstract values, but only by the practice of the real 'form of life'. According to Adorno, a Kantian universal justice necessarily runs counter to the structures of modern society; its incommensurability with the vertical and the horizontal differentiation of society turns the moral impulse of justice into its opposite: its practical orientation becomes irresponsible and its good intentions produce negative consequences.

In contemporary debates, social fragmentation finds its expression in Lyotard's distinction between *litige* and the *différend* of hermetically closed discourses, Foucault's ruptures between incompatible *épistémès* and Luhmann's plurality of closed self-referential systems.[13] Other theories are closely related: Michael Walzer's spheres of justice and Nelson Goodman's ways of worldmaking.[14] Especially theories of legal pluralism and pluralist versions of neo-materialism point to the relation between societal fragmentation and the insurmountable differences between various legal orders.[15] In their view, irreconcilable incompatibilities result from colliding social practices, each of them endowed with its own rationality and normativity and with an enormous potential for mutually inflicted damage. The highest degree of abstraction has been reached by Gotthard Günther, who radicalises polycentricity into a more threatening polycontexturality, that is, a plurality of mutually exclusive perspectives which are constituted by binary distinctions. They are not compatible with one another and can be overcome only by rejection values which in their turn lead to nothing but other binary distinctions.[16] All these accounts, despite their differences in other respects, concur in one point – that the collision of today's idiosyncratic worlds of meaning makes it impossible for them to be reconciled by a justice that is applicable across society as a whole.

The consequences for a concept of justice today are drastic. Under contemporary conditions of social fragmentation, an Aristotelian or Kantian concept of a just society has lost its plausibility. So it is only to the social fragments that the attribute of justice can be ascribed today. Even if we applied Rawls or Habermas under contemporary conditions, if we universalised reciprocity between human beings, we would have to start with fragmented reciprocal relations and we would end up with a fragmented, not a comprehensive justice. Suppose, for example, we apply the 'veil of ignorance' or the 'ideal speech situation' to an economic exchange between two rational actors governed by the efficiency principle within an ideal market. We end up with a universalised justice which is, however, only economic in its nature and does injustice to the moral, legal and political aspects of our life, not to mention the ecological issues involved. Rawls purposely confines his concept of justice to politics, developing a model of distributional processes that applies exclusively to institutionalised politics and not to the social fabric as a whole. And when he attempts to move beyond political institutions into broader social structures, his model of society as a 'social union of social unions' turns out to be sociologically untenable.[17]

Even if we were to restrict justice to the fragments, under conditions of polycontexturality, the reciprocity relation between human actors fails as a starting point. The injustices committed by fragmented institutions do not occur only in relation to their internal members. If this were the case, it could be corrected by the principle of generalised reciprocity. Fragmented institutions are unjust towards external constituencies that are exposed to their actions without being members. The justice or injustice of a fragmented institution thus becomes asymmetrical, the relation of a partial rationality to its society-wide public. Justice would therefore have to be reformulated as a super-norm for a highly developed partial rationality in its asymmetric relation to this public, rather than as a relation of reciprocity. In the language of systems theory: if justice relies on the reflexivity of social systems, then the reflexivity of interaction, with reciprocity as its core, is not suited as a model for formal organisations and functional subsystems. They need different forms of reflexivity which are based on their internal logic, but at the same time push them to go beyond this internal logic. A reflexivity that focuses on justice would thus depend crucially on the institutions' ability to recognise and explore the restrictedness of their specialised perspective and to infer self-limitations for their expansionist course of action.[18]

Thus, a sociological account will register a paradigm lost – justice as the ideal of a good society. But this does not mean, as Kelsen suggested, that legal sociology has to abandon the idea of justice *tout court*.[19] It needs to reformulate the old idea under new conditions and to distinguish carefully between different mono-contexts of justice, between moral justice, political justice, economic justice and, especially, juridical justice. It is in vain that one searches for the one pan-contexture where the principles of a just society can be formulated. To be sure, the quest for a just society is as relevant today as it ever was, perhaps more so, but the cause of societal justice has no forum, no procedure, no criteria through which it could be litigated. The search for a just society cannot follow one ideal path. From the beginning it is split into different avenues. Each different concept of justice is realised in one specific social practice, obeys one partial rationality and one partial normativity. These cannot be fused into common principles of justice. In his brilliant book on *Spheres of Justice*, Michael Walzer has demonstrated in relation to property how different social contexts necessarily produce different principles of justice.[20] This needs to be generalised. Political justice deals with the accumulation of power and consensus for producing collective decisions and forms the basic institutions of the political constitution as a precarious relation between power compromises, interest aggregation and policy considerations on the one hand and the claims of external social configurations on the other. Rawls and Habermas do indeed make important contributions to this kind of political justice. But they have little to say in support of a specific juridical justice that deals with the authoritative resolution of individual conflicts, with litigation and the application of rules to concrete cases, with the infinite singularity of persons and situations and with the decentralised normative order that is created by myriads of judicial decisions. No wonder that Rawls's *Justice as Fairness* had great success in political contexts but turned out to be a failure in law in action. If justice in litigation means taking careful account of the singularities of the case, of the specific claims of the parties, of the particularity of the underlying conflict and of the concrete infinity of the individuals involved, then in the final analysis Rawls's veil of ignorance is counterproductive.[21] Legal sociology needs to develop a concept of justice which is specific to the law, that is, a juridical justice. This does not mean, of course, that law monopolises justice; rather, that in contemporary society, different concepts of justice co-exist in different contexts, with no meta-principle that could give them unity.

Equality, the main conceptual basis of justice on which both Habermas and Rawls rely has a fundamentally different meaning in law and in politics. Political equality results from the aggregate equality of the citizens. Juridical equality, in contrast, results from an individualisation process that looks for the (in)equality of new cases and old cases. Juridical equality differs from ethical generalisation and from political aggregation. In a first approximation, it can be described as the recursive application of legal operations to the results of legal operations in numerous litigation processes, which creates the artificial network of juridical concepts, rules and principles and simultaneously shapes concepts of justice. The never-ending practices of equal or unequal treatment are the mechanism which makes legal equality differ from political equality. To treat what is equal equally and what is unequal unequally triggers a self-propelling series of distinctions. It is a generative mechanism, a 'historical machine', as von Foerster would call it, which relentlessly increases complexity in the world of legal constructs.[22] Precedent, *stare decisis* and treating like cases alike are less interesting here. Rather, it is the deviation from the precedent, the 'distinguishing' and 'overruling', the unequal treatment of what is not equal, that provokes the search for more and more elaborate legal constructs and the search for a specific juridical justice.

Of course, one gives only a partial account if one relates juridical justice to litigation, that is to the internal self-reference of the law in applying past decisions and rules to new factual situations. The missing part regards the permanent irritation of the law by external social processes, which permanently redirects the juridical semantics of justice. The typical incongruence between legal rules and doctrines and the particular conflict, which is due to their co-variation with changing social structures, becomes apparent at this point.[23] The closed network of legal operations reacting to external irritations takes place in contexts far away from the irritations of individual cases which are brought before the judge. This second source of external irritations creates an independent dynamic which drives the law into an inevitable incongruence between individual conflicts, legal criteria for their resolution and principles of justice. Various independent machineries of social norm production intrude from the periphery into the domain of law by transforming social norms into legal rules. The most prolific extra-legal rule-making machines are installed in various formal organisations, in informal networks and in standardisation and normalisation processes which today compete with the legislative machinery and the contractual mechanism.[24] The search for juridical justice cannot reject these externally produced rules as alien to the conflict at hand. Instead, in the judicial reconstruction of these rules, it draws from them the very criteria which are supposed to resolve the particular conflict, while simultaneously reviewing them in the name of the *ordre public* of law – thus developing, step by step, both new and shifting substantive aspects of justice.

In this way, principles of juridical justice are permanently changing in their recursive confrontation with these two dynamics: case-by-case litigation and social norm production. This sets the semantics of juridical justice on a different track from that of both political and moral justice. The latter follow their own, idiosyncratic paths of universalisation. The modern experience entails not just their difference, but also their mutual contradiction. Legislation driven by concerns of political justice undermines the juridical justice of litigation and vice versa. Likewise, the principles of moral justice, developed on the basis of mutual respect in daily interaction and systematised by philosophical ethics, stand in a similar relation of mutual contradiction to the claims of juridical justice.

Against consensus theories: ecological justice

Niklas Luhmann offers a sociological concept of justice, under the conditions of polycontexturality, as 'law's contingency formula'.[25] The concept is difficult and it is easily misunderstood. Invoking justice incites disturbing social dynamics, beginning with the emergence of social conflicts, in their translation into the artificial language of law, in the practice of litigation, in the tactical manoeuvring of lawyers, in the controversies concerning the interpretation of rules, in judicial decision-making, in the enforcement of law, in people's compliance and – most importantly – in their non-compliance with legal rules and decisions, in their protest and revolt against unjust law. How does justice work in these practices? Neither as a legal rule, nor as a principle, nor as a value, nor as a criterion for decision-making within the law. Justice does not appear as something external to the law against which legal decisions can be measured, nor as a moral virtue, nor as a political objective, nor as a regulative idea. All these could be weighed against other internal rules, principles, values, criteria, and against other external virtues, objectives and ideals. Within the boundaries of law, justice cannot be weighed against anything. In this respect, juridical justice differs from its counterparts in morality, politics and economics. For them, justice is one normative programme among many – legitimacy, welfare, efficiency – while within the law, justice is invoked as the central incontestable orientation formula. As the programme of programmes of law, justice will not compete with any other legal or extra-legal formula. As the contingency formula of law, justice has a similar status to that of other contingency formulas in other fields: legitimacy in politics, God in religion, scarcity in the economy, *Bildung* in education, limitationality in science.[26] A contingency formula means prohibition of negation, canonisation, incontestability. And its dynamics reveal a paradox. The necessary search for incontestability again and again reproduces new contingencies: necessary contingency, contingent necessity.

As the contingency formula of law, justice is a necessary 'search scheme for reasons or values which can become legally valid only in the form of programmes'.[27] It is not a principle that is internal or external to the law, but a social process, a process of self-observation of the unity of law on the basis of its programmes, a legal self-control which operates via the above-mentioned 'historical machinery' of law in the never-ending practices of equal or unequal treatment. Thus Luhmann arrives at the definition of justice as 'adequate complexity of consistent decision-making'.[28]

In subsequent debates within the sociology of law, this definition has been met with scepticism.[29] If justice is unable to furnish substantive criteria for individual decisions, if it does not identify a legal value or principle, if it produces no external ethical or political maxim, then it is reduced to a purely formal justice which boils down to the simple demand for conceptual consistency. Then it does not differ from the logic of *stare decisis* and the systematicity of legal doctrine. This critique misses the point, however. It ignores the element of 'adequate complexity'. Justice as the contingency formula of law explicitly goes beyond internal consistency. It is located at the boundary between the law and its external environment and means both the historical variability of justice and its dependence on this environment. Invoking justice – and this is the core of the contingency formula – makes explicit the dependence of law on its ecologies, on its social, human and natural environment. Thus, beyond formal consistency, substantive aspects of orientation come into play. In the definition 'adequately complex consistency of legal decisions', the crucial aspect is ecological adequacy in its relation to internal consistency.[30] The intention of justice is not to maximise doctrinal consistency, but to respond sensitively to extremely divergent external demands and to strive at the same time for high consistency. Justice as a contingency formula is not a justice that is immanent to the law, but a justice that transcends the law. Internal consistency plus responsiveness to ecological demands: that is the double requirement of juridical justice.[31]

In contrast to neo-Kantian theories of justice, which refine various formal and procedural requirements of consensus and universalisation further and further, a sociological concept concentrates on the substantive relation of law to its ecology: Does the law, in the way it tests the equality or inequality of cases, do justice to contemporary polycontextural society? Does it do justice to the natural environment? Does it do justice to individual minds and bodies? Such an ecological orientation of the law in the broadest sense is probably the most important contribution systems theory, with its insistence on the system/environment distinction, makes to the debate on justice. Justice redirects the attention of the law to the problematic question of its adequacy in relation to the outside world.

But there is a qualification to be added here. This is because it is at this very point that systems theory, with its (in)famous insistence on the self-referential closure of the law, reveals a strong contradiction within the ecological orientation of justice. The extreme hetero-referentiality of the law, which would be required by justice as proof of the adequacy of the law in relation to society, people and nature, cannot be achieved by the law reaching into the outside world. Rather, hetero-referentiality exists only within the law, which remains caught in the chain of its self-referential operations. This contradiction lies at the core of the practice of justice today: How is justice possible as a transcendence of the boundaries of law, when it is inescapably caught in the self-referential closure of the legal system? Justice as the necessary but impossible self-transcendence of the closure of law – this seems thinkable only as the *coincidentia oppositorum* of law.

How can justice ever transcend the closure of law, if the transfer of validity on the basis of the binary code legal/illegal takes place exclusively in recursive chains of court judgements, legislative and contractual acts? Justice is confronted with the primary closure of law: operational closure by the concatenation of legal acts – legal structures – legal acts. In the tautological self-reference and radical insulation of the law from its social environment,[32] operative closure has become in itself a major source of injustice. With good reason communitarian critics of modern law ask for radical change in order to break open the boundaries of the law, to re-integrate law into society and to establish alternative fora, procedures and criteria of 'communal justice'.[33] Yet as we know, the practices of justice in the modern world have taken a different course. Juridical justice does not break open operational closure and return to the social embeddedness of the primary operations of law.

Instead, paradoxically, it 'transcends' positive law via its second closure, i.e. via legal self-observation.[34] From the moment of the crucial transformation of the law, when legal argumentation in court proceedings, legislation and contracting began to exclude arguments ad hoc and ad hominem and to refer to specialised legal materials (precedents, rules, principles), the discourse on justice has become that part of legal self-observation which focuses on the boundaries of law and attempts to transcend them. Whenever the closure of legal operations has been complemented by the closure of legal self-observation, the practices of justice have concentrated on the adequacy of the law in relation to its environment.

Why should justice as a self-observational practice within the law be able to overcome the primary closure of law? The reason is the 're-entry' of the extra-legal into the legal. While legal operations create the boundary between law and non-law, between legal communication and other types of social communication by virtue of their sequentialisation, legal self-observations use this very distinction of legal/non-legal within the symbolic space of the law.[35] Whenever the distinction between legal and non-legal (in the sense of extra-legal, not illegal!) re-enters the sequence of legal operations, legal argumentation acquires the capacity to create an 'enacted' environment,[36] by distinguishing between norms and facts, between internal legal acts and external social acts, between legal concepts and social interests, between internal reality constructs of the legal process and those of social processes. That is the moment in which the discourse on justice passes judgement on these distinctions and raises the question of whether legal decisions are doing justice to their 'enacted' ecologies. This is the paradoxical achievement of double closure – operational and observational. Both rule-producing legal acts and rule-connecting arguments remain in their closed circuit of internal concatenations. But by virtue of the internal distinction of self-reference and hetero-reference, justice relates law to its (enacted) social environment and asks for its ecological adequacy.

Justice as a discursive practice within the law works on the drastic consequences that the re-entry of its ecologies has created. It makes use of the epistemic confusion (à la Magritte: 'This is not a pipe') about the reality status of the hetero-referential observations of law. One result of this re-entry is the above-mentioned imaginary space within the law, which takes itself for reality.[37] In its judgement on the ecological adequacy of law, justice cannot but create fictions about the outside world which it must treat as solid realities. Justice thus appears only within this imaginary space within the law which is created by the re-entry of the ecology of the law into the law, i.e. by the internal reconstruction within the law of external demands emanating from society, people and nature.

As the contingency formula of law, justice is dependent upon the great historical principles of social differentiation. At this point a theory of justice is directly subsidised by social theory. In their claim to be expressions of justice, the criteria for the consistency of the law are not simply subject to historical change in a random way. They co-vary with the varieties of social differentiation mentioned above. In a stratified society it is accepted as a natural and necessary requirement of justice that the judge takes full account of the social rank of the litigating parties. Justice is not blind. The famous formula of *suum cuique*, which today seems rather hollow to us, makes sense to people living in legitimate hierarchies of social stratification. Each person receives something different, according to his social rank. As Lawrence Rosen has shown in his empirical studies on the anthropology of justice, this is true for traditional Islamic law where justice demands that the social position of the parties and their social networks are meticulously reconstructed within the trial and are explicitly taken into account in the final decision.[38] Max Weber got it wrong when he referred to this pejoratively as 'qadi-justice', which in his view did not live up to the most basic demands of universal justice.[39] It was also true for the society of old Europe, where it was natural and legitimate that the law treated members of the nobility differently from clergymen, town people and peasants. It is only on the threshold of modernity that Michael Kohlhaas protests violently against the way the law privileges aristocratic horse thieves over him, the common horse dealer.[40] While the *justitia mediatrix* of the Middle Ages mediated in a vertical-hierarchical mode between divine, natural and human law,[41] the justice of modernity mediates in a horizontal-heterarchical mode between the proper normativity of the law and the proper normativity of its social, human and natural ecologies. Today, the law searches for its peculiar criteria of justice, i.e. criteria for treating like cases alike and unlike cases differently, in its environment, i.e. in different social discourses, in educational, scientific, medical, political and economic discourse. It validates them after a complicated process in which it legally reconstructs them. In spite of the equality clause in the constitution, constitutional law legitimates unequal treatment when it is legitimised according to pedagogical, scientific, medical and other 'reasonable' criteria.

Is this a new natural law that replaces God, nature and reason by differentiation principles of society, as it were a sociological concept of natural law? In fact, this concept of justice undercuts the distinction between positivism and natural law and declares them both simultaneously right and wrong. With natural law, it shares the impulse to search for justice in an extra-legal orientation. But in common with positivism it finds that the search for justice can only be carried out by the law itself, not by external authorities, be they God, nature or natural reason. Justice turns against natural law when it refutes the idea that outside authorities will furnish substantive criteria of justice. But it also turns against positivism insofar as justice is not something that can be produced by a legal decision.

Neither natural law nor legal positivism, then: instead, justice sabotages legal decisions. Against law's relentless desire for certainty, juridical justice creates a vast space of uncertainty and indeterminacy. Justice reopens the space that has been closed by the routine of legal decisions and asks obstinately whether, in the light of external demands on the law, the case needs to be decided differently. Justice works as a subversive force with which the law protests against itself. Justice protests against the natural tendencies of the law towards *stare decisis*, towards routine, security, stability, authority and tradition. Against the inbuilt tendencies of the law towards orderly self-continuation, it infuses into the legal order a tendency towards disorder, revolt, deviation, variability and change. It protests in the name of society, people and nature but does so from within the law. Subversive justice stirs up the law. Mutiny on the *Bounty* – this is what sociology has to say about juridical justice.

Against rationalism: the irrational in the self-transcendence of law

But why mutiny? Why not just external attacks on the law in the name of society? That people who have put their hopes into the law will blame the law for its injustice once they lose their case is to be expected. But that the resistance should originate in the inner *arcanum* of law – that is the scandal. The cause for the internal revolt, for the subversion from within the law in the very name of justice, lies in the glaring failure of law to live up to its own promise – to supply convincing reasons for its decisions, to produce a legitimate basis of rational argumentation that people accept as just. Legal reasoning does not and cannot justify legal decisions – anyone who has had to decide a legal case has been exposed to this disturbing experience. In other words, law cannot in principle stop the intrusion of irrationality into its rational world of norm-oriented decision-making and reasoned argument. This is why practitioners of law have always been sceptical of rational theories of justice in the style of Rawls and Habermas. The philosophers of justice, of course, are aware of the irrational element in legal decisions, but they are desperately practising a kind of exorcism. By ever more aggrandising the role of rational argument in law in order to give a firm basis to their judgement, they try to get rid of the devil, to exorcise the paradox of self-reference.[42] In vain, of course.

By contrast, the most provocative recent analyses of the fundamental failure of law have been formulated by Jacques Derrida, pointing to the aporias of justice, and by Niklas Luhmann, pointing to the paradox of legal decisions.[43]

To be sure, they are re-analysing a centuries-old experience of the law, which has resorted to the time-honoured double formulas of *ratio et voluntas* and *ratio et auctoritas* in order to cope with the limits of reason in legal decisions. Even analytical jurisprudence, which in contrast to deconstruction or autopoiesis is not under suspicion of irrationalism, has to acknowledge the limits of rational argument in law and admit that the logical application of norms to cases will work only when the judge introduces additional ad hoc assumptions into the syllogism.[44] Proponents of analytical jurisprudence also have to admit that, in the last instance, any attempt to justify rules by rules and principles inevitably ends up in Münchhausen's trilemma: infinite regress, arbitrary rupture or circularity.[45] The failure of reason to ground legal decisions is driving critical legal studies further into their obsession with the indeterminacy of law. It is driving Carl Schmitt into his obsession with decisionism. No wonder that all kinds of interdisciplinary analyses step in with their specific remedies to cure the law of its disease: psychology with the affective element, psychoanalysis with the unconscious, economics with efficiency, sociology with class structure, political science with policy considerations or social antagonisms and so on. But what, today, is law's own reaction to its fundamental failure?

The discourse of justice is the reaction to the failure of law. As I have said, it is a social dynamic within the law and cannot be identified with a philosophical construct or with a criterion for legal decisions. To put everything that follows into one short formula, juridical justice is an idiosyncratic process by which the self-observation of law interrupts, blocks and sabotages the routinised recursivity of legal operations. After rendering law self-transcendent, justice forces the law to return to its immanence and to continue its operations under massive constraints, thus creating new injustice – hence the term 'self-subversive justice'.[46]

In other words, after 'journeying through the desert', i.e. after an 'irrational' experience of self-transcendence, justice is compelled to reconstruct this infinite experience under the restrictive conditions of the legal system – under the triple constraint of decision, rule-making and justification. As a consequence of this pressure to continue its rule production, justice produces new injustice against which it protests, only to find itself in its turn under the renewed constraints of the legal process. And so on and so on – in a permanent self-tormenting oscillation.

As a discursive practice, justice not only subverts positive law in the name of its ecologies, but also subverts itself in a self-propelling cyclical process. Justice becomes self-subversive when, after protesting against positive law, it returns to legal positivisation. Obviously, this circularity disappoints the hopes of legal philosophy. It cannot produce just results, nor can it perfect an imperfect value of justice, nor does it approximate asymptotically to an ideal of justice. What it does is permanently to reconstruct both positions – positive legal decisions and the infinite experience of justice – in order to at once destruct them. This practice creates and annihilates justice in a permanent cyclical movement from the immanence of law to its transcendence back to immanence. At the very end it does nothing but re-incite the inner restlessness of law, the great legal nervousness, the permanent oscillation between two poles, the necessary contingency of law.

This self-observation of law should not be confused with a diffuse yearning for justice that shadows the rational legal process and from time to time incites it to produce a better legal rule. Instead, juridical justice can be analysed theoretically and identified empirically as an ongoing discursive process within legal practice itself. Of course, what is meant by legal practice is not just organised litigation and legislation by the legal profession. Rather, it means the whole range of serious communication about law, wherever it happens in society, including protest by citizens against the law. In a Derridean manner, one could speak of 'justiciance' in order to characterise the iterative movements, the permanent changes, the deferment and displacement of meaning, the incompleteness of justice and its futurisation.

What is more, the search for juridical justice takes place under severe restrictions. The search formula itself contains a strange combination of high indeterminacy and high structuration. This combination has nothing to do with mediation, compromise, the middle ground or 'relative indeterminacy'. Instead, it radicalises both to the extreme. 'Bringing chaos to order' – the double meaning of Theodor Adorno's famous formulation reveals the radical character of juridical justice: to derange the orderly legal process, to create temporary order out of this chaos, to derange it again ...[47]

Juridical justice as a discursive process cannot be separated from the initial conditions or from the subsequent constraints that are both dictated by the historical situation of modern law. This excludes from the outset a societal or historical universalisation of the concept of justice. A detailed analysis of these constraints would be the task of a socio-legal theory of justice. The differences between juridical justice and a diffuse yearning for justice can be described by reference to the following four characteristics.

1 Initial conditions

As against a general desire for justice in the world, juridical justice is invoked in a specific situation. Whenever legal procedure and argumentation stumble across the 'hiatus' of law, the ongoing legal process comes to a sudden halt.

In terms of systems theory, the hiatus opens up a gaping chasm in the recursive sequentiality of operation – structure – operation (legal act – legal rule – legal act). Against fantasies of legal autopoiesis as automatic social machinery,[48] systems theory has stressed again and again that the chain of communicative self-production is interrupted in virtually every transition from structure to operation (expectation to communication). Operations produce structures, but structures cannot in their turn produce subsequent operations. They can only create a condensed space of possibilities, a space in which the new operation 'happens'. The new operation needs to overcome a moment of fundamental indeterminacy.[49] Within the law every legal act (legislative, judicial and contractual decisions) changes the legal situation by producing a legal rule. But these rules cannot produce new legal acts, only more or less condensed references to possible new legal acts.[50]

This is the point where, in order to overcome the hiatus, legal argumentation begins its relentless work – with considerable success, yet in vain. Legal reasoning never decides a conflict, but nevertheless achieves something decisive. Legal argument transforms differences. It transforms the original choice to be made into a new one, it transforms a social conflict into a technical legal question. Legal reasoning does not determine, it does not justify, nor does it hide something else. It merely transforms differences, but it does so drastically. Either way, a decision is necessary, both before and after argumentation, but the concrete alternative that has to be decided will be a different one. It is the job of legal reasoning to lure lawyers into a situation where they have to decide a question which differs from the litigants' original question.[51]

Which new legal act will happen remains mysterious. It is at this point, at the transition from structure to operation, from legal rule to legal act, from argument to decision, that the hiatus gapes, that the interstice between rule and decision cannot be bridged by argumentation. The aporias of legal decision cannot be overcome by rational discourse, neither by legal reasoning nor by moral or political justification. They are in themselves neither just nor unjust. However, if justice is to be done, the hiatus cannot be leapfrogged by Carl Schmitt's pure decisionism, nor can it be plastered over by Jürgen Habermas's continuous rationalisation. The discourse of justice invokes the rejection value of the alternative between decisionism and rationalisation. By a reflexive act of self-observation the rejection value brings the aporia to the attention of legal consciousness. It does not attempt to circumvent or to negate it. It simply articulates it as the limit of rational reasoning, transforming it into a painful, almost unendurable experience.[52] This attempt to overcome the aporias of the legal process by intensifying reflexivity to the point where the law transcends itself is the necessary initial condition for the discourse of juridical justice. No philosophical theory of justice or other external authority can dictate its normative content. It is law itself that puts the law on trial.[53]

2 *The self-transcendence of law*

The most difficult question to be answered is what is meant by the self-transcendence of law in its exposure to the hiatus between structure and operation. A first answer was attempted above by reconstructing Niklas Luhmann's ecological concept of justice which, via the re-entry of the external into the internal, can go beyond the operative closure of law while remaining within it. The criteria for ecological justice are not found outside the law. Rather, the law transcends itself by 'enacting' its ecologies – society, people, nature – and developing adequate legal concepts. This excludes the importation of external material. Instead, law constructs criteria of ecological justice from its own world knowledge. It is this re-entry into the equal/unequal decisions of law which establishes the special traits of juridical justice as opposed to popular images of justice, to collective decisions of political justice and to reciprocal recognition in moral justice. Law's search for justice cannot externalise its criteria, cannot put its hope in either democracy or morality, not to mention rational choice, but is thrown back onto itself. By enacting its ecologies, law alone bears the responsibility for its criteria of justice.

In three bold steps, Jacques Derrida moves far beyond Niklas Luhmann's ecological concept of justice. His ideas have given exceptionally strong impulses to the current debate on justice. In his first step, Derrida experiments with new modes of dealing with the paradox of law. Luhmann, after identifying the decisional paradox of law, demands its de-paradoxification, i.e. he demands that the paradox be hidden whenever it emerges and that a new and more robust distinction be introduced instead. But Derrida directs juridical thought to face up to the disturbing experience of the paradox. He drives the law into an obscure world where Luhmann would anticipate only paralysis and horror. Justice, according to Derrida, is more than a mere consistency formula, more than a contingency formula, it is the transcendence formula of law – 'invocation, abyss, disruption, experience of contradiction, chaos within the law'.[54] This excess has profound consequences for legal decision-making: it changes the situation into a decision *sub specie aeternitatis*, not just *sub specie societatis*.

Derrida's second step radicalises the meaning of the self-transcendence of law. Luhmann claims that justice transcends the law in the direction of its enacted ecologies and stops there. He thus gives in to the deficiencies of the re-entry. If re-entry means nothing more than an internal reconstruction of the external, if it cannot mirror, but only 'enact' the outer world, then what it means is a simultaneous inclusion and exclusion of the outer world. But that which is excluded from the law relentlessly demands to be let in, as a matter of justice. This perturbation, and the confusion and the shock it creates, remain strangely neglected in Luhmann's analyses. It is the distinction directrice between system and environment that produces its own blind spot, which does not permit an analysis of the in-between of perturbation. Luhmann can only see what happens within the boundaries of the law and he focuses only on those distinctions that are drawn after the perturbation. Derrida, however, transgresses this boundary as well and expects of justice a transcendence beyond any meaning – a journey through the desert which in his words opens the 'necessarily indeterminate, abstract, desert-like experience that is confided, exposed, given up to its waiting for the other and for the event'.[55] This is a deeply alienating style of thought for contemporary scholarship: a reference to the transcendence of any signification, to mystical violence in Walter Benjamin's sense and to alterity in Emmanuel Levinas's sense. Derrida challenges the cold spheres of modern rationality by invoking their transcendent counterparts: 'pure' justice, generosity, friendship and forgiving.

In a third step, he constructs an idiosyncratic juridical transcendence, which he separates strictly from religious transcendence. While Luhmann concentrates the experience of transcendence in one world of meaning, namely religion, thus implicitly excluding other social spheres, Derrida's deconstructive thought liberates it from this isolation and brings back the disquieting awareness of transcendence into the highly rationalised and secularised worlds of the economy, of science, politics, morality and law. With this bold idea, Derrida thinks through the consequences of a phenomenon which Luhmann also knew well: despite all division of labour, specialisation and functional differentiation, knowledge is produced everywhere in society, not only in the sciences. In spite of the monopoly of the state, power also emerges outside of institutionalised politics. In spite of the formalisation of the law, the distinction legal/illegal is made in many different social contexts. Similarly, the experience of transcendence on which religious practices focus their energies cannot be limited to the world of religion and theology, but emerges in other worlds of modernity and creates effects that are quite different from the effects of its religious counterpart. Max Weber's strange formula of a 'new polytheism' in modernity gains a more profound meaning if transcendence is seen to have an influence on the various spheres of rationality. It gets lost if the plurality of rationalities is reduced to a mere polycentrism of reason. A plurality of gateways to transcendence – this is how one could read Max Weber's new polytheism. Indeed, the achievement of the old polytheism consisted in using differences in transcendence to legitimise differences in immanence, in particular social roles, competences and functions – a situation which repeats itself under different conditions in modernity. I suggest that it is possible to interpret Derrida as identifying idiosyncratic modes of self-transcendence in diverse modern rational institutions. His astonishing theses refer to the strange paradoxical effects of transcendence in fragmented spheres of rationality, of the 'pure gift' as against the profit-led economy, of 'friendship' as against professionalised politics, of 'forgiveness' as against secularised morality and of 'justice' as against highly formalised law.[56] All of these are the excesses of reference which originate in the distinct logic of each institutional context and, tending towards transcendence, reactivate utopian energies in secularised discourses.

If one continues along those lines, then the search for justice opens up a space of juridical transcendence which can in no way be identified with that of religion and theology. In what respect do they differ? What is the peculiarity of the transcendence of law? The answer, I submit, lies in the peculiarity of the legal paradox. Justice begins where the law ends. This is the point where the hiatus between structure and operation gapes, where the legal paradox emerges and where the discourse of justice is forced to overstep the limits of legal signification. The legal paradox is not empty, it is different from the paradoxes of other institutions. It poses the question: Is it lawful to apply the distinction between lawful and unlawful to the world? Thus, as soon as the law encounters its own paradox, it is exposed to the question of justice. This in its turn is separate from any other transcendence formula, from generosity, from friendship, from forgiving, not to mention from salvation.

The peculiarity of the legal paradox – questioning the lawfulness of the legal code – is ever-present in the process of transcending the law. This question is necessary when law over-reaches the limits of its own signification, but it can no longer be expressed in the rational language of legal argumentation. It can only be expressed in an enigmatic language, in unreal idealisation, in parables, symbolisation, literature, delirium, utopia. No wonder that this is the very moment of the much-criticised romantic rupture in the Michael Kohlhaas novella. The gipsy woman, endowed with powers of witchcraft and fortune telling, takes charge in managing the conflicting demands on justice, giving him the amulet as a clue to justice which will never be known to the world: 'An amulet, Kohlhaas, the horse dealer; take good care of it, some day it will save you your life.'[57]

To summarise the argument up to this point: the discourse of juridical justice can no longer hope to identify any criteria of justice, neither within the law itself, nor in any social world, nor in the world of religion. It has to go beyond the law in order to make the experience of transcendence, under the impression of which it has to go back to the immanence of law. However, is any experience of transcendence possible if Nietzsche is right in saying that 'God is dead'? In a secularised society, can one think the transcendence of law without religion? Is this not a natural law without God, and also a natural law without reason? And finally, is there any meaning left in the most enigmatic formulation of justice, which is found in St John: 'Of righteousness, because I go to my Father, and ye see me no more'?[58]

Can there be a transcendent concept of justice without religion? This is the point of departure for Emmanuel Levinas in determining a 'philosophical transcendence' in contradistinction to a purely religious one. Levinas contrasts the totality of meaning with the exteriority of transcendence, in which the infinite demands of alterity and of justice appear.[59] Here one needs to be aware of the radical difference of alterity in Levinas's as well as in Derrida's thinking. Alterity is misunderstood if it is conceived only as the principle of solidarity with the other or as the singularity of the individual perspective.[60] Alterity means something else, the non-linguistic, non-phenomenological concrete experience of the other, an experience of the transcendence of consciousness and communication in the face of the other. As against reasoned justification, as against the rationality of public speech, the experience would be the non-justifiable, non-rational other of justice. Justice would be located at the boundary between the immanence and the transcendence of law. In the last instance, justice is the attempt to overcome the rupture between immanence and transcendence – to transform the immanence of law in a non-conceivable manner. Justice is not a standard of 'impeccable ideality', but a 'process of transformation of injustice into law'.[61]

There is an additional, more profound meaning to the first part of John's formula. Justice is realised only after actually enduring injustice, suffering and pain. Justice is the transformation of pain, the self-sacrifice which alone can transform immanence into transcendence. When Michael Kohlhaas refused to reveal the content of the mysterious amulet to the Elector of Saxony, he paid with his life, but this earned him the reverence of the people because he had been prepared to die for the sake of justice. In this sense, 'going to the Father' would mean ending the separation of immanence and transcendence via the transformation of injustice. Suffering would originate in the search for justice – a search in vain which realises itself only in the non-perfect order of immanence. In short, justice would be a process of transforming the law which is possible only by going through the real experience of injustice. This idea is echoed in Emile Durkheim's *colère public* and also in those legal theories that stress a sense of injustice as the underlying cause for legal norms. The second part of St John's formulation, invisibility, means not only the non-accessibility of transcendence but also a 'liberation of every individual's rights from the finite conditions of human norm production'.⁶² However, only in a world with spiritual authority could such a hope for salvation exist. If in a secularised society transcendence can only be thought as transcendence without God, then salvation through justice is impossible.

What remains is nothing but a desperate searching which produces the permanent inner restlessness of law. It ceaselessly invents new criteria of justice and constructs new legal arguments, and these very constructions destroy the possibility of justice. The search for justice becomes a mere addiction of the law, destructive and inventive at the same time.

3 Constraints of positivity

The most important differences between a diffuse desire for justice and a specifically juridical justice surface when the drastic constraints which modern law imposes on its contingency formula become visible after the experience of self-transcendence. Juridical justice cannot deal with the totality of injustice in the world, but must bridge the hiatus with its own mechanisms – however unsatisfactorily. Here is the point of difference with the 'legal pietism' of the German free law school which denied any possibility of 'treating like cases alike and any possibility to generalize concrete duties into universal norms'.⁶³ It is at this point that infinite juridical justice is exposed to three differently operating, harsh constraints.

Juridical justice is under pressure to make a decision which connects structure and legal act within the limiting framework of the binary code of law and its existing programmes, even if this decision contradicts its own experience – this is the constraint of decision-making. Even if, after a long and painful process of soul searching and debate, the judge knows that both parties to the case are right, even if he knows that whatever he decides will do injustice to one of the parties, he must decide in favour of one or the other.⁶⁴ *Tertium non datur.*

At the same time the legal system imposes heavy cognitive constraints on the search for justice. It is not free to indulge in the irrational sentiment of injustice or in the vague desire for justice. The aporias of justice which have led into the experience of alterity, into irrational legal sentiment, into human suffering and pain, and into the wealth of transcendence, force the law to transform these experiences into rational reasons, technical arguments and doctrinal concepts – this is the constraint of rational justification. Once again this is the difficulty Luhmann described, of answering responsively and with rational arguments to the extreme demands of the ecologies of law and of simultaneously satisfying the internal requirements of normative consistency.

Finally, the options of juridical justice are drastically reduced by the poverty of law's own instruments. In aspiring to justice, law does not have at its disposal much power or influence. It has comparatively impoverished operations and structures: legal acts and legal rules. No arbitrary exercise of sovereign power, no generous distribution of monetary resources, no precise prediction of future events, no dark oracle, no mystic revelation. It must reduce the overwhelming experience of alterity, that is, the experience of the infinity of the other, to an absurdly simplified form, the formulation of a legal rule which claims to be adequate to the social conflict – this is the constraint of rule-making.[65]

One cannot overestimate the disciplining effects that these three constraints have on juridical justice. The constraint of decision-making means that the conflict cannot possibly be suspended: one party has to be right, the other wrong. The constraint of rational justification means that the decision must be founded on reasons which pretend to combine consistency and responsiveness. The constraint of rule-making means that the decision reduces the complexity of the conflict to an over-simplified rule. In such conditions, how can responsive legal structures be created? How is the leap that overcomes the hiatus possible? In the face of the infinite demands of juridical justice, only a modest secular order is established.

However, theories of justice that attempt to ignore these constraints – and there are more than a few of these, all among the most responsive ones – do nothing but discredit themselves. They take justice to be a radical self-transcendence of law, but they close their eyes to the countervailing claims of legal transcendence to an immanent realisation of justice in the name of omnipresence.[66] Such theories exclude themselves from the discourse on juridical justice, which forces its participants both to transcend the law and to translate this experience into legal decisions, arguments and rules. Theories that escape from such constraints may continue to work as philosophical theories of justice. They may even become a thorn in the flesh of the law. But the pain will fade. After a certain amount of time it will not register any more. Critical theories of law in particular suffer from this growing irrelevance. They collapse before the iron law of deconstructibility: Critique without an alternative proposal does not count.[67] A 'juridical negativism' can establish itself only as a temporary phenomenon. Eventually, it must formulate the conditions under which legal prohibitions will be enacted.[68] The constraints of juridical justice produce a situation different from Theodor Adorno's alternative in moral philosophy and his preference for a 'concrete denunciation of the inhuman' and against a 'non-committed abstract identification of human being'.[69] The passionate engagement of critical legal studies merits a detailed sociological case study to demonstrate the self-marginalisation of gifted and committed jurists. And a Heideggerian waiting game cannot cope at all with the juridical *'Hic Rhodus hic salta'*, whether this be Giorgio Agamben's hopes for a new community, or Philippe Nonet's patient waiting for ... .[70] Both Luhmann and Derrida insist on this point. Derrida, in his critique of Walter Benjamin, even goes as far as to blame legal philosophy for complicity with evil if it refuses to return to the immanence of positive law and instead is content with the distinction between mythical and mystical violence, the criteria of which remain inaccessible.

But there are positive aspects to the disciplining constraints. They put the law under enormous pressure to innovate. Against the double imperative to 'bring chaos to order', no legislative act, no judicial decision and no doctrinal construct can resist: the discourse on juridical justice subjects them all to scrutiny. However, to fulfil the simultaneous requirement of formulating alternative proposals is much more demanding. It puts juridical justice under permanent pressure to invent new legal rules, judicial judgements and doctrinal constructs. This introduces a comparative dimension into the law that allows or even compels us to distinguish between higher and lower degrees of juridical justice. A legal order would dispose of a higher degree of juridical justice if it allows for the self-transcendence of its boundaries and at the same time produces decisions, arguments and rules that claim to be more just than those of comparable legal orders. At the same time, pressure for innovation means chances of improvement. The peculiarity of the contingency formula of law, namely the combination of high indeterminacy and high structuration, favours creative energies. In the 'imaginary space' of the re-entry, institutional imagination finds new opportunities. It is not by chance that the *longue-durée* inventions of the juridical person, the consensual contract and the construct of the state count as achievements of the first order. And the often retold parable of the 'twelfth camel and the qadi' points to hidden affinities between artistic and juridical creativity.

4 Effets pervers

But strangely, in the last instance those legal theoreticians who refuse to find alternative proposals are right. They are not ready to pay the price for the triple constraint of justice. The price for reducing the infinite experience of justice to a binary-coded decision, to its rational justification and to its conditional programming is high: new injustice. Owing to the poverty of legal formalisation, but also, as Levinas has stressed again and again, to the insensitivity of philosophical norm universalisation, the search for juridical justice itself produces new injustice which in its turn provokes its renewed self-transcendence and new constraints. Levinas: 'General and generous principles can be inverted in their application. Every generous thought is threatened by its own Stalinism.'[71] At this moment the difference between self-subversive justice and a universalising rational justice is painfully felt. It reveals that one of the highly praised virtues of justice, its reliance on rational decisions, justifications and norms, is actually one of the most pernicious origins of injustice.

The darkest side of juridical justice, however, is its relentless drive towards universalisation. The temptation towards the 'justicialisation' of the world means that the binary logic of justice – the self-transcendence of law and its legal re-disciplining – is extended to society as a whole. Instead of limiting itself to equal/unequal judgements in conflict resolution, as opposed to the different requirements of political distributional justice and of the justice of recognition in morality, it attempts, in an 'acute fever of righteousness', to establish a just society by applying the instruments of juridical justice. It is just to decide the problems of the world with the help of the binary code of law – this is the *summum jus, summa injuria* of functional differentiation. This expansionist drive can be observed in other contingency formulas as well, in that of the economy, which describes all the problems of the world as a question of scarcity to be solved only by economic means, in the legitimacy formula of politics and in the limitationality formula of science. All these contingency formulas promise to be able to produce a good society, although in fact they can give only partial answers for their limited sector. 'Justicialisation' as an attempt to bring the whole of society to justice with juridical instruments is disastrous. It is the imperialism of legal rationality, with parallels to economic, political and scientific expansionisms – a unidirectional growth of juridical justice that needs to be resisted politically. This imperialism of a partial rationality is dangerous because it meets the human desire for a non-divisible justice. Knowing full well that under the conditions of modernity, this desire cannot be fulfilled, juridical justice as societal justice continues to offer the false promise of salvation. Both produce a dangerous mixture of unanswerable questions and hypocritical answers. Human rights ideology as the ideal of a just society, today's imperialism of a juridical justice unleashed, produces the totalitarian seeker of justice who projects the limited juridical justice of the law onto the whole of society, the Michael Kohlhaas of our times – 'one of the most upright and at the same time one of the most terrible men of his day'. [72]

Notes

This chapter was previously published as 'Self-subversive justice: contingency or transcendence formula of law?', *Modern Law Review*, 72:1 (2009), 1–23. For critical comments on an earlier draft, I would like to thank Sonja Buckel, Eva Buddeberg, Neil Duxbury, Andreas Fischer-Lescano, Rainer Forst, Roger Friedland, Malte Gruber, Vagias Karavas, Fatima Kastner, Martin Loughlin, Richard Nobles, Soo-Hyun Oh, Andreas Philippopoulos, Marcus Pöcker, Hubert Rottleuthner, David Schiff, Anton Schütz, Fabian Steinhauer, Thomas Vesting and Rudolf Wiethölter. My thanks for careful editorial help go to Chris Foley.

1 Kleist, *Michael Kohlhaas*, p. 3.
2 Even Roger Cotterrell takes a cautious stance: 'Social theory has no direct link with the promotion of justice': Cotterrell, *Law's Community*, pp. 2, 60.
3 Derrida *et al.*, 'Préjugés: devant la loi'; Derrida, 'Force of law'; Derrida, *Specters of Marx*; Luhmann, *Rechtssystem und Rechtsdogmatik*; Luhmann, 'Gerechtigkeit in den Rechtssystemen'; Luhmann, *Law as a Social System*, pp. 211 ff.
4 Derrida, 'Force of law', p. 959.
5 For different nuances, see Koselleck, 'Begriffsgeschichtliche Probleme', pp. 365 ff.; Derrida, 'Force of law', p. 919; Luhmann, 'Subjektive Rechte', pp. 48 ff.
6 Luhmann, *Law as a Social System*, pp. 218–19, 221 ff., 225 ff.
7 For the concept of re-entry, see Spencer Brown, *Laws of Form*, pp. 56–7; 69 ff.
8 For a detailed discussion of paradoxes in law, see Teubner, 'Dealing with Paradoxes'.
9 Rawls, *A Theory of Justice*; Habermas, *Between Facts and Norms*. For an insightful analysis of their concepts of justice, see Forst, 'Rechtfertigung der Gerechtigkeit'.
10 For the concept of polycontexturality, see Günther, 'Cybernetic Ontology' and Günther, 'Life as Poly-Contexturality'.
11 For a reformulation of reciprocity under conditions of polycontexturality, see Wiethölter, 'Zur Argumentation im Recht', p. 119.
12 Durkheim, *Division of Labor*, pp. 111 ff.; Weber, *Gesammelte Aufsätze zur Wissenschaftslehre*, pp. 603 ff.; Wittgenstein, *Philosophical Investigations*, pp. 225 ff., 572; Adorno, *Negative Dialectics*; Adorno, *Problems of Moral Philosophy*, pp. 75–6, 84–5.
13 Lyotard, *The Differend*, ch. 2; Foucault, *Order of Things*, chs 2, 3, 7; Foucault, *Discipline and Punish*; Luhmann, *Theory of Society*, vol. 2, pp. 1 ff.
14 Walzer, *Spheres of Justice*; Goodman, *Ways of Worldmaking*, ch. 7.
15 For example, Petersen and Zahle (eds), *Legal Polycentricity*; Teubner, 'Altera pars'. For neo-materialism, see Buckel, *Subjektivierung und Kohäsion*, pp. 226 ff.
16 Günther, 'Cybernetic Ontology' and Günther, 'Life as Poly-Contexturality'.
17 For his pre-sociological concept of society, see Rawls, *A Theory of Justice*, pp. 528 ff.
18 See Chapter 5 in this volume.
19 Kelsen, 'Problem der Gerechtigkeit'.
20 Walzer, *Spheres of Justice*. For a contextualisation of justice in relation to equality, see Pauer-Studer, *Autonom leben*, p. 25.
21 Thorough analyses of this conflict between political equality and individual justice can be found in Menke, *Reflections of Equality*, pp. 107 ff.
22 Foerster, 'Through the Eyes of the Other'.
23 For social processes irritating law, see Teubner, *Law as an Autopoietic System*, pp. 47 ff., 64 ff.; Luhmann, *Law as a Social System*, pp. 464 ff.
24 Teubner, 'Altera pars', pp. 150 ff.
25 Luhmann, *Law as a Social System*, pp. 214 ff.; cf. Dreier, 'Niklas Luhmanns Rechtsbegriff', pp. 315 ff.

26 Luhmann, *Theory of Society*, vol. 1, pp. 282 ff.
27 Luhmann, *Law as a Social System*, p. 218.
28 Luhmann, 'Gerechtigkeit in den Rechtssystemen', pp. 388 ff.; Luhmann, *Law as a Social System*, p. 219.
29 For example, Esser, *Vorverständnis und Methodenwahl*, pp. 201 ff.; Raiser, *Grundlagen der Rechtssoziologie*, pp. 139 ff.; Röhl, *Allgemeine Rechtslehre*, 2nd edn, § 53.
30 The line of reasoning is close to David Nelken's 'ecological approach to law': Nelken, 'Law in action or living law?', pp. 174–5.
31 For such an ecological concept of justice, see Teubner, *Law as an Autopoietic System*, pp. 100 ff., 121–2; Teubner, 'Altera pars', pp. 175–6; Chapter 5 in this volume, pp. 105–127; Teubner, 'Alienating Justice', pp. 28 ff.; Teubner, 'Dreiers Luhmann', pp. 201 ff.
32 Teubner, *Law as an Autopoietic System*, pp. 13 ff.; Luhmann, 'Closure and Openness'; Luhmann, *Law as a Social System*, pp. 76 ff.
33 Cotterrell, *Law's Community*, pp. 65 ff., 91 ff., 315 ff. For a critique of operational closure, see also Kerchove and Ost, *Le droit ou les paradoxes*, pp. 101 ff.
34 For double closure as a necessary condition of self-organisation in general, see Foerster, *Observing Systems*, pp. 288 ff., 305 ff.; and in formal organisations, Luhmann, *Organization and Decision*, ch. 7.
35 Luhmann, *Law as a Social System*, pp. 98 ff., 305 ff.
36 Weick, *Social Psychology*. On enaction as an alternative to representation, see Varela, 'Whence Perceptual Meaning?', pp. 235 ff.
37 Spencer Brown, *Laws of Form*, pp. 56–7; 69 ff.
38 Rosen, *Anthropology of Justice*, pp. 58 ff.
39 Weber, *Economy and Society*, pp. 213 ff.
40 Kleist, *Michael Kohlhaas*.
41 Placentinus, 'Quaestiones de iuris subtilitatibus', p. 53.
42 Typical for this strategy are Habermas, 'Vorbereitende Bemerkungen zu einer Theorie der kommunikativen Kompetenz', pp. 123 ff. and Habermas, 'Wahrheitstheorien', pp. 255 ff.
43 Derrida, 'Force of law', pp. 961 ff.; Luhmann, *Law as a Social System*, pp. 281 ff.
44 Consider just one example: Alexy, 'On balancing'.
45 Albert, 'Problem der Begründung'.
46 This concept of self-subversive justice is the subject of a recent debate: see Clam, 'Wie dicht sind die Opfer?'; Ladeur, 'Das subjektive Recht als Medium der Selbsttransformation'; Schütz, 'Von einem neuerdings erhobenen gerechten Ton'; Steinhauer, 'Derrida'.
47 Wiethölter transferred the famous formula from art to law: Wiethölter, 'Zur Argumentation im Recht', p. 107. See also Adorno, *Minima Moralia*, part 3, p. 222.
48 Rottleuthner, 'Biological Metaphors in Legal Thought', p. 117.
49 Luhmann, *Social Systems*, ch. 8.
50 Luhmann, *Law as a Social System*, pp. 85–6.
51 Teubner, 'Alienating Justice', pp. 27 ff.; Luhmann, *Law as a Social System*, pp. 305 ff.
52 Derrida, 'Force of law', pp. 961 ff.; Luhmann, *Law as a Social System*, pp. 281 ff.
53 Wiethölter, 'Just-ifications', p. 73.
54 Derrida, 'Force of law'.
55 Derrida, *Specters of Marx*, p. 90.

56 Derrida, 'Force of law'; Derrida, *Given Time*, vol. 1; Derrida, *Politics of Friendship*; Derrida, 'Le siècle et le pardon', English translation in Derrida, *On Cosmopolitanism and Forgiveness*.
57 Kleist, *Michael Kohlhaas*, p. 106.
58 John 16: 10. For a subtle interpretation, see Folkers, 'Johannes mit Aristoteles', pp. 68 ff.
59 Levinas, *Otherwise than Being*; Levinas, *Totality and Infinity*, section I.C.3.
60 But see Honneth, *Das Andere der Gerechtigkeit*, pp. 154 ff., 165 ff.
61 Folkers, 'Johannes mit Aristoteles', pp. 71–2.
62 Ibid., pp. 76–7.
63 Wieacker, *History of Private Law*, § 29 III 3 c, n. 57.
64 See the famous paradox of the rabbi, retold by Atlan, *Enlightenment to Enlightenment*, p. 17.
65 Fikentscher, *Methoden des Rechts*, pp. 201 ff.
66 Folkers, 'Johannes mit Aristoteles', pp. 76–7.
67 Luhmann, *Law as a Social System*, p. 428.
68 Wiethölter, 'Recht und Politik', p. 158; Wiethölter, 'Just-ifications', pp. 20–1.
69 Adorno, *Problems of Moral Philosophy*, p. 261.
70 Agamben, *Homo Sacer*, pp. 166 ff.; Agamben, *State of Exception*, pp. 74 ff.; Nonet, 'Time and law', pp. 322 ff.
71 Levinas, *Otherwise than Being*.
72 Kleist, *Michael Kohlhaas*, p. 81; see also Ogorek, 'Adam Müllers Gegensatzphilosophie', pp. 121 ff.

2

The economics of the gift – the positivity of justice: the mutual paranoia of Jacques Derrida and Niklas Luhmann

I System versus *différance*

Niklas Luhmann and Jacques Derrida have made the same diagnosis as regards the sober world of lawyers and economists.[1] Where other people observe rational decisions based on cost–benefit calculations and on rule–fact subsumptions, their diagnosis is that of the madness of decision. In contrast to all analyses of rational choice, games theory and decision theory and to all promises of normative argumentation and discursive rationality, the protagonists of autopoiesis and deconstruction insist that the everyday routines of legal and economic decisions contain a component of madness, irrationality, mystery and even sacredness. The irrational is not to be viewed as a negligible remainder in a process of increasing rationalisation, but as the driving force of the decision. According to Luhmann:

> The mystery of the decision and the mystery of the hierarchy mutually support each other. Both exhibit an unspeakable (dare one say, religious) element, which makes them into what they are.[2]

According to Derrida law and justice works

> ... without calculation and without rules, without reason or without rationality ... we can recognise in it, indeed accuse, identify a madness.

And perhaps another sort of mystique. And deconstruction is mad about this kind of justice. Mad about this desire for justice.³

The deconstructive consensus held by the opponents goes even further. It is not just in the fleeting, ecstatic moments of decision that the irrational erupts into the world of calculation. Rather, it reaches the very foundations of formal rationality in law and in the economy. Derrida and Luhmann are in agreement that arbitrariness, inconsistencies, antinomies, paradoxes and even violence lie at the bottom of the most refined constructs in economic and legal action. However, exposing the irrational is not where the analysis ends, in the spirit of Carl Schmitt's decisionism, but where it begins.⁴ Neither theory is aimed simply at denouncing the elaborate practices of justification and calculation in economics and law as being merely an ideological mystification of power constellations.⁵ On the contrary, in the face of their paradoxicalities, Derrida and Luhmann drastically raise expectations regarding the quality of economic and legal calculations. According to both authors, exposing the irrationality of a decision does not mean suspending the question of social justice, but on the contrary implies taking the normative requirements of justice even more seriously.⁶

However astonishing the convergence of autopoiesis and *différance* may be, the crucial point is not the uncovering of isomorphies, analogies and secret affinities.⁷ Usually, systems theorists prefer a selective incorporation technique. They decorate the facades of their autopoietic palaces with deconstructive fragments of *différance*, of *itération*, of *trace*. This is certainly attractive for theory building, but it ultimately leads only to an involution of architectonics without altering the foundations. This decorative incorporation is as irrelevant as the rigorous confrontation of deconstruction and autopoiesis preferred by Derrideans, which in the end leads only to reciprocal immunisation.

By contrast, I would prefer a reading that uncovers a reciprocal paranoia in Derrida's and Luhmann's writing, a dynamic of mutual persecutions between the theories. In fact, this dynamic begins with a common analysis of foundational paradoxes in law and economy which ties the theories to each other. But this changes abruptly when incompatible reality constructs render each theory blind to and distrustful of the other. We ought to abandon all hope of restoring sight to the blind and trust to the distrustful. Rather, we should exploit the paranoid dynamic itself, by definition a 'form of delirium characterised by convictions which despite being apparently similar are in reality conflicting and are not capable of being altered either through logic or through experience, e.g. delusions of grandeur or fears of persecution'.⁸ Autopoiesis and deconstruction – what knowledge do we gain from their reciprocal fears of persecution, which end in a hectic whirl of deconstructive moves and systemic counter moves, in an ascending relation of stabilisations and destabilisations, in a dance of mutual retribution? This reading of paranoia becomes productive when the closed world of the fictions of one theory reappears in the fictitious world of the other. Thus: autopoietic systems as Jacques Derrida's nightmare, the gift of justice as Niklas Luhmann's redemption.

II Foundational paradoxes

First, it is amazing how radically both Derrida and Luhmann depart from common assumptions, challenging the consensus on the foundations of legal and economic institutions. One needs to be courageous, not to say eccentric, if, like Derrida, one seeks to ground a social theory of the economy not in the structures of exchange and in the reciprocity of the mutual satisfaction of needs, but, of all things, in the structure of the gift.[9] The relation of a pure gift in Derrida's conceptualisation is totally asymmetrical, it means giving without gratitude, a radical non-reciprocal generosity that is destroyed by the existence of mere trace elements of symmetry, of reciprocity, even of recognition or of the social bond of gratitude. Such courage is also necessary if, like Luhmann, one refuses to conceive of the foundation of law in terms of a *Grundnorm*, of an ultimate rule of recognition, of substantive and procedural principles of legal validity, or in terms of its socio-political legitimation, but instead thinks of it in terms of the extreme borderline case of the pure self-referentiality of legal operations, which fall into paradoxical confusion through their self-application.[10] It is precisely the radicalism of deconstruction and of systems theory which offers a new perspective on the foundations of legal and economic institutions, a perspective which has previously been rejected as based on flawed reasoning.[11] Legal and economic institutions, Derrida and Luhmann insist, are not based on rational principles but on dangerous antinomies and paradoxes which not only destroy their legitimacy, but also paralyse each operation and calculation through their self-contradictory structures.

Their approach to the founding paradox of law reveals how, despite far-reaching agreement between their respective analyses, their initial consensus suddenly turns into complete incompatibility between their lines of thinking. Both commence with a critique of the violence of law which is informed by Walter Benjamin.[12] While they reject as superficial the customary critique of law in terms of ideology and power, which seeks to expose it as the expression of economic or political interests, at a deeper level, both authors view the law as something that is caught in the paradoxes of its own self-referentiality.[13]

Since the origin of authority, the foundation or ground, the position of the law can't by definition rest on anything but themselves, they are themselves a violence without ground. Which is not to say that they are in themselves unjust, in the sense of 'illegal'. They are neither legal nor illegal in their founding moment.[14]

Luhmann identifies the same phenomenon.[15] At the bottom of the hierarchies of legal rules, he sees 'the paradox of the binary code applied to itself'. For both authors, all efforts of the law towards legitimacy, a normative foundation or even justice are, in the end, useless, since they are ultimately based on the violence of the primordial distinction between legal and illegal. This is a distinction that cannot show itself to be legal, legitimate or just, but turns out to be nothing but arbitrary and indiscriminate.

The foundational paradox is the point where the bifurcation of deconstruction and autopoiesis begins. Derrida does not shy away from the precipice of the legal paradox and attempts to enter its dark worlds with a bold interpretation of the original violence of law which leads him to a mysterious distinction between different legal forces.[16] Reinterpreting Benjamin's famous essay on law and violence, he distinguishes between a mythical foundational violence, which establishes the positivity of the state and the law only through bloodshed, and a divine foundational violence, which, while being destructive and even annihilating, avoids bloodshed and supports life, thereby establishing justice. It is at this stage that Derrida formulates the most provocative paradox: the distinction between positivity and justice is itself indecipherable; there are no criteria which might distinguish between mythical and divine violence, not only before the decision, but also after the decision. The question is merely postponed to an indeterminate future, and thus delegated to an infinite responsibility.

Luhmann shies away from such precipices; for him, these results of deconstructive analysis merely confirm once more the paralysing effects of the paradox, which intensify the more one attempts to shed light on the darkness of the legal paradox. The result is mere Derridean 'verbal acoustics', obscurities of speech and the typical deconstructive gesture of frightening people with dark paradoxes: '... a mixture of arbitrariness and paralysis'.[17] Luhmann explicitly moves in the opposite direction: while it is fruitless to develop a theory which only repeats the inconsistencies, the unruliness, the darkness of the legal paradox in a different language, a creative use of the paradox becomes possible once theory enquires into the possibilities of de-paradoxification. De-paradoxification means inventing new distinctions which do not deny the paradox, but temporarily displace it and thus deprive it of its paralysing force. This leads Luhmann to historical and sociological analyses that detail how institutionalised distinctions between natural and positive law in European legal history or current distinctions between legislation and adjudication have produced their impressive cultural achievements despite or precisely because of the legal paradox.[18]

Thus, contrary to first appearances, the foundational paradox of law is not a common object of analysis for Derrida and Luhmann, but merely a common runway, which they use to take off in opposite directions: the autopoietic escape from and the deconstructive search for the paradoxes of law. If one turns one's attention to the foundational paradox of the economy, the divergence of their approaches shows that it is, however, not sufficient to identify the difference between paradoxification and de-paradoxification as merely one of cognitive interest, analytical direction and conceptual apparatus. Their formulations of the economic paradox are already so different that a common starting point is barely recognisable; instead, a more fundamental difference between autopoiesis and deconstruction comes into view.

For Luhmann, the circular movement of the economy is made possible at the historical moment when economic institutions successfully circumvent the paradox of scarcity, according to which a more ample supply for one is the greater need of another, or, more abstractly, every taking of scarce goods which serves to lessen scarcity increases scarcity. Only by rendering this blockage invisible is it possible to overcome this paradox and to set the circular movement of the economy going. This occurs when the effects of the taking of rare resources are bifurcated and effectively institutionalised as a binary code in economic action.

> For the person who takes something, the scarcity which is assumed in the act of taking something lessens. For all others, it increases ... Condensed scarcity thus appears as the difference between 'having' and 'not having'.[19]

Derrida thinks about the possibility of the circular movement of the economy from a different starting point, not from that of the paradoxes implied in taking scarce goods, but that of the impossibility of the pure gift. The gift relation is the exact opposite of the economic exchange relation, but at the same time it is the gift which first sets off the circular movement of the economy. The founding paradox of the economy reveals itself in the moment when the relation of the pure gift, which exists before any reference to subjectivity, constitutes the subject:

> a subject as such neither gives or receives a gift. It is constituted, on the contrary, in view of dominating, through calculation and exchange,

the mastery of this *hubris* or of this impossibility that is announced in the premise of the gift.[20]

And yet, both versions of the economic paradox coincide in the concept of property. The bifurcation of the effects of the act of taking, their coding as property, i.e. as the difference between having and not having, and the construction of the corresponding semantic artefacts of property owners and non-property owners in Luhmann's view leads away from the blockades of the scarcity paradox and into the dynamics of the economy. According to Derrida, the constitution of the subject as a giver and receiver and the recognition of the property of the subject destroy the purity of the gift and render the calculations of the economy possible.

But Derrida's interest in the circular flows of the economy is not informed by Luhmann's concerns with de-paradoxification and with the social construction of order by means first of the property code and then of the money code and the programmes of the economy. Instead he analyses the way in which the continuous provocation of the gift permanently interrupts and transcends the circular movement of the economy. What we are dealing with thus are not two competing social theories on the economy which illuminate the same subject matter from different perspectives and with different cognitive interests. Rather, even according to their own self-understanding, this is a clash between two alternative worlds which oppose each other in a way that cannot be understood as the competition of different methods, theories or paradigms. Luhmann is engaged in an ambitious attempt to construct a scientific theory of society as a phenomenology of communication, in strict analogy to Edmund Husserl's phenomenology of consciousness. This stands in stark contrast to Derrida's explicit refusal to develop a scientific theory of the gift. Theory, Derrida insists, would be incapable even of thinking the gift. Instead, he seeks to make use of an analogy with the opposition between thought and epistemology, between the noumenal and the phenomenal, in order to conceive of a 'transcendental illusion' of gift which 'exceeds the limits of experience, knowledge, science, economy – and even philosophy'.[21]

Thus, although they initially agree on the paradoxical foundation of law and of the economy, the two schools of thought in fact have nothing to say to each other. Luhmann asks how de-paradoxification techniques construct the immanence of social institutions and build a world of autopoietic social systems, their coding and programming. By contrast, Derrida's thought aims at the transcendence of social institutions through their re-paradoxification and proposes a counter-world of *différance*, in which the deconstructive double movement permanently exposes the founding antinomies of social institutions as well as the paradoxical paralysis of concrete legal and economic decisions.

Luhmann's world and Derrida's counter-world are closed off against each other and one cannot directly influence the other. It is, however, precisely their mutual closure that makes them threaten, persecute and haunt each other.

III Derrida's nightmare: autopoietic social systems

Yet why is their relation not simply one of indifference? Why should Niklas Luhmann of all people stalk Jacques Derrida, following his deconstructive movements step by step? And why should systems theorists be under continuous threat of intellectual harassment from deconstructionists? While the opposing features of de-paradoxification and re-paradoxification, of empirical institutional analysis and transcendental illusion, of the immanence of social systems and their transcendence by *différance* can render plausible the way in which they exclude each other, they do not explain how and why they rely on each other and even haunt each other.

To do this, one needs a whole different set of interconnections. The thesis proposed here is that there is indeed an interlocking between autopoiesis and deconstruction. The institutional analyses of systems theory and of deconstruction interlock in such a way that they cannot let go of each other. Each move made by one results in a corresponding move of the other, without, however, the ability to spell this out, let alone control it. The effects of this interlocking are felt constantly in their respective analyses of legal and economic institutions. But the interlocking itself occurred in their basic concepts, or rather in the *distinctions directrices* of their theoretical architectures. More specifically, Derrida's distinction between writing and speech is drawn in such a way that it is necessarily blind towards Luhmann's distinction between consciousness and communication, but, at the same time, continuously provoked by it. On another level, precisely the reverse happens. Luhmann's autopoiesis is permanently provoked by Derrida's *différance*, but at the same time unable to conceptualise it. There is a reason why these *distinctions directrices* are so important for the legal and economic themes under consideration. In the end, they decide on the way the social is perceived and thus, implicitly, on the possibility of being just towards or of giving to another.

Derrida and Luhmann start with the same question: can Edmund Husserl's phenomenology of consciousness do justice to social institutions? Or rather, why can it not? Their attempt to delete (or rather illuminate) Husserl's blind spot concerning society is shared by other contemporary theories of 'Justice towards the Other', such as those of Lyotard, Habermas or Levinas.[22] There is general agreement that Husserl's attempts to integrate society into the philosophy of consciousness – the (in)famous *Monadengemeinschaft* – have failed.[23] His distinction between consciousness and the outer world has no room for the social. The fundamental inaccessibility of the outer world and the merely phenomenal construction of the world inside consciousness is the reason for a fundamental injustice towards the other. Husserl's phenomenology cannot adequately conceive of society, in fact it cannot even do justice to the multiplicity of conscious individuals. Communication becomes a mere declaration of signs and the production of meaning takes place only within consciousness. This cannot do justice to the other: for all intents and purposes, the other has a mere phenomenological (consciousness-dependent) existence. As if to make up for this, the distinction transcendental/empirical (ideal/psychological) is introduced. But while this makes a universal, objective and ideal sphere of meaning beyond a single consciousness possible, it has inherited all the difficulties associated with transcendentalism: it is ahistorical, a priori, unempirical, undynamic, highly abstract, 'pure', etc.

Lyotard's phenomenology of language games attempts the exact opposite. However, this is bound to repeat Husserl's problems in inverted form. Here, the world exists only as the construct of a particular discourse.[24] Consciousness, inner speech and introspection are accordingly taboo. Since language games are self-referentially constituted, they do justice only to themselves, not to the inner infinity of subjective consciousness. Actors are merely pale linguistic constructs of the language game. Lyotard's blind spot is situated in precisely the same place as Husserl's. It is just that they find themselves on opposite sides of the principal distinction between inner and outer: on the side of consciousness in one case, on that of discourse in the other. Husserl's exclusion of the social is paralleled by Lyotard's exclusion of consciousness. The issue of particular interest here, that of justice, according to Lyotard is not a question of doing justice to the originality, the infinity and depth of the other, but merely a problem in the conflictual relation between different closed discourses. The *différend* can never become a *litige*. The *différend* necessarily results in injustice, in the violence of one language game towards another.

Now, Derrida and Luhmann both attempt to overcome the alternative between consciousness and discourse as monopolists in the production of meaning. With his thesis of the primacy of writing over speech and his polemic against the philosophy of consciousness, Derrida aims specifically at the blind spot between consciousness and speech.[25] Writing is the supplement of this distinction; it undermines it; it embraces 'inner' and 'outer' processes of meaning, which leave a trace. This is the point where Derrida's *distinction directrice* interlocks with Luhmann's. Derrida doubly deconstructs the hierarchy of speech and writing, into a tangled hierarchy and into a secret reversal of the hierarchical relation.²⁶ This ingenious idea matches the originality of Luhmann's conceptual move, which seeks to escape the sterile juxtaposition between the philosophy of consciousness and language game theory by duplicating the production of meaning, locating it separately both in psychological systems and in social systems. Each *distinction directrice*, however, inhabits precisely that place where the other has its blind spot. The juxtaposition of writing and speech and that of communication and consciousness are mutually irreconcilable *distinctions directrices* that cannot be integrated into a synthesis. What remains for the outside observer is a continuous 'switching' from one distinction to the other, resulting in an almost simultaneous observation of the world from two contradictory, but supplementary perspectives. Yet the precondition for this supplementarity, at least if it is to become productive, is that the distinctions are capable of reciprocally illuminating their blind spots.

Derrida's writing/speech difference has an unavoidable blind spot when it comes to the peculiarities of social institutions. The distinction is responsible for the (in)famous asociological character of deconstruction. Because it imposes writing on the difference of consciousness and speech as the excluded third in this difference, deconstruction in its turn excludes society from the difference of intertextuality. Deconstruction cannot do 'justice' to the autonomy of the social. But for the same reason it cannot do 'justice' to the unfathomable depths of individual consciousness, given that writing cannot distinguish communication and consciousness. To make up for this, deconstruction instead draws on Levinas's philosophy of alterity. This, however, is itself only another correction of the Husserlian blindness to the social. The totality of consciousness and its production of meaning is juxtaposed by Levinas with the infinity of transcendence, and the reality of the other and his or her experience is placed in the realm of infinity.²⁷ In this 'premature' sacralisation of the social, any experience of society disappears in the blind spot of the distinction between totality and infinity.

This is where Derrida's nightmare begins. Social systems operate in the blind spot of his *distinction directrice*. He can deconstruct economic and legal institutions, but only as texts and intertextualities, not as social systems. Their restless autopoietic self-reproduction continues to haunt him, without ever being seen in the daylight of deconstruction. The secret of autopoiesis is that social systems are no longer threatened by the paradoxes of their deconstructive reading. Autopoietic self-reproduction means that in routine operations, they are constantly de-paradoxifying their foundational paradox. Thus, they are capable of deconstructing deconstruction. Not, of course, in the sense that they can exclude it on a long-term basis, but in the sense that they postpone, displace, disseminate, historicise deconstruction itself, and thus drastically alter the conditions of its possibility.[28] Luhmann's concepts are Derrida's 'unconcepts', autopoietic monsters in the world of deconstruction, which constantly pursue his deconstructive efforts with their relentless de-paradoxification. This is particularly true of Luhmann's central concepts of social autopoiesis, polycontexturality and second-order cybernetics.

What is the paradox that is dealt with by social autopoiesis? It is the paradox of alterity, the paralysing self-contradictions that occur in the primordial encounter with the other. Action is paralysed whenever ego makes her action dependent on alter and vice versa. The encounter with the other and the unfathomable abyss which this opens up are, of course, Derrida's continuous theme in his philosophy of the gift and in his philosophy of justice.[29] In the guise of the paradox of double contingency, they are equally central to Luhmann's theory.[30] But there is a decisive difference in the way they are treated. In Luhmann's account, the paradox of the encounter with the other is resolved by the emergence of autopoietic social systems. Social systems do not abolish the original paradox, but transfer it to a new sphere of meaning, namely, that of communication. The double contingency of two self-referential systems in their internal infinity is made bearable when communication emerges as an autonomous system for the production of meaning. Communication eliminates the paralysing effects of the paradox because '... the self-reference of social systems requires an immanent duality to allow a circle to form whose interruption can permit structures to develop'.[31]

To be sure, the paradox of alterity remains. But it changes its form; it is reconstructed and homogenised within the sphere of communication. It loses its power to paralyse two self-referential systems that are reconstructing each other in an infinite and unresolvable circularity, and it reappears as the precarious but manageable social interdependence of two communicative constructs, ego and alter. When they are reconstructed in communication, the paradoxical effects of their encounter are as it were rendered harmless. But there is a price to pay. While the paradoxes of the encounter with the other disappear, the foundational paradoxes of social systems emerge. To render them invisible in their turn becomes the permanent problem of communication.

While Derrida does delve relentlessly into the paradoxies in the constitution of subjectivity and intersubjectivity, the instruments of deconstruction are designed in such a way that they cannot thematise the crucial transformation of the paradox of alterity into the foundational paradoxes of communicative worlds, among them the paradoxes of law and of the economy. Thus, deconstruction remains wedded to the original paradoxes of alterity. This also helps to explain Derrida's deficit as regards historical and sociological analysis, as can be seen, for example, in *Specters of Marx*, which is frighteningly strong as far as all kinds of spectrologies are concerned, but remarkably weak when it comes to concrete analyses of contemporary society.[32] The transformation of the paradox of double contingency into the foundational paradoxes of the emerging third, i.e. the social system, also entails its historicisation. Even if the basic structures of the paradox remain the same, the particular mode of its invisibilisation and the threatening moments of its re-emergence now depend on historical contingencies. The paradox itself is 'necessary knowledge, a transcendental necessity, the successor of the transcendental subject'.[33] By contrast, the distinctions which are used for de-paradoxification are dependent on socio-historical conditions of plausibility and of acceptability, are compatible knowledge, are contingent. This is how the social construction of systems, their continuous deconstruction and their recurrent reconstruction become a subject for the sociology of knowledge. What kind of society makes particular de-paradoxifying distinctions plausible? What kinds of *choques exogènes* will once more expose the paradoxical foundations of a social institution? The activity of deconstruction itself is thereby thoroughly socialised and historicised. The possibility of invoking the paradox of alterity does always remain present. But strangely, it has no consequences,[34] whereas the successful re-paradoxification of specific social systems, which must vary each time in accordance with concrete historical conditions, constitutes the actual threat.

The next autopoietic monster – polycontexturality[35] – gives rise to other deconstructive nightmares, because it again drastically changes the historical situation. The emergence of a multitude of autonomous spheres of meaning within society, each of which is founded on its own particular codes and programmes, and, particularly, their operational and observational closure against each other produce a new anti-deconstructive immunity. They become resistant to the paradoxes of other spheres of meaning. The legal system, for example, deals extensively with economic conflicts, but remains indifferent towards the economic paradox of scarcity, the resolution of which is declared to be an economic problem, not a problem of law. Similarly, when constitutional lawyers construct self-referring rules, actually a logical impossibility, they do not care about the Cretan paradox that haunts logicians. With cool indifference, they apply self-referring rules in legislative and judicial practice.[36] In law, deconstruction counts only if it touches on the legal paradox itself and threatens legal practice in its application of the binary code legal/illegal. Then and only then do the conceptual machineries of legal doctrine begin their relentless search for 'saving distinctions'. The collapse of natural law at the beginning of the modern age and the effect of globalisation today attest to this real threat to the operations of the legal system.[37] While natural law hierarchies have been safely replaced by the institutionalised practices of legal positivism, the threats of globalisation are still provoking modern law. Up to now, no saving distinctions are in sight.

Here also, however, polycontexturality has the power to deconstruct deconstruction. Polycontexturality makes it possible for social systems to externalise their foundational paradoxes and to render them harmless by shifting them to other social systems. The politicisation of the legal paradox of validity and of the economic paradox of scarcity are striking historical examples. Both social systems successfully externalised these problems when they institutionalised a differentiation between 'levels' of decision-making (between the level of adjudication and legislation in law, between decisions concerning the allocation of money and the actual amount of money in the economy) and defined the 'higher level' as something that was no longer an issue for legal or economic action, but a political question to be dealt with by the political system (legislation and central banks as political institutions).[38]

However, the highest degree of deconstruction resistance is attained when second-order cybernetics and the difference between operation and self-observation are firmly institutionalised in social systems. At that point, the operations of legal systems (judicial precedents, legislative decisions, contracts) establish an autonomous network of decisions, the validity of which is not necessarily dependent on the validity of legal argumentation (concepts, doctrines, principles, policies), but merely structurally coupled to them in a loose way. Such an institutionalised separation of self-observation and operation creates problems for deconstructive practice, given that the latter does not systematically distinguish texts from social institutions, i.e. from materialised, long-lasting normative structures which are based on a presumed consensus. Contradictions, antinomies and paradoxes, which regularly arise in the line of legal argumentation, do not necessarily have an effect on the operational decision-making of law. Only when deconstructive moves affect the validity of legislative, judicial or contractual decisions, something which has recently started to happen as a consequence of the globalisation crisis of law, does the hectic search for new bases of normative validity begin.[39]

As should have become clear, the nightmarish effects of social systems do not consist merely in the fact that they immunise the production of meaning against deconstruction. Taken together, autopoiesis, polycontexturality and second-order cybernetics do this quite successfully, even if this immunisation works only temporarily, given that social systems are regularly overtaken by their own paradoxes. What is far more irritating about social systems is the fact that their continuous transformation subjects deconstruction itself to a process of historical evolution. The result of this almost rhythmical play of paradoxification, de-paradoxification and re-paradoxification is an evolutionary dynamics in which deconstruction, permanently provoked by its autopoietic subversion, is bound to change its character. Variation, selection, retention – should the evolutionary mechanisms that give rise to the proliferation of monkeys and social systems also direct the hectic iterational movements of *différance*? But even a deconstructive Darwinism is not yet the worst nightmare for deconstruction. Its real incubus is the amazing productivity in the interplay of deconstruction and autopoietic reconstruction. Paradoxes do not just threaten the structures of social systems (legal rules, economic routines), something against which they must defend, insulate and protect themselves. More important and astonishing is that paradoxes are used creatively to produce new worlds of meaning. The true deconstructive obsession seems to be not with defensive, conservative systems maintaining their original structures, but with the insatiable systemic impulse to invent new differences, with the birth of autopoiesis from the spirit of deconstruction.

IV Luhmann's redemption: the gift of justice

It is often asserted that the blind spot in Luhmann's systems theory is where other people see the person, the individual, the subject.[40] The assertion is plainly wrong. The destruction of the subject, personless systems, anti-humanism – this criticism is justified when levelled against discourse theories, or against deconstruction (which, for its part, can be additionally criticised for a resubjectification of *différance* after the deconstruction of the traditional subject), but not when directed at systems theory. Luhmann explicitly attributes the dynamics of autopoiesis not only to society, but also to consciousness. As mentioned above, he circumvents the complementary failures of the philosophy of consciousness and of language theory by duplicating the production of meaning. In contrast to Derrida, who simply silences the distinction between mind and society with his comprehensive concept of writing, Luhmann separates communication and consciousness and treats them as mutually inaccessible, but constructs both as autonomous worlds of meaning. In a sense, Luhmann combines Husserl with Wittgenstein: he combines the phenomenology of language games with that of consciousness, without, however, merging them (as Derrida's *différance* or Habermas's intersubjectivity attempt to do) into one. The blind spot of autopoiesis lies elsewhere: not in the absence of a subject, but precisely in the distinction between two 'subjects', in the distinction between communication and consciousness, society and individual, outer and inner, system and system.

One ought not to view this as a flaw in his theory. Rather, it is its greatest achievement. So far, Luhmann is the one who has offered the most plausible construction of the autonomy of the social. Society is a web of communications, nothing else, and human beings are part of the environment of society. Its greatest achievement, however, necessarily makes his theory blind to the symbolic space where the *monades* of communication and consciousness meet each other. This is the weak point which Habermas has attacked successfully as the 'artificial' separation of psychological and social system.[41] Of course, Luhmann has worked ceaselessly on the blind spot of his theory and has attempted again and again to compensate for the violence of the mind/society separation. Emotionally loaded concepts such as 'structural coupling' or 'interpenetration' were introduced to reconnect psychological and social systems. But the inner logic of the theory forces him time and again to shift structural coupling and interpenetration into the interior of the participating systems and to minimise, if not to eliminate, the interaction, the translation, the interrelation between consciousness and communication. True, Luhmann submits, systems are irritated by their outside world, but the irritation is something that is done by the irritated system itself in its internal reconstruction of the outside world.

For Luhmann, relation is an 'unconcept', not only in an intersubjective, but also in an intersystemic regard, and it can only be dealt with through compensatory observations of the synchronisation of systems. The same compensatory mechanism is also at work in the inner sanctum of the super-theory – in the distinction between system and environment. Autopoiesis theory is not able to conceptualise the relation between system and environment, a shortcoming for which secondary constructs of structural coupling are meant to compensate.[42] And it is precisely in this inner sanctum that autopoiesis begins to be troubled by deconstruction. The unity (!) of *différance* begins to haunt the irrevocable multiplicity of autopoietic systems. In Derrida's view, the constitution of meaning appears as nothing like the multitude of separate, but parallel recursive processes of mutually closed systems – let alone the separation of psychological and social systems. The Derridean dynamics of *différance* are a differential, paradoxically constituted, changing, context-dependent and permanently contingent, yet interconnected movement. They resist a clear separation, let alone a mutual systemic closure, of legal, economic, political and religious aspects, interactional and organisational patterns, social and psychological components.[43] It is proposed that while such a concept of *différance* is incompatible with autopoiesis, it is, at the same time, its necessary supplement. It can articulate the open dance of heterogeneous systemic operations itself, the infinite network of relations, the coordination and interplay of the various aspects, but without transferring these in turn to a closed system of interlinked, homogenous operations. This understanding of *différance* cannot be systematically integrated into autopoiesis, it can only appear as a threatening visitation of the closed system from without.

The necessary blindness of the system/environment distinction has important consequences for a systems-theoretical concept of justice. In contrast to popular prejudice, Luhmann does not dismiss justice as a hackneyed old European idea, but gives it a central position in his theory of law. But under modern conditions, justice can no longer serve as an internal criterion for the decision of individual cases. Nor is justice the highest internal norm of law, nor an external political or moral value which positive law must comply with. Instead, justice serves as the contingency formula of law, problematising the relation between law and its social environment. According to Luhmann, justice means adequate complexity of the law and a maximum of internal consistency in the face of the extremely diverse environmental demands made on it.[44] But here again systems theory cannot deal with the environmental relation 'as such'. It can only treat it asymmetrically, either from the inner perspective of the legal system or from the external perspective of an observer. The interrelations between law and society, the processes of translation from one system into the other, again disappear in the blind spot of the system/environment distinction. At best, this formulation of justice does adequately reflect the internal requirements of modern positivised law. Under conditions of extreme functional differentiation, the internal consistency of decision-making in law is strained by polycontexturality – a difficult problem, to which the contingency formula of justice reacts. But Luhmann's concept of justice is less adequate when it comes to institutions in the environment of law, as they appear only as external disturbances that endanger consistency, and to which one can do 'justice' only through a new kind of consistency.

Most importantly, however, this concept of justice is not at all commensurate to the relation between the law and its 'world', defined as the unity of the difference between law and non-law, the unity of the difference between system and environment. This is the most difficult issue for an autopoietic theory of justice. Luhmann concedes that

> the intention to observe the unity of the difference remains possible and makes sense in the world of meaning. But this sense takes on the form of a paradox, the form of the basic paradox of the identity of that which is different.[45]

Based on this premise, for Luhmann the unity of the difference between law and non-law can never be a suitable theme for justice, a theme for the contingency formula of a social system. But it is precisely at this vulnerable point, this blank, this missing piece, this paradox that Derrida aims his difficult and unstable distinction between justice and positive law:

> a distinction between justice and *droit*, between justice (infinite, incalculable, rebellious to rule and foreign to symmetry, heterogeneous and heterotropic) and the exercise of justice as law or right, legitimacy or legality, stabilizable and statutory, calculable, a system of regulated and coded prescriptions.[46]

Derrida's conception of justice is distinguished from Luhmann's

> ... just because of this infinity and because of the heteronomic relation to others, to the faces of otherness that govern me, whose infinity I cannot thematize and whose hostage I remain.[47]

This conception of justice – which draws on Levinas's philosophy of alterity – is, similarly to Luhmann's, not an internal legal norm. Nor is it an external social, moral or political demand on the law. Rather, it is – unlike Luhmann's conception – aimed directly at the transcendence of law, which legal operations can never attain, but to the demands of which they are nevertheless permanently exposed. By emphasising the insurmountable difference between positive law and such a form of justice, deconstruction formulates the transcendent dimension of law, ironically precisely in Luhmann's sense of an observation of the world of law as the unity of the difference between law and non-law, an observation which necessarily ends in paradoxes.

This is Derrida's central thesis: justice as transcendence, in irreconcilable, sharp contrast to the immanence of positive law, yet for ever haunting the law. And it is here that parallels become visible with the relationship between the gift and the circular movement of the economy. The gift is not, as in Marcel Mauss's *Essai sur le don*, merely an ethical or political counter-principle to the cold economic logic of capitalism. The gift transcends every social relation and provokes it – as in the metaphor of the beggar – as an unconditional demand from the other.[48] The gift, too, is not pure transcendence, without any connection to the circular movement of the economy, but stands in the same contradictory relation of irrevocable separation and simultaneous connectedness by way of permanent provocation. Hence also Derrida's repeated calls for political engagement, which are provoked by the insatiable demands of a transcendent justice and a transcendent gift.[49]

Luhmann's sociology refuses to address this question. Instead, it is solely concerned with the immanence of law, the positivity of legal acts and legal rules, and the relation of law to the social environment. Luhmann goes beyond this only in one point. Were the law to be confronted with its own paradox, then indeed it would – also and particularly from the perspective of systems theory – be exposed to its own transcendence. But systems theory, with its insistence on the de-paradoxification of law, strictly prohibits this exposure. If one is to prevent legal decision-making from being blocked, one needs to invisibilise the paradox, not to confront it. Social autopoiesis, for the sake of self-continuation, needs to suppress the relationship of social systems with transcendence. Admittedly, the relation between society and transcendence is not declared to be generally meaningless. It is, however, concentrated within religion as an autonomous social system, where it is treated as an idiosyncratic way of dealing with paradoxes: as the symbolisation of the excluded third of the difference between system and environment.[50]

By contrast, Derrida's gift of justice pursues systems theory with uncomfortable questions, for present purposes above all with the question of whether there can be a religious experience that is specifically one of law. From this perspective, the legal paradox would no longer be observed only with a view to its avoidance, but with regard to the question of whether legal language is able to symbolise that which lies 'behind' it as the utopia of law.[51] While it remains correct that positive law can only arise out of the invisibilisation of the legal paradox, 'justice' would in that case become the formula for confronting the paradox of law, and thus more than merely an internal consistency formula or a formula for the adequacy of the law in relation to its environment. Instead of being the contingency formula of law, justice would be its transcendence formula. Questions of justice would not be concerned merely with esoteric speculations of legal or economic theory, but with experiences that have practical relevance, even if no criteria of justice are provided at the same time: the sight of a limitless justice, the extreme, but justified demands of which can never be realised; the unbearable experience of an infinite responsibility in the face of the impossibility of decision; the sense of a fundamental failure of law; the encounter with *tragic choices* which end in injustice and guilt whatever decision one takes. The symbolisation of transcendence would then no longer be limited to religion as a specialised social system in accordance with the schema of functional differentiation, but would be an authentic experience for the legal system itself, as it would be also for the economic and other social systems, whose contingency formulas are based around their specific experiences of paradox. It has already proved impossible to centralise the reflexive theories of partial systems, for example legal theory and economic theory, in the knowledge system, and the reflection of social identity must therefore be seen as a decentralised practice within the partial systems themselves. Given this, how likely is it that the transcendence formulas of social institutions are dealt with exclusively within the system of religion and not within these institutions themselves? Justice is too important to be left to the priests (let alone to the lawyers). Is it not even the case – and this is the question I shall end with – that Derrida's profound and demanding analyses of the gift and of justice, as the transcendence and not the contingence formulas of the economy and of the law, should be viewed as new, idiosyncratic and in a true sense historically and socially adequate forms of religious experience in a time of extreme polycontexturality?

Notes

This chapter was previously published as 'Economics of gift, positivity of justice: the mutual paranoia of Jacques Derrida and Niklas Luhmann', *Theory, Culture and Society*, 18:1 (2001), 29–47. Copyright © 2001 by the author. Reprinted by permission of SAGE Publications, Ltd.

1. Luhmann's and Derrida's most relevant texts on law and economy are Derrida, *Specters of Marx*; Derrida, *Given Time*, vol. 1; Derrida, 'Force of law'; Luhmann, *Law as a Social System*; Luhmann, 'Legal argumentation'; Luhmann, *Wirtschaft der Gesellschaft*; Luhmann, *Sociological Theory of Law*.
2. Luhmann, 'Paradoxie des Entscheidens', p. 287.
3. Derrida, 'Force of law', p. 52.
4. Schmitt, *Concept of the Political*; Schmitt, *Political Theology*.
5. Derrida is quite explicit on this point, e.g. Derrida, 'Force of law', p. 933.
6. In his analysis of the precarious relation between positive law and justice, Derrida asks explicitly for a 'compromise between two incommensurable and radically heterogeneous dimensions', ibid., p. 1004; cf. on the same issue, Derrida, *Specters of Marx*, pp. 73–5. Luhmann argues for a difficult balance within contemporary justice, rendering 'adequate complexity of law ... compatible with internal decisional consistency': Luhmann, *Law as a Social System*, pp. 219–20.
7. For the ongoing debate between deconstruction and systems theory, see Koschorke and Vismann (eds), *Widerstände der Systemtheorie*; Hahn, 'Vom Kopfstand des Phonozentrismus'; Stäheli, 'Latent Places'; Berg and Prangel, *Kommunikation und Differenz*; Cornell, 'Relevance of time'.
8. Felici and Trifone, *Dizionario Garzanti*, p. 1432.
9. Derrida, *Given Time*, vol. 1, ch.1.
10. Luhmann, *Law as a Social System*, pp. 459–60; Luhmann, 'Third question'.
11. Fletcher, 'Paradoxes in legal thought', p. 1279.
12. Benjamin, 'Critique of Violence', pp. 277–300.
13. On paradox and self-reference in general, see Dupuy and Teubner (eds), *Paradoxes of Self-Reference*. On the paradoxes of legal self-reference see Teubner, *Law as an Autopoietic System*, ch.1.
14. Derrida, 'Force of law', p. 943.
15. Luhmann, 'Third question', p. 154.
16. Derrida, 'Force of law', pp. 1027 ff.

17 Luhmann, 'Sthenography', p. 134. His most explicit critique of Derrida's work can be found in Luhmann, 'Deconstruction as second-order-observing'.
18 On various social practices of de-paradoxification in general, see Luhmann, 'Paradoxy of observing systems'; Luhmann, 'Why does society describe itself as postmodern?'; on the institutional history of de-paradoxification in law, Luhmann, 'Third question'.
19 Luhmann, *Wirtschaft der Gesellschaft*, p. 181.
20 Derrida, *Given Time*, vol. 1, p. 24.
21 Ibid., p. 30.
22 Lyotard, *The Differend*; Habermas, *Between Facts and Norms*; Levinas, *Totality and Infinity*.
23 Husserl, *Cartesian Meditations*, pp. 128 ff.
24 Lyotard, *The Differend*.
25 Derrida, *Writing and Difference*; Derrida, *Of Grammatology*.
26 On this double movement, see Dupuy, 'Deconstructing deconstruction'.
27 Levinas, *Totality and Infinity*.
28 Luhmann, 'Paradoxy of observing systems'; Luhmann, 'Observing re-entries', p. 490.
29 Derrida, 'Force of law', p. 959; Derrida, *Given Time*, vol. 1, pp. 1 ff.
30 Luhmann, *Social Systems*, ch. 3.
31 Luhmann, *Theory of Society*, vol. 1, p. 200.
32 Derrida, *Specters of Marx*, pp. 77 ff., where more or less journalistic impressions of globalisation are meant to revitalise the ambitious claims of Marx's social theory.
33 Luhmann, *A Systems Theory of Religion*, pp. 93–5.
34 Fish, *Doing What Comes Naturally*, pp. 155–6.
35 On this concept, see Günther, 'Life as Poly-Contexturality'.
36 On the legal and logical problems of self-referring rules, especially in constitutional law, see Suber, *Paradox of Self-Amendment*; Hart, 'Self-Referring Laws'; Ross, 'On self-reference'.
37 Teubner, 'King's many bodies'.
38 For this externalisation technique in law, see Luhmann, 'Verfassung als evolutionäre Errungenschaft'; in the economy, Luhmann, *Wirtschaft der Gesellschaft*, p. 100.
39 Wiethölter, 'Social Science Models', p. 53; Heller, 'Legal Discourse in the Positive State', p. 185.
40 E.g. Frankenberg, 'Down by Law', p. 336.
41 Habermas, *Philosophical Discourse of Modernity*, ch. 12.
42 Luhmann, *Theory of Society*, vol. 1, pp. 49 ff.
43 Derrida, *Margins of Philosophy*.
44 Luhmann, 'Observing re-entries', pp. 214 ff.; Luhmann, *Ausdifferenzierung des Rechts*, pp. 274 ff.; Luhmann, *Rechtssystem und Rechtsdogmatik*, p. 23.
45 Luhmann, 'Sinnform Religion', p. 16.
46 Derrida, 'Force of law', p. 959.
47 Ibid., p. 959.
48 Derrida, *Given Time*, vol. 1, pp. 31 ff.
49 Derrida, 'Force of law', p. 933.
50 Luhmann, 'Society, Meaning, Religion'; Luhmann, 'Religion and ultimate paradox'; Luhmann, *Religious Dogmatics*.
51 Blecher, *Zu einer Ethik der Selbstreferenz*.

3

Dealing with paradoxes of law: Derrida, Luhmann, Wiethölter

grandiosity of law in the ruins
Duncan Kennedy on Rudolf Wiethölter[1]

I Conflicts of laws under suspicion of paradox

Twenty-five years ago, when the great paradoxologists of our times were still quite differently engaged – Jacques Derrida was organising grammatological exercises and Niklas Luhmann kept reducing complexity – Rudolf Wiethölter already had that disquieting phenomenon, the paradox of law, in his sights.[2] When in 1977 he wrote a *punctatio* in the *Festschrift* for his academic teacher Gerhard Kegel, consisting of a list of points for and against Kegel's concept of conflict of laws, it was still a nagging suspicion. Could it be that instead of the social theory Wiethölter was passionately seeking *above* the conflicts of laws, there was only a grandiose paradox *behind* them? In 2002, in a *punctatio* for his academic disciples – *punctatio* now signifying a non-binding pre-contractual commitment as well as a medieval practice, deriving from the Orient, of interpreting the future from points distributed randomly in the sand – the suspicion had turned into certainty. After discussing various critical, deconstructive and systems approaches, Wiethölter describes the primary task of the jurist with the riddling formula:

> 'administration of justice' as cultivation of the paradox of law itself, of simultaneously its preservation and its treatment.[3]

An antonym substitution has taken place here: the counter-concept to the conflict of laws is no longer social theory, which produces identity, but the paradox of law, which produces confusion.[4] In this chapter, I wish to explore the consequences of this substitution of a different opposite, a substitution which encapsulates the searching and learning processes of the last twenty-five years.

It was the ambitious project of the Kegel *Festschrift* to detach the mode of thought which is characteristic of the conflict of laws from private international law and to make it serve not only other areas of law, but also and especially a social theory of law. The point was no longer merely to reflect conflicts between national legal systems theoretically and to cope with them in practice, but to generalise conflict-of-laws thinking itself so as to make it yield results for conflicts between sets of norms, areas of law and legal institutions, as well as for those between social systems, indeed even for divergences between competing social theories. The twofold recourse to the historical experience of private international law and to competing social theories managed to establish 'conflict of laws' as the central category for a legal reconstruction of social contradictions.[5]

With this sort of generalised conflict-of-laws thinking, Wiethölter was able to build on the classics of social theory and to draw selectively on ideas in Hegel's dialectic of negation, Marx's real social contradictions, Weber's polytheism and Simmel's productivity of conflict. Social contradictions as the driver of social dynamics was the guiding theme. But in Wiethölter's thought, social contradictions did not appear as such, but only after a specifically legal metamorphosis. In a complicated process of translation, social contradictions were transformed into conflicts of legal norms. The multiplicity of different kinds of social conflict was thereby reduced to the necessity of having to take a legal decision, which requires venues, procedures and criteria. The concepts of the sociology of conflict were replaced by conflict-of-laws doctrine (connecting factors, characterisation, reference, *renvoi*, *ordre public*, adaptation, internal and external consistency). Wiethölter built up towering hierarchies of norms, convoluted interlacings of rules of conflict and of substantive rules, themselves overarched in turn by still higher rules of both kinds. There was a continuing search for ultimate justifications, supreme norms, supreme courts. The 'self-righteous substantive norm' criticised by Kegel was outdone twice over, first by his characterisation of the 'self-righteous conflict of laws' created by Kegel himself, and then in a critique of Kegel through a 'self-righteous meta-systemic law'.[6] But the secret judge of the whole conflict-of-laws affair was to be social theory, itself an arena of conflict between different approaches and thus for its part searching for a super-theory to guide it.[7]

An exemplary illustration of this conflict-of-laws style of thought can be found in Wiethölter's critique of the current synthesis between the protection of subjective rights and that of legal institutions. In this context, Ludwig Raiser had formulated the famous conciliatory formula of 'the private actor as a functionary of the overall legal system', which postulates that the exercise of subjective rights has to be seen as oriented towards institutions. The protection of individual rights by the law is always already serving the protection of important social and legal institutions. The formula was, for the time being, the last and most important outcome of a long debate between various dualisms of private/public, subjective rights/objective law, entitlements/infrastructures, contract/organisation, individual/institution, and had become widely accepted in contemporary doctrine in both private law and public law.[8] For Wiethölter, however, the formula of subjective right and legal institution was by no means the solution, but that which constituted the problem in the first place. It could serve neither as a substantive nor as a conflict rule; it was itself the conflict. Moreover, in 1977, it seemed to Wiethölter that there was a clear trend towards a left-Kegelian 'paradigm shift'. Turning away from the conciliatory formula, Wiethölter advocated a 'politicisation of private law' in the form of a 'transformation from *contractual constitutional law*, i.e. classical 'private law', into *organisational constitutional law*, i.e. 'modern' non-private law,'[9] in which the common good resulted not from the institution-oriented exercise of subjective rights by private actors, but from political conflict and consensus within legally constituted social organisations.

II Changing the mode of thought: from conflicts to paradoxes

Yet even in 1977 nagging doubts were already visible, which would grow stronger as time went on. Scarcely had Wiethölter developed his own formula of a 'self-righteous meta-systemic law' than he was already placing it under suspicion of paradoxicality. He himself allowed the mutual outbidding of conflictual and substantive norms to founder on the Münchhausen trilemma of norm justification: infinite regress, arbitrary rupture or circularity.[10] At that point, he fell back on 'social practice', in which the hierarchical levels of conflict rules and substantive rules are blurred, as a last-ditch stop-gap solution.[11] Behind it all, though, it becomes increasingly clear that that which is called conflict of laws on the outside means paradoxes of law on the inside. Conflicts of laws are nothing but epiphenomena of legal paradoxes. Ultimately, it is the antonym substitution already mentioned that is happening here: the opposition identity/difference, which in Wiethölter's work appears in the relation between the theory-led decision that produces identity and the conflict of norms that produces difference, is converted into the opposition paradox/difference.

This conversion is exemplified in the way Wiethölter is reformulating the rights versus institution issue today. First, a conflict resolution which tends to be one-sided and which, in transforming a contractual constitution into an organisational constitution, proceeds by way of a politicisation of conflict guided by social theory is (implicitly) withdrawn. The conflict itself is then interpreted as an expression of an underlying paradox, a problem that cannot be got at with decisions on the basis of venues, criteria or procedures:

> It is no surprise that our legal semantics of 'legal protection' (with guaranteed subjective rights at the centre) and 'institutional protection' (with temporal, material and social infrastructural guarantees at the centre) does neither 'good' nor 'justice' to the contemporary requirements of the timeless paradox of law (in brief, of a law of conflict of laws about (legally) right and wrong admitted into the law).[12]

These are no mere semantic adaptations to fashionable paradoxologies, but thought-out, dense formulations expressing word for word the structural differences between conflict of laws and paradox. What this means is no longer a reference to 'social practice', but a change in thinking. Listed in outline, this involves the following:

(1) Conflicts of laws are contradictions between different claims of validity: either A or not-A; law or non-law; one norm or the other; one social model or the other. Paradoxes can of course manifest themselves as contradictions, but they have a more complicated structure, due to their self-referentiality or to their 'self-righteousness':[13] A because not-A and not-A because A; legal because illegal, and illegal because legal. Is the Cretan lying when he says about himself that he is lying? Is the law itself legal, i.e. is it legal or illegal to judge conflicts on the criteria of legal/illegal?

(2) This is the reason for the differences in outcome. Conflicts can be resolved by deciding between alternatives, or they allow for a compromise. Both these ways are barred in the case of paradoxes. One cannot escape the oscillation between their poles by deciding, since each decision sets the self-referential circle off again. The situation is one of undecidability in principle. The result of paradox is paralysis.[14] This is why paradoxes are ordinarily either ridiculed or tabooed.[15]

(3) Conflicts require criteria, venues, procedures in order for a decision to be possible. Paradoxes cannot be overcome that way. There is no *via regis* towards a 'solution' for them, at most a *via indirecta*. It is not the decision of the conflict that they call into question, but the very conflict itself. At any rate one has to leave the beaten track. That is what makes dealing with them so hard, and the comparison of Wiethölter with Derrida and Luhmann so rewarding.

But why this fascination with paradoxes of all things? Why is Wiethölter, the proponent of a conflict-of-laws theory, who after all openly expresses a preference for the theory of rational discourse, interested in systems theory and deconstruction, which are obsessively engaged in revealing paradoxes? After all, Derrida's thought amounts to a 'deconstructive putrefaction of private law doctrine', as Habermas might put it if he were present and polemically minded: disclosing the ambivalences, uncertainties and paradoxes of law by formal logical operations and genealogical investigations. Is it, he might, present or absent, go on to ask, worth participating in a legal 'twilight of the gods'? And as regards the internal logic of systems theory, the idea that it should place paradoxes at its centre seems downright absurd. This means a self-abandonment of the approaches that had been guiding it so far: compatibility of structure and function, possibilities of cybernetic control, dealing with environmental complexity through requisite variety. Nothing is more anti-systemic than paradoxes. They lead only to contradiction, inconsistency, chaos, paralysis and horror.

It is tempting to conflate these destructive tendencies of both theories with a resigned, pessimistic, melancholic undertone that is perceptible more than occasionally in Wiethölter's analyses of present-day private law, to the tune 'everything is possible, but nothing can be done'.[16] Wiethölter had indeed already embarked on deconstructing the law before the word even existed in Germany: his merciless revelations of ostensible uncertainties in the doctrines of private law, which made him so unpopular within the profession, show this, as does his ruthless disclosure of inconsistencies in legal and social theory.[17] Another entirely deconstructive aspect is Wiethölter's 'legal negativism',[18] his refusal to give specific answers to specific legal questions, be it to 'solve' cases, 'discover' doctrinal constructions or 'decide' disputed questions of legal theory – something which he rigorously sustained for decades. In its ascetic severity, his stance of refusal confirms Derrida's famous aporias of law, in which, with unsparing inevitability, every legal argument leads into a position of suspension, of *epoche*, of undecidability.[19]

Yet this interpretation is probably still too facile. For ultimately it is not their undeniable critical and destructive potential that drives the interest in paradoxes.

What is really fascinating about them are the productive possibilities of working with them.[20] Here lies, as even cultural theorists admit, the advantage of systems theory over the resigned pathos of deconstruction in the work of Paul de Man and his epigones, an advantage which is hard to dispute. This is because systems theory sees in 'the paradoxes arising from self-reference not an end point, but the starting-point for further evolution. That confers upon this theory, compared to other recent post-metaphysical constructions, a relatively high degree of comprehensiveness.'[21] Not only do worlds of meaning necessarily lead one into paradoxes, but paradoxes bring forth new worlds of meaning. Not only does the conflict of laws produce Kegelian aporias, but these aporias produce new conflicts. Paradoxes are not logical errors that have to be extirpated if one is to advance. How much they are needed today as a ubiquitous and central moment of social dynamics is demonstrated in the following extreme formulation: Paradoxes take the place of the transcendental subject; typical structures are historically contingent phenomena.[22] Applied to the law, this means:

> The legal paradox in a nutshell: The law assumes that which it is meant to effect, this included, excluded third, which ensures at once that the conditions for its own possibility will be exhausted and that they can be regenerated, in other words that justifications are both unfeasible and enacted.[23]

Taking the example of human rights, this is what the thought pattern of paradox-driven legal development looks like:[24] The paradoxical circular relationship between society and individual (society constitutes individuals, who in turn constitute society) is, as it were, the a priori that underlies all historically varying human rights concepts. Constituted communicatively as persons, people of flesh and blood irritatingly make themselves felt also as non-communicatively constituted individuals/bodies, despite all their socialisation, and insist on their 'rights'. This tension in the relation between individual and society brings forth various socially adequate structures of meaning that are deconstructed anew again and again in the course of historical development (schematised in historical phases: human nature in old natural law, the agreement of individuals in social contract, the entry of persons endowed with natural rights into the state of civilisation, the a priori validity of subjective rights, the political positivisation of individual fundamental rights, the scandalisation of human rights breaches in world society). Is it possible, then, that this obsessive interest is due to the fact that it is precisely paradoxes – and no longer social contradictions or clashes of rationality – that constitute the motive force of legal development? And could this be the reason for Wiethölter's puzzling formula according to which the administration of justice is not simply the elimination of the legal paradox for the sake of legal order, but on the contrary its 'maintenance and treatment'?

A comparison with the contradiction-driven dynamics in classical social theory clarifies the specific features of a paradox-driven dynamics. Not unlike the contradiction in dialectics, the paradox

> is founded on an initial irreconcilable disruption. In common with the Hegelian concept it is dynamic, but it exceeds his conception of the original contradiction as a strict bipolar one. The signified and its unmarked other are not given in an a priori correlation. They cannot be deduced 'logically' from each other, but originate in contingent distinctions, which can draw the frontier between signification and non-signification differently each time.[25]

The interplay of de-paradoxification and re-paradoxification is therefore anything but a cumulative sequence of negations, a 'transcending' of the contradiction, a progress of the spirit.[26] It is more a case of the return of the same, a continual oscillation between paradox and structure, a dialectic without synthesis. The successive relation between paradox and difference shows an experimenting, incremental, exploratory production of orders that almost needs to stumble over contingencies in order to construct new differences. And, ever-present, there is the permanent haunting of the worlds of meaning by their deconstruction, which time and again brings irruptions of chaos into civilisation.

Like Marx's 'real contradictions', paradoxes, too, appear as turned on their heads, since they do not occur as disturbances in the ideal world of thought, but, as 'real paradoxes', force social relations to dance. But, unlike them, paradoxes do not suggest that there is an implied logic of decay in the primary and secondary contradictions of the social order which would then enable the revolutionary Big Bang. Real paradoxes are highly ambivalent. They have the potential to be destructive and paralysing, but they simultaneously contain productive, creative possibilities. Both options are open: paralysis or structural innovations? It is not some sort of determinism that is at work here, but sheer contingency. Catastrophe or a productive new order that is itself threatened by catastrophe – both are equally likely. This ambivalence can serve as a plausible explanation for the oft-noted, enormous pressure to innovate which is experienced by today's societies.

At the same time, the quality of the de-paradoxification is also strangely pathological. It promises no solution of the crisis, but at most its temporary postponement, concealment, invisibilisation, suppression, repression.[27] It is only a matter of time before crisis breaks out again. Not by chance this recalls theories of repression, in which repression leads to the repeated symptomatic manifestation of that which had been repressed. 'Something is rotten in the state of Denmark' – this is the permanent condition of such societies, even if the temporary de-paradoxification were to be 'well-done'. And unlike in psychoanalysis, there is no therapy that promises success. Direct confrontation with the paradox does not bring about liberation, but paralysis. At best, our society relies on a rationality of repression.

The question then arises, however, whether it is possible that the fascination with paradoxes might be not just an intellectual fashion, but could have something to do with their adequacy to the object. Does the shift from classic theories of contradiction to paradoxologies reflect the twentieth-century experiences of totalitarianisms, two world wars and ecological and psychological catastrophes in the midst of advanced civilisation? Does it offer a plausible interpretive model for the experience that precisely the highly developed rationality patterns of economics, politics and the law are exposed to the incursions of arbitrariness, irrationality, indeed violence, in the performance of their most mundane operations? And, what is more, not from the outside, but from their inmost *arcana*? Does it also serve as a plausible interpretive model for the dominance of a cognitive style that no longer appears in the guise of a great, consistent social project, but of a groping experimentation in conditions of radical uncertainty? The following argument from Jean Clam may make the current search for non-teleological strategies of de-paradoxification plausible:

> The problem of this teleological form of de-paradoxification is that it sets off a dynamic which radically negates the paradox (as an evil to be eliminated). The modern experience of this dynamic has shown that the more hopeful the enthusiasm for attaining or imposing the *telos*, in other words, the more thorough the destruction of the foundations of the paradox, the stormier and more damaging the return of that which had been negated. De-paradoxification by way of utopian teleologies is akin to treating the original paradoxes as if they were something that can be reconciled and overcome, rather than something that cannot be transcended and that generates systems. This in turn justifies shifting the certainty of reconciliation along the temporal dimension, which is given a macrohistorical format for this purpose. Confidence in the possibility of transcending the paradox, together with a postponement of any corroboration thereof to the distant future, protects blind raging at the paradox from the possibilities of learning from failure.[28]

III Luhmann: sociologising deconstruction

Thus, the question of how society deals with paradoxes moves into the foreground. Regardless of how systems theory and deconstruction analyse the syntax of paradoxes, or describe their semantics within the context of textuality and society, the real question is their pragmatics.[29] Here it is probably Luhmann who has set the tone against a merely destructive paradoxology, against a resigned and simultaneously provocative presentation of the inconsistencies, against settling for a mere legal negativism:

> It could well be that our society is the outcome of a structural and semantical *catastrophe* in the sense meant by René Thom – that is, the result of a fundamental change in the form of stability that gives meaning to states and events. If this is so, the deconstruction of our metaphysical tradition is indeed something that *we* can do *now*. But if so, it would be worthwhile to choose the instruments of deconstruction with sufficient care so that by using them we could gain some information about our postmetaphysical, postontological, postconventional, postmodern – that is, *postcatastrophical* condition.[30]

'By their fruits ye shall know them.' Compared to the systems theory of law and to legal deconstructivism, what insights into the postcatastrophical condition of the law does Wiethölter's conflict-of-laws thinking provide? If the aim is to gather information for the law of today, what standards of 'sufficient care' must be respected in choosing the instruments of deconstruction? In the careful handling of paradoxes, Wiethölter initially follows in Luhmann's footsteps, but then parts ways with him at particular points to pursue search interests that are decidedly his own.

First step – paradoxification: Even in the second-order observation that first discloses the paradoxes, the instruments employed must be chosen with sufficient care. For this observation is more than an information-free deconstruction of configurations of meaning, since it can go beyond the destruction of illusions to say something about their socio-historical significance. Why does the legal system need illusions, and which ones? Luhmann demonstrates this with regard to the illusion of the binary legal code, which is exposed to the paradoxes of its own self-reference. Behind the distinction between legal/illegal he finds both the foundational paradox of law and the decisional paradoxes of daily legal practice, and he then asks about the social meaning of this context of delusion, in which the legal code has remained astonishingly stable in spite of its manifest artificiality, whereas the forms of de-paradoxification in the programmes of law have constantly changed.[31]

At first, Wiethölter follows this analysis. But then he looks for the central paradox of law elsewhere: not behind the binary code of legal/illegal, but behind the law of the conflict of laws applicable to the conflict between law and non-law. What is at issue now are no longer the empty paradoxes of the legal system's self-reference, the problems of mere self-legitimation of the Münchhausen trilemma, but the much more substantial paradoxes of the law's hetero-reference, the question of the law's relation to the world. In his very formulation of the fundamental legal paradox, Wiethölter thus already raises the normative question of whether and how the law does the world justice.

Second step – de-paradoxification: Since each and every distinction can be paradoxified, with the result of paralysing thought and decision, the truly productive achievement of the paradox consists in also provoking that which promises delivery from this danger, the counter-forces of de-paradoxification. According to Luhmann, the law only arrives at autopoietic system formation by converting the paradox into a difference, by misunderstanding the endless oscillation between legal and illegal as a conditionable contradiction, indeed by technicalising the paradox into a programmable binary code.[32]

Wiethölter follows the argument with polite interest. Of burning concern to him, however, is the question of how the paradoxes in the relation of the law to the world can be transformed into decidable conflicts of norms. This seems to offer a more productive explication of the paradox, because it directs the search not just towards the enabling conditions for the self-reproduction of legal practice, but towards venues, procedures and criteria of conflict decision that 'do justice' to the world. And this is not all: the form of the conflict itself changes in line with changing social conditions of de-paradoxification. Hence Wiethölter's eloquent silence in response to the request to name the entities in conflict, the question of what it is that is clashing: Is it norms, principles, social models, theories, rationalities?

Third step – sociologising the paradox: What is at issue here is the choice of the observer who is to carry out the de-paradoxification. Luhmann chooses social communication and not mental acts or physical distinctions. This consistent sociologisation of deconstruction is where he differs so much from Derrida. Beset by ambivalences, uncertainties and breakdowns, the social systems of communication observed by systems theory each invent their specific new distinctions which they are able to stabilise for a while.

Wiethölter, however, selects a more awkward observer's viewpoint. At first, in setting his sights on the 'law of the conflict of laws applicable to the conflict between law and non-law', he seems to be choosing the legal system, which internalises the opposition of law and society in a re-entry, to be the observer. This is where the translation of social aporias into decidable conflicts between norms takes place. But this is followed by the typical Wiethölter gesture of referring to a trinitarian authority as the observer of this re-entry, namely the magic triangle of great social theories: critical theory, autopoiesis theory and economic institutionalism. This is where Wiethölter's normativism differs from the cognitivism of Luhmann, according to which sociology should confine itself to noting what decisions are made in the conflict of laws. For in the translation of conflicts between legal norms into models of social theory, Wiethölter glimpses a great opportunity to acquire normative criteria for the decision of conflicts of law.

But this is not enough. Wiethölter avoids deciding the dispute between rival social theories, all of which make some claim to be authoritative. Despite personal sympathies for Habermas's discourse theory, he scrupulously keeps all three at an equal distance, and gives any overly close contact with them a wide berth. This does in no way entail a non-committal theoretical relativism. Nor is there any claim of providing a super-theory, but only of marking a puzzling void in the Bermuda Triangle of social theories, of creating a space of suspension within the bounds of which the cancelling out of the rival theories' validity claims is the condition for putting the law on trial. Wiethölter places his hopes in mutual irritation, even in reciprocal learning by the rival theories involved, but without identifying this meta-process with the rationality of discourse, of systems or of the market. This, it seems, is how his breathless to-and-fro translations of conflicts of laws into the language of discourse theory, of systems theory and of economic institutionalism must be understood. In the course of translation, they are meant to create a normative surplus value. And it is only provisionally, only tentatively that he recommends drawing the initial distinction within critical theory, and then, in the light of this distinction, to continue with the other theories as subsequent distinctions. But in seeing the relation between the theories as one where they illuminate each other's weak points, he continually stresses the provisional nature of this decision.[33]

Fourth step – return of the paradox and its renewed concealment: According to Luhmann, social catastrophes occur in the correlations between social structure and semantics when change in social structures ruins the semantics. What characterises today's problems is that the fundamental structural change of functional differentiation has completely destroyed the old European semantics, and even the hectic *polysémies* of postmodernity can be understood only as a restless search for socially adequate self-descriptions. A pulsating historical rhythm of continually repeated destruction and reconstruction is at work here: paradoxifications provoke the search for new, socially adequate distinctions, and under specific conditions these in turn are forced to confront their own paradoxes. But what conditions determine the recursive revelation and concealment of the paradox? Systems theory identifies two: the pressure of social problems and communicative plausibility. New differences, which are themselves deconstructable, are accepted by social communication if they are plausible, i.e. compatible with other valid distinctions. At the same time, social communication prohibits their ever-possible re-paradoxification when the pressure of social problems is too great.[34]

Wiethölter himself has always been on this sort of 'relativist' search for de-paradoxifications that are historically and socially appropriate, and he regards systems theory, as the most advanced social theory to date, as perfectly suitable to assess them. Yet he cannot content himself with a 'cool' systems-theoretical analysis that merely notes pressure from social problems and registers plausibilities. Behind pressure and plausibility he energetically seeks their preconditions, which, in ever-changing enigmatic formulations, he calls the 'surplus value of law', the 'factor X' of judicial activism, or 'non-law as law'.[35] Plausibilities are not simply to be noted, but provocatively to be doubted. And what is required is not dispassionate observation, but active commitment to increasing social problem pressure. This political mobilisation of sociologically crystallised structures seems to me to be the real message of his misleading formula of a 'political theory of law' in contradistinction to a non-political social theory of law. Here Wiethölter seems to be coming close to more recent deconstructivist versions of systems theory, according to which the way paradoxes are dealt with has to be seen as a genuinely political issue in all social systems (not just in institutionalised politics).[36] Even outside the political system, the 'political' thus appears as the making of decisions in a context of undecidability: as the dissolution of semantic ruptures into antagonistic arrangements, enciphered à la Wiethölter as the dissolution of the paradox of law into conflicts between law and non-law.

What Wiethölter finds acceptable in systems theory is therefore the fundamental challenge of real paradoxes, inevitably recurring in the course of structural change and demanding the construction of new social identities. Equally acceptable are the 'relativist' criteria regarding the historical, substantive and social adequacy of these new identities, which are thus compatible with other social distinctions and respond to the pressure of social problems.

What is to be criticised, however, is the strange void in the architecture of systems theory, an architecture which does present us with an impressive hierarchy of levels of reflection, but ultimately fails to complete it. At a first level, basic self-reference is at work (the self-reference of elementary events): one legal act is referring to the next legal act, and reflexively to itself. At a second level, the reflexivity of processes applies: the creation of legal norms is itself made subject to norms (constitution, procedural law, secondary norms). At a third level, reflection operates as self-referential reflection in the norm theories and validity theories of law, on the one hand, and as reflection of system–environment relations, on the other. Here legal theory appears as social theory, as legal theories of the person and the individual, and as ecological legal theory.[37] Thus all the boundaries of law are reflected in legal theory – except one. What is excluded from the reflection of law are the boundaries of the meaning of law itself, not the questions as to the meaningless, nor those as to the negation of meaning, which is itself meaning, but those beyond meaning. While Luhmann asks about how and whether the law does justice to its environment, he does not ask about whether and how it does justice to the world. According to Luhmann's system of law, in the concept of justice, the law does possess a contingency formula, but it does not have a transcendence formula. And this is what Wiethölter is looking for.

His criticism of systems theory is likely to focus on the exclusive way it localises the reflection of transcendence in only one differentiated system. According to Luhmann, in traditional society, transcendence was reflected at various loci in society. The dimension of the religious was present everywhere, including in the law (natural law and justice had religious connotations as a matter of course). But in Luhmann's theory, secularisation entails the de-transcendentalisation of all social subsystems and a concentration of the reflection of transcendence in only one system of meaning, that of religion.[38] But is this not at variance with the tough resistance to secularisation displayed by social utopias (socialism, fascism, neo-liberal doctrines of salvation), a resistance which is palpable also and especially in the highly rationalised subsystems of politics, law, the economy and science? Is there not an otherwise inexplicable manifestation of doctrines of salvation here, of eschatological hopes that find expression not only in pop religion and New Age movements, but precisely within the secularised systemic rationalities? Max Weber's characterisation of social rationalities as a new absolute polytheism attests this for theory, just as the ideological wars of the twentieth century, which had precious little to do with religion as a differentiated system of meaning, do for practice.

A parallel has to be drawn here to the differentiation of knowledge. It is true that the production of knowledge is concentrated in the knowledge system (universities), but along with this, the production of knowledge and the reflection of this production also happen in other social subsystems (legal theory, political theory, economic theory). And the reflection remains specific to the relevant subsystem, even when it is conducted at universities in academic form. The argument against the way Luhmann ignores the question of doing justice to the world runs as follows: If, in the course of social differentiation, academia has not managed to monopolise the reflection of the relation between the subsystems and their environments, but instead is forced to leave it to these subsystems themselves, why should religion succeed in monopolising the reflection of the boundaries of meaning? The empirical test for this would consist in asking where in society social utopias are designed.

It is here, in regard to this transcendence of positivity, that Jacques Derrida's idiosyncratic contribution to the handling of the paradox of law begins. His more recent analyses, in which he turns deconstructive thinking towards social institutions, seem to be not just about the mere disruptions of deconstruction, but about bringing a disquieting awareness of transcendence back into the highly rationalised worlds of the economy, of science, politics and law. His astonishing theses concern the paradoxical effects of the 'pure gift' as against the profit-led economy,[39] of 'friendship' as against professionalised politics,[40] of 'forgiveness' as against secularised morality[41] and of 'justice' as against highly technicised law.[42] All of these are referential excesses that reactivate utopian energies from quite different sources. How far can the 'political theory of law' identify with this?

IV Derrida: theologising deconstruction

Luhmann is certainly doing Derrida an injustice when he accuses him of simply staying in the ambivalence of deconstruction; of merely frightening people with his paradoxes; of producing no insights into the new world with his verbal acrobatics.[43] Luhmann is constructing a false alternative here between staying in deconstructive ambivalence on the one hand and creating systemic eigenvalues on the other. At any rate as far as his late work is concerned, this alternative does no longer do justice to Derrida. For since 'Force of law: the mystical foundation of authority', Derrida in particular has been seeking practical political ways out of the paralysis of deconstruction. In deconstructing law, only the first step proposed by him consists in reducing the law to paradoxes. This means, firstly, the paradox of decision – there is no determinable meaning of law, but only *différance*', the continuing transformation and deferment of the meaning of law – and secondly, the paradox of ultimate justification, the founding of law on arbitrary force. But this does not lead to a paralysis of thought; instead, it is only in these unfathomable abysses that justice as a problem becomes conceivable at all: 'Justice as the possibility of deconstruction'.[44] The next step of deconstructive thought leads to a 'journey through the desert'. And this is indeed a reference, disconcerting for today's style of academic thinking, to transcendence, to mystic force, to encounters with the other as in Levinas's philosophy of otherness, to the challenge to modern rationalities posed by 'pure' justice, the gift, friendship, forgiveness. This is followed by the third step, however, a step one would not expect after a deconstruction of law and a reference to transcendence: a 'compromise' of transcendence with immanence, a serious and detailed reengagement of deconstruction with the calculation of rules and legal argumentation – but in the light of the unending demands of otherness.

Thus, we must reconsider the way in which systems theory and deconstruction differ in their circumvention of paradox. It is not that one theory persists in paralysis while the other seeks new eigenvalues in de-paradoxification, but rather that both are looking for different ways out of paradox. It may be more appropriate to indicate their directions: sociologisation versus theologisation of paradox.[45]

How far will the political theory of law go along with this? Wiethölter likes to cite Adorno: *'Chaos in Ordnung bringen'*[46] – an ambiguous formulation which can be read both as 'sorting out chaos' and as 'introducing chaos into order'. Luhmann's de-paradoxification stresses only one side of this ambiguous formula, in doing everything to avoid looking at the paradoxes and in converting the threatening chaos into a new order. By contrast, Derrida chaoticises order in that he seeks to plumb the dark worlds of the paradox through a critique of the foundational violence of law, but subsequently looks for a compromise with the arguments and calculations of legal practice. According to this, justice is not an aim, not a consistency formula, not a contingency formula, but invocation, abyss, disruption, experience of contradiction, chaos within the law. This has thoroughly practical consequences for legal knowledge and legal decision-making: changing the situation as a decision *sub specie aeternitatis*, not just *sub specie societatis*.

As much as Wiethölter, the poetic non-systemist, may feel attracted to such chaoticisations of legal order, he is unlikely to be able to reconcile himself to the theologisation that Derrida favours. His strictly secularist understanding of state and law as opposed to religion requires that binding legal criteria be developed in immanence only. Specifically German experiences with mysticism and religiosity in the public sphere, with neo-paganism and with political theology, are likely to immunise him against a legal theology renewed in the name of deconstruction, at any rate in the public institutions of politics and law. The fairly explicit accusation Derrida directs against Benjamin in regard to his puzzling distinction between mystical and mythical force, a distinction which moreover is supposedly beyond human comprehension,[47] Wiethölter is likely to bring against Derrida himself with a *Tu quoque*: namely that by having recourse to 'mystic violence', one may be promoting complicity with evil.

The central quotation 'Deconstruction is justice'[48] should be able to bring into focus the common features of deconstruction and the political theory of law as well as their differences. Both agree that deconstructive analysis is anything but a mere nihilistic disintegration. In their view, it is looking for more than a *non-foundationalism* which proves the impossibility of providing the law with a foundation. For all the logical and doctrinal acuteness it employs, it is not aimed at a mere analytical dissection or logical critique of the law, or at an academic, politically non-committal criticism of concepts, constructs, norms and justice. Both emphatically claim to be looking for the rightness of law,[49] in Derrida's formulation

> to aspire to something more consequential, to change things, and to intervene in an efficient and responsible, though always, of course, very mediated way, not only in the profession but in what one calls the *cité*, the polis and more generally the world. Not, doubtless, to change things in the rather naive sense of calculated, deliberate and strategically controlled intervention, but in the sense of maximum intensification of a transformation in progress ... [that is occurring specifically in] ... an industrial and hyper-technologized society.[50]

In parallel, both theories also distance themselves cautiously but resolutely from a critique of power in the tradition that runs from Marx to Foucault. A critique of law from the standpoint of political economy, revealing the law to be an instrument for maintaining power, is regarded by both as obsolete, as is an obsessive micro-analysis of power. Political economy and micro-analysis of power, while useful, are not considered essential enough, not complex enough, not close enough to the interior of the law. Deconstruction, by contrast, means revealing the immanent violence at the core of the law itself.[51]

The relation of both to the modern rationality-based critique of law is somewhat more doubtful. It is true that both are engaged in disclosing the arbitrary nature of law and in criticising the lack of legitimacy of positive law. But both take a rather more sceptical view of Habermas's project to re-found law upon discursive rationality. In this regard, Derrida is emphatic in his deconstruction of a communicative rationality, because it closes its eyes to the unavoidable moment of violence in the foundational paradox and in the decisional paradox of everyday law. The violence of the founding act of law and the aporias of legal decision-making are not themselves accessible to rational discourse, not foundable, not justifiable, neither just nor unjust. Wiethölter is much more cautious here and retains critical theory's claim to found and legitimise law. Yet he distances himself from all optimistic advocates of a fundamental capacity of the law to be grounded in rational discourse, by insisting doggedly and deconstructively on the undecidability of conflicts of laws and hence their paradoxicality.

A definite parting of the ways between deconstruction and political legal theory is likely, however, when it comes to the mystical foundation of the authority of law. This is especially true of Derrida's recourse to Levinas's philosophy of otherness, which counterposes the totality of meaning with the exteriority of transcendence wherein justice appears as an infinite demand of the other. Political legal theory, which 'does not have some other law, nor something other than law, in mind, but the other (one possible other) of law',[52] may perhaps respect this course, but it is unlikely to follow it. At most it might reconstruct this way of speaking of the transcendence of the law in the shape of a temporalisation, a futurisation that cannot be made present, whereby justice can always only mean a postponement to the future. Derrida says 'justice remains, is yet to come, *à venir*'.[53] Wiethölter's formulation that a constitutional law of the law 'does not have some other law, nor something other than law, in mind, but the other (one possible other) of law, its redeemable surpluses of enabling rather than its unredeemed ones of promise'[54] shows his proximity to ideas of temporalisation and his sceptical distance from the ideas of otherness and transcendence in Levinas and Derrida.

V Wiethölter: reciprocity and (im)partiality

If, then, we have more or less grasped the eigenvalues of political legal theory as opposed to systemic and deconstructive paradoxologies, what are the consequences of the shift from the conflict of laws to paradox? What happens to the predominating conflict between the protection of rights and the protection of institutions?

As already indicated, Wiethölter not only distances himself from Ludwig Raiser's conciliatory formula of the private person as a functionary of the overall legal system, in which the protection of individual interests through subjective rights is simultaneously invoked for institutional protection, but he also retracts the conflict-of-laws norm of an 'organisational constitutional law' which he had initially had in view. Why? Because the underlying conflict is itself increasingly deconstructed. Again it is the two great deconstructors that are at work: problem pressure and communicative plausibility. The pressure of today's social problems renders the time-honoured distinction between the protection of rights and institutional protection implausible to such an extent that it can no longer evade its re-paradoxification. In the confrontation of the law with global social problems – such as ecological risks, the consequences of reproductive medicine or the exclusion of entire population groups as a result of worldwide functional differentiation, to mention just a few key points – it becomes clear that the law is facing social problems that can no longer be overcome through oscillation between subjective rights and objective law under the guidance of meta-norms.

That, however, means that the search for new de-paradoxifications becomes critical. Which new distinctions should fill the deconstructed void left behind by the *collision directrice* between the protection of rights and that of institutions? Wiethölter's formulations are extremely cautious in this regard:

> Perhaps the most exciting hope might come from the kind of 'law', *a portiori* the kind of 'constitutional law' or 'constitutional law of the law', that deals with conflict-of-laws principles at the level of law versus morality, law versus politics, law versus the economy, etc., or more exactly and more generally, law as a 'structural coupling' of 'life-world systems'. The 'protection of rights' and the 'protection of institutions' in contemporary translation would then become the protection of justifications for the functions of freedom.[55]

Still more cautiously formulated is his attempt to establish a new leading distinction: reciprocity versus (im)partiality. Both sides of this distinction have little to do with their traditional meaning, however. 'Reciprocity' is now understood as the mutual interlocking of autonomies and '(im)partiality' now means acceptance of autonomy subject to reserved controls.[56]

Overall, Wiethölter has drawn up *punctationes* that constitute a highly risky contractual offer. In conclusion, I maybe should try to respond, point by point, with suggestions for amending the preliminary contract, leaving it to others' interpretive skills to decide whether these amount to declarations of acceptance or new offers.

Point 1: conflicts between law and society: Wiethölter demands that the central distinction of law versus non-law be dissolved into various 'conflict-of-laws principles at the level of law versus morality, law versus politics, law versus the economy, etc.' This definitely shifts the focus of the law onto a radical pluralism of social autonomies. A whole bundle of distinctions now serves the purpose of de-paradoxification and becomes a substitute for de-plausibilised dichotomies of private versus public, subjective rights versus objective law, entitlements versus infrastructures, contract versus organisation, individual versus institution. At the centre of the 'constitutional law of the law', cutting across the obsolete dichotomy of private and public law, is the relation of the law to extremely varied social autonomies and their intrinsic rationalities and normativities.

The consequences of this shift are hard to foresee. At any rate this means finally taking leave of the triangle of politics/economy/law and accepting a polygon of social rationalities, all equally originary, that the law has to take into account. This makes the dispute over the social primacy of any one sub-rationality – under headings such as 'the economic society', 'the knowledge society', 'the organisational society' or 'the network society' – obsolete. The equation 'private law as economic law' has to be dissolved into the new equation 'private law as law of society', with 'law of society' implying from the outset not a law that is applicable to society as a whole, but a multiplicity of socially autonomous kinds of law. From the beginning, a constitutional law of the law must abandon any hopes for the totality of a societal constitution, for a locus where the identity of society as a whole can be defined, and adapt to an irreducible multiplicity of 'laws of society'. The challenge now consists no longer in 'economic constitutional law I, II, or III', but in a multiplicity of civil constitutions which do not merely bring a third sector of non-profit organisations and concerned citizens within the compass of the law, but in which the respective intrinsic normativities of social autonomies assert their claims.[57]

This should be accompanied by a reassessment of the traditional sources of law, where political-legislative law is devalued, while plural laws of society, in being the result of internal social conflicts, and judge-made law, in its ability to sense and reflect social normativities, are valorised. However, the priority goal for such civil constitutions would have to be to focus more decisively on the legal protection of non-economic and non-political normativities in society. The law must primarily confront the issue of 'institutional externalities', the 'environmental damage' caused by autonomisation processes.[58]

Point 2: sacrificium intellectus: The shift from a legal thinking modelled on the conflict of laws to one that is paradox-based, which is supposed to result in an 'updated translation' of the leading conflict between the protection of rights and institutional protection into that of reciprocity versus (im)partiality, has consequences for a style of legal thinking that academic moralists would rightly have to rebuke as intellectual dishonesty, obdurate dogmatism or, at the least, *pensiero debole*. If, however, it is true that each and every distinction can be deconstructed, that each and every last decision ends in undecidabilities, that each and every conflict of laws ends in paradoxes, then new distinctions, even those that can be upheld only temporarily, e.g. reciprocity versus (im)partiality, can be introduced only at the cost of renouncing criticism.

That is likely to be particularly difficult for such an astute lawyer and passionate enlightener as Wiethölter. But, having once given an inch to deconstructive, paradoxical thinking, one must, on pain of total paralysis, make the paradoxes of the newly proposed distinctions invisible, keep their latencies latent, repress their aporias, renounce their deconstruction, limit one's astuteness, refrain from criticism, set up delusions, lie to one's students. At any rate, that is, if the pressure of social problems requires it and plausibility within the network of socially accepted distinctions suggests it.

It follows from the deconstructibility of all institutions that critique without an alternative proposal does not count. 'Communication can be critical about every norm, but if it is critical, it must offer a substitute suggestion.'[59] This is not easy to reconcile with Wiethölter's suspension of the necessity of making a decision. Admittedly, this *sacrificium intellectus* is different from that demanded of the theologian in the name of faith, or the lawyer in the name of legal doctrine. For the pressure of social problems and plausibility are themselves not stable quantities, but historically variable, so that there can only ever be historically and socially adequate and therefore fluctuating justice. And both are in turn exposed to public reflection and dispute, as befits the programme of a political legal theory. Critical thinking must therefore focus on this level, the level of exhaustive analysis and discussion of social problems and social consistency, in order to be able to assess whether newly introduced distinctions such as reciprocity versus (im)partiality should be deconstructed again with all speed, or whether they may claim an at least temporary validity. And Sisyphus must at the same time beware of letting the arduously raised boulder, which might in the proper circumstances rest stably on the hilltop for a while, roll back down for lack of sufficient care in deconstruction.

Point 3: blind experimentalism: The groping character of a de-paradoxification of the distinction law versus non-law that suggests new distinctions only experimentally and exposes them to the test of social compatibility corresponds to a way of proceeding that not long ago was disparaged as 'muddling through', namely to a radical incrementalism, an experimentation in conditions of extreme uncertainty, a 'blind' stumbling of the law from case to case, a stumbling of politics from scandal to scandal. This implies a renunciation of grand designs, of the implementation of grand social projects – but not a renunciation of social theory. Theory now changes its role. It moves closer once more to the medieval divinatory practice of *punctatio*. It arbitrarily places points in the sand for the purpose of daring interpretations and predictions, in order to acquire points of reference from their retrospective confirmation or non-confirmation.

Legally, this calls for a reassessment of case law. The experience of the particular case and case-by-case law are to have primacy over the overhasty generalising of the universal law. But this would have to be accompanied by a decided politicising of case law which aims not merely to balance individual interests in an individual case of conflict, but which sees itself explicitly as a social-institutional experiment. If this was to be more than an empty formula for reviving the quiescent civil law, it would have to be reflected in procedural changes to the law, changes ranging from the collectivisation of the right of action, to public rights of participation and of being heard, to more sophisticated evidential procedures and to an *ex post*, learning way of regarding *res judicata*.

Point 4: society-wide reciprocity: This concept is equally far removed from the feudal relation of loyalty between prince and vassal and from the mutuality of market exchange. Seeking to create individual contractual parity using individual judicial corrections looks like naive recourse to outmoded concepts of *jus* as a balancing relation between individuals or of the autonomy of the bourgeois subject. What is sought is rather a way of compensating for asymmetric individual relations which restores balanced social relations by an extremely circuitous route across several system boundaries. The point is, then, reciprocity as mutual dependence of sub-autonomies, something that applies not just to the autonomy of social systems, but also to that of individuals, collectives, institutions and formal organisations. It is a thoroughly normative concept and therefore has much more in common with Durkheim's notion of solidarity and the social division of labour than it does with Luhmann's concept of the structural linkage of areas of social autonomy.

It is likely that the consequences of this sort of integration achieved by way of society-wide reciprocity will tend in the direction of a greater dissociation between law and institutionalised politics. If it is true that the leading role of politics in the integration of society as a whole has been, if not completely lost, at least significantly reduced, then reciprocity can no longer be described as an exclusively political project in which the law has to follow legislative action and, especially, legislative omission with thinking obedience, but should be seen as one where the law itself must engage responsively with emerging forms of reciprocity in society. In this context, proponents of a normative sociology such as Lon Fuller or Philip Selznick, but also François Ewald or Roger Friedland and Robert Alford are likely to be the protagonists of an intra- and inter-institutional 'morality' taking shape in society, the intrinsic potential of which the law can take up and, in thinking obedience, develop further.[60] It is not an accident that quite a number of network phenomena come into play at this point, overlying if not replacing the integrative effects of institutionalised politics. Wiethölter's scepticism in regard to the fashionable network debate is likely to disappear if it could indeed be shown that networks are not just hybrid legal formations between the law of contract and company law, but that intersystem networks can contribute decisively to creating society-wide reciprocity because they obey different logics of action.[61]

Point 5: impartial partiality: Through this openly paradoxical formula, political legal theory definitively distances itself from systems-theoretical or deconstructive paradoxologies. If the formula is meant to describe the relation between the law and social autonomy, as the following quotation suggests,

> [i]t simply is not the case that an asserted autonomy has ever by itself amounted to a guarantee for a decentralised and sectoral 'general good'. Rather, it has been itself a party, to which one can permit activities only in exchange for criteria which are formed in a way that is 'objectively justified', venues which are kept open and fairness procedures which are adhered to, in short, a 'relative impartiality' and capacity for universalisation,[62]

then it entails neither a sociologisation of law nor its theologisation, but a release of social potentials for normativity, a sort of maieutics.

Adopting a participatory perspective on legal discourse, this formula differs from Luhmann's systems sociology and its celebration of impartial academic detachment in its partiality, in a threefold sense: first, partiality for the normativity criteria of the legal tradition and the further development of law, which are rightly demanded, quite impartially, from the autonomous sectors of society; second, partiality for the normativity criteria of the autonomous sectors themselves, whose part the law will take in cases of conflict in order to resolve disputes impartially; finally, partiality for one of the strangest of Wiethölter's puzzling formulas, for 'society as society', which, though explicitly building on Luhmann's deconstruction of society, remains committed to the latter as it were in a counterfactual, utopian manner.[63]

The formula of impartial partiality also contains a dissociation from deconstruction, which in its concept of justice refers to a transcendent otherness of law. One of Wiethölter's most radical ideas is to be found here, and accordingly, he does formulate it with appropriate caution:

> Perhaps the emancipation of such law from law in the rival social theories, which, no doubt, as 'other than law' or 'other law', does not (yet) seem out of date, into an 'other of law' contains a step towards chances of realisation, and perhaps then as 'universal' general (not solely private) law. 'Law' would then not be bowing to social theory designs, but itself be one, and therefore at any rate not 'system', not 'discourse', not an 'undertaking'.[64]

Such a far-reaching autonomisation of law, a 'grandiosity of law in the ruins', which, quite in contrast to earlier formulations, moves away from a dependence on social theories and promotes the law itself to the position of a social theory design, would indeed transgress the boundaries of the law, though not in the direction of a transcendence of otherness, but of the immanence of a quasi-therapeutic relationship, which uses the healing normativity of medicine as its reference, not in the sense of externalisation in the direction of public health and biopolitics, but of a 're-entry' of the logic of wounding and healing into law.[65] In the end, the question that remains open in regard to this therapeutic relationship between law and society is this: Which is the therapist, and which the patient?

Notes

This chapter was previously published as 'Dealing with Paradoxes of Law: Derrida, Luhmann, Wiethoelter', trans. Iain L. Fraser, in Oren Perez and Gunther Teubner (eds), *On Paradoxes and Inconsistencies in Law* (Oxford: Hart, 2006), pp. 41–64. Reprinted by permission of Bloomsbury Publishing plc.

1 Kennedy, 'Comment on Rudolf Wiethölter', p. 516. The following texts by Wiethölter are available in English: Wiethölter, 'Materialization'; Wiethölter, 'Social Science Models' (1986); Wiethölter, 'Proceduralization'; Wiethölter, 'Just-ifications'.
2 Wiethölter, 'Begriffs- oder Interessenjurisprudenz'.
3 Wiethölter, 'Just-ifications', p. 73.
4 The fact that this antonym substitution represents a relevant social process and not a mere fallacy of thinking is stressed by Holmes, 'Poesie der Indifferenz', pp. 25 ff., 28.
5 By generalising the thinking used in the conflict of laws, Wiethölter set a precedent, explicitly followed by: Walz, *Steuergerechtigkeit*, pp. 199 ff.; Joerges, *Verbraucherschutz als Rechtsproblem*, pp. 123 ff.; Joerges, 'Zur Legitimität der Europäisierung des Privatrechts'; Teubner, *Law as an Autopoietic System*, ch. 6; Teubner, 'Altera pars'; Ladeur, 'Helmut Ridders Konzeption der Meinungs- und Pressefreiheit', pp. 281 ff.; Amstutz, *Evolutorisches Wirtschaftsrecht*, pp. 326 ff.
6 Wiethölter, 'Begriffs- oder Interessenjurisprudenz', pp. 246, 248, 256.
7 Ibid., pp. 229–30.
8 Raiser, 'Rechtsschutz und Institutionenschutz'.
9 Wiethölter, 'Begriffs- oder Interessenjurisprudenz', p. 260.
10 Ibid., p. 216; Wiethölter, 'Zum Fortbildungsrecht', p. 1.
11 Wiethölter, 'Begriffs- oder Interessenjurisprudenz', p. 213.
12 Wiethölter, 'Just-ifications', p. 67.
13 On paradoxes in a philosophical perspective, see Probst and Kutschera, 'Paradox'. On the distinctions between contradictions and paradoxes in a pragmatic perspective, see the classic treatise by Watzlawick *et al.*, *Pragmatics*. On dealing with paradoxes in law, see Fletcher, 'Paradoxes in legal thought'; Suber, *Paradox of Self-Amendment*. Cf. also Ross, 'On self-reference'; Hart, 'Self-Referring Laws'.
14 See Gumbrecht and Pfeiffer (eds), *Paradoxien, Dissonanzen, Zusammenbrüche*.
15 Watzlawick *et al.*, *Pragmatics*.
16 Wiethölter, 'Zur Argumentation im Recht', p. 100.
17 Since Wiethölter, *Rechtswissenschaft*.
18 Explicitly Wiethölter, 'Recht und Politik', pp. 155, 158.
19 Derrida, 'Force of law', pp. 959 ff.

20 Krippendorff, 'Paradox and Information', pp. 51–2; Luhmann, 'Sthenography', pp. 135 ff.; Watzlawick et al., *Pragmatics*, ch. 7.
21 Koschorke, 'Grenzen des Systems', p. 56.
22 The whole quotation reads: '... paradoxes are the only form in which knowledge is given *unconditionally*. They take the place of the transcendental subject whom Kant and his successors expected to have direct access to a knowledge that is unconditional, a priori valid, and insightful in and of itself. ... That conclusion does not by any means exclude questions about typical structures in which paradox resolutions gain relatively stable forms which are historically preserved ...'. Luhmann, *A Systems Theory of Religion*, p. 94.
23 Wiethölter, 'Ist unserem Recht der Prozeß zu machen?', p. 803.
24 Luhmann, 'Paradox der Menschenrechte'.
25 Clam, 'Grundparadoxie des Rechts', p. 138.
26 On the relation Luhmann–Hegel, cf. Luhmann, *Social Systems*, ch. 9, para. I.
27 See the articles collected in Gumbrecht and Pfeiffer (eds), *Paradoxien, Dissonanzen, Zusammenbrüche*.
28 Clam, 'Grundparadoxie des Rechts', p. 129.
29 In addition to the references in n. 13, see Krippendorff, 'Paradox and Information'; for legal paradoxes, Luhmann, *Law as a Social System*, pp. 459 ff.
30 Luhmann, 'Deconstruction as second-order-observing', p. 777 (emphasis in the original text).
31 Luhmann, *Law as a Social System*, pp. 173 ff.
32 Ibid.
33 Wiethölter, 'Zum Fortbildungsrecht', pp. 25 ff.
34 Luhmann, *Law as a Social System*.
35 Wiethölter, 'Zum Fortbildungsrecht', p. 1.
36 Stäheli, *Sinnzusammenbrüche*.
37 Luhmann, *Law as a Social System*, pp. 423 ff.
38 Luhmann, *A Systems Theory of Religion*, pp. 232 ff.
39 Derrida, *Given Time*, vol. 1.
40 Derrida, *Politics of Friendship*.
41 Derrida, 'Le siècle et le pardon'.
42 Derrida, 'Force of law'.
43 Luhmann, 'Deconstruction as second-order-observing', pp. 765 ff.
44 Derrida, 'Force of law', p. 945.
45 For an instructive comparison of the theories, see Barjiji-Kastner, *Ohnmachtssemantiken*, which also contains a detailed discussion of theological and non-theological transcendence in the interpretation of Derrida, with further references.
46 Wiethölter, 'Zur Argumentation im Recht', p. 107.
47 Benjamin, 'Critique of Violence'.
48 Derrida, 'Force of law', p. 945.
49 Wiethölter, 'Zum Fortbildungsrecht', p. 1.
50 Derrida, 'Force of law', pp. 931–2.
51 Ibid., pp. 925–6.
52 Wiethölter, 'Just-ifications', p. 72.
53 Derrida, 'Force of law', p. 969.
54 Wiethölter, 'Just-ifications', p. 72.
55 Wiethölter, 'Zur Argumentation im Recht', p. 119.
56 Wiethölter, 'Just-ifications', p. 71.
57 First steps in this direction can be found in Teubner, 'Contracting worlds'.

58 On the analysis of institutional externalities see Sciulli, *Theory of Societal Constitutionalism*.
59 Luhmann, *Law as a Social System*, p. 428.
60 Fuller, *Morality of Law*; Selznick, *Law, Society and Industrial Justice*; Selznick, *Moral Commonwealth*; Ewald, *L'État providence*; Friedland and Alford, 'Bringing Society Back In'.
61 For this view of networks, see Ladeur, 'Towards a legal theory of supranationality'; Teubner, 'Hybrid Laws'; Krebs and Rock, 'Unternehmungsnetzwerke'.
62 Wiethölter, 'Zum Fortbildungsrecht', p. 21.
63 Wiethölter, 'Zur Argumentation im Recht', pp. 117–18.
64 Wiethölter, 'Just-ifications', p. 73.
65 'Law, which can draw its force of validity neither from eternal ideas nor from itself, verges more on "medicine" and "biology" than on theology and technology, and is – as "poiesis" – more of an "art" than a "science".' Wiethölter, 'Verrechtlichung', unpublished manuscript, Frankfurt, 1995, p. 9.

4

The Law before its law: Franz Kafka on the (im)possibility of Law's self-reflection

The man from the country

Let us imagine that the man from the country in Kafka's parable 'Before the Law' is not the human individual who has been delivered up to the force of institutionalised legalism (power, morality, religion, etc.), as we find in numerous Kafka interpretations with their somewhat over-hasty role fixation. Let us suppose instead that he is a judge 'from the country', who – back there, in the country – has to deal with a legal case according to the law, and who now, in the torment of decision-making, cannot find what is right according to the law. Or to put it another way: let us imagine that it is the individual legal procedure itself, or more generally the *decision-making practice of the legal process*, in all the confusion of life, that stands before its own law and has no idea what it is doing. In that case it would not be the accused person who has to give an account of himself before the law in criminal proceedings, or the party seeking its rights before the law, but the Law itself, in a desperate search for a law by which it can make its decision. If we now place the protagonists that emerge from this dual role change in confrontation with each other – i.e. it is not a specific individual that stands 'before the law', but legal discourse, and the law for its part is not a generalised and distant authority, but (at a much more trivial level) the positive law of the land – then we have to address the question: What happens within the mysterious relationship between 'Law AND law' when that relationship is subjected to the nightmarish logic in Kafka's universe?

This is not meant to dispute the validity of the individual perspective in its own right. In complementing it, however, our institutional perspective allows very different things to come to the fore in Kafka's world. I am encouraged in my somewhat far-fetched interpretation by Jacques Derrida's whirlwind of associations concerning Kafka, in which he summons literature 'before the law'.[1] And Kafka himself, who sends his observers through a wide variety of institutions, through power, the military, the circus and through medicine, always designates them not simply as outsiders, but as part of professional-institutional life: the land surveyor, the country doctor, the researcher, the new lawyer, the bank clerk, the advocate. Last but not least, Kafka's own negative experiences as an insurance clerk dealing with the absurd internal laws of the insurance companies were certainly used by him in his literary output. It seems entirely reasonable, then, not only that in Kafka's parables flesh-and-blood human beings are dragged before the law, but that at the same time the legal institutions of modernity are subjected to an agonising self-examination.

The legal discourse that seeks to make certain of its law is tormented by nightmares that are different from those experienced by the person who is subject to the law and who is exposed to the arbitrariness of the judicial system. Kafka's parable renders visible the abysses that are faced by any collective self-reflection of the epistemic community of the Law. If the Law is standing 'before' the law, then it is on a desperate search for its origin in time, for justification of its content, and for the social basis of its norms and judgements. And the insoluble question of priority arises: Does Law perhaps take precedence over law? So that law definitely does not take precedence over Law? Should the chain of events that constitutes legal procedure precede, in a temporal sense, the law or the norm that is supposed to assist that chain of events in reaching a decision? Should that chain of events be the origin of the law in a substantive respect also? And from a social perspective: should the decision in the individual case have hierarchical precedence, by departing from the general law? And in the triangular relationship that exists between the man, the doorkeeper and the law, the question becomes even more complicated: where does the precedence lie – with the law, or with the spokesman for the law, or with the legal procedure? With which of these three does the origin of the norms lie?

The man from the country – from an institutional perspective, the meaning of this indication of origin becomes multi-layered, and no longer simply refers to the rustic layman who comes to grief when faced with the guiles of legalistic sophistry. The implied contrast between town and country opens up a wealth of different dimensions. These cannot all be discussed here, only hinted at by means of the following distinctions: (1) law versus life, more generally: culture versus nature, (2) statutory norm vs. the process of norm application, more generally: structure versus process, (3) statutory text versus legal interpretation, more generally: norm versus decision, (4) law versus legal case, more generally: universality versus singularity. The man from the country – this is no longer only a human being as a party in proceedings, but the entire complex process of the application of the Law, a process which is played out before the door, directly on the threshold that separates life from the law.

Self-slander

The 'Someone' who must have slandered Josef K. in *The Trial* is none other than Josef K. himself. With this bold assertion, Giorgio Agamben makes a plausible case that it is not a separate outside authority that is accusing a person 'before the law'; instead, the man from the country is accusing himself.[2] If we follow the role change that has been proposed, then the self-accusation of a person is transformed into the *self-accusation of the Law*. The Law is putting itself on trial.[3]

The Law cannot escape its self-accusation, for if (in the same way as the man from the country 'insatiably' asks the keeper of the law about the general law) it follows its implacable inner urge towards universalisation, then of necessity it is no longer asking the question 'legal or illegal?' solely in respect of the one legal case in the present instance, but also in respect of all human actions. It raises – for all events in the world – the question of their legal position (*Rechtslage*). Indeed, historically speaking, the Law of modernity underwent this development of universalising its categories when it moved from a thinking about *actiones* that was fixated on legal procedures to a thinking about legal positions that relates to society as a whole, and in doing so it has 'juridified' the entire world. Inevitably, then, legal procedure comes up against itself and asks the self-tormenting question: Applying the difference between legal and illegal – is this in itself legal? But at that point the Law becomes caught up in the paradoxes of self-reference. As with the lying Cretan, whose true statements become false and vice versa, what we are faced with is no longer a simple contradiction, but an infinite oscillation within the paradox: If legal, then illegal. If illegal, then legal … This is the fundamental paradox of the Law, which in response to the question as to its foundation does not get a clear yes or a clear no, but an almost mocking interchange between the positive and negative value of a viable justification.

The fact of having actually brought the legal/illegal distinction into the world in the first place, and thus of constantly producing anew not only that which is legal, but also that which is illegal – therein lies the original sin of the Law. The Law is in a position of guilt vis-à-vis the world, because in the very creation of this distinction it does harm to the world, not only when it inflicts punishment on a condemned person, but also when it simply raises the *quaestio juris*, when it cuts through the world's innocence with its 'either legal or illegal' (*tertium non datur*) binary code. The Law thus places all people, all events and even itself under a 'Kafkaesque' general suspicion which even the humanistic law of the Enlightenment, with its presumption of innocence, cannot remove. The inexorable compulsion to keep scanning the world according to this criterion produces more and more 'wrong'. And it is precisely the much-vaunted general nature of the law, which is supposed to do away with arbitrariness in individual cases, that in turn creates new 'wrong', because with its violent abstractions it can never do justice to singularity in its infinite manifestations.

Kafka's law compels legal practice to generate life a second time, by generating a 'legal reality' which is fictive, yet is very real in its fictiveness, almost monstrous. The entire novel *The Trial*, in which Josef K. in his imagination transforms the banal reality of his life as a bank clerk into a persecution situation, bears nightmarish witness to the world of madness into which the modern juridification of life leads us.[4] Kafka's law palace is one of the many 'iron cages of the slavery of the future' which Max Weber prophesied for modern society – Kafka's castle would be another such, also the penal colony, the circus and America. The compulsion that is exercised in Law's palace reduces flesh-and-blood human beings to juridical persons acting on compulsion, whose characteristic quality consists exclusively in having rights and duties, whose activities are limited to only being able to commit a right or a wrong, whose sole quality is being either guilty or innocent. The propagating of this second world – that is the evil deed committed by the Law. It is an act of violence against life, in respect of which the Law (if it applies its own categories to itself) accuses itself. This, after all, is the curse of the wrong deed, 'that propagating still, it brings forth wrong'.

But we shall have to go a step further: not just self-accusation, but *self-slander* by the Law. This would be the third interpretation of the dispute in the cathedral between Josef K. and the court chaplain, concerning the question as to whether the doorkeeper has deceived the man or whether the doorkeeper himself is the one who is deceived.[5] In its search for the law, the legal practice of modernity becomes a victim of self-deception – in judging itself, it deceives itself, and does so not out of negligence or by *dolus eventualis*, but by *dolus directus*. In the clear awareness that it is using false categories for its self-accusation, the Law slanders itself. Not only when the Law judges men, but also when the Law puts itself on trial, it cannot do otherwise than expose itself to its own slanderous categories. This is where Kafka's critique of modern Law, with its pride in its autonomy and formality, comes into play for the second time. This critique is now aimed not at the practice of application, but at its self-reflection. By contrast with the Law of traditional societies, which was able to classify and assess its law in an all-embracing cosmology in whose moral, religious and political connections it is indissolubly bound up, the highly specialised Law of our functionally differentiated society cannot comprehensively assess its law and decide whether it is true or untrue, good or evil, beneficial or damaging, beautiful or ugly, healthy or sick, just or unjust.

The loss of criteria of positive law, of our legal norms that are established only through decision – that is the disease from which Law in the modern age suffers. Modern Law only has its constricted, inadequate (for the purposes of describing the world), context-free, ultimately meaningless legal/illegal binary code – this 'cant' of modern legality – at its disposal. And the Law can only reflect on itself with the aid of its own life-falsifying constructs. Its self-assessment is caught within the narrow-mindedness of its criteria, its processes, its fora. The original sin of the Law consists not only in the fact of its doing wrong to the human beings who are subject to it through the violence of its binary coding, but also in that even in its best moments, in the moments of critical self-reflection, it has done itself this wrong, the wrong of self-slander, and continues to do so over and over again. The way in which modern Law deceives itself – the doorkeeper deceives the man, the man deceives the doorkeeper and the law deceives both – is something that 'you don't have to consider ... true, you just have to consider it necessary',[6] as the court chaplain in the cathedral rightly says, just as Josef K. is right when he says of the total juridification of the world: 'Lies are made into a universal system.'[7]

Excesses of ambivalence

Yet the *Kalumnia* by which Agamben sees Josef K. as being for ever marked is not the whole story, for this attaches a strictly negative value to the Law. Agamben sees only the violence the Law does to human beings. Agamben's history of Law is a story of harm that starts with *homo sacer* and of necessity ends in the prison camps, concentration camps and refugee camps of modernity – in Kafka's penal colony. But Kafka's parable 'Before the Law' has a more complex structure: *not pure negativity, but excessive ambivalence*. The Law always produces both at the same time: it puts some people in the wrong, others in the right. With its condemnations, it causes pain, suffering and torment, but at the same time, it also creates certainty of expectation and trust, something on which people can construct their life plans. Kafka, in his own life, suffered under the absurdity of insurance law, but he made bold proposals as to how this absurd law could bring about more justice.[8] Because the Law is only able to generate legal fictions, it is permanently producing lies, but it is precisely legal lies that can be rather helpful, as the well-known Islamic legal parable of the twelfth camel shows. Kafka's Law causes the torments of the permanent awareness of guilt, and it arouses the hope of redeeming acquittal. In the success of modern Law lies its failure, and in its failure lies its success.

It is this simultaneity that makes the torment truly unbearable. This is because in the purely negative context that Agamben presents to us, the escape to freedom would be open: (self-)destruction of the Law. The man from the country would not remain sitting in front of the doorkeeper, not knowing what to do. He would – indeed he would have to – protest against the evident wrong, either by fighting it or by simply going away. Voice or Exit. In protest or in flight, Law would finally free itself from the law. That was the message of the Free Law Movement: disregard the law when you give a judgement. Kafka's legal world has nothing to do with any such legal pietism. 'Before the law', in response to the threatening question of whether it is doing something legal or illegal when it applies the law, the legal process gets the paradoxical answer: with the application of the law, you are always simultaneously acting legally and illegally.

The self-evident certainty of Agamben's pre-judgement in regard to the Law – *Kalumnia* – is transformed by Kafka into an existential uncertainty: *Kalumnia* – or perhaps truth? If one observes the observer 'Up in the gallery', the excessive ambivalence of Kafka's universe is made even more clear. 'If some frail, consumptive equestrienne *were* to be urged around and around' helplessly by the cruel rituals of the circus operation, 'then, *perhaps*, a young visitor to the gallery *might* race down ... and yell: Stop! ... But since that *is* not so', he '... *weeps* without knowing it'.[9] The horror is not simply the reality behind the beautiful appearance, neither do horror and appearance have the same 'reality status'. The appearance is expressed in the indicative mood of that which is really happening, and the horror is expressed in the subjunctive mood of that which is merely possible. This remarkably asymmetric ambivalence gives the lie to the negativism of Agamben, who can only see the horror in the law of the modern age. It is infinitely more difficult to deal with excessive ambivalence than with absolute horror.

The paradox makes it inevitable that even the self-accusation of the Law can never stop oscillating between the values of legal and illegal. The accusation is never followed by a judgement, nor even by a guilty verdict pronounced against the law by Agamben's higher Law. The judgement on the guilt or innocence of the Law is indefinitely deferred. And it remains impossible to decide whether the mere existence of the Law itself is its guilt – or, on the contrary, its merit. And this is what makes for the Kafkaesque situation par excellence – not the certainty that the self-accusation is a deliberate slander, as Agamben would have it, and that the intrinsic guilt of the Law is thereby established a priori, but instead the tormenting uncertainty as to whether the self-accusation is the slander of an innocent party or a self-reflection promising truth and justice.

And it is this paradox that first explains the strangely activist passivity of the man towards the doorkeeper. The paradox paralyses legal practice, and robs it of the courage to decide in favour of resistance to the law, to either flee or stand, to choose voice or exit. But that is only one side. The other side is that the paradox drives the Law to try to de-paradoxify the law by continuously introducing new distinctions, like those which the legal man from the country almost submissively offers to the doorkeeper of the law. While Agamben's negativity calls for the abolition of law, Kafka's paradox provokes the 'insatiable', continuously re-attempted creation of distinctions which are intended to get closer to the law in adopting a 'thinking obedience'. But what is the quality of these distinctions?

The judgement

The sheer bafflement of the man from the country in the face of the inaccessibility of the law (i.e. from the perspective we have adopted, the paralysis of the self-reflection of the Law that is triggered by the foundational paradox and by the decision-making paradox of the law) is not the end of the story. Like flashes of lightning, three sudden and devastating events happen to the man at the moment of his death. First: an inextinguishable shining light breaks forth. Then: the entrance was intended only for him. Then: the entrance is closed. After such a Damascene experience, no one can hold out any longer in the suspension that has been caused by the paradoxes.

'... *this entrance was meant solely for you.*' With these words, a harsh judgement is pronounced: he who stands before the law is condemned to the freedom of decision. This judgement sheds a new light on the earlier ambiguous answers given by the doorkeeper – that entrance is forbidden, but may be deferred until later; that the entrance is left open, but with a warning concerning the more powerful doorkeepers. Only the man can – and must – decide. Neither the universality of the law, from which he might get help in his decision-making, nor the support provided by others who are seeking access to the law will give him any indications as to how he is to decide. This absolute necessity of having to make a decision means, as far as the individual perspective is concerned, that a radical switch is necessary from the objective law of an external legislator, whose commands have to be obeyed by the subject, to the subjective right of the individual, i.e. to the Law-making power which is nevertheless subject to the law. In terms of the institutional perspective, this 'only for you' means that the individual legal trial has no other recourse than itself in its decision-making. Only the singular legal trial itself which is actually proceeding, and no outside authority, not even the general law that is held in such great esteem by all, can be responsible for establishing the norm on which the decision will be based. The law only has form as empty validity without any meaning.

The law as a concrete structure, as a defined, binding behavioural standard, has absolutely no existence of its own in relation to the legal event. It exists only insofar as it is invoked by a legal event, and continues to exist only insofar as this legal event invokes the expectation of future legal events. The law has to be continually re-invoked by legal events. If the Law as a chain of events dies, then the door to the law will also be 'closed'. Law books themselves are not the law, they are at best doorkeepers, or, in another form of words, they are merely sediments of meaning that are reawakened to a new meaning only by the invocation of each legal event. The invocation has to be continually renewed.

But this norm-setting autonomy stands 'before' the law, i.e. it remains bound by the law. Without the law and its infinite 'worlds behind worlds', which create the 'normative space', no freedom to set norms, no further development of the Law, no justice is possible. The freedom to which the law condemns the Law is not simply unstructured chaos, but freedom to set norms, a freedom which is preformed by the structures of the law. As Derrida rightly says, it is only the conditions that make legal cognition possible, conditions that are guaranteed by the law, which

> ... give the text the power to *make the law,* beginning with its own. However, this is on condition that the text itself can appear *before the law* of another, more powerful text protected by more powerful guardians.[10]

The fact that this is circular or tautological does not have to be understood as a criticism. On the contrary. In Kafka's novel *The Trial*, the tautology becomes autological, because the text in the 'Cathedral' chapter applies the circularity of the normative to itself: The parable 'Before the law' stands before the law of the entire *Trial* novel, just as the novel also stands before the law of the parable. Not only do the two works constitute a reciprocal interpretation of each other, but each is a precondition for the other. The specific 'guilt normativity' of the two texts does not arise from any outside norm-setting authority which is independent of them, but from the self-referential, free-floating, self-supporting interrelation between the two texts.

Yet there is a particular contradiction in this duty to establish norms. The powerful doorkeepers forbid the man from gaining entrance to the law. And at the same time the entrance is intended only for him. In this, he is exposed to the confusions of a 'double bind': he is obliged to obey the law, and at the same time he is obliged to break it. Act in such a way that the maxim of your will is to obey the law at all times and simultaneously to break the law at all times. This 'double bind' provides him with absolute freedom and at the same time entangles him in permanent guilt: the obligation to decide and the guilt of deciding.

Regardless of which alternative he chooses, he is always embroiled in guilt. The individual either becomes guilty of having broken the law or becomes guilty of not rebelling against the law. Was it right to bribe the first doorkeeper, or should the man have found the courage to take up the fight for the Law?

The currently prevailing legal theory refuses to contemplate such paradoxical and unreasonable demands. The foundational paradox of the law, the decision-making paradox of the application of the law, the 'double bind' of the subjective right are banned from legal theory. Some simply deny their existence, others forbid any paradoxical figures of thought on logical grounds, yet others ridicule and dismiss them as mere philosophical fancies. Against the background of the nightmarish suggestivity of Kafka's texts, however, all three responses appear merely as helpless gestures. Only a few present-day legal theoreticians take these paradoxes seriously: Niklas Luhmann, Giorgio Agamben and Jacques Derrida.

Contexts of delusion

Luhmann builds his legal theory upon the bold thesis that the place of the transcendental subject is now occupied by the paradox.[11] In exactly the same way as Kafka, Luhmann sees the Law, insofar as it has developed an extreme autonomy in the process of modernisation, as being from the outset entangled in the paradoxes of self-reference, so that its self-observations are threatened with paralysis. For Luhmann, too, the way out of this paralysis is: '... *this entrance was meant solely for you.*' The doorkeeper's astonishing revelation leads us out of the paralysis, the suspension, the twilight. 'Draw a distinction' – this is what Luhmann requires of legal practice, so that it may circumvent the paradoxes. To demand that legal discourse itself, and only legal discourse, must draw a new distinction – that is the strategy of de-paradoxification, which provides protection against the unfathomable depths of the paradoxes. Even if the new distinction in turn is necessarily founded on a paradox, it nevertheless has a self-supporting power which is based on its plausibility and its capacity to solve problems – albeit only for a limited time.

This is certainly an elegant solution, but it cannot do justice to what happens in the death scene. It does not react to the two other sudden events, indeed it has to disregard them. Luhmann's de-paradoxifying solution cannot close the door on the law and the paralysis it induces: it must constantly expect the return of law's paradox. And Luhmann's 'praise of routine' certainly does not cause any inextinguishable shining light to break forth from the door of the law. It only continues the previous routine of pedantic legalistic distinctions, the permanent recursiveness of legal operations. The new distinction only conceals the paradox in a rather insecure place from which it will soon re-emerge.

Agamben, on the other hand, does actually read two of the events together: '... *this entrance was meant solely for you. I'm going to go and shut it now.*' The closing of the door – this, for Agamben, is the key message. He gives us a surprising interpretation. The fact that the door to the law is closed is not a defeat, not a failure for the man, but on the contrary is the result of his patient strategy of waiting, and the intensive, indeed intimate continuing encounter solely with the keeper of the law, rather than the impossible ingress into the law itself. The strategy is aimed at compelling the doorkeeper to lock the entrance to the law. The man finds his freedom precisely at the moment when the entrance to the law is locked, when the law is cancelled, its empty validity interrupted, the law itself abolished.[12]

However, Agamben cannot come to terms with the shining light. In Agamben's reading, the shining light which the man recognises in the darkness plays almost no part at all. But this 'radiance that streams forth inextinguishably from the door of the Law' is the moment of the greatest intensity in the parable, 'outshining' the two other events in the death scene. In this light, everything is different. Derrida even speaks of the 'most religious moment'.[13] And what does the parable say about the origin and intensity of the light? The light comes 'from the door of the Law', that is, its origin lies nowhere else than in the law itself, and it 'streams forth inextinguishably', that is, its intensity is linked to the permanent existence of the law. That is the exact opposite of the abolition of the law, as argued by Agamben. It is impossible to have the experience of the light without the law, without its empty claim to validity, without its lying, without its paradoxes, without its obscenity. No law – no light. The absence of law which Agamben hopes for will never be able to generate the light. This is because the desperation which Kafka evokes does not relate to the grand delusion of the law, which Agamben would like to destroy because it prevents justice. That is too simple. In that case one could indeed set the law aside, switch it off, abolish it. This possibility always remains open. Instead, the man makes the astonishing discovery that it is precisely the grand delusion of the law that is necessary in order to render the prospect of justice at least momentarily possible. Or to put it another way: justice is dependent upon the obscenities of the law. Justice cannot be had without the law.

It is only on the basis of the *inseparable connection between all three events* that the death scene can be interpreted – inextinguishable light, singular intention, closing of the door. In the shining light that appears, the closing of the door does not signify the abolition of the law, or its cancellation in any future community. Neither can the fact that the light appears simultaneously with the closing of the door be reduced to the opposition between a doom-laden present and the promise of a distant good future, as Agamben would suggest. That would be Manichaeism, which expects the future community only from 'the *Muselmann*', i.e. from the deepest humiliation.[14] And which makes the salvation of the 'coming community' conditional on the abolition of the law. But in the present event the light and the darkness coincide. In the darkness shortly before the closing of the door, the light appears as *the fleeting illumination of a chance that in the failure of Law before the law, justice is possible.*

In an individual perspective, this would mean that the man, at the end of his torments, experiences the subjective recognition of individual justice. An institutional perspective would go one step further, and could relate (and restrict) this possibility to the single legal procedure. It is only for this singular conflict, and not for other conflicts, that this door to the law is intended, and it is only for this singular conflict that a view opens up onto the justice meant for it alone. A justice which is strictly limited to the individual case is possible, but there is no possibility whatsoever of any generalisation to other cases. The justice associated with the individual trial has no continuing effect; on the contrary, the door of *res judicata* will shut: It must be opened anew in each trial and will always shut again afterwards.

These are two possible interpretations. We may ask, however, whether the text does not allow of a reading that takes Kafka's critique of legal modernity to an extreme level. On such a reading, autonomous legal discourse itself would be the collective subject before the law, which is able to experience the shining light only in its self-transcendence in the face of the law intended for it alone. This self-transcendence would entail neither a future in which the Law is abolished nor a return to the embedded Law of traditional societies. The fact that Kafka is not in any way nostalgic about the Law of the pre-modern age is demonstrated by the encounter of the land surveyor in *The Castle* with the repressive structures of the village community, against which he is constantly rebelling. 'Meant solely for you' would then mean the exclusively *juridical justice of modern autonomous Law*, a justice which can be developed from the overcoming of the law only by the Law itself, without having recourse to any other institutions – not politics, not science, not morality, not religion. In modernity, a justice that might apply to the whole of society is impossible, there is only a particular justice that is peculiar to and intended for the Law, a justice which is clearly distinct from other particular justices (those peculiar to politics, morality or economics). The specific self-transcendence of modern Law would then mean that for the Law as a singular institution there is a separate path to justice which only the Law itself and no other institution can follow. It is only in the blindness in which modern decontextualised Law is imprisoned that it is able to see the shining light of its self-transcendence. It is not the entrance of an individual conscience to transcendence that is intended, but a collective entrance to transcendence, albeit one that does not concern society as a whole, but the self-transcendence of legal discourse itself.[15]

Bifurcation

If we think of the three events together in this way, then two mutually contradictory ways of judging the man's behaviour are revealed.

In one interpretation, it is precisely the mere fact of sitting there, this not particularly glorious 'activist passivity' of the man, that allows him to perceive justice. Not only the man's patient waiting, but also his insatiable questions have not been in vain. He acquires powers of judgement in the final moment of his endeavours. And he does so because he has decided not to penetrate into the infinite emptiness of the law and instead is trying, in one continuing endeavour, to establish a bridge between different worlds. He is not 'in' the law, but remains out of doors, 'before' the law, outside the law, on the threshold, in the permanent confrontation with the doorkeeper, in order to mediate between life and the law from that position. Judgement proves its worth not simply in the subsumption of the particular within the general, but in the bridging of two irreconcilable worlds.[16] Kafka radicalises the opposition that has to be bridged: not merely in the direction of reason versus emotion, but of legal argument versus irrational decision, of the order of the law versus the chaos of life, and ultimately of immanence versus transcendence.

This interpretation approaches the sophisticated manoeuvre by which Jacques Derrida brings his impressive deconstruction of the Law to its conclusion.[17] After a radical transcendence of the positive law, after the journey through the desert, after the delirium of infinite justice, there must come about (as Derrida surprisingly demands) a 'compromise', a compromise of infinite justice with the most trivial calculation of legal consequences, of banal subsumption under a rule of law. According to Derrida, the shattering experience of justice ought not to serve as an alibi for the composure with which a possible future is expected.

> Left to itself, the incalculable and giving (*donatrice*) idea of justice is always very close to the bad, even to the worst for it can always be reappropriated by the most perverse calculation. ... And so incalculable justice *requires* us to calculate.[18]

To penetrate ever deeper into the paradoxes of the law, and to wish to remain there in post-structuralist quietism – this would then be the culpable error. Instead, the humiliating continuing compromise with the obscene doorkeeper must be demanded of him. The shining light appears only in the re-closing of the door, in the final refusal of entry. That would be not simply fulfilment in failure, but fulfilment only after the labours of the encounter, the compromise with calculation, the humiliation, the bribery, the Sisyphean work of legal discourse. Not the praise of mystical violence, but the praise of the compromise between the mystical experience of justice and the banal calculation of legal consequences – that would be the one interpretation that would justify the man's waiting.

The other interpretation is revealed if the parable is read alongside another text by Kafka. This interpretation does not accept that the toilsome confrontation with the doorkeeper results in justice. On the contrary, the man is forced to realise in the shining light that he could have obtained justice if he had not allowed himself to become involved in the meaningless questioning of the first doorkeeper, but if he had only found the courage to do battle with the other more powerful doorkeepers and to penetrate into the law as far as his strength would take him. This obedience that leads the man to remain sitting in front of the door, his fulfilment of duty, is his violation of duty. Instead of only bribing the first keeper, the man should have found the courage to break the entrance ban and to take up the fight for the Law. In this reading, too, the shining light is an experience that comes over him here and now. This is because at this point, he 'recognises' justice – but only as a justice that is other, not his, and of which he has failed to avail himself.

But the question of how this other justice might be attained is expressed only negatively 'before the law', only as the disappointing experience of having missed the big opportunity. That the positive establishment of justice appears possible in Kafka's work, and the way in which this might come about, is more readily seen in 'An Imperial Message'. Here also, we have the triangular situation between a distant authority, a subject of that authority, and an intermediary, although in this case the direction of movement is reversed. Here also there is a go-between, not a doorkeeper but an imperial messenger who makes superhuman efforts to ensure that the message from the authority reaches the subject. And here too there is the bitter disappointment of discovering that any real mediation between the two worlds is impossible, and the communication via the messenger is a vain hope. Instead: 'Nobody could fight his way through here even with a message from the dead man.' Then, however, comes the all-deciding sentence: 'But you sit at your window when evening falls and dream it to yourself.'[19]

The question of which of the two readings is appropriate – whether justice is to be found in the patient, self-tormenting, humiliating confrontation with the obscene keeper of the law, or conversely in the collective imagination of the legal discourse that takes place before the law and that is bent on penetrating into the law – must remain open. For both readings, however, the same applies: even when the shining light illuminates everything, there is no triumph of justice. Kafka's excessive ambivalence does not stop even at the light that shines inextinguishably out of the law. Kafka refuses to answer the question as to 'whether it's really getting darker around him or if his eyes are merely deceiving him'. Is this really the shining light of justice? Of transcendence? And if so, is it then a light that comes from outside – from God, from science, from politics, from morality or from natural law? Or does it come from within, as a self-transcending from the arcanum of the law itself? Or is it merely some kind of reflected light? A mere shimmering illusion concealing the dark emptiness? A hypocritical self-deception on the part of modern Law, which has become blind in its formal autonomy? It is impossible to escape from this ambivalence, because there is no criterion available to us by which we can distinguish between a collective imagination of justice and a collective self-deception.

Law and literature

All in all, Kafka appears to be a sensitive observer of modern Law, whose insights provide legal sociology and legal philosophy with much food for thought. The accuracy with which Kafka portrays the excessive ambivalence of the Law seems to be at a higher level than that of many social theoreticians who reveal to us the dilemmas of Law in the modern age. Max Weber defined this dilemma in terms of the internal 'formal' rationality of the Law being at risk from 'material' irrational outside influences emanating from economic and political interests. Kafka's response is that it is precisely the inmost formal rationality of the Law that is most deeply irrational. Hans Kelsen's attempts to preserve the 'purity' of Law's normativity against impure empirical influences fail in light of Kafka's observation that it is precisely from its purity that the obscenity of the Law springs. The conversation in the cathedral between Josef K. and the chaplain gives the lie to all attempts at a rational argumentation theory of the Law such as those of Habermas or Alexy. In terms of scholarliness, interpretative skill, equality of opportunities for articulation, honesty and authenticity of the participants in the discussion, this conversation certainly meets the requirements of rational discourse. And yet it does not end in a liberating consensus, but in uncertainty, paralysis, anxiety and a sense of oppression. And Luhmann has to concede to Kafka that his 'de-paradoxification' strategies, which swiftly invent a new distinction when faced with the paradox, will never see the inextinguishable shining light breaking forth from the door of the law, because these strategies do not expose themselves to the paradox, but stop 'before the law' and its paradoxes, and commence their withdrawal back into routine as quickly as possible.

But why, then, the literary form? Why does the experienced insurance law practitioner Dr. jur. Franz Kafka not simply write a work of well-organised legal sociology? Is the whole point of Kafka's parable to provide legal theory or indeed legal practice with suggestions as to how they could deal with the paradoxes of the Law? Or does legal literature have an added value, over and above the benefits it provides for legal theory?

The key may be found in certain peculiarities of a legal practice 'from the country'. In the long conversations between the man and the doorkeeper, and between Josef K. and the chaplain, the communication is at a much more complex level than could ever be reconstructed by rational academic disciplines. It is true that legal doctrine, jurisprudence and the sociology of law describe, in great detail, the rational dimensions of the legal system, the ordering of the proceedings, the logic of argumentation, the construction of legal doctrine and the structure of *stare decisis*. But they pay no attention to what they term the 'non-rational' elements of legal practice and normally exclude these from analysis – indeed must exclude them. The dark urge for justice, the convoluted pathways of the sense of justice, the arbitrary elements in the judge's professional judgement, the decision-making torments of the jury trial, the obscene elements in legal procedure, the foundational and the decision-making paradoxes of the Law – generally speaking, the particular excesses of legal ambivalence – cannot be reconstructed by the academic disciplines, at least not in any depth. What can logical or theoretical analyses of the legal paradoxes say about the painful experience of the paralysis, and about its ecstatic resolution in the shining light, that are experienced by the man from the country at the moment of his death? In the intricacies of the court trial, in the *arcana* of administrative bureaucracies and in the practitioners' complicated contractual constructions, legal practice creates for itself a second version of reality, rather as art or religion create their own worlds, which can only be perceived to a limited extent by the rational approach of the academic disciplines that observe them. And even legal doctrine, which in turn represents a peculiar abstraction of legal practice that, measured by the standards of social science, cannot be regarded as scientifically legitimate, is not capable of controlling Law's *arcana* by means of its conceptual tools. Social science and legal doctrine can only qualify the deeply hidden areas of legal practice as irrational, and condemn them as such. The same happens when legal sociology investigates the pre-judgements of the judiciary, and when argumentation theory analyses judgements. This second reality is not just the legal process with its various roles, its norms, concepts and principles, but also an entire creation of a legal world, a world which looks completely different from the everyday world or the world of academic disciplines.

Yet literary reconstructions can attain an independent insight into the secret worlds of legal practice. Assuredly, they do not have any direct access to the inmost recesses of the law either, but literary observation produces an added value that goes beyond the most highly advanced sociology of the legal paradox to date, such as that presented, for instance, by Luhmann. This added value can be indirectly described as the experiential access to the paradoxes of the Law, an affective understanding of the practice of judgement, and the emotional import of injustice. Art, in dealing with the Law, communicates messages about legal events that cannot be communicated in words (see Michelangelo's Moses). As far as the literature of the Law is concerned, this seems counter-intuitive, for ultimately, it does of course communicate about law in words; in a way that is comparable to legal doctrine, it conveys a peculiar knowledge about the legal world. But its actual literary message is not made up of the content, but of something that is verbally non-communicable but is nevertheless communicated together with the words (see Kleist's *Michael Kohlhaas*, Kafka's *The Trial*, Borges's 'Deutsches Requiem'). 'Art functions as communication although – or precisely because – it cannot be adequately rendered through words (let alone through concepts).'[20] This is by no means intended to reduce the role of legal literature to the psychological sense of justice (*Rechtsgefühl*), to the mere fact of its being a trigger of affect in mental processes. Rather, as a consequence of the duplication of meaning production in consciousness and in communication, there exists in legal literature a genuine communication about what cannot be communicated in words. The added value of Kafka's parable is this: the non-communicable aspects of the Law are made communicable by the literary form, and only by the literary form. It is neither in legal doctrine nor in legal theory that we are able to experience the arcanum of the Law, but in the story 'before the law'.

Appendix: Kafka, 'Before the Law'

Before the Law stands a doorkeeper. A man from the countryside comes up to the door and requests admittance to the Law. But the doorkeeper says that he can't grant him admittance now. The man thinks it over and then asks if he'll be allowed to enter later. 'It's possible' says the doorkeeper, 'but not now.' Since the gate to the Law stands open as always, and the doorkeeper steps aside, the man bends down to look through the gate into the interior. When the doorkeeper sees this he laughs and says: 'If you're so drawn to it, go ahead and try to enter, even though I've forbidden it. But bear this in mind: I'm powerful. And I'm only the lowest doorkeeper. From hall to hall, however, stand doorkeepers each more powerful than the one before. The mere sight of the third is more than even I can bear.' The man from the country has not anticipated such difficulties; the Law should be accessible to anyone at any time, he thinks, but as he now examines the doorkeeper in his fur coat more closely, his large, sharply pointed nose, his long, thin, black tartar's beard, he decides he would prefer to wait until he receives permission to enter. And the doorkeeper gives him a stool and lets him sit down at the side of the door. He sits there for days and years. He asks time and again to be admitted and wearies the doorkeeper with his entreaties. The doorkeeper often conducts brief interrogations, inquiring about his home and many other matters, but he asks such questions indifferently, as great men do, and in the end he always tells him he still can't admit him. The man, who has equipped himself well for the journey, uses everything he has, no matter how valuable, to bribe the doorkeeper. And the doorkeeper accepts everything, but as he does so he says: 'I'm taking this just so you won't think you've neglected something.' Over the many years, the man observes the doorkeeper almost incessantly. He forgets the other doorkeepers and this first one seems to him the only obstacle to his admittance to the Law. He curses his unhappy fate, loudly during the first years, later, as he grows older, merely grumbling to himself. He turns childish, and since he has come to know even the fleas in the doorkeeper's collar over his years of study, he asks the fleas too to help him change the doorkeeper's mind. Finally his eyes grow dim and he no longer knows whether it's really getting darker around him or if his eyes are merely deceiving him. And yet in the darkness he now sees a radiance that streams forth inextinguishably from the door of the Law. He doesn't have much longer to live now. Before he dies, everything he has experienced over the years coalesces in his mind into a single question he has never asked the doorkeeper. He motions to him, since he can no longer straighten his stiffening body. The doorkeeper has to bend down to him, for the difference in size between them has altered greatly to the man's disadvantage. 'What do you want to know now,' asks the doorkeeper, 'you're insatiable.' 'Everyone strives to reach the Law,' says the man, 'how does it happen, then, that in all these years no one but me has requested admittance.' The doorkeeper sees that the man in nearing his end, and in order to reach his failing hearing, he roars at him: 'No one else could gain admittance here, because this entrance was meant solely for you. I'm going to go and shut it now'.

Kafka, *The Trial*, pp. 215–16.

Notes

This chapter was previously published as 'The Law before its law: Franz Kafka on the (im)possibility of Law's self-reflection', trans. Ancilla Juris (anci.ch) 2012, 176–203, www.anci.ch/_media/beitrag/ancilla2012_176_teubner.pdf

1 Derrida, 'Before the Law', p. 186.
2 Agamben, 'K', p. 13.
3 Wiethölter, 'Ist unserem Recht der Prozeß zu machen?'
4 Concerning the madness of the Law, careful diagnoses are to be found in Kiesow, *Alphabet des Rechts*.
5 Kafka, *The Trial*, pp. 215–16.
6 Ibid., p. 223.
7 Ibid.
8 Banakar, 'In search of Heimat', p. 467; Corngold (ed.), *Franz Kafka: The Office Writings*, p. ix.
9 Kafka, *Complete Short Stories*, pp. 401–2 (my emphasis).
10 Derrida, 'Before the Law', p. 214.
11 Luhmann, *A Systems Theory of Religion*, pp. 93–5.
12 Agamben, *Homo Sacer*, pp. 55 ff.

13 Derrida, 'Before the Law', p. 208.
14 Agamben, *Homo Sacer*, pp. 185–6.
15 For more detail on this subject see Chapter 1 in this volume.
16 As is well known, Kant located the power of judgement not in the sphere of pure reason, nor in the sphere of practical reason, but defined it as a means of combining the two parts of philosophy into a single whole, Kant, *Critique of Judgment*, pp. 15–18.
17 Derrida, 'Force of law', pp. 969 ff., 1044–5. This triggered great irritation in the deconstructivist camp: Vismann, 'Das Gesetz "DER Dekonstruktion"'.
18 Derrida, 'Force of law', p. 971.
19 Kafka, *Complete Stories*, p. 8.
20 Luhmann, *Art as a Social System*, p. 19.

Part II

Juridical epistemology: reconstructing the horizontal effects of human rights, the private–public dichotomy and contracting

5

The anonymous matrix: human rights violations by 'private' transnational actors

I *HIV/AIDS v. TNC*

The disastrous AIDS epidemic, which has killed more people worldwide than all the civil wars of the 1990s,[1] took a special turn in South Africa with the legal case *Hazel Tau v. Glaxo and Boehringer*.[2] The case translates the multidimensional social issues involved into the following narrower *quaestiones juris*: has the pricing policy of transnational pharmaceutical enterprises violated fundamental human rights? Can AIDS patients assert their right to life directly against transnational corporations? Does 'Access to medication as a human right' exist in the private sector?[3] More generally, do fundamental rights obligate not only states, but also private transnational actors directly?[4]

In October 2003, the national Competition Commission had to decide whether the complainants had an actionable right of access to HIV medications against the firms GlaxoSmithKline and Boehringer Ingelheim. From a technical legal viewpoint, the claimants based their legal position on the point that the pharmaceutical firms had breached Art. 8(a) of the Competition Act 89 of 1998 by charging excessive prices for antiretrovirals, to the detriment of consumers. They accused private collective actors of violating human rights: 'The excessive pricing of ARVs is directly responsible for premature, predictable and avoidable deaths of people living with HIV/AIDS, including both children and adults.'[5] The surprising outcome was that even though the South African

Competition Commission acknowledged the firms' right to amortise their development costs, it basically found for the complainants.[6]

The 'horizontal' effect of fundamental rights, i.e. the question whether they impose obligations not only on governmental bodies, but also on private actors directly, is taking on much more dramatic dimensions in the transnational sphere than it has ever had nationally. The issue arises not only in regard to infringements of human rights by pharmaceutical enterprises in the worldwide AIDS epidemic,[7] but has already caused a stir in several scandals in which transnational corporations were involved.[8] To name but a few conspicuous cases, these include: environmental pollution and inhuman treatment of local population groups, e.g. by Shell in Nigeria;[9] the chemical accident in Bhopal;[10] disgraceful working conditions in 'sweatshops' in Asia and Latin America;[11] child labour connected with IKEA and NIKE;[12] the suspicions of having footballs produced in China by forced labour levelled against sports goods manufacturer Adidas;[13] the use of highly poisonous pesticides in banana plantations;[14] disappearances of unionised workers;[15] and environmental damage arising from big construction projects.[16] The list could easily be extended. The scandalous events fill volumes. At their core is the accusation that transnational corporations do lasting, irrecoverable damage to the environment and to people.[17]

In the transnational sphere, it is extremely difficult to fall back on familiar patterns of solutions drawn from national constitutional law. While these solutions have dealt with the horizontal effect of fundamental rights, they usually dodge the tricky question of whether private actors are subject to direct obligations to respect fundamental rights, by developing a host of doctrines whereby fundamental rights have only 'indirect' effects in the private sector.[18] Very broadly speaking, there are two constructions to be found, albeit in numerous variants. Under the state action doctrine, private actors are excluded as a matter of principle from the binding effect of fundamental rights, unless some element of state action can be identified in their actions, which may be discovered either because state bodies are somehow involved or because the private actors perform some public functions.[19] Alternatively, under the doctrine of the structural effect of fundamental rights, those rights do impact on the whole legal system, so that fundamental rights must be observed whenever state law is applied in the private sector. But the restriction of obligations to the *legal* system simultaneously implies that the private actors themselves are not subject to any direct obligation arising from fundamental rights.[20]

In the transnational private sector, the question whether collective actors are themselves bound by fundamental rights is much more acutely significant than in the law of nation states. In this sector, the otherwise omnipresent state and national law are almost absent, so that the state action doctrine and the doctrine of the structural legal effect of fundamental rights are applicable only in few situations. On the other hand, transnational private actors, especially transnational corporations, regulate whole areas of life through private governance regimes of their own, so that the question of the applicability of fundamental rights can no longer be evaded.

This situation confronts legal policy and constitutional legal theory with enormous problems. Yet it would be simplistic to politicise the question directly, to reduce it to the political bifurcation between neo-liberal and social-democratic conceptions of fundamental rights, hegemonic and anti-hegemonic strategies, or Empire versus Multitude.[21] That would be tantamount to a political decision between either an exclusively state-oriented validity of fundamental rights, or else their enforcement throughout society.[22] Instead, I propose to leave the well-beaten tracks of these debates and to take a roundabout route through somewhat obscure territories of legal and social theory. The detour commences with what I call divisional concepts of fundamental rights and ends with ecological ones. This journey will open up a different perspective on fundamental rights in the transnational private sector. This view may be presented as a question: Can the horizontal effect of fundamental rights be rethought by framing it no longer in terms of interpersonal conflicts between individual bearers of fundamental rights, but rather in terms of conflicts between anonymous matrices of communication, on the one hand, and concrete individuals, on the other? Can we understand human rights in the private sector in such a way that individuals may assert their rights against the structural violence of impersonal communicative processes?

II Divisional concepts of fundamental rights

What does one gain and what does one lose by taking this detour? What happens if we no longer see questions about fundamental rights as a problem of balancing the rights of concrete actors, but rather as an 'ecological' problem: as an injury that an expansive social system does to its social, human and natural ecologies? Considering our general question, what do we gain from this perspective for understanding and analysing the horizontal effect of human rights in globalised sectors of society, outside of institutionalised politics?

In its search for just institutions, the European tradition has always aspired to construct an 'appropriate' balance between society as a whole and its parts. It has oscillated between experiences of a divided society and abstract conceptions of the appropriateness of its internal balance. The justice of institutions vis-à-vis people was the heuristic formula by which legal semantics reacted to changes in the social structure.[23] The concept responded anew in each case to the painful experience of society's internal divisions.

Can a fair balance be found between the individuals among themselves, as well as between the individual and society, in spite of these divisions? Or, in non-individualist versions, can there be a fair balance between parts of society – estates, classes, strata, interest groups, ethnic and cultural identities, social spheres, sub-rationalities – and between the parts and society as a whole? Or can institutional justice only be achieved once society's divisions have been overcome and a new unity of society has been brought about?

On this view, which I shall call *divisional*, the justice of institutions vis-à-vis people was seen as a problem of society's internal division into unequal parts – or, more dramatically, of its destructive rifts, its power and distribution struggles and its antagonistic conflicts. How is an equitable unity of society to be guaranteed despite its self-destructive fragmentation? The classical answer was: Do not eliminate the divisions, but equilibrate them through *suum cuique*! Neutralise the dangerous divisive tendencies by assigning to the parts their due place in the overall order! Actual human beings were regarded as components of society; and justice was done to them through the familiar formulas of *justitia distributiva* – the whole allotting to the parts (individuals, groups, sectors) their due share – and *justitia commutativa* – the equitable relation of the parts (individuals, groups, sectors) to each other.

Though the divisional view always predominated, the relation of the whole to its parts and the fair balance between them has been perceived in different ways over the course of history. Feudal society primarily regulated the relations of the estates with each other. It guaranteed justice as the natural hierarchy between the *partes majores*, which at the same time represented the whole of society, understood as *corpus*, and the *partes minores*. Human individuals were always transcended in the estate or in the corporation.[24] There were no subjective rights, still less fundamental rights, in the modern sense of unilateral entitlements. Instead, the prevailing conception was that of *jus* as a complex relation of divisional balance, fair in itself, between parts of different kinds; an example would be the relation between feudal lords and vassals as one of loyalty and care in asymmetrical (hierarchical) reciprocity.[25]

The bourgeois revolution rebelled against the injustice of distributive relationships between the estates. It responded to the divisional injustice by calling for the equality of all parts of society. In particular, fundamental rights followed a new logic, which, however, remained divisional: freedom of the parts in relation to the whole of society, equality among them and solidarity as mutual support. Liberal theories followed the new divisionalism through to its logical conclusion. Society consists only of individuals. Fairness is to be guaranteed by self-regulating invisible hands that, underpinned by fundamental rights, coordinate the autonomous spheres of individuals: economic markets, political elections, the competition of opinions and the free play of scientific knowledge. Interventions of compensatory justice are to be admissible only in order to keep regulation among the parts running smoothly.

The proletarian revolution propounds a contrary theory of society, but one that again takes a divisional approach. The totality of society consists of the social classes that spring from economic structural contradictions. Justice will only become possible once the classless society is born out of their antagonistic conflicts. In social-democratic welfare-state conceptions, the parts of society, that is the classes, are transformed into socio-economic strata. Here, too, a divisional view dominates, especially in regard to second-generation fundamental rights. Social and participatory rights are aimed at harmonising the living conditions of different strata, as a political, state-guaranteed justice.[26]

Ultimately, the great social theories also follow divisional patterns. This is clearest in concepts of a social division of labour that discovers a fair balance in organic rather than mechanical solidarity.[27] In classical functionalism, the divisional element is to be found in the fact that a balance comes about through exchange relations among different functional spheres, and ultrastability is achieved by compensatory mechanisms when there are occasional disruptions, if necessary through state compensation out of the proceeds of growth.[28] In conflict theories, insoluble permanent conflicts replace the just balance among the parts. In the modern polytheism of different spheres of rationality, the hope for a lasting fair balance has given way to a resigned acquiescence in a chain of tragic decisions.[29]

The specific consequence of these divisional theories of society for human rights is that the latter are conceived as the subjective rights of the parts against the state, which represents society as a whole. Doctrines on the horizontal effect of fundamental rights in the private sector are framed accordingly.[30] They are concerned with the distribution of the unevenly divided resources of a society – power, wealth, knowledge – according to the pattern of *justitia distributiva* or *commutativa*. This programme requires either an extension of the state–citizen distributive pattern into society, or else resource allocation on the commutative pattern: fundamental rights as rights of the parts of society against each other. Thus, one ends up with a weighing-up of the individual fundamental rights positions of private actors against each other.[31] In the final analysis, however, it remains unclear how far and on what terms fundamental rights can claim validity in non-political sectors of society.

III Ecological concepts of fundamental rights

There is a deeper question, however: Is it really appropriate to view the justice of institutions as a divisional (distributive) justice between the whole and the parts (or between the parts themselves) and to regard human rights as guarantees – formal, material or procedural – granted to individuals against society as a whole and against the state as its organisational embodiment (or as reciprocal guarantees by and to each of the parts)?

Social theory poses a different question here: Is the internal division of society which creates injustice as inequality among people not just a secondary phenomenon? It understands the main significance of the internal differentiation of society differently, namely as a result of the confrontation of communicative networks with their environments. This is perceived most acutely by systems theory, which analyses the autonomisation of communicative networks in terms of a radical exclusion of people from society. Actual people are not at the centre of these networks, nor can they get back inside them. People are the *environment* for communicative networks to whose operations they are exposed without being able to control them.[32] Here, systems theory takes up theorems of social alienation from the social theory tradition and gives them a contemporary form.[33] At this point there are secret contacts with officially hostile theories: with Foucault's analyses of disciplinary power, Agamben's critique of political exclusion, Lyotard's theory of closed discourses and Derrida's deconstruction of justice,[34] even if these contacts are officially denied on all sides.[35] This proximity can only be indicated here, not enlarged upon.

The legal question which follows is this: If people are not parts of society, but for ever banished from it, how are human rights to be reformulated? Whereas the European political tradition perceived the question of just institutions as a problem created by the internal differentiation of society, and therefore aimed at *institutional justice in spite of difference*, today it looks like there is much to be said for distinguishing the social system from its natural and human environment and hence for describing *institutional justice as difference*: as the unbridgeable gap between social institutions and actual people. The reaction to this difference cannot be inclusion, but at best responsiveness. Human rights are thus not a reaction to distribution problems within society, but an answer to problems of ecological sensitivity in communication – problems which transcend society. Human rights achieve justice towards human beings only insofar as they transcend the boundaries of communication – a simultaneously impossible and necessary task.[36] And another question follows from this: Does not the far-advanced fragmentation of society in turn create new internal boundaries between individual subsystems within society, on the one hand, and new external boundaries between these systems and their environments outside society, on the other, so that the fairness of specialised social institutions also can only be posed properly as an ecological problem, and no longer as a (re)distribution problem?

Such an ecological understanding of fundamental rights as 'just' boundaries between social systems and their various internal and external ecologies takes on two new dimensions if we compare it with divisional theories that see people as parts of society and justice as a problem of inequality. The first dimension concerns the insurmountable difference between communication and its environment. Is communication even capable of ever doing justice to the people in its extra-societal environment? Can it ever meet the non-egalitarian obligations which flow from a consideration of that which is particular and individual? The second dimension is that the question is no longer one of the distribution, among the parts of society, of social resources in the broadest sense, i.e. power, wealth, knowledge or life chances. Instead, the point is to restrict the acts of institutions in such a way that they do justice to the intrinsic rights of their social and human ecologies. The overcoming of inequality between people and the fair distribution of resources are replaced by two quite different demands as regards social institutions: (1) the internal and external limitation of their expansive tendencies; and (2) a sensitive balancing between their intrinsic rationality and the intrinsic rights of their ecologies, reformulated internally as ecological demands.

The human rights tradition is thereby accused of not taking human individuals seriously.[37] This is not despite, but because of its basic humanistic approach, which leads it – against its better knowledge – to place human beings at the centre of the institutions. The category error of the divisional tradition could be formulated using Magritte's familiar caption: *ceci n'est pas une pipe*; or in the fundamental rights context: *la personne n'est pas un être humain*. By understanding fundamental rights as areas of personal autonomy, traditional thought brings about a fatal equation of 'mind/body' on the one hand and 'person' on the other.[38] But if one takes the difference seriously by seeing the 'person' as a mere semantic artefact of social communication on the one hand, and mind and body as living, breathing entities in the environment of this communication, on the other, it becomes clear that it is precisely the humanistic equation of semantic artefacts with actual human beings that does people an injustice.

The fact that people are not parts of society, but insuperably separate from it, has one inexorable consequence:[39] society and mind/body are not communicatively accessible to each other. Mind and body are each independent, self-sustaining (mental or organic) processes. While it is true that both have certainly brought about communication, they cannot control it. Communication becomes autonomous from people, creating its own world of meaning separate from the individual mind. This communication can be used by people productively for their survival, but it can also – and this is the point at which fundamental rights become relevant – turn against them and threaten their integrity, or even annihilate them. Extreme examples are: killing by a chain of command; sweatshops as a consequence of anonymous market forces; martyrs as a result of religious communication; and political or military torture as a destruction of identity.

It is these negative externalities of communication, their potential to threaten mind and body, that are at the core of the human rights problem – and not social inequality among human beings, as has been traditionally supposed! The environment-threatening potential of society seen as a communicative ensemble is by no means in contradiction with its operative closure; on the contrary, it is its consequence. To be sure, their mutual closure makes society and people inaccessible to each other. Communicative processes cannot penetrate body and mind; the latter are external to communication. But communication can irritate psycho-physical processes in a way that threatens their self-preservation. Or it may simply destroy them. This is where the body and mind of individuals (not of 'persons') demand their 'pre-legal', 'pre-political', even 'pre-social' (i.e. extra-societal) 'latent intrinsic rights'.[40] Body and mind insist on their identity and their self-preservation against destructive perturbations of communication – and they do this without any forum before which they could assert these 'rights'.[41] And human rights in the strict sense should in fact be restricted to this 'stark' issue of mental and bodily integrity in the face of communicative processes, and not be burdened with problems of social communication that have an entirely different structure. This is not to deny the relevance of such problems for fundamental rights in the broader sense, but rather to emphasise it.[42]

These latent 'rights' only become overt, however, if bodily pain and mental suffering no longer remain unheard in their speechlessness, but succeed in irritating the communication of society and in provoking new distinctions within it.[43] The resistance of ill-treated bodies and souls can be 'heard' only if it is expressed within communication itself – in the social messages of physical violence as anti-hegemonic communication and the messages of suffering souls in complaint and protest. It is only then that there is a chance that from this, communicative conflicts concerning the core area of human rights will develop. It needs to be emphasised, however, that these communicative conflicts can only ever be proxies and are thus only able to re-present the real environmental conflicts in communication, not present them directly. These communicative conflicts are by no means identical to the real conflicts that the communication provokes in relation to its ecologies of mind and body.

Nor do these communicative conflicts reflect them accurately. Rather, they are merely intra-societal resonances of external conflicts, mere reconstructions within communication of ecological conflicts. Accordingly, the results of these communicative conflicts are once again merely internal communicative norms, which can neither regulate nor protect mind and body. But, in a roundabout way, they can become relevant for both, if social norms develop from these conflicts which ultimately set limits on communication, delineating its boundaries with that which is extra-communicative. This is where the law's central figure – the legal prohibition: thou shall not – becomes effective beyond the limits of the communicative: prohibitions of particular communications (a ban on killing, a ban on torture). Thus 'latent rights' (i.e. intrinsic claims by people of flesh and blood to their bodily and mental integrity) are reconstructed socially as 'living rights' in Eugen Ehrlich's sense, that is as 'human rights' in the strictest sense, which can be fought for and won anywhere in society, not just in law or in politics.[44]

That argument explains why it makes no sense to frame human rights as a decision of the political sovereign (whether a prince or the self-governing people) promulgated by positive law. While human rights are not like natural law in the sense of having some kind of pre-political absolute validity, they are pre-social (extra-social) in a very different sense, in that they are based on the 'latent rights' of bodily and mental entities to their integrity. At the same time, they are 'pre-political' and 'pre-legal', in being built on the 'living law of human rights' which arises out of communicative conflicts in politics, morals, religion or law, and the results won in those conflicts. To positivise them as technical law is not the free decision of the democratically legitimated legislator, but based on this double foundation of self-sustaining processes outside society and conflicts within it.

IV Fundamental rights as a problem of modernity: the expansion of political power

The problem of 'latent human rights' thus always arises whenever there is communication at all: as the 'intrinsic rights' of organic life and of mental experience, in situations where their integrity is endangered by social communication. In old Europe, this was not 'translated' into the semantics of human rights, however, but rather into the semantics of the perfection of man in imperfect nature, or of the soul's salvation in a corrupt world. The original Fall of Man happened under the Tree of Knowledge: the material meaning-producing force of communication, with its ability to distinguish good and evil, destroyed the original unity of man and nature, made man god-like and led to the loss of Paradise. The origin of alienation goes back to the very first communication.

Human rights in their specific modern sense appear only with the second Fall. This does not coincide with the emergence of private property, as Marx would have it, but with the autonomisation of a multiplicity of separate communicative worlds. First of all, and clearly visible everywhere from Macchiavelli's time onwards, the matrix of politics becomes autonomous. It becomes detached from the diffuse moral, religious and economic ties of the old European society and infinitely extends the usurpation potential of its particular medium, i.e. power, without being restrained any longer by immanent bonds. By means of its operative closure and its structural autonomy, it creates new environments for itself and then develops expansive, indeed downright imperialist, tendencies towards them. Absolute power releases unsuspected destructive forces. The centralised power to make legitimate collective decisions, which develops a special language of its own, indeed a high-flown rationality of the political, has an inherent, boundary-transgressing totalising tendency.[45]

Its expansion proceeds in two divergent directions. First, it crosses the boundaries with other social sectors. Their response is to insist on their communicative autonomy, free from intervention by politics. This response is the birth of fundamental rights, either as personal or as institutional rights to autonomy. Fundamental rights demarcate areas of autonomy from politics which are allotted either to social institutions or to persons as social constructs.[46] In both cases, fundamental rights set limits on the totalising tendencies of the political matrix within society. Secondly, and with particular vehemence, politics expands beyond the outer boundaries of society in its endeavours to control the human mind and body. Their resistance becomes effective only once it can be communicated as protest in the form of complaints and violence, once it has been translated into social form as the political struggles of the oppressed against their oppressors and finally, via historical compromises, has resulted in political guarantees of the self-limitation of politics vis-à-vis people as psycho-physical entities. Unlike the aforementioned institutional and personal fundamental rights, these political guarantees are human rights in the strict sense.

The fundamental rights tradition has not separated these 'latent' human rights distinctly from personal and institutional rights to autonomy, but has always translated them in an undifferentiated manner into individual fundamental rights that do not distinguish sufficiently between institutional, personal and individual rights, through a re-entry of the external into the internal.[47] Communication cannot guarantee or regulate the autonomy of the mind, nor even describe it appropriately with any prospect of a correspondence between perception and object. The difference between communication and mind is unbridgeable. But this difference is repeated within communication by means of a re-entry. The same applies to the difference between communication and the body. The external human beings (mind and body), who are not accessible to communication, are modelled within the law as 'persons', as 'bearers of fundamental rights', without there being any guarantee that the constructs of persons within society will correspond to the people outside it. It is to these artefacts of communication that actions are attributed and areas of freedom granted as fundamental rights. This is where the tradition effects the pernicious equation of person and human being in the unitary concept of individual fundamental rights, something which has already been criticised above. It does not distinguish sufficiently between guarantees of communicative freedoms on the one hand and guarantees of psycho-physical integrity on the other. Against this, we must insist on the difference between personal fundamental rights and human rights in the strict sense. Human rights in this sense do also rely on the technique of re-entry and thus on their attribution to communicative constructs, but they must be understood as semantically different from personal communicative freedoms, namely as intended guarantees of the integrity of mind and body. This is where the clash between the egalitarian perspective of the person and the non-egalitarian perspective of the individual human being becomes the subject of moral, political and legal discourse.

V The fragmentation of society: multiplication of expansive social systems

This model of fundamental rights, which is oriented towards politics and the state, works only as long as the state can be identified with society, or, at least, as long as the state can be regarded as the organisational form of society and politics as its hierarchical coordination. However, as other highly specialised communicative media – money, knowledge, law, medicine, technology – gain autonomy, this model loses its plausibility. At this point, the horizontal effects of fundamental and human rights become relevant. The fragmentation of society multiplies the boundary zones between autonomised communicative matrices and human beings. The new territories of meaning each draw boundaries of their own between themselves and their human environments. Here new dangers arise for the integrity of body and mind. These are the issues to which the 'third-party effect' of human rights in the strict sense should be confined. Another, no less important, set of issues concerning constitutional rights would be the autonomy of institutional communicative spheres vis-à-vis their 'private' subjugation, and a third set of issues would concern the autonomy of personal communicative freedoms.[48]

Thus, human rights cannot be limited to the relation between state and individual, or the area of institutionalised politics, or even solely to phenomena of power in the broadest sense.[49] The specific danger to physical and mental integrity posed by a self-sustaining communicative matrix emanates not only from politics, but in principle from all autonomised social sectors that have expansive tendencies. As regards the matrix of the economy, Marx has clarified this, especially through such concepts as alienation, fetishisation, the autonomy of capital, the commodification of the world and the exploitation of man by man. Today we see – most clearly in the writings of Foucault, Agamben and Legendre[50] – similar threats to human integrity from the matrices of the natural sciences, of psychology, of the social sciences, of technology and medicine, and of the information media. For example, the experiments carried out on people by Dr. Mengele were once regarded as an expression of a sadistic personality or as an enslavement of science by totalitarian Nazi policy. Subsequent research suggests that the experiments are better regarded as the product of the expansionistic tendencies of science to seize every opportunity for the accumulation of knowledge, especially under the pressure of international competition, unless it is restrained by external controls.[51]

By now it should have become clear why it makes no sense to talk about the 'horizontal effect' of political fundamental rights. There is no translation of state guarantees of individual freedoms into the 'horizontal' relations between private actors. Something else is needed instead. It is necessary to develop new types of guarantee that enable a limitation of the destructive potential of social communication for body and mind. This is why the state action approach is too limited in allowing fundamental rights to operate in the private sector only if trace elements of state action can be identified. And this is also why the economic power approach is misleading in seeing fundamental rights exclusively as a response to power phenomena. This is much too narrow, for, while it does account for social power, it does not take into consideration the more subtle dangers to integrity posed by other communicative matrices, as for example by the monetary mechanism.

Accordingly, it is the fragmentation of society that is central to the human rights question today. There is not just a single boundary between *political communication* and the *individual*, guarded by human rights. Rather, the same problems arise in numerous social institutions, each forming its own boundaries with its human environment: *politics/individual, economy/individual, law/individual, science/individual, medicine/individual* (never as a whole/part relation, but understood as the difference between communication and mind/body). It thus all comes down to identifying the different border points, in order to recognise the border violations that endanger human integrity by their specific characteristics. Where are these border posts? In the extremely varied constructs of persons in the subsystems: *homo politicus, oeconomicus, juridicus, organisatoricus, retalis*, etc. While these are mere constructs within communication which enable classification, they are also real points of contact with people 'out there'.[52] It is through the mask of the 'person' that social systems make contact with people; while they cannot communicate with them, they can irritate them very significantly and be irritated by them in turn. In tight perturbation cycles, communication irritates consciousness by its selective 'enquiries' that are conditioned by assumptions about rational actors, and is irritated by the 'answers' which are themselves conditioned in a highly selective way. It is in this recursiveness that the 'exploitation' of human beings by social systems (not by other human beings!) comes about. The social system as a specialised communicative process concentrates its irritations of human beings on its person constructs. It 'sucks' mental and physical energies from them for the sake of the self-preservation of the difference marking it off from its environment. It is only in this highly specific way that Foucault's disciplinary mechanisms develop their particular effects.[53]

VI The anonymous matrix

If violations of fundamental rights stem from the totalising tendencies of partial rationalities, there is no longer any point in regarding the horizontal effect of fundamental rights as if it concerned relations between private actors whose rights need to be weighed up against each other. The origin of the infringement of fundamental rights needs to be examined more closely. The simple part-whole view of society continues to make itself felt in the use of the imagery of 'horizontality'. This takes the sting out of the whole human rights issue to an almost unbearable extent, as if it were just a question of individuals infringing the rights of other individuals.

The violation of the integrity of individuals by other individuals, whether through communication, mere perception or direct physical action, constitutes a completely different set of problems, however, which arose long before the radical fragmentation of society in our days. It must be systematically separated from the fundamental rights question as such.[54] In the European tradition, it (alongside other constructions) was translated in social terms by investing persons, as the communicative representatives of actual human beings, with 'subjective rights' against each other. This was elaborated philosophically by the theory of subjective rights in the Kantian tradition, according to which citizens' spheres of arbitrary freedom ideally are demarcated from each other in such a way that the law can take a generalisable form. Legally, this idea has been most clearly developed in the classical law of tort, in which not merely indemnifications, but violations of subjective rights are central. Now, 'fundamental rights' in their institutional, personal and human dimensions, as here proposed, differ from 'subjective rights' in private law. They do not concern the mutual endangerment of private individuals, i.e. intersubjective relations, but rather the dangers to the integrity of institutions, persons and individuals that are created by anonymous communicative matrices (institutions, discourses, systems). Fundamental rights are not defined by the fundamental nature of that which they protect, or by their privileged position in constitutional texts, but as counter-institutions opposing the expansionist tendencies of social systems.

The Anglo-American tradition does not differentiate here and speaks of 'rights' in both cases, thereby overlooking from the outset the fundamental distinction between subjective rights and fundamental rights, while being able to deal with them together. By contrast, criminal law concepts of macro-criminality and criminal responsibility of formal organisations come closer to the pertinent issues being considered here.[55] These concepts concern norm violations that do not originate with human beings, but with impersonal social processes which use human perpetrators as their functionaries.[56] But they are confined to the dangers stemming from more easily visualised 'collective actors' (states, political parties, business firms, groups of companies, associations) and miss the dangers stemming from the anonymous 'matrix', that is from autonomised communicative processes (institutions, functional systems, networks) that are not personified as collectives. Even political human rights should not be seen as relations between political actors (state versus citizen), i.e. as an expression of person-to-person relations. Instead, political human rights are relations between anonymous power processes, on the one hand, and tortured bodies and hurt souls, on the other. In communication, this notion is expressed only very imperfectly, not to say misleadingly, as the relation between the state as a 'person' and the 'persons' of the individuals.

It would be repeating the fatal category error of the tradition were one to treat the horizontal effect of fundamental rights in terms of subjective rights between individual persons.[57] That would just end up in the law of tort, with its focus on interpersonal relations. And we would be forced to apply the concrete state-oriented fundamental rights wholesale to the most varied interpersonal relations, with disastrous consequences for freedom of choice in private life. Here lies the rational core of the excessive protests of private lawyers against the intrusion of fundamental rights into private law, though these complaints are in turn exaggerated and overlook the genuinely societal nature of the fundamental rights issue.[58]

The category error can be avoided. Both the 'old' political and the 'new' polycontextural human rights question should be understood in terms of people being threatened not by their fellows, but by anonymous communicative processes. These processes must in the first place be identified. Foucault has seen this most clearly, in radically depersonalising the phenomenon of power and in understanding today's micro-power relations in the capillaries of society as the expression of the discourses/practices of 'disciplines'.[59]

We can now summarise the outcome of our abstract considerations. The human rights question in the strictest sense must today be seen as the endangerment of the integrity of the body and mind of individuals by a multiplicity of anonymous and by now globalised communicative processes. The fragmentation of world society into autonomous subsystems creates new external boundaries on the outside of society between subsystem and human being and new internal boundaries within society between the various subsystems. The expansive tendencies of the subsystems aim in both directions.[60] The new 'equation' which is to replace the old 'equation' of the horizontal effect now comes into clearer view. The old one was based on a relation between two private actors – private perpetrator and private victim of the infringement. One side of the new equation is now no longer occupied by a private actor as the violator of fundamental rights, but by the *anonymous matrix of an autonomised communicative medium*. On the other side there is no longer simply the undifferentiated individual. Instead, owing to the presence of new boundaries, the protection of the individual, hitherto seen in unitary terms, splits up into several dimensions. On this other side of the equation, the fundamental rights have to be systematically divided into three or even four dimensions:

Firstly, there are *institutional rights* which protect the autonomy of social discourses – the autonomy of art, of science, of religion – against their subjugation by the totalising tendencies of the communicative matrix. By protecting them against the totalitarian tendencies of science, media or economy, fundamental rights take effect as 'conflict-of-laws rules' between partial rationalities in society.[61]

Secondly, there are *personal rights* which protect the autonomy of communications, attributed not to institutions, but to the social artefacts called 'persons'.

Thirdly, there are *human rights* as negative bounds on societal communication, where the integrity of the body and mind of individuals is endangered by a communicative matrix that crosses boundaries. (Also to be mentioned, albeit not systematically discussed here, are ecological rights, where society endangers the integrity of natural processes).

It should be stressed that specific fundamental rights are to be allocated to these dimensions not on a one-to-one basis, but with a multiplicity of overlaps. Some fundamental rights are mainly to be attributed to one or another of these dimensions (e.g. freedom of art, freedom of science, and property primarily to the institutional rights dimension, freedom of speech primarily to the personal rights dimension, and freedom of conscience primarily to the human rights dimension). Some display all three dimensions (e.g. religious freedom). It is all the more important, therefore, to distinguish the three dimensions carefully within the various fundamental rights and to take into account the fact that they have very different legal forms and very different requirements for their implementation.

VII Justiciability?

Let us now concentrate on the third dimension, that of human rights in the strictest sense, that of the protection of mental and physical integrity. The ensuing question for lawyers is this: can the issue of the 'horizontal' effects of fundamental rights be reformulated by shifting the focus from conflicts within society (person versus person) to conflicts between society and its ecologies (communication versus body/mind)? In other words, can the 'horizontal' effect be transplanted from the paradigm of interpersonal conflicts between individual bearers of fundamental rights to that of ecological conflicts between anonymous communicative processes on the one hand, and concrete people on the other?

The difficulties are enormous. To list only a few:

How is it even possible for communication to address destructive system/environment relations 'between' the symbolic universes of Communication and of Consciousness as a conflict – as a social conflict, let alone a legal conflict? This is a real Lyotard-style problem: is this possible, if not as *litige*, then at least as *différend*? In the absence of a supreme court for meaning, all that can happen is either that the mental experience endures the infringement and then fades away unheard, or that the infringement is 'translated' into communication. But in the latter case, the paradoxical and highly unlikely demand will be for the infringer of the right (society, communication) to punish its own crime! That is indeed to make the poacher into a gamekeeper. It is by institutionalising political fundamental rights that several nation states have already managed precisely this kind of gamekeeper-poacher self-limitation – however imperfectly.

How can the law describe the boundary conflict, when after all it has only the language of the 'rights' of 'persons' available to it?[62] In this impoverished rights language, is it even able to construct the difference between interpersonal conflicts inside society and the communicative endangerments of individuals outside society via external social conflicts? Here we reach the limits not only of what is conceivable in legal doctrine, but also of what is possible in court proceedings. In litigation there must always be a claimant suing a defendant for infringing his rights. In this framework of a mandatory binarisation in the form of person/person conflicts, can human rights ever be asserted against the structural violence of anonymous communicative processes? The only way to do this – at any rate in litigation – is simply to continue to utilise the category error so harshly criticised above, but, being aware of its falsehood, to correct it immanently as far as possible by introducing a difference. That means individual lawsuits against private actors, in which human rights are asserted – not the rights of persons against persons, however, but those of flesh-and-blood human beings against the structural violence of the matrix. Or, in traditional terms, the confrontation with institutional problems that is really intended has to take place within individual forms of legal action. We are already familiar with something similar from existing institutional theories of fundamental rights, which recognise as their bearers not only persons, but also institutions.[63] Whoever enforces individual freedom of expression simultaneously protects the integrity of the political process. But what is at issue here are not the rights of impersonal institutions against the state but, in a multiple inversion of the relation, the rights of individuals outside society against social institutions outside the state.

While it is quite plausible in itself, is this distinction clear enough to be justiciable? Can person-to-person conflicts be separated from individual-against-individual conflicts, on the one hand, and from conflicts between a communication system and an individual, on the other, if communication, after all, is made possible only via persons? Translated into the language of society and of law, this becomes a problem of attribution. Whodunnit? Under what conditions can the concrete endangerment of integrity be attributed not to persons or individuals, but to anonymous communication processes? If this attribution could be achieved, a genuine human rights problem would have been formulated even in the impoverished rights talk of the law.[64]

In an extreme simplification, the 'horizontal' human rights problem can perhaps be described in familiar legal categories as follows. The problem of human rights in private law arises only where the endangerment of body/mind integrity emanates from social 'institutions' (and not just from individual actors). In principle, institutions include private formal organisations and private regulatory systems. The most important examples here would be business firms, private associations, hospitals, schools, universities as formal organisations; and general terms of trade, private standardisation and similar rule-setting mechanisms as private regulatory systems. We must of course be clear that the term 'institution' represents only imperfectly these chains of communicative acts, characterised by a specialised medium, which endanger the integrity of mind and body – something which is referred to here by the metaphor of the anonymous 'matrix' – and understand that it conveys very little of their expansive tendencies. But for lawyers, who are oriented towards rules and persons, it has the advantage of defining the institution as a bundle of norms and, at the same time, allowing it to be personified. The concept of the institution accordingly could point the way for a re-specification of fundamental rights in social sectors (corresponding, as it were, to the definition of the state as an institution and as a person in the field of politics). The outcome would be a formula of 'third-party effect' which could seem plausible even to a black-letter lawyer. It would not regard horizontal effect as a weighing of individuals and their fundamental rights against each other, but instead as the protection of human rights, personal rights and the rights of discourses against expansive social institutions.

VIII *HIV/AIDS v. TNC*

Now that our expectations have been both heightened and lowered, let us take another look at the HIV catastrophe in South Africa. I cannot offer a solution, but at best suggest directions in which thinking about human rights might develop. It should be fairly clear how inadequate it is to weigh a patient's individual fundamental right to life against the transnational corporation's individual property right in court proceedings. This is not an issue of corporate social responsibility, with a single corporate actor infringing the fundamental rights of AIDS patients through its pricing policy. A human right of access to medication can become a reality only if the 'horizontal' effect of fundamental rights is reformulated and its focus shifted from interpersonal conflicts (person versus person) to system/environment conflicts (communication versus body/soul, or institution versus institution).

In the institutional dimension, the conflict needs to be set in its social context, which requires us to observe that the AIDS catastrophe is ultimately due to a clash of incompatible logics of action.[65] The critical conflict arises in the domain of patent rights to medicines and is the contradiction between norms of economic rationality and norms formed in the health context.[66] It is then a matter not of imposing price controls on particular pharmaceutical firms, but of developing abstract and general rules on incompatibilities between the business sector and the health sector, and of preparing WIPO, WTO and UN law, as part of a transnational patent law, to respond to destructive conflicts between incompatible logics of action by building health concerns into the norms of economic rationality. Since there is no higher authority that can decide the conflict, it can only be solved from the viewpoint of one of the conflicting regimes, here the WTO. But the competing logic of action, here the principles of the health sector, has to be brought into the international economic law context as a limitation.

It is, however, to be feared that this will not adequately take into account the dimension of genuine human rights. In other words, if access to medication is not lastingly improved by the measures now decided and by the planned WIPO treaties, the transnational development of patent law in relation to pharmaceutical products will have to be adjusted again, whether by granting, in a transparent, procedurally simplified and low-cost fashion, the right to compulsory licensing, or by a licence or patent exception system graded according to economic capacity, or finally by the radical cure of a general settlement that would completely remove certain medicines from the protection of transnational patent law for a period.[67]

This sketch of possible legal approaches to the AIDS catastrophe shows how misplaced the optimism is which holds that the human rights problem will surely be amenable to a solution using the resources of legal policy. Even institutional rights confront the law with the boundaries between it and other social subsystems. Can one discourse do justice to the other? The dilemmas connected with this question have been analysed by Lyotard.[68] But at least this is a problem located within society, one to which Luhmann tried to respond with the concept of justice as socially adequate complexity.[69] The situation is even more dramatic as regards human rights in the strict sense, located at the boundary between communication and the individual human being. All the tentative efforts to juridify human rights cannot hide the fact that this is a strictly impossible project. How can society ever 'do justice' to real people if people are not its parts but stand outside communication, if society cannot communicate with them but at most about them, indeed not even reach them but merely either irritate or destroy them? In the light of grossly inhuman social practices, the justice of human rights is a burning issue, but one which has no prospect of resolution. This has to be stated quite bluntly.

If a positive concept of justice in the relation between communication and human being is definitively impossible, then, short of succumbing to post-structuralist quietism, the only option left to us is some kind of second best. In the law, we have to accept that the problem of the integrity of body and mind can only be experienced through the inadequate sensors of irritation, reconstruction and re-entry. At best, the law can only guess at the deep dimension of the conflicts between communication on the one hand and mind and body on the other. The only remaining source of direction is the legal prohibition, through which a self-limitation of communication seems possible.[70] But even this prohibition can describe the transcendence of the other only allegorically. This programme of justice is ultimately doomed to fail. It cannot, with Derrida, console itself that it is 'to come, à venir',[71] but has to face up to its being in principle impossible. The justice of human rights can, then, at best be formulated negatively. It is aimed at removing unjust situations, not creating just ones. It is only the counter-principle to communicative violations of body and soul, a protest against inhumanities of communication, without it ever being possible to say positively what the conditions of a 'humanly just' communication might be.

Nor do the emancipatory programmes of modernity help to take us any further. The criteria of democratic involvement of individuals in social processes do not tell us anything, since it is only persons that take part, not bodies or minds. From this viewpoint, one can only be amazed at the naivety of participatory romanticism. Democratic procedures are no test of the human rights justice of a society.[72] Equally uninformative are universalisation theories that proceed transcendentally via a priori characteristics or via the a posteriori universalisation of expressed needs. What do such philosophical abstractions have to do with actual human individuals? The same criticism applies to economic theories of individual preferences aggregated through market mechanisms.

Only the self-observation of mind/body – introspection, suffering, pain – can judge whether communication infringes human rights. If these self-observations, however distorted, gain entry to communication, then there is some chance of a humanly just self-limitation of communication. The decisive thing is the "moment": the simultaneity of consciousness and communication, the cry that expresses pain: hence the closeness of justice to spontaneous indignation, unrest and protest, and its remoteness from philosophical, political and legal discourses.

Notes

This chapter was previously published as 'The anonymous matrix: human rights violations by private transnational actors', trans. Iain L. Fraser, *Modern Law Review*, 69:3 (2006), 327–46.

1. United Nations General Assembly, *A More Secure World*, Nos 44, 48.
2. South Africa Competition Commission, *Hazel Tau et al v. GlaxoSmithKline, Boehringer Ingelheim et al* (16 December 2003), available at www.compcom.co.za/.
3. See Hestermeyer, 'Access to medication'.

4 See Bass, 'Implications of the TRIPS Agreement', p. 192.
5 *Hazel Tau et al. v. GlaxoSmithKline, Boehringer Ingelheim et al.*, Complaint to the South Africa Competition Commission, para 17, available at www.tac.org.za/Documents/DrugCompaniesCC/HazelTauAndOthersVGlaxoSmithKlineAndOthersStatementOfComplaint.doc.
6 On the case, see: Law and Treatment Access Unit of the AIDS Law Project & Treatment Action Campaign, *Price of Life*; J. P. Love, 'Expert Declaration' (Center for Study of Responsive Law, 2003), available at www.cptech.org/ip/health/cl/cl-cases/rsa-tac/love02032003.doc.
7 Details in Chapter 10 in this volume.
8 Wood and Scharffs, 'Applicability of human rights standards', p. 539.
9 See e.g. Saro-Wiwa, *Flammen der Hölle*.
10 Hoering, 'Bhopal und kein Ende'.
11 Fung et al., *Can We Put an End to Sweatshops?*.
12 See e.g. Cleveland, 'Global labor rights', pp. 1551 ff.; Ashagrie, 'Statistics on Working Children'.
13 Holtbrügge and Berg, 'Menschenrechte und Verhaltenskodizes', p. 179.
14 Yozell, 'The Castro Alfaro Case'.
15 Weber, *Die Verschwundenen von Mercedes-Benz*; Fischer-Lescano, *Globalverfassung*, pp. 31 ff.
16 Perez, *Ecological Sensitivity and Global Legal Pluralism*.
17 Baker, 'Tightening the toothless vise'.
18 For a comparative view, see Friedman and Barak-Erez, 'Introduction'; Anderson, 'Social democracy'; for England, see Tomkins, 'On Being Sceptical about Human Rights'; for Israel, see Barak, 'Constitutional human rights', for South Africa, see Cheadle and Davis, 'Application of the 1996 constitution'.
19 See the comparative analysis of Anderson, 'Social democracy'.
20 This implication becomes obvious in Canaris, *Grundrechte und Privatrecht*, pp. 30–62; for a critique of this approach, see Brüggemeier, 'Constitutionalisation of Private Law'.
21 On the political strategies of societal constitutionalism see Anderson, 'Social democracy', pp. 33 ff.; Hardt and Negri, *Multitude*, pp. 202 ff.; Davis et al., 'Social Rights, Social Citizenship, and Transformative Constitutionalism'.
22 This suggestion is from Anderson, 'Social democracy', pp. 33 ff.
23 On the relationship of legal semantics and social structures, see Luhmann, 'Subjektive Rechte'.
24 Gierke, *Wesen der menschlichen Verbände*, pp. 26 ff.
25 Villey, *Leçons d'histoire*, pp. 249 ff.
26 For example Rothstein, *Just Institutions Matter*.
27 Durkheim, *Division of Labor*, pp. 68–87.
28 Parsons, *System of Modern Societies*, pp. 4–28.
29 Weber, *Gesammelte Aufsätze zur Wissenschaftslehre*, pp. 605 ff.; on this, see Schluchter, *Religion und Lebensführung*, vol. 1, p. 302.
30 Alexy, *Theory of Constitutional Rights*, ch. 10. Symptomatic for an individualistic understanding of the effects of human rights is Lessard, 'Idea of the "private"'.
31 See a decision by the German Federal Constitutional Court which is representative of this approach: BVerfGE 89, 214 et seq.; see also Alexy, *Theory of Constitutional Rights*, ch. 10; Brüggemeier, 'Constitutionalisation of Private Law'. Very critical towards the subjective rights view is Ladeur, *Kritik der Abwägung*, pp. 61 ff.

32 Luhmann, *Social Systems*, pp. 176–209; Luhmann, 'Individuality of the Individual'; Luhmann, 'Individuum und Gesellschaft'; Luhmann, 'Die Form "Person"'.
33 Mead, *Mind, Self and Society*, pp. 135 ff.
34 Agamben, *Homo Sacer*, pp. 15–29; Foucault, *Discipline and Punish*; Derrida, 'Force of law'; Lyotard, *The Differend*.
35 It is unnecessary to point this out to the *cognoscenti* among those scornful of systems theory: they see these secret convergences, especially Schütz, 'Thinking the law'; Schütz, 'Sons of the Writ'.
36 Here the argument comes close to positions on justice of which Derrida, 'Force of law', is the most forceful exponent.
37 Luhmann, *Law as a Social System*, p. 74, n. 47.
38 When talking about human beings, Luhmann refers to a self-organising individual in its whole individuality, in its empirical incommensurability, and no longer to something that could have been integrated into the normative structure of society as an abstraction, as 'the human being'. Luhmann, *Introduction to Systems Theory*, pp. 180 ff.
39 On the division of communication and mind see, in addition to Luhmann, *Social Systems*, pp. 176–209: Luhmann, 'Individuality of the Individual'; Luhmann, 'Individuum und Gesellschaft'; Luhmann, 'Die Form "Person"'; also Fuchs, *Eigen-Sinn des Bewußtseins*; Wasser, 'Psychoanalyse als Theorie autopoietischer Systeme'; Stenner, 'Is autopoietic systems theory alexithymic?'
40 To be enjoyed with extreme caution! These are not rights in the technical legal, political or moral sense, but self-preserving tendencies shown by a chain of differences against its environment.
41 Without mentioning the law, Fuchs, *Eigen-Sinn des Bewußtseins*, p. 22, uses similar formulations to characterise the claims of the psyche against communication.
42 Luhmann, *Law as a Social System*, p. 485.
43 Fuchs, *Eigen-Sinn des Bewußtseins*, p. 17, speaks of social addresses as the 'scheme of schemes by which communication equips itself with the possibility of irritations (in principle, with guidance) in regard to units in the environment appearing as mental or social "agencies" which in principle are identifiable and can be accessed through communication'.
44 This is not to be confused with the distinction in legal philosophy between rights in the state of nature and in the civil state.
45 Luhmann, *Grundrechte als Institution*, p. 24.
46 On the transformation of individual into institutional fundamental rights, see Ladeur, *Kritik der Abwägung*, p. 77.
47 See again Alexy, *Theory of Constitutional Rights*.
48 The institutional aspect is emphasised by Ladeur, *Kritik der Abwägung*, p. 64: 'Fundamental rights can contribute to the self-reflection of the private law in those situations where the protection of non-economical interests and goods is at issue – as is the case with the third-party effect of communicative freedom.'
49 In labour law, the horizontal effect of fundamental rights is commonly reduced to 'social power' along the lines of political power. In the face of organisational power, this seems reasonable, but it reduces the question of fundamental rights to a mere issue of the balance of power. See Gamillscheg, 'Grundrechte im Arbeitsrecht'. Explicitly political concepts concerning the horizontal effect of fundamental rights exhibit similar reductions, e.g. Anderson, 'Social democracy', p. 33.
50 Agamben, *Homo Sacer*, pp. 15–29; Foucault, *Discipline and Punish*; Legendre, *Le crime du caporal Lortie*.

51 See Schmuhl, *Grenzüberschreitungen*; Böll, *Lost Honor of Katharina Blum*.
52 For details see Fuchs, *Eigen-Sinn des Bewußtseins*, pp. 16–33.
53 For details on person constructs as the junction between communication and mind, see Hutter and Teubner, 'Homo Oeconomicus'.
54 Certainly people can do great evil to each other by violating rights of the most fundamental kind (life, dignity). But this is not (yet) a fundamental rights question in the sense intended here. Rather, it concerns one of the Ten Commandments, fundamental norms of the criminal law and the law of tort. Fundamental rights in the modern sense are not directed against perils emanating from people, but against perils emanating from the matrix of social systems.
55 See e.g. Jäger, *Makrokriminalität*; Gómez-Jara Díez, *La culpabilidad penal de la empresa*.
56 For clarification it should be emphasised that this is not to say that individual responsibility disappears behind collective responsibility. Rather, both can exist in parallel.
57 Very critical towards the consideration of subjective rights in the range of the horizontal effect is Ladeur, *Kritik der Abwägung*, pp. 58 ff.
58 Medicus, 'Grundsatz der Verhältnismäßigkeit'; Zöllner, 'Regelungsspielräume'; Diederichsen, 'Selbstbehauptung des Privatrechts'; Diederichsen, 'Bundesverfassungsgericht als oberstes Zivilgericht'.
59 Foucault, *Discipline and Punish*. Foucault's problem, however, is his obsessive fixation on the phenomenon of power, which leads him into a senseless inflation of the concept of power. As a consequence, he cannot discern the more subtle effects of other communication media.
60 In more detail see Chapter 10 in this volume, pp. 237 ff. Not the therapy, but the diagnosis is followed by Koskenniemi, 'Global Legal Pluralism'.
61 Ladeur, *Kritik der Abwägung*, pp. 60, 69 ff., 71; Graber and Teubner, 'Art and money'; Teubner, 'Ein Fall von struktureller Korruption?'; Teubner, 'Expertise as Social Institution'.
62 Glendon, 'Rights Talk'.
63 See the impersonal concept of fundamental rights by Ridder, *Soziale Ordnung des Grundgesetzes*; Ladeur, 'Helmut Ridders Konzeption der Meinungs- und Pressefreiheit'.
64 This problem is comparable to the demarcation of sovereign and fiscal actions in public law or of actions of agents and personal actions in private law.
65 Cf. Teubner, 'Ein Fall von struktureller Korruption?'
66 On the details of the current conflict and perspectives of possible resolutions see Chapter 10 in this volume.
67 Correa and Musungu, 'WIPO Patent Agenda'; see also Helfer, 'Regime shifting'; generally on regulation in the domain of bio-technology: Stoll, 'Biotechnologische Innovationen'.
68 Lyotard, *The Differend*, paras 1 ff.
69 Luhmann, *Rechtssystem und Rechtsdogmatik*, pp. 20–3; Luhmann, *Ausdifferenzierung des Rechts*, pp. 374 ff.; Luhmann, *Law as a Social System*, pp. 214 ff.
70 This may explain the high value that is ascribed to the prohibition in law by authors with different theoretical backgrounds, Wiethölter, 'Just-ifications', p. 66; Legendre, *Le crime du caporal Lortie*, ch. 5.
71 Derrida, 'Force of law', p. 969.
72 Even if there is no doubt that democratic procedures might increase political sensitivity concerning human rights issues.

6

After privatisation? The many autonomies of private law

> The logic of the market is insufficient for society. It has conquered social sectors for which it is wholly inadequate.
>
> Speculator George Soros (1998)[1]

I A perennial oscillation?

What is the price of efficiency? The last twenty years have seen an important shift in the pattern of public service provision throughout the countries of the OECD. Across a whole range of services – higher education, research and development, utilities, transport, telecommunications, the media, health and social services, security and law enforcement – there has been a transfer of responsibility from the public to the private sector.[2] Pressures of globalisation and technological changes, combined with the neo-liberal policies of national governments, both conservative and progressive, have created a transnational wave of privatisation. Political and legal resistance at a national level seems to be powerless against this overwhelming movement. The crucial question seems to be: After privatisation, what now? What will market mechanisms do to the public interest aspects of these services, which previously had been protected – more or less successfully – by public law principles, democratic legitimation, fundamental rights and the *Rechtsstaat*?

If they are not to be sacrificed on the altar of market efficiency, so the argument goes, then, paradoxically, privatisation of public services will lead to a massive intrusion of public law principles into private law regimes. In the course of privatisation, the private law of advanced industrialised societies will need to pay a part of the price for the loss of the democratic and political dimensions and incorporate public law elements to a hitherto unknown degree.[3]

I would like to contest this emerging consensus on a new compensatory political justice. The social theory underlying this view is so reductive as to obscure many of the most important dimensions of these changes. The privatisation phenomenon, accordingly, is observed only along one dimension, as a move in a perennial oscillation between the public and private sector, swinging like a pendulum from the old *Polizeystaat* of the eighteenth century to nineteenth-century liberal society and then, in the twentieth century, first to the modern welfare state and finally back to the future of the new private globalised regimes. While agreeing that private law will indeed undergo a massive transformation after privatisation, I shall put forward an alternative hypothesis consisting of two different claims:

(1) The crucial problem is not how to compensate for the loss of the public interest in privatisation. Rather, it is how to move out of the reductive public/private dichotomy itself and how to make private law responsive to a plurality of diverse 'private' autonomies in civil society.
(2) The adequate reaction to privatisation is not to impose public law standards on private law, but rather to transform private law itself into the constitutional law of diverse private governance regimes, something which will ultimately lead to its far-reaching fragmentation and hybridisation.

II Deconstructing the public/private divide

It has almost become a ritual these days to deconstruct the private/public distinction. The problem is: nobody knows how to dis-place it, let alone how to re-place it.[4] Social theorists have analysed the breakdown of the boundary between state and society time and again, but in its place, they envision merely a diffuse politicisation of society as a whole.[5] Similarly, the distinction between public law and private law has been repeatedly attacked by legal scholars, but what is put forward in its stead is no more than a vague assumption that private law is pervasively political.[6] The ideology of privatisation has profited from this de(con)struction without re(dis)placement by presenting the old dichotomy as the only institutional choice available. Privatisation is then welcomed as an efficiency-enhancing movement from rigid governmental bureaucracies to dynamic markets.

In spite of all critique, the public/private distinction has maintained a remarkable viability over the centuries. This is due to its chameleon-like character, which, in its long history, has adapted swiftly to structural changes in society. It changed its appearance from the juxtaposition *polis* versus *oikos* in the old European society[7] to that of state versus society in the bourgeois era,[8] and survives in the contemporary distinction between the public and the private sector. In this formula two distinctions are successfully merged: political versus economic rationality on the one hand and hierarchical organisation versus market coordination on the other. Responsiveness, flexibility and efficiency are, of course, associated with the second part of both distinctions.

Not only is it argued here that the public/private distinction is an oversimplified account of contemporary society. More controversially, I argue that any idea of a fusion of the public and private spheres is equally inadequate. *As an alternative conceptualisation, it is proposed that the public/private divide should be replaced by polycontexturality.*[9] What does this mean? How can yet another continental neologism be of any help to our understanding? The claim is this: Contemporary social practices can no longer be analysed using a single binary distinction; the fragmentation of society into a multitude of social sectors requires a multitude of perspectives of self-description. Consequently, the simple juxtaposition of state and society, which translates into law as the distinction between public law and private law, needs to be replaced by a multiplicity of social perspectives that are simultaneously reflected in the law.[10] A dialectical *Aufhebung* of the distinction can serve to maintain and even to strengthen law's responsiveness to the public/private divide if this divide is understood as the difference between political and economic rationality. But at the same time the dualism needs to be broken up and replaced by a multiplicity of social perspectives, which then needs to be translated into law. The simple dualism of private law versus public law, which reflects the dualism of political versus economic rationality, cannot grasp the peculiarities of social fragmentation. Is a research project public or private in its character? And surely there is more to a doctor–patient relationship than a market transaction regulated by a few governmental policies.

Neither public law, as the law of the political process, nor private law, as the law of economic processes, has the capacity to develop adequate legal structures in relation to the many institutional contextures of civil society.[11] But, at the same time, it is by no means safe to assume that there is a new fusion of private and public law as suggested by such seductive slogans as 'private life is public' or 'everything is politics'. Rather, private law needs to reinforce its elective affinity to the contemporary plurality of discourses – not only its affinity to the economy as it is predominantly understood today, but also the close relation between private law and the many contexts of intimacy, health, education, science, religion, art and media. This would lead to a thoroughgoing reflection within private law of the distinctive eigenlogics of these various realms of discourse – a reflection which would encompass their internal rationality as well as their inherent normativity.

The point of strengthening these various relations is to de-politicise and to de-economise private law at the same time, to distance it not only from the public sector, but also from the private sector. It has become commonplace today to stress the difference between an efficiency-driven private law and the regulatory policies of the welfare state, and to emphasise the autonomy and decentralised rule production of the former as opposed to the central legislative intentions of the latter. But it is much less well understood that private law cannot be identified simply with the juridification of economic action. Indeed, this has been the great historical error of private law doctrine: contract law is increasingly reduced to the law of market transactions; the law of private associations has been restricted to the law of business organisations. We have increasingly come to view property law only as the basis for market operations and to shape tort law as the set of policies and rules that internalise economic externalities and eradicate third-party effects.[12] These are understandable errors, of course. Legal doctrine had to adapt to the double Great Transformation of our century, the victorious imperialism of both the economic and the political system, which has divided the social world between them into two spheres of influence. On the one hand, economic action developed totalising tendencies in its society-wide expansion and transformed non-commercial social relations, e.g. the relationships of the classical professions with their clients, into profit-oriented economic relations. Private law followed this ongoing commercialisation of the social world – sometimes reluctantly, but always obediently. On the other hand, there was the apparently unstoppable growth of the welfare state, transforming social activities into public sector services. Accordingly, private law abdicated its responsibilities for the legal regulation of these social activities in favour of public law principles. And this error has been the common starting point for the great influential ideologies, liberalism and Marxism, in their countless variations and combinations, including social democracy and New Labour. For both ideologies, private law is identical with the law of the economy – witness the slogans of the German debate: the *'Privatrechtsgesellschaft'* (private law society) of the ordo-liberals versus the *'Privatrecht als Wirtschaftsrecht'* (private law as the law of the economy) of the political interventionists. The only point of disagreement was thus whether private law should reflect economic efficiency or governmental policies, principles of economic autonomy or of political intervention. *Tertium non datur.*

Both political ideologies have assisted in creating legal institutions which stress, albeit in different forms, the interplay of the political and the economic sector, but at the same time – and this is my central point today – they have neglected or instrumentalised other sectors of civil society.

A non-reductive concept, however, would identify private law in many social spaces: wherever spontaneous norm formation is the source of law. The astonishing pluralism of new forms of voluntarily chosen intimacy relations and the abundance of new contracts about intimate partnerships provide one example of non-economic private law in civil society. Spontaneous rule-making processes in civic movements and in non-profit private organisations are another. Traditional legal doctrine is quite right when it identifies 'private autonomy' as the centre of private law, but in its obsessive drive towards the doctrinal unity of private law[13] it misses the crucial point – the discursive pluralisation of contemporary society into many private autonomies. The main challenge for private law theorising today, it seems to me, is to rethink the one (de facto: economic) autonomy of the free individual into the many autonomies of different social worlds – the autonomy of intimate life, healthcare, education, research, religion, art, the media – to which private law needs to be responsive. The core function of private law is to juridify diverse processes of decentralised spontaneous norm formation in civil society that are fundamentally different from processes of political regulation by the central authority of the state. The task of private law in this broader sense is to constitutionalise spaces of social autonomy: not only economic forms of action, but in particular non-economic forms of contracting and other modes of consensual action, idiosyncratic private ordering, standardisation, normalisation, codes of practice, formal organisations and loosely organised networks in different contextures of civil society.[14]

If there is one lesson that private law could learn from contemporary social theory, it is the lesson that social autonomy, i.e. the capacity of a social field for self-regulation, is not confined to the market mechanism of the economy, but is realised via different forms in many other social worlds of meaning. While there is broad consensus among competing social theories about this pluralisation of social worlds, arguments about how to identify the social fragments, how to draw the boundaries between them, how to characterise their specific rationality and their proper normativity and how to design legal-political institutions that are responsive to their eigenlogics are all highly controversial. And a crucial question for private law is how, for its own purposes, it should identify and, even more importantly, how it can adequately constitutionalise different private autonomies in a way that responds to this discourse plurality.

One group of theories explores the bewildering diversity of conflicting rationalities. Theories of discourse plurality à la française celebrate le différend between conflicting *genres* of hermetically closed language games based on different grammars and life practices.[15] The more sober Anglo-American New Institutionalism distinguishes a plurality of governance regimes that produce specific routines, normative patterns and institutional requirements and analyses the resulting politics of interinstitutional conflicts.[16] German neo-romantic autopoiesis imagines a rich plurality of self-producing contextures in which specific operations, codes and programmes emerge and shape the rich tapestry of the many social worlds, but wholly without a pre-established harmony.[17] Private law urgently needs to redirect the rather confused debate about its conceptual and normative unity and to focus attention on how to calibrate its conflict-resolving doctrines and procedures to the politics of collision between different discourses, institutions and systems.[18]

Yet another group of theories attempts to draw normative conclusions from this discursive pluralisation. Critical theory takes for granted a plurality of different life-world discourses with different logics of argumentation and develops normative arguments for rendering them compatible with each other.[19] Postmodern social and legal theory discusses a plurality of structural places, of autonomous sites of power, knowledge and law production, making a case for local micropolitics.[20] Theories of directly deliberative polyarchy observe the emergence of hybrid public-private governance regimes which operate autonomously as problem-solving units and which, if suitably institutionalised, will generate new forms of deliberative coordination and social learning.[21] Communitarian theories distinguish between different 'spheres of justice' which institutionalise diverse moral ideas about equality. They postulate that political legal institutions need to abandon their universalist ambitions and draw upon this particularistic norm formation.[22] Since private law is intimately linked to spontaneous norm production, private law theory should make use especially of those theories that stress the aspect of spontaneous self-organisation, the autonomous setting of boundaries and the emergence of genuine forms of normativity within social fields.

There is, however, one crucial normative conclusion to be drawn from the pluralism of private autonomies. The remarkable responsiveness private law has developed in the past towards economic markets by elaborating complex commercial contracts, forms of business organisation, economic property rights and business standards can serve today as the great historical model for its relation to other autonomous discourses in civil society. The precarious balance between self-regulation and intervention which private law has maintained in its relation to economic markets needs to be institutionalised in other sectors of civil society. The respect of private law for the autonomy of the market sector needs to be expanded to other autonomous spaces. As Rudolf Wiethölter, probably the most sensitive observer of these developments, puts it:

> To take autonomy seriously is to rely on self-determination and at the same time on inevitable externalisation (outside control). The latter should be understood not as hetero-determination, but as a potential outside support in situations where self-help is impossible, similar to therapeutic help and to supportive structures outside the law.[23]

This, however, leaves open the crucial question: What are the conditions under which the responsiveness of the law becomes possible? Under what circumstances will private law develop a similar but different sensitivity towards spontaneous norm making in other social worlds like education, research, media, art or health? And particularly important for the present situation: how does the contemporary trend towards their privatisation affect the conditions for this responsiveness?

III Old and new mismatches

Privatisation itself appears in quite a different light if one abandons the private/public dichotomy in favour of the notion of polycontexturality, i.e. if one realises that the one private autonomy is in fact many private autonomies of spontaneous norm formation. What one sees then is more than the mere transfer of activities from the state to the market. Privatisation does not, as is usually assumed, redefine the distribution between political and economic action. Rather, it transforms the character of autonomous social systems – which I call activities – by changing the mechanisms of their structural coupling with other social systems – which I call regimes.[24] In contrast with a process in which genuinely political activities oriented towards the public interest are transformed into profit-oriented economic activities, one sees a set of distinctive and autonomous activities such as research, education or health, which are each displaying their proper principles of rationality and normativity and which in the process of privatisation are undergoing changes to their institutional regime. Thus, instead of a bipolar relation between economics and politics, one has to think of privatisation in terms of a triangular relation between these two and the public service activities involved. The traditional view sees them either as political or as economic in character. Only by overlooking the distinctive rationality of the third vertex, the activity (which may be facilitated or obstructed by different institutional or political regimes), does it become plausible to claim that it is privatisation that unleashes the potential which is blocked by the old public regime. But at the same time new blockages appear. Old mismatches between activities and regime are replaced by new mismatches.

What do these old and new mismatches look like? Before privatisation, the specific rationalities of diverse social sectors were dealt with in the political arena by public law regimes – albeit to a degree which varied from country to country. The broad qualification 'political' and 'administrative' was able to cover quite diverse logics of action. However, this did not mean that politics had actually taken over those autonomous social sectors, transformed their rationality into power politics and made them an integral part of the political system. While this may have been true of fascism and real socialism, which attempted to politicise diverse sectors of society completely, liberal-capitalist regimes adopted a different technique: that of expanding the public sector into civil society. The modern welfare state carefully avoided destroying the autonomy of diverse social rationalities, but created a relation of dependency by means of their tight structural coupling to the political-administrative system. Basically, this involved tolerating their operational autonomy while channelling contacts with their social environment exclusively via the political system. The political system attempted to regulate their external contacts in such a way that their main sources of influence came from politics, while the direct irritation produced by other sectors of society was reduced, filtered, mediated and controlled by the political process. Social problems were first translated into political issues and then brought to the attention of the welfare state services only in this politicised form.

But at the same time, the public sector itself changed its character. It responded to the immense diversity of welfare state activities by internal differentiation according to the pattern of centre/periphery. At the periphery, it created special administrative fields and specialised agencies which enjoyed a certain insulation from the influence of the political centre.[25] Administrative law theory developed doctrines of public sector self-regulation, '*mittelbare Staatsverwaltung*'[26] or '*besondere Gewaltverhältnisse*',[27] which respected the eigenlogics of different sectors and shaped the public law accordingly.

The perennial problem of this tight structural coupling, however, has been a profound structural mismatch between social activities and their political-administrative regime.[28] Economists have not ceased to analyse and criticise the costly mismatches of the interventionist state. In the deregulation debate they were able to demonstrate the inadequacy of political regulation by command and control in matching the internal logic of social action, and to highlight the immense costs the resulting mismatches produced.[29] Similarly, transaction cost economics has analysed the economic costs which were produced by frictions between social activities and their governance regimes.[30] The intrusion of political influence (in the narrow sense of the party–political power game) into the integrity of the 'civil service' was one of the primary motives for privatisation. Political meddling with research, education, health, etc. was a central problem of the public regime. Another was the economic inefficiency and professional incompetence which resulted from governance by rigid hierarchical bureaucracies. Structurally, it was the selectivity of the political-administrative process that filtered the contacts between welfare state services and the rest of society and thus made these services more sensitive to the signals of politics than to anything else in society. To a considerable degree, the stifling of progress in those cultural fields was the price paid for a tight coupling to administrative politics. Privatisation means not only the unleashing of market forces, but also the unleashing of professional energies in diverse fields that had been blocked by the political–administrative process.

After privatisation, the internal rationalities of research, education, health and art are becoming liberated from their tight coupling to party politics and administrative bureaucracies. Usually, however, they do not devolve into autonomous regimes of their own. Rather, under the predominant logic of privatisation, tight structural links to politics have been replaced by similarly tight links to the economy. Again, their operational autonomy – this needs to be stressed – remains untouched. But their contacts with the rest of society are filtered through economic mechanisms. The institutions governing public services are transformed into economic enterprises, guided by monetary mechanisms and exposed to market competition.

Here is the irony. Having fought against the inefficient mismatches of public provision and state-owned enterprises, the privatisers are now creating new mismatches between activities and their economically efficient regimes. While the new market regime liberates a whole set of sociocultural activities that had been stifled within the old regime of public service provision, in the long run privatisation tends to create fatal mismatches with the economically non-viable aspects of these activities, even if they are central to the full achievement of the activities' proper rationality and normativity.

However, the creation of these new mismatches generates resistance from the inner dynamics of the public services themselves. In the long run, conflictual dynamics will emerge that raise the question whether institutional changes will respond to the new mismatches. What institutional responses will this provoke? My suggestion is that we should look for these along five different trajectories:

(1) To what degree will the market regime change itself so as to 'tolerate' economically non-viable activities within privatised regimes? Historical

experience with private universities, private science foundations or private art institutions confirms that under certain institutional conditions, the market regime is capable of developing flexible forms of economic action – displaying a long-term rather than a short-term orientation, leaving spaces for cultural autonomy within economically efficient organisations, cross-subsidising non-profitable activities – which, up to a point, are able to adapt it to non-economic rationalities.

(2) To what degree will the third sector of non-governmental and non-profit activities take over and create governance regimes that facilitate and cultivate social activities of a non-political and non-economic character (charities, not-for-profit organisations, donations, voluntary associations, leisure activities)?

(3) To what degree will the public sector maintain or regain control over privatised activities in a way that would further their autonomy and protect them against the logic of the market (traditional governmental administration, newly created regulatory agencies, quangos)?

(4) To what degree will individual markets or the economy as a whole develop a political system of their own which protects and facilitates non-economic activities (business associations, informal networks between large enterprises, professional associations)?

(5) To what degree will mixed regimes emerge that cut through the public/private divide and develop forms of coordination in which political and economic rationalities, hierarchies and markets are closely intertwined?

Which of these alternative directions of possible development will be realised depends to a large degree on the specific production regimes which are institutionalised, given today's 'varieties of capitalism'.[31] Along all these trajectories, private law, the law of contract, property, tort and associations certainly would only have a limited role to play. But this would be a new and different role, neither responsive exclusively to the private autonomy of economic actors, nor a mere continuation of the policy-oriented private law of the interventionist state that has become dependent upon institutionalised politics. Rather it would be a private law that is acting under the constant challenge of new mismatches between public services and their economic regimes.

In this context, it is misleading to identify mismatches with market failures if these are defined by reference to the results of an ideal market (zero transaction costs, perfect information, free entry and exit, fully internalised costs and benefits) which produces Pareto-efficient results. Even an ideal market is bound to produce mismatches in relation to the internal rationality of privatised public services. An economic analysis approach to legal regulation that merely attempts to mimic an efficiently operating market is blind to such mismatches.[32] But it is equally misleading to use the old public law standards of the welfare state services as a yardstick for distinguishing match/mismatch. This would be a similarly illegitimate privilege for institutionalised politics and their idiosyncratic perception of social conflicts and problems.

More recently, it has become common to distinguish between economic and social regulation or to develop a typology of several regulatory rationales – the regulating of natural monopoly, regulation for competition, social regulation.[33] These formulas still seem to be trapped in the public/private divide. They assume a centralised political perception of the mismatches involved. In addition, the contrast between allocative and distributive policies on which they are founded does not sufficiently grasp the crucial multi-dimensionality of perspectives.[34] The distinction between economic and social regulation in itself seems to be a modern repetition of the old private/public divide, reconstructed from the perspectives of regulatory agencies. The polycontexturality of social sectors and their idiosyncratic perspectives appear only in a reductive economic or political translation. And it is telling that social regulation is itself sub-divided into governmental policies and consumer protection, which in its turn is the reappearance of the private/public divide in new disguises (note the change of antonym: not government/citizen, but government/consumer).

As an alternative to this re-constitution of the old forms of public and private, we need to develop the criteria for regulation – to take up the famous formulation by Michael Walzer – within the diverse 'spheres of justice' themselves. It is at these structural sites, it is in the plurality of social sectors that internal controversies and conflicts about their proper identity in society take place. The politics of reflection within different social worlds and the 'politics of institutional contradiction' in their relation to the larger public thematise the mismatches between activities and regimes.[35] It is in regard to these conflicts within different social discourses that private law – in doctrine as well as in procedure – needs to develop a high degree of responsiveness. To be sure, the criteria cannot be derived from ready-made rationality principles in the social subsystems and then simply incorporated into private law. Rather they emerge as a result of conflicts between diverse social actors. Private law needs to participate in this definition of criteria for the conflict between social activities and the economic regime.

IV Colliding rationalities

Of course, the mismatch between public service and its economic regime in the health sector will look different from that in education, research or in the media. There is no general formula according to which the logic of economic action necessarily contradicts the internal logic of other socio-cultural activities. However, there are some structural problems which repeat themselves in the binding arrangements which connect the service activities with the economy.[36] What are these structural conflicts that are exposed to private law after privatisation? What are the interdiscursive tensions on the basis of which social conflicts are emerging, conflicts that in some cases are brought to the courts and to which private law has to find an answer, even at the price of changing its fundamental structures?

To stress this point again, the search is not one for conflicts between the political rationality of the good old public services and the economic rationality of their cynical privatised successors, but rather one that aims to identify areas of conflict where the logic of the market collides with fundamental principles of the social subsystems involved. I shall deal with some of the most conspicuous conflicts in some detail in as far as they are of concern to private law, while just mentioning a few others.

(1) *Structural corruption*: In the dark corners of some of the most prestigious private universities in the Western world there are lurking so-called 'pink' and 'super-pink' students (children of alumni and generous donors who are a bit less gifted than their parents). In some cases, they are said to take up to 15 (!) per cent of the available admission slots.[37] This is only one of the most drastic examples of structural corruption in private public services. It is structural because there is no personal corruption of university administrators or selectors involved; they are, of course, driven by noble motives of institutional patriotism. In this situation, educational standards of excellence, equality of admission and meritocratic treatment are in sharp conflict with the legitimate concerns of rich families to perpetuate the *splendor familiae* and the equally legitimate concern of cost-conscious university managers to take advantage of these opportunities. However, the courts show a remarkable reluctance to interfere in the internal concerns of private universities precisely because they are private.[38] The example shows quite drastically how inappropriate it is to work with the private/public distinction in this context. Fundamental principles of higher education stand in an orthogonal relation to the private/public divide. And these conflicts are not as easy to resolve as they seem at first sight; educational principles of equality have, of course, to be weighed against the advantages of cross-subsidising poorer students from this source of revenue.

Similar conflicts crop up in the recently privatised parts of the media, where the logic of the market is structurally corrupting journalistic integrity. Again, once upon a time, when radio and television were public services, a similar structural corruption was endemic as party politics were closely involved in their supervision, under the cover of pluralistic representation. And the BSE saga has been a paradigm for a new public-private partnership in the structural corruption of research in the natural sciences. Selective funding of research projects, corporate influence on research priorities, lobby pressures on the interpretation of scientific findings, the dismissal of over-zealous scientists employed by government and, last but not least, the secretive politics of European Community comitology – all these have been used successfully in order to exclude or to manipulate research and to compromise the integrity of the scholarly process.

It comes as a relief, however, that structural corruption after privatisation is a field where a modern public morality seems to coincide with autonomy-enhancing tendencies of private law. It has become an almost uncontested point of contemporary moral consensus that the core rationality of a social domain like research, health or education should not be allowed to be distorted by economic rationality. This is seen not only as a technical matter, but as a moral issue.

> The sabotaging of binary codes has become a moral problem – corruption in politics and in law, doping in sports, the purchasing of love, or cheating with regard to the data of empirical research.[39]

Business ethics teaches that the economy needs to respect the integrity of the methods of research, education, medical treatment and other autonomous fields of knowledge if it is not to sacrifice long-term objectives to short-term advantages.[40] Systems sociology recommends that economic action should keep out of the specific eigenlogics of diverse social systems and that it must resist the temptation presented by its decentralised decision structure: that of obtaining advantages through special deals.[41] Normative sociology urges that economic action be restrained, that it be effectively channelled in its influence on different institutions in such a way that these institutions can actually take on responsibility for the consequences of their actions.[42]

Such an ethics of boundaries coincides with what is typically the main concern of private law institutions – that of creating Chinese walls between different spaces of action as in property law, of prohibiting incompatibilities of roles as in contract law, of establishing spaces of autonomous decision-making as in the law of associations. Safeguarding boundaries between different spaces of action can be effectively utilised against structural corruption in the media, in research or in the health sector after their privatisation.

(2) *Social exclusion*: Every day, we can read in the newspapers of a series of new conflicts in health, utilities, transport, social security, insurance and telecommunication, where profit-driven privatised services discriminate against poor, disabled or homeless people or completely exclude them from their provision. In principle, the economy is itself based on the rule of universal

inclusion, just like those other social systems. Each member of society is supposed to have access to their activities. But the specific conditions of universal inclusion are in sharp conflict. Under the old public regime, political inclusion via universal suffrage had served as a relatively reliable guide for inclusion into public services, although one should keep in mind the degree to which discrimination on purely political grounds in terms of voting blocks and interest group influence has been the rule. The new economic regime discriminates sharply and visibly in terms of buying power, which creates one of the most conspicuous mismatches with inclusion claims in regard to health, social security or telecommunication.

The foreseeable reaction of private law to these conflicts of different inclusion conditions is to impose strict rules of universal service on profit-driven private regimes.[43] Against the market logic of freedom of contract, a counter-principle needs to be established right at the centre of private law regimes which guarantees – in the formulation of the Green Paper on telecommunication in the European Union:

> access to a defined minimum service of specified quality to all users at an affordable price based on the principles of universality, equality and continuity.[44]

We are indeed witnessing a strange phenomenon. Under postmodern conditions, there occurs a revival of old, even medieval common law duties. It is not by chance that duties dating from time immemorial which applied to ferrymen and other common carriers, to common callings, to prime necessity, to business affected with a public interest had been discarded as 'arcane' in nineteenth-century England. It is no more by chance that after their take-over of the welfare state, contemporary law will treat private government regimes as the new ferrymen.[45] In the creation of these duties of universal service there is an interesting division of labour between regulatory agencies and the courts. Where regulation by the politically governed regulatory bodies is light-handed, common law principles are reappearing in private litigation and the courts are challenged to spell out legal principles of universal service. Where the regulatory agencies take a more active approach, the courts tend to support these developments by incorporating universal service duties into their interpretation of contracts.[46]

Again, one should not misunderstand this as an intrusion of political into economic rationality. Rather it is the institutional rationality of the particular social sector involved – health, telecommunication, social services – whose specific inclusion principle is in conflict with that of the economy. As a consequence, private law is faced with the task of simultaneously incorporating contradictory logics of action. Private law has to bring non-profit principles of *Kontrahierungszwang* (obligation to conclude contracts) and universal service to bear on profit-oriented transactions, provide for the judicial rewriting of standard contracts, the fair distribution of cross-subsidies between competitors, the establishment of non-profit organisations administering private funds and the imposition of non-economic, non-political socio-cultural standards on profit-driven enterprises. Against the market logic and against the legal principle of contractual freedom it will have to impose systems of private taxes and cost subsidisation in order to provide financial resources for the special inclusion principle of the social sector involved. And the institutional imagination of private law is required when it comes to shaping, interpreting and adjudicating the constitutional law of profit-oriented private service providers and their rules of universal service.

(3) *Contracting privity*: Privatisation translates public services into the language of private contracts, with the result of an enforced bilateralism which cuts off broader social structures. A large public service project, for example, which requires the cooperation of diverse medical, social service, scientific, financial and political skills, will be organised by the contracting and subcontracting schemes of diverse public and private organisations. If things go wrong and the courts have to apply contract law to these projects, they will, of course, follow the logic of market transactions and will tend to resolve conflicts by isolating each of those individual contracts in legal terms. They thus speak the language of economics, which translates the complex unity of a project into a multiplicity of bilateral economic transactions. Contract law resolves conflicts without taking into account that the artificial isolation of bilateral transactions is actually incompatible with the network structure of interdependent social, technical and political relations. The new economic analysis of law which formulates normative criteria for the resolution of legal conflicts would drive this dependency of the law upon economic translation even further. The criteria – allocative efficiency and transaction cost reduction – translate the whole productive world of projects into the language of the economic costs and benefits of bilateral transactions and – what is worse – make this translation binding for the law.

Hugh Collins has systematically exposed this distortion of social relations by their economic contractualisation within four categories: (1) enforced bilateralisation; (2) highly selective performance criteria; (3) the inadequate externalisation of negative effects; (4) the imposition of power relations.[47] It is an open question to what degree the contractualisation of public services will, in addition, lead to a distortion of judicial review, especially when it comes to the representation of group interests in private litigation. Since contractualisation introduces privity of contract into complex, multilateral service relations, these relations might be constructed by the judiciary as a multitude of unrelated bilateral relations. To quote Mark Freedland:

> Government by contract may involve a comparable network of contracts, so that there can be an interlocking of service procurement contracts on the one hand, and consumer or customer contracts with the service provider on the other. In such arrangements, the doctrine of privity of contract ensures that the consumer has no direct contractual relation with the service procurer. It would not be wholly surprising to find that, by extension of that reasoning, there were many situations in which the citizen as consumer had no sufficient interest to seek judicial review of the actions or policies of the government department which had procured the service in question.[48]

Viewed from a more optimistic perspective, this might create new pressures on private law to take the network character of interrelated contracts seriously and encourage public law to re-conceptualise the notion of sufficient interest for judicial review. The conflict between multilateral social networks and bilateral economic transactions will in the long run force the law to account for the third-party effects of contracting, even if this contradicts the sacred privity of contract, reduces allocative efficiency and increases transaction costs.

(4) *Limits to monetarisation*: Privatisation reignites an old conflict about the limits of what money can buy. Historically, the emergence of Protestantism and the outbreak of religious wars had a lot to do with the intrusion of the money mechanism into traditionally sacred fields. Dr. Martin Luther protested fiercely against commercialising personal salvation and public offices, and this finally succeeded in establishing their social definition as *res extra commercium*. Today, when we read the shocking news in the papers that a certain – *nomen est omen* – Dr. Seed is going to privatise the production of human clones, it is mainly the privatisation of the health sector and the commercialisation of bio-medical research that once more provoke the old conflict about the limits of economic colonialism. And again, some of these conflicts inevitably will be fought out in private litigation, where courts will have to be prepared to deal with them by means of the general clauses of contract law. It will be by applying private law principles that the courts – with or without the support of the legislator – will have to decide about the limits of commercialisation.[49]

(5) *Dumbing down*: Especially in the arts and in culture, but also in the media and even in the universities, heated controversies about the decline of professional quality have emerged that put the blame on market mechanisms.[50] Witness the controversy regarding the BBC and BSkyB, where one and the same person, now Media Professor at Oxford, has forcefully advocated

both extreme positions! Have you recently listened to Radio 3 and Classic FM and discovered first-hand what has happened to classical Austro-German music under the influence of competition? The famous Anglo-Austrian Friedrich von Hayek would have to call this 'competition as a process of discovery'!

A corrective institutional imagination is pinning its hopes on market-independent standards and assessment procedures, on all kinds of auditing practices,[51] on the creation of a professional and cultural reputation to be incorporated in private law standards, on the establishment of a right to diversity[52] and the pluralisation of financial sources which would create a certain autonomy of standards.[53]

(6) *Perverse selectivity*: The remarkable evolutionary success of 'fat cats' in the privatised utilities is only one indicator for the tendency of the economic system for perverse selectivity: Small distinctions create huge inequalities. These inequalities do not only offend the popular culture of envy; more importantly, they contradict the publicly perceived differences of achievement in different public service sectors and effectively undermine the meritocratic claims of the new private governance regimes. Can private law litigation successfully fight the reproduction of such strange beasts in social evolution? As regards pink students, the answer is probably yes – as regards fat cats, it is probably no.

V Reaction I: fragmenting private law

Can one anticipate structural patterns that will appear in private law after privatisation? Since legal evolution depends to a large degree on the direction that the privatisation process as a whole will take, one must think in alternative scenarios. What are possible scenarios for the reaction of private law to these structural conflicts? I would suggest distinguishing two main scenarios: one is fragmentation, the other hybridisation. Borrowing the distinction between tight and loose coupling from organisational sociology, we could say that private law patterns would differ according to the intensity of the services' structural coupling to the economy.[54] In cases where they are loosely coupled to economic processes, fragmentation will be the reaction of private law to the emergence of a multitude of social autonomies, while hybridisation would be its response when faced with situations of tight economic coupling. Ironically, in both scenarios it is privatisation itself which dashes the hopes of legal doctrine for a renewed unity of private law under the market regime. It is privatisation that drives private law into higher and higher degrees of differentiation, where increasingly special areas of private law incorporate specific rationalities of different spheres of justice that are non-economic in their character.

Of course, the fragmentation of private law is a long-term historical process which has taken on many forms and is due to many causes. And many modern phenomena of a fragmented private law, for example labour law, consumer law, the law of intellectual property and environmental law, are not at all related to privatisation. It is not clear what the underlying factors for this multiple fragmentation are: the dominance of particular social groups, the emergence of special professions, the prominence and political urgency of policy arenas, the pressure of social problems, the internal requirements of specialised legal doctrines or the establishment of special court jurisdictions. However, there is one crucial criterion for a genuine fragmentation of private law into an externally induced autonomous area: spontaneous norm formation in a social field which is used as a source of law. Whenever the autonomy of a social system expresses itself in the existence of a machinery of norm production – agreements, formal organisation, standardisation – a field of special private law emerges, with an accompanying juridification.

The paradigmatic case of this can be seen in developments in the new law of intimate relations.[55] The dramatic transformations that traditional family law is undergoing can be seen to be connected to a peculiar privatisation of private life. Today, people are choosing a bewildering variety of intimate relations and idiosyncratic lifestyles outside the traditional forms of family law (non-formalised partnerships, same-sex relations, loosely organised forms of life sharing, group living, new forms of child raising, enlarged families). Withdrawing reluctantly from the monopoly of heterosexual marriage and other regulations of intimate life, the state responds increasingly to a radical contractualisation of family law. The traditional regulation of marriage and family retreats to merely framing the autonomy of self-regulation in intimate life and providing for conflict resolution in case of crisis. Here we have an exemplary case where the law relies on a private autonomy which is not at all based on profit-oriented economic exchanges under market conditions, but on a long-term personal, intimate relation which stabilises itself based on the instabilities of mutual affection. The rationality of intimate life to which the law responds is no longer the old one of economic subsistence (the role of the *oikos*), nor is it political (the family as the smallest cell of society or the object of population policies), rather, its rationality is unique: to provide the only space in contemporary life where the person as a whole in all its role aspects finds its legitimate expression. And the rules and principles of the new family law are responding almost exclusively to such an extravagant rationality of intimate life and its spontaneous norm formation.

Can we expect parallel developments of privatisation in other social subsystems where a highly developed rationality of a non-economic character governs? Is there a future for an elaborate 'private' education law, research law, health law or art law which will reflect the genuine rationality of these areas in relative distance to both political and economic rationality? What would such a law look like, a law which has to deal with governance structures that some observers of the privatisation process describe as

> ... functionally specified 'problem-solving units'. These units are neither conventionally public, since they operate independently of state command and control, nor conventionally private, because they do exercise a problem-solving function and have reflexive capacities concerning the interests of society as a whole.[56]

This might be a somewhat over-optimistic view of their capacities of reflexive monitoring. But in each of these fields there exist elaborate mechanisms of spontaneous norm formation that play a constitutive role similar to that played by the market transaction in the law of commercial contracts. If, for example, an ongoing practice of contracting with private not-for-profit educational institutions is exposed to extensive litigation and legislative lobbying, the resulting law of educational contracting will differ enormously from classical contract law. The contractual freedom of the educational institution to choose its pupils will be sharply limited by educational principles of academic merit, a strict prohibition of discrimination and positive rules of equal treatment that will in the long run lead to the extinction of the species of pink students. Internal relations would be governed by a broad 'educational judgement rule' which would be subjected to judicial scrutiny of whether or not, in the exercise of professional discretion, educational principles have actually governed the decision. And the rights of choice for parents, pupils and teachers would be defined in a legal process that concretises them, combining due process with pedagogical principles.[57] As Philip Selznick notes, educational institutions, after their privatisation, have the constitutional obligation

> to take account of public concerns, including, among much else, the quality of basic education, teacher preparation, equality of opportunity, racial integration, care for the handicapped, education for civic responsibility.[58]

The extent to which such autonomous fragments of private law emerge depends crucially on the direction that the politics of privatisation will take. The open question is whether they result in a tight or loose coupling with market processes, and in what proportions they do so. There are numerous methods of privatisation.[59] Some of the former public services have actually been reorganised in the non-profit sector, in charities, foundations, trusts and voluntary organisations. Others have been handed over to the family and the so-called community. The more privatisation will result in the transfer of social activities to the non-profit sector, the more private law will fragment into autonomous fields. There is a direct correlation between the growth of a private non-profit sector and the growth in private law fragmentation.

But private law is not merely the dependent variable in this context. Much depends on the conceptual readiness of the law to take advantage of the opportunities offered by social structures: Is the private law of contract, association, property and tort capable of constructing legal forms that are systematically open to opportunities for a third sector, for the institutionalisation of non-economic rationalities? The more private law offers regimes of non-profit organisation for formerly public services, the greater the chances that political pressures will exploit structural tensions between their inner rationality and economic rationality and attempt to move them into the non-profit sector.

VI Reaction II: hybridisation

But for many, if not most public services, privatisation today means tight structural coupling with the economy. How, then, will private law react when social services have fully 'commercialised' their spontaneous norm formation, transformed their special agreements into commercial contracts, their service institutions into profit-oriented business organisations, their standardisation procedures into market standards?

In such a situation, when adjudicating disputes in private law, the courts will have only a narrow view of privatised services. Through the filter of contract law, they receive information about these activities almost exclusively as cost–benefit calculations. Private litigation is exposed to a typical asymmetry in the structural links between the law, the economy and the social system involved. The situation is very nearly a repetition of the former dominant position of institutionalised politics in relation to the old public services. Every element of the service itself, whether research, education, technology, art or medicine, will be first filtered into the market dimension of economic calculations, allocative efficiency and transaction costs and presented to the law for conflict resolution in this form. For private litigation, this creates a serious distortion of social relations because a lot of information about the social system involved will be inevitably lost due to its reconstruction in economic terms.

A corrective change in private law would amount to restructuring the links with its non-economic environment. Private law needs to perceive the newly privatised services fully in their hybrid character. They are hybrids not in the usual sense of mixed regimes of private and public law,[60] or of political and economic aspects. The idea of polycontexturality *leads* to a different sense of hybridisation. Privatised public services are simultaneously part of two social systems, the economic system and the social system where they realise their services. Private law has to break the monopoly of structural linkages to the economy on both sides and instead establish direct links with the concrete social field involved. In practice, this means enforcing its non-economic aspects, by law, against the logic of economic calculation.

The sources of private law would then no longer to be found exclusively in economic contracting, organisation and standardisation, but actually in two parallel and often contradictory processes of spontaneous norm formation. The terms of a legal contract would be based on two equally important mechanisms of social self-regulation: (1) an economic transaction and (2) a productive agreement. Contract law would reconstruct contracting not only as an entrepreneurial project or as a profit-seeking monetary transaction under more or less competitive market conditions, producing economic expectations on both sides. Of equal importance would be its legal reconstruction as a 'productive' project in one of the many social worlds, in distribution, production, services, engineering, science, medicine, journalism, sports, tourism, education or art, which produces normative expectations of a different kind. And the coordination of this conflict would not be left automatically to the cost/benefit language of the monetary transaction, but would be a matter of contract law. It is probably a euphemism to speak of a balancing of two different rationalities. Rather, in view of the self-enforcing dynamics of economic calculation, what is meant is that private law takes a partisan stance for the 'other', the diverse social rationalities involved, and imposes their standards on economic action. In this context I can only mention, but not elaborate, the concept of Discourse Rights, which would serve here as an authoritative legal basis.[61] These are the impersonal rights of certain spheres of communication, founded in constitutional law and directed in a horizontal effect against the intrusions of any social system with hegemonic tendencies.

What is different about this post-privatisation legal regime? How does it differ from modern private law, the law of mixed economies which aims to correct market failures via policy interventions – consumer protection, public policy clauses, an expansion of good faith? The differences are twofold. First, this is no longer the more or less marginal post hoc correction of an essentially economic transaction. Instead, from the very beginning, contract is seen as constituted by two equally important social dynamics and the job of the law is not just correction, but a thoroughgoing reconciliation of conflicts. Secondly, the non-economic aspects of the private law relation are no longer filtered and distorted by the political process and translated into legal policies in this distorted form, as tended to be common practice in the private law of the welfare state. Rather, private law turns directly to the spontaneous norm production in the social field involved. It counts on a division of labour between the dynamics in the social field involved and the dynamics of private law litigation which could be described as learning by mutual anticipation.[62]

Similarly, the law of private associations would perceive private organisations not just in economic terms, with some marginal corrections in terms of governmental policies. Where non-economic associations are in a relation of tight coupling with the market regime, the task of private law is to coordinate, *ab initio*, the requirements of two different social systems. The role of private law would then be to constitutionalise spaces of professional autonomy within those organisations, ring-fencing them against direct intrusions of the market.

Finally, standardisation would no longer be seen as a process in which private law follows economic calculation by weighing the costs of prevention against the expected costs of damage discounted by its probability. Instead, it would be institutionalised as a process in which the law reconstructs the emergence of professional standards according to the logic of action of the public service involved.

Altogether, post-privatisation private law would no longer accept at face value the economic reconstruction of social relations, rather it would perceive them as genuinely hybrid relations. This would change the two main methods of law-making in private law: perturbation and mimicking.

The perturbations of private law's environment which trigger the development of new rules would come not just from market mechanisms via economic transactions. The law would directly observe and juridify intrinsic standards and agreements in the social field involved (expanding good faith in the form of mandatory rules, advancing non-economic criteria of negligence as opposed to the economistic Learned Hand formula).

Legal simulation is a technique used in the formula of hypothetical contracting and the reasonable person. The point would be to use not only the market test as mimicking the outcomes likely to be produced by an efficient market, as legal economics recommends, but a social discourse test which develops concrete standards by simulating micropolitical processes in one of the many 'spheres of justice' involved.

VII Re-importing conflicts?

The problem for this analysis is this: where are the social dynamics that could possibly irritate private law to undergo such far-reaching structural changes? To a considerable degree, the dynamics of privatisation itself threaten to produce these *effets pervers*[63] in the form of certain self-defeating tendencies. If it is true that the previous expansion of welfare state services liberated the market from political conflicts, absorbing them more or less successfully into the political-administrative system,[64] then it can be expected that privatisation has the effect of re-importing these conflicts into the economic arena. Paradoxical as this may sound, after privatisation, political conflicts about public services are indeed increasing. As one observer of the privatisation process in Britain summarises:

> ... the structures adopted for nationalisation had never required a resolution of the problems of conflicting regulatory rationales, but privatisation and the creation of new regulators flushed this question out into the open.[65]

Privatisation has created new tensions which have had recourse to private litigation as one arena for conflict resolution.[66] Explosive political conflicts that were formerly absorbed within the diverse regimes of public law do not vanish after privatisation as if by a gracious gesture of the invisible hand. After the take-over by the market, these conflictual energies re-emerge in new forms and the new private regimes of governance have to cope with them. They will not be resolved by market mechanisms alone. In their turn, the privatised services will be driven into a new politicisation. And this repoliticisation is not necessarily limited to the establishment of public law regulatory agencies, but entails in addition the politicisation of private governance itself, its different modes of self-regulation and conflict resolution via private litigation.

The sources of these conflicts can be identified in the privatised public services themselves, which have to bear the structural tensions between their proper rationality and economic calculation. Professionals as well as clients suffer from those tensions. It is this resistance of social practices to their new economic regime that is the source of all kinds of new quasi-political conflicts now taking place within the 'private' spheres. A good indicator for this change is the growing intensity of the political struggles between regulatory agencies, consumer groups, regulated companies and their shareholders which we are currently experiencing.[67] Another gauge of this new conflictual situation is the extent to which protest movements and other forms of civic resistance are switching their targets from political to economic institutions. And there is the strange alliance between civic protest movements and the mass media, speaking up, in the name of ethics, against a comprehensive economisation of public services which damages their integrity. For the future of private law, it is crucial not only that its doctrinal-conceptual structures are prepared for such conflicts, but also that different litigation procedures are introduced to make private law responsive to the new types of conflict caused by privatisation itself – including, but not limited to, rules of standing for groups, collective representation, multilateralisation of the adversary two-party process and elements of public interest litigation.[68]

Notes

This chapter was previously published as 'After privatization? The many autonomies of private law', *Current Legal Problems*, 51 (January 1998), 393–424. For critical comments, I would like to thank Julia Black, Hugh Collins, Oliver Gerstenberg, Colin Scott and Lindsay Stirton.

1. 'Die Reichen hauen ab', *Der Spiegel*, 6 April 1998, p. 121.
2. Privatisation is understood here in a broad sense, including in particular a change of public ownership and the introduction of market elements into governance structures. For a useful classification (privatisation, contracting out, introduction of market elements into the public sector), see Freedland, 'Government by contract', pp. 86–7.
3. This perspective is well elaborated with regard to common law principles of public utilities in Taggart, 'Public Utilities and Public Law', and with regard to the new regulation of privatised public services in Prosser, *Law and the Regulatory Process*.
4. For an influential argument, see Horwitz, 'History of the public/private distinction'.
5. The *locus classicus* is Habermas, *Structural Transformation of the Public Sphere*; considerable refinements of analysis in Habermas, *Between Facts and Norms*, ch. 8, III.
6. Engle, 'After the Collapse of the Public/Private Distinction'; Olsen, 'Constitutional law'.
7. Spahn, 'Oikos und Polis'.
8. Riedel, 'Gesellschaft, bürgerliche'.
9. This concept has been coined by Günther, 'Life as Poly-Contexturality', and has become one of the central elements of autopoietic social and legal theory, see for example Luhmann, 'Coding of the Legal System'; Teubner, 'King's many bodies'.
10. For a similar argument in different theory contexts, see Friedland and Alford, 'Bringing Society Back In'; Santos, *Toward a New Common Sense*, pp. 416 ff.; Gerstenberg, *Bürgerrecht und deliberative Demokratie*, p. 346; Wilhelmsson, 'Private Law 2000'.
11. The extremely vague concept of civil society shall be used here in a more precise systemic sense, comprising all those social communications that are not part of the political or the economic system. This is similar to Habermas's use of the concept. However, it includes not only diffuse (life-world) communication

but – unlike Habermas's usage – communication in any other social system. Cf. also Cohen and Arato, *Civil Society and Political Theory*, ch. 3.
12 'Private law has become the domain of property and economic relations': Röhl and Röhl, *Allgemeine Rechtslehre*, p. 434.
13 E.g. Weinrib, *Idea of Private Law*; Zöllner, *Privatrechtsgesellschaft*.
14 For a similar perspective, especially in tort law, see Wilhelmsson, 'Private Law 2000'.
15 Lyotard, *The Differend*; Lyotard, *Lessons on the Analytic of the Sublime*, ch. 5.
16 Most explicitly, Friedland and Alford, 'Bringing Society Back In'; see also Powell and DiMaggio (eds), *New Institutionalism*; Scott, *Institutions and Organizations*.
17 Luhmann, 'Differentiation of Society'; Luhmann, 'Paradox of System Differentiation'.
18 See Teubner, 'De collisione'; Teubner, 'Altera pars'.
19 Habermas, *Between Facts and Norms*, ch. 4.
20 Bauman, *Postmodern Ethics*; Santos, *Toward a New Common Sense*, pp. 416–55.
21 Cohen, 'Procedure and Substance'; Gerstenberg, *Bürgerrecht und deliberative Demokratie*, pp. 345–6.
22 Walzer, *Spheres of Justice*; Selznick, *Moral Commonwealth*, pp. 229 ff.
23 Wiethölter, 'Zum Fortbildungsrecht', pp. 27–8.
24 See Friedland and Alford, 'Bringing Society Back In', p. 256.
25 Cf. Habermas, *Between Facts and Norms*, ch. 8, III.
26 'Indirect state administration'.
27 'Special status in relation to the public authority of the state'.
28 For a critique of the shortcomings of nationalised industries in Britain, see National Economic Development Office, *Study of UK Nationalised Industries*.
29 For this debate, see Mitnick, *Political Economy of Regulation*; Wilson, *Politics of Regulation*; Breyer, *Regulation and its Reform*.
30 Particularly Williamson, *Economic Institutions of Capitalism*; Williamson, 'Comparative economic organization'; Williamson, *Mechanisms of Governance*.
31 See Hall and Soskice (eds), *Varieties of Capitalism*; for an application to comparative law, see Teubner, 'Legal irritants'.
32 E.g. the exclusively economic approach to privatisation in Littlechild, *Regulation of British Telecommunications' Profitability*; Littlechild, *Economic Regulation of Privatised Water Authorities*.
33 Prosser, *Law and the Regulatory Process*, pp. 5–6.
34 Here, despite all its merits, lies the problem of the non-economic approach to regulation: Stewart, 'Regulation and the Crisis of Legalization'; Sunstein, 'Paradoxes of the regulatory state'.
35 For a similar perspective, under the heading of communitarianism, see Walzer, *Spheres of Justice*; Selznick, *Moral Commonwealth*, pp. 291–345; under the title of interinstitutional conflicts, Friedland and Alford, 'Bringing Society Back In', pp. 256 ff.; using the formulation of deliberative polyarchy, Cohen, 'Procedure and Substance'; Gerstenberg, *Bürgerrecht und deliberative Demokratie*; under the description of postmodern law, Wilhelmsson, 'Private Law 2000'.
36 For a general formulation of colliding social systems, see Luhmann, *Theory of Society*, vol. 2, pp. 309–10.
37 Gossip (1998), *passim*.
38 In the US, there is a recent trend towards greater judicial intervention in private universities; see the contrast between *Greene v. Howard University*, 271 F. Suppl. 609 (1967) and *Harvey v. Palmer College of Chiropractic*, 363 N.W.2d 443. For

the British debate on judicial intervention in private associations, see Black, 'Constitutionalising self-regulation'; Swann, 'Private into Public Law'.
39 Luhmann, *Theory of Society*, vol. 2, p. 281.
40 E.g. the programmatic statement by De George, 'Status of business ethics'.
41 Luhmann, *Grundrechte als Institution*, p. 115.
42 Selznick, *Moral Commonwealth*, pp. 289 ff.
43 See Mueller, 'Universal service in telephone history'; Sauter, 'Universal service obligations'.
44 COM (94) 440 and COM (94) 682.
45 Taggart, 'Public Utilities and Public Law', pp. 257 ff.; for a comprehensive analysis of the common law duties that apply to universal service, see Haar and Fessler, *Wrong Side of the Tracks*.
46 Scott, 'Juridification of Regulatory Relations'.
47 Collins, 'Sanctimony of Contract', pp. 76–7.
48 Freedland, 'Government by contract', p. 100.
49 For the use of private law for public purposes, see Wightman, 'Private Law and Public Interests'.
50 See the recent study by Hogan, 'Publish and Be Damned!'
51 For a discussion of diverse aspects of the 'audit society', see Power, *Audit Society*.
52 Stewart, 'Regulation in a liberal state', p. 1568.
53 For the pluralisation argument, see 'It's Us against Them', *The Guardian*, 1 May 1997, p. B7, concerning the freedom of science, and Graber and Teubner, 'Art and money', concerning the freedom of art.
54 Weick, 'Educational organizations'; Perrow, *Normal Accidents*.
55 For recent developments, see Allert, *Die Familie*.
56 Gerstenberg, *Bürgerrecht und deliberative Demokratie*, p. 352.
57 For a context-sensitive explication of due process, see Winston, 'Self-incrimination'; Selznick, *Moral Commonwealth*, pp. 516–17.
58 Selznick, *Moral Commonwealth*, p. 517.
59 Stark, 'Privatisation'.
60 Black, 'Reviewing Regulatory Rules', p. 157, defines the hybridity of self-regulatory agencies in terms of private/public, but expresses doubts concerning the viability of this distinction: '... we should rather start by looking at the type of function being exercised, asking what duties and responsibilities should accompany the exercise of such functions and to whom should they be owed, what degree of autonomy should those exercising them have and what degree of judicial supervision should be exercised over them ...'.
61 For an elaboration, see Teubner, 'Contracting worlds'; Graber and Teubner, 'Art and money'. The idea of impersonal discourse rights is an extension of the systemic theory of constitutional rights, Luhmann, *Grundrechte als Institution*; Willke, *Stand und Kritik*.
62 See Teubner, 'Ist das Recht auf Konsens angewiesen?'
63 Boudon, *Effets pervers*.
64 Habermas, *Legitimation Crisis*.
65 Prosser, *Law and the Regulatory Process*, p. 3.
66 Wilhelmsson, 'Private Law 2000', makes this argument with particular reference to tort law.
67 Prosser, *Law and the Regulatory Process*, pp. 3–4.
68 A recent account of public interest litigation is Micklitz and Reich (eds), *Public Interest Litigation*.

7

In the blind spot: the hybridisation of contracting

I The 'contractual gap' in late modernity

My starting point is the transformation of the contract – the most fundamental institution of private law – in modern times: its hybridisation. I want to focus on the consequences of the following argument, which is one that I have developed at length elsewhere.[1] Today, contract is no longer the consensual exchange relationship between two legal subjects to which the judge grants legal force as long as the *nudum pactum* can at least be endowed with a *causa*.[2] Within the dynamics of social fragmentation, where one and the same contract appears as the simultaneous expression of different and divergent rationalities, the old two-person relationship of the contract has metamorphosed into a polycontextural relationship, which, though consensual, is impersonal. And the binding force of the contract disappears in the 'in-between' of the contextures. So what are the consequences of this fragmentation?

Today's individual contract typically breaks down into several operations within different contexts: (1) an economic transaction that is recursively interconnected with other transactions and that changes the market situation in accordance with the intrinsic logic of the economy; (2) a productive act that changes the productive situation in accordance with the intrinsic logic of the relevant social context (e.g. technology, medicine, media, science, art and other social areas where goods and services are produced); and (3) a legal act that is recursively interconnected with other legal acts and that changes the legal situation in accordance with the intrinsic logic of the law.[3] The prevailing extreme social differentiation results in the real (not just analytical) splitting of the one contract into three acts, a legal act, an economic transaction and a productive act, and the enabling of their simultaneity ('*uno actu*'). The single contract is fragmented into a multiplicity of different operations that occur in different, mutually closed discourses. It is at once transaction, production and obligation – but at the same time it is a fourth thing, the 'in-between', the interdiscursive relation between the various performative acts.

An expert contract may serve as an example to illustrate the importance of distinguishing among these three dimensions.[4] There is a whole array of concrete projects of considerable scale that involve contracts for expert advice or opinions: complex acquisitions of property, large credit operations, construction projects, high-risk financial transactions and the like. Usually there is a triangular situation: the *expert* and two partners to a project, one of them the *mandator* contracting with the expert who is supposed to give expert advice on the project, the other the *beneficiary*, the third party, who, as a rule, is not a party to the expert contract. In many legal orders, there is considerable controversy as to whether the expert is contractually liable not only to the mandator, but also to the beneficiary. The explanation for this controversy is that the expert contract participates in three different contracting worlds: (1) in the contractual interaction of mandator and expert; (2) in the economic context of monetary operations; and (3) in the social context of producing the expert report. Each of these contracting worlds imposes a different 'privity' on the transaction, that is, different boundaries, different rules of membership, different principles of exclusion and inclusion. The worlds involved display variations of bilateral, trilateral and multilateral obligations. While in many types of contract, the implied configurations share more or less identical boundaries, it is the peculiarity of the expert report transaction that it is exposed to a conflict of different privities, which contract law is asked to decide. In expert contracts, a fundamental clash, the direct collision between the principles of contractual loyalty and expert impartiality, comes to the fore. Experts are held to professional standards of scientific objectivity and neutrality. Bilateral contracting, by contrast, imposes legitimate obligations of cooperation, trust, interdependence and loyalty towards the economic interests of the mandator on the expert. The question underlying the aforementioned controversy is whether liability to a third party, in this case that of the expert to the beneficiary, provides an adequate solution to this conflict.

What 'is' this interdiscursive contractual relationship? How do the dynamics of the conflict work and how are the various contractual acts attuned to one another? This would seem to be one of the thorniest problems deriving from the contemporary disintegration of the unity of the contract.

Can we still discern some operational, structural or systemic 'unity' of the contract that can be a suitable substitute for the exchange between two people? The different disciplines involved affirm this emphatically: they base the unity of contract on either legal consensual obligation or on economic efficiency or on productive transformation and then superimpose their specific perspectives on the other aspects. Contract is thus economised or legalised or socialised. But this is a false, 'imperialist' interdisciplinarity.[5] In contrast, a social theory which deserves that name will not let itself be taken over by any of these partial perspectives, but will instead elucidate the social multidimensionality of the single contract in a transdisciplinary fashion. The sobering consequence is that a unity of the contract can no longer be construed. A contract is neither a unitary process (of social transactions in the broadest sense which would be capable of comprehending the relational essence of contract),[6] nor a unitary structure (usually perceived as an ensemble of norms enacted by private autonomy),[7] nor a unique event/operation/act (such as, in legal doctrine, the agreement of the contracting parties).[8] The single contract is always already a multiplicity of differing processes, structures, operations.

Its unity, if any, consists then only in the interconnection, in the so-called structural coupling of the economy, the productive context and the law (parallels would be property and the constitution, as institutions linking the law to different social worlds).[9] While this does mean that the systems involved mutually adapt to each other according to laws of perturbation, it certainly does not mean that the separation of the systems is suspended, or even that the contractual operations of the systems involved partly overlap. The hybrid (ambivalent, polyvalent) nature of the contract finds its basis in the inescapable hermeneutic differences between the different social contexts in which the individual contract is situated.

Correspondingly, no unitary meaning of the one specific contract spanning the hermeneutic boundaries can be discerned. The overall meaning of a contract is always produced only relatively and differentially, only in mutual reconstruction of the diverse (partial) agreements, whether in the language of costs, or in the language of legal expectations, or in the language of the relevant production standards.[10] It is their mutual observation that enables the re-entry of the system/environment distinction into each system. That creates an imaginary space within the legal agreement for the representation of the legally relevant facts of business and production. At the same time, an imaginary space of legal obligations and productive processes is created in the economic transaction, but of course only in the language of cost factors, profit expectations, economic property rights and preferences. And finally, an imaginary space for the reconstruction of resources and obligations appears within the productive act. But even such a re-entry of one system into the other leaves us with the insurmountable hermeneutic difference between the contractual languages of legal norms, production standards and transaction costs. None of them is in a position to rightfully claim interpretive predominance.

Can we, then, at least see the unity of contract in the dynamic interactions among those three autonomous contractual chains? In principle, the answer is no, since they are not directly accessible to each other – a condition that would make interaction possible. What occurs is only a mutual irritation of economic transaction, production relationship and legal relationship, which sensitises each to external noise and creates an internal readiness for change. Correspondingly, there is no common history of the three concatenations of contractual operations, since they each have a past and a future of their own in their different respective social contexts. In this sense, one can speak only of the co–evolution of three autonomous perspectives, which are, however, each controlled by evolutionary mechanisms of their own and, in principle, stay separate. Any unitary narrative of the contract fails because of the differences in the various 'path-dependent' evolutionary dynamics.

Our first interim finding is that social differentiation splits the formerly unitary contract into three autonomous concatenations of events in the respective legal, economic and production contexts. This difference is – despite (or even because of) mutual observation, structural coupling, re-entry and co-evolution – always reproduced anew as an insurmountable hermeneutic dissonance. The 'in-between' continually dissolves again into phenomena that must perforce be assigned to one system or the other. The gaps between law, production and the economy – gaps that it might have been the proper role of the modern contract to fill – remain unfilled. If that is so, the question arises as to whether elsewhere in modern society, outside the operationally closed systems, there are social mechanisms that are located 'in-between' these systems and that materialise the binding force of the contract. What we are looking for is the social site where the 'transformation of a distinction into a Möbius strip', which is what the contract actually accomplishes, comes about.[11]

Does such binding force attach to some pan-socially institutionalised communication 'between' the systems of the economy, production and the law? Can we identify some emergent discourse consisting of 'interdiscursive' operations of a new kind? This locus of pan-social identity finding is just what several authors have often sought.[12] A vain search! Empirically, communication bridging the economy, law and production does, indeed, happen, but definitely not in the sense of an independent communication system emerging among collective actors.[13] There is only a 'diffuse' communicative linkage of legal acts and productive acts to acts of payment, and vice versa. The reason for this absence is the difference institutionalised in modernity between society as a whole and functional subsystems. While this difference supplements the difference among subsystems, it in turn creates a new unbridgeable 'gap'.

Might not, then, 'life-world' communication in Habermas's sense restore the unity of the contract? In fact, the contract is not only a transactional, productional and juridical relationship, but also an exchange in the life-world, indeed a 'relational contract'. Yet looked at more closely, this is either its reconstruction in intimate relations (family, friendship, etc.), that is, into yet another functional subsystem, so that it is again merely a new intersystem relation that is thereby created, or else the contract is reconstructed in diffuse communication 'outside' the functional subsystems, which then raises the question of whether the contractual unity is restored at quite different levels, those of interaction or of organisation.

Can, then, the 'integration' of legal, productional and economic aspects be restored in the living social relation called 'contract'? If we change the perspective from functional subsystems to interaction and organisation,[14] then, indeed, the contract can be seen as a unitary, self-reproducing social process. And in fact, the concrete interaction of the contracting parties and the formal organisation of the contract do 'integrate' legal, economic and productional aspects, the coordination of which they effect with every successful operation as a 'contractual act' (negotiations, conclusion of the contract, performance, amendment, breach of contract, etc.). But once more they do this only as autonomous discourses, which, again each under the laws of its own internal perspectives and maintaining its own autopoiesis, reconstruct legal, productional and economic aspects. Instead of transcending the hermeneutic differences between the three contractual chains emerging in different social contexts, they only add yet another difference to the set: the one between different social levels (society, organisation, interaction). They thus only exacerbate the initial problem of how mediation among the various autonomous processes in the unitary contractual constellation is possible.

In an act of ultimate despair, we may still try 'humanising' the contract. After all, integration of the various social aspects of contract takes place in the consensus of real flesh-and-blood people. But even this only adds yet another internal perspective to the already multiply fractured contractual *Gestalt*, tending to further disintegrate rather than integrate it. For in that case, a further twofold reconstruction of the communicative *consensus* (or, better yet, of several communicative *consensūs*) in the consciousness of the individuals involved is added on top of the multiple social reconstructions of the one contract. The set of differences within society is further augmented by the difference between society and mind, without any unity being created thereby.

At the centre of the contractual phenomenon, there is thus a void, the central absence in the modern contract. Altogether, the contract 'as such' remains a mere configuration with no operative substrate of its own, an invisible dance of mutual adaptation, a secret coordination of consent, a grandiose relation consisting in the structural coupling of a multiplicity of meaning-processing systems. However one tries to frame it, the contract's unity (of meaning) disappears in the black hole of compatibilities, synchronisations, resonances, co-evolutionary processes. Its content, its dynamics, its decisions, its binding energies are scattered over the closed systems involved. The contract itself only momentarily 'bridges' differences of the most varied nature: differences between society, functional systems, organisations, interactions, consciousnesses. The contract 'as such', however, is a nothingness in the dark space between the systems. It always lies in the blind spot of the distinction between system and environment.[15] Is this a failing of modern society or a failing of its theory? Is it the reality of functional differentiation or its self-description that is at fault here? Under conditions of functional differentiation, can the contractual differences no longer be bridged? Or is it only that contract theory no longer has anything to say about bridging, about harmonisation, about binding force? Perhaps here the logic of the blind spots and their various compensations can help us.

II In the blind spot

Every distinction creates a *tertium non datur*. The excluded *tertium*, which is nevertheless present, must, however, remain latent for the distinction itself, since otherwise the very distinction would be called into question. As a recursive concatenation of distinctions, every social system – not only the contract – is based on a flaw: on the violence of the initial distinction that constitutes its unity. The flaw is, accordingly, not a flaw at all, but an advantage: without it, no construction is possible. That implies the renunciation of perfection. The eye that sees everything is no longer able to see anything.[16]

Even this sketch of the logic of the blind spot assists with an initial insight, namely, that the interdiscursive gap is ineluctable in the genesis of the contract. That which, in the vain search for the binding force of the modern contract, seems to be a flaw in its practice or an error in its theory is actually a latency that is simply necessary for constructional reasons. What follows from this for the modern contract 'as such', however, is that the contract's interdiscursive binding effect must remain invisible to contemporary society as a whole and to its self-description. It can be observed only in its effects on the economy, on law and on production, but not in itself as the relationality between them.

In the dance of the mutual adaptations of the diverse contractual projects, while the movements of the individual bodies can be seen, the dance itself remains invisible.

The latency is not only necessary, but needs to be secured against its actualisation. Both the (constructed) object and the latency itself need to remain invisible in the blind spot, to avoid the collapse of the construction. This may, but need not, be bound up with corresponding intentions. In contractual thought, it was no doubt the humanistic concept of the legal contract that safeguarded this latency. As agreement between people, as harmony of two declarations of will, as binding promise between persons, as common source of binding norms, it carefully avoids seeing the multiplicity of hermeneutic differences described above. The full consent of two people overcomes all distinctions, and one's word alone, given by one person to another, is considered capable of keeping the divergent projects together. In this role of covering the blind spots of the differential genesis of contracts, the otherwise rather obsolete legal concept of the contract with its celebration of individual private autonomy has managed to make itself indispensable even in modernity. Or, to put it in a different conceptual tradition: 'The unknownness of the abstraction of exchange is thus a constitutive component of the exchange action itself.'[17]

Yet even when latency is safeguarded, it does not put the unruly question of the binding nature of contract to rest. For the very attraction of the gap lies not only in the constant effort to conceal it, but also in the effort to fill it. There is a constant suspicion that the real point lies in the gap. In the contractual context, there is a permanent gnawing sense that the agreement of the contracting parties is not capable of binding the diversifying projects.[18] And it is not just this suspicion that lies concealed here, but the actual, continually reopening difference between the various types of consent. If contractual consent means something different for the contracting parties involved, for the contractual relationship, for law, for the economy and for production,[19] how are these various consensūs brought into harmony? Here lies the reason for the persistent unrest in the imperfect order of the interdiscursive contractual complex.

Hence the ongoing efforts to ensure the 'unity' of the contract in operational practice and reformulate it in various self-descriptions. New compensatory manoeuvres are continually thought up to re–integrate the lost unity of the contract: imperialist interpretation by one specialised discipline (law, economics, sociology), re–entry of the initial distinction, the repeated making of further, new distinctions, the incorporation of other perspectives. What happens is a grandiose complexification of operations and of observations of the contract around the blind spot. This becomes particularly clear in a theory perspective that discloses the polycontextural dimensions of the contract in their radicality, while, at the same time, complexifying the binding aspects that have been discussed above: contract as intersystemic structural coupling, contract as pan-social integration, contract as organisation or as interaction (see Part I). The result is a never-ending process of creating differences, and of compensating for their blind spots by the invention of a false unity.

Is there an alternative? Perhaps. We may imagine a way of increasing the compensation of blind spots in a different direction. One might think of this as akin to two diametrically contradictory theories, each of which is, however, positioned exactly in the other's blind spot, so that they cannot be integrated into a synthesis. The inspiration is taken from the 'particle–wave' theoretical dispute in quantum physics, which has shaken our ideas of the one right theory.[20] Neither theory is 'right'; it is the conflict between them that makes both 'right'. Constant switching from one to the other gives an almost simultaneous observation from two contradictory but complementary perspectives. But there is a strict condition for complementarity: each must be able to illuminate the other's blind spot.

Can this yield a generalisable model for polycontextural observation that could work in our contractual context? The trick would be not simply to postulate theoretical pluralism, postmodern arbitrariness, dependence on the observer's viewpoint – an 'anything-goes' approach whenever a theory seems to have reached its limits.[21] Theoretical multiplicity as such in principle contributes nothing at all towards throwing light on the blind spots of competing theories. Nor is it enough for one theory to focus on aspects that the other neglects. Instead, we need strict complementarity of two theories precisely fitting in with each other in their contradiction relating to the relevant blind spot. The procedure would have three steps: (1) choose an ambitiously constructed theory; (2) identify the blind spot in its initial distinction; and (3) choose a second, strictly complementary non-congruent theory, with a leading distinction 'orthogonal' to the first theory's distinction and, accordingly, focusing on its blind spot, and vice versa. Systems theory versus deconstruction, systems theory versus discourse theory – would these be possible candidates for this sort of negative symbiosis of theories? And does the focus on the other's latencies establish the mutual attraction between the two? Or would systems theory first have to invent its own complement anew? At any rate, this sort of switching between orthogonal perspectives might supply more interesting insights than the otherwise usual technique of mutual incorporation of theories, which then only continue to cultivate their blind spots, albeit at a different place. In the relation of the competing theories to each other, the switching would be neither a one-sided incorporation nor an overlapping integration, nor a disconnected pluralist co-existence. It would be more of a case of dialectic without synthesis. The complement is the 'negation' of the difference; both are necessarily dependent on each other. But no integration of complement and difference is possible, since each buries the other in its difference technique.

III Contract as 'wave and particle'?

Where does the metaphor of the contract as particle and wave lead us? Particles – those would be the various contractual projects as discrete units: transactions in the economy, contract conclusions in law, productive acts in the various other worlds of meaning, exchanges in organised social relations, and the pursuit of interests by the individuals involved. Wave would denote the dynamic relation between law, the economy and the productive social context, between various levels of social formation – interaction, organisation, society – between states of mind and socially constructed consensūs. And the trick would be not to resolve the dynamic contractual complex into either a theory of social particles or a theory of social waves, but to leave it in its contradictoriness and seek surplus value in that very contradictoriness. What on one view of the contract disappears as a multiplicity of discrete operational chains between the systems becomes visible in the complementary perspective as a binding dynamic. And that which in this view, in turn, appears only as an undifferentiated unitary occurrence is brought into focus in the other in its multiplicity of meanings.

This leads directly to the (latent) dispute between Luhmann and Latour about the non-modernity of modernity, or about the relationship between differentiation and hybridisation.[22] Both systems theory and actor–network theory agree that hybridisation and differentiation are neither mutually exclusive nor reciprocally restrictive, but that the relation between them is one of mutual enhancement. Hybrids are not simply compromises or mediations that weaken the differentiations of modernity through integration, but rather arise only once differentiation has produced and stabilised differences; indeed, they base their very existence on the stable persistence of the difference.[23] It is only the combination of both sides of the difference that brings out the special nature of the hybrid: neither mediation nor synthesis, but extremely ambivalent (or polyvalent) unity.

What is in dispute, however, is the relationship between differentiation and hybridisation. Latour starts by insisting on the mutual reinforcement of modernity and non-modernity, but ultimately, in the last instance as it were, decides in favour of non-modernity. In the parliament of things, it is the politics of the hybrid that wins. In the end, Latour gives priority to hybridisation over differentiation.[24] The contract would thus be a hybrid that combines economic, productional and legal aspects. Luhmann, by contrast, opts for late modernity. In the sophisticated conceptual manoeuvring of operational closure and structural coupling, production of difference, and re–entry, ultimately the differences always prevail. The outcome is the dissolution of the unity of the hybrid in the difference of the systems involved. The contract then has a legal, a productional and an economic side facing one another in structural coupling.

The so-called third position would be to accept the dispute itself as the solution, without deciding it. The productive condition for this, however, is that the dispute be capable of making the blind spots of both positions visible. In fact, hybridisation *à la* Latour is located exactly in the blind spot of systems theory, since its initial distinction between system and environment blinds it to everything that might occur 'between' system and environment. That is why Luhmann has to dissolve the hybrid completely and without remainder in the difference of the systems. From his viewpoint, nothing else is 'thinkable'. Latour, by contrast, decides in favour of the unity of the hybrid, or of a 'mediation' between the opposites, and correspondingly renders himself blind to the system/environment differentiations. The fruitful complementarity of the two positions is retained, however, if two prohibitions are upheld: Avoid the decision between differentiation and hybridisation! But also avoid any mediation, let alone synthesis! The alternative is a continual switching between 'wave and particle', between difference and hybrid, between closed systems and integrating networks. Can this sort of double vision be kept up? Can we, using two mutually contradictory, equally valid theories, neither reducible to the other, see the contract as a multiplicity of systems and simultaneously as a unitary network?

Moreover, where can a theory of the contract be found which is complementary to systems theory and which illuminates the blind spot of functional differentiation? Its focus would be on the 'binding' force of the contract, which, invisible to systems theory, not only acts between the contracting parties, but in the dynamic of the contractual complex also holds together the individual aspects in the law, the economy and the productive system, in society, organisation and interaction, in social and mental systems. It would be naive to assume that such a complement to systems theory already exists among the available range of theories. Neither Habermas nor Derrida nor Foucault developed their constructs to be strictly complementary to Luhmann. A complementary theory does not simply exist, but must be sought precisely in the blind spot of functional differentiation, if not indeed first of all invented.

Systems theory – like any other well-constructed theory – is entitled to its very own complement. Its self-confirming self-rejection is, moreover, only the autological consequence of the polycontexturality it so highly favours, from which it will except not even itself.[25] For the complement to systems theory there are, however, only fragments available in today's theoretical spectrum. We shall attempt an initial survey of them below.

Contract as '*différance*' (Derrida)? On Derrida's view, the contract would definitely not appear as a multiplicity of separate and parallel system recursions or discourse narrations.[26] Instead, the contractual dynamic would be a differential, paradoxically constituted complex chain of distinctions, changing according to context and constantly deferring its meaning, but nonetheless cohesive (and not discursively/systemically or mentally/socially split) and embracing in its relationality the legal, economic, political, interactional and organisational, as well as the social and mental, aspects of the contract and holding them together. My guess is that this concept of the contract, not compatible with systems-theory conceptualisation but complementary to it, can articulate the open dance of the heterogeneous operations themselves, the net of relations, the coordination, the interplay of the various aspects, without, in turn, converting it into a closed system of interlinked operations of similar type.

Contract as '*actant*' (Latour)? The contract would appear as a binding force, as energy between the systems, which, however, is not, as in systems theory, converted into system events and expectations, but floats freely between the systems. These energies may even arise out of the differentiation itself, as tectonic tensions between the 'continents' separated by institutionalised differentiation. My guess here is that the contract lets the tectonic forces of continental drift work for it, as it were, by noting, coordinating and thus mutually strengthening and accelerating randomly arising opportunities for coordination between the continents. Energy, force, drive, desire, power are concepts of only very limited use in systems theory. Expectation (versus action), medium (versus form), complexity difference (versus evolution) are the few 'energy-containing' phenomena; the rest of the forces 'hold sway' outside the systems, as a blind spot.

Contract would then appear as a hybrid, an activating relation of tension between the various poles, developing its own force of attraction, of push and pull. The focus is directed at the 'unconscious' of functional differentiation, which brings about the mediation of the separated aspects. On this view, the contract would appear as an 'integrator', albeit in sharp contrast to usual notions of the integration of a functionally differentiated society, not as compromise or mix, not as de–differentiation, not as superdiscourse or metadiscourse, but as a brief flash of tangential, ad hoc agreement between divergent dynamics.

And finally, contract as 'the task of the translator' (Benjamin)? The contract must convert legal, economic, political and life-world aspects into each other in such a way as to 'succeed', to create the room for compatibility that must exist between the various aspects if the contract is to come into being and to be fulfilled. The symbol of unity is the 'object of the contract', meaning not one of the system aspects in isolation, but the compatibility complex responsible for its success. Benjamin's 'pure language' appears in the translation process not as possible reality or even just as a desirable goal, but as an unattainable 'regulatory idea' of a permanent, yet at the same time impossible translation process: 'bringing the seeds of pure language to maturity in translation seems never achievable'.[27] The obligation to restore the 'break', the fragmentation, the social estrangement, exists despite the impossibility of fulfilment.[28] The contract is then to be read as a single text written in three languages (law, economy, production) – an extremely improbable translation accomplishment. At the same time, however, this is what constitutes the added value of contractual practice as the added value of translation: by momentarily 'translating' social discourses for each other in an ad hoc manner, the contract enables these discourses to extract an added value they could never have accessed individually out of their own intrinsic dynamics.[29]

It would be the 'task of the translator' to seek between the systems the binding force of the contract that keeps the centrifugal dynamics of the functional systems together within limits that are highly determined in temporal, social and substantive terms: the brief flash of a momentary, narrowly circumscribed agreement affecting a small number of actors. This binding effect can no longer be supported by the classical theories of binding by contract: neither by factual prior performance by one party, nor by the word given in a promise, nor by the consent of the contracting parties. For that would presuppose an integration of the various aspects of the contract that today no longer exists. Instead, binding is produced by a mutual connecting of the contractual performances which proceeds independently in each social context: as a price–performance relation on the market, as synallagmatic linkage of contractual rights and obligations in law and as the reciprocal dovetailing of perceived needs in the productive context. These separate performances of various realms of meaning are accessible to a system/environment perspective; indeed, only a fully elaborated systems theory can make them visible at all. But what remains invisible to this sort of perspective is the dynamic of the conflictual harmonisation of these binding mechanisms: the dance of reciprocities that is precisely what binds these reciprocities to each other.[30]

Here, an analysis orthogonal to the system/environment perspective must step in which looks at the mutual impact which the binding forces of the contract have on each other between the systems, on the contractual 'transformation of a distinction into a Möbius strip'.[31] The focus is on the ongoing translation process between various reciprocities in the contractual complex, their conflicts, their rapprochements. The interesting thing about this translation process seems to be its highly particularistic nature: the very renunciation of a general transformational grammar in the relation between the discourses involved, the very non-generalisable idiosyncratic nature of any contractual agreement, make the analysis of the dynamic of the transformation process itself (and not only its outcomes) so important. This process has to clarify whether and how it can be possible to render economic exchange equivalence, legal synallagma and productive reciprocity compatible in an ongoing translation process.

IV Contract as constitution

This subtle interplay of different worlds of meaning, the fractured dissemination and distortion of meaning in the contractual ultracycle, however, depends fundamentally on a fragile symmetry of chances of translation.[32] It is built upon the non-translatable multiplicity of the language games, on their separation, their autonomy, their actual freedom, and on their ability to overcome the translation paradox by their own and specific kind of productive misunderstanding. This opens up new normative perspectives. The freedom of contracting individuals is transformed into the freedom of translating discourses. It is no longer just the freedom of economic actors to choose their partners in the market and to strike a voluntary agreement of their own choosing under market conditions. This would be only a partial aspect, which would reduce freedom of contract to the freedom of the economic discourse to translate other discursive projects into the economic language but not vice versa. Freedom of contract today means the freedom of all three discourses to translate, to transfer, to reconstruct operations of other discourses in their context, the freedom of their productive misunderstanding according to their internal logic. To cite Derrida, who developed his ideas on interdiscursivity and translation in a discussion of Kant and Schelling on academic freedom in relation to the state, this freedom 'presupposes separation, heterogeneity of codes and the multiplicity of languages, the non-trespassing of boundaries, the non-transparence'.[33]

This freedom is threatened whenever totalising, if not totalitarian, tendencies of one social system attempt to impose its version of translation on the other worlds of meaning. While modern freedom of contract was limited to the protection of free choice in the market against fraud, deception, and particularly against political interference, the new freedom of contract would need to extend to a protection of contract against the free market itself whenever this language game begins to monopolise the right to interdiscursive translation and imposes the economic translation on the other discourses. Freedom of contractual translation is directed against an economic imperialism, against tendencies of the economic discourse to erect a new tower of rationality. In contrast to such tendencies, a new Babylonian confusion of tongues would destroy the project of an economic rationalisation of the world and introduce the obligation of a necessary and simultaneously impossible translation between the different languages of the social world.

Private law today is, of course, not living in splendid isolation from its environing society, but rather in close structural coupling, via the mechanisms of contract, with the economic subsystem of society.[34] But this is where the problem lies. Private law thus receives information about the rest of society quasi-automatically and almost exclusively through the cost–benefit calculations of the economic discourse. Any other discourses in society, whether research, education, technology, art or medicine, are first translated into the world of economic calculation, allocative efficiency and transaction costs and then, in this translation, presented to the law for conflict resolution. This means a serious distortion of social relations. This distortion of social relations by their economic contractualisation has four dimensions: (1) bilateralisation – complex social relations are translated into a multitude of closed bilateral relations; (2) selective performance criteria; (3) externalisation of negative effects; and (4) power relations.[35]

This shows how urgently private law needs to rid itself of this monopoly of economic calculation and to make direct contact with the many other social subsystems in society that have different criteria of rationality than the economic discourse. To be sure, this does happen today – at least to a limited degree – whenever contract law uses the famous general clauses of 'public policy' to invalidate an economically viable contract due to non-economic criteria, or those of 'good faith' to balance economic criteria against other social criteria of performance. But these are merely marginal corrections of the dominant economic worldview that is imported into the law by myriads of economic transactions. These marginal corrections need to be replaced by a condition of full symmetry within the triangle of discourses in contract.

What does this mean in concrete terms? Coming back to our initial example of an expert contract, the consequences of such an approach become visible more clearly.[36] As we saw earlier, in the expert contract a fundamental conflict, the direct collision between the principles of contractual loyalty and expertise impartiality, comes to the fore.[37] Expert advice, if it is supposed to work properly, needs to be guided strictly by principles of scientific enquiry. The application of rigorous methodical standards, an orientation towards a comprehensive body of concepts and theories, reliance on intersubjective consensus in the community of experts, strict insulation against interference of outside political or economic interests, neutrality and impartiality in relation to the interests of the clients involved – all are of primary importance.[38] Bilateral contracting, by contrast, imposes a legitimate obligation of cooperation, trust, interdependence and loyalty towards the economic interests of the mandator on the expert. The expert is under a contractual obligation to further the interests of his client, to use his scientific-methodical instruments to advance the position of the party with whom he has entered into a contract and who, after all, finances the expert report.

Thus, private law faces a sharp collision between two legitimate self-regulatory institutions: contract and expert advice. In the private expert report, the ethos of contract – privity, particularism, interest orientation, utility and loyalty – clashes directly with the ethos of scientific enquiry – public knowledge, universalism, disinterestedness, originality and scepticism.

Judicial intervention is needed if the integrity of independent expert advice is to be maintained within the private sector. More abstractly, it is needed to facilitate an internal reflective balancing of its institutional benefits to social actors (the mandator, beneficiary, others) against its social function (the advancement of knowledge in non-scientific sectors of society). This is the reason why it is an important matter of public policy to declare that expert advice should constitute a legally 'protected sphere' within civil society. Thus, 'the state in essence buffers these enterprises "artificially" from all other spheres' more "natural" condition, that of immediate competition within economic and political market places'.[39]

The task at hand is to search for spaces of compatibility between contract and expertise, to search for a legal regime of expert advice that furthers an internal reflection on the balance of function and contributions. This is where liability to third parties enters the picture. It appears as an adequate means to create a space of compatibility. It provides a solution for a typical collision of contracting worlds. It does so by redefining 'privities', i.e. the external boundaries of interpersonal relations. While the concrete project, whether in the technological, social, scientific or medical sector, requires one comprehensive multilateral relationship, which formalises the agreed cooperation of several actors, the concrete contract and the economic market relation are fragmenting the multilateral complex into various strictly bilateral relations. The 'privity' of the relation is defined differently by the contract and by the project. Liability to third parties dissolves this conflict of different privities in favour of the multilateralism inherent in the expert advice. Via liability law, the social institution of expert advice forces the bilateral contract to transform itself into a multilateral obligation. The conflict between multilateral social networks and the bilateral economic transactions forces the law to account for third-party effects of contracting, even if this contradicts the sacred privity of contract, reduces allocative efficiency and increases transaction costs.

If, then, as a matter of law, a responsibility to third parties is included in the contract, the one-sided contractual duty of loyalty is counterbalanced by a liability supplement towards the other participant in the project. Thus, despite its contractual loyalty, private expert advice can regain its requisite neutral and impartial orientation. Independent expertise as an institution, as a complex of social expectations, thus represents one of the non-contractual elements of contract that – as a matter of law – the private autonomy of the parties has to respect. Whenever expert advice is organised under a private law regime, the requirement that it be complemented by liability to third parties is a necessary implicit dimension of this regime.

To express the result in one formula: *liability to third parties symbolises the transformation of interest-bound expert advice into project-bound expert advice*. The existence of this liability is a highly visible threshold that separates two institutions. It draws a limit between partisan expertise where knowledge is (legitimately) used for the pursuit of one-sided private interests and independent expertise where knowledge is applied in an disinterested way with built-in controls of reliability and where it is independent from personal loyalty and reciprocity considerations. Expert liability to third parties marks the boundary between the fields of economic rationality and scientific rationality.

To generalise from this example, contract as translation raises the issue of authenticity, of the integrity of the text, of its survival in the free play of translation. Freedom of translation within the triangle of contractual projects requires that each text have a right to its autonomy. Violations of this right have been committed by the diverse totalitarianisms of the twentieth century. Totalising regimes control the meta-rules of translation between discourses. They monopolise the right of the ultimate translation, which they then impose upon other discourses as binding.

These 'rights' are social phenomena, incipient and inchoate normative constructs that emerge from social practices as compelling claims so important to an institutionalised practice as to make legal recognition plausible.[40] But this presupposes a conceptual readiness of the law to respond to the pressures of social development. For the law, the conceptualisation of contract as interdiscursivity raises the issue of constitutional rights, of fundamental rights for discourses. Yet these rights can no longer be seen as protecting only the individual actor against the repressive power of the state, but, in the situation of today's polycontexturality, need to be reconstructed as 'discourse rights'. The normative correlate of contract as translation would be an extension of constitutional rights into the context of private governance regimes. This, however, requires a fundamental rethinking of the horizontal effect of constitutional rights.[41]

Notes

This chapter was previously published as 'In the blind spot: the hybridization of contract', trans. Iain L. Fraser, *Theoretical Inquiries into Law*, 8:1 (2007), 51–71.

1. Teubner, 'Contracting worlds'. Some consequences for legal doctrine are suggested in Teubner, 'Expertise as Social Institution'.
2. On the social history of contracting in the continental law area, see Wieacker, *History of Private Law*; cf. Abegg, *Die zwingenden Inhaltsnormen*; Grimm, *Soziale, wirtschaftliche und politische Voraussetzungen der Vertragsfreiheit*. For the common law, see Atiyah, *Rise and Fall*; Friedman, *Contract Law in America*.
3. Abegg, *Die zwingenden Inhaltsnormen*; Amstutz, 'Verfassung von Vertragsverbindungen'; Crone, *Rahmenverträge*; Müller, *Verwaltungsverträge*.
4. For details, see Teubner, 'Expertise as Social Institution'.
5. Most clearly visible in the economic analysis of law, for example, Craswell, 'Contract Law'.
6. This is, however, the trend in relational contracting theory, which views the contract as a 'socially embedded' legal relationship. See Macneil, 'Relational contract: what we do know'; Gordon, 'Unfreezing legal reality'; Eisenberg, 'Relational Contracts'. See also the critical comments on Teubner, 'Contracting worlds', in Gerstenberg, 'Justification (and justifiability) of private law'; Macneil, 'Relational contract theory: challenges and queries'; Campbell, 'Limits of concept formation'.
7. As in legal institutionalism. Cf. MacCormick and Weinberger, *Institutional Theory of Law*.
8. As in the still dominant legal doctrine. See, e.g., Medicus and Petersen, *Bürgerliches Recht*, p. 19, para. 24.
9. Luhmann, *Law as a Social System*, p. 395.
10. On this reciprocal reconstruction of the contract in the different contracting worlds as a productive misunderstanding, see Teubner, 'Expertise as Social Institution'; Teubner, 'Contracting worlds'; Teubner, 'Two faces of Janus'.
11. Baecker, *Form des Unternehmens*, p. 207 (describing the binding force of the contract as a replacement of difference (firm/environment) by identity (transaction)). In light of our discussion, this should be amended to 'differences'.
12. Particularly significant in this respect is Bendel, 'Funktionale Differenzierung', with his concept of 'intersystemic discourse'. Similar advances also can be found in Preuss, 'Rationality Potentials of Law'; Jessop, 'The Economy, the State and the Law'.

13 In this context, see Willke, 'Societal Guidance', p. 353. Nor is there any socially institutionalised communication system that might be able to restore the unity of the contract through the medium of values, see Luhmann, *Theory of Society*, vol. 1, p. 204.
14 Luhmann, 'Interaction, Organization, and Society'.
15 More precisely, in the blind spots of the re-entries, i.e. the contractually relevant system/environment distinctions, each of which is repeated within the system as system/system distinctions: from the viewpoint of a contracting party as one party versus another, from the viewpoint of law as legal contract versus transaction, etc.
16 On the metaphor of the 'blind spot' in the context of constructivism, see Luhmann, 'Wie lassen sich latente Strukturen beobachten?'; Foerster, 'Gleichnis vom blinden Fleck'.
17 Zizek, *Enjoy Your Symptom!*, p. 16.
18 This is one of the motives for interdisciplinary attempts to find the contractual binding force outside the law, for example, in the 'relational contract' or in economic (!) structures.
19 One spectacular case of the divergence of consensus between law (or legal doctrine) and economics (theory) is 'efficient breach of contract'.
20 For a discussion of particle–wave dualism as incompatibility or complementarity of theories in an observer-dependent perspective, see Bitbol, 'En quoi consiste la "Révolution Quantique"?', pp. 225 ff.
21 Feyerabend, *Against Method*.
22 Latour, *We Have Never Been Modern*; Latour, *Politics of Nature*; Luhmann, *Social Systems*.
23 Hutter and Teubner, 'Parasitic role of hybrids'.
24 Latour, *Politics of Nature*; Latour, *We Have Never Been Modern*.
25 Luhmann, *Theory of Society*, vol. 2, p. 338.
26 An implicit concept of the contract can be found in Derrida, 'Force of law'; on law in general, see Derrida, *Given Time*, vol. 1.
27 Benjamin, *Gesammelte Schriften*, vol. 2, p. 15.
28 For a deconstructive perspective on translation, see Hirsch (ed.), *Übersetzung und Dekonstruktion*.
29 For more on this, see Teubner, 'Contracting worlds'.
30 This refers to Wiethölter's concept of reciprocity: Wiethölter, 'Just-ifications', pp. 65–75.
31 Baecker, *Form des Unternehmens*, p. 207.
32 For more details on the following normative argument, see Teubner, 'Contracting worlds'.
33 Derrida, 'Des tours de Babel'.
34 Luhmann, *Law as a Social System*, p. 395.
35 Collins, 'Sanctimony of Contract', pp. 75–81.
36 For more details, see Teubner, 'Expertise as Social Institution'.
37 For the larger historical and social background of these conflicts, see Sciulli, *Theory of Societal Constitutionalism*, p. 40.
38 For a recent comprehensive reformulation of the fundamental social norms in the scientific community, see Ziman, *Real Science*, p. 28.
39 Sciulli, *Theory of Societal Constitutionalism*, p. 207.
40 For incipient and inchoate law as a result of social practices that press for legal institutionalisation, see Selznick, *Law, Society and Industrial Justice*, p. 32. In less

normative language, a similar argument for the emergence of constitutional rights as a social institution has been developed by Luhmann, *Grundrechte als Institution*, p. 186.

41 For an attempt to spell out what the implications of such an approach are for the freedom of art in private contexts, see Graber and Teubner, 'Art and money'; Graber, *Zwischen Geist und Geld*. For the debate on constitutional rights in private contexts, see Chapter 5 in this volume; Anderson, 'Social democracy'; Barak, 'Constitutional human rights'; Clapham, *Human Rights in the Private Sphere*; Collins, *Justice in Dismissal*.

Part III

The dark side of functional differentiation: the normative response of societal constitutionalism

8

A constitutional moment? The logics of 'hitting the bottom'

I Collective addiction?

Is there such a thing as collective addiction? Do we recognise addiction as a genuine social phenomenon? What does it mean to speak of the addictive society? The usual answer would be binge drinking or the herd instinct of bankers before the crisis. In fact, these are social amplifiers of addictive behaviour: they influence obsessive behaviour in the form of peer-pressure, imitation, social norms or mob mentality. But what they are concerned with is ultimately only the addiction of individuals.

Through the lens of systems theory, we look for and find something rather different. It is possible that social processes as such might exhibit the properties of addictive behaviour quite independently of the dependence syndromes of individual human beings. Josef Ackermann is clearly not an addict, and yet Deutsche Bank is in urgent need of detox therapy. This would amount to collective addiction in the strict sense. For Alan Greenspan, its discovery was a shock: 'those of us who have looked to the self-interest of lending institutions to protect shareholders' equity, myself included, are in a state of shocked disbelief'.[1] He would never have believed that banks would act against their own interests by high-risk 'gambling' practices to the point of self-destruction.

That rational organisations could act so irrationally, against their own interests, brought Greenspan to a painful realisation: his 'whole intellectual edifice', based entirely on rational choice, 'collapsed'.

The addiction syndrome of a collective actor would be one manifestation of genuine social addictive behaviour. The other would be communication chains that exhibit an intrinsic compulsion to grow, which would not require the involvement of a collective actor. Independently of the addiction of individuals, communications would concatenate such that they become caught up in compulsive engagement in an activity despite lasting self-destructive consequences. If there is such a thing as non-individual, and thus collective or communicative, compulsions to grow, then the greed of individual bankers is not the main problem. Instead we must look for the specific social addiction mechanisms that cause such impersonal addiction phenomena.

What does this fascinating phenomenon have to do with constitutional moments? My intention is to draw a line from self-harming growth compulsions of social systems, through the moment of near-catastrophe, to new orientations, which cannot be effected from the outside but only through the transformation of their 'inner constitution'. With Derrida, we might talk of the 'extreme *capillarity* of discourses' at which the transformation must direct itself; since it is they – and not the capital constitutions of the world of states – that regulate the inner life of the social body, down to the very finest blood vessel.[2] Thus: constitutions beyond the state.

These are my hypotheses:

(1) In order to understand the recent global financial crisis, we should not rely on factor analysis alone. Instead, we should look for the underlying self-destructive growth compulsions of information flows – in other words, for phenomena of collective addiction.
(2) 'Hitting the bottom' refers to the constitutional moment when either a catastrophe begins or societal forces for change of such intensity are mobilised that the 'inner constitution' of the economy transforms under their pressure.
(3) Plain money reform is one of several examples that illustrate a capillary constitutionalisation of the global economy, the effects of which could not be achieved through either national or transnational interventions of the world of states.
(4) The dichotomy constitutional/unconstitutional develops into a binary meta-code within the structural coupling between the economy and law, and is set above both the legal code and the economic code.

II Growth compulsions and the financial crisis

1 *Causal factors or the compulsion to grow?*

A variety of regulations have been proposed in reaction to the global financial crisis: the abolition of bankers' bonuses, enhanced equity funds for the banks, a Tobin tax, quality control of financial products, tightened national and international state supervision of financial institutions, particularly hedge funds, tightened control of capital flows and stock market transactions, and improved rules of accounting and risk assessment.[3] Typically, these proposals are based on factor analysis, in which individual causes are isolated, through the attribution of causality, and held responsible for the crisis. The aim of regulation, then, is to introduce counter-factors to the causal chain in order to prevent a repetition of the crisis. Their chances of success shall not be disputed here; however, they do have one problem in common: *fatta la legge trovato l'inganno*. No sooner has a law been passed than the loophole appears. The Achilles heel of such regulation is that national or international rules can always be effectively avoided; in the face of such enormous efforts at avoidance, *ex ante* regulation is impossible.[4]

A deeper understanding of the crisis is offered by an analysis which regards the factors of factor analysis simply as interchangeable activating conditions and which attempts to discover the underlying dynamic. This dynamic, which fuels the development of ever new avoidance strategies, should be tamed through transforming the 'internal constitution' of the global financial economy. One among several instructive examples is provided by the so-called plain money reform currently recommended by a number of finance experts.[5] This reform goes right to the heart of the economic constitution – the money mechanism. Money creation ceased, long ago, to be the prerogative of central banks acting to generate a money supply through paper money not tied to the gold standard. The widespread circulation of non-cash money in current accounts, the circulation of moneyless payment transactions, new communication technologies and – of particular importance – the globalisation of money and capital transactions have prised the money-creating monopoly out of the hands of the national central banks.[6] By virtue of these developments, it is now the globally active commercial banks which *de facto* have assumed the capacity to create money – in principle independently of the central banks. And this is the case even if non-cash money is euphemistically referred to only as quasi-money. In Europe, the ratio of non-cash money to cash money is 4:1. In the UK, non-cash money accounts for 92% of the total. The main source of money creation today is the provision of credit guarantees by commercial banks (active money creation): the debtor is given a sight fund (sight deposit) to the value of the borrowed sum and, as a result, the money supply of the national economy is directly increased. What is happening here is *creatio ex nihilo*. It is absolutely not the case that existing saving deposits of the banks cover the credit provided by commercial banks by way of non-cash money. Rather, credit is provided more or less freely according to the independent risk calculations of the individual banks. Public central banks can influence this private money creation only indirectly through the regulation of interest rates.

It is this massive creation of money by private banks that is responsible for the current excesses of the compulsion to grow in the global financial sector. It serves, through advance financing, to compel the real economy to grow to an extent that is socially harmful. At the same time, this private money creation is exploited for an unforeseen increase in self-referential financial speculation. Citing Huber:

The banks act like every other economic actor: procyclically and in their own interest, without any concept of the whole economy and without any political or social accountability. As a consequence, the creation of money by the banks proceeds procyclically, overshooting the mark. In this way, extremely exaggerated business and stock market cycles can be created:

- in the up-and-up, an oversupply of money and consequent price inflation, increasingly also capital market stock price inflation (investment bubbles, asset price inflation),
- in the down-and-down of crisis phases – due to imploding stock market capitalisation/asset values and payment defaults – a scarcity of money and a monetary shrinking of the economy. The financial institutions themselves are as exposed as the state, the economy and society beyond them.[7]

The point of the theory, however, is as follows: the alternative cannot lie with zero growth, but rather with attacking the excesses of the compulsion to increase. 'Stability and zero growth are impossible in today's monetary system.'[8] Through the creation of value, the creation of money perforce leads to an increase in profits – and, in turn, the increase in profits forces further money and value creation. This necessarily results in a growth spiral. The alternative would be a shrinking of the economy that, in the long term, would be incompatible with today's money-centric economic system. A functioning monetised economy is reliant on a certain compulsion to grow. That said, it is not the compulsion to grow as such which occupies centre stage, but rather the difference between necessary growth and self-destructive growth excesses with undesirable consequences.[9]

2 *Self-destructive growth dynamics in communication*

This distinction between necessary growth dynamics and pathological growth excesses is of theoretical and practical interest. If growth-inducing mechanisms cause an excessive triggering of social processes that in themselves are not pathological, then an analogy with individual addiction phenomena is appropriate.[10] As stated above, however, the common conception of addiction syndromes as psychological problems (and, correspondingly, of therapies aimed at individuals) leads us up a blind alley. To identify genuine social equivalents of individual addictive behaviour becomes crucial. A systems-theoretical analysis may assist us in this task. The starting point for such an analysis is a strict division of psychological processes from social processes, both of which are held accountable for the production of meaning in their own right. Luhmann's greatest achievement was to complement the Husserlian phenomenology of consciousness with an independent phenomenology of communication (not to replace the former with the latter!). This led to a typical doubling of phenomena, which hitherto had been understood only psychologically. Memory, for example, is not only a psychological dynamic, but in addition a socially institutionalised, purely communicative process. Even for complexes that were hitherto understood exclusively as phenomena belonging to individual consciousness – such as intention, strategy, interest, preference or understanding – a distinction must be made according to whether they occur in the individual consciousness, or proceed as communication processes independent of consciousness.[11]

The definition of individual addiction – compulsive engagement in an activity despite lasting negative consequences – must be rethought for social systems in general, and for collective actors in particular. Which 'addiction mechanisms' are responsible for the fact that the autopoietic self-reproduction of a social system through the recursivity of system-specific operations reverts into a communicative compulsion to repetition and growth, bringing self-destructive consequences in its wake? Communication can be understood to suffer from an addiction syndrome when its irresistible attachment to exogenous factors engenders a compulsion to grow. Returning to our example, we might understand the non-cash money created *ex nihilo* by the commercial banks to be an addiction mechanism: the payment operations concatenate such that an excessive growth compulsion is released in the financial and real economies. The increased expectations of profit inherent in the supplementary creation of money through credit guarantees by the commercial banks then cause a compulsion to grow in the real economy, which further increases the expectations of profit. This releases a dynamic which can no longer be regarded as a steady circular flow within the economy, but instead must be understood as a rapidly accelerating growth spiral. Parallel to this, within this dynamic of money multiplication, bank loans are taken out that are not intended to finance productive investments, but are used instead to purchase speculative assets. If the interest payable on the bank loan exceeds the expected increase in the value of the assets, the result is the collapse of speculation, financial crisis and eventually economic crisis. Both communicative growth compulsions can occur quite independently of individual greed and addictive behaviour; even addiction-resistant individuals must play along with these compulsions, to a great extent, or risk exclusion from the game. That said, it does remain the case that individuals with certain corresponding psychological dispositions are attracted by the game, so that individual and social addictive behaviour mutually strengthen each other.

Such a dynamic raises a fundamental question for autopoietics: how are we to conceive of the relationship between social self-reproduction and the compulsion to grow? Notions of a self-producing communication cycle which, so to speak, flows back into itself, might appear to offer an answer; however, these are much too harmless and may even be misleading. The theory of autopoietic systems has already broken with the axiom of classical structuralist-functionalist theory, that is, with the imperative of self-preservation. Connectivity (*Anschlussfähigkeit*) of recursive operations is the new imperative – autopoiesis proceeds or not, as the case may be.[12] Yet the disquieting question remains of whether autopoiesis is not secretly dependent on the logic of growth. Is there an affinity between the self-reproduction of social systems and their implacable compulsion to grow? And, particularly relevant to our discussion, does the recursivity of autopoiesis have inherent tendencies, over and above such normal growth, towards a socially harmful compulsion to repeat and grow? And by what means is such a 'turbo-autopoiesis' triggered? The famous-infamous expansion tendencies of the functional systems – the tendencies towards a comprehensive politicisation, economisation, juridification, medialisation or medicalisation of the world – may well indicate such a compulsive growth dynamic. And it seems likely that a moment of excessive expectations, a type of high-risk 'credit' in future communications, may lie hidden in the motivations to accept a communication created by the media money, power, law, truth and love. This credit can then only be 'cashed in' by means of ever higher payments and the effects these in turn have on increasing 'credit' expectations, so that a necessary increase dynamic, a growth spiral develops. If this is the case, the pathological growth spiral can no longer be regarded as a phenomenon particular to the money medium, but instead must be seen as a general characteristic of functional systems. Such a dynamic goes well beyond the acceleration cycle in modern societies diagnosed by Hartmut Rosa.[13] It is to do not only with a transformation of time structures, contingent on social structures, which leads to an acceleration dynamic. Generally speaking, it is a question of advance 'payments' generating expectations of an increase in 'payments' which, in turn, compel the next advance 'payment' – in other words, an initially stabilising dynamic which tends to tip into socially harmful excesses.

There is, I submit, an inherent compulsion of ever higher production in functional systems other than the economy – an inherent compulsion which on the one hand is a necessary condition of self-reproduction, but on the other can be propelled by identifiable growth-inducing mechanisms to the point of transition into destructive tendencies. Can the difference between 'normal' growth and its 'pathological' forms – in other words, their addiction phenomena – be clearly identified? In the case of law, it is quite clear that law does not simply resolve conflicts and then just returns to a neutral, inactive position. Law itself creates conflict through its own regulations, which in turn require more regulation. As the example of drug-related legislation strikingly shows, through its regulatory intervention in daily life, law itself produces situations that provoke conflicts.[14] And at the same time, every norm brings with it difficulties of interpretation that cause conflicts. Ultimately, the sheer volume of norms produces internal conflicts of norms requiring legal solutions. Is the price for the autonomy of law the fact that it necessarily contributes to an increase in conflict? This would still be normal for a moderate inflation of legal norms. What should be seen critically, however, is a type of addiction syndrome of the law in which norm production exhibits a dependency on external stimuli – political legislation and economic contractual mechanisms – producing, at national and transnational level, the much-criticised pathologies of the excessive juridification of the world. Might these be the 'legal excesses' of late modernity?[15] In politics, the excessive growth compulsions of the welfare state are the obvious candidate. In science, research creates ever deeper uncertainties, which can only be dispelled by further research which again causes new uncertainties. In each of these contexts we need to differentiate between a growth imperative that is necessary for continuation, and excessive rates of increase, which threaten the normal state of things.

III The constitutional moment

1 *Hitting the bottom*

It is, then, a case of identifying the dynamics that accelerate the growth spiral of a social sector to the point where it tips over into destructiveness by colliding with other social dynamics. Such growth accelerations of the functional systems burden these systems themselves, society and the environment with serious 'problems ensuing from their own differentiation, specialisation and high achievement orientation'.[16] Three areas of collision can be identified: (1) the collision of the growth imperative of one system with the integrity of other social subsystems; (2) the collision with a comprehensive rationality of world society; and (3) the collision of the growth acceleration of a system with its own self-reproduction. The evolutionary dynamics of these three collisions certainly have the potential to lead to social catastrophes. But the collapse is not, as Karl Marx had postulated, a matter of necessity, and nor is there anything necessary about Max Weber's 'iron cage' of modernity. Niklas Luhmann is more plausible: the occurrence of catastrophe is contingent. It depends on whether growth-inhibiting countervailing structures emerge to prevent the positive feed-back catastrophe within the growth dynamic.

Only the experience of near-catastrophe, as opposed to the mere experience of contingency as such, may be regarded as the 'constitutional moment'.[17] This is not the moment when the self-destructive dynamic causes the abstract danger of a collapse to appear: that is the normal state of things. Rather, it is the moment when the collapse is directly imminent. Functionally differentiated society appears to ignore earlier opportunities for self-correction; to ignore the fact that sensitive observers point out the impending danger in warnings and entreaties. The endogenous self-energising processes are so dominant that they allow self-correction only at the very last moment. The similarity with individual addiction phenomena is again obvious: 'Hit the bottom!' It is not until the eleventh hour that there is a chance that the understanding will be lucid enough, and the will to change strong enough, to allow a radical change of course. And that applies not only to the economy, where warnings about the next crisis are regularly ignored. It also applies to politics, which does not react when experts criticise undesirable developments, but waits instead until the drama of a political scandal unfolds – and then reacts frantically. In science, the Kuhnian paradigm shift would seem to be a similar phenomenon, where aberrations from the current dominant paradigm are dismissed as anomalies until the point where the 'theory catastrophe' forces a paradigm shift.

The constitutional moment is the direct experience of crisis; the experience of a liberated social energy, yielding destructive, even self-destructive, consequences that can only be overcome by their reflection and by the decision for self-limitation. The passage of social systems through the 'dark side' of their promise of progress is ultimately no departure from the healthy normal course of things, no error to be avoided. Quite the opposite: the experience of the dark side is almost a necessary condition of the transformation of the inner constitution. It is ultimately, then, the pathologies that herald the constitutional moment: the moment in the catastrophe in which a decision is made between a total destruction of the energy and its self-limitation.

In functional differentiation, a risky experiment is entered upon: that of renouncing the unity of society and of liberating a variety of fragmented social energies – each of which, since it is not limited by any inbuilt counter-principles, produces a massive internal growth dynamic. The great achievements of civilisation in art, science, medicine, economics, politics and law only became possible by virtue of this process. But the dark side of these increase principles potentially leads to moments of catastrophe, the constitutional moments which make collective learning experiences of self-limitation possible. 1945 is the paradigm. It was the constitutional moment for a worldwide proclamation of human rights in the wake of a political totalitarianism; the moment in which political power worldwide was willing to self-limit. Similarly, 1789 and 1989 were moments in which, in the wake of destructive expansion tendencies, politics limited itself by guaranteeing the separation of powers and fundamental rights within political constitutions.[18]

Constitutional moments are not limited to politics. In the course of functional differentiation, all subsystems develop growth energies which are highly ambivalent both in their productivity and in their destructivity. In many areas of society, a new constitutional question develops: 'How many inward expansions does society produce thereby, how much monetarisation, juridification, scientification, politicisation can it produce and cope with, and how many of these at the same time (rather than, for example, monetarisation alone)?'[19] In the late phase of functional differentiation, this becomes the central problem of societal constitutionalism. This is the real experience of late modernity following the triumphant victory of the autonomy of different sub-rationalities. The question is no longer: What are the institutional preconditions of their autonomy? Instead, it is: Where are the limits of the expansion of the functional systems? The economy, celebrating its triumphs and defeats in global turbo-capitalism, is paradigmatic here.

2 *Capillary constitutionalisation*

When the excessive growth processes of a social subsystem spin out of control, the following alternative exists: either state intervention or inner constitutionalisation. Following the experiences of political totalitarianism in the last century, a permanent subordination of the subsystems to the state is no longer a valid option. The political regulation of social processes through global regulatory regimes is much more viable; however, the meaning of such regulation is ambivalent. For what are the options today? Either the administrative steering of global communication processes or the externally compelled self-limitation of the system's options. If it is correct that it is of central importance to defend against the three possibilities of collision – self-destruction of the system, environmental damage in the widest sense (endangering the integrity of the social, human and natural environments) and threats to world society – then the second option is to be preferred. This is the message of a societal constitutionalism. The problem to be solved by a global constitutional order is this: how can external pressure of such force be exerted on the subsystems that self-limitations of their options for action will take effect in their internal processes?

Why self-limitation and not external limitation? Does experience not teach us that self-limitation strategies put the fox in charge of the henhouse? That excesses can only be prevented by the external exercise of control, backed by massive sanctions? Yet does it not also show that attempts to steer internal processes by means of external interventions are bound to misfire?[20] Here, societal constitutionalism attempts to steer a difficult path between external interventions and self-steering.[21] A 'hybrid constitutionalisation' is required, in the sense of external social forces, which include not only state instruments of power, but also legal rules and countervailing forces from other civil society contexts such as the media, public discussion, spontaneous protest, intellectuals, social movements, NGOs or trade unions, applying such massive pressure on the functional systems that internal self-limitations are configured and become truly effective. In the economy, for example, arrangements against indefensible working conditions must be found which

> ... combine[s] external (countervailing) pressure – be it from the state, or unions, or labor-rights NGOs, comprehensive and transparent monitoring systems, and a variety of 'management systems' interventions aimed at eliminating the root causes of poor working conditions.[22]

It is only possible to invent these limitations from within the system-specific logic, and not from without. '[E]ach functional system determines its identity itself ... through an elaborate semantics of self-interpretation [*Selbstsinngebung*], reflection, autonomy.' The dependence of the subsystems 'can no longer be specifically normativized, can no longer be legitimated for society as a whole as an essential condition for order'.[23] The difficult task of mutually aligning the function of a social system and its contribution to the environment at a sufficiently high level can only be attempted by a system-internal reflection, which may be initiated or mandated externally, but cannot be replaced.[24] It is for this reason that an external political determination of transnational social sub-constitutions is not feasible. Only constitutional irritants, i.e. political impulses to constitutionalise, are possible. The knowledge of which type of self-limitation can be chosen does not even exist as such in advance. It cannot simply be accessed, but must be internally created. The endogenous growth compulsions themselves can only be fought with endogenous growth inhibitors. The necessary knowledge cannot be built up from an external observation point as centrally available know-how; instead, it must be built up through the cooperation of external pressures and internal processes of discovery.

High cognitive demands are nevertheless thereby placed on national and international interventions by the world of states and by other external pressures, for the very reason that they cannot simply arrange behaviour, but must instead create irritations in a selective manner. 'The state must not intervene directly so as to achieve particular desired situations or the assessment of "results"; rather, it must observe the social systems and direct its intervention precisely at their self-transformation.'[25] When subsystemic rationality develops self-destructive tendencies, external political interventions are indeed unavoidable; however, they need to be aimed at 'creating new possibilities through the breaking open of self-blockades; but not at superimposing a different, state-centred rationality'.[26] Political-legal regulation and external social influence are only likely to succeed if they are transformed into a self-domestication of the systemic growth dynamic. This requires massive external interventions from politics, law and civil society: specifically, interventions of the type suited to translation into self-steering.

The task would be, with a bit of luck, to combine external political, legal and social impulses with changes to the internal constitution. Speaking once more with Derrida, changes to the 'capillary' constitution of discourses itself are necessary, down to the very arteries of communicative circulation, 'where their fineness becomes microscopic' and where they cannot be touched by the influences of the 'capital' constitution of the state.[27] It seems that Derrida was inspired here by the Foucauldian reformulation of the concept of power: the problem of today's societies lies not with the excesses of juridical power wielded by the political sovereign, but rather in the phenomenon of 'capillary power', achieved through progress in scientific disciplines and dependent on technology. This capillary power permeates the social body through to its very microstructures.[28] Nobody knows how such a capillary constitutionalisation could be achieved in concrete terms. *Ex ante* prognoses are, as a matter of principle, impossible. And, for that reason, there is no alternative but to experiment with constitutionalisation. The application of external pressure means that the self-steering of politics, law or other subsystems creates such irritations of the focal system that ultimately the external and internal programmes play out together along the desired course. And that cannot be planned for, but only experimented with.[29] As has been mentioned, the desired course for social sub-constitutions consists in limitations of the endogenous tendencies towards self-destruction and environmental damage. This is the core of the constitutional problem: the difficult task of dealing with the self-transformation of the focal subsystem and that of its environmental systems.

3 Devil and Beelzebub

What is remarkable is that it is the political system, of all things, which has assumed an historic role as a precursor, in its own sphere, for exactly this paradoxical undertaking: subjecting its own expansion to its own self-limitation. Only Beelzebub can cast out the devil! The history of the political constitutions of nation states teaches us a lesson regarding the way in which a social system can limit its own possibilities, increased immensely by functional differentiation, through relying on its own resources. It cannot be stressed enough that these self-limitations did not arise automatically by reason of functional imperatives, but only under immense external pressure, as the result of fierce constitutional battles. In this auto-limitative role, politics as developed in the nation state has set the benchmark of how constitutions can assist a social system to limit, for itself, its own growth compulsions.

These limitations had different lines of attack, of course, depending on the expansion tendency of the political system. As a counter-movement to political absolutism in the early modern period, the political separation of powers was intendfed to divide absolute power, and to restrain the sub-powers through their mutual control. *Rechtsstaat* principles were intended to place normative limits on the prerogative of the all-powerful sovereign. Following the separation of politics, administration and justice, the politicisation tendencies within administration and justice were supposed to be restricted. And, finally, fundamental rights were intended as the great civilising achievement by which politics would prevent itself from politicising individual and institutional spheres of autonomy within society. In today's changed conditions, new self-limitations are added to these classical limitations. On the one hand, fierce competition among Western industrialised states and the enforced modernisation politics of developing states have transformed the threat to the natural environment into an urgent problem of the political constitution, which can only be addressed through transnational constitutionalisation. On the other hand, politics has to respond with constitutional self-limitations to the infamous 'growth acceleration laws' of the welfare state. To guarantee the independence of the central banks and to impose effective limits on national debt is quite clearly to engage in matters of constitutional importance.[30] The constitutional importance of the question of whether subsidies and other excessive state expenditure should be subjected to a test of sufficient connection with public welfare is, in contrast, rather more hidden. Social-scientific and political performance reviews by authorities independent of the state (similar to audit courts) which render errors visible and avoidable could be among the currently urgent constitutional self-limitations of the politics of the welfare state.

What does this mean for the constitutions of other social sub-spheres, in particular for the economic constitution? In order to inhibit pathological compulsions to grow, stimuli for change which follow the historical model of the self-limitation of politics need to generate permanent counter-structures that will take effect in the payment cycle down to its finest capillaries. Just as power is used in political constitutions to limit power, the system-specific medium must turn against itself. Fight fire by fire; fight power by power; fight law by law; fight money by money. Such a medial self-limitation would be the real criterion differentiating the transformation of the 'inner constitution' of the economy from external political regulation.

An important achievement of constitutional law for its constitutive and limitative role is to maintain the possibility of dissensus as a precondition of an independent selectivity dispersed in society. According to classical *Rechtsstaat* principles, this is guaranteed by the protection of property and freedom in society. Today, this is no longer sufficient. What is required is a strengthened politics of reflection within the economy that is supported by constitutional norms. Historically, collective bargaining, codetermination and the right to strike have already enabled new forms of societal dissensus.[31] In today's transnational organisations, ethics committees and codes of conduct fulfil a similar role.[32] Societal constitutionalism sees its point of application wherever it turns the existence of a variety of 'reflection centres' within society, and in particular within economic institutions, into the criterion of a democratic society.[33] Candidates for a capillary constitutionalisation exist not only in the organised sector of the global economy, in corporations and banks, but also in its spontaneous spheres:[34]

Politicisation of the consumer: Instead of being taken as a given, individual and collective preferences are openly politicised through consumer activism, consumer campaigns, boycotts, product criticism, eco-labelling, eco-investment, public interest litigation and other expressions of ecological sustainability. *De gustibus est disputandum!* Such politicisation represents not simply an external intervention in the self-steering economy, but rather a transformation of the inner constitution, touching the most sensitive area of the circulation of money, namely, the willingness of consumers and investors to pay. And this becomes a question of constitutional importance, or more precisely, a question of fundamental rights in the economy: how to protect the formation of social preferences against their restrictions through corporate interests. It is at this point, and for good reason, that courts developed the doctrine of the 'horizontal effect of fundamental rights' – in cases of product criticism, of the exposure of unsafe working conditions and of ecological protests against corporate policies. These legal developments protect the fundamental rights of the economic citizen from repeated attempts by economic organisations to silence critics of corporate policies. In the era of global information networks – keyword 'companynamesucks' – such fundamental rights in the economy are set to become even more important and to require greater legal protection.[35] And in the future, these constitutional rights should not be oriented one-sidedly towards market efficiency, as is suggested by the concepts of market failure, information asymmetry, or incomplete contracting,[36] but instead towards social and ecological sustainability.

Ecologisation of corporate governance: What is meant here is not a new managerial ethics, but rather a transformation of internal company structure, compelled by external pressures from parliaments, governments, trade unions, social movements, NGOs and the media; a transformation which limits the tendencies to speculation and compulsions to grow necessarily associated with the emergence of modern corporate structures.[37] Such a company constitution, oriented towards sustainability, would demand respect for environmental concerns – nature, society, human life – accompanied by internal implementation and external controls.

Plain money: Finally, a plain money reform of the kind that has been proposed to combat growth excesses would penetrate the *arcanum* of the global financial constitution:

> The measure that is most important in the long term for the prevention of speculation excesses in financial markets damaging to the public good consists in putting an end to the multiple creation of money by the commercial banks. This would prevent the pro-cyclical excessive expansion and contraction of the money supply and replace it with a sustainable money supply policy, orientated towards the real economy.[38]

In other words, the addictive drug, the creation of non-cash money, must be withheld from the commercial banks. This promises to be an effective detox therapy. Commercial banks should be prohibited from creating new money through current account credit and limited, instead, to offering loans that are based on existing credit reserves. The creation of non-cash money should be the sole prerogative of national and international central banks. Plain money reform aims, therefore:

(1) at allowing only central banks to create money, including cash money and non-cash money assets,
(2) at having this money brought into circulation through public issue, free of debt (without interest and redemption),
(3) at prohibiting the creation of money by the banks by way of current account credits.[39]

Such reform would require a simple but fundamental amendment of the law of the central banks at national, European and international level. In the Statute of the European Central Bank, the current Article 16 would need to be changed (as marked in italics):

> The Governing Council shall have the exclusive right to authorise the issue of legal tender within the Community. Legal tender shall include coins, bank notes *and sight funds*. The ECB and the national central banks may issue such forms of currency. Coins, banknotes *and sight funds* issued by the ECB and the national central banks shall be the only forms of currency to have the status of legal tender with the Community.[40]

There is good reason for plain money reform to be instituted from the outset at European level. Given the global mobility of capital, the reform of money creation becomes the task of an emergent transnational economic constitution. It is no longer appropriate today to talk of a constitutional vacuum in the transnational sphere that requires to be constitutionalised. This is refuted not only by social science analyses of the 'new constitutionalism', but also by economists and commercial lawyers, whose long-standing investigations of emerging institutions in the global economy indicate the exact opposite to be the case: today, constitutional institutions have already established themselves in the transnational sphere with an astounding density.[41] Despite the failure of the constitutional referendum, it is now only rarely disputed that the European Union has its own independent constitutional structures.[42] But other international organisations, transnational regimes and their networks also are not only highly juridified by now; they have become part of a global – if thoroughly fragmented – constitutional order. The global institutions that emerged from the agreements of the 1940s – the Havana Charter, GATT, Bretton Woods; the new arrangements of the Washington consensus – IMF, World Bank, WTO; and the recently initiated public debate concerning a 'global finance market constitution' all speak the language of a real-life societal constitutionalism on a worldwide scale. It is not the creation *ab ovo* of new constitutions in a constitution-free globality that is at stake, but rather the transformation of an already existing transnational constitutional order.

Given the existence of transnational financial markets, plain money reform requires constitutional solutions on a transnational scale. Yet even the proponents of plain money believe the chances of a global unitary solution to be low, given the likely opposition of leading nation states. What appears much more realistic is that some nation states might go it alone or that some might cooperate, at least if these states are relatively strong with a stable government, a strong economy and a stable, convertible currency. Regional solutions within economic blocks are most likely in the Eurozone, less so in the US or Japan. Currently, the best possible solution would lie with the creation of a global financial constitutional regime through the cooperation of central banks in a 'coalition of the willing'.

In what follows, my arguments shall focus on plain money. This is a matter, as Huber has rightly said, 'of constitutional importance'[43] – though not of the political constitutions of nation states, but rather of the constitution of the global economy. I do not intend to express a preference for transforming the monetary system as opposed to changing corporate governance or strengthening fundamental rights of consumers. Neither should plain money be presented as a cure-all for the financial crisis.[44] A plethora of external political regulations as well as internal changes to the economic constitution would be required for an adequate response to the crisis (particularly attractive candidates are the prohibition of proprietary trading for banks and the institutional division of powers between commercial banks and investment banks). Rather, I intend to use plain money as an example to illustrate clearly what the current paradox of societal constitutionalism looks like: without the state, but at the same time highly political. Plain money reform aims at the centre of the economic constitution because it configures – 'constitutes' – the self-limitation mechanisms of the economy, the economic medium, money, and the transnational cash flows themselves: it is not an indirect attempt at regulating the economy externally by means of political power, legal rules, moral imperative, discursive persuasion or public opinion. While it is presumed that external authorities have an important role to play in such a process of self-discipline, this role is limited to influencing the external conditions of success of the self-limitation of money by money. In what follows, it will be shown whether and to what extent plain money reform involves constitutional functions, constitutional processes and constitutional structures, in a strict rather than a metaphorical sense.

IV Plain money – an amendment to the 'capillary constitution'?

1 Constitutional functions: constitutive/limitative

From the perspective of constitutional sociology, political constitutions have the constitutive function of protecting the autonomy of politics, first achieved in modernity, from 'foreign' sources of power (religious, economic or military). They do this by formalising the power medium.[45] Other social sub-constitutions – the constitutions of the economy, science, the media and public health – perform the same constitutive function by securing for each sphere the relevant medial autonomy, something which, moreover, happens today on a global scale. With the help of constitutive rules, each sub-constitution regulates the abstraction of a communicative medium – power, money, law or knowledge – as an autonomous social construct within the functional system.[46] At the same time, the various sub-constitutions ensure, under differing historical conditions, that the society-wide effect of their media is secure. They develop organisational rules, procedures, competences and rights within the subsystem, codify the separation from the other interpenetrating social spheres and, in this way, reinforce the functional differentiation of society.[47]

Would plain money reform play a role in this constitutive function? Legal rules for money creation configure actors, organisational rules, competences, procedures and modes of functioning of the communication media of the economy. The decision in favour of plain money corrects the 'invisible' historical transformation of the global economic constitution which has been caused by the development of non-cash money.[48] The introduction of paper money, as opposed to coins, had been clearly a 'visible' official constitutional decision. The monopoly of the central banks with respect to money creation had been introduced through constitutional decisions, by rendering money creation a decision of the national central banks to create cash money. But this was followed by an 'invisible' constitutional development. The rapid development of cashless payment transactions and, more importantly still, the globalisation of the financial markets relocated control over the supply of money from governments and central banks into the hands of globally active private financial institutions. In the course of this creeping constitutional change, the autonomously developing money mechanism was institutionally privatised to 80%. Without any explicit political decision, the commercial banks established themselves as the real constitutional centre of money creation, marginalising the money creation of the national central banks. Now, plain money reform places the money-creating competences of private constitutional subjects back into the hands of the public (not necessarily state-organised) constitutional subjects. Plain money reform does, then, play a role in the constitutive function of an economic constitution.

That said, the limitative constitutional function fulfilled by plain money may be more important still. Following the recent financial crisis, limitations of the excesses of economic commerce are high on the agenda. We could even talk of a secular displacement of constitutive constitutional functions in the direction of limitative constitutional functions. This is a necessary consequence of the global autonomous positioning of the functional systems: 'We cannot pre-suppose that society will be able to exist with the environment that it creates.'[49] Plain money reform participates in two antinomic thrusts to constitutionalise global markets. Following Karl Polanyi's analysis of the transformation of modernity, we might speak here of a double movement of transnational constitutionalism: first the expansion of subsystems is supported by constitutive norms, and then it is inhibited by limitative norms.[50] In the development of the financial constitution, too, expansion along purely economic lines causes counter-movements on a global scale, aiming at a reconstruction of the 'protective covering of *cultural institutions*'.

If we look at the political constitutions of the world of states, it becomes clear that their societal and ecological roles are the result of the functional differentiation into autonomous subsystems:

> The fact that they belong to society means that all sub-systems are placed under conditions of structural compatibility with respect to their own function and ability to vary. For the political system, the constitution fulfils the function of reformulating such conditions of social compatibility for its own internal use, i.e. for collective decisions.[51]

Creating structural compatibility with society in this way is not a problem particular to politics, but common to all social subsystems.[52] Similarly, the conditions of compatibility may be imposed externally, but cannot be decided in their entirety from without, since they must, to a great extent, be produced internally within the system. Considerable differences between the political constitution and other social constitutions arise with regard to the respective conditions of self-reproduction. Only politics constructs its constitution on a pattern of building power and consensus for the production of collectively binding decisions, and only politics has to look primarily to power for its self-limitation. Other social systems organise their own constitutions and limitations according to their own internal logics – the economy via payment transactions, science via cognitive operations and the mass media via news operations. These logics shape both the constitutive and limitative rules. The original meaning of 'constitutio', initially a medical expression for the state of the body – ill or healthy – is still present in every constitution: engagement with the inner constitution always involves both the healthy functioning of the internal organs and the suitability of the body for living in its environment.[53]

As for authorities to judge whether the systems are in a healthy state, the theory of societal constitutionalism has identified 'collegial institutions' in the various social sectors which cultivate the relevant logics of action and has required them to be constitutionally institutionalised.[54] Collegial institutions are reflection centres for social self-identification, in the sense both of the rationality and normativity of the relevant social sector, and, simultaneously, that of rendering it compatible with society. The collegial institutions function as a type of think-tank for the relevant constitution, which is to be understood, for its part, as the benchmark for system–environment relations.

Plain money reform relocates the weight of such collegial institutions from the commercial banks to the central banks. This may be regarded as a significant self-limitation of the growth compulsions of the economic payment cycle. Proponents of plain money reform proclaim it to be an effective withdrawal therapy directed against the excessive addictive behaviour of the credit sector. Three expansion-limiting effects are prominent:

(1) The expansionist tendencies of private banks will be limited if they are prohibited from creating money *ex nihilo*. It is to be expected that the speculative use of current account credit will abate as a result.
(2) The expansionist tendencies of global financial markets in relation to the real economy will be limited if their relationship is regulated by central banks and no longer by private banks. The coordination of the financial and real economies will no longer be dependent on the profit motives of commercial banks, but on the central banks' circumspect weighing-up of consequences for the whole economy.
(3) The expansionist tendencies of the economy in relation to other social sectors and the natural environment will be limited if current account credit can no longer force the increase of growth compulsions. 'It is not a question of renouncing growth, but rather of minimising the exponential compulsions to grow.'[55] The most important aspect of this externally compelled self-limitation is that money creation by the central banks which incorporates careful consideration of its societal and ecological effects will block the socially harmful compulsion to grow.[56]

2 Constitutional processes: double reflexivity

If it is true that plain money reform performs important constitutional functions via constitutive and limitative rules, the question remains whether such reform would also institutionalise genuine constitutional processes and structures.

Though lawyers may not like to admit it, law does not play the primary role in state constitutions and other sub-constitutions. The primary aspect of constitutionalisation is always the self-constitution of a social system: of politics, the economy, the communications media or public health.[57] Law plays a necessary but subsidiary role. An exacting definition of economic constitutionalism would have to realise that constitutionalisation is primarily a social process and only secondarily a legal process. A useful definition of social constitutions puts it as follows:

> ... constitutions can be understood as instruments which, in their political function, frame the body of rules and norms which establish the formal structure, decisional competences, and a hierarchically based locus of authority within a given social entity at the same time as [they], in [their] legal function, establish principles for the structuring of conflicts between norms within such an entity. Constitutions are in this sense laying down the enabling and the limitative rules guiding social entities.[58]

A constitution serves, first and foremost, to self-constitute a social system. Politics, the economy, science, art, the health sector and the mass media all constitute themselves as social systems autonomous from one another.[59] Constitutional processes are an example of 'double closure' in the sense suggested by Heinz von Foerster.[60] They are triggered when social systems develop a second-order closure, in addition to their operative first-order closure, by applying their operations reflexively to their operations. Science secures its autonomy when it succeeds in establishing a second level of cognition in addition to the first-order operations oriented towards the binary true/false code. The first-order operations are then tested against the truth values of the second level – the level of methodology and epistemology. Politics becomes an autonomous power sphere of society when it directs power processes via power processes and produces a double closure of politics through the provision of electoral procedures, modes of organisation, competences, the separation of powers and fundamental rights. And what about the economy? It becomes autonomous when, in the money cycle, payment operations are employed in order to control the money supply itself.[61] The subsystems define their exterior limits and interior identities by means of this double closure;

this determines their autonomy in the strict sense. This procedural reflexivity produces for every functional system the 'form in which the medium acquires distinctness and autonomy'.[62]

It needs to be stressed that this medial reflexivity, together with associated cognitive and normative reflections on its social identity, does not yet generate constitutions in the technical sense. It serves the purpose, in the first instance, of self-constituting systems rather than self-constitutionalising them. Epistemology, the overpowering of power or the monetary steering of the money supply do not amount, as such, to a social constitution, but rather are reflexive operations. Constituting social autonomy is not to be equated with its constitutionalisation. We should only speak of a constitution in the narrow sense when the subsystemic reflexivity of a social system – be it politics, the economy or another sector – is simultaneously supported by law or, more precisely, by the reflexivity of law. Constitutions do not emerge until phenomena of double reflexivity appear: reflexivity of the self-constituting social system *and* reflexivity of the supportive legal system.[63]

Constitutions in the strict sense emerge when a structural coupling of the reflexive mechanisms of law (i.e. secondary rules, in which rules are applied to rules) with reflexive mechanisms of the relevant social sector occurs. This definition shares a starting point with Luhmann's definition; both assume that the state constitution involves the structural coupling of politics and law.[64] But structural coupling is only a necessary and not a sufficient condition: a whole swathe of political-legal phenomena, such as legislation or judicial review of political decisions, amount to structural couplings of politics and law. To define constitutions more precisely, one should determine the coupling relationship both more specifically and more generally. One should determine it more specifically because not every coupling of politics and law generates constitutional qualities, e.g. regulative rules, which attempt to achieve political aims via law. Only the coupling of reflexive processes within both systems does so. And one should determine it more generally because a constitution emerges not only in politics, but rather in every social system, insofar as its reflexivity couples with secondary legal norms. In addition, a particular density and permanence of the structural coupling is likely to be required before it will conform to the definition of a constitution. In other words, we should distinguish between a constitution and mere loose and occasional couplings of law and social sector. Only when the structural couplings have achieved a particular density and permanence does the developmental path typical of a constitution appear as the institutionalised co-evolution of the two social systems. In order to identify constitutions, as against other instances of structural coupling, we might wish to speak of a 'binding institution' of law and social subsystem when referring to the former.

Every constitution requires secondary legal norms. Primary rules within a social sector result only in its juridification and not in its constitutionalisation.[65] In fact, no social constitutions would ever be created if there existed only primary rules prescribing behaviour; similarly, only a straightforward juridification would result if there were only rules aimed at conflict resolution or rules aimed at the implementation of particular policies. The critical point is not reached until secondary norms regulate the identification, setting and amendment of rules which determine the competence to issue and to delegate primary norms.[66] Political or social constitutions establish themselves where these two reflexive processes connect with one another. We should speak of a constitution only when this interaction of social processes and legal processes comes into play: in the language of systems theory, when permanent and strict (as opposed to temporary and loose) structural couplings of a social system and the law are established. Only then do we find the curious duplication of the constitutional phenomenon: a doubling which excludes the widely held idea that legal orders and social orders will merge into a unitary constitutional phenomenon. A constitution is always the connection of two real, ongoing processes. From the point of view of law, it is the production of legal norms, which typically is intertwined with the basic structures of the social system. From the point of view of the social system, it is the generation of basic structures of social order, which simultaneously inform the law and are regulated by it. Under these conditions, it makes sense to talk, in the sociological and the legal sense, of elements of a political constitution of the transnational world, of a constitution of the world economy, of a global constitution of science or of a digital constitution of the Internet.[67]

But what is the reason behind this double reflexivity? Law enters the process of self-constituting a social system at the point where the above-mentioned closure of the social system through its own first- and second-order operations no longer suffices, where reflexive social processes cannot stabilise themselves and, in particular, where they threaten to become paralysed by paradoxes. Where this is the case, the self-constituting social autonomy needs to be supported by additional closure mechanisms. Law is one of them – though not the only one. In the case of politics, the self-description 'state' plays this role. 'The political system is only capable of differentiation once it describes itself as the "state".'[68] Without the formal limitation to a collective actor exercising public authority, the closure of institutionalised politics in relation to other power processes in society cannot be realised. Politics' structural coupling with law serves a similar role in its autonomisation. Since the reflexive application of power processes to power processes is exposed to the continual fluctuations of power, legal rules must stabilise the second-order operations that apply to the acquisition and exercise of power. Even more important is the role of law in disarming the paradoxes of political power. While the debilitating paradox of a sovereign power bound by its own acts is not, historically, solved by the creation of the *Rechtsstaat*, it is normalised by it.[69]

The supportive institutions which facilitate self-constitution vary greatly from system to system. In its achievement of autonomy, science can do almost entirely without external stabilising influences. Methodology, philosophy of science and epistemology can act by themselves to set limits to the 'empire of science'.[70] In order to guarantee the scientificity of knowledge, science does not need to describe itself as a collective – the scientific community – or even to institutionalise the incorporation of that community in parallel to the formal organisation of the state. Law plays a relatively minor role in the constitution of science. It is necessary only for the guarantees of scientific freedom and for the formal organisation of scientific activities.

The economy, in contrast, requires massive interventions from the law in order to achieve self-constitutionalisation, though not to the comprehensive extent characteristic of politics. As is well known, the institutions of property, contract, competition and currency constitute the cornerstones of an economic constitution. Each of these relies on double reflexivity: on applying economic transactions to economic transactions and on applying legal rules to legal rules. Double reflexivity is particularly apparent in the financial constitution. In the banking sector, the ability to pay and the inability to pay are generated simultaneously. The banking system relies on the paradox of self-reference, on the unity of the ability and inability to pay. 'The banks have the core privilege of being able to sell their own debts for profit.'[71] This paradox is disarmed where payment operations become reflexive, that is, where operations of money supply are applied to operations of money supply. But this reflexivity of economic operations is unstable. It has been stabilised through an internal hierarchisation of the banking sector, supported by a 'hard' regulation by means of binding law. In this way, the law, with its procedural and organisational norms that regulate central banks in their relation to the commercial banks, contributes to the process of coping with the paradoxes of the economic cycle.

Coping with paradoxes by means of a constitution is precarious: the danger of the reappearance of paradoxes always remains. The possibility of a paralysis of the financial system has not been excluded for good by the constitutionally supported hierarchy of payment operations in the relation between central banks and commercial banks.

> The logical and empirical possibility of a collapse of the whole system, a reappearance of the paradox and a total blockage of all operations by the primordial equation able to pay = unable to pay cannot thereby be excluded. It can, however, be rendered sufficiently improbable.[72]

That it is not in fact 'sufficiently improbable' was evidenced by the recent financial crisis. The excessive growth dynamic in global financial transactions made the possibility of an inability to pay on the part of the banking sector apparent. Plain money reform addresses this directly with double reflexivity. Without such a reform, the central banks have insufficient control of the money markets. They can only indirectly 'stimulate or destimulate' them 'by means of intervention events'.[73] They have the ability to steer the money supply indirectly by amending prime rates and thereby rendering borrowing more or less difficult. As regards direct steering of the money supply, they are limited to creating paper money and have no power over the current account money that is globally dominant today. Plain money reform transforms economic reflexivity by restricting the secondary payment operations of money creation, generated by non-cash money, to central banks. The secondary payment operations of the central banks – their money supply decisions, their creation of cash and non-cash money, their payments to the state, to citizens or to the banks – are applied reflexively to the primary payment operations (buying and lending). Plain money reform transforms juridical reflexivity, by prohibiting financial banks via secondary rules from creating money through credit account money and by establishing a monopoly on money creation in favour of the central banks. Through the restriction of money-creating competences, the law takes on the limitative function of an economic constitution and at the same time stabilises the self-reflexive relations of payment operations, relations which would dissolve again if they were not legally anchored in this way.

3 *Constitutional structures: a binary meta-code*

In the end, the crucial question is whether plain money reform also creates specific constitutional structures capable of channelling the constitutional functions and processes outlined above. This is disputed by constitutional lawyers who acknowledge genuine constitutional phenomena only in the nation state and greet the idea of a transnational or even a societal constitutionalism with scepticism.[74] According to them, what goes by the name of 'constitutionalisation' in public or private global orders is merely a juridification of social spheres, partly by international law and partly privately and autonomously – but certainly not a creation of constitutions.

In order to identify truly constitutional structures, we must move beyond the understanding of constitutions developed so far, which sees them as the structural coupling of law and social systems.[75] The end point of constitutionalisation – be it in politics, science or other social sectors – is not reached until an independent constitutional code – a binary meta-code – develops within the very structural coupling of law and the relevant social system: until, moreover, the internal processes of the system orient themselves towards that code. The constitutional code is binary. It oscillates between the values 'constitutional/unconstitutional'. And it functions at the meta-level, for the reason that it subjects decisions that have already been tested as legal/illegal to an additional test, namely, whether they correspond to constitutional requirements. What emerges here is the hierarchy between simple law and constitutional law, 'the law of laws', typical of all constitutions – constitutions of states, of other functional systems, of organisations and of networks. The constitutional code (constitutional/unconstitutional) is set above the legal code (legal/illegal). The crucial point of the meta-code, however, is its hybridity: it is set not only above the legal code, but at the same time also above the binary code of the relevant social system. It exposes the binary-encoded operations of the latter to the additional test of whether or not they conform to the principles of public responsibility of the social system.

This connection between structural coupling and its hybrid meta-code can most readily be observed in the state constitutions of modernity. There, the distinction constitutional/unconstitutional is explicitly adopted as the binary meta-code of law and of politics, i.e. of two systems that are themselves binary-coded. This happens, however, without this meta-coding resulting in a merging of law and politics into one single system and without the constitution itself developing into an autonomous social system.

The constitution of the global economy also operates with such a hybrid meta-code. It serves as a fictitious unitary formula for two quite different constitutional operations within the economy. The meta-code requires that it be set above the legal as well as the economic binary code. In each of the two sides of the economic constitution, the meta-code generates different meanings depending on whether it is attempting to control economic code operations or legal code operations. On its economic side, it serves the reflection of the societal function of the payment operations and searches for forms of economic activity that are environmentally viable. On its legal side, it institutes the separation of simple law from superior constitutional law and judges legal acts according to whether they correspond to constitutional values and principles.

Although the constitutional code appears to the economy as the one and only *distinction directrice* 'constitutional/unconstitutional', it is operating either as an economic meta-code or as a legal meta-code, depending on the context. Here we have an interesting example of an 'essentially contested concept', characterised by the fact that the same term is interpreted in different and highly controversial ways in different contexts.[76] The Janus-headed character of the meta-code has to do with the above-mentioned fact that the economic constitution (as the structural coupling of two social systems closed off from one another, i.e. economy and law) is not in itself a social system, but a distinct discursive process either within the law or within the economy. Constitutional operations – i.e. decisions and arguments of central banks on the one hand and constitutional courts on the other – do not merge the two systems into a single economic constitution but remain, instead, tied to their respective operational contexts, that is, to the law or to the economy. Correspondingly, the distinction 'code-compliant/code-non-compliant' is only a common umbrella formula for all kinds of constitutional decisions and arguments, capable of assuming completely different meanings depending on their respective context. The constitutional code is an observation scheme that takes on different forms in the law and in the economy.

These differences necessarily lead to the emergence of distinct programmes under the direction of the constitutional code in legal and in economic practice. These two types of programmes irritate one another to the point where they create a specific co-evolutionary path of legal and economic structures within the economic constitution.[77] Where the differential legal/illegal is subordinate to the meta-code of the economic constitution, a re-entry of the distinction law/economy into the legal system occurs. Fundamental principles of the economic system are reconstructed as legal constitutional principles (according to the particular historical situation: property, contract, competition, social market economy or ecological sustainability). Law 'translates' the fundamental principles of the economy into legal principles and concretises them as legal rules of constitutional law. Here we find the reason why constitutional law cannot be reduced to particular decision-making procedures, but instead demands substantive legitimation through inner constitutional principles. Without the re-entry of fundamental principles of the focal social system into the legal system, this would be incomprehensible or, worse, would be seen as 'natural law' in the age of positivism. Whether and how constitutional law is bound to the values of the relevant social system is clearly not pre-determined by natural law. Rather, it is the historically variable result of reflexive processes in the constitutionalised social system, reconstructed in law as an ensemble of constitutional principles.[78]

In the opposite direction, something comparable occurs: the meta-code allows the re-entry of law into the economic system (again historically variable: mandatory rules of contract law, social obligations of property, the limits of competition, rule-of-law principles in economic decisions or fundamental rights within corporations). In this way, economic operations are bound by constitutional law.

The mutual re-entry opens up two different 'imaginary spaces' of the economic constitution:[79] two different (but interrelated) constitutional programmes, one in the economy, one in law, which are both oriented, albeit separately, towards the constitutional code. This double meaning is particularly apparent in property and contract, the traditional institutions of the economic constitution. Economically, property means the interruption of consensus requirements for particular communication results. Legally, property is defined as a subjective right, for example in Germany in Sections 903 and 906 of the Civil Code and Article 14 of the Constitution. And, although they are closely interrelated, an economic transaction is not identical to a legal contract. Transaction and contract are not just two sides of the same coin, but distinct social phenomena.[80] The economic constitution as such can be understood as one language game with a particular double structure under the control of the *distinction directrice* of a meta-code. But the language game does not strengthen into an independent social system with its own unitary language acts, structures and boundaries. Rather, it forms what one can call a 'binding institution' in which law and the economy are closely structurally coupled and permanently irritate one another. In this way, a 'bi-lingualism' develops which requires continual efforts at 'translation'.

Now, plain money reform would transform constitutional programmes both in the law and in the economy. In the economic context, it would formulate anew the public principles of money creation for the central banks: To which ends should the central banks direct the creation of money, those of combating inflation or those of limiting excessive growth compulsions? In the legal context, it would transform the legal principles of the economic constitution: Under a plain money regime, money creation by the private banks would be economically unconstitutional and not simply illegal.

To summarise, plain money reform would reach deep into the capillary constitution of the global economy. In all three respects, it corresponds to the definition of a constitution outlined above. First, plain money fulfils constitutional functions, both constitutive and, particularly, limitative ones. Secondly, it takes part in the double reflexivity of the legal and the economic system by issuing rules governing money creation. Thirdly, it subjects the activities of commercial and central banks to the hybrid meta-code of the economic constitution by transforming economic as well as legal constitutional programmes.

V The politics of societal constitutionalism

1 *Constitutionalisation by the state?*

But does a societal constitutionalism aiming at extensive autonomy of the social subsystems not imply an extensive de-politicisation of society?[81] In that case, is the constitutionalisation of the economy, for our purposes through the introduction of plain money, not itself a politically explosive matter? To both questions, the definitive answer is: 'Yes and no'. As indicated above, societal constitutions are paradoxical phenomena. They are not part of the political constitution of society, but at the same time they are highly political social issues. The paradox can be solved with the help of a double conception of the political. This is understood in a variety of ways,[82] but here, the double meaning of the political is understood as follows. Firstly, 'the political' can be taken to refer to institutionalised politics: the political system of the world of states. In relation to this notion of 'the political', the social sub-constitutions keep their distance; they require extensive autonomy against the political constitution. Moreover, as regards the participation of the political system in the process of the social sub-constitutions, particular 'political restraint' is required. Secondly, the concept can also indicate the political in society, outside of institutionalised politics. It can indicate, in other words, the internal politicisation of the economy itself and of other social spheres, that is, the politics of reflection on the social identity of the social system involved. In this respect, the particular social constitutions are highly political, but beyond the state.[83]

Let us return to plain money. As early as 1813, Jefferson demanded that the right to issue money should be taken from the banks and restored to the people.[84] But who are 'the people' when it comes to money? How can the creation of money be restored to the people? After everything that has been said so far, the answer can only be that money creation belongs in the public sphere, though not in the domain of the state. Ought we to subject the creation of money to state control? No. Ought we to place it in the public sphere? Yes. Public sphere in this context does not refer to an intermediate sphere between state and society.[85] An accurate definition of 'the public' today requires that the public/private distinction as a means of delimiting social sectors be deconstructed and simultaneously reconstructed within each of these social sectors.[86] Money creation is clearly among the most important public functions of the economy. It is part of the public infrastructure of the economic sector. It is a public good. Money creation is a genuine component of the constitution of the economy because it takes part in determining the public function of the economy. It follows, then, that money creation ought to be removed from private profit-oriented commercial banks and restored to the monopoly of a public, though non-state, institution: the central bank.

But why should the political constitution not assume control of this task of regulating the internal structures of social sub-spheres?[87] This has already been discussed above in the context of internal versus external regulation. Now it arises as a question of democratic theory regarding the overall responsibility of democratic politics for society. If, after all, the greatest privilege of the democratic sovereign is that of granting a constitution to society, why favour auto-constitutionalisation of social sectors and not political dictate? The answer can only be hinted at here. The basic social structures of modernity make it necessary to redefine the relationship between representation, participation and reflection. In a functionally differentiated society, the political constitution cannot fulfil the role of defining the fundamental principles of other subsystems without causing a problematic de-differentiation – as occurred in practice in the totalitarian regimes of the twentieth century.[88] In the age of modernity, the only way in which society can be constitutionalised is by every subsystem acting reflexively to develop its own constitutional principle for itself, without these principles being prescribed by politics. Such decentred reflexivity is necessary because it is no longer accurate to say that the *maiores partes* represent the whole of society while the *minores partes* participate, as was the case in the old society. Instead, modern society regards participation and representation as identical and abolishes them at the same time. We must give up the notion that politics represents society in the state and that other social spheres – people or sub-spheres – participate in it. No social subsystem, not even politics, can represent society as a whole. Instead, it is characteristic of the current state of social development that psychic and social systems must develop their own reflexive processes of structure selection – processes of thinking about thinking, or of loving love, of researching into research, regulating regulation, financing the use of money or overpowering the powerful.[89]

And their democratic legitimation must indeed relate to society as a whole – though it need not proceed through the channels of institutionalised politics.[90] Space does not allow me to elaborate further.[91] It must suffice to indicate the participation of the general public in the decision-making of transnational private regimes. For example, the Aarhus Convention made an impact by declaring three principles of public participation: (1) access to information; (2) public participation in decision-making procedures; and (3) access to justice in environmental matters. This allows the anchoring of the administrative apparatus of public and private regimes

> in its social substrate, that is, in global society itself (and not its political system, i.e. the international community [of states]), to be integrated into the development of new categories of legal acts, and for decision-making (in the legislative, executive and juridical apparatuses) and discussion (in the global sub-publics) to be structurally coupled with one another

in such a way that the duality of spontaneous and organised areas of social constitutionalisation, which is significant in terms of democratic theory, can be established.[92]

2 In the shadow of politics

The state should not prescribe the constitution of the economy and other social subsystems, but it should produce constitutional irritations for them. As has been said above, institutionalised politics, together with other actors, particularly civil society actors, must exert massive external pressure in order to compel changes in the capillaries of the payment cycle of the economy. That would be the appropriate division of labour. Social systems have the best constitutional chances where they can develop their own constitutions in the shadow of politics.[93]

In this context, Renner proposed that the economic constitution should be conceived of not just as a binding institution of the economy and the law, but as a trilateral structural coupling of economy, law and politics.[94] Indeed, numerous structural couplings of institutionalised politics and the economy and law do exist, for example the taxation system or the lobbying of economic organisations. Typically, however, these do not achieve the density of what we described above as 'binding institutions' and which distinguishes constitutions from all other structural couplings. If we look closer at how politics works its way into economic constitutions, then we can see that there is, in truth, no real trilateral coupling, but rather two sets of bilateral coupling: one in the relationship economy–law, involving the institutions of property, contract, competition and currency referred to above, and the other in the relationship law–politics, involving constitutional legislation and adjudication. In the relation politics–economy, the existing structural couplings are not so tight that they assume the quality of binding institutions. The constitutionally relevant political interventions are never directly performed as a conversion of power into money, but instead proceed almost always indirectly via the legal system by way of legislative acts. And even these do not create a permanent bond in the institutionalisation of constitutions, but only an occasional one, which is dissolved again by the decoupling of the economy from politics. Political interventions in the economic constitution, which of course do exist, ought not to be understood, then, as genuine operations of a binding institution, but rather as external constitutional impulses.

The most important external impulses come from the political system during the foundational act of the relevant constitution, but are usually transmitted by the legal system. To establish a financial constitution would require political impulses, which would have to work their way into the internal structure of the economy. Generally, an autonomous economy requires a strong political system. The mafia-like conditions in Russia after 1989 offer ample illustration of the negative effects that ensue when a capitalist economy is introduced in a 'big bang' without rule-of-law constraints. To date, transnational politics has reacted most convincingly when, at the moment of the financial crisis, an international coordination of 'first aid' measures was put into effect. To that extent, it can be concluded that social constitutions are politically imposed. However, the internal reconstruction of the political impulses is decisive for the sustained functioning of a specific constitution. Without this, the constitutional irritations of politics and society fade; without it, there is no chance of a sustained transformation of the economic constitution. It is not the 'big decision', the mythical foundational act, that is relevant for the existence of a constitution, but rather 'long-lasting chains of interconnected communicative acts of successfully anchoring a constitution as the "highest authority"'.[95] The political irritations produced by legislative decisions must be absorbed in such a way that they are channelled into the capillaries of the payment cycle. Only then can a specific constitution 'take effect' beyond its formal validity. The political impulse is limited to the foundational act and to fundamental changes; over and above that, a high degree of constitutional autonomy vis-à-vis politics is needed.

The phrase 'in the shadow of politics' has an additional meaning. Societal constitutionalism always depends on law; law, for its part, depends on the physical monopoly of politics on power. Economic and social sanctions alone are not sufficient to stabilise constitutional norms. Plain money reform, too, requires politically backed legal sanctions in order to prohibit, as forgery, the unauthorised creation of money by commercial banks and to counteract avoidance strategies.[96] Such political support, however, does not transform the economic constitution into a state constitution. It is only the instruments of state power that law mediates, de-politicises and places at the disposal of the economic constitution.

Yet the shadow must remain a shadow. A high degree of autonomy for the central banks in relation to politics is essential. Discretionary interventions by politics in concrete decisions regarding money creation must be excluded. The political independence of the central banks is, indeed, a requirement of constitutional importance.[97] The reason why the power games of institutionalised politics must be excluded from money creation is the acute danger of inflation emanating from the long-term temptation of politics and, in particular, democratic politics. 'Where democratic governments have unlimited political power in respect of money, it is impossible to resist inflationary pressures.'[98] Unusually, this observation of Friedrich Hayek's is correct, though the conclusion which he draws from it, namely that the creation of money must be totally privatised, is not.

3 Politicising the economy

In contrast, the politicisation of the economy itself is high on the agenda of societal constitutionalism. Above, we have already seen the political dynamic released in the market by the politicisation of consumer preferences and by the ecologisation of corporate governance.[99] With a monopoly on the creation of money, the central banks perform an important political role. Politicising the economy means intense reflections on the social consequences of the extension or limitation of the money supply among academic experts and the general public, by consumers and corporations, ending in decisions of the central banks. This is where fierce discussions take place and final decisions are taken on whether, in a concrete situation, the growth compulsions released by the creation of money are excessive or not. The political decision of whether to subject the financial system to withdrawal therapy cannot be allowed to depend on private profit motives. It can only be decided by the central banks, guided exclusively by reference to the monetary system and its compatibility with society as a whole.

Obviously central banks make wide-ranging political decisions regarding the creation of money. But they do not thereby become part of the political system. They do not participate in the production of power and consensus for the making of collective decisions. Neither are they part of the power cycle of politics, which runs from the public through parliaments, the administration, interest groups and back again to the public. Their position can most readily be compared with that of constitutional courts, standing right at the hierarchical summit of the legal system, responsible for making highly political decisions without thereby becoming part of the political system.[100] 'Guardians of the constitution' – that is the appropriate metaphor. And just as constitutional assemblies and constitutional courts are the guardians of the political constitution, so the central banks and the constitutional courts are the guardians of the economic constitution. And their constitutional politics requires a high degree of autonomy.

Central bankers tend to present themselves as apolitical experts, strictly bound by mandate when taking decisions *lege artis*. It is nonetheless obvious that central banks make genuinely political decisions within the economic system. Decisions regarding the supply of money cannot be reduced to a straightforward technocratic implementation of arithmetical calculations. Central banks have a great deal of political discretion; they are exposed to the risk of great uncertainty; they are reliant on deliberative justifications before the public; and they are responsible for the correctness of their decisions. This is the eminently political content of reflexive processes within the economy that balance the relation between social function and contribution to the environment. For that reason, a politics of money, especially one that is independent of institutionalised politics, must be transparent and accountable.

Yet the taboo must not be broken.[101] No discretionary interventions by the political system! Even if that system does possess greater democratic legitimation. The autonomy of the central banks in respect of politics is a necessary precondition of the functioning of plain money reform. Alongside the traditional executive, legislative and judicative powers, the central banks act, as a neologism nicely puts it, as the 'monetative' power, as the constitutional institution of the economic system.[102] Here, the meaning of an autonomous financial constitution is revealed, which has to obey its own logic and, despite its highly political character, must not be surrendered to the power processes of institutionalised politics. The analogy with constitutional courts is again appropriate. This is a principle not of the political, but of the societal separation of powers.

While decisions on money creation as such are the exclusive prerogative of the central banks, the related question of how profits generated by money creation should be used is clearly a matter for the political system. Whether these quite considerable sums (accrued, to date, by the commercial banks without any *quid pro quo*) should be paid to the Treasury, made available to the banking system or used to finance tax cuts or individual earnings is not a question for the central banks, but for the political process.[103]

The dynamics of external political impulses and the internal politics of the 'capillary constitution' are, as we stated above, not an automatic consequence of functional imperatives. They develop only in phases of crisis, which are themselves caused by excessive growth compulsions. These are the constitutional moments during which social energies of such intensity may be activated that catastrophe can be averted. From an historical perspective, it is clear that the Great Depression in 1929 was such a moment. At that time, the nation states were faced with a constitutional decision: to abolish the autonomy of the economy via totalitarian politics of either a socialist or fascist inclination, or to inaugurate the 'New Deal' and the welfare state as a limitative constitutionalisation of the national economies. And today? Was the banking crisis of 2008 system-relevant? Was it so threatening that it amounted to a new constitutional moment, of the global economy this time, bringing its self-limitation through a global financial constitution into the realm of the possible? Or had 'the bottom' not yet been reached? Will the fading of the crisis herald the global return of the old addictive behaviour, which is resistant to withdrawal treatments at the nation state level?

Notes

This chapter was previously published as 'A constitutional moment? The logics of "hitting the bottom"', in Poul F. Kjaer, Gunther Teubner and Alberto Febbrajo (eds), *The Financial Crisis in Constitutional Perspective: The Dark Side of Functional Differentiation* (Oxford: Hart, 2011), pp. 3–42. Reprinted by permission of Bloomsbury Publishing plc.

1. 'Greenspan concedes flaws in deregulatory approach', *New York Times*, 24 October 2008, p. B1.
2. Derrida, *Other Heading*, p. 42.
3. 'Der Erreger lebt weiter', *Der Spiegel*, 14 September 2009, p. 108.
4. Streeck, *Re-Forming Capitalism*, pp. 236 ff.
5. The classic is Fisher, *100% Money*. Today's protagonists are Binswanger, *Wachstumsspirale*; Huber and Robertson, *Creating New Money*. See also Creutz, 'Vollgeld und Grundeinkommen'; Zarlenga, *Lost Science of Money*; Robertson, 'National and International Financial Architecture'; Senf, 'Bankgeheimnis Geldschöpfung'.
6. Thus, in further development of the ideas of Schumpeter, *Theory of Economic Development*, p. 153, Graziani, *Monetary Theory of Production*, pp. 82–3.
7. Huber, 'Geldordnung II'.
8. Binswanger, *Vorwärts zur Mäßigung*, p. 21. This argument marks the difference from theories of zero growth, which focus on the social and ecological limits of growth, i.e. scarcity of resources, aging processes and increasing state debts: cf. Miegel, *Exit*.
9. Binswanger, *Vorwärts zur Mäßigung*, pp. 11 ff., differentiates between a necessary compulsion to grow and a socially destructive urge to grow.
10. Freyberger *et al.*, *Kompendium*.
11. This is particularly clear in Luhmann, *Social Systems*, pp. 107 ff.; Luhmann, 'Zeit und Gedächtnis'; Luhmann, 'Individuum und Gesellschaft'.
12. Luhmann, *Social Systems*, p. 54.
13. Rosa, *Beschleunigung*, esp. pp. 295 ff.; Rosa, 'Speed of global flows'.
14. Luhmann, *Law as a Social System*, p. 153.
15. As opposed to the legal excesses of modernity that Michael Kohlhaas exhibited in his violent fights against the feudal order: Kleist, *Michael Kohlhaas*.
16. Luhmann, *Theory of Society*, vol. 2, p. 125.
17. The term is used differently here, of course, from Ackerman, *We the People*.
18. For a thorough analysis from this perspective, see Thornhill, 'Towards a historical sociology'.
19. Luhmann, *Theory of Society*, vol. 2, p. 95.
20. On the debate regarding the limits of political regulation, see Braithwaite, 'Enforced self-regulation'; Ogus, 'Rethinking self-regulation'; Gunningham and Rees, 'Industry self-regulation'; Ayres and Braithwaite, *Responsive Regulation*.
21. The general formulation regulation of self-regulation is the result of an extended debate regarding the chances of social steering by politics and law. See Hoffmann-Riem (ed.), *Regulierte Selbstregulierung als Steuerungskonzept*.
22. Locke *et al.*, 'Does Monitoring Improve Labour Standards?'
23. Luhmann, *Theory of Society*, vol. 2, p. 88.
24. Ibid., p. 95.
25. Ladeur, 'Methodische Überlegungen zur gesetzlichen "Ausgestaltung" der Koalitionsfreiheit', p. 657.

26 Ladeur, *'Abwägung'* – *ein neues Paradigma*, p. 60.
27 Derrida, *Other Heading*.
28 Foucault, 'Prison Talk', p. 39.
29 External attempts at irritation and internal reactions must converge in the direction of a common minimising of difference. See Luhmann, 'Limits of steering'; Luhmann, 'Steuerung durch Recht?'
30 Luhmann, *Law as a Social System*, p. 412.
31 Luhmann, 'Politische Verfassungen im Kontext', p. 182 and n. 94.
32 From a legal-theoretical point of view, see Calliess, *Prozedurales Recht*, pp. 224 ff.
33 Sciulli, *Theory of Societal Constitutionalism*; Sciulli, *Corporate Power in Civil Society*.
34 On the differentiation of spontaneous spheres and organised spheres of functional systems and their relevance for the democratisation of (global) social sub-spheres, see Teubner, 'Global Private Regimes'.
35 Generally on the economic horizontal effect of fundamental rights in the transnational sphere, see Ladeur and Viellechner, 'Transnationale Expansion staatlicher Grundrechte'. On the protection of fundamental rights on the Internet, see in particular Karavas, *Digitale Grundrechte*. And on criticism of corporations, see Karavas and Teubner, 'www.companynamesucks'.
36 In the context of international private law, such arguments are made by Rühl, 'Party Autonomy', pp. 177 ff.; Schäfer and Lantermann, 'Choice of Law', p. 104.
37 This context is referred to explicitly by Binswanger, *Vorwärts zur Mäßigung*, pp. 150 ff., 157 ff.
38 Huber, 'Geldordnung II', p. 4.
39 Ibid.; Fisher, *100% Money*; Binswanger, *Vorwärts zur Mäßigung*, pp. 139 ff.
40 Huber and Robertson, *Creating New Money*, p. 24.
41 On the new global constitutionalism, see, for example: Schneiderman, *Constitutionalizing Economic Globalization*; Tully, 'Imperialism of Modern Constitutional Democracy', pp. 328 ff. On the global economic constitution, see Behrens, 'Weltwirtschaftsverfassung'.
42 On this debate, see Weiler, *Constitution of Europe*; Weiler and Wind (eds), *European Constitutionalism*; Walker, 'Post-Constituent Constitutionalism'.
43 Huber and Robertson, *Creating New Money*, pp. 38 ff.
44 On its chances of success, see ibid., pp. 61 ff.
45 Thornhill, 'Towards a historical sociology', pp. 169 ff.
46 For Lindahl and Preuss, too, the role of constitutive norms represents an opportunity to release the term 'constitution' from its narrow relation with the state and to apply it to the constitution of a whole series of social institutions: Lindahl, 'Constituent Power and Reflexive Identity', pp. 14 ff.; Preuss, 'Disconnecting Constitutions from Statehood', pp. 40 ff.
47 This generalises, for all sub-constitutions, Thornhill's analyses of the political constitutions. See Thornhill, 'Towards a historical sociology', pp. 169 ff.
48 On this point, see Binswanger, *Wachstumsspirale*, pp. 114 ff.; Binswanger, *Vorwärts zur Mäßigung*, pp. 141–2; Huber and Robertson, *Creating New Money*, p. 38.
49 Luhmann, *Wirtschaft der Gesellschaft*, p. 169.
50 Polanyi, *Great Transformation*, pp. 138 ff.
51 Luhmann, 'Politische Verfassungen im Kontext', p. 6.
52 Prandini, 'Morphogenesis of Constitutionalism', pp. 312 ff.
53 Luhmann, 'Politische Verfassungen im Kontext', p. 178.
54 Sciulli, *Theory of Societal Constitutionalism*; Sciulli, *Corporate Power in Civil Society*.

55 Binswanger, *Vorwärts zur Mäßigung*, p. 12.
56 Fisher, *100% Money*; Binswanger, *Wachstumsspirale*; Huber and Robertson, *Creating New Money*; Creutz, 'Vollgeld und Grundeinkommen'; Zarlenga, *Lost Science of Money*; Robertson, 'National and International Financial Architecture'; Senf, 'Bankgeheimnis Geldschöpfung'.
57 This aspect is emphasized in constitutional sociology: Prandini, 'Morphogenesis of Constitutionalism', pp. 316 ff.; Thornhill, 'Towards a historical sociology', pp. 169 ff.
58 Kjaer, 'Metamorphosis of the functional synthesis', p. 532.
59 Prandini, 'Morphogenesis of Constitutionalism', p. 310.
60 Foerster, *Observing Systems*, pp. 304 ff.
61 Luhmann, *Wissenschaft der Gesellschaft*, pp. 289 ff.; Luhmann, *Politik der Gesellschaft*, p. 64; Luhmann, *Wirtschaft der Gesellschaft*, pp. 117–18, 144 ff., 209.
62 Luhmann, *Theory of Society*, vol. 1, p. 224.
63 On the double reflexivity of constitutions, see Kuo, 'Between fragmentation and unity', pp. 465 ff.; Chapter 10 in this volume, pp. 237 ff.; Teubner, 'Corporate Codes of Multinationals'. Kjaer also presumes double reflexivity in his definition of a transnational economic constitution: Kjaer, 'Metamorphosis of the functional synthesis'.
64 Luhmann, 'Verfassung als evolutionäre Errungenschaft'.
65 This is a response to Dieter Grimm's argument against a transnational constitutionalism: Grimm, 'Gesellschaftlicher Konstitutionalismus'.
66 Primary and secondary norms in the sense proposed by Hart, *Concept of Law*, pp. 77 ff.
67 The development of a societal constitutionalism in the transnational sphere is observed by Calliess and Zumbansen, *Rough Consensus and Running Code*; Kjaer, 'Metamorphosis of the functional synthesis', pp. 532–3; Prandini, 'Morphogenesis of Constitutionalism', pp. 316 ff.; Renner, *Zwingendes transnationales Recht*, pp. 229 ff.; Backer, 'Governance without Government'; Joerges and Rödl, 'Zum Funktionswandel des Kollisionsrechts II', pp. 767, 775 ff.; Kuo, 'Between fragmentation and unity', pp. 456 ff.; Wielsch, 'Epistemische Analyse des Rechts', pp. 69 ff.; Preuss, 'Disconnecting Constitutions from Statehood', pp. 40 ff.; Brunkhorst, 'Legitimationskrise der Weltgesellschaft', pp. 68 ff.; Tully, 'Imperialism of Modern Constitutional Democracy'; Chapter 10 in this volume, pp. 237 ff.; Karavas, *Digitale Grundrechte*, passim; Schepel, *Constitution of Private Governance*, esp. pp. 412 ff.; Teubner, 'Societal Constitutionalism', pp. 5 ff.; Walter, 'Constitutionalizing (inter)national governance'.
68 Luhmann, 'Staat als historischer Begriff', p. 144.
69 Luhmann, 'Zwei Seiten des Rechtsstaates', pp. 497–8; Luhmann, *Politik der Gesellschaft*, pp. 35, 334 ff.
70 Illuminating on this point is Stichweh, 'Einheit und Differenz'.
71 Luhmann, *Wirtschaft der Gesellschaft*, p. 145.
72 Ibid., p. 146.
73 Ibid., p. 117.
74 Grimm, 'Gesellschaftlicher Konstitutionalismus'.
75 Luhmann, 'Verfassung als evolutionäre Errungenschaft'.
76 This much-discussed expression originates with Gallie, 'Essentially contested concepts'. In our context, it is used to indicate that different social systems use the term 'constitution' and at the same time ascribe to that term rather different meanings.

77 On such a connection between structural coupling and co-evolution, using the example of the production regime, see Teubner, 'Idiosyncratic Production Regimes'. More generally on the co-evolution of law and the economy, see Amstutz, *Evolutorisches Wirtschaftsrecht*.
78 Here we find the explanation for Kumm's important hypothesis that (transnational) constitutional law must legitimate itself by means of internal constitutional principles and not just by means of procedures. Kumm is unable to explain, however, how these principles in turn legitimate themselves. That requires recourse to the reflexive practices in the social system itself. The removal of paradoxes by means of a constitution again takes effect here. See Kumm, 'Best of Times', pp. 214 ff.
79 On the connection between re-entry and imaginary space, see Spencer Brown, *Laws of Form*, pp. 56–7, 69 ff.
80 On the double character of institutions in the structural coupling of law and the economy, see Teubner, 'Legal irritants'.
81 This is the most important critique raised against societal constitutionalism, emphasised in particular by Brunkhorst, 'Legitimationskrise der Weltgesellschaft', pp. 76 ff. Other authors use the critique to flatly deny the existence of constitutions outside the state: see e.g. Wahl, 'In Defence of "Constitution"', pp. 240–1.
82 On the extensive debate regarding *le politique* and *la politique* see Christodoulidis, 'Against Substitution', pp. 191 ff.
83 Kjaer, 'Metamorphosis of the functional synthesis', pp. 522 ff., attempts a careful explanation of the political dimensions of the social sub-constitutions.
84 Jefferson, 'Thomas Jefferson to John Wayles Eppes', pp. 297 ff.
85 Ridder, *Soziale Ordnung des Grundgesetzes*; Rinken, 'Geschichte und heutige Valenz des Öffentlichen'.
86 On this point in more detail, see Teubner, 'State policies in private law?'; Chapter 6 in this volume.
87 This would be the consequence of conceptions of constitutionalisation that admit a variety of social sub-constitutions, but then postulate a primacy of the political constitution: e.g. Joerges and Rödl, 'Zum Funktionswandel des Kollisionsrechts II', pp. 767, 775 ff. For the nation state this might be more or less realistic, but it ceases to be so for transnational relations: e.g. Kjaer, 'Metamorphosis of the functional synthesis', pp. 517 ff.
88 On this point from a constitutional-theoretical perspective, see Thornhill, 'Towards a historical sociology', pp. 188 ff.
89 Luhmann, *Theory of Society*, vol. 1, p. 223.
90 This would correspond to the views of the early Habermas, who, after a fundamental critique of parliamentarianism, called for the democratic potential of societal processes outside institutionalised politics to be tested. Apparently this insight has been lost by the later Habermas (and his followers): Habermas, *Structural Transformation of the Public Sphere*, ch. 25.
91 For an informative account, see Bredt, *Demokratische Legitimation*, pp. 248 ff.
92 Fischer-Lescano and Renner, 'Europäisches Verwaltungsrecht und Völkerrecht'; on spontaneous and organisational spheres, see Teubner, 'Global Private Regimes'.
93 This formulation is close to the position adopted by Grimm, 'Gesellschaftlicher Konstitutionalismus', p. 81, who allows societal constitutionalism a limited chance of success only 'in the shadow of public power'. Nevertheless, there remain important differences in assessing the primacy of institutionalised politics.
94 Renner, *Zwingendes transnationales Recht*, pp. 233 ff.
95 Vesting, 'Politische Verfassung?', p. 613.

96 On questions of detail regarding avoidance and the means of combating it, see Huber and Robertson, *Creating New Money*, pp. 51 ff.
97 Thus also: Binswanger, *Vorwärts zur Mäßigung*, p. 147; Huber and Robertson, *Creating New Money*, pp. 38–9.
98 Hayek, *Denationalization of Money*, pp. 22–3.
99 This extraordinary political dynamic outside of institutionalised politics, which is becoming increasingly noticeable at present, must cause authors such as Brunkhorst or Wahl to reconsider their vehement criticism of societal constitutionalism on the grounds that it de-politicises society: Brunkhorst, 'Legitimationskrise der Weltgesellschaft', pp. 76 ff.; Wahl, 'In Defence of "Constitution"', pp. 240–1.
100 As a matter of fact, where they are highly dependent on politics, they transform themselves into hybrid institutions. At that point, the central banks practise a double politics. Their promise of an independent reflection politics is contradicted by the fact that they are enmeshed in the power games of the political system. They are similar, then, to the politicised constitutional courts that commonly exist where the separation of powers is not sufficiently developed.
101 Ladeur, 'Autonomie der Bundesbank'.
102 Senf, 'Bankgeheimnis Geldschöpfung'; Binswanger, *Vorwärts zur Mäßigung*, p. 147.
103 Binswanger, *Vorwärts zur Mäßigung*, pp. 147–8.

9

Global Bukowina: legal pluralism in the world society

The center of gravity of legal development therefore from time immemorial has not lain in the activity of the state, but in society itself, and must be sought there at the present time.[1]

I

Who is right – Bill Clinton or Eugen Ehrlich? Both the US President and the almost forgotten law professor from Czernowitz, Bukowina, who developed his idea of a 'living law' in the far east of the Austrian Empire, have a utopian vision of a global legal order. But they do not agree on how to get to this global legal order. In Bill Clinton's New World Order it is the *Pax Americana* which will globalise the rule of law. His global law will be based on the worldwide hegemony of a political-military-moral complex. In Eugen Ehrlich's 'Global Bukowina', it is civil society itself that will globalise its legal orders, distancing itself as it does so from the political power complex in the Brave New World's Vienna. Although Eugen Ehrlich's theory turned out to be wrong as regards the national law of Austria, I believe that it will turn out to be right, both empirically and normatively, as regards the newly emerging global law. Empirically, he is right because the political-military-moral complex will lack the power to control the multiple centrifugal tendencies of a civil world society.

And normatively he is right because for democracy, it will in any case be better if politics is as far as possible shaped by its local context.

Lex mercatoria, the transnational law of economic transactions, is the most successful example of global law without a state.[2] But the significance of a Global Bukowina extends far beyond economic law. It is not only the economy, but also various other sectors of world society that are developing a global law of their own. And they do so – as Giddens has put it – in relative insulation from the state, official international politics and international public law.[3] Among the initial candidates for such a global law without a state are the internal legal regimes of multinational enterprises.[4] A similar combination of globalisation and informality can be found in labour law in cases where enterprises and labour unions as private actors are dominant law-makers.[5] Technical standardisation and professional self-regulation have tended towards worldwide coordination with minimal intervention by official international politics. Human rights discourse has become globalised and is pressing for its own law, derived from sources that are not just independent of national legal orders, but directed against the practices of national states.[6] Especially in the case of human rights, it would be 'unbearable if the law were left to the arbitrariness of regional politics'.[7] Similarly, in the field of ecology, there are tendencies towards legal globalisation in relative insulation from state institutions. And even in the world of sports, people are discussing the emergence of a *lex sportiva internationalis*.[8]

Thus, we see several kinds of global legal order that are no longer merely rudimentary and that have emerged independently both of national legal orders and of traditional *jus gentium*. With regard to these kinds of global legal order, I would like to put forward three arguments:

(1) Global law can only be adequately explained by a theory of legal pluralism and a corresponding, pluralistically oriented doctrine of the sources of law. The theory of legal pluralism has only recently undergone a successful transformation by turning its attention from the law of colonial societies to the laws of diverse ethnic, cultural and religious communities in modern nation states. It now needs to shift its focus once more – from the law of groups to the law of discourses. Similarly, jurisprudential enquiry into the sources of law should direct its attention to new, spontaneous processes of law creation that have emerged in multiple sectors of a global civil society, independently of state-based national and international law.

(2) The emerging global (not inter-national!) law is a legal order in its own right that should not be measured by the standards of national legal orders. It is not an underdeveloped body of law that retains certain structural deficiencies in comparison to national law, as is usually assumed. Rather, this in most respects fully developed legal order has peculiar characteristics

that distinguish it from the traditional law of nation states. These characteristics can be explained by differentiation within world society itself. For while global law lacks political and institutional support at the global level, it is closely coupled with globalised socio-economic processes and receives important impulses from them.

(3) Its relative distance from international politics and *jus gentium* will not protect global law from its re-politicisation. On the contrary, the very reconstruction of social and economic (trans)actions as a global legal process undermines its non-political character and forms the basis for its re-politicisation. However, this re-politicisation is likely to proceed in new and unexpected ways.[9] We can expect global law to become politicised not via traditional political institutions, for example of a quasi-parliamentary kind, but via the very processes by which law engages in structural coupling with highly specialised, isolated discourses.

II

Bill Clinton has an intellectual mentor whom he rightly cites as an authority for his ideas: Immanuel Kant from Königsberg. Kant's philosophical design *Zum Ewigen Frieden* (eternal peace) is the legitimate predecessor of the new *Pax Americana*, even if this latter *Pax* has violated some of Kant's fundamental principles – the minor ones, of course, such as the principle of non-intervention.[10] For Kant, the globalisation of law, a 'transcendental formula of public law', is simply a consequence of the legalisation of international politics. If the sovereign states were to agree to certain legal principles enshrined in a binding international agreement, a new and just legal order for all mankind would develop.[11] America's New World Order is supposed to grow out of these same roots: global law is to follow a globalisation of politics, or more precisely the globalised politics of the United States, a politics which after all is well known for being based on the 'rule of law'. Presumably Immanuel Kant would consider the image of his book's title quite fitting as a symbol of the new order: the sign of a Dutch inn-keeper depicting a cemetery and carrying the inscription 'Eternal Peace'.

Yet history has refuted the political philosophers Kant and Clinton, whereas it has already become possible to discern the outlines of Eugen Ehrlich's Global Bukowina. Today, globalisation is no longer a utopia, but a mundane reality.[12] However, its dynamics are very different from those anticipated by Kant and Clinton. For Kant, it was a necessary precondition of world peace that the nation states should form a political federation under a republican constitution. Only then would a uniform globalisation of other aspects of society be possible – for example, a right to hospitality as a *jus cosmopoliticum*.[13] The modern experience, however, is one of fragmented globalisation processes in civil society rather than of a uniform globalisation of society under the guidance of politics. Today's globalisation is not the gradual creation of a world society by inter-state politics, but a highly contradictory and highly fragmented process driven at different speeds by different social systems. Not only has politics lost its leading role in this process, it has clearly receded in importance compared to other sectors of society. Despite the importance of international relations and international private and public law, the centre of gravity for politics and law still lies in the nation state. In fact, strong and increasing counter-tendencies towards a strengthening of regional and local politics can be observed. The other social sectors have clearly overtaken politics and law on the road to globalisation. Each of them is on the way to its own global village, and these villages are getting ready for a staunch defence of their autonomy against the hegemonic claims of politics. This is particularly true of the globalisation of law.

While thus far, the argument presented here does follow Wallerstein's critique of international relations, it diverges from it in preferring the idea of worldwide fragmented discourses as an alternative to his model of worldwide economies. Non-political globalisation does not occur exclusively as a consequence of the internal logic of a capitalist economy, but results from the internal dynamics of a multitude of social subsystems.[14] Capital has never allowed its aspirations to be determined by national boundaries: this claim to globality is also made by the other cultural provinces, as Karl Mannheim called the autonomous sectors of society. These days, not only the economy, but also science, culture, technology, health systems, social services, the military sector, transport, communication media and tourism are self-reproducing world systems in Wallerstein's sense, successful competitors of the politics of nation states. And while the political process has reached only a proto-globality in international relations, that is, no more than intersystemic relations between national units with rather weak transnational elements, the other social subsystems have already begun to form an authentic global society, or rather a fragmented multitude of diverse global societies.

What does this multi-paced scenario of globalisation imply for the law? At the global level, Eugen Ehrlich seems to be vindicated in his opinion that a centrally produced political law is marginal compared with the lawyers' law in practical decision-making and especially with the living law of Bukowina.[15] Therefore, political theories of law are likely to be of little use in understanding legal globalisation. This is true of positivist theories which stress the unity of state and law just as much as of those critical theories which tend to dissolve law into power politics. Staring obsessively at power struggles in the global political arena of international politics – where legal globalisation occurs at best to a limited extent – they overlook dynamic processes in other arenas where global legal phenomena are emerging in relative insulation from politics. The crucial point is that 'the structural coupling between law and politics via constitutions has no correspondence at the level of world society'.[16]

What about theories of autonomous law? Can globalising dynamics be identified in Ehrlich's *Juristenrecht* (lawyers' law)?[17] Are we experiencing something like a globalisation of autonomous law, as a development of Wallerstein's ideas within a model of global systemic differentiation might suggest? The historical evidence is poor. There are few signs of a strong, independent, large-scale, global development of genuine legal institutions, especially international courts.[18] The experience of The Hague is not very promising, and recent attempts to continue the Nuremberg tradition of world tribunals seem destined to end in financial and political disaster. Because of the restrictions of international public law and the regionalism of politics, worldwide legislation is a cumbersome process. There is no global administration to speak of, despite the existence of numerous international organisations. Perhaps the most interesting and dynamic phenomenon within law's empire itself is the development of private worldwide law offices, of multinational law firms which tend to take a global perspective of conflict regulation.[19]

Thus, if neither Ehrlich's state law nor his lawyers' law points the way to legal globalisation, his living law seems to be the best candidate. To repeat the famous statement: 'The center of gravity of legal development therefore from time immemorial has not lain in the activity of the state, but in society itself, and must be sought there at the present time.'[20] Ehrlich, of course, is romanticising the law-creating role of customs, traditions and practices in small-scale rural communities. But in the globalisation processes of the present, his living law seems to take on a different and quite dramatic significance, based on cold, technical social processes rather than warm communal bonds. Since it is not politics, but civil society itself that drives the globalisation of its various fragmented discourses, the globalisation of law is bound to follow suit by way of a spill-over effect of those developments. This brings us to our main thesis: global law will grow mainly from the social peripheries, from the areas of contact with other social systems, and not in the political centres of nation states and international institutions. A new living law growing out of fragmented social institutions which followed their own paths to the global village seems to be the main source of global law. This is why, for an adequate theory of global law, neither a political theory of law nor an institutional theory of autonomous law will do; instead a – renewed – theory of legal pluralism is required.[21]

However, there are important differences between the above and Ehrlich's living law of Bukowina. As mentioned above, new theories of legal pluralism have turned away from examining colonial situations and are now focusing on the interrelation between nation-state law and the diverse laws of ethnic, cultural and religious communities.[22] There will have to be yet another turn if the theories are to prove adequate in coping with worldwide legal pluralism. The new global living law does not draw its strength from the law of ethnic communities in the way that the old local living law was assumed to do and the more recent law of a patchwork of minorities supposedly still does. Clearly, the life-world of different groups and communities is not the principal source of global law. Theories of legal pluralism will have to reformulate their core concepts, shifting their focus from groups and communities to discourses and communicative networks.[23] The social source of global law is not the life-world of globalised personal networks, but the proto-law of specialised, organisational and functional networks, which are forming a global, but sharply limited identity. The new living law of the world does not draw on stores of tradition to maintain itself, but on the ongoing self-reproduction of highly technical, highly specialised, often formally organised and rather narrowly defined global networks of an economic, cultural, academic or technological nature.

Thus, we can expect global law to have characteristics that differ significantly from our experience of the law of the nation state:

(1) *Boundaries*: Global law does not define its inner boundaries on a territorial nation-state basis which is preserved even during the gradual development of federal elements, as Kant had envisaged. Instead, global law becomes internally differentiated by forming invisible colleges, invisible markets and lines of business, invisible professional communities and invisible social networks that transcend territorial boundaries, but nevertheless press for the emergence of genuinely legal forms. A new law of conflicts is emerging on the basis of intersystemic, rather than international, conflicts.[24]

(2) *Sources of law*: General legislative bodies will become less important with the development of globalisation. Global law is more likely to be produced in self-organised processes of structural coupling between the law and ongoing globalised processes of a highly specialised and technical nature.[25]

(3) *Independence*: While the legal process within nation states, or at least within some of them, has developed a rather high degree of institutional insulation, global legal orders will probably remain, for the foreseeable future, in a relation of diffuse but close dependency on their respective specialised social fields, with all the attendant problematic side effects

of this kind of 'corruption'. Examples of such side effects are a pronounced dependence on outside interests and a relative weakness of due process and the rule of law. Obviously, this creates strong political demands for legal reform.

(4) *Unity of the law*: For state-building processes in the past, the unity of the law was one of the highest political goods – a symbol of national identity and simultaneously a symbol of (almost) universal justice. A worldwide unity of the law, however, is more likely to become a threat to legal culture. For legal evolution, the main problem will be how to ensure that there continues to be a sufficient variety of legal sources in a globally unified law. We may even anticipate conscious political attempts to institutionalise legal variation, for example at regional levels.

III

A war of religion is raging in the field of international economic law. Since the sixties, international lawyers have fought their own Thirty Years' War over the independence of a global *lex mercatoria*. Is it positive law in its own right?[26] Or is it an ensemble of social norms which can be transformed into law only by the juridical decisions of the nation states involved?

This is, however, a proxy war. The controversy has model characteristics. It is important not only for the law of global trade itself, but also for other fields of global law which are emerging in relative insulation from official international politics (see cection I above): the internal law of multinational corporations, employment law, environmental law, human rights law, the law of professional organisations. For these new areas of global law without the state, *lex mercatoria* represents a paradigmatic case. In its long history, stretching back to the old medieval law merchant, it has accumulated a rich experience as an autonomous non-national body of law.[27] What lessons can other bodies of global law learn from *lex mercatoria*?

The debate on *lex mercatoria* is one of the rare cases in which practical legal decision-making becomes directly dependent on legal theory. But it is astonishing how poor its theoretical foundation actually is. The entire debate is trapped in the categories of those defunct legal theories which legal practitioners seem to remember from their undergraduate jurisprudence courses. But if key concepts of contemporary legal theory are introduced, are there insights to be gained for *lex mercatoria* and other forms of global law without the state?

On the one side we find lawyers (mainly French) for whom the new *lex mercatoria* qualifies as an emerging global legal order. For them, this positive law has its sources in worldwide commercial practices, unitary directives, standardised contracts, the activities of global economic associations, codes of conduct and the awards of international arbitration courts. This legal order, they claim, is independent of any national sovereign.[28]

The theoretical arguments developed by these advocates of *lex mercatoria*, however, are of an intellectual poverty which is matched only by the conceptual narrowness of their opponents. One line of thought tries to revitalise theories of customary law.[29] But what are the operational criteria proposed for the discovery of empirical evidence of *consuetudo longa*? No adequate conceptualisation of *opinio juris* at the global level is provided and no attempt is made to demonstrate the legitimacy of customary law under modern conditions of legal positivism.[30] A second line of thought tries to utilise the kinds of institutionalism developed in early twentieth-century Italy or France.[31] Its proponents construe a *droit corporatif* of global economic actors, vaguely resembling medieval merchant law.[32] This institutionalist vision regards the close-knit world community of merchants – a *societas mercatorum* – almost as a formal organisation. Some even liken it to a Rotary Club, others to the old merchants' guilds, and they ascribe to it a sense of solidarity or an 'inner law of associations' with a disciplinary code and organisational sanctions such as blacklisting and exclusion from membership. For the competitive dynamics of today's world markets, such corporatism on a global scale seems somewhat antiquated, to put it mildly. A third line of thought has developed the adventurous construct of *contrat sans loi*, supposedly founded on self-regulatory contracts without any basis in national or international law. This construct is, however, bound to fail when it tries to reconcile itself with the traditional doctrine of legal sources. According to this view, it is national laws that are supposed to grant freedom of contract in the form of the choice of a non-national global law.[33]

On the other side we find mainly British and American lawyers who evoke the sovereignty of the nation state in order to attack *lex mercatoria* as law fiction, as a phantom conjured up by a few speculative Sorbonne professors.[34] Their arguments are based on the nineteenth-century notion of the unity of law and state: so-called a–national law is unthinkable! Seen from this standpoint, any legal phenomenon in the world necessarily has to be rooted in a national legal order; it needs at least a minimal link to national law. *Lex mercatoria* will never develop into an authentic legal order because it does not have a basis in an exclusive territory where it can be enforced by the use of coercive power. Commercial customs by themselves are incapable of creating law; they can only be transformed into law by a formal act of the sovereign state. The same is true for standardised contracts; they should be subordinated to the political control of national legal orders. Private associations, in turn, may create their own quasi-laws, but these are without binding force. Finally, according to this view, international arbitration cannot develop an authentic body of case law that has precedential value because arbitration awards can always be questioned by resort to national courts and by the *exequatur* procedures within nation states. Only the received doctrines of the classical law of conflicts, private international law, are capable of adequately dealing with any international legal conflict in economic affairs. If legal globalisation is really necessary, then, so say proponents of this line of thought, the only legitimate sources are international treaties and conventions under the authority of international public law.

The bitterness of the controversy indicates that we are in the vicinity of a taboo, deeply rooted in practices, doctrines and theories of law. It demonstrates the tremendous resistance confronting Ehrlich's Global Bukowina in a legal world still conceptually dominated by the nation state. Just how deeply this taboo is rooted is demonstrated by the almost apocalyptical tone of the critique of *lex mercatoria*:

> It is difficult to imagine a more dangerous, more undesirable and more ill-founded view which denies any measure of predictability and certainty and confers upon the parties to an international commercial contract or their arbitrators powers that no system of law permits and no court could exercise.[35]

Lex mercatoria does indeed break a double taboo concerning the unity of state and law. It does so firstly by claiming that merely private arrangements (contracts and associations) produce valid law without authorisation and control by the state. From Savigny onwards, contract has been denied the dignity of a legal source and, perceived as a mere factual phenomenon, it has been shifted to the domain of empirical sociology.[36] Since *lex mercatoria* is contract without law, it is in this sense a *lex illegitima*. But secondly, *lex mercatoria* also breaks the taboo by claiming to be valid outside the nation state and even outside international relations. How can authentic law 'spontaneously' emerge on a transnational scale without the authority of the state, without its sanctioning power, without its political control and without the legitimacy of democratic processes? Where is the global *Grundnorm*?[37] Where is the global 'rule of recognition'?[38]

IV

How would the contemporary sociological theory of law approach *lex mercatoria* and other forms of global law without the state? It goes without saying that legal theory cannot bind the legal practices of *lex mercatoria* by its definition of what is legal and what is not. And there are, of course, many legal theories that come up with idiosyncratic definitions of what law is.[39] There is, however, one type of legal theory that makes itself explicitly dependent upon legal practices. It observes law as a self-organising process that autonomously defines its boundaries. This is called second-order observation,[40] and it observes how legal practices themselves observe the world. The theory does not itself, in a supposedly analytical manner, attempt to delineate what is inside and outside the law. Instead, it produces instruments of observation. The law is at once object and subject of observations, and the theory observes the observations of legal practice. In its turn, legal practice might gain by being informed about the mode of its own observations, and redefine its validity criteria.

Such a theory would not reject positivist accounts outright that make the existence of *lex mercatoria* dependent on the formal legal acts of a nation state. The war of religion could come to a peaceful end – on the condition that the global reach of law is no longer treated as a question of doctrinal definition, but as an empirical question which allows for variation. Our decisive question would be: where are concrete norms actually produced? In national politics and in international political relations? In judicial processes within nation states and in international courts? Or in global economic and other social processes? Legal experience seems to bear out the hypothesis that a global economic law is developing along all three dimensions.[41] Of course, this presupposes a pluralistic theory of norm production which treats political, legal and social law production on an equal footing.[42]

However, taking into account the fragmented globalisation of diverse social systems, this theory would have to give a different relative weight to these norm productions. A theory of legal pluralism would perceive global economic law as a highly asymmetric process of legal self-reproduction. Global economic law is law with an underdeveloped centre and a highly developed periphery. To be more precise, it is a law whose centre is created by the peripheries and remains dependent on them.[43] *Lex mercatoria*, then, represents that part of global economic law which operates on the periphery in direct structural coupling with global economic organisations and transactions. It is a law stemming from paralegal rules which are produced at the margin of law, at its boundary with economic and technological processes.[44]

This would allow us to identify numerous phenomena within a global commercial law which – in accordance with traditional positivist theories – have a clearly national and international basis. Attempts at the unification and harmonisation of commercial law by international treaties, as well as by the acts of national agencies and courts that adapt their domestic law to global requirements, would be cases in point. But what about *lex mercatoria* itself, that is, the more difficult case of a pluralist law production on a non-political and non-national basis?

What we see there is a self-reproducing, worldwide legal discourse which closes its boundaries by the use of the legal/illegal binary code and which reproduces itself by processing a symbol of global (not national) validity. The first criterion – binary coding – distinguishes global law from economic and other social processes. The second criterion – global validity – distinguishes global law from national and international legal phenomena. Both criteria are instruments of second-order observation, as mentioned above. They observe how the law observes itself, in our case how a global law observes itself in its environment of national legal orders and global social systems.

With this definition we pay tribute to the linguistic turn in sociology and apply it to the concerns of law and society. Accordingly, rule, sanction and social control, the core concepts of the classical sociology of law, recede into the background. Speech act, *énoncé*, coding, grammar, transformation of differences, and paradox are the new core concepts utilised in the contemporary controversies on law and society.[45] They promise a deeper understanding both of *lex mercatoria* and of global legal pluralism.

The sanction is losing the place it once held as the central concept for the definition of law, for the delineation of the legal from the social and the global from the national. Of course it has played an important role in the tradition, in John Austin's theory of law (commands backed by sanctions), in Max Weber's concept of law (administration by legal professionals), in Eugen Ehrlich's distinction of legal and non-legal norms and in Theodor Geiger's behaviouralism (alternative compliance/sanction).[46] In contemporary debates, sanctions are only seen as one among many symbolic supports for normativity.[47] In these debates, the symbolic reality of legal validity is not defined by sanctions.

In the *lex mercatoria* debate, the fact that this kind of law is dependent upon the sanctions of national courts has been used as an argument against its authentically global character.[48] If a specialised legal discourse, such as the commercial one, claims worldwide validity then it does not matter where the symbolic backing of its claims by means of sanctions comes from, be it local, regional or national institutions. It is the phenomenological world constructions within a discourse that determine the globality of the discourse, and not the fact that the source of the use of force is local.

Similarly, rules lose the strategic position they once had as core elements of law.[49] In the switch from structure to process, the central elements of a legal order are *énoncés*, communicative events, legal acts and not legal rules. It has proved hopeless to search for a criterion delineating social norms from legal norms. The decisive transformation cannot be found in the inherent characteristics of rules, but in their insertion in the context of different discourses. Rules become legal rules once they are applied to the binary code of legal/illegal by communicative events and produce microvariations in the legal structure.

As mentioned already, the fact that its rules are rather indeterminate has been used as an argument against the independent existence of *lex mercatoria*.[50] But the determinacy of rules is a misleading criterion. The existence of an elaborate body of rules is not decisive. What matters is the mutual constitution of legal acts and legal structures in a self-organising process.[51]

The concept of social control is likewise insufficient as a means for identifying the elements of an independent legal discourse. Today's legal pluralists tend to replace the legal proprium with social control.[52] In their account of *lex mercatoria* as a form of social control, they include within legal pluralism global commercial customs and practices as well as transactional patterns and the organisational routines of multinational enterprises. They even go so far as to include purely economic exigencies and the naked use of power in global markets. However, if legal pluralism entailed everything that serves the function of social control, it would be identical with a comprehensive pluralism of social constraints of any kind.[53]

Why should legal pluralism be defined only by the function of 'social control'[54] and not the function of 'conflict resolution', as theories of private justice would suggest?[55] Why could the function of 'coordinating behavior', 'accumulation of power' or 'private regulation', which theories of private government would emphasise,[56] not be taken to define legal pluralism? And why not 'discipline and punish', which would tend to include any mechanism of disciplinary micro-power that permeates social life?[57] Each of these functions would bring the diverse social mechanisms in global markets and multinational organisations into the realm of legal pluralism. Functional analysis of this kind is not suited to providing criteria for the delineation of the legal and the non-legal in *lex mercatoria*.

Now, if we follow the linguistic turn, we will not only shift the focus from structure to process, from norm to action, from unity to difference, but, most importantly for identifying the law in its specificity, from function to code.[58] This move brings forward the dynamic character of a worldwide legal pluralism and at the same time clearly delineates the 'legal' from other types of social action. Legal pluralism is then defined no longer as a set of conflicting social norms in a particular social field, but as the co-existence of diverse communicative processes that observe social action using the binary code of legal/illegal. Purely economic calculations would be just as excluded from this as the norms of political logic, mere conventions, moral norms, transactional patterns or organisational routines. But whenever such non-legal phenomena are communicatively observed using the *distinction directrice* legal/illegal,[59] they play a part in the game of legal pluralism. It is the implicit or explicit invocation of the legal code which constitutes phenomena of legal pluralism, ranging from the official law of the state to the unofficial laws of world markets.

To avoid misunderstanding, I hasten to add that the binary code legal/illegal is not peculiar to the law of the nation state. This view has nothing to do with a 'legal centralism'.[60] It categorically repudiates any claim by the official law of the nation states, of the United Nations or of international institutions to a hierarchically superior position. Instead, it assumes a heterarchy of diverse legal discourses whose genuinely legal character needs to be recognised not only by sociology and legal theory, but also by legal doctrine.

A global merchants' law would thus form part of the multitude of fragmented legal discourses which, in the form of state law, of rules of private justice or of the regulations of private government, have a role in the dynamic process of the mutual constitution of actions and structures in the global social field. And it is not the law of nation states, but the symbolic representation of validity claims which determines whether they are of a local, national or global nature. The different legal orders within legal pluralism continuously produce normative expectations, but at the same time exclude merely social conventions and moral norms, since these are not based on the binary code legal/illegal. And they may serve many functions: social control, conflict regulation, reaffirmation of expectations, social regulation, coordination of behaviour or the disciplining of bodies and souls. It is neither structure nor function, but the binary code which defines the legal proprium in local or global legal pluralism.

V

So far, we have shown that a theory of legal pluralism is capable of identifying authentic legal phenomena operating at the global level. But this leaves the following question unanswered: given the absence of a unified global political system and the absence of unified global legal institutions, how has it been possible to establish a global legal discourse, based on the binary code of the law and a global symbol of validity, without its being rooted in national law? The answer is that there is a paradox underlying the creation of global economic law – the paradox of a self-validating contract. If this paradox of contractual self-reference is successfully de-paradoxified, a global legal system in economic affairs can get off the ground.

In *lex mercatoria* it is the practice of contracting that transcends national boundaries and transforms a merely national law production into a global one

– numerous international business transactions, standardised contracts of international professional associations, model contracts of international organisations and investment projects in developing countries. However, as soon as these contracts claim transnational validity, they are cut off not only from their national roots, but from their roots in any legal order. This may be fatal. It is not only lawyers who declare contracts without law unthinkable. The idea that every contract needs to be rooted in a pre-existing legal order is not merely a legal axiom. Sociologists, too, will protest against *contrat sans loi*. From the work of Emile Durkheim onwards, the great sociological objection to any autonomous contractualism has been that the binding force of contract needs to be rooted in broader social contexts.[61] Of a purported contractual *lex mercatoria*, sociologists would ask the famous Durkheimian question: where are the non-contractual premises of global contracting?

Why not in the contracts themselves? Apparently this is a dead end. Any self-validation of contract leads directly into the paradox of self-reference, into the contractual version of the Cretan liar paradox.[62] In the positive version (We agree that our agreement is valid), it is a pure tautology. In the negative version (We agree that our agreement is not valid), it is the typical self-referential paradox which leads to nothing but endless oscillation (valid – not valid – valid ...) and blockage. The result is undecidability. This underlying paradox is the principal reason why lawyers, as well as sociologists, declare self-validating contracts unthinkable and consider this to amount to a *reductio ad absurdum* of *lex mercatoria*.

Social practice, however, is more creative than legal doctrine and social theory. *Kautelarjurisprudenz*, the practice of drafting international contracts, has found a means of concealing the paradox of self-validation in such a way that global contracts have become capable of doing the apparently impossible. Global contracts are creating their non-contractual foundations themselves. They have found three ways of de-paradoxification – time, hierarchy and externalisation – that mutually support each other and make it possible, without the help of the state, for a global law of the economic periphery to create its own legal centre.

Empirically, we find the most perfect de-paradoxification in those commercial contracts that construct a so-called 'closed circuit arbitration'.[63] This is a self-regulatory contract that goes far beyond one particular commercial transaction and establishes a whole private legal order with a claim to global validity. Apart from substantive rules, it contains clauses that refer conflicts to an arbitration tribunal which is identical with the private institution that was responsible for creating the model contract. This is the 'closed circuit'.

In the first place, these contracts establish an internal hierarchy of contractual rules. They contain not only 'primary rules' in the sense established by Hart,[64] which regulate the future behaviour of the parties, but also secondary rules that regulate the recognition of primary rules, their identification, their interpretation and the procedures for resolving conflicts. Thus, the paradox of self-validation still exists, but it is concealed in the separation of hierarchical levels, the levels of rules and meta-rules. Unlike the rules, the meta-rules are autonomous, although both have the same contractual origin. The hierarchy is 'tangled', but this does not prevent the higher echelons from regulating the lower ones.[65]

Secondly, these contracts temporalise the paradox and transform the circularity of contractual self-validation into an iterative process of legal acts, into a sequence of the recursive mutual constitution of legal acts and legal structures. The present contract extends itself into the past and into the future. It refers to a pre-existing standardisation of rules and it refers to the future of conflict regulation, and thus turns itself into one element in an ongoing self-reproduction process in which the network of elements is continuously reproduced by ever new elements of the system.

Thirdly, and most importantly, the self-referential contract uses the de-paradoxification technique of externalisation. It externalises the fatal self-validation of contract by referring conditions of validity and future conflicts to external non-contractual institutions which are nevertheless contractual in the sense that they are merely internal products of the contract itself. The most prominent of these self-created external institutions is arbitration, which has to judge the validity of a contract, even though its own validity is based on the very contract the validity of which it is supposed to be judging. Here, the vicious circle of contractual self-validation is transformed into the virtuous circle of two legal practices: contracting and arbitration. An internal circular relationship is transformed into an external one. In the circular relationship between the two institutional poles of contract and arbitration, a 'reflexive mechanism', as Stein puts it,[66] we find the core elements of the emerging global legal discourse: use of the specialised binary code legal/illegal and processing of a non-national and even non-international — which is to say global — symbol of validity. An additional externalisation of this reference to quasi-courts is the reference to quasi-legislative institutions, to the International Chamber of Commerce in Paris, the International Law Association in London, the International Maritime Commission in Antwerp and to all sorts of international business associations.[67] Thus, transnational contracting has created an institutional triangle of private adjudication, legislation and contracting *ex nihilo*.

Why is this externalisation so important for the creation of an authentically global law? The answer is: not only because it supports the de-paradoxification of contractual self-validation, but also because it creates dynamics of interaction between an official legal order and a non-official one, something that is constitutive for a modern legal system. It introduces an internal differentiation between organised and spontaneous law production, which creates the functional equivalent of the distinction in domestic law between the law of contract as applied by the state through the courts and the private autonomy of contractually structured relations.[68] Thus, arbitration bodies and private legislation dramatically change the role of the international contract itself. Although arbitration and standard contracting are themselves based on contract, they transform the contractual creation of rights and duties into a kind of unofficial law which is then controlled and disciplined by the official law of the arbitration bodies. Private arbitration and private legislation become the core of a decision system which begins to build up a hierarchy of norms and of decision-making authorities. This is what makes the reflexivity of *lex mercatoria* possible.[69]

In this way, the global legal discourse is founded on the paradox of contractual self-validation and differentiated into an official and a non-official legal order. Contrary to the claim of the defenders of a *lex mercatoria*, this has nothing to do with customary law, since even empirically speaking, it is not based on practices ennobled by *opinio juris*.[70] Like other forms of non-customary law, it is based on decisions of positive law-making. It is positive law in the form of private legislation, adjudication and contracting. Of course there are customs which are incorporated into contracts as commercial practices, and they do play a role, but it is a rather limited one.

Nor should *lex mercatoria* be equated with a *droit corporatif*. In the world market, something like a corporation of merchants with the ability to discipline its members does not exist. Clearly there are formally organised professional organisations, but there is no formally organised business community which could produce an internal law of associations via the mechanism of membership, entry and exit. The formal sources of legal validity are individual transactions of the world market, which is structurally different to a formal organisation.

Finally, *lex mercatoria* has little in common with the *contrat sans loi* of some international lawyers.[71] It is true that the decisive mechanism of validity transfer is the contract, and not national law, commercial custom or a kind of global corporatism. But these authors still attempt to find the legitimation of the self-regulatory contract in national law:

> If national laws permit the parties to an international contract to choose the law applicable to their contract, then it is only logical [sic] that they must also allow the parties to create contractual conditions that are so complete in themselves that there remains no room at all for the application of national law.[72]

This obviously is not 'logical'. To permit a choice of law, that is, a choice among existing national laws, in no way includes the permission to create a new law outside any national legal order. The comity of sovereign nation states refers to other national laws, but not to an a–national legal order. In contrast, our concept of global legal pluralism works on the basis of two assumptions which are more radical than an implied delegation of state power. The first assumption relates to traditional theories of the sources of law. The global context, in which no pre-existing legal order can be said to be the source of the validity of global contracts, compels us to define contracting itself as a source of law, as a source on an equal footing with judge-made law and with legislation. In our case, contracting is even the primary source of law and the basis for its own rudimentary quasi-adjudication and quasi-legislation. The second assumption refers to theories of legal legitimacy. Rules of recognition need not necessarily be produced hetero-referentially by an independent public legal order and then applied to private contractual arrangements. What we face here is a self-legitimating situation, comparable only to authentic revolutions in which the violence of the first distinction is law-creating. 'In ogni violenza vi e un carattere di creazione giuridica.'[73] Clearly, the silent revolution of *lex mercatoria* – like any law based on revolutionary acts – needs recognition by other legal orders. But this is only a secondary consideration. Recognition is not constitutive of the existence of a legal order.

VI

It would be a momentous misunderstanding if a comparison of *lex mercatoria* with a national legal order led one to describe the differences between the two as deficiencies inherent in *lex mercatoria* and to conclude that the latter is an as yet underdeveloped legal order on the global scale.[74] The asymmetries of a weak institutional centre which depends on a strong economic periphery are not a merely transitory phenomenon. They are due to their global environment, that is, globalised markets and enterprises with a global reach on the one hand, and regional politics that are interconnected merely by international relations, on the other. Thus it can be anticipated that the discourse of global economic law will find a dynamic stability by itself and develop its own specific logic, which must be understood in its own right.

1 *Structural coupling with global economic processes*

This is the overriding characteristic of *lex mercatoria*. It is a law that grows and changes according to the exigencies of global economic transactions and organisations.⁷⁵ This makes it extremely vulnerable as regards the interests of and the power exercised by economic actors. Since there is little institutional insulation of its quasi-legislation and its quasi-judiciary, the relative autonomy and independence which national legal orders have historically been able to attain will probably not be achieved here. For the foreseeable future, *lex mercatoria* will be a corrupt law – in the technical sense of the word. At the same time, lack of institutional autonomy makes this law vulnerable to political attacks on its political legitimacy.⁷⁶

2 *Episodic character*

Self-reproductive legal orders consist of interacting episodes that are linked to each other in a second communicative circle (precedents, legal doctrine, codification) which is the locus of the evolutionary mechanism of stabilisation.⁷⁷ This is *lex mercatoria*'s weak point, since it consists of episodes with rather weak communicative links. We find myriads of highly sophisticated contractual regimes which – as in the case of investment projects in developing countries⁷⁸ – can be of extreme economic and political importance for a whole region. However, the links between these regimes of contractual feudalism are rather flimsy, so that the global empire of law is a little like the Holy Roman Empire of the German Nation, an uncoordinated ensemble of many small domains, a patchwork of legal regimes. The principal links between them are still being supplied by private associations which are responsible for the formulation of model contracts.⁷⁹

Arbitration tribunals are likewise strong in producing episodes and weak in linking them with one another. There are some signs of a system of precedents in arbitration matters, beginning with the publication of reasoned arbitration awards and a practice of using old awards as precedents.⁸⁰

> The constant flow of arbitration awards is nourishing a new legal order that is born of, and particularly suited to, regulating world business. Trade usages and custom, as well as professional regulations, will attain the status of law as they become embodied in arbitral decision making.⁸¹

Yet there are structural obstacles to the systematic development of an authentic case law, let alone a hierarchy of arbitration courts that could close the second communicative circle. Thus, the chances that an autonomous legal evolution of *lex mercatoria* will occur are rather slim. While legal variation and selection mechanisms are indeed in place, its stabilisation mechanism is so underdeveloped that in the foreseeable future the development of this law is likely to follow the external evolution of the economic system, but fail to develop an internal evolution of its own.[82]

In the long run, *lex mercatoria* may very well develop certain institutionalised linkages of its episodes that would make its own path-dependent evolution possible. However, as one can extrapolate from contemporary tendencies, these linkages will look quite different from their main national counterparts – court hierarchies and parliamentary legislation. As already mentioned, there is an inchoate practice of precedent and *stare decisis* in commercial arbitration. However, the lack of any institutionalised court hierarchy which could guarantee a certain normative consistency is compensated by an increasing reliance on mutual observation and adaptation of arbitration bodies and by the increasing reliance on the 'Big Three' in international commercial arbitration – the Chambre de Commerce International, the Iran–United States Claims Tribunal and the International Centre for Settlement of Investment Disputes.[83] A reputational hierarchy will substitute for an organisational hierarchy. Similarly, the political linkage between episodes of adjudication and legislative-parliamentary bodies familiar from the traditional nation state will not be repeated in global economic law. Rather, the reference will be to the legislators of private regimes: economic and professional associations, and a whole heterarchical network of international organisations, private and public. Through these multiple circular linkages of its episodes, *lex mercatoria* may gain the ability to develop not only mechanisms for variation and selection, but also independent mechanisms for retention, the interplay of which might result in an autonomous path of legal evolution.

3 *Soft law*

The normative substance of *lex mercatoria* is extremely indeterminate. Instead of sophisticated rules of private law, it consists of broad principles that change in their application from case to case.[84] This is one of the reasons why some lawyers negate its existence as law altogether.[85] From the preceding discussion, we know why they are wrong: they are seeking a body of rules as the essence of an autonomous legal order, instead of looking to the communicative processes that transfer the symbol of validity according to the binary legal code. Although there have been several attempts to codify rules of global economic law (UNIDROIT 1994),[86] the softness of *lex mercatoria* is remarkable. It is more a law of values and principles than a law of structures and rules.[87] But is softness a weakness or is it a strength? Again, we should not see this as a deficiency, but as a typical characteristic of global law. It compensates for the lack of global enforceability; it makes this law more flexible and adaptive to changing circumstances; it makes it better suited to a global unification of law.[88] And it makes it relatively resistant to symbolic destruction in the case of deviance. Stability is the result of softness. *Lex mercatoria* is soft law, not weak law.

VII

In the long run its de-politicised origin and its apolitical character cannot protect *lex mercatoria* from repoliticisation. On the contrary: the juridification of economic relations provokes political interference. While it is extremely difficult for any political process in national politics or international relations to intervene in global economic transactions or in multinational organisations, juridification drastically changes things. Once the contractual mechanism stabilises the structural coupling between law and the economy, political processes tend to use the result of this coupling for their own purposes. This is observable in the case of *lex mercatoria*, which has been unable to protect itself from the maelstrom of international politics. It will be less and less able to do so in the future.[89]

There are two reasons why the *lex mercatoria* will not be able to retain its idyllic status of a privately created legal order. The re-nationalisation of *lex mercatoria* is one reason. For the more the issue of the competitiveness of national economies or regional blocks in the global economy comes to the fore in international politics, the more *lex mercatoria* will be under pressure to bend to national economic policies. The development of intellectual property law on an international scale is a good case in point.[90] In any case, *lex mercatoria* will become an openly politicised sphere of law in which the political role of international organisations moves centre stage.

The North–South divide is the other reason. The discussion of a New Economic World Order has already had an impact on global economic law. The UN codification of sales or the Standard Contracts of UNECE are good examples of the repoliticisation of *lex mercatoria*.

However, as far as the *lex mercatoria* is concerned, these mechanisms of repoliticisation are still merely part of its external environment. The politics of *lex mercatoria* itself will undergo substantial change only when the inner mechanisms of this global law-production process are politicised as well: when the internal structures and processes of the law-creating mechanism – the law-making authorities in international private associations and the composition and procedures of arbitration tribunals – become the subject of public scrutiny and debate.

Notes

This chapter was previously published as 'Global Bukowina: legal pluralism in the world society', in Gunther Teubner (ed.), *Global Law without a State* (Aldershot: Dartmouth, 1997), pp. 3–28.

1. Ehrlich, *Fundamental Principles of the Sociology of Law*, p. 390.
2. See Mertens, 'Lex Mercatoria'.
3. Giddens, *Consequences of Modernity*, p. 70.
4. See Robé, 'Multinational Enterprises'; Muchlinski, '"Global Bukowina" Examined'.
5. See Bercusson, 'Globalizing Labour Law'.
6. See Bianchi, 'Globalization of Human Rights'.
7. Luhmann, *Law as a Social System*, pp. 482 ff.
8. Simon, *Puissance sportive*; Summerer, *Internationales Sportrecht*.
9. Especially in the re-definition of the global–local distinction as resistance against globalisation. For a discussion of these issues, see Wilder, 'Local Futures?'; Schütz, 'Twilight of the Global Polis'.
10. Kant, *Perpetual Peace*, pp. 7–8.
11. Ibid.
12. The term 'globalisation' is somewhat misleading. It suggests that a multitude of nationally organised societies are now moving towards a single world society: see Giddens, *Consequences of Modernity*, pp. 12 ff. It is more appropriate, however, to date the existence of one world society from the historical moment in which communication became worldwide. Nation states thus do not represent societies of their own, but exist according to a principle of territorial differentiation of one world society. Globalisation, as we experience it today, means a shift of prominence in the primary principle of differentiation: a shift from territorial to functional differentiation at the world level. On this, see Luhmann, 'World society as a social system'; Luhmann, *Law as a Social System*, pp. 479 ff.; Stichweh, 'Zur Theorie der Weltgesellschaft'; Schütz, 'Twilight of the Global Polis'.
13. Kant, *Perpetual Peace*, pp. 28 ff.
14. Wallerstein, *Capitalist World Economy*; Giddens, *Consequences of Modernity*, pp. 65 ff.; Luhmann, 'Coding of the Legal System'.
15. Ehrlich, *Fundamental Principles of the Sociology of Law*, pp. 446 ff.
16. Luhmann, *Law as a Social System*, pp. 487–8.
17. Ehrlich, *Fundamental Principles of the Sociology of Law*, pp. 122 ff.
18. Higgins, *Problems & Process*.
19. Flood, 'Cultures of Globalization'.
20. Ehrlich, *Fundamental Principles of the Sociology of Law*, p. 390.
21. See Robé, 'Multinational Enterprises'.
22. Santos, 'Modes of production of law'; Santos, 'Law: a map of misreading'; Fitzpatrick, 'Law and societies'; Henry, *Private Justice*; Henry, 'Construction and Deconstruction of Social Control'; Macaulay, 'Private Government'; Griffiths, 'What is legal pluralism?'; Merry, 'Legal pluralism', pp. 873 ff.
23. Teubner, 'Two faces of Janus', pp. 1456 ff.

24 Teubner, *Law as an Autopoietic System*, ch. 5; Teubner, 'De collisione'.
25 See Teubner, 'Autopoiesis and Steering'.
26 Stein, *Lex mercatoria*, pp. 179 ff.
27 For its history, see Baker, 'Law merchant and the common law'; Berman, 'Law of International Commercial Transactions', pp. 3 ff.; Meyer, *Bona fides and lex mercatoria*, pp. 48 ff.
28 Goldman, 'Frontières du droit'; Goldman, 'La lex mercatoria dans les contrats'; Goldman, 'Applicable Law'; Goldman, 'Nouvelles réflexions sur la Lex Mercatoria'; Fouchard, *L'arbitrage commercial international*; Fouchard, 'La loi régissant les obligations contractuelles'; Kahn, 'Droit international économique'; Kahn, 'La lex mercatoria'; Loquin, 'L'application des règles anationales'; Osman, *Principes géneraux de la lex mercatoria*.
29 Goldman, 'Applicable Law', p. 114.
30 See Esser, 'Richterrecht'; Freitag, *Gewohnheitsrecht und Rechtssystem*; Zamora, 'Is there customary international economic law?'
31 Romano, *L'ordinamento giuridico*; Hauriou, *Aux sources du droit*.
32 Goldman, 'Frontières du droit'; Fouchard, *L'arbitrage commercial international*; Fouchard, 'La loi régissant les obligations contractuelles'; Kahn, 'Droit international économique'.
33 Schmitthoff, 'Das neue Recht des Welthandels'; Schmitthoff, 'Nature and Evolution'; Cremades and Plehn, 'New lex mercatoria', pp. 328 ff.
34 Mann, 'Internationale Schiedsgerichte'; Mann, 'England rejects "delocalised" contracts'; Kassis, *Théorie générale des usages du commerce*; Mustill, 'New Lex Mercatoria'; Delaume, 'Comparative analysis as a basis of law in state contracts'; Highet, 'Enigma of the lex mercatoria'; see also Bar, *Internationales Privatrecht*, vol. 1, pp. 76 ff.; Sandrock, 'Fortbildung des materiellen Rechts', pp. 77 ff.; Spickhoff, 'Internationales Handelsrecht'.
35 Mann, 'Internationale Schiedsgerichte', p. 127.
36 Savigny, *System of the modern Roman law*, p. 10.
37 Kelsen, *Pure Theory of Law*.
38 Hart, *Concept of Law*, pp. 92 ff.
39 Mertens, 'Lex Mercatoria'.
40 Luhmann, *Law as a Social System*, pp. 93–4.
41 Cf. the classification of international economic law by Schanze, 'Potential and Limits'.
42 Teubner, 'Two faces of Janus'; Luhmann, *Law as a Social System*, pp. 131 ff., 291 ff.; Robé, 'Multinational Enterprises'.
43 For the internal differentiation between centre and periphery, see Luhmann, *Law as a Social System*, pp. 291 ff.
44 Braeckmans, 'Paralegale Normen'.
45 Despite the differences between various post-structuralist legal theories, it is striking to observe how much their analytical tools resemble each other. For postmodern theories, see Lyotard, *The Differend*; Derrida, 'Force of law'; Arnaud, 'Legal interpretation'; Ladeur, *Postmoderne Rechtstheorie*; Douzinas and Warrington, *Justice Miscarried*; for discourse theory, see Jackson, *Law, Fact and Normative Coherence*; for critical theory, see Habermas, *Between Facts and Norms*; Wiethölter, 'Proceduralization'; and Lenoble and Berten, *Dire la norme*; for systems theory, see Luhmann, *Law as a Social System*; Schütz, 'Desiring society'; for game theory, see Kerchove and Ost, *Le système juridique*; Kerchove and Ost, *Le droit ou les paradoxes*.

46 Austin, *Province of Jurisprudence*, pp. 13 ff.; Weber, *Economy and Society*; Ehrlich, *Fundamental Principles of the Sociology of Law*; Geiger, *Vorstudien zu einer Soziologie des Rechts*, pp. 68 ff.
47 E.g. Luhmann, *Sociological Theory of Law*, ch. 2, section 3.
48 E.g. Kassis, *Théorie générale des usages du commerce*, pp. 332 ff.; Bar, *Internationales Privatrecht*, vol. 1, pp. 80–1; Schlosser, *Recht der internationalen Schiedsgerichtsbarkeit*, pp. 152 ff.
49 Hart, *Concept of Law*; Kelsen, *Pure Theory of Law*.
50 Langen, *Transnational Commercial Law*; Berman, 'Law of International Commercial Transactions', p. 51; David, 'Le droit du commerce international', p. 17; Bar, *Internationales Privatrecht*, vol. 1, p. 79.
51 Teubner, 'Two faces of Janus'.
52 Griffiths, 'What is legal pluralism?', p. 50, n. 41.
53 Cohen, 'Social-Control Talk', p. 101.
54 Griffiths, 'What is legal pluralism?', p. 50.
55 Henry, *Private Justice*.
56 Macaulay, 'Private Government'.
57 Foucault, *Discipline and Punish*; Fitzpatrick, 'Impossibility of popular justice'.
58 Ladeur, *Postmoderne Rechtstheorie*; Luhmann, *Law as a Social System*, pp. 76 ff.; Teubner, *Law as an Autopoietic System*.
59 Luhmann, 'Coding of the Legal System'.
60 Griffiths, 'What is legal pluralism?', pp. 2 ff.
61 Durkheim, *Division of Labor*, pp. 200 ff.
62 Dupuy and Teubner (eds), *Paradoxes of Self-Reference*.
63 Cremades and Plehn, 'New lex mercatoria'.
64 Hart, *Concept of Law*, pp. 77 ff.
65 Hofstadter, *Gödel, Escher, Bach*, pp. 684 ff.; Hofstadter, 'Nomic', pp. 70 ff.; Suber, *Paradox of Self-Amendment*.
66 Stein, *Lex mercatoria*, pp. 164 ff.
67 Schmitthoff, *Export Trade*.
68 Cf. Luhmann, *Law as a Social System*, pp. 291 ff.
69 Stein, *Lex mercatoria*, pp. 164 ff.
70 Berman, 'Law of International Commercial Transactions', pp. 50 ff.
71 Schmitthoff, 'Das neue Recht des Welthandels'; Schmitthoff, 'Nature and Evolution'; Cremades and Plehn, 'New lex mercatoria', pp. 328 ff.; Mertens, 'Lex Mercatoria'.
72 Schmitthoff, 'Das neue Recht des Welthandels', p. 69.
73 Resta, *L'ambiguo diritto*, p. 10. See also Resta, 'Struttura autopoietica del diritto', pp. 59 ff.
74 Virally, 'Un tiers droit?', p. 385; Siehr, 'Sachrecht im IPR', p. 117.
75 Braeckmans, 'Paralegale Normen'.
76 Joerges, 'Rechtssystem der transnationalen Handelsschiedsgerichtsbarkeit', p. 41; Bonell, 'Das autonome Recht des Welthandels'.
77 Teubner, 'Episodenverknüpfung'; Teubner, *Law as an Autopoietic System*, ch. 3.
78 See Schanze, 'Potential and Limits'.
79 Schmitthoff, *Export Trade*; Stein, *Lex mercatoria*, ch. 3.
80 Carbonneau, 'Rendering arbitral awards with reasons'; Paulsson, 'Lex mercatoria dans l'arbitrage'; Berger, 'International arbitrator's applications of precedents'; Stein, *Lex mercatoria*, pp. 165 ff.
81 Cremades, 'Impact of international arbitration', p. 533.

82 On the external and internal evolution of law, see Teubner, *Law as an Autopoietic System*, ch. 4.
83 Stein, *Lex mercatoria*, p. 167.
84 Mustill, 'New Lex Mercatoria', pp. 174 ff.; Hoffmann, 'Grundsätzliches zur Anwendung der "lex mercatoria"', pp. 220 ff.
85 Bar, *Internationales Privatrecht*, vol. 1, p. 79.
86 International Institute for the Unification of Private Law, *Principles of International Commercial Contracts*.
87 Meyer, *Bona fides and lex mercatoria*, pp. 128 ff.
88 See Mertens, 'Lex Mercatoria'.
89 Joerges, 'Rechtssystem der transnationalen Handelsschiedsgerichtsbarkeit', p. 41; Bonell, 'Das autonome Recht des Welthandels'; Karnell, 'Will the consumer law field be the Waterloo of the new lex mercatoria?'; Béguin, 'Le développement de la *lex mercatoria*'; Stein, *Lex mercatoria*, pp. 247 ff.
90 Nimmer and Krauthaus, 'Globalization of law'.

10

Regime-collisions: the vain search for legal unity in the fragmentation of global law

Andreas Fischer-Lescano and Gunther Teubner

I The fragmentation of global law: two reductionisms

Predictions of future events tend to be a rarity within the social sciences. It is an even less frequent occurrence for predicted events to come to pass. Niklas Luhmann's prediction on the future of global law is a memorable exception. In 1971, while theorising on the concept of world society, Luhmann ventured the 'speculative hypothesis' that global law would experience a radical fragmentation, not along territorial lines, but along those between different social sectors. The reason for this would be a transformation from normative (politics, morality, law) to cognitive expectations (economy, science, technology); a transformation that would be effected during the transition from nationally organised societies to a global society.

> At the level of global society, this means that norms (in the form of values, stipulations, goals) will no longer pre-programme recognition patterns; rather, and in stark contrast, the problem of learning adaptation will gain structural primacy, so that the structural conditions for learning within each social system must be supported through normatisation.[1]

Subsequent analyses added a complementary prediction: should the law of a global society become entangled within sectoral interdependences, a wholly new form of conflicts law will emerge; an 'inter-systemic conflicts law', derived not from collisions between the distinct nations of private international law, but from collisions between distinct global social sectors.[2]

And indeed, a quarter of a century later, an almost explosive expansion of independent and globally active, yet sectorally limited, courts, quasi-courts and other forms of conflict-resolving bodies did occur.[3] The Project on International Courts and Tribunals[4] has identified an astonishing number of around 125 international institutions in which independent authorities reach final legal decisions. Among others, this international jurisdiction comprises the International Court of Justice, the International Tribunal for the Law of the Sea, various tribunals for reparations, international criminal courts and tribunals, hybrid international-national tribunals, trade and investment judicial bodies, regional human rights tribunals and convention-derived institutions, as well as other regional courts, such as the European Court of Justice, the EFTA Court and the Benelux Court.[5] With the inauguration of the WTO Appellate Body, the ICTY, the ICTR and the ICC at the latest, this trend, which had been ongoing behind the scenes for quite some time, was made clearly visible and immediately provoked a lively discussion on the risks posed by a proliferation of international courts and the fragmentation of international law. How to combat what traditional international lawyers view as a 'pathological' *relativité normative*,[6] as well as all the problems of contradictions between individual decisions, rule collisions, doctrinal inconsistency and conflict between different legal principles, is increasingly an issue of concern to case law,[7] expert committees,[8] ICJ presidents[9] and academic controversies.[10] The open question that remains is whether traditional, nation-state oriented modes of tackling collisions of law will suffice, or whether a radical rethinking of conflicts law is necessary.

However, a characteristic legal reductionism may also be observed here: a reductionism which both oversimplifies the manner in which norm conflicts are understood, and which narrows the possible range of their solutions. In principle, lawyers register only a confusing variety of autonomous legal fields, self-contained regimes and highly specialised tribunals. They identify a danger to the unity of international law on the grounds that the conceptual-doctrinal consistency, the clear hierarchy of norms and the effective judicial hierarchy that was developed within nation states is lacking.[11] Accordingly, they direct themselves to a hierarchical solution to the problem, which, while not wholly reproducing the ideal of the legal hierarchies of the nation state, at least comes somewhere close to doing so. One far-reaching suggestion argues that as soon as a new tribunal is established, the ICJ should be given an appellate function with regard to that tribunal.[12] Alternatively the ICJ, whose advisory opinions would preserve the unity of international law, should be invoked in the case of conflicts between jurisdictions.[13] One even more far-reaching suggestion entails not only that new international conventions should be submitted at the draft stage to the International Law Commission (ILC) for comment, in line with the process envisaged by Article 17 of its Statute,[14] but also promotes a certification procedure:

> The Commission could be asked to devise a general 'check-list' to assist States in preventing conflicts of norms, negative effects for individuals and overlapping competencies with regard to existing subsystems that could be affected by the new regime. In the course of reviewing ongoing negotiations, the Commission could even issue 'no-hazard'-certificates indicating that the creation of a specific new subsystem has no negative effects on existing regimes.[15]

Quite apart from the fact that such hierarchical schemes have a minimal chance of success, it is clear even from a politically oriented perspective alone that they understate the problem of norm collision.[16] Such a perspective locates the cause for fragmentation not within the lack of jurisdictional hierarchy, but identifies the basis of the norm collisions in the underlying conflicts between the policies pursued by different international organisations and regulatory regimes. In this political perspective, collisions between legal norms are merely a mirror of the strategies followed by new collective actors within international relations, who pursue power-driven 'special interests' without reference to a common interest and give rise to drastic 'policy conflicts'. Neither doctrinal formulas of legal unity, nor the theoretical ideal of a norm hierarchy, nor the institutionalisation of a jurisdictional hierarchy provide adequate means to avoid such conflicts. Instead, the only possible perspective for dealing with such policy conflicts is the explicit politicisation of legal norm collisions through power mechanisms, negotiations between relevant collective actors, public debate and collective decisions.

This observation is certainly correct. Its dramatic nature should likewise not be underestimated.[17] Yet even this political foundation for legal norm collision is not deep enough and in its turn a political reductionism. Both legal and political approaches offer only a one-dimensional explanation for collisions and, as a consequence, seek similarly one-dimensional solutions either at the legal or the political meta-level.[18] Global legal pluralism, however, is not simply a result of political pluralism, but instead the expression of deep contradictions between colliding sectors of a global society. At its core, the fragmentation of global law is not simply about legal norm collisions or policy conflicts. Its origin lies in contradictions between society-wide institutionalised rationalities, which law cannot solve, but which demand a new legal approach to colliding norms.

This thesis will be developed in more detail along three lines of argument:

(1) The fragmentation of global law is more radical than any single reductionist perspective – legal, political, economic or cultural – can comprehend. Legal fragmentation is merely a secondary effect of a more fundamental, multi-dimensional fragmentation of global society itself.
(2) Any aspirations to a normative unity of global law are thus doomed from the outset. A meta-level at which conflicts might be solved is wholly elusive both in global law and in global society. Instead, we may expect intensified legal fragmentation.
(3) Legal fragmentation itself cannot be eradicated. At the best, a weak normative compatibility of the fragments might be achieved. However, this is dependent on the ability of a new kind of conflicts law to establish a peculiar type of network logic that can help to establish a loose coupling of the colliding units.

II Legal collisions from the perspective of social theory

Various social theories on legal globalisation allow us to paint a clearer picture of how legal fragmentation depends on more fundamental processes of fragmentation within global society. The Stanford School's institutionalist theory of 'global culture', postmodern concepts of global legal pluralism, discourse analysis of the global nature of law and politics, various models of a 'global civil society' and, in particular, systemic concepts of a differentiated global society have all propagated an understanding of a polycentric form of globalisation which places legal fragmentation in a different light.[19] To arrive at such an understanding, however, one must give up a series of popular conceptions in social and legal theory – six, to be precise – and replace them by ideas of a rather unfamiliar kind. Much of this has been already dealt with at length elsewhere, so it is just the conclusions that will be reiterated below.[20] What do need to be discussed in more detail here are the particular consequences this has for the fragmentation of global law.

1 Rationality conflicts in a polycentric global society

A first conception that must be dispensed with is the widespread assumption that global legal fragmentation is primarily a result of the internationalisation of the economy. The economic steering mechanisms of the nation state have supposedly been unable to keep pace with the creation of distinct global markets; instead, a variety of competing global regulation regimes have been established, each with their own legal decision-making authorities.[21] The alternative to such an economy-led form of globalisation can be termed 'polycentric globalisation'.[22] The primary motor for this development is an accelerated differentiation of society into autonomous social systems, each of which transcends territorial confines and constitutes itself globally. This process is not confined to markets alone. Science, culture, technology, health, the military, transport, tourism and sport, as well as – albeit with some significant delay – politics, law and welfare, have all become autonomous global systems in their own right by following their own specific developmental trajectories.

What are at issue in the present context are the external relations of these autonomous global villages: their relations with one another and with their other social, human and natural environments. These are anything but harmonious. If anywhere, it is here that the notion of a 'clash of cultures' is appropriate. Through their own operative closure, global functional systems create a sphere for themselves in which they are free to intensify their own rationality without regard to other social systems or, indeed, to their natural or human environments. They do this for as long as they can; that is, for as long as it is tolerated by their environments.[23] Ever since the pioneering analysis of Karl Marx,[24] repeated proof has been furnished for the destructive potential of a globalised economic rationality.[25] Max Weber deployed the concept of modern polytheism in his efforts to identify this potential within other areas of life and to analyse the resulting, and threatening, rationality conflicts.[26] Today one is more likely to speak of discourse collisions.[27] By now, the social, human and ecological risks posed by other highly specialised global systems, such as science and technology, have become readily apparent even to a broader public.[28] Similarly, and especially where the position of countries within the southern hemisphere is considered, it is clear that real dangers are posed less by the dynamics of international politics and more by economic, scientific and technological rationality spheres that instigate the 'clash of rationalities'. According to Niklas Luhmann's central thesis, the underlying cause for postmodern risks is found within the rationality maximisation pursued by different globally active functional systems, which entails an enormous potential for endangering people, nature and society.[29] Seen in this light, the problems of global society, namely environmental degradation, spectacular social under-provision and stark discrepancies in life and development potential, have an underlying cause that must be analysed in terms of functional differentiation and autonomous systems dynamics; by the same token, it is simply inappropriate to downplay the significance of the problems produced by global finance markets, hedge funds, financial speculation, pharmaceutical patents, the drugs trade and reproductive cloning by framing their explanation and their political-legal solution solely with reference to political conflicts. It is the fragmented and operationally closed functional systems of global society in their expansionist fervour that create the real causes for the problems of global society, and at the same time employ global law for the normative reinforcement of the highly refined, particular logics of their own spheres.[30] It is doubtful whether the creation of judicial hierarchies can ever overcome a form of legal fragmentation that derives from structural social contradictions. However, a return to the idea of public international law as a law of coordination[31] and a resurrection of old myths is also impossible: '[T]he sin of differentiation can never be undone. Paradise is lost.'[32]

2 *The global legal system and inter-legality*

In order to better understand the connection between processes of legal evolution and social differentiation, it is also necessary to give up the idea that a legal system in its strict sense exists only at the level of the nation state. Instead, one must proceed from the assumption that, in line with the logic of functional differentiation, the law, too, has established itself globally as a unitary social system outside of national legal systems. However, the unity of global law no longer relies in a structural manner on an institutionally secured normative consistency, as in the case of the nation state with its court hierarchies. Instead, it has a procedural basis in the mode of connection between legal operations, which transfers binding legality even between highly heterogeneous legal orders.[33] This is an indirect result of the globalisation of societal differentiation. In this way, the operative unity of the legal system is accomplished at the global level, too. But this unity for its part will also have to deal with a multitude of fundamental normative conflicts. Legal unity within global law is redirected away from normative consistency towards an operative 'inter-legality'.³⁴ What, however, are the unifying features of this inter-legality?

3 The co-evolutionary internal differentiation of global law

In order to answer this question, we must correct perceptions about the internal differentiation of law. Here, we are confronted with the first direct impact of social differentiation on law. For centuries, the internal differentiation of law had followed the political logic of nation states and manifested itself in the multitude of national legal orders, each with their own territorial jurisdiction. Even international law, which viewed itself as the contract law of nation states, did not depart from this model. The final break with such conceptions was only signalled in the last century with the rapidly accelerating expansion of international organisations and regulatory regimes, which, in sharp contrast to their genesis within international treaties, established themselves as autonomous legal orders. The national differentiation of law is now overlaid by sectoral fragmentation.³⁵ It is therefore not true that the appearance of global regimes entails the integration, harmonisation or at least convergence of legal orders, as lawyers in particular continue to claim; what it does instead is transform the internal differentiation of law. The impact of societal fragmentation on the law consists in the way in which a success-oriented political regulation of differently structured societal spheres requires the parcelling out of issue-specific policy arenas, which in their turn undergo an intense self-juridification.³⁶ The traditional differentiation in line with the political principle of territoriality into relatively autonomous national legal orders is thus overlaid by a sectoral differentiation principle: the differentiation of global law into transnational legal regimes, which define the external reach of their jurisdiction along issue-specific rather than territorial lines, and which claim a global validity for themselves.³⁷

4 Autonomous 'private' legal regimes

This nonetheless is still not sufficient to furnish us with a comprehensive understanding of legal fragmentation. Global regulatory regimes certainly give us a picture of the fundamental transformation of global law from a territorial to a sectoral differentiation, but only insofar as it is induced by those forms of legal regimes which derive from international agreements. No light whatsoever is shed on the equally rapid growth in the number of non-state 'private' legal regimes. It is these regimes that give birth to a 'global law without the state', which is primarily responsible for the multi-dimensionality of global legal pluralism.[38] A full understanding of this legal pluralism is only possible if one abandons the assumption that global law derives its validity exclusively from processes of state law-making and from state sanctions, whether these flow from domestic sources of law or from officially recognised international sources of law. This leads to a further impact of societal fragmentation on law, which requires us both to extend our concept of law to encompass norms lying beyond the legal sources of national and international law, and, at the same time, to reformulate our concept of the regime. As Berman's formulation indicates, one of the central and as yet unsolved future tasks of international law will be that of:

> recognizing and evaluating non-state jurisdictional assertions that bind sub-, supra-, or transnational communities. Such non-state jurisdictional assertions include a wide range of entities, from official transnational and international regulatory and adjudicative bodies, to non-governmental quasi-legal tribunals, to private standard-setting or regulatory organizations.[39]

'Transnational communities', or autonomous fragments of society, such as the globalised economy, science, technology, the mass media, medicine, education and transportation, are developing an enormous demand for regulatory norms which cannot, however, be satisfied by national or international institutions. Instead, such autonomous societal fragments satisfy their own demands through a direct recourse to law. Increasingly, global private regimes are creating their own substantive law.[40] They have recourse to their own sources of law, which lie outside the spheres of national law-making and international treaties.[41]

The most prominent contemporary private legal regimes are the *lex mercatoria* of the international economy and the *lex digitalis* of the Internet.[42] To these, we must, however, also add numerous private or private-public instances of regulation and conflict resolution, which are making autonomous law with a claim to global validity.[43] In their character as 'private' regimes, such institutions must be distinguished clearly from the understanding of regimes common in international relations theory, which defines them as 'principles, norms, rules, and decision-making procedures around which actors' expectations converge in a given area of international relations'.[44] This definition necessarily entails an extraordinary collapsing of both political and legal elements. The politically centred perspective that this reflects, however, is not adequate in regard to autonomous private regimes. Nor can it be replaced by an economically centred perspective, as often adopted within a theory of private ordering which achieves its goals with the aid of the simple equation of private law with the economy.[45] An alternative is offered by the notion of postnational formations that evolve in divergent social spheres:

> [T]hese formations are now organized around principles of finance, recruitment, coordination, communication, and reproduction that are fundamentally postnational and not just multinational or international.[46]

The *differentia specifica* separating postnational formations from the classical regime is the fact that so-called private regimes result from the self-juridification of highly diverse societal fragments. The notion of postnational formations allows a regime concept that has been attaching itself too closely to political processes to be generalised such that it might capture the manner in which apolitical autonomous social spheres of many different kinds produce conflicting legal norms.

5 *Centre and periphery*

This, however, also renders the breakdown of the classical legal hierarchy of norms inevitable. While it was still possible, albeit with great effort, to accommodate political regulatory regimes within a normative hierarchy of state-induced law, constituted in line with Kelsen's and Merkl's methodology[47] as a hierarchical legal structure made up of national legal acts, national legislation, national constitutional law and international law, with an international constitutional law as a conceivable next higher level, this hierarchy collapses with the emergence of autonomous non-state regimes.[48] And what will take the place of a hierarchy of legal norms? – The centre–periphery divide.[49] While courts occupy the centre of the law, the periphery of the diverse autonomous legal regimes is populated by political, economic, religious and other organisational or spontaneous, collective or individual subjects of law which, at the very boundaries of the law, establish themselves in close contact with autonomous social sectors. Once again, it is the fragmentation of global society that establishes the new fault lines – this time between the legal centre, the legal periphery and the social environments of law. In the zones of contact between the legal periphery and autonomous social sectors, an arena for a plurality of law-making mechanisms is established: standardised contracts, agreements of professional associations, routines of formal organisations, technical and scientific standardisation, normalisations of behaviour, and informal consensus between NGOs, the media and social public spheres. By virtue of their independent secondary norms, which differ fundamentally from those of national or international law, genuinely self-contained regimes can establish themselves, in line with the following technical definition:

> A regime is a union of rules laying down particular rights, duties and powers and rules having to do with the administration of such rules, including in particular rules for reacting to breaches. When such a regime seeks precedence in regard to the general law, we have a 'self-contained regime', a special case of *lex specialis*.[50]

Since such regimes are structurally coupled with the independent logic of the social sectors, they inevitably reproduce within the law the structural conflicts that exist between the various functional systems, albeit in a different form. Standard contracts within the *lex mercatoria* that reflect the economic rationality of global markets collide with WHO norms that derive from fundamental principles of the health system. The *lex constructionis*, the worldwide professional code of construction engineers, collides with international environmental law. The WTO Appellate Panel is confronted with cases encompassing collisions between human rights regimes, environment protection regimes and economic regimes.[51] International law dedicated to the maintenance of peace, more particularly its normative ban on the use of force, has a highly uneasy relationship with international human rights law.[52] Meanwhile, the same is true of international humanitarian law and environmental protection regimes,[53] general human rights law and environmental law,[54] etc. Indeed, these rationality conflicts are so vehement that they have fragmented even the very centre of global law, where courts and arbitration tribunals are located. In this core, they act as a barrier to the hierarchical integration of diverse regime tribunals, and prevent a conceptual-doctrinal consistency within global law.

If the courts of developed nation states were still able to guarantee their legal unity by means of creating hierarchical appeal processes and, in particular, constitutional courts, the courts, tribunals, arbitration panels and alternative dispute resolution bodies proliferating at the global level are so closely coupled with their own specialised regimes in the legal periphery, both in terms of organisation and self-perception, that they inevitably contribute to the fragmentation of global law. These new conflicts are a result of the polycontexturalisation of the function of law. They are created by the different internal environments of the legal system, which in turn depend on different paradigms of social ordering.[55]

6 Auto-constitutional regimes

The ultimate intensification of these legal collisions occurs as a result of the constitutional entrenchment of the regimes. The fragmentation of global society has ramifications for constitutional theory as well. At a global level, the locus of constitutionalisation is shifting away from the system of international relations to different social sectors, which are establishing civil constitutions of their own.[56] According to the concept of constitutional pluralism, it is appropriate to speak of the 'constitution' of collective bodies outside the confines of the nation state when the following preconditions have been fulfilled:

> (i) the development of an explicit constitutional discourse and constitutional self-consciousness; (ii) a claim to foundational legal authority, or sovereignty, whereas sovereignty is not viewed as absolute; (iii) the delineation of a sphere of competences; (iv) the existence of an organ internal to the polity with interpretative autonomy as regards the meaning and the scope of the competences; (v) the existence of an institutional structure to govern the polity; (vi) rights and obligations of citizenship, understood in a broad sense; (vii) specification of the terms of representation of the citizens in the polity.[57]

'Polity' in this context should not be understood in the narrow sense of institutionalised politics; it refers as well to non-political configurations of civil society, in the economy, in science, education, health, art or sports, in all those social areas where constitutionalising takes place.[58] Thus, self-contained regimes become entrenched as auto-constitutional regimes. As noted before, the defining feature of self-contained regimes is not simply that they create highly specialised primary norms (substantive rules in specific fields of law), but also that they produce, in contrast to the generalised secondary norms of international law, their own procedural norms on law-making, law recognition and legal sanctions.[59] Such reflexive norm production is not yet, however, constitutional norm production in the strict sense. It becomes constitutional only when it achieves a position that is exactly parallel to that of political constitutions, which must be understood not simply as higher legal norms given positive legal form, but as the structural coupling of the reflexive mechanisms of law with those of politics.[60] What distinguishes auto-constitutional regimes is the fact that they link legal reflexive processes with reflexive processes of other societal spheres.[61] Reflexive in this context means the application of specific processes to themselves, the 'norming' of norms, the application of political principles to the political process itself, epistemology as theorising theories, etc. Auto-constitutional regimes are defined by their duplication of reflexivity. Secondary rule-making in law is combined with the definition of fundamental rationality principles in an autonomous social sphere. To make the distinction between such societal constitutions and simple regimes even clearer: regimes unite primary and secondary legal norms, and their primary rule-making is structurally coupled with the creation of substantive social norms in a specific social sector. Societal constitutions in addition establish a structural coupling between secondary rule-making in law and reflexive mechanisms in another social sector. A non-state, non-political, civil-society-led constitutionalisation thus occurs in as far as reflexive social processes, which determine social rationalities through their self-application, are juridified in such a way that they are linked with reflexive legal processes. Under these conditions it makes sense to speak of the existence of constitutional elements – in the strictest sense of the term – within economic regimes, within the academic system and within digital regimes of the Internet. In such diverse contexts we find typical elements of a constitution: provisions on the establishment and exercise of decision-making powers (organisational and procedural rules) on the one hand, the definition of individual freedoms and societal autonomies (fundamental rights) on the other.[62] Clearly, societal constitution making at the same time intensifies conflicts between legal regimes, since it reinforces the independence of the legal regime from other distinct legal regimes through reflexive mechanisms.

Only when these various conceptual changes are taken to their logical conclusion does one gain an adequate understanding of legal fragmentation, an understanding which differs starkly from the day-to-day perspective of lawyers who locate the genesis of legal fragmentation in the lack of a judicial hierarchy and characterise fragmentation as merely a matter of jurisdictional conflicts. To sum it up in a single formula: the fragmentation of law is the epiphenomenon of real-world constitutional conflicts which, mediated via autonomous legal regimes, have their ultimate origin in the rationality collisions institutionalised in global society.

III Selective networking of colliding regimes

Our interim result: Lasciate ogni speranza. Any aspiration to the organisational and doctrinal unity of law is likely to be a vain hope. This is because global society is a 'society without an apex or a centre'.[63] Following the decentring of politics, there is no authority in sight that would be in a position to undertake the coordination of societal fragments. The law especially is not able to fulfil this role, not even indirectly through the integration of its global fragments.

Following the collapse of legal hierarchies, the only realistic chance lies in the development of strictly heterarchical forms of law that limit themselves to creating loose relationships between the fragments of law. This is only possible by way of a selective process of networking that normatively strengthens already existing factual networks between the legal regimes: externally by the linkage of legal regimes with autonomous social sectors; and internally by the linkage of legal regimes with one another. Recent developments of network theory may be relevant for international law. This theory has identified the paradoxical logic of action in networks, the *unitas multiplex* of hierarchical configurations.[64] As 'highly improbable reproductive connections of heterogeneous elements',[65] networks are selectively operative counter-institutions to the differentiation of autonomous systems. Connecting different, autonomous logics of actions, they fulfil a coordinating role between autonomous functional systems,[66] between formal organisations[67] or, as in our case, between autonomous regimes. Three guiding principles for the decentralised networking of legal regimes may be identified in the abstract:

(1) Simple normative compatibility instead of hierarchical unity of law;
(2) Law-making through mutual irritation, observation and reflexivity of autonomous legal orders;
(3) Decentralised modes of coping with conflicts of laws as a legal method.[68]

If hierarchical thinking is abandoned, a normative concept of networks between legal regimes needs to be included within the law's self-description. Such a normative reorientation can build on various tentative efforts within legal practice and doctrine, some of which will be discussed below.

1 *From international conflicts to inter-regime conflicts*

Two questions are typically posed in this context. First, how should we act in the absence of legal hierarchy, that is, in the absence of collectively binding decisions, centralised competences and hierarchically ordered legal principles? In the abstract, the answer is: by strengthening mutual observation between network nodes.[69] The final binding decision is replaced by a sequence of decisions within a variety of observational positions in a network; a process in which network nodes mutually reconstruct, influence, limit, control and provoke one another, but which never leads to one final collective decision on substantive norms. In this context, transparency and mutual accessibility are the primary requirement; participation and deliberation are imbued with a new significance. The second question is how decisions are to be taken when transnational conflicts cannot be attributed to one national law in areas like copyright, cyberlaw, human rights and environmental law because there is no relationship that is most significant. Once again in the abstract, the answer is to stop attempting the most authentic possible reconstruction of national norms. Rather, the choice of national law must be superseded by an orientation to regimes that are transnational, but sectoral, and lead to different principles of conflicts law. Both reactions are highlighted in the example of copyright law.

First example: transnational copyright

Conflicts decisions within international copyright law have traditionally been taken in line with the territoriality principle. The definitive expression of this principle is found in the Berne Convention of 1886.[70] However, the Convention is no match for the cyber-revolution, for technical innovations in transmission media and for the transnationalisation of science and art. Even though there were contemporary attempts to do so, the Convention did not establish a harmonised copyright law, but instead focused on the mutual recognition of differing territorial systems. Article 5 of the Convention furnishes the primary norm:

> Authors shall enjoy, in respect of works for which they are protected under this Convention, in countries of the Union other than the country of origin, the rights which their respective laws do now or may hereafter grant to their nationals, as well as the rights specially granted by this Convention.[71]

Certainly, states have attempted to match the transnational law-making process by founding the World Intellectual Property Organization (WIPO), which has long administered almost all multinational agreements on intellectual property, by means of the Agreement on Trade Related Aspects of International Property Rights (TRIPS) concluded during the GATT Uruguay Round in April 1994,[72] through various cooperation efforts between the WTO and WIPO,[73] through the European Convention relating to questions on copyright law,[74] through 'WIPO Internet Treaties'[75] and by means of European measures,[76] as well as related law-making acts.[77] However, there is still no harmonised international copyright. Territorially bound and nationally divergent copyright guarantees remain determinative. International agreements simply mediate between different protection standards and establish reciprocal national entitlements to the implementation of minimum levels of protection. As Dinwoodie has indicated, the new situation means that the 'facade of copyright rules based upon territoriality needs to be stripped away, and a new approach constructed. Some uncertainty is an inevitable, but worthwhile, short-term cost.'[78]

What might this 'new approach' look like? Essentially, this entails an effort to avoid a race to the bottom, not by assuming that the full range of relevant norms is exclusively to be found within partial, national legal orders, but instead through a consideration of the possible spill-over effects within other territorial legal orders. It follows that further transnational law-making mechanisms, over and above national legal norms, are also included within the equation. In substance this would include reorienting traditional conflicts law away from conflicts between national legal orders, and refocusing it on conflicts between sectoral regimes, such as is the case in the context of collisions between ICANN and national courts, ICTY and ICJ, WTO and WHO, WTO and EAS.[79] As Dinwoodie and Berman have suggested, a shift from territoriality to functional regime affiliation would mean that the division of jurisdictional competences and the normative preconditions for substantive decisions could no longer be inferred from each local legal order.[80]

The question of jurisdiction would not be answered by mechanically subsuming the case under the rules of the forum coincidentally addressed; rather, it would be dependent on the characteristics of the functional regime. The particular jurisdiction would then no longer be dependent on the issue of whether some form of legal link to the national law of a forum might be established, but would rather be determined by the question of whether the forum addressed can be understood as a part of a sectoral legal order. Any 'mechanical counting of contacts with a geographically based sovereign entity'[81] would be dispensed with and replaced by the connecting rules of a regime jurisdiction.

In conflicts law, when it comes to determining the applicable substantive law via conflict rules, it is equally important to apply this logic of functional connection to each set of conflict rules. The problems that arise out of the judicial reconstruction of the other national legal order in cases of transnational legal questions can be overcome through a form of conflicts law that is not based on the determination of the one territorial law with the closest connection to the conflict, but seeks instead to identify the functional regime to which the legal issue in question belongs. One therefore needs to investigate the substantive rules within this regime and other regimes, and to cope with the plurality of substantive law-making by national, international and transnational regimes.

This results in the creation of new forms of conflict rules, whose determination of the applicable law would choose not between nations, but between functional regimes. In their character as conflict rules in the technical sense, however, they would still work with the classical methods of conflicts law, and as such would be required to decide between legal orders and to apportion the legal issue in question to one of the orders involved, be they nations or be they regimes. A far more dramatic step, however, is the reorientation from conflict rules to substantive rules. Traditional private international law knows such a substantive law approach in only very few exceptional cases, in which the transnational nature of the contested subject matter is so overwhelming that it is virtually impossible to apportion the legal issue in question to one or another legal order.[82]

In our case of inter-regime conflicts, however, the exception becomes the rule. Conflicts whose core content might be exclusively apportioned to one regime are, by contrast, exceptional. Only exceptionally can a conflict that has economic and ecological implications be said to have its one most significant relation to either the economy or the ecology; usually both relations are equally significant. Overarching regime conflicts that have relevant effects within both regimes are the rule. This leaves only one possible solution: developing substantive rules through the law of inter-regime conflicts itself. This, however, would take place in the absence of hierarchically superior decision-making bodies judging at a neutral distance from the legal orders involved. We face a paradoxical situation, where the legal decision-making authority within each regime, which is also a party to the legal conflict, must create substantive norms that claim validity for both regimes involved. Transnational substantive norms are created, within a kind of mixed-law approach, with an eye both to one's own and to the other legal regime, but also with an eye to third-party legal orders.[83] In a mirror of the methodology applied by international customary law, different law-making mechanisms are to be included in the determination of the applicable rule.[84] In any case, however, care must be taken to overcome the limitations imposed by political law-making and the related hierarchy established between national and international orders.[85] Instead, the goal would be a strange legal Esperanto of regimes within which national, international and transnational legal acts clamour for attention. The courts involved – national courts and transnational conflict resolution authorities – would be required to meet the challenges of creating transnational substantive norms out of this chaos, seeking appropriate legal norms for the individual case at hand beyond their territorial, organisational and institutional legal spheres and taking responsibility for combining these norms in order to develop a transnational body of law.

2 *From policy conflicts to rationality collisions*

As noted, the collisions arising in such cases cut right across traditional politics, which builds power and consensus to produce binding collective decisions.

Accordingly, the famous governmental interest approach developed within conflicts law, which has successfully overcome the formalistic view of mere norm conflicts through the attention it pays to the substantive policy conflicts existing between the states involved, is not helpful in the case of regime collisions.[86] As intimated above, the colliding units are only in part political-regulatory regimes that are constituted by international treaties and pursue explicit policies. They are to a large extent made up of autonomous private governance regimes – producing global law without the state – that have their roots in a variety of non-political sectors of world society. Thus, we are no longer confronted with social conflicts translated into institutionalised politics – with power conflicts, ideology debates and policy controversies – but instead with very specific forms of social conflict which, for their part, provoke the establishment of private governance regimes. It is only in some cases that these conflicts may invite a reaction from international politics in the form of issue-specific regulatory regimes. The result is a collision between private governance regimes on the one hand and political-regulatory regimes on the other. All the jurisdiction conflicts that ICJ presidents and international legal experts have warned us about, conflicts between ICANN and national judges, between the ICTY and the ICJ, between the WTO and WHO, between the ICJ and the International Maritime Court, between the *lex mercatoria* and human rights, between the *lex constructionis* and ecological concerns, differ fundamentally in form from mere policy conflicts. Consequently, it is simply not enough to reduce the conflicts law that must be developed to a matter of reconstructing the different policies and political interests that are found in conflict constellations and finding accommodations between them.[87] Instead, law must concern itself with the underlying social conflicts themselves.

This means primarily that law needs to understand the legal norm collisions of the regimes involved – that is, political regulatory bodies, or international organisations, or, indeed, affected states – as an expression of the fundamental conflicts between the organisational principles of social systems. Conflicts law then would have as its main objective the establishment of compatibility between colliding rationality principles of global sectors. Normative expectations are established within the global spheres of science, art, technology, economy, education and religion and are juridified within specific legal orders. Transnational law in the form of a specific functional regime is thus anything but a nation-state enterprise, even though transnational law-making is subject to massive political pressures. Regime expectations are only binding on partial segments of global society, and the substitution of functional regime affiliation for territorial differentiation is dependent on each decisional forum evolving a sufficiently refined understanding of its own regime logic. If we look again at transnational copyright law this would mean that the legal reformulation of collisions between

WIPO, WTO, EU and national laws must to this extent be redrawn. Transnational copyright law should concern itself with the underlying collisions between distinct rationalities, i.e. conflicts between the rationales of science, technology, art and the economy. In the final analysis, this involves establishing a measure of compatibility between them and an end to the practice of simply orienting law in line with the policies of organisations and states. This compatibilisation technique, which differs from policy analysis and interest weighing, is sketched below with reference to the example of patent protection for medicines.

Second example: patent protection for medicines

In 2001, the US requested the establishment of a WTO Panel to investigate the legal situation as regards patents within Brazil. Although Brazil had, under pressure from the US, overhauled its patents law in 1997,[88] it had nonetheless retained its potential competence to grant obligatory licences should the patent owner not be engaged in local production within Brazil. Beginning with Article 68, the Brazilian Patent Law[89] thus allows for domestic production of so-called generics,[90] that is, copies of patent-protected medicines; but limits this to cases where the population is threatened by an epidemic and the price of the medicine on the world market is too high. The law refers to 'abuse of economic power' ('praticar abuso de poder econômico') on the part of pharmaceutical concerns. Further, Articles 68 *et seq.* of the Brazilian Patent Law provide for domestic production of patented medicines should a foreign firm have been selling a drug within Brazil for longer than three years without having established a local production plant. 150,000 people have died of AIDS in Brazil since 1981. In 1997, the annual number of new infections stood at over 20,000, but could be reduced through preventative measures to less than 5,000. The annual cost to the Brazilian Government of treating AIDS-infected patients was around US$300 million.[91] The two components Efavirenz and Nelfinavir, patented by the US concern Merck and the Swiss company Roche, accounted for over a third of this sum. Since neither company was engaged in local production, the Brazilian Health Minister announced the domestic production of generic copies. The US Government considered Articles 68 *et seq.* of the Brazilian Patent Law to be potentially discriminatory in regard to US patent owners and accordingly requested the commencement of bilateral consultations in May 2000.[92] Once these had, in the opinion of the US, failed, the US requested commencement of panel proceedings on 9 January 2001.[93]

There are three possible ways of reading the conflict. The first would be to regard it as a conflict between Brazilian national law and the rights of the patent owners (in international law terms mediated by the US). Being in possession of rights – much in the manner of the 39 pharmaceutical concerns who, represented by the Pharmaceutical Manufacturers' Association of South Africa (PMASA), entered into judicial proceedings in the light of a similar constellation within South Africa[94] – they attempted to protect their property rights against Brazilian assault. This perspective would thus require us to determine the content of, and limits to, international patent protection. This effort is quickly confronted with the provision of Article 30 of TRIPS:

> Members may provide limited exceptions to the exclusive rights conferred by a patent, provided that such exceptions do not unreasonably conflict with a normal exploitation of the patent and do not unreasonably prejudice the legitimate interests of the patent owner, taking account of the legitimate interests of third parties.[95]

Moreover, Article 31 of TRIPS allows its members to use a patented material, even without a necessary authorisation from the patent owner, if:

> prior to such use, the proposed user has made efforts to obtain authorization from the right holder on reasonable commercial terms and conditions and that such efforts have not been successful within a reasonable period of time. This requirement may be waived by a Member in the case of a national emergency or other circumstances of extreme urgency or in cases of public non-commercial use. In situations of national emergency or other circumstances of extreme urgency, the right holder shall, nevertheless, be notified as soon as reasonably practicable. In the case of public non-commercial use, where the government or contractor, without making a patent search, knows or has demonstrable grounds to know that a valid patent is or will be used by or for the government, the right holder shall be informed promptly.[96]

The question would accordingly be one of whether Articles 68 *et seq.* of the Brazilian Patent Law infringe the TRIPS Agreement, even though they make explicit reference to the notion of an 'abuse of economic power' and the conflict erupted as the Brazilian regime attempted to give effect to its national programme to combat AIDS. However, the parties concerned are united in their critique of the porous nature of TRIPS norms: on the one hand, because TRIPS does not give rise to a sufficient level of protection for intellectual property and does not pay adequate regard to the economic interests of patent holders;[97] and on the other, because it does not pay sufficient attention to the economic interests of the countries of the southern hemisphere.[98] In this regard, patent laws share the same fate as copyright laws: in the case of both legal institutions, international law-making is 'out of touch with modern times and the changing norms of an innovative community'.[99] How the Panel itself might have decided remains a hypothetical question, since the US and Brazil gave the Chairman of the DSB notice, in line with DSU Article 6, of their having reached a mutually satisfactory solution to the problem on 5 July 2001.[100] What had happened?

This relates to the second reading of the conflict: the Brazilian conflict was a conflict between the WTO and WHO; an institutional conflict between the policies of two international organisations,[101] the WTO on the one hand, and, on the other, the WHO belonging to the UN family.[102] This would not be an unusual constellation and a brief review of the Alston-Petersmann controversy[103] will provide ample information about both perspectives, which entrust either only the UN (Alston) or principally the WTO (Petersmann) with the task of finding an adequate balance between colliding freedoms and rights.[104] The really unusual facet of the case was thus not the regime collision as such, but rather the fact that the US did not wait for it to unfold. There could not have been a more inopportune moment for WTO proceedings on patent protection for AIDS medicines in view of the scheduling of a UN Special General Assembly on the combating of HIV/AIDS for a few months later.[105] Special General Assemblies are not everyday occurrences. Instead, they are concerned with portentous questions, are prepared over many years and encompass both civil society and state actors. The machinery of civil society mobilisation went into immediate action, leading to outrage among AIDS sufferers everywhere against the protectionist orientation of US economic policy. Brazil was not slow in taking advantage of this surge of feeling and was able to achieve the acceptance of a Resolution at the next sitting of the UN Commission on Human Rights.[106] The Resolution, adopted by 52 votes to none, with one abstention (that is, against the will of the US), sets out, among other things, a desire:

> (a) to facilitate, wherever possible, access in other countries to essential preventive, curative or palliative pharmaceuticals or medical technologies used to treat pandemics such as HIV/AIDS or the most common opportunistic infections that accompany them, as well as to extend the necessary cooperation wherever possible, especially in times of emergency;
>
> (b) to ensure that their actions as members of international organizations take due account of the right of everyone to the enjoyment of the highest attainable standard of physical and mental health ...[107]

The Resolution was explicitly directed towards the growing conflict and was a diplomatic barometer of the fact that the pressure on the US Government was growing ever stronger. It is thus not surprising that, punctually on the first day of the UN General Assembly Special Session on AIDS, the US Government joined with Brazil to lodge its written intention to set the conflict on patent protection for AIDS cocktails aside.[108]

The third reading of the conflict is neither rights related, nor institutional, but instead conceives of the collision as a conflict between competing rationalities. The political compromise between Brazil and the US, which forced patent owners to offer the states concerned affordable licences,[109] was complemented by the so-called Doha Declaration of the WTO:

> We stress the importance we attach to implementation and interpretation of the Agreement on Trade-Related Aspects of Intellectual Property Rights (TRIPS Agreement) in a manner supportive of public health, by promoting both access to existing medicines and research and development into new medicines and, in this connection, are adopting a separate declaration.[110]

This 'separate declaration', the 'Declaration on the TRIPS Agreement and Public Health',[111] provides an incisive reconstruction of the problem and refers to a conflict that is deeper than a simple policy conflict between two international organisations. The question of patent protection for AIDS medicines furnishes the arena in which the fundamental principles of two global operational spheres, economy and health, collide. Each conflict constellation can be traced back to this collision: *Brazil v. US, WTO v. WHO, US v. UN, Pharmaceutical Manufacturers' Association of South Africa v. South Africa*. Each appearance of the constellation before each legal forum was concerned with reaching agreement between the conflicting demands of each system (patent protection versus effective health protection). Any potential WTO panel decision of the DSB would be confronted with three issues:

- The question is not one of deciding between the reach of opposing territories or between different institutional solutions to the patents problem. Instead, the argument sketched in the first case must be taken to its full conclusion, such that the substantive norms of a global patent law are evolved in a quasi-judicial process.
- It is not sufficient merely to refer to the contemporary policies pursued by international organisations, such as the WTO or WHO. Instead, the conflict-resolving legal authority must, in the final analysis, revisit underlying rationality conflicts and attempt their compatibilisation.

- Since no central authority for deciding the conflict exists, the problem can only be solved from the decentralised perspective of one of the conflicting regimes; in this case, the WTO. However, the competing rationality principles – in this case, that of global health protection – must be introduced as a logical limitation within the specific institutional context – in this case the economic context of WTO law.

In addition to reserving a national competence to define emergency situations,[112] the Doha Declaration establishes a 2016 deadline for less developed countries: their rules will take precedence only up until that date. At the same time, the General Council has now established a detailed regulatory framework for the issuing of compulsory licences.[113] In our reading, the economically oriented WTO regime has created an internal limitation on its own logic through the reformulation of a principle of health protection. This compatibilisation technique allows it to build responsive external linkages within its own perspective of economic rationality. Such a re-entry of conflicting law within one's own legal system allows for the translation of rationality collisions into an aspect of the question of law that falls to be decided by the court or tribunal; it avoids the unfortunate situation in which external cognition can only take place on the collapse of a regime.[114] Regarding the example of the WTO, this means that the re-entry of environmental rationalities within the self-organisation of this regime should be promoted; that is, a re-entry extending far beyond the very narrow terms of Articles 7, 11 and 3.2 DSU.[115] The reconstruction of non-WTO law within the WTO legal system would then not be an external imposition of limits, but the internal achievement of the WTO regime itself, and would reflect a process of mutual constitution.[116]

The literature is full of controversies on the status and role of general international law within the WTO regime. Such controversies, however, tend to derive from the concepts of direct/indirect effect,[117] prevailing/overriding application[118] and the international conformity of legal interpretation,[119] which have developed within the conflicts between international and national law, and between EU and national law. It is thus not only too narrow, especially with regard to its fixation on international public law,[120] but also chooses the wrong starting point for analysis through its over-emphasis on colliding state-derived normative commands.[121] Rather, the re-entry of non-WTO law within WTO law means the identification of colliding social realities, the re-entry of alien sectoral regime orders within a legal regime, the reformulation of the conflict within the legal issue to be decided and the internal compatibilisation of legally reformulated systemic rationalities. In the concrete case, this entails that health protection measures must in certain cases be themselves protected from economic pressures. Respect for this would thus suggest an extensive interpretation of the exceptional provisions of Article 31 of TRIPS in situations in which health measures are necessary 'which promote broad access to safe, efficient and affordable preventive, curative or palliative pharmaceuticals and medical technologies'.[122] While patent protection rules may answer economic rationality demands, they nonetheless contradict demands of the health system. Resolution 2001/33 of the UN Human Rights Commission foresees such a conflict solution.[123] Measures such as the Brazilian AIDS programme must thus be exempted from economic logic to the degree that the normal standard for patent protection is not to be applied in such cases. The critical conflicts issue would thus be one of identifying collisions between the norms of economic rationality and norms formed within the context of the protection of health.[124] In this concrete case, the matter is one of the evolution of abstract and general incompatibility norms within the context of the economic and health sectors and the priming of WTO as well as UN law (seen as part of a transnational patents law) to deal with destructive conflicts between incompatible rationalities.

3 *From a common* jus cogens *to regime-specific* ordres publics

If one takes the realistic stance that there is no final hierarchical decision-making authority within regime conflicts law, the question remains whether or not common legal principles can be assumed within the heterarchical order of diverse autonomous regimes. The existence of *ius cogens* within transnational law is not merely a problem for political regulatory regimes established by international treaties; it poses particularly acute problems for autonomous private governance regimes, for the *lex mercatoria* or the *lex digitalis*, for example. Here we face a seemingly insoluble dilemma: if the private governance regimes originate in contractual relations between private global players, where is the legal source of a mandatory law which would need to be created and enforced against the wishes of the parties to the contract? Accordingly, the mere existence of mandatory law within private governance regimes has been doubted. It is important here to avoid two extreme positions. On the one hand, binding norms are not like some kind of natural law possessing a priori validity; accordingly, mandatory law cannot simply be created following the logic of a higher *ius cogens* in the sense of Article 53 of the Vienna Convention,[125] or of the UN constitution in its guise as a global constitution that reaches into all societal regime spheres by means of Article 103 of the UN Charter.[126] On the other hand, however, an interpretation founded in the potential 'hijacking' and 'Hayeking'[127] of human and environmental rights by a regime with a highly particularist agenda, which has haunted the debate on the constitutionalisation of the WTO, is also inadequate. Neither interpretation has fully plumbed the depths of the problem of *jus cogens* posed by a heterarchical order. A hierarchical elevation and subordination of legal orders is equally anathema to a polycentric global law as is the assumption that an emergent functional regime is an autarkical system operating within a global societal vacuum. Beyond the alternative of either central coordination or the autarky of closed regimes, we are left with the option of a network logic. It is characterised by combining two conflicting demands with one another. On the one hand, one finds in networks the autonomous and decentralised reflections of network nodes which seek compatibility with their human and natural environments. On the other, linkages exist in networks between these decentralised reflections, in the sense that nodes observe each other closely. Thus, in spite of their autonomy, regimes can build on the assumption of common reference points, which is of course nothing more than an operative fiction. Building on this fiction, each of them can subordinate itself to a, necessarily abstract, seemingly common philosophical horizon, to which it orients its own rule-making. This horizon of mandatory rules possesses no common founding text; a common grammar has not been found. The only clear fact is that Article 53 of the Vienna Convention cannot give clear expression to the *unitas multiplex* of autonomous regimes since its provisions and legal consequences are subject to debate even within the international law regime itself.[128] Yet more significantly, Article 53 has its place within international public law and international politics; a semantic that would be without function in other societal contexts in which formulations such as 'international *ordre public*',[129] '*mandatory rules*',[130] '*ordre public trans-national*'[131] are in circulation.

These concepts represent the legal expression of the common good in highly diverse social contexts. Clearly, while a global *jus non dispositivum* has no common written philosophical horizon, the unity of the diverse concepts derives from the paradoxical situation that the linguistic diversity of the global Esperanto of mandatory law does make subordination to the fiction of a common validity core possible, in a process that the French philosophers Deleuze and Guattari might have characterised as being 'rhizomorphic' in nature.[132] Nurturing different common good formulas within different regime contexts certainly creates a problem. But the problem is not one of harmonising these reference points, but instead one of prompting regimes to engage in internal self-organisation so as to establish their own grammars for their version of a global *jus non dispositivum*. A large variety of processes assume the prompting role: the scandalising of sectors of public opinion,[133] pressure from international politics[134] and co-operation between autonomous regimes.[135]

Third example: lex constructionis

The *lex constructionis* and its standard contracts on transnational construction projects are dominated by a small number of well-organised private associations: the International Federation of Consulting Engineers (FIDIC), the International European Construction Federation (FIEC), the British Institution of Civil Engineers (ICE), the Engineering Advancement Association of Japan (ENAA) and the American Institute of Architects (AIA). In addition, the World Bank, UNCITRAL, UNIDROIT and certain international law firms also contribute to developing legal norms of the *lex constructionis*. Article 4.18 of the FIDC Model Contract, which is fundamentally the same as the Construction, Installation and EPC Model Contracts,[136] furnishes us with the typical formula deployed – where the issue is considered at all[137] – to give recognition to environmental issues in private construction contracts:

> The Contractor shall take all reasonable steps to protect the environment (both on and off the Site) and to limit damage and nuisance to people and property resulting from pollution, noise and other results of his operations. The Contractor shall ensure that emissions, surface discharges and effluent from the Contractor's activities shall not exceed the values indicated in the Employer's Requirements, and shall not exceed the values prescribed by applicable Laws.[138]

A fleeting glance suffices to show that the contractual agreement aims to externalise the environmental costs of the entire project and that contractual duties relate only to the concrete measures that the contractual parties should take to 'limit' their own emissions. In general, such contracts do not concretise human rights or general duties to the environment. Oren Perez notes:

> The response of the lex constructionis to the construction-environmental dilemma is, then, based primarily on a strategy of deference, which seeks to externalize the responsibility for regulating the environmental aspects of the construction activity to the 'extra-contractual' realm of the law of the host-state. This is achieved through the employment of 'compliance' provisions, which appear in most of the standard forms. … The notion of 'efficient risk-allocation' further illustrates how this logic of externalization operates. In order to maximize its economic value

the contract is expected to provide the parties with an efficient risk-allocation scheme. This should be achieved by allocating particular risks to the party best able to manage them.[139]

Among the large number of legal questions that this example gives rise to, the following concentrates upon global mandatory law. Although the notable case of Furundčija[140] saw the ICTY extend the jurisdictional reach of the *jus cogens* principle to the degree that national law contradicting Article 53 Vienna Convention would be invalid – a conclusion that would also seem to suggest itself in relation to the UN[141] and to the WTO[142] – the operational capacities of the principle would surely be overtaxed were it also to be afforded direct effect within private regimes such as the *lex mercatoria*, *lex digitalis* or *lex sportiva*. By the same token, the potential for the substantive extension within international law-making processes of the legal rights protected by Article 53 of the Vienna Convention is also limited. Only segments of the International Bill of Rights have been afforded the international legal quality of *jus cogens*, while a further clarification of Article 30 of the Vienna Convention within inter-regime processes is hardly to be counted on.[143] The establishment of hierarchies within global law is clearly regime-dependent.[144] As the ICTY has made clear for itself and thus also for others:

> In International Law, every tribunal is a self-contained system (unless otherwise provided).[145]

Rather than engage in a wholly unrealistic attempt to create a hierarchy within the fragmentation of global law, efforts should thus be focused instead on intra-regime responsiveness to the immediate human and natural environment; that is, functional regimes must each evolve their own *jus non dispositivum*. In this respect, we should not forget that the UN regime has, to date, had much difficulty establishing its own *jus cogens*.[146] Legal control of Security Council resolutions by the ICJ, the 'principle judicial organ' of the UN, is very limited.[147] The dysfunctional separation of powers within the UN disadvantages UN self-organisation, forms a barrier to the development of an autonomous *jus non dispositivum* and in part also contributes to a double is-ought fallacy, whereby the room for manoeuvre afforded the Security Council under Article 39 of the UN Charter is such that the way it is controlled appears to be 'through public opinion, but not through law'.[148] This position, however, both underestimates the legal dimension of scandalising public opinion,[149] and does not recognise the mutual dependency between the regime and its environment; an environment whose normative expectations have an impact 'if the special regime fails to function properly'.[150] Absent both an autonomous *jus non dispositivum* and a functioning, regime-internal, structural link between law and politics, analysis must proceed from an assumption of the indirect effect of the *jus cogens* of Article 53 of the Vienna Convention within the UN regime.[151] In the words of Justice Lauterpacht:

> The concept of *jus cogens* operates as a concept superior to both customary international law and treaty. The relief which Article 103 of the Charter may give the Security Council in case of conflict between one of its decisions and an operative treaty obligation cannot – as a matter of simple hierarchy of norms – extend to a conflict between a Security Council resolution and *jus cogens*. Indeed, one only has to state the opposite proposition thus – that a Security Council resolution may even require participation in genocide – for its unacceptability to be apparent.[152]

By contrast, economic, scientific, technological, health-based and religious regimes each need to establish their own reference points for mandatory law. This can also be observed in the *lex mercatoria* and the *lex constructionis*. Quite independently of the choice of laws made by individual contracts within the *lex constructionis*, and notwithstanding all 'national interests' – which representatives of the so-called special connection theory would like to see taken into account even outside the contractual structure[153] – a *lex-mercatoria*-specific *erga omnes* law that no longer bases itself within national public policy is emerging. We could come to the conclusion that arbitration tribunals must move beyond concrete contractual terms in order to take environmental consequences and human rights complications into account as part of a specific mandatory law;[154] equally, courts of arbitration must apply their own *ordre public*:

> It is generally recognized that the arbitrator can, in the name of 'truly international public policy', refuse to give effect to certain agreements of the parties. Likewise, if the object of a law is to guarantee the respect of principles the arbitral tribunal considers as forming a part of transnational or 'truly' international public policy, it must find that such law prevails over the will of the parties. Because of the transnational character of these norms, a connection between the state that enacted the mandatory rules and the dispute is not necessary.[155]

At the same time, if arbitration courts fail to take into account *jus cogens*, it may well be that national courts will not enforce their decision.[156] Even more significant than these external pressures is the regime-internal juridification of the duty of courts of arbitration to take binding laws into account.[157] The potential of this liability of arbiters for the generation of a *jus non dispositivum* has barely been explored within the *lex mercatoria*. Accordingly, it is very possible to imagine a situation where a failure by courts of arbitration to consider the norms of the *jus non dispositivum* could result in third parties raising liability claims, modelled on national prototypes, against arbiters.

4 From stare decisis *to default deference*

By contrast to the binding nature of the judgments of superior courts, it belongs to the logic of networks that autonomous regimes enter into relations of mutual observation.[158] Legal certainty within this polycentric legal system cannot be furnished by a hierarchically superior decision-making authority placed at the centre of the law. Rather, what can be realistically expected is uncertainty absorption in a process of iterative connection of legal decision to legal decision that recalls the strict precedent tradition, but also departs from it in various significant ways.

Fourth example: desaparición

Around 30,000 people disappeared (the *desaparición*) during the Argentinian military dictatorship of the years 1976–83. During its transition back to democracy, Argentina initially applied amnesty laws exempting wrongdoers from prosecution. In 2003, however, the Argentinian National Congress declared both amnesty laws passed by the Alfonsin regime to be invalid.[159]

What is of interest here is the manner in which the global legal system has dealt with the Argentinian *desaparición*. The case raises important issues, involving a whole host of non-territorial courts, although many would prefer to see these Gordian knots severed by the sword of politics.[160] The legal challenges can be distilled down to a question of what crimes can be judged under what jurisdictional rules in what systems and under what treatment of the immunity question. The entire discussion has been dealt with elsewhere.[161] The case of the disappeared, however, is also an instructive example of how contingent issues can be transformed into international criminal law under conditions of iteration and the absorption of uncertainty.

The first case that explicitly dedicated itself to the crime of disappearance[162] was the decision of the United States District Court in the case of *Forti v.*

Suarez-Mason, 672 F. Suppl. 1531 (N.D. Cal. 1987). The court first ascertained that no precedent existed for its decision:

> However, plaintiffs do not cite the Court to any case finding that causing the disappearance of an individual constitutes a violation of the law of nations. ... Unfortunately, the Court cannot say, on the basis of the evidence submitted, that there yet exists the requisite degree of international consensus which demonstrates a customary international norm.[163]

Nonetheless, the plaintiffs were not satisfied with this judgment and a few months later the court dared to give a fresh judgment on the basis of academic literature and political resolutions alone:

> The legal scholars whose declarations have been submitted in connection with this Motion are in agreement that there is universal consensus as to the two essential elements of a claim for 'disappearance'... Plaintiffs cite numerous international legal authorities which support the assertion that 'disappearance' is a universal wrong under the law of nations.[164]

Subsequently, scores of judgments were handed down on the crime of disappearance. For a variety of reasons, this issue was dealt with by very different regimes: national courts, the American Human Rights Court, the European Court for Human Rights and the Human Rights Commission for Bosnia-Herzegovina.[165] The case proved remarkable not only for the emergence of a transnational criminal norm on the 'disappeared' – indeed, even a *jus cogens* norm in the sense of Article 53 of the Vienna Convention – and the reception of these decisions by Argentinian judges,[166] but also for the manner in which judges from very different regimes entered into a relation of mutual observation with other regimes. The networking in this process is not always explicit.[167] Rather, it consists in an informal reference to a given process of transformation, building on the individual aspects dealt with in past cases. Thus, for example, the ICJ decision in the arrest warrant case – a case which saw the ICJ rely on national immunity rules for state functionaries which distinguish between crimes committed in a private or an official function – can only be understood against the backdrop of Argentinian cases and the *Pinochet* case; it can only be explained where the observer is aware that this differentiation is owing to a normative concept that refuses to afford human rights crimes an official state character and thus classifies them as private acts. The House of Lords in the *Pinochet* case, in particular, transformed the question of 'a *ratione materiae* exception to immunity for persons who, *ratione personae*, are to be regarded as immune' into one of a public/private distinction.[168] It was this distinction which the ICJ employed,[169] even though in the concrete case before them – the case of an official functionary carrying out his official functions – they held the arrest warrant to be contrary to international law.

Were the fragmentation discussion within international law to concentrate on potential hierarchical solutions, it would tend to miss the point. Instead, it needs to re-focus on the issue of precedent. Is there a middle way here between the Scylla of a legally binding effect achieved through strict precedent and the Charybdis of a concept of precedent founded in simple persuasion or even the harmonisation of methodological approaches? In fact, default deference presents one possibility; that is, the rebuttable presumption that the decisions of international regime courts do have the character of precedent for one another.[170] There is a connection to the issue of uncertainty absorption within networks and formal organisations;[171] that is, the acceptance of previous decisions, with a continuing potential for variation. The ICTY made it clear in the *Čelebici* judgment that

> the operation of the desiderata of consistency, stability, and predictability does not stop at the frontiers of the Tribunal. The Appeals Chamber cannot behave as if the general state of the law in the international community whose interests it serves is none of its concern.[172]

By the same token, however, the ICTY itself was correct, in the case of *Tadic*,[173] to expand the ICJ 'effective control test'[174] through a new distinction and to declare the ICJ criteria to be non-applicable to the concrete case, since it concerned organised military groups rather than unorganised individuals, as had been the case in the *Nicaragua* judgment. Equally, the judgment cannot be termed provocative in terms of its treatment of the legal question. The ICTY surely had good reason,[175] within the concrete context of individual responsibility in the realm of humanitarian law, to afford a more extensive interpretation to a restrictive reading of causality that is wholly appropriate for exceptions given for the use of force within the context of Article 51 of the UN Charter.[176] The prominence that a fragmentation discussion affords differences between the ICJ and ICTY is thus unjustifiable in substantive terms,[177] and, indeed, seems to be more concerned with the fact that while in its *Tadic* decision, the ICTY stated 'with respect' that, in view of the concrete case matter, it 'does not hold the *Nicaragua* test to be persuasive',[178] the *Čelebici* decision saw it insist upon its status as an 'autonomous judicial body' without a 'hierarchical relationship' to the ICJ.[179] This, however, is neither a provocation, nor a judicial revolution, but rather a form of judicial networking at the global level that is suited to complexity.

IV From legal unity to normative regime compatibility

What impact does all this have on the self-perception of law in view of the fragmentation of transnational law into autonomous regimes? The immediate consequence is that high expectations of our ability to deal adequately with legal fragmentation must be curbed since its origins lie not in law, but within its social contexts. Rather than secure the unity of international law, future endeavours need to be restricted to the achievement of weak compatibility between the fragments. In the place of an illusory integration of a differentiated global society, law can only, at the very best, offer a kind of damage limitation. Legal instruments cannot overcome contradictions between different social rationalities. The best law can offer – to use a variation on an apt description of international law – is to act as a 'gentle civilizer of social systems'.[180] In the words of Ladeur, contradictions 'cannot be avoided, but a new form of self-observation and self-description of the legal system is in fact charged with the task of maintaining compatibility between different legal arenas and of making them permeable to each other'.[181] A realistic option is that legal 'formalisation' might be able to dampen the self-destructive tendencies apparent within rationality collisions. If all goes well, as our examples show, it might be possible to translate a – limited – portion of these rationality conflicts into the *quaestio iuris* and thus offer one among several fora for peaceful settlement. However, even then, law does not act as a superior coordinating instance; much would already have been achieved were it able to furnish forms of legal guarantees for autonomy in the face of totalising tendencies and domination by one system. In the context of societal fragmentation, law will be forced to limit itself to its classical role: that of providing compensation for mutually inflicted damage and of curbing harm to human and natural environments.

Notes

This chapter was previously published as 'Regime-collisions: the vain search for unity in the fragmentation of global law', *Michigan Journal of International Law*, 25:4 (2004), 999–1046.

1 Luhmann, *Soziologische Aufklärung 2*, p. 63.
2 Teubner, *Law as an Autopoietic System*, p. 100.

3 Abi-Saab, 'Fragmentation or unification', p. 923; for proposals of categorisation, see Buergenthal, 'Proliferation of international courts'; for documentation of collisions, see Oellers-Frahm, 'Multiplication of international courts'; Alford, 'Federal courts'.
4 The Project on International Courts and Tribunals (PICT) was founded in 1997 by the Center on International Cooperation (CIC), New York University and the Foundation for International Environmental Law and Development. From 2002 onwards, PICT has been a common project of the CIC and of the Centre for International Courts and Tribunals, University College London. See PICT, www.pict-pcti.org.
5 PICT has gathered good documentation on legal frameworks and explicatory literature. For Dinah Shelton's instructive account of the area of human rights, see Shelton, *Remedies*, pp. 137–82; regarding 'hybrid courts', see Dickinson, 'Promise of hybrid courts'.
6 Along these lines, see the early critique by Prosper Weil. See Weil, 'Towards relative normativity', p. 440.
7 Among the *loci classici* on the question of state responsibility are *Prosecutor v. Duško Tadić*, Judgements International Tribunal for the Prosecution of Persons Responsible for Serious Violations of International Humanitarian Law Committed in the Territory of the Former Yugoslavia since 1991, Case No. IT-94-1-A, at paras 115–45 (15 July 1999) (hereinafter *Prosecutor v. Tadić*); Military and Paramilitary Activities (*Nicar. v. US*), 1986 ICJ 14, 62, paras 109–16 (27 June 1986) (hereinafter *Nicar. v. US*).
8 See Report of the Study Group on Fragmentation of International Law: Difficulties Arising from the Diversification and Expansion of International Law, UN General Assembly Official Records, 55th Sess., Suppl. No. 10, at 237, UN Doc. A/CN.4/L.628 (2002); see also ILC Reports, UN General Assembly Official Records, UN Doc. A/CN.4/L.644 (2003); Study on the Function and Scope of the *lex specialis* Rule and the Question of 'Self-Contained Regimes', Preliminary Report by Martti Koskenniemi, Chairman of the Study Group of the ILC, at ILC(LVI)/SG/FIL/CRD.1 (4 May 2004) (hereinafter Koskenniemi Preliminary Report); see further Martti Koskenniemi, Outline of the Chairman of the ILC Study Group on Fragmentation of International Law: The Function and Scope of the Lex Specialis Rule and the Question of 'Self-Contained Regimes', available at www.un.org/law/ilc/sessions/55/fragmentation_outline.pdf, at 2–10 (2003) (hereinafter Koskenniemi Outline).
9 Report of Stephen M. Schwebel, President of the International Court of Justice, UN General Assembly Official Records, 54th Sess., Agenda Item 13, at 3–4, UN Doc. A/54/PV.39 (1999) (hereinafter Schwebel); see also Report of Gilbert Guillaume, President of the International Court of Justice, UN General Assembly Official Records, 55th Sess., Agenda Item 13, at 7, UN Doc. A/55/PV.42 (2000) (hereinafter Guillaume Report), which warns of an 'unwanted confusion' and a 'risk of conflicting judgments', and accordingly supports Schwebel's suggestion that the ICJ should be given the jurisdiction to provide advisory opinions at the request of international tribunals. See also Guillaume, 'Future of international judicial institutions', pp. 861–2.
10 See Charney, 'Impact on the international legal system'; Romano, 'Proliferation of international judicial bodies'; Petersmann, 'Constitutionalism and international adjudication'; Dupuy, 'Danger of fragmentation'; Treves, 'Conflicts'; see also Charney, 'Is international law threatened'; Koskenniemi and Leino, 'Fragmentation of international law?'; Shahabuddeen, 'Consistency in Holdings'; Abi-Saab, 'Fragmentation or unification', p. 923.
11 See Gerhard Hafner, *Risks Ensuing from Fragmentation of International Law*, UN General Assembly Official Records, 55th Sess., Suppl. No. 10, at 326, UN Doc.

A/55/10 (2002). (Hafner's study provided the impetus for the creation of the ILC Study Group.)
12 Oellers-Frahm, 'Multiplication of international courts', p. 67.
13 Schwebel (see n. 9 above), at 4; Guillaume Report (see n. 9 above); Hafner (see n. 11 above), at 335; Dupuy, 'Danger of fragmentation', p. 801.
14 Hafner (see n. 11 above), at 335–9.
15 Ibid., at 399.
16 Koskenniemi and Leino, 'Fragmentation of international law?'
17 This is so even though Martti Koskenniemi makes a subtle attempt to lessen postmodern anxieties (ibid.), and has by now taken the opportunity during his leadership of the ILC Study Group to change its self-description from 'Risks ensuing from fragmentation of international law' to the more soothing formula 'Fragmentation of international law: difficulties arising from the diversification and expansion of international law': UN General Assembly Official Records, ILC, 55th Sess., at 1, UN Doc. A/CN.4/L.644 (2003). However, this view underestimates the problematic issue of consistency, resulting from the fragmentation phenomenon, for legitimacy, efficiency and credibility of law; the deficiencies of postmodern theories are similar, even if they describe the legal fragmentation in its social context. See, e.g., Santos, 'Law: a map of misreading'; Fitzpatrick, 'Law and societies'.
18 Berman, 'Globalization of jurisdiction', p. 371, provides a similar critique of legal and political (and economic) reductionism, but then falls into the trap of cultural reductionism himself.
19 On global culture, see Meyer *et al.*, 'World society and the nation-state'. On discourse analysis, see Schütz, 'Twilight of the Global Polis'. On global legal pluralism, see Santos, *Toward a New Legal Common Sense*, passim. On global civil society, see Held, *Democracy and the Global Order*, passim; Günther and Randeria, *Recht, Kultur und Gesellschaft*, pp. 63 ff.; Brunkhorst, 'Ist die Solidarität der Bürgergesellschaft globalisierbar?' On global society, see Luhmann, 'Staat des politischen Systems', p. 373; Stichweh, *Weltgesellschaft*, passim; Willke, *Heterotopia*, p. 13. See also the contributions in Albert and Hilkermeier (eds), *Observing International Relations*.
20 See Chapter 9 in this volume; Fischer-Lescano, *Globalverfassung*, pp. 41 ff.
21 For Dahrendorf's argument, see Dahrendorf, 'Anmerkungen zur Globalisierung', p. 41.
22 Held, *Democracy and the Global Order*, p. 62.
23 Luhmann, *Theory of Society*, vol. 1, p. 76.
24 Marx, *Capital*.
25 Most impressively by Polanyi, *Great Transformation*, pp. 138 ff.
26 Weber, *Gesammelte Aufsätze zur Wissenschaftslehre*, pp. 586–97; on Weber, see also Schluchter, *Religion und Lebensführung*, vol. 1, pp. 299–302.
27 See Lyotard, *The Differend*.
28 Literature which is influential in this area includes: Beck, *Risk Society*; Beck, 'Umweltpolitik'.
29 Luhmann, *Theory of Society*, vol. 2, pp. 309 ff.
30 Teubner, 'Altera pars'.
31 See, e.g., Böckenförde, *Staat, Nation, Europa*, p. 123; Weil, 'Towards relative normativity', p. 440.
32 Luhmann, *Wirtschaft der Gesellschaft*, p. 344.
33 For systems-theoretical concepts of a global legal system, see Luhmann, *Law as a Social System*, pp. 479 ff.; Chapter 9 in this volume; Fischer-Lescano,

Globalverfassung, pp. 62 ff.; Calliess, 'Reflexive transnational law'; D'Amato, 'International Law as an Autopoietic System'.
34 See Santos, 'State transformation, legal pluralism and community justice'; Amstutz, 'Contract collisions'.
35 For discussions of regimes, see Hasenclever *et al.*, *Theories of International Regimes*; Hasenclever *et al.*, 'Integrating theories of international regimes'; Kratochwil and Ruggie, 'International organization', p. 759; Mitchell, 'Sources of transparency'; Nadelman, 'Global prohibition regimes'; Young, 'International regimes'.
36 On the juridification of international organisations, see Abbott *et al.*, 'Concept of legalization'.
37 With specific reference to ICANN as a 'global regulatory regime', see Lehmkuhl, 'Resolution of domain names vs. trademark conflicts', p. 71; Mueller, *Ruling the Root*, pp. 211–26; Walter, 'Constitutionalizing (inter)national governance', p. 186. On different aspects of the Internet regime, see Perritt, 'Economic and other barriers to electronic commerce'; Post, 'Anarchy, state, and the Internet'; Post, 'The "unsettled paradox"'; Post, 'Of black holes'.
38 Teubner (ed.), *Global Law without a State*. On the discussion of legal pluralism, see Berman, 'Globalization of jurisdiction', pp. 325–71; Merry, 'Legal pluralism'; Weisbrod, *Emblems of Pluralism*; Petersen and Zahle (eds), *Legal Polycentricity*; Berman, 'World law'.
39 Berman, 'Globalization of jurisdiction', p. 325. See also Aleinikoff, 'Sovereignty studies', pp. 201–2.
40 Princen and Finger, *Environmental NGOs in World Politics*, p. 10; Shaw, *Global Society*, pp. 5–9; Darcy de Oliveira and Tandon, 'Emerging Global Civil Society'; Wapner, 'Politics beyond the state', pp. 312–13.
41 Young, *International Governance*, pp. 184–211.
42 On the *lex mercatoria*, see McConnaughay, 'Rethinking the role of law', pp. 471–7; Maniruzzaman, 'Lex mercatoria and international contracts', pp. 672–4; Friedman, 'Erewhon', pp. 356–9. On the *lex digitalis*, see Perritt, 'Dispute resolution in cyberspace', pp. 691–2.
43 Berman notes: 'Elsewhere, we see the widespread use of international non-governmental regulatory frameworks. For example, the Apparel Industry Partnership, a joint undertaking of non-governmental organizations, international clothing manufacturers, and American universities, has established its own quasi-governmental (but non-state) regulatory regime to help safeguard public values concerning international labor standards. The partnership has adopted a code of conduct on issues such as child labor, hours of work, and health and safety conditions, along with a detailed structure for monitoring compliance (including a third-party complaint procedure). In the Internet context, the "TRUSTe" coalition of service providers, software companies, privacy advocates, and other actors has developed (and monitors) widely adopted privacy standards for websites. Similarly, the Global Business Dialogue on Electronic Commerce has formed a series of working groups to develop uniform policies and standards regarding a variety of e-commerce issues. And, of course, ICANN, discussed previously, is a non-state governmental body administering the domain name system.' Berman, 'Globalization of jurisdiction', pp. 369–70 (citations omitted).
44 Krasner, 'Structural causes and regime consequences', also available in Krasner (ed.), *International Regimes*, pp. 1–22. For a position that is critical of Krasner's approach, see Hasenclever *et al.*, 'Integrating theories of international regimes';

Hasenclever et al., *Theories of International Regimes*; Kratochwil and Ruggie, 'International organization', pp. 759–61; Young, 'International regimes', pp. 104–8.
45 See Ellickson, 'Bringing culture and human frailty to rational actors'; Posner, 'Decline of law'; Hadfield, 'Bias in the evolution of legal rules'; Bernstein, 'Law & Economics'.
46 Appadurai, *Modernity at Large*, p. 167.
47 See Kelsen, *Pure Theory of Law*; see further the collected articles of Hans Kelsen and Julius Merkl in Klecatsky et al. (eds), *Wiener rechtstheoretische Schule*.
48 Teubner, 'Global Private Regimes'.
49 Luhmann, *Law as a Social System*, pp. 291 ff.; Teubner, *Law as an Autopoietic System*, pp. 36–42; Fischer-Lescano, 'Emergenz der Globalverfassung', p. 737.
50 Koskenniemi Outline (see n. 8 above), at 9; see also Preliminary Report by Martti Koskenniemi, Chairman of the Study Group of the ILC, at ILC(LVI)/SG/FIL/CRD.1/Add.1, at para. 105 (4 May 2004).
51 A vast literature addresses this collision constellation. For an especially pointed review, see Pauwelyn, 'Role of public international law'. On the collision of TRIPS and Convention on Biological Diversity, see Bodeker, 'Traditional medical knowledge'; see also Consultative Opinion on the Compatibility between Certain Provisions of the Convention on Biological Diversity and the Agreement on Trade Related Aspects of Intellectual Property Rights as to the Protection of Traditional Knowledge, International Court of Environmental Arbitration and Conciliation, EAS – OC 8/2003 (19 November 2003) (hereinafter International Court of Environmental Arbitration and Conciliation), available at http://iceac.sarenet.es.
52 See Koskenniemi, 'Police in the temple'; see also Cassese, 'Ex iniuria ius oritur'; Simma, 'NATO, the UN and the use of force'.
53 See Vöneky, *Fortgeltung des Umweltvölkerrechts*. For further information on regime pluralisms in human rights law, see Bothe, 'Historical Evolution of International Humanitarian Law'.
54 See Hanschel, *Environment and Human Rights*.
55 Ladeur, *Postmoderne Rechtstheorie*, pp. 59–167.
56 On the concept of 'societal constitutionalism' from a social theory perspective, see Sciulli, *Theory of Societal Constitutionalism*; Sciulli, *Corporate Power in Civil Society*. For plural constitutionalism, see Walker, 'Idea of constitutional pluralism'; Walter, 'Constitutionalizing (inter)national governance', p. 186; Fischer-Lescano, 'Luhmanns Staat'; Teubner, 'Societal Constitutionalism'; Brunkhorst, *Solidarity*, pp. 151–62; Calliess, 'Reflexive transnational law'; Cottier and Hertig, 'Prospects of 21st century constitutionalism'.
57 Walker, 'The EU and the WTO', p. 33.
58 This is emphasised by Sciulli, *Theory of Societal Constitutionalism*; Teubner, 'Societal Constitutionalism'; Brunkhorst, *Solidarity*, pp. 151–62; Fischer-Lescano, 'Luhmanns Staat'.
59 Simma, 'Self-contained regimes'; see generally Koskenniemi Preliminary Reportand Koskenniemi Outline (see n. 8 above).
60 Luhmann, 'Verfassung als evolutionäre Errungenschaft'.
61 On a systems-theoretical concept of regimes, see Teubner, 'Contracting worlds'; Albert and Hilkermeier (eds), *Observing International Relations*, pp. 292–306.
62 See Fischer-Lescano, 'Globalverfassung'.
63 Luhmann, *Political Theory in the Welfare State*, ch. 3, n. 9.
64 On the 'network society', see Powell, 'Neither market nor hierarchy'; Castells, *Rise of the Network Society*, pp. 67–150.

65 Baecker, *Organisation und Gesellschaft*, p. 14.
66 Willke, *Ironie des Staates*, pp. 183–210; Luhmann, *Theory of Society*, vol. 2, p. 115; Brodocz, 'Strukturelle Kopplung durch Verbände', p. 366.
67 Kämper and Schmidt, 'Netzwerke als strukturelle Kopplung', p. 227.
68 For the European context, see Joerges, 'Impact of European integration on private law'.
69 Ladeur, *Postmoderne Rechtstheorie*, p. 82.
70 Berne Convention for the Protection of Literary and Artistic Works, 9 September 1886, S. Treaty Doc. No. 99-27, 1980 United Nations Treaty Series 31.
71 Ibid., art. 5(1), at 35.
72 Agreement on Trade-Related Aspects of Intellectual Property Rights, 15 April 1994, Marrakesh Agreement Establishing the World Trade Organization, Annex 1C, Legal Instruments – Results of the Uruguay Round, vol. 31, 33 International Legal Materials 81 (1994) (hereinafter TRIPS Agreement).
73 Agreement between the World Intellectual Property Organization and the World Trade Organization, 22 Dec. 1995, 35 International Legal Materials 754, 756–7 (1996).
74 European Convention Relating to Questions on Copyright Law and Neighbouring Rights in the Framework of Transfrontier Broadcasting by Satellite, opened for signature 11 May 1994, European Treaty Series No. 153, available at http://conventions.coe.int/Treaty/EN/CadreListeTraites.htm.
75 WIPO Diplomatic Conference of 20 December 1996 on Certain Copyright and Neighboring Rights Questions: WIPO Copyright Treaty, available at www.wipo.int/documents/en/diplconf/distrib/pdf/94dc.pdf; Diplomatic Conference of 20 December 1996 on Certain Copyright and Neighboring Rights Questions: WIPO Performances and Phonograms Treaty, available at www.wipo.int/documents/en/diplconf/distrib/pdf/95dc.pdf.
76 Council Regulation 40/94 of 20 December 1994 on the Community Trademark, 1994 *Official Journal of the European Union* (L 11) 1; Proposal for a European Parliament and Council Regulation on the Community Design, COM(93)342; Council Directive 93/83/EEC of 27 September 1993 on the Coordination of Certain Rules Concerning Copyright and Rights Related to Copyright Applicable to Satellite Broadcasting and Cable Retransmission, 1993 *Official Journal of the European Union* (L 248) 36, 1; Council Directive 91/250/EEC of 14 May 1991 on the Legal Protection of Computer Programs, 1991 *Official Journal of the European Union* (L 122) 34, 1.
77 See generally Dinwoodie, 'Development and incorporation of international norms', p. 748.
78 Dinwoodie, 'New copyright order', p. 573; Berman, 'Globalization of jurisdiction', p. 371.
79 See International Court of Environmental Arbitration and Conciliation (see n. 51 above).
80 Dinwoodie, 'New copyright order', p. 573; Berman, 'Globalization of jurisdiction', p. 371.
81 Berman, 'Globalization of jurisdiction', p. 496.
82 See Kegel and Schurig, *Internationales Privatrecht*, p. 65; Steindorff, *Sachnormen*.
83 Christian Joerges develops a similar approach in EU law. The colliding entities are not identified in autonomous national legal systems, not in hierarchic levels of federal orders, but in semi-autonomous levels of European multi-level governance. The solution is thus the development of substantial norms at one level

while observing the *altera pars* of other levels. See Joerges, 'Zur Legitimität der Europäisierung des Privatrechts'.
84 See, e.g., Rousseau, 'De la compatibilité des normes juridiques', p. 151 (speaking of different legal norms 'd'égale valeur juridique', but, of course, referring only to the traditionally non-hierarchical international law existing prior to the Vienna Convention on the Law of Treaties).
85 This approach is different from Philip Jessup's 'transnational law', which conceives of a principle of international law primacy. See Jessup, *Modernes Völkerrecht*, p. 21.
86 See Brilmayer, 'Role of substantive and choice of law policies'.
87 For this approach, see Martinez, 'Towards an international judicial system', p. 472.
88 Braune and Menezes, 'Patentability'.
89 Regula direitos e obrigações relativos à propriedade industrial, Decreto No. 9.279, 14 May 1996, *Diário Oficial da União* (Federal Law), 15 May 1996 (Br.) (in force since May 1997).
90 See also Decreto No. 9.787, 11 February 1999, *Diário Oficial da União*, 11 February 1999.
91 For recent developments, see: 'Após negociações "duras" com laboratórios: Ministério vai economizar R$ 229 milhões', *O Estado de São Paulo*, 26 January 2004.
92 WTO Dispute Settlement Body, Brazil-Measure Affecting Patent Protection- Request for Consultations by the United States, WTO Doc. WT/DS199/1 (8 June 2000).
93 WTO Dispute Settlement Body, Brazil – Measure Affecting Patent Protection- Request for Consultations by the United States, WTO Doc. WT/DS199/3 (9 January 2001). The DSB received this request during its meeting on 1 February and, following representations from the US and Brazil, decided to establish a Panel in accordance with art. 6 DSB. See WTO Settlement Dispute Body, Minutes of the Meeting, WTO Doc. WT/DSB/M/97 (27 February 2001).
94 Bass, 'Implications of the TRIPS Agreement', pp. 192–3.
95 TRIPS Agreement (see n. 72 above), at art. 30.
96 Ibid., at art. 31.
97 Lewis, 'Patent protection for the pharmaceutical industry', pp. 841–2.
98 Bass, 'Implications of the TRIPS Agreement'.
99 Romano, 'International Conventions and Treaties', p. 539.
100 WTO Dispute Settlement Body, Brazil-Measures Affecting Patent Protection – Notification of Mutually Agreed Solution, WTO Doc. WT/DS199/4 (19 July 2001).
101 On the political instrumentalisation of regimes, see Helfer, 'Regime shifting'.
102 On the battle against AIDS, see World Health Organization, *Treat 3 Million by 2005 Initiative*. Principal responsibility in the battle against Aids has been given by the UN institutions to UNAIDS, which acts as a network-coordinating node among a whole variety of secondary and special UN organisations.
103 On current cases affecting the UN and WTO equally, see Fidler, 'Global outbreak of avian influenza'.
104 Petersmann, 'Time for a United Nations "global compact"'; Alston, 'Resisting the merger'.
105 Declaration of Commitment on HIV/AIDS, UN General Assembly Official Records, Special Session, 25–7 June 2001, available at www.un.org/ga/aids/coverage.
106 Commission on Human Rights Res. 2001/33, UN Economic and Social Council Official Records, 57th Sess., Suppl. No. 3, UN Doc. E/2001/23 – E/CN4./2001/167 (2001), at 169 ff.

107 Ibid., at 171.
108 Letter from Peter Allgeier, Executive Office of the President, Deputy United States Trade Representative, to the Chairman of the Dispute Settlement Body of the World Trade Organization, WT/DS199/4 (25 June 2001), available at http://docsonline.wto.org.
109 On the connection between the Brazilian and South African cases, see Bass, 'Implications of the TRIPS Agreement', p. 206.
110 WTO Ministerial Conference, 4th Sess., Ministerial Declaration, WT/MIN(01)/DEC/1, para. 17. (20 November 2001).
111 WTO Ministerial Conference, Declaration on the TRIPS Agreement and Public Health, WT/MIN(01)/DEC/2 (20 November 2001); on the implementation of the Declaration, see WTO General Council, General Council Chairperson's Statement, WT/GC/M/82 (13 November 2003).
112 See WTO Ministerial Conference, Declaration on the TRIPS Agreement and Public Health, at para. 5(c): 'Each member has the right to determine what constitutes a national emergency or other circumstances of extreme urgency, it being understood that public health crises, including those relating to HIV/AIDS, tuberculosis, malaria and other epidemics, can represent a national emergency or other circumstances of extreme urgency.'
113 WTO General Council, Implementation of Paragraph 6 of the Doha Declaration on the TRIPS Agreement and Public Health, WT/L/540 (2 September 2003); on details, see Sun, 'Road to Doha'.
114 This, for example, is how Marschnik understands the significance of the regime-external environment, which, for example, would see international common law applied on the failure of an international legal regime. See Marschik, *Subsysteme im Völkerrecht*, p. 162.
115 See Böckenförde, 'Zwischen Sein und Wollen', p. 979.
116 See Lauterpacht, 'Restrictive interpretation and the principle of effectiveness', p. 76: 'It is the treaty as a whole which is law. The treaty as a whole transcends any of its individual provisions or even the sum total of its provisions. For the treaty, once signed and ratified, is more than the expression of the intention of the parties. It is part of international law and must be interpreted against the general background of its rules and principles.'
117 Böckenförde, 'Zwischen Sein und Wollen'.
118 Pauwelyn, 'Role of public international law', p. 566 ('prevails', 'overrides', etc.).
119 Betlem and Nollkaemper, 'Giving effect to public international law'.
120 See Koh, 'Transnational legal process', pp. 183–4.
121 For a similarly narrow approach characterised by conflict avoidance, see WTO Panel on Korea, Measures Affecting Government Procurement, WTO Doc. WT/DS163/R, para. VII.918 (19 June 2000).
122 Commission on Human Rights Resolution 2001/33, UN Economic and Social Council Official Records, 57th Sess., Suppl. No. 3, at 171, UN Doc. E/2001/23 – E/CN4./2001/167 (2001).
123 On the implications of the human rights covenants, see Yamin, 'Not just a tragedy'.
124 Fischer-Lescano, 'Odious Debts'.
125 Tomuschat, 'International Law'.
126 Fassbender, 'United Nations Charter as constitution'.
127 Both formulations are used by Phillip Alston in the Alston/Petersmann controversy: see Alston, 'Resisting the merger'.

128 On the conflict regarding a narrow versus a wide and a meaningful versus a less meaningful interpretation, see Paulus, *Internationale Gemeinschaft im Völkerrecht*, pp. 352–8.
129 Kälin, 'Menschenrechtsverträge'.
130 Voser, 'Mandatory rules of law'.
131 Grigera Naon, *Choice-of-Law Problems*, p. 65.
132 Deleuze and Guattari, *On the Line*.
133 Brunkhorst, *Solidarity*, pp. 157–8.
134 See especially UN Norms on the Responsibilities of Transnational Corporations and Other Business Enterprises with Regard to Human Rights, Sub-Committee for the Promotion and the Protection of Human Rights, 22nd Sess., Meeting 55, UN Doc. E/CN.4/Sub.2/2003/12/Rev.2 (2003).
135 See UN Global Compact, at www.unglobalcompact.org; for a preliminary stocktaking, see Rieth, 'Deutsche Unternehmen, Soziale Verantwortung und der Global Compact', available at www.uni-tuebingen.de/gk.globale-herausforderungen/papers/rieth/052003_Lothar_Rieth_SV_Dt_Unt_GC.pdf.
136 EPC stands for 'engineering, procurement and construction'.
137 The ENAA's Model Form and the New Engineering Contract devised by the ICEdo not even include such a limited provision.
138 Art. 4.18 of the FIDC Model Contract.
139 Perez, *Ecological Sensitivity and Global Legal Pluralism* (especially the details on contractual techniques within the *lex constructionis*).
140 *Prosecutor v. Furundžija*, International Criminal Tribunal for the Former Yugoslavia, Case No. IT-95-17/1-T, 28 International Legal Materials 317, 349, para. 155 (1999) (decided 10 December 1998): 'The fact that torture is prohibited by a peremptory norm of international law has other effects at the inter-state and individual levels. At the inter-state level, it serves to internationally de-legitimise any legislative, administrative or judicial act authorising torture. It would be senseless to argue, on the one hand, that on account of the jus cogens value of the prohibition against torture, treaties or customary rules providing for torture would be null and void ab initio, and then be unmindful of a State say, taking national measures authorising or condoning torture or absolving its perpetrators through an amnesty law. If such a situation were to arise, the national measures, violating the general principle and any relevant treaty provision, would produce the legal effects discussed above and in addition would not be accorded international legal recognition.'
141 See, e.g., Herdegen, '"Constitutionalization" of the UN security system', p. 156; Scott *et al.*, 'Memorial for Bosnia', p. 59.
142 See Pauwelyn, 'Role of public international law', p. 565.
143 Sinclair, *Vienna Convention*, pp. 94–6; on the WTO, see Böckenförde, 'Zwischen Sein und Wollen'; on the issue within the context of the Hague Convention, see Schulz, 'Relationship between the Judgments Project and Other International Instruments'.
144 Helfer, 'Constitutional analogies'.
145 *Prosecutor v. Tadić* (see n. 7 above), International Criminal Tribunal for the Former Yugoslavia, Case No. IT-94-1-AR72, 35 International Legal Materials 32, 39, para. 11 (1996) (decided 2 October 1995).
146 Interpretation and Application of the 1971 Montreal Convention Arising from the Aerial Incident at Lockerbie (*Libyan Arab Jamahiriya v. United States*), 1992 ICJ

114–217 and Concerning Application of the Convention on the Prevention and Punishment of the Crime of Genocide (*Bosnia and Herzegovina v. Yugoslavia (Serbia and Montenegro)*), 1993 ICJ 3–30.
147 On the lack of a Marbury moment within the UN regime, see Watson, 'Constitutionalism', p. 45; Franck, '"Powers of appreciation"', pp. 519 ff.
148 Martenczuk, *Rechtsbindung und Rechtskontrolle*, p. 275.
149 Fischer-Lescano, 'Emergenz der Globalverfassung', pp. 750–3.
150 Koskenniemi Outline (see n. 8 above), at 10; Marschik, *Subsysteme im Völkerrecht*, pp. 162–3.
151 Reaching the same conclusion, see Herdegen, '"Constitutionalization" of the UN security system', p. 156; Scott *et al.*, 'Memorial for Bosnia', pp. 58–9; Watson, 'Constitutionalism'.
152 Application of the Convention on the Prevention and Punishment of the Crime of Genocide, Provisional Measures, Order of 13 September 1993, ICJ Reports 1993 (Separate Opinion of Judge Lauterpacht), 407–48, at 440, para. 100.
153 Voser, 'Mandatory rules of law', pp. 323–5.
154 Mayer, 'Mandatory rules of law', pp. 274–87; Bucher and Tschanz, *International Arbitration in Switzerland*, pp. 102–5.
155 Voser, 'Mandatory rules of law', pp. 349–50.
156 See: United Nations Convention on the Recognition and Enforcement of Foreign Arbitral Awards, 10 June 1958, 330 UNTS 38, 42 art. V(1)(c); see also Posner, 'Arbitration and harmonization', p. 651.
157 See Guzman, 'Arbitrator liability', pp. 1316–17.
158 Slaughter, 'Global community of courts'; Burke-White, 'Community of courts'.
159 Law No. 23.492, 24 December 1986, 1986-BLA 100 (Argentina); Law No. 23.521, 8 June 1987, 1987-ALA 260 (Argentina). See also *Boletín Oficial*, 3 September 2003.
160 For arguments against universal jurisdiction, see Kissinger, 'Pitfalls of universal jurisdiction'; for arguments against immunity exceptions, see Kahn, 'On Pinochet'.
161 Fischer-Lescano, *Globalverfassung*, pp. 62 ff. For an instructive summary of the doctrinal questions of *desaparición* and *desiderata* from a *lex ferenda* perspective, see Manfred Nowak, Report for the Human Rights Commission, UN Doc E/CN.4/2002/71, at 8, 25 (8 January 2002).
162 The decision of the Nuremberg Tribunal was not explicitly concerned with disappearances, but saw Hitler's Night and Fog Decree ('Nacht- und Nebel-Erlass'; see 'Night and Fog' Decree, Doc. 090-L, 37 IMT-Nuremberg 570–75 (1945)) as demonstrating the characteristics of systematic ill-treatment, brutality in the sense of art. 6(b) of the Nuremberg Statute and art. 46 of the Convention on the Laws and Customs of War on Land: see Proceedings of the 218th Day, 1 IMT 485–530 (1 October 1946).
163 *Forti v. Suarez-Mason*, 672 F. Suppl. 1531, 1542–3 (ND Cal. 1987).
164 *Forti v. Suarez-Mason*, 694 F. Suppl. 707, 710 (ND Cal. 1987).
165 See Velásquez Rodríguez Case, Inter-American Court of Human Rights, OAS/ser. C/no. 4, at para. 153 (1988). For later cases, see *Palić v. Bosnia and Herzegovina and Republika Srpska*, Case No. CH/99/3196, Human Rights Chamber for Bosnia and Herzegovina (2001); *Unković v. Bosnia and Herzegovina*, Case No. CH/99/2150, Human Rights Chamber for Bosnia and Herzegovina (2001).
166 For the decision of the Argentine federal judge Cavallo, see Simón Julio y del Cerro, Juan Antonio s/sustracción de menores de 10 años, Case No. 8686/2000, Juzgado Nacional en lo Criminal y Correccional Federal No. 4 de la Capital Federal,

Secretaría No. 7, published in *Revista Argentina de Derecho Constitucional*, 2:3 (2001), 129 ff., at 252.
167 The decision mentioned in n. 165 above referred to political declarations and conventions. See, e.g., Velásquez Rodríguez Case (see n. 165 above), at para. 151.
168 There are in total four decisions of global remedies in the Pinochet case: see Cassese, 'When may senior state officials be tried', p. 869.
169 Arrest Warrant of 11 April 2000 (*Congo v. Belg*ium), 2002 ICJ, p. 3, at p. 25, para. 61 (14 February 2002).
170 Martinez, 'Towards an international judicial system', p. 487.
171 Luhmann, *Politik der Gesellschaft*, p. 189.
172 *Prosecutor v. Zejnil Delalić* (hereinafter Čelebici Case), International Criminal Tribunal for the Former Yugoslavia, Case No. IT-96–21-A, at para. 26 (20 February 2001), available at www.un.org/icty/indictment/english/cel-ii960321e.htm; this decision quotes the separate opinion of Judge Shahabuddeen in the case *Laurent Semanza v. Prosecutor*, International Criminal Tribunal for Rwanda, Case No. ICTR-97–23-A, at para. 25 (31 May 2000).
173 *Prosecutor v. Tadić* (see n. 7 above), at paras 115–45.
174 Ibid., at para. 115.
175 That is, good reason in the same manner that national jurisdictions give voice to different causality concepts in civil and criminal law.
176 This was the same reason given for departure from the ICJ's effective control test in the case of *Prosecutor v. Kvočka*, Case No. IT-98–30/1, T.Ch. (5 December 2000).
177 Koskenniemi and Leino, 'Fragmentation of international law?', p. 566.
178 *Nicar. v. US* (see n. 7 above), at para. 15.
179 Čelebici Case (see n. 172 above), at paras 24, 26.
180 See Koskenniemi, *Gentle Civilizer of Nations*.
181 Ladeur, *Postmoderne Rechtstheorie*, pp. 159–60.

11

Horizontal constitutional rights as conflict-of-laws rules: how transnational pharmaceutical groups manipulate scientific publications

Isabell Hensel and Gunther Teubner*

But where are the pictures of the people who drowned?[1]

I Publication bias: the manipulation of clinical studies in the pharmaceutical network

The 'Edronax' case: In 1997, the anti-depressant Edronax, which was manufactured by the pharmaceutical company Pfizer and contained the ingredient Reboxetine, was licensed in Germany and other EU countries, although an attempt to have the drug licensed in the US had failed. In 2010, the *British Medical Journal* revealed that less than two thirds of the studies actually carried out, specifically those with positive results, had been duly published by Pfizer, while no mention was made of those studies which showed that in comparison with placebos, the drug was not only ineffective, but also had harmful side effects. This was confirmed in later studies by the Institut für Qualität und Wirtschaftlichkeit im Gesundheitswesen (IQWiG – Institute for Quality and Efficiency in Healthcare).[2]

The case of BASF and Betty Dong: Boots Pharmaceuticals (now the Knoll Pharmaceutical Company, a subsidiary of BASF) commissioned the research scientist Prof. Betty Dong of the University of California in San Francisco to investigate the effectiveness of Synthroid, the most frequently prescribed thyroid medication in the US, in return for a research subsidy of a quarter of a million dollars. Dong had to sign a contract stating that she would not publish any negative study results without Boots' agreement. In fact, Synthroid was found not to have any advantages over comparable and cheaper generic products in terms of its effectiveness. On the basis of the contractual clause, and by making defamatory statements concerning Dong and her scientific methods, Boots then prevented publication for seven years. As a result, by claiming that Synthroid was a superior product, the Group was able to further expand its market share. When the *Wall Street Journal* made the case public in 1996, BASF had to face class actions from approximately 5 million claimants for inadmissible suppression of the study, unfair competition practices and violation of consumer protection regulations. The company ultimately agreed to a settlement.[3]

The hormone replacement therapies case: Alongside many other pharmaceutical companies which had been in competition with each other since the 1940s over the prevention of symptoms of menopause by hormone replacement therapies, Wyeth (now Pfizer) organised marketing campaigns well into the 1990s. Without any basis in terms of the results of solid scientific studies, Wyeth promoted the preventive effect of the treatments. Only when an external randomised study was carried out in 1998, with further follow-up studies and a Women's Health Initiative in 2002, was the preventive effect refuted and evidence produced concerning the health risks to women who had used these treatments, and who had developed breast cancer, strokes, thrombosis, dementia and incontinence more frequently after receiving the treatment. Media such as *PLOS* and the *New York Times* obtained court decisions forcing the disclosure of the marketing documents by the manufacturer Wyeth, in parallel with the compensation claims filed by the women whose health had been damaged. In the course of all this, it emerged that the majority of the scientific articles on which the marketing campaign was based had been written in cooperation with communications agencies and ghostwriters.[4]

There is a long list of such scandals involving the big pharmaceutical companies. Over and over again, scientific findings concerning the harmful consequences of medicinal products for health, or the total absence of any consequences whatsoever for health, do not reach the public, or do so only on a selective basis. These manipulations take many different forms, including selective publication,[5] censorship clauses in research contracts, the use of ghostwriters, pressure put on researchers to prevent studies from being carried out[6] and even the dismissal of researchers by financially dependent research institutions.[7] Underlying these cases is a conflict of incompatible rationalities[8] that ultimately leads to publication bias.[9] This term is used to describe the statistical distortion of data when research data are suppressed or manipulated in scientific publications. This is not merely a matter of a few regrettable, isolated cases that give rise to public concern because they cause scandals in scientific research and healthcare. Numerous empirical studies have shown that publication bias is a worldwide problem which is due to the substantial conflicts of interest that exist between research institutions, the pharmaceutical industry, the healthcare system, the publishing world, investors and political regulation bodies. For example, a study which compared the protocols and subsequently published articles relating to 102 studies of medicinal products showed that in 62% of cases, the published article seriously deviated from the study protocol.[10] Increasingly, negative (i.e. unwelcome) study results, which will not be effective in terms of the marketing of the substances concerned, are withheld or manipulated, and only the positive results are published in the specialist journals. Thus, only a portion of the clinical studies carried out reach the public domain. These drastic external selections are due to the immense interest of the pharmaceutical industry in positive clinical results, because these will exert a positive influence on licensing and marketing. By financing research, the pharmaceutical industry tries to satisfy this need, thus intervening, more or less subtly, in the process of scientific research itself. These manipulations are damaging not only to scientific research, but also to the provision of healthcare generally.

It is not sufficient to describe publication bias as a consequence of individual corruption, which can be controlled by the regulatory bodies of national governments. In light of the worldwide activities of the big pharmaceutical companies and the globalisation of academic research, this is a conflict with transnational dimensions.[11] At the same time it points to a structural conflict within society which political control will only be able to correct in isolated cases, but which it cannot manage effectively. Underlying the circumstances of the individual cases is a problem of constitutional rights – the conflict between different social rationalities.

II The third-party effect of constitutional rights: a critique and some alternatives

Can constitutional rights be used as conflict-of-laws rules to overcome this multidimensional conflict, which is being played out both in a national and a transnational context? There is obviously a massive clash here between the interests of transnational pharmaceutical groups in the successful marketing of their products and the interests of the research community in publishing their results without hindrance, as well as the interest of patients in having effective health protection. What is legally relevant in this context is the third-party effect of constitutional rights, according to which actors can assert their constitutional rights (academic freedom and the right to health being the relevant rights here) not only vis-à-vis governmental bodies, but also vis-à-vis private actors.[12] The term 'third-party effect' implies a transfer of public-law constitutional rights into relationships under private law. A central concern in this transfer is that the principles of private law should not to be violated in the process. For this reason, a direct third-party effect is usually rejected and only an indirect third-party effect accepted, whereby the value system of constitutional rights is transformed by the general clauses of private law and addressed to the judiciary. In parallel with this, the doctrine of a responsibility to protect serves to impose a duty on the legislator in regard to constitutional rights in private relationships. In essence, all concepts of a third-party effect envisage a balancing of the opposing rights of private law subjects on a case-by-case basis.

By comparison with the long-standing traditional understanding of constitutional rights, which thought exclusively in terms of the relationship between the individual and the state, the third-party effect represents a significant change. It responds to the emergence of intermediary social forces by transferring public-law norms into private-law relationships. Yet it is precisely in the image of a transfer that the problem lies. The differences between the sender's context and the recipient's context are so great as to make any transfer of norms in the strict sense impossible. Instead, what is needed is a separate reconstruction of constitutional rights which is dependent on the recipient's context. The transfer metaphor may still be convincing as a kind of transitional semantic, according to which constitutional rights asserted against the state are 'transferred' to private-law relations and endowed with a 'third-party effect' vis-à-vis social actors. In the long term, however, intra-societal constitutional rights can only be understood in the context of their origin in intra-societal conflicts. This is because the threats emanating from within society are fundamentally different from those emanating from the state. And the differences are just as great in regard to the circumstances in which the violation of a constitutional right takes place and in regard to the appropriate sanctions, so that the simple idea of a third-party effect of constitutional rights that were originally directed against the state is misleading.

The challenge consists in releasing third-party effects in private law from their clandestine attachment to the state, and in basing the development of their standards on the specific features of intra-societal conflicts from the outset. Below, we will thus critically examine four central aspects of third-party effect theory and develop alternatives, using publication bias as a paradigmatic case.

Theses:

(1) The third-party effect has so far been configured in an individualist perspective only, as balancing individual constitutional rights of private actors against each other. However, in order to deal with substantial structural conflicts within society, constitutional rights in private relations have to be reformulated in their collective-institutional dimension.
(2) Instead of being limited to the protection against state-equivalent power in society, the third-party effect must be widened and directed against all communication media with expansive tendencies.
(3) The contextualisation of constitutional rights must not be confined to adapting these rights to the particularities of private law. It must go further than this and take into account the particular normativities of the autonomous social institutions at risk.
(4) Instead of imposing a responsibility to protect on state actors only, third-party effects must address the societal threats to constitutional rights directly and activate societal counter-forces.

1 *Constitutional rights as collective institutions*

An initial critique is directed against the prevailing understanding of the third-party effect as a balancing of individual constitutional rights.[13] If the third-party effect is seen as a transfer of public constitutional rights into private relationships, this ignores the fact that a mere transfer will alter the structure of the rights and reduce legal protection. The question of the possible unlawfulness of any interference is not examined; instead, legal subjects under private law are classified as 'violators' and 'violated' and their equally justified positions as regards their constitutional rights are brought into 'practical concordance' in the individual case.[14] This does not provide anything but a purely formal additional value compared to the protection of subjective rights in tort law. On the contrary, legal protection is reduced, since violations of constitutional rights are much more difficult to establish, the balancing dimensions multiply, and the political leeway for balancing expands.[15] And the fact that the decision concerning violations of constitutional rights is made dependent on the circumstances of the individual case makes it impossible to formulate general norms for issues as significant as these. This amounts to a level of casuistry that is conceptually uncontrollable.

However, the most important objection to such an exclusive focus on individual rights is that by doing so, one fails to address the central problem of intra-societal violations of constitutional rights. While it has long been recognised in public law that constitutional rights serve to protect both individual rights and social institutions,[16] the third-party effect in private law as a rule has so far been concerned only with individual protection and has neglected the protection of institutions. The German Federal Constitutional Court (Bundesverfassungsgericht, BVerfG) sees only a conflict between the individual subjective rights of 'equal-ranking holders of constitutional rights' here, between 'conflicting constitutional rights positions' 'in their interdependency'.[17] And its private-law critics respond at the same level, i.e. the level of individual rights.[18] In doing so, both ignore the fact that in this context, the collective-institutional dimension of constitutional rights is acutely relevant.

It is the conflict between collective institutions, however, that constitutes the really controversial aspect of the third-party effect. The term 'collective-institutional' distances itself from Carl Schmitt's institutionalism and refers explicitly to Helmut Ridder's theory of 'non-personal constitutional rights', according to which 'constitutional rights are aimed at the specific freedom of a social field through the organisation of that field' – freedom of science or freedom of art, for example.[19] In particular, it should be emphasised that in contrast to politically conservative preconceptions, 'institution' is to be understood not as a legal guarantee for the permanent existence of social structures against tendencies of political change – in Carl Schmitt's definition: 'that which is present, formally and organisationally existent and available'[20] – but as a socio-legal normativisation process which is subject to constant change.

Admittedly, in the case of publication bias it is perfectly possible for scientists to assert individual defence claims against the censorship imposed by the big pharmaceutical companies, or to plead the nullity of contracts that prevent publication, or for patients to sue for damages. But any private litigation by individual actors fails to take account of the collective-institutional dimension, and therefore also of the societal conflicts which are the real difficulty. This is because the manipulations of the big pharmaceutical companies do not merely violate individual rights of scientists and patients, but also – and in a more profound way – the integrity and therefore the functioning of the socially autonomous institutions of scientific research and of the provision of healthcare.[21]

It needs to be stressed that the collective-institutional dimension is significant not only for the victims of rights violations, but on both sides of the horizontal constitutional-rights relationship. If there are institutions as well as individuals on the victims' side, on the perpetrators' side not only persons, but also anonymous social processes must be held responsible for the violation of constitutional rights. This two-sided aspect of the collective-institutional relationship is often overlooked. However, the discussion in criminal law concerning so-called macro-criminality and the criminality of formal organisations, which has its background in the sociological debate on 'structural violence',[22] has developed such a collective-institutional perspective in regard to the perpetrators, too.

In such cases, violations of constitutional rights are ultimately attributable to non-personal social processes that use human actors as their agents.[23] Structural violence emanates from an 'anonymous matrix', that is, not only from the rather more visible 'collective actors' (states, political parties, commercial companies, groups of companies, associations), but also (with an equal if not greater intensity) from anonymous communicative processes (institutions, functional systems, networks) which are difficult to address for the very reason that they are not personified as collective actors.[24] The hazards originating in the digital processes of the Internet are a particularly clear example.[25] At the centre of the conflict is the clash between irreconcilable rationalities: economically rational action has a structurally corrupting effect on the particular rationalities of science and of the healthcare system. And a particular feature of the clash is its asymmetry. Constitutional rights have to be protected in such asymmetrical situations, in which the expanding economic dynamic disables the fragile internal operating mechanisms of scientific research and healthcare.

Constitutional rights as a collective institution: this means, therefore, a two-sided relationship in which guarantees of autonomy are given to social processes in order to prevent them from being overwhelmed by the totalising tendencies of other social processes.[26] In this collective-institutional dimension, constitutional rights function as conflict-of-laws rules that operate within the conflict between the opposing rationalities of different parts of society. They seek to protect the integrity of art, of the family and of religion in the face of the totalising tendencies at work in society, that is, in technology, the media and the economy. It is obvious that we will not advance any further in this context if we try to balance individual constitutional rights against each other.

Instead, the horizontal protection of constitutional rights must be rigorously refocused on organisation and procedure. Institutional protection for areas of social autonomy has been implemented for some time in public law, particularly in media law.[27] In the field of the mass media, freedom of opinion cannot be effectively protected by means of subjective rights for individual actors, but only through organisation and procedure.[28] This insight needs to be applied more generally, particularly in regard to the horizontal effect of constitutional rights in different social areas.

Ultimately, it is the contextual adequacy of any such collective-institutional protection of constitutional rights that is decisive. Organisation and procedure must be selected in such a way as to be oriented to the specific contexts on both sides of the violation – the violators as much as the violated.[29] In the case of publication bias, the guiding question is therefore: under what conditions is the economic exploitation of research results intrusive in such a way that it violates the core integrity of research, on the one hand, and that of healthcare, on the other? The search for criteria must thus proceed in two different directions: (1) What determines the specific risk potential of the processes that violate constitutional rights when the publication of research results is subjected to economic pressure? (2) How are we to define, in this context, the core area of scientific research and of the healthcare system which is violated by the manipulation of results? Only when these two questions have been answered with sufficient accuracy can we determine how organisation and procedure must be structured in order for them to be capable of restoring the violated integrity of scientific research and the healthcare system.

2 Expansionary tendencies of the communication media

A second weak point of traditional third-party effect doctrines is that they concentrate exclusively on protection against social power.[30] This is shown particularly clearly by the state action doctrine[31] in the US: a third-party effect of constitutional rights is established if socio-economic power equivalent to state power emanates from private actors.[32] However, theories of third-party effect prevalent in Germany also take structural imbalances and hazards as their starting point and see social power phenomena only.

Indisputably, legal protection in the face of socio-economic power is an important area of third-party effect, but here, too, the weakness of the transfer principle is noticeable. For only if it were a question of transferring state-oriented constitutional rights to intra-societal conflicts would it be plausible to restrict constitutional rights to cases where private power has developed within society that is comparable to state power in its intensity. In fact, this is why the third-party effect has been exceptionally successful in labour law, as in that context, private property is transformed into the organisational power of private government, which in terms of its impact is in no way inferior to the exercise of state power.[33]

Yet if we focus exclusively on socio-economic power, we fail to see other, subtler causes of constitutional rights violations. As appropriate as it is for constitutional rights to be directed against power phenomena in the state sector, it is entirely inappropriate to limit constitutional rights to the communication medium of power in cases of societal violations of constitutional rights. In principle, constitutional rights are put at risk not only from power, but from all communicative media as soon as autonomous subsystems develop expansionary dynamics. In today's world, that primarily means the expansionary tendencies of the economy, of technology, of medicine and (particularly relevant at the present time) of the information media. Social power is thus only a partial phenomenon of the societal risks to which constitutional rights are exposed. The essential differences between social and political constitutional rights always result from the specific internal conditions of reproduction of the social sector in question. In politics, constitutional rights are primarily directed against the dangers of power. In other social systems, constitutional rights are directed against risks emanating from the specific communication media of the social system in question, that is, from monetary operations in the economy, from cognitive-technical operations in science and technology and from information flows in the media system.[34]

In the case of publication bias, power certainly plays an important role. In particular, the censorship contracts forced on scientists by the pharmaceutical industry indicate an asymmetric power distribution. Yet we ought not to focus solely on the power phenomenon. We must also guard against the subtler ways in which economic influence is exerted, which – without any manifest exercise of power – 'substitute extra-scientific values and standards for intra-scientific relevance'.[35] In particular, we must take into consideration the corruptive influence of funding streams, above all when these are not transformed into organisational or contractual power. The technique of influence exercised by the pharmaceutical companies is not 'prohibitive or repressive, but seductive ... it leads its victims astray rather than telling them what they must not do'.[36] Its motivating force is based not on the power of negative sanctions, but on the vast financing requirements of scientific research, towards which the seductive techniques of the pharmaceutical companies are geared with pinpoint accuracy. 'Because research is so intensive in terms of staff and resources, the financing of scientific activity is the "nerve centre" of its freedom.'[37] This is another reason why constitutional rights can achieve little against the influences exerted by the money medium if they are structured only as defensive rights against power. Effective protection against these seductive techniques thus becomes the challenge that has to be addressed by the concept of a third-party effect.[38]

Of course, not every economic influence that is brought to bear on scientific research is necessarily a violation of constitutional rights. The contact between science and industry takes many different forms, including marketing of scientific results, influence over the choice of research topics as a result of companies sitting on university supervisory committees, the financing of profitable projects, the practice of industrial research, applied research generally and the close cooperation between industry and science in Silicon Valley contexts.[39] All of these may give rise to political regulation, but as long as the core autonomy of science is not affected, they do not constitute a violation of constitutional rights.

It is only when the external influences systematically manipulate the scientific code itself, that is, when they seek to determine from the outside what is true and what is false – as in the case of the politically inspired theories of Lysenko in the Soviet Union – that the core area of scientific research is violated.[40] When economic rational choice usurps the role of scientific rationality, when it replaces the scientific code with the economic code, the violation of academic freedom is obvious. But this is just what normally does not happen in the context of publication bias. The pharmaceutical industry is wary of directly interfering in research processes and telling scientists what results they are to produce.[41] Given an established practice of scientific research, any such crude external interference in the binary code of scientific research or its programmes would – as the Lysenko disaster demonstrated – simply invite ridicule. The manipulation in question here is very much subtler and therefore more dangerous, because the way in which it becomes inscribed into the research process itself and gives rise to publication bias is almost imperceptible.[42] This is also why it is extremely difficult to provide evidence of such bias. Only time-consuming empirical and statistical research (as described at the beginning of this paper) has finally been able to prove the systematic falsification of the publication process.

This makes a precise determination of how scientific autonomy is being put at risk even more difficult in such situations. The thesis pursued here is as follows: *The reason why the manipulations encroach on the core area of science is not that they directly violate the binary code of science or its programmes, methods and theories. Rather, they interfere with the evolution of science by systematically falsifying its fragile selection mechanism.* The precarious interconnections between variation, selection and retention of scientific evolution are exposed to the economically motivated manipulations of the publication mechanism. This has dramatic consequences for the autonomy of the scientific system. At the same time, in the interplay of autonomous areas within society, the economic infiltration of science violates the integrity of the healthcare system.

(a) Violation of the publication mechanism

In publication, the evolution of the science system has developed a selection mechanism[43] that selects system-relevant results from among the variations of ongoing research activity. Initial publication in relevant specialist journals has the function of filtering out, from among the many different variations of the internal research process, the results that will determine the direction of further development. By making new knowledge visible, publication makes a selection from among the variations of the scientific process that occur via the binary code and the programmes, and makes it possible for research results to be stabilised as the current 'state of knowledge' in educational literature and manuals; this stabilisation stimulates new variations in its turn.[44] The practice of publication establishes scientific objectivity and impartiality because it makes it possible for scientific findings to be verified according to the criteria of connectivity with other areas of research and of openness to criticism.[45] Thus the social institution of a functioning publication practice is as much part of the protection of scientific freedom as is the principle of freedom of publication itself. Here we can see the interplay between the individual and the collective-institutional level of constitutional rights. Constitutional rights relate not only to individuals but also to 'collective institutions ... which cannot be defined in contradistinction to the subject because they are involved in the (re)production of the subject, without being a macro-subject'.[46] Far from limiting individual constitutional rights, collective institutions serve as a space for their realisation.[47] Conversely, enforceable individual constitutional rights have an advocacy function in regard to the protection and further development of collective institutions.

Economically motivated manipulation impairs this mechanism both directly and indirectly. By contractual rights of disposal and exploitation and by censorship clauses, the pharmaceutical networks may not be intervening directly in the 'production' of scientific results, but they are certainly intervening directly in their 'presentation'.[48] Negative studies are withheld and study results are manipulated so that the population of publication records is increased in the direction of profitable results, that is, the frequency distribution of positive and negative research results is significantly shifted in favour of positive results.

By contrast, indirect impairment occurs if financing pressure supersedes the internal cognitive interest of science. When this happens, the publication of positive study results becomes more lucrative and more interesting for the researchers than the publication of negative study results.[49] 'Good scientific practice', in the sense of a behavioural standard internal to science that would have regarded any such selective publication as scientific misconduct, becomes less relevant.⁵⁰ An imperceptible change thus occurs in the way in which the scientific world itself understands what the purpose of publication is. Symptomatic of this development is the increasing and not very transparent use of so-called communications agencies and ghostwriters. Prominent researchers seeking to enhance their reputations are falsely named as the authors of studies that have in fact been written by anonymous ghostwriters, consultancy companies or employees of the big pharmaceutical companies.⁵¹

Some publishers also encourage such manipulations when, by accepting mainly positive results, they adapt their publication methods to the expectations of the big pharmaceutical companies and the financial pressures they impose.⁵² Not infrequently, agreements are reached between widely circulated specialist medical publishers and the big pharmaceutical companies who co-finance them through drugs advertising. Such agreements can concern both the orientation of the specialist journal and the publication criteria.⁵³ In the pharmaceutical sphere, there is the additional problem of finding independent experts to carry out peer reviews so as to avoid conflicts of interest capable of influencing results.

Where economic interests influence the practice of scientific publication in this way, the internal selection criteria by which scientists operate will be replaced by criteria that have nothing to do with science. Peer review processes will be ineffective, as negative data do not appear. The possibility of integration with subsequent and parallel research is put at risk, or, worse still, the falsification is incorporated into subsequent research.⁵⁴ If false data are used as a basis for follow-on research, this will ultimately affect how the values of the 'truth code' of science itself are allocated. The repercussions of publication bias for research practice tend towards an undoing of the connection between research and publication. The core of scientific self-reproduction is put at risk.

(b) Violation of the healthcare system

At the same time, this practice violates the right to health, in both a collective-institutional and an individual sense. The collective institutions of politics and of the health system rely on full disclosure of all studies carried out in regard to a medical product, as do the doctors who treat patients. If findings on negative consequences for health are withheld or manipulated, the effects of substances cannot be objectively recorded because of the selective nature of the data in specialist journals. This leads to serious errors in decision-making, because the positive effects are overestimated both in the context of drug licensing and of patient treatment.⁵⁵ In accordance with §§ 21 ff. of the German Medical Products Act (AMG), clinical studies serve as a basis for drug licensing.

Hence, the regulatory authorities for medical products no longer investigate such products independently, and thus these manipulations lead directly to incorrect evaluations of the efficacy and usefulness of drugs. The result, as demonstrated by the Edronax case, is that incorrect efficacy information is provided in package leaflets and incorrect reimbursement decisions are made by health insurance funds. Treatment guidelines drawn up by professional associations are incorrect. Statutory control bodies such as the IQWiG and ethical commissions cannot fulfil their function, since they have to rely on defective data.[56]

The risks to patients and trial participants are obvious. The distortion of studies exposes patients to useless or even harmful treatments. Drugs that are in fact effective remain hidden from view and are withheld from patients. When studies that have already been carried out are suppressed, trial participants are unnecessarily subjected to new studies.[57]

3 *Contextualisation*

There is a third weak point in the traditional third-party-effect doctrine. It, too, is connected to a misguided reliance on the idea of a transfer. Since the third-party effect is generally understood simply as the transfer of constitutional rights from public law to private-law relations, care supposedly needs to be taken to ensure that the basic principles of private law are not violated. Accordingly, the theory of an indirect third-party effect considers that the adaptation to private law is most likely to be assured if constitutional rights are incorporated into private law indirectly through general clauses. The theory of a responsibility to protect seeks to involve the legislator as an intermediary, who, for the same reasons, is meant to formulate only such standards as are compatible with the principles of private law.

It is of course true that societal constitutional rights need to be adequate to their context. But their context is understood in a manner which is decidedly too narrow if it is merely defined as the world of private law. The call 'to maintain the fundamental independence and autonomy of civil law vis-à-vis the system of constitutional rights under constitutional law'[58] only describes a first step of contextualisation. The second step leads to a much more difficult challenge: state-oriented constitutional rights need to be modified not only in accordance with the context of private law, but also in accordance with the different contexts of society in which they are applied. They have to be newly calibrated in order to protect the particular rationality and normativity of each different area of society in which constitutional rights are at risk.[59]

This is where the transfer principle shows its limitations. While it may be possible to transfer individual constitutional rights from public law into private-law relationships, any transfer of institutional constitutional rights, that is, a transfer of a previously defined organisation and of already established procedures, is bound to fail because of the variety and specificity of particular social normativities.[60] An adequate protection of constitutional rights cannot be obtained by a uniform conception of what it means to protect constitutional rights which is applied to all areas of society;[61] it has to be ensured 'locally' by a careful and sensitive contextualisation.

The question of which kind of organisation and which procedures will protect the constitutional rights of the collective institutions of scientific research and healthcare against the harm that can be done by economic action must be answered primarily via the normative self-understanding of the social practices that are at risk.[62] In their own codes and programmes, science and healthcare develop normative orientations that are not the same as commonly held opinions of individuals, but have a collective-institutional character.[63] Such collective-institutional norms, which build up into historically evolved structures, are discussed, criticised and reformulated in the reflective discourses of science and healthcare, before the law examines them according to its own criteria and establishes new legal norms.

As far as publication bias is concerned, the reflective discourses of science and healthcare have in fact developed a collective-institutional alternative to individual protection, which it would be advisable to implement in law:[64] trial registration as the third-party effect of academic freedom and of the right to health by way of organisation and procedure.[65] Publicly accessible registers of studies and results are set up on a binding basis. They fully record studies from their inception in order to ensure transparency and scrutiny for the entire research process.[66] This protection of constitutional rights only becomes effective with the cooperation of the specialist journals, which make registration of all studies carried out a precondition for publication.[67] Results for drugs that are intended for distribution on the market are only allowed to be published if the clinical studies on which they are based have been entered in the clinical trial register and if all results have been included, both positive and negative.[68]

Trial registration is particularly well adapted to dealing with the conflict between economic and scientific rationality. The duty of registration takes effect precisely at the point where (as has been described above) manipulations falsify the evolution of scientific knowledge. Unlike other possible sanctions, the duty of registration is aimed exactly at the critical selection mechanism where the interests of industry, science and healthcare come into conflict. Trial registration does not counteract repressive or prohibitive power techniques applied by the big pharmaceutical companies, but operates instead as a corrective against their 'seductive' manipulation techniques.[69] It ensures transparency, but – even more decisively – it stabilises and protects the act of publication, by no longer restricting publication to results, but expanding it to include the entire research project. And it does so before any results are known. It thus forces the parties to define their publication conduct under a veil of ignorance. Research projects have to be made accessible to the medical public already at a point when there is still uncertainty as to the results. The contingent nature of the research project is thereby made public, and publication practice faces systematic pressure in regard to the frequency distribution of positive and negative results.

The duty of registration therefore takes effect precisely at the point of the selection mechanism of scientific evolution, a mechanism which (unlike individual court actions) does not operate solely in the individual case, but exerts a continuing influence on the joint development of industry, scientific knowledge and medical practice. The duty of registration strengthens the scientific selection criterion of novelty without regard to positive or negative results, and weakens the economic selection criteria that give rise to publication bias. And at the same time it strengthens the selection criteria for medical practice, for which knowledge concerning harmful side effects or indeed the lack of efficacy of a drug is just as important as information about positive curative effects. This tends towards a restoration of the intimate connection between research and publication which is constitutive of the self-production of scientific knowledge and which the seductive manipulation techniques of the pharmaceutical companies seek to sabotage.

4 Beyond the state's responsibility to protect: alternatives to state regulation of publication practice

In the generally accepted concept of the responsibility to protect, we find the fourth weakness of the third-party-effect doctrine. Its exclusive focus on the state is bound to be misleading: although it is private actors that are violating constitutional rights, the concept imposes an obligation on the state and not on the private actors themselves. This is particularly problematic in science, since the autonomy of the scientific community to some extent resists governmental responsibilities to protect. By contrast, trial registration targets the social processes themselves in order to protect science from being abused by industry. It takes the particular dynamic of the conflict as its starting point and protects the integrity of science from the inside, by motivating large numbers of private actors to become involved on the basis of their respective functional rationalities. In so doing, it mobilises social forces to combat the expansionary tendencies of the pharmaceutical networks. It almost functions like an immune system that identifies and combats elements that are foreign to science.[70] There is certainly a political element here, but it does not operate as external state control, but instead alters the internal self-reproduction of academic activity. State-based concepts of the responsibility to protect which, in the name of academic freedom, impose duties of publication developed by legislative bodies reduce the potential of autonomous scientific processes.[71] Legislative standard setting underestimates the scientific community's need for autonomy and fails to connect with its evolutionary mechanisms. It is bound to miss the mark when trying to meet social needs because it regards the actors involved as mere objects to be regulated. But these actors are responsible (co-)authors in the protection of the autonomy of 'their' particular social areas.[72] As an alternative to a comprehensive regulatory responsibility of the state, therefore, a procedurally based reconnection of constitutional rights to society is proposed. To set standards relating to constitutional rights is not an exclusive task of state policy, but primarily a function of societal self-organisation. The ultimately decisive reason for this is 'that no superior information is available outside an emergent systematisation context about the possibilities of and the needs for systematisation in that context'.[73] The state thus ought not to elaborate comprehensive responsibilities of protection; instead, its role should be limited to more indirect forms of control by way of organisation and procedure.[74]

Trial registration is a way of managing conflict which is adequate to the needs of science because it protects academic freedom by means of a procedure of scientific self-regulation. It represents an alternative to previous proposals of a 'plurality of financial sources' as a scientific third-party-effect mechanism, an alternative that takes into account the particular nature of the conflict situation.[75] Trial registration has one outstanding feature: because the structurally coupled publishers organise trial registration, they encourage the tendency to develop a specific (self-)control network as a counter-force to the pharmaceutical networks.[76] In this way, it confronts the difficult and frequently discussed problem of how networks can be regulated when their decentralised structure means that they lack an addressee.

This network consists of various social actors who, each having their own motives for doing so, are able to effect the protection contained within the register mechanism. The specialist journals, with their dependence on reputation, play a central role if they make registration a precondition for publication. In addition, they can accord special weight to studies with negative results, either by publishing negative studies separately or by establishing a duty to take them into consideration in peer review. The specialist journals are self-motivated, since they aim to maintain their function as a neutral medium of scientific knowledge, in contradistinction to the mass media, and to avoid being used as a mere tool for advertising.[77]

Universities, research funding institutions, scientific councils and medical associations can contribute to the success of trial registration.[78] By creating their own registers, internal registration obligations, ethics commissions and ombudsman proceedings, they reinforce the duty of registration created by the publishers.[79] Within science, the duty of registration raises the standard of care, because it requires the details of studies to be disclosed. Within healthcare, doctors will have a personal responsibility to stay informed about study results published in the registers and to correlate this information with the specialist journals. In addition, transnational control mechanisms are able to prevent any attempts at circumventing trial registration, if transnational actors such as NGOs, the media and public interest litigation with their 'public outcry' strategies become involved with trial registration.[80] In 2007, WHO set up the registration network International Clinical Trials Registry Platform (ICTRP) in order to coordinate private and public activities relating to the registration of clinical studies on a worldwide scale.[81] Private and public registers, which have to fulfil certain quality standards, feed their data into the meta-register on a regular basis. The aim is to ensure the quality of the register entries. The meta-register serves as a seal of quality in particular for smaller, private registers, and removes the burden of a standard international public register.

III Conclusion: constitutional rights as conflict-of-laws rules

A clear distinction needs to be made between constitutional rights in state–citizen conflicts and constitutional rights in intra-societal conflicts. Seen from this perspective, traditional state-oriented constitutional rights provide a normative safeguard for the relationship between citizen and state, but cannot claim to constitute a comprehensive value system for society or even a 'common frame of reference'. Standing in contrast to the dogmatic system of state-oriented constitutional rights, there is a multitude of societal conflicts between constitutional rights that have no need for external grounds to justify spheres of protection and evaluation.[82] Specific clashes between constitutional rights give rise to idiosyncratic conflict rules, which are distinguished not by priority rules or burdens of justification, but by the specific autonomy requirements of the social areas in question.

Like the 'hard won' defensive role of state-oriented constitutional rights in the relationship between citizen and state, the conflict-based self-constitution of academic freedom sketched above is a long-term process of boundary drawing. Just as state-oriented constitutional rights have historically been won as a result of state–citizen conflicts, academic freedom constitutes itself in the conflict with other social rationalities, in particular with the rationality of economic action. The clash becomes a productive process because it challenges science to define itself in the conflict.[83] This is the deeper reason why it is not sufficient to see the horizontal effect of constitutional rights as a transfer of the content of positivised (state-oriented) constitutional rights. The historical experience of state-oriented constitutional rights is certainly an element to be taken into consideration, and the level of protection achieved by way of a horizontal effect must be measured against this. Governmental responsibilities of protection are therefore not superfluous, but occupy a legitimate position alongside the solution-generating capacity of the global regime conflict between industry, scientific research and the healthcare system.[84]

Within these conflicts, science has an opportunity to reformulate the limits of its autonomy under the pressure exerted by society's conflicting rationalities. Niklas Luhmann's statement regarding the paradox at the very origin of human rights also applies to the emergence of transnational constitutional rights:[85] it is in the direct experience of their violation, in instances of acute disappointment, that constitutional rights acquire their shape and form. It is only when the selection mechanism of publication is violated that its significance for the way science operates is defined. This is where social conflict solutions as experiments in law-making have their origin.

Constitutional rights as collective institutions – the formula emphasises their dual character as social process and legal process at one and the same time. Legal positivism must not be allowed to put the social dynamic of constitutional rights at risk. Only in that case will they be able, in their collective-institutional dimension, to operate as conflict-of-laws rules and to fulfil their function of reinforcing social differentiation. It is for that very reason, however, that they elude a unifying objectivisation by formal legal means. Instead of defining common constitutional rights standards that apply to both state and society,[86] the law needs to continue to react to the formation of normativity in diverse social discourses in a context-sensitive manner.[87] The law can facilitate the creative development of the dynamics of social areas by acting as a moderator, but it must not prescribe their content.[88] Understood in this way, legal responsibilities to protect owed in regard to the self-regulation mechanisms of society are directed not towards content, but towards procedures. The task of the law would be to set up areas of protection in which social counter-institutions – in our case, trial registration – are able to develop.[89] By mobilising and multiplying dissenting voices, trial registration ensures that research results which go against economic interests cannot be manipulated. It provides a more appropriate counter-institution to publication bias than any state regulation could achieve. By moving to a facilitating law, trial registration has the potential to strengthen the scientific world against the expansionary tendencies of the economy.

Notes

This chapter was previously published as 'Horizontal fundamental rights as conflict of laws rules: how transnational pharma-groups manipulate scientific publications', trans. Cornelia Moser, in Kerstin Blome, Andreas Fischer-Lescano, Hannah Franzki, Nora Markard and Stefan Oeter (eds), *Contested Regime Collisions: Norm Fragmentation in World Society* (Cambridge: Cambridge University Press, 2016), pp. 139–68.

1. The poet Diagoras of Melos poses this provocative question when, as a proof for the existence of the gods, a priest shows him the votive pictures of people who have been saved by prayer from shipwreck. Diagoras was subsequently sentenced to death. Cicero, *De natura deorum*.
2. Eyding *et al.*, 'Reboxetine for acute treatment of major depression'; Institut für Qualität und Wirtschaftlichkeit im Gesundheitswesen, 'Bupropion, Mirtazapin und Reboxetin', available at https://www.iqwig.de/de/projekte_ergebnisse/projekte/arzneimittelbewertung/a05_20c_bupropion_mirtazapin_und_reboxetin_zur_behandlung_der_depression.1132.html#berichte.
3. Cf. US Court of Appeals, 7th Cir. (2008) *BASF AG v. Great American Assurance Co.*, 522 F.3d 813, 816. See Krimsky, *Science in the Public Interest* (2003).
4. Fugh-Berman, 'Haunting of medical journals'.
5. Cf. also the criticisms made in the case of the Vioxx study (involving Merck as manufacturer), in which the myocardial infarction risk was concealed (Bombardier *et al.*, 'Comparison of upper gastrointestinal toxicity') and in the case of the study on the licensed swine flu drug Tamiflu, manufactured by Roche (Jefferson *et al.*, 'Neuraminidase inhibitors').
6. See the case of the so-called MIDAS study of the efficacy of calcium blockers (involving Sandoz, subsequently Novartis, as manufacturer), in which the researchers successfully defended themselves: Applegate *et al.*, 'Multicenter Isradipine Diuretic Atherosclerosis Study'.
7. For example, the dismissal of the research scientist Nancy Olivieri from the University of Toronto when she wanted to issue warnings about negative study results; her employer was receiving research grants from Apotex, the manufacturer of the drug under investigation. See Viens and Savulescu, 'Introduction to the Olivieri Symposium'.
8. For conflicts between incompatible rationalities in modern society, see Weber, *Gesammelte Aufsätze zur Wissenschaftslehre*, pp. 605 ff.; Luhmann, *Theory of Society*, vol. 2, ch. 5, para.18.
9. See the early use of this term by Smith, 'Publication bias'.

10 Chan *et al.*, 'Empirical evidence for selective reporting'. See also a German study: Schott *et al.*, 'Finanzierung von Arzneimittelstudien 1'; Schott *et al.*, 'Finanzierung von Arzneimittelstudien 2'.
11 Petryna, *When Experiments Travel*.
12 For the current discussion in Germany, see Rüfner, 'Grundrechtsadressaten'; in a historical perspective, see Stolleis, *Geschichte des öffentlichen Rechts*, vol. 4, pp. 216 ff. On the legal position in Europe, see Clapham, *Human Rights Obligations of Non-State Actors*. For international law, see Gardbaum, '"Horizontal effect" of constitutional rights'; Ruggie, 'Protect, Respect, and Remedy'. On academic freedom, see Schmidt-Assmann, 'Wissenschaftsplanung im Wandel', p. 653.
13 Ladeur, *Kritik der Abwägung*; Fischer-Lescano, 'Kritik der praktischen Konkordanz'. For a critique of the legal situation in the US, see Mathews and Stone Sweet, 'All things in proportion?'
14 The principle is defined by Hesse, *Grundzüge des Verfassungsrechts der Bundesrepublik*, para. 72; Alexy, 'Verfassungsrecht und einfaches Recht'. For an early formulation, see BVerfGE 83,130 – Mutzenbacher.
15 For a critical view on state duties of care in the 'risk society', see Christensen and Fischer-Lescano, *Ganze des Rechts*, pp. 311 ff.
16 In general, see Dreier, *Dimensionen der Grundrechte*, pp. 27 ff.
17 BVerfGE 89, 214 – Bürgschaft.
18 Zöllner, 'Regelungsspielräume'.
19 Ridder, *Soziale Ordnung des Grundgesetzes*, pp. 90–1; Ridder, *Freiheit der Kunst*. A concise definition of the term is provided by Steinhauer, 'Grundrecht der Kunstfreiheit'. Steinhauer introduces the term 'collective-institutional' and uses it to describe Ridder's constitutional rights theory in contradistinction to Carl Schmitt's 'institutional' constitutional rights theory.
20 Schmitt, 'Freiheitsrechte', p. 155.
21 The fact that academic freedom is put at risk not only through governmental interference, but also by social (in particular industrial) influences, and accordingly requires effective protection of its constitutional rights, is emphasised by Augsberg, 'Subjektive und objektive Dimensionen', p. 74. The same is true for the global health system: see Krajewska, 'Bioethics and human rights'.
22 The *locus classicus* on structural violence is Galtung, 'Institutionalized conflict resolution'; on macro-criminality, Jäger, *Makrokriminalität*.
23 For clarity, it should be stressed that this does not mean that individual responsibility is eclipsed by collective responsibility, but rather that both exist side by side at all times, although they are subject to different preconditions.
24 More details in Chapter 5 in this volume. Steinhauer, 'Grundrecht der Kunstfreiheit', p. 4, also stresses that the collective-institutional dimension is not properly grasped if the term refers only to legal entities and collective actors. For an institutional interpretation of the horizontal effect of constitutional rights in the transnational arena, see Viellechner, *Transnationalisierung des Rechts*, pp. 217 ff.
25 Cf. 'Im digitalen Panoptikum: Wir fühlen uns frei. Aber wir sind es nicht', *Der Spiegel*, 6 January 2014, p. 106.
26 This formulation goes beyond Luhmann's concept of constitutional rights insofar as it deals not only with the totalising tendencies of politics, but also with those of other systems: Luhmann, *Grundrechte als Institution*.
27 BVerfGE 57, 295, 320–3 – Rundfunkentscheidung.
28 Vesting, *Tagesschau-App*; Ladeur, *Medienrecht und die Ökonomie der Aufmerksamkeit*, pp. 255 ff., 268 ff.

29 For details, see Teubner, *Constitutional Fragments*, pp. 142 ff.
30 A survey can be found in Schwabe, *Die sogenannte Drittwirkung*, pp. 12 ff.
31 Cf. US Supreme Court (1883), Civil Rights Cases, 109 US 3. For a critical response, see Gardbaum, '"Horizontal effect" of constitutional rights'.
32 Clapham, *Human Rights Obligations of Non-State Actors*; Nowrot, 'Den "Kinderschuhen" entwachsen'.
33 Gamillscheg, 'Grundrechte im Arbeitsrecht'; Conrad, *Freiheitsrechte und Arbeitsverfassung*.
34 As emphasized by Wheatley, 'Deliberating Cosmopolitan Ideas'; Verschraegen, 'Differentiation and Inclusion'.
35 Stichweh, *Wissenschaft, Universität, Professionen*, p. 28.
36 The formulations which were coined for digital manipulation apply equally to manipulation in the context of publication bias: see 'Im digitalen Panoptikum: Wir fühlen uns frei. Aber wir sind es nicht', *Der Spiegel*, 6 January 2014, p. 106. It is doubtful whether this should be referred to in terms of a 'technology of power', as currently often occurs under Foucault's influence. This is because in this case the medium of communication is not power, but money, and risks to constitutional rights arise without the translation of money into power.
37 Schmidt-Assmann, 'Wissenschaftsplanung im Wandel', p. 657.
38 See section 3 ('Contextualisation') for further detail on this point.
39 On the commercialisation of science, see Bumke, 'Universitäten im Wettbewerb'.
40 See Medwedjew, *Fall Lyssenko*.
41 Admittedly this does not always apply. In many cases industry (which depends on market innovations) attempts to control the actual scientific output directly and even to cause scientists to openly falsify the allocation of the values of the science code.
42 According to Niklas Luhmann, massive external pressure on the scientific research system leads to an inflation of the truth medium. 'Much value is placed … on commitments to truth, without any adequate guarantee that these commitments can be fulfilled. The possibility of internal integration, empirical verification and the precision of concepts are neglected in order to meet the widespread interest in research results. Like a fever, inflationary phenomena of this kind are a clear symptom that the system is defending itself against external influences by accommodating them.' Luhmann, *Wissenschaft der Gesellschaft*, p. 623.
43 See ibid., pp. 576 ff.; Stichweh, 'Einheit und Differenz'.
44 Concerning the complex relationship between variation, selection and stabilisation in the evolution of science, see Luhmann, *Wissenschaft der Gesellschaft*, pp. 583, 587–8.
45 On the 'communicative constitutional right' of academic freedom, see e.g. Lenski, *Personenbezogene Massenkommunikation*. But see also Schmidt-Assmann, 'Wissenschaft – Öffentlichkeit – Recht'.
46 Steinhauer, 'Grundrecht der Kunstfreiheit', p. 4.
47 On the institutional dimension of academic freedom, see for example BVerfGE 35, 79, 112; Augsberg, 'Subjektive und objektive Dimensionen', pp. 77–80.
48 See Nowotny, 'Changing Nature of Public Science'; Lexchin *et al.*, 'Pharmaceutical industry sponsorship'.
49 Easterbrook *et al.*, 'Publication bias'; Dickersin *et al.*, 'Factors influencing publication'.
50 Cf. Fanelli, 'Do pressures to publish increase scientists' bias?'; Dickersin, 'Existence of publication bias'; Gelling, 'Negative results'. Regarding time-lag bias, see Stern

and Simes, 'Publication bias'. Concerning the distorting effect of multiple publication, see Tramèr *et al.*, 'Impact of covert duplicate publication'.
51 The *PLOS Medicine* Editors, 'Ghostwriting revisited'.
52 See Franzen, *Breaking News*, pp. 73 ff., 88 ff.
53 Cf. the study by Becker *et al.*, 'Association between a journal's source of revenue and the drug recommendations made'; see also Kesselheim, 'Covert pharmaceutical promotion'. For the independence initiative by the International Society of Drug Bulletins and WHO, see Schaaber *et al.*, 'Warum unabhängige Arzneimittelzeitschriften und Fortbildungsveranstaltungen wichtig sind'.
54 See Ahmed *et al.*, 'Assessment of publication bias'.
55 Tonks, 'Clinical trials register for Europe'.
56 An analysis of defective conclusions can be found in Sutton *et al.*, 'Empirical assessment'.
57 Horton, 'Medical editors trial amnesty'.
58 Dürig, 'Grundrechte und Zivilrechtsprechung', pp. 158–9.
59 Concerning the reformulation of constitutional rights in the business context, see the classic study by Selznick, *Law, Society and Industrial Justice*, pp. 75 ff., 259 ff.; more recently, see Schierbeck, 'Operational Measures', p. 168.
60 Luhmann, *Grundrechte als Institution*, p. 188: The special nature of social spheres deserves protection against the levelling effect of politicisation.
61 Although this view is maintained on the basis of human dignity as the supreme constitutional principle of objective law by Dürig, 'Art. 1 GG'.
62 This corresponds to the German Constitutional Court's practice of referring to a social sphere's self-understanding when defining science, art and other areas in legal terms; BVerfGE 111, 333, 354. For a comprehensive account of this subject, see Augsberg, 'Subjektive und objektive Dimensionen', pp. 74–5, 84.
63 Vesting, *Rechtstheorie*, pp. 95 ff., speaks in this context of 'social conventions and implicit knowledge'. For science, see Augsberg, 'Subjektive und objektive Dimensionen'; for the health sector, Krajewska, 'Bioethics and human rights'.
64 Here one might refer to Wiethölter's concept of proceduralisation as the liberation of social normativity: Wiethölter, 'Just-ifications', pp. 71 ff., 75.
65 The US has provided a model in the form of the FDA Amendments Act of 2007: Food and Drug Administration, FDA Amendments Act (FDAAA) of 2007, public law No. 110–85 § 801, available at www.gpo.gov/fdsys/pkg/PLAW-110publ85/pdf/PLAW-110publ85.pdf).For the situation in Europe, see Quack and Wackerbeck, 'Verpflichtung zur Registrierung'.
66 Initial attempts are being made by the US governmental study register ClinicalTrials.gov or the German Clinical Studies Register at the University Hospital of Freiburg (www.germanctr.de). The impact of this issue is such that at the European level, too, public databases such as Eudra Pharm and the Clinical Trials Register are becoming established (www.eudrapharm.eu/eudrapharm/clinicaltrials.do and www.clinicaltrialsregister.eu), in addition to the EudraCT database (which is limited to access by the authorities of the Member States).
67 De Angelis *et al.*, 'Clinical trial registration'. There are also a few online journals that primarily publish negative results, for example the *Journal of Negative Results in Biomedicine* (www.jnrbm.com/). See Pfeffer and Olsen, 'Editorial'.
68 Journals can similarly counter the practice of ghostwriting, by making publication conditional on the provision of details of the persons taking part in the study and its financing.

69 Han makes reference to this decisive difference: 'Im digitalen Panoptikum: Wir fühlen uns frei. Aber wir sind es nicht', *Der Spiegel*, 6 January 2014, p. 106. Constitutional rights against the 'anonymous matrix' must therefore be structured differently from constitutional rights against state power: see Chapter 5 in this volume.
70 'Social systems need contradiction for their immune system, for the continuation of their self-reproduction under difficult circumstances.' Luhmann, *Social Systems*, p. 385; see also Luhmann, *Wissenschaft der Gesellschaft*, p. 623.
71 This is a problem with the new EU regulation on clinical studies (available at http://register.consilium.europa.eu/doc/srv?l=EN&t=PDF&gc=true&sc=false&f=ST%20 17866%202013%20INIT). Its implementation was decided by the European Council of Ministers on 20 December 2013. Insofar as the new regulation formulates a duty of registration in regard to clinical studies, it is reacting to social pressure, emanating from medical associations, ethics commissions, numerous NGOs and the Member States, to maintain the level of protection provided by societal trial registration. An initial draft regulation by the EU Commission of July 2011 was exclusively aimed at the liberalisation and stabilisation of the pharmaceutical market in Europe. However, if the regulation goes beyond the duty of registration and standardises specific publication duties in regard to the nature and method of clinical study reports, it will infiltrate the differentiated publication forms of the scientific world, with unforeseeable consequences as far as the science community is concerned.
72 Gerstenberg, 'Private Law, Constitutionalism and the Limits of the Judicial Role'; Karavas, *Digitale Grundrechte*, pp. 87 ff., 99.
73 Stichweh, *Wissenschaft, Universität, Professionen*, p. 84.
74 Augsberg, 'Subjektive und objektive Dimensionen', p. 80.
75 On the plurality of financial sources as an institutional support of academic freedom, see Graber, *Zwischen Geist und Geld*, pp. 227 ff.
76 A similar transformation of the academic world from the inside is described by Wagner, *Arzt und seine Kritiker*.
77 Cf. Dirnagl and Lauritzen, 'Fighting publication bias'. On initiatives within scientific publishing, see Franzen, *Breaking News*, pp. 246 ff.
78 Thus the World Medical Association Declaration of Helsinki, following the extensions of 2000 and 2008, establishes the duty 'to register each clinical study … in a publicly accessible database before recruitment of the first subject' (art. 35) and to publish negative studies (art. 36), available at www.wma.net/en/30publications/10policies/b3/index.html.
79 Such as the Ethical Commission of the Freiburg Medical Faculty (www.uniklinik-freiburg.de/ethikkommission/live/antragstellung/gemaessMPG.html#Publikationsvorhaben). Generally on this point, see Jull *et al.*, 'Clinical trials in NZ'.
80 Concerning the role of the media and scandals in the uncovering of publication bias, see the examples above.
81 World Health Organization (2012) International Clinical Trials Registry Platform (ICTRP) (2012), available at www.who.int/ictrp/en.
82 This is an extension of Luhmann's argument; see Luhmann, *Grundrechte als Institution*, p. 36.
83 An analysis concerning the autonomy of science is provided by Augsberg, 'Subjektive und objektive Dimensionen', pp. 74 ff.; for the autonomy of the health sector, see Krajewska, 'In Search of the Holy Grail'.
84 For the concept of a transnational regime, see Chapter 10 in this volume.

85 Luhmann, 'Paradox der Menschenrechte', p. 222.
86 This is, however, the view underlying (for example) the understanding of European constitutional rights as an expression of a common belief in constitutional rights. See Terhechte, *Konstitutionalisierung und Normativität*, pp. 3 ff.
87 Selznick, *Law, Society and Industrial Justice*, pp. 32 ff.; Luhmann, *Grundrechte als Institution*, p. 192.
88 On the structural primacy of learning in world society and a shift in the law towards facilitating cognitive expectations, see Luhmann, 'World Society as a Social System'.
89 Concerning such an impartially 'partisan' law, which is in favour of social autonomy but which exercises this 'partisanship' on an impartial basis, see Wiethölter, 'Justifications'. On facilitating law, see Christensen and Fischer-Lescano, *Das Ganze des Rechts*, p. 316.

12

The project of constitutional sociology: irritating nation-state constitutionalism

I The new constitutional question

Once again, Google has become the target of a passionate political debate.[1] The global search engine's 90 per cent market share, its questionable handling of users' private data and its massive expansionist tendencies into other sectors of the Internet raise not only political but also constitutional questions in the strict sense. Experts are warning the public about a 'social–private gap' and a 'distortion effect' in Google's activities: A dominant search engine may have incentives to distort its results in ways that increase its own profits but harm society.[2] However, it is not easy to determine which constitution is actually being affected by Google's market power. What is certain is that, due to their territorial boundaries, nation-state constitutions would constitute too narrow a focus here. However, Google's market power is not solely a problem of the global economic constitution, either. Google's information monopoly becomes a problem for the constitution of the new media that cannot be reduced to economic issues. Its worldwide digital networking activities, which have enabled massive intrusions into rights to privacy, informational self-determination and freedom of communication, represent typical problems for the constitution of the global Internet. And the lack of transparency in Google's governance structures raises constitutional questions of democracy and of public controls.

This is a constitutional rather than a merely regulatory matter. While legal-political regulation tries to influence actors' behaviour externally, here it is the internal structures of the Internet and of its collective actors that need to be changed. In the case of Google, a constitutional change would imply something akin to a separation of powers, by dividing 'software' and 'service' and subjecting them to different legal regimes. A regulatory change would imply the introduction of a regulatory agency to monitor results, with confidential access to the search machine's algorithms.[3] What is needed is a transformation of the constitution of the Internet in its *capillarité*,[4] which extends to the finest ramifications of digital processes.

Moreover, it is not just the juridification, but the constitutionalisation of a legal vacuum that is the challenge. And this entails a complex interlacing of social and legal processes at the meta-level of the Internet and its collective actors. It is not the information processes themselves that form the digital constitution, but rather their architecture – the famous 'digital code'.[5] And this constitution includes not only the digital code *per se*, but also its interplay with legal norms, which for their part are not primary, behaviour-controlling rules but secondary rules, that is, constitutional norms of a higher rank.

Google is exemplary of the new constitutional question, which is prompted by the tendencies of a globalisation, privatisation and digitalisation of the world. Compared to the old constitutional question of the eighteenth and nineteenth centuries, different yet no less severe problems become apparent today. While then the focus was on the release of the nation state's political energies as well as their effective limitation by the rule of law, today's constitutionalisation concentrates on constraining the destructive repercussions that result from the unleashing of entirely different social energies, which are especially noticeable in the economy, but also in science and technology, in medicine and the new media.[6] Constitutionalisation beyond the nation state occurs as an evolutionary process moving in two different directions: constitutions evolve in transnational political processes outside the nation state and, simultaneously, in global society's 'private' sectors outside of international politics.[7]

When the sociology of law addresses these problems, it returns to the beginnings of sociology as such. According to leading constitutional sociologist Chris Thornhill, the narrow perspectives of constitutional law, which confined the constitutional phenomenon to the state, were rejected by sociology from the outset in favour of a focus on the constitution of modern society as a whole and its various sub-constitutions.[8] Today, transnationalisation confronts constitutional sociology with three different challenges:

- the empirical analysis of ongoing constitutionalisation processes beyond the nation state,

- the development of a theory of transnational societal constitutionalism, and
- the formulation of sociological preconditions for normative perspectives in politics and law.

Whether and how constitutional lawyers will respond to these sociological irritations remains an open question. What is certain is that such irritations are being met with considerable resistance. Can transnational regimes become suitable constitutional subjects, that is, are they social institutions capable of having their own constitution? Constitutional lawyers have raised this question and answered it with a resounding 'No!'[9] In their view, only nation states can be constitutional subjects – not international organisations or transnational regulatory regimes, and certainly not 'private' transnational regimes. So-called constitutions beyond the nation state, they argue, lack a social substrate that could provide a suitable object for a constitution. The norms of transnational regimes perform only regulatory functions, not genuine constitutional ones. It is asserted that they are unable to create the kind of interplay between different arenas of public opinion and binding decision-making processes that one sees in the political sphere. Furthermore, it is claimed that the transnational understanding of the term 'constitution' merely refers to hierarchies of legal norms, without, however, being able to anchor them in democratic processes. These arguments are not legal arguments in the strict sense, but rather sociological theses within the discourse of constitutional law. How does legal sociology respond to them?

II Empiricism: constitutionalisation processes

First and foremost, this is a matter of empirical social research. In which areas, in which types of social conflict and with what institutional results do actual constitutionalisation processes take place in the transnational sphere? This is clearly not merely a task for the future, since recent research has shown that constitutional norms have already evolved in different transnational contexts. Thus, future empirical studies can build upon these findings:

Transnational human rights: Especially against non-state collective actors, the horizontal effects of human rights have become a prominent legal issue, particularly in public interest litigation. In environmental scandals in Nigeria, in the AIDS debacle in South Africa and in incidents of child labour, land grabbing and biopiracy in developing countries, it has become apparent that transnational corporations have again and again committed serious human rights violations.[10] Inter-state human rights conventions are of a certain relevance here, but it is global civil society that has proved to be the driving force when it comes to imposing sanctions for these human rights violations. Transnational human rights have only a limited effect against states when they are guaranteed by inter-state conventions. They do not apply automatically to international organisations or transnational regimes.[11] This changes only when, as in the WTO, an independent judiciary begins to develop on the basis of international treaties, and when mere panels of conflict negotiation are transformed into genuine court institutions in which constitutional rights are recognised. Then those courts themselves, in a procedure similar to the common law, are able to determine which standards of fundamental rights should apply within transnational regimes.[12] Similarly, private arbitration tribunals of the International Chamber of Commerce (ICC), the International Corporation for the Settlement of Investment Disputes (ICSID) and the Internet Corporation for Assigned Names and Numbers (ICANN) decide human rights issues. It is they who actually decide the scope of human rights when they are faced with the choice between different standards of fundamental rights and determine which constitutional rights are legally binding in their regimes.[13] Furthermore, protest movements, NGOs and the media are involved in the creation of constitutional rights when they express outrage at violations of human rights by transnational collective actors.[14]

The global economic constitution: Social science analyses of the 'New Constitutionalism',[15] economic studies of an emerging global economic constitution[16] and international law studies on the growing significance of constitutional norms[17] have identified constitutional institutions of astonishing density in the transnational sphere. Today, only very few authors continue to deny that the European Union – despite the failure of the constitutional referendum – has developed a genuine constitution.[18] In the transnational sphere the Washington Consensus gave political momentum to the constitutionalisation of the global economy, which is based on the autonomy of world markets. It triggered not only political regulation, but also the standardisation of constitutional principles. These principles were designed to provide an unlimited scope of action for global companies, abolishing government participation in businesses, combating trade protectionism and freeing commercial enterprises from political regulation.[19] The guiding principle in the constitution of the International Monetary Fund as well as that of the World Bank was the opening of national capital markets. The constitutions of the World Trade Organization (WTO), of the European internal market, the North American Free Trade Agreement (NAFTA), the Mercado Común del Sur (MERCOSUR) and the Asia-Pacific Economic Cooperation (APEC) were directed at the constitutional protection of the freedom of world trade and the promotion of direct investment.[20] The production of limitative rules, as a replacement for national regulations, was not part of the political agenda, however, and in fact was even combated for years as counterproductive.

Only today, due to the experience of near catastrophe in the recent corporate and financial crises, do collective learning processes appear to be emerging which seek constitutional limits at the global level.[21]

Transnational regime constitutions: International organisations, transnational regimes and global networks today are not only strongly juridified, but also constitutionalised. Despite their fragmentation, they have become part of a worldwide constitutional order. To be sure, this constitutional order does not attain the density of a national constitution. The global institutions that were born out of the agreements of the 1940s – the Havana Charter, GATT, Bretton Woods; the new institutions of the Washington Consensus – the IMF, the World Bank, WTO; but also the recent public debate about a global 'financial market constitution' and pleas for a worldwide 'democratic constitutionalism', speak the language of actual, existing global sub-constitutions.[22]

Lex mercatoria: Above its contractual norms, this self-created law of the global economy has created a layer of constitutional norms. In the *lex mercatoria*, a hierarchy of norms exists, with the constitutional norms, principles, procedural rules and human rights making up the so-called *ordre public d'arbitrage international* at its apex. Detailed analyses of arbitration tribunals have identified a variety of such self-created constitutional norms of international arbitration. Private arbitration tribunals transform the property principle, freedom of contract, competition rules and human rights into positive norms that are part of a transnational public policy.[23]

Corporate constitutionalism: A dynamic sector of transnational constitutionalisation has emerged that deals with the internal structure of corporations. Triggered by a first wave of 'neo-liberal' constitutionalisation, corporate constitutions focused on procuring a high degree of autonomy for transnational companies.[24] The corporate governance principles of multinational companies promoted business autonomy, capital market orientation and the establishment of shareholder values. This emerging global corporate constitutionalism was aimed at two things: first, to loosen the strong structural linkage between transnational companies and nation-state politics and law; and secondly, to strengthen the rule of law structurally to the extent that this is needed for the worldwide networking of their functionally specific communications. Following the large number of corporate scandals in recent years, however, the so-called Corporate Codes of Conduct are involved in a second wave of constitutionalisation, which is aimed at limiting companies' activities. By means of private ordering, they attempt – for the benefit of various stakeholders in society – to break the shareholder orientation and to engender social responsibility in the areas of work, product quality, the environment and human rights.[25]

Global administrative law: This is the most recent candidate for a constitutionalisation of transnational sectors.[26] Today, there are more than 2,000 global regulatory agencies in the form of international and intergovernmental organisations.[27] In contrast to the administrative law of the UN and general international law, which apply only within the internal space of institutionalised politics, the norms of this administrative law directly regulate the various sectors of global society affected by them. Through regulation of the social environment, forms of 'private ordering' are emerging that cannot be captured by the categories of traditional 'public' administrative law. This development emphasises the 'societal' character of global administrative law. Regulatory competences are shifting vertically from nation states to international regimes and horizontally from states to non-public actors – transnational companies and collective actors in civil society.[28] The constitutional norms that are being developed here include, in particular, due process of regulation, notice-and-comment rules, compulsory consultation with experts, the principle of proportionality and respect for human rights.

Constitutionalisation of international law: This much-debated phenomenon also plays a role in the constitutionalisation of global subsystems.[29] Here, three complexes of norms that indeed possess constitutional qualities move to the fore: *jus cogens*, norms claiming validity *erga omnes* and human rights.[30] As expressions of universal values they waive the element of state consensus and develop legally binding force even against states that have not given their consent. Such genuine constitutional norms are developed by changing the basic structure of international law. In the past, this basic structure consisted in an ensemble of contractual relations between sovereign states. Now it has been transformed into an independent legal order that, in the *ordre public transnational*, creates its own foundation with its own constitutional norms. Only this constitutionalisation allows international law to do what seems unthinkable for a mere contractual order that is not supported by a comprehensive legal order: to impose, even against the explicit will of contracting parties, legally binding norms that are legitimised not through (contractual) state treaties, but through the orientation of the legal order towards the common good.[31]

In all these sectors, the task of socio-legal analysis is to identify the specific features of global constitutionalism as compared to its national counterparts.[32] The search for transnational equivalents to the traditional constitutional subject, the nation state, is given priority. What are the new constitutional subjects under the conditions of globality? The system of international politics itself? Global functional systems? International organisations? Transnational regimes? Global networks? New assemblages, configurations or ensembles? The answer depends on whether such non-state institutions enable sustainable analogies to the *pouvoir constituant* of the nation state, to the self-constitution of political collectives, to democratic decision-making and to organisational rules of a political constitution in the strict sense.[33]

Which collective actors and which power relations are the driving forces behind the constitutionalisation of transnational configurations? This question forms the focus of much legal sociological research, especially following the recent financial crisis. In particular, the question arises as to the role played by the nation states in the constitutionalisation of global societal institutions. Are they the constitutional legislator for other sectors of world society? Or only participating observers of autonomous societal constitutionalisation processes? Or coordinators of conflicting systemic dynamics? It is possible that societal forces are more relevant than nation states.[34] Counter-forces within civil society – the media, public debate, spontaneous protest, intellectuals, social movements, NGOs, trade unions, professions – exert considerable pressure on the internal constitutionalisation of transnational regimes.

To identify idiosyncratic constitutional principles that, in contrast to the traditional political principles of state constitutions, reflect the different underlying social systems: this may well be the specific contribution of legal sociology to the constitutional debate. When legal practice re-specifies transnational human rights in different social fields, this does not amount merely to an adjustment of originally state-oriented human rights to the peculiarities of private law, as legal scholars usually assert. An approach founded purely in legal doctrine, which traces the so-called objective value order of the constitution to its supposed concrete embodiment in the normative order of private law, misses the peculiarities of the different social contexts for which private law provides its general norms. Human rights need to be released from their state orientation and newly calibrated to the specific threats that are produced by other social systems. If the constitutions of the economy, science, the mass media and the health system now legally formalise their communicative media on a global basis, fundamental rights must be redirected towards them.

III Theory: the ubiquity of the constitutional phenomenon

1 A multidisciplinary debate

Constitutions are too important to be left to constitutional lawyers and moral philosophers. Within widely different disciplines, theoretical traditions have developed that have criticised the restriction of constitutionalism to the nation state and that have posed the constitutional question for various sectors of society.

The renowned historian Reinhart Koselleck has been fiercely critical of constitutional lawyers for their continued exclusive focus on nation states.[35] He demands recognition of the historical reality that even in the era of the nation state, there was not only a nation-state constitution, but also a more comprehensive societal constitution that subjected economical, societal and cultural institutions to constitutional demands. At the same time, Koselleck emphatically draws attention to the new transnational constitutionalisation. Due to the state-centred nature of conventional constitutionalism, he fears that it is impossible 'to address the post-statal, in a way supranational, phenomena of our times'.[36]

In a similar vein, classical sociology already posed the constitutional question not only for the state, but also for all societal sectors. Emile Durkheim established a link between basic societal structures – segmental differentiation versus division of labour – on the one hand, and societal constitutional norms – mechanic versus organic solidarity – on the other.[37] In the sociology of organisations, pioneering work has been done by the theory of 'private government' by revealing the genuinely political character of commercial enterprises and other private organisations which required the transfer of political principles to private organisations.[38] Within organisations that are apparently exclusively centred around economic efficiency, genuine political power processes could be discovered and analogies to the larger political systems could be drawn. The theory claimed that in analogy to constitutional state-political governments, private governments establish legitimacy through an explicitly political configuration of organisational rules and secure their members' freedoms through constitutional rights.

That the demands for constitutionalisation expand to encompass the entire economy as well as other social processes has long been the theme of more broadly based theories of a welfare-state-oriented societal and economic constitution. At the beginning stood the political 'idea of a Labour Constitution', that is, a social order which grants workers participatory rights via statute law or collective agreements and thus limits exclusive shareholder rights.[39] With time, this idea has become more generalised. The political constitution is understood as a 'societal' overarching institution, with the consequence that democratic co-determination and guarantees of constitutional rights are to be extended from the political process to all socially relevant organisations.[40] Such programmes postulate constitutions for all social sectors, following the model of democratic politics. These programmes are based on theories of societal transformation, such as Polanyi's, which register the unstoppable economisation of society, but at the same time also identify social counter-movements that reconstruct the 'protective covering of cultural institutions' against the total economisation of society.[41]

Theories of economic constitutionalism acquired greater depth and precision in an exemplary controversy whose representatives in Germany are Hans-Joachim Mestmäcker and Rudolf Wiethölter. Ordo-liberal theory claims that property, contract, competition and monetary institutions form an autonomous economic constitution that emerges not merely from the constitutional law of the state, but from the interplay of economic self-regulation, economic theories and legal-political norms. The legitimacy of economic constitutionalism is based not on the political decisions of the legislature, but primarily on the autonomy of economic action.[42] In contrast, the 'political theory of law' focuses on a '*Rechtsverfassungsrecht*' for all social sectors with the aim of institutionalising the political in 'society as society'. The latter is formed 'not simply of the "democratic" unified sum total of such citizens, but also "organises" institutionalisations for decision-making, communication and education processes'.[43]

Theories of neo-corporatism that identify a variety of societal sub-constitutions have become very influential, both in practice and in theory.[44] Politico-economic theories about the 'varieties of capitalism' have clarified the peculiarities of neo-corporatist regimes.[45] The theory of this kind of societal constitutionalism, in which organised interests from different social sectors exert quasi-public functions, was particularly influential in the 1970s until it was reduced in significance by the emerging wave of liberalisation. However, following the great financial crisis, it regained currency.

A mature theory of societal constitutionalisation was eventually presented by David Sciulli.[46] Taking Max Weber's dilemmas of modern rationalisation as his starting point, he poses the question whether there are any forces opposing the existing massive evolutionary drift towards increasing authoritarianism in modern societies. According to Sciulli, the only social dynamic that has effectively counteracted this drift in the past and that can offer resistance to it in the future is to be found in the institutions of 'societal constitutionalism'. In his view, what really counts here is the social institutionalisation of the 'collegial formations' identifiable in specific forms of organisation adopted by the professions and in other norm-producing deliberative institutions.

2 *A constitutional concept for the transnational context*

The current challenge for constitutionalism consists in taking up these different theoretical strands and in reformulating them in accordance with the new global situation. Primarily it is a matter of developing a constitutional concept that is adequate for transnational regimes. How far must the principles of nation-state constitutions be generalised in order to avoid the fallacies of methodological nationalism? And how do they need to be re-specified for the peculiarities of diverse societal institutions in a globalised world? Such a method of generalisation and re-specification will have to answer the following question: Is it possible to identify a transnational equivalent to nation-state constitutions in terms of functions, arenas, processes and structures?

It should be self-evident nowadays that a 'formal' constitutional concept is too narrow. Instead, even constitutions outside the state need to satisfy the requirements of a 'material' concept, according to which a constitution establishes a distinct legal authority that in turn structures a *societal* process (and not merely a political process, as in nation-state constitutions) and is legitimised through this process.[47] In order to qualify as constitutional norms, the norms of transnational regimes have to pass the following quality tests:

(1) *Constitutional functions:* Do transnational regimes produce legal norms that perform more than merely regulatory or conflict-solving functions, i.e. that act as either 'constitutive rules' or 'limitative rules' in the strict sense?

Regime constitutions fulfil the constitutive function if they formalise the autonomy of their own communication medium, and if today, they do this on a globalised scale. By means of constitutive rules,[48] the constitution in question regulates the abstraction of a uniform communicative medium – power, money, law, knowledge – as an autonomous social construct within a worldwide constitutive functional system. To that purpose, organisational rules, procedures, competences and subjective rights are developed, the separation between different social spheres is codified, and, in that way, the functional differentiation of society is supported.

Regime constitutions fulfil the limitative function, which is of particular significance today, if they develop norms of constitutional self-restraint. This is not a peculiar problem belonging to the political system, but one faced by all sectors of society.[49] Differences exist only as a result of the specific internal reproductive conditions in each case. It is only politics that constructs its constitution along the lines of an aggregation of power and consensus for collective decisions and that therefore must act through the medium of power in its self-limitation. Other social systems have to align their constitutional limitations to their own communicative media.

(2) *Constitutional arenas:* Is it possible to identify different arenas of constitutionalisation within regimes, comparable to the interplay of the arenas of organised political processes and of the spontaneous process of public opinion regulated in the organisational part of state constitutions?

Societal constitutionalism turns the existence of a variety of 'reflection centres' within society, and in particular within economic institutions, into the main criterion of a democratic society.⁵⁰ The internal differentiation of functional systems into an organised professional sphere and a spontaneous sphere plays a key role in the interplay between these reflection centres. Within the organised professional sphere, a further differentiation can be observed between decentralised organisations and centralised self-regulating institutions. Historically, the corresponding internal differentiation of politics has already been elaborated into detailed sets of norms by the political constitutions of states in their organisational part: norms regarding voting rights and political fundamental rights, on the one hand, and procedural rules for parliamentary, governmental and administrative decisions, on the other. Yet even the other functional systems constitutionalise different internal arenas: not only their organised professional arenas (i.e. corporations, banks, Internet intermediaries, health organisations, professional associations and universities), but also their spontaneous arenas (i.e. the various function-specific constituencies).

(3) *Constitutional processes*: Do the legal norms of regimes develop a sufficiently close connection to their social context or their 'nomic community' – comparable to that between constitutional norms and the 'nomic community' of nation states?

This connection to a nomic community is incorporated into the constitutional concept as the criterion of a 'double reflexivity'. The primary aspect of constitutionalisation is first of all always the self-constitution of the communication medium of a social system: of politics, of the economy, of the media or of public health.⁵¹ While the law does play an indispensable role in these processes, it is nevertheless a subservient one. An ambitious constitutional theory for a global societal constitutionalism must remember the fact that constitutions are primarily social processes and only secondarily legal processes. However, such medial reflexivity does not yet generate constitutions in the technical sense; it enables only the self-foundation – not yet the constitutionalisation – of social systems. Whether in politics, economics or in other sectors, one can only speak of constitutions in the strict sense when the reflexivity of a social system is structurally linked to the reflexivity of law, that is, to secondary rules. Constitutions emerge when such phenomena of double reflexivity appear – the reflexivity of the self-constituting social system and the reflexivity of the law that supports its self-foundation.

Constitutional structures: Do regimes produce the typical constitutional structures familiar from nation states, in particular the priority of constitutional rules and the judicial review of ordinary law?

The endpoint of constitutionalisation (be it in politics, in the economy or in other social spheres) is not reached until an autonomous constitutional code – or, to be more precise, a *hybrid binary meta-code* – arises which guides the internal processes of both the systems involved. The code is *binary* because it oscillates between the values 'constitutional/unconstitutional'. The code functions at the *meta-level* because it subjects decisions that have already been subjected to the binary 'legal/illegal' code to an additional test. Legal decisions are tested for whether they comply with the constitution. This is where the typical constitutional hierarchy emerges: the hierarchy between ordinary law and constitutional law, 'the law of laws'. The constitutional code of the social sphere under consideration (constitutional/unconstitutional) is given precedence over the legal code (legal/illegal). What is special about this meta-coding, though, is its *hybridity*, as the constitutional code takes precedence not only over the legal code, but also over the binary code of the functional system concerned. Thus it exposes the binary-coded operations of the functional system to an additional reflection concerning the question of whether or not they take into account the subsystem's public responsibility.

Only on condition that a transnational configuration possesses all these characteristics can one speak of it as having a transnational constitution in the strict sense.

IV Politics and law: self-limitation of societal growth compulsions

If constitutional law was going to be receptive to sociological analyses of transnational constitutionalisation, it would at the same time need to keep a sufficient distance from its neighbouring discipline. On no account can constitutional sociology prescribe legal principles for transnational constitutions, let alone individual constitutional rules. Instead, constitutional law should focus on an interdisciplinary division of labour, in which each discipline makes an autonomous contribution from its own perspective. What this means is that constitutional sociology examines the intrinsic logic of transnational configurations, discovers the characteristics of transnational constitutionalisation processes and develops alternatives for structural solutions outside national, state-based constitutions. In its turn, constitutional law responds to these irritations and, based on its own intellectual traditions, develops independent concepts, principles and rules for transnational constitutions that can be regarded as appropriate legal solutions for the new kind of constitutive and limitative problems facing them.

Today, constitutional law needs to concentrate on developing *limitative rules* for transnational regimes. This is because sociology has identified massive growth compulsions with destructive consequences in various functional systems. Inherent pressure towards an ever-increasing production is a precondition for the self-reproduction of the economy, but this pressure can be heightened by identifiable mechanisms of intensification to such an extent that a descent into destructive tendencies is the consequence.[52] However, this pressure is found not only in the economy, but also in other functional systems. Such growth compulsions go beyond the acceleration circle of modern society diagnosed by Hartmut Rosa and William Scheuerman.[53] The issue here is not just the social alteration of time structures, which amounts to an acceleration of social processes. That is merely the temporal dimension of a general dynamic. Attention needs to be paid to its material and social dimensions as well. In its material dimension, this dynamic manifests itself as the growth imperative of symbolic production, that is, as a tendency to multiply operations of the same kind.[54] In its social dimension, it occurs as a problem in social epidemiology, that is, as manifesting itself through imitation, spreading and contagion, in a way that has been studied in particular in analyses of the 'herd instinct' in financial markets.[55] Overall, this is a question of advance contributions that generate expectations of an increase in performance, which in turn exact further advance contributions. In other words, something that begins as a dynamic necessary for system maintenance has a tendency to slide into socially harmful excess.

Constitutional law is confronted with the task of developing constitutional rules that are in a position to respond to the motivation–competence dilemma faced by transnational regimes. This dilemma consists in the fact that while civil society movements, the spontaneous areas of functional systems, the courts and state politics are highly motivated to limit the expansive tendencies of the regimes, they lack the knowledge, the capacity for action and the power of implementation that are required to achieve such changes successfully. In contrast, in transnational regimes these capacities are highly developed; however, due to their interest in self-maintenance, their motivation for self-limitation is mostly missing. In this situation, aptly characterised by Habermas as 'the new obscurity', the only remedy left is a 'siege' of the organised professional regimes by a political general public.[56] It is only changes in the internal constitution of transnational regimes that can increase their ability to be irritated by the demands of civil society, the courts and state politics.

How such a capillary constitutionalisation can succeed in a concrete manner, no one can predict. *Ex ante* prognoses are, as a matter of principle, impossible. There are thus no alternatives to an experimental constitutionalisation. Political interventions are indispensable in countering the self-threatening elements of subsystemic rationality. Their aim must be to introduce new possibilities into this rationality by breaking down self-blockages, not to counter it with a different, state-based rationality. Political and legal regulation and external societal influence are only likely to succeed if the practical form they take is the self-domestication of systemic growth dynamics. This calls for considerable external interventions from politics, law and civil society – but only those designed to translate into self-transformation and those whose translation into internal processes of change actually succeeds.

Notes

This chapter was previously published as 'The project of constitutional sociology: irritating nation state constitutionalism', *Transnational Legal Theory*, 4:1 (2013), 44–58.

1. Pollock, 'Is Google the next Microsoft?'; Manne and Wright, 'Google and the limits of antitrust'.
2. Pollock, 'Is Google the next Microsoft?', p. 38.
3. See ibid., p. 39.
4. Derrida, *Other Heading*, p. 42.
5. Lessig, *Code and Other Laws*.
6. Allott, 'Emerging universal legal system', p. 16, goes so far as to describe the new constitutional question as 'the central challenge faced by international philosophers in the 21st century'.
7. For a detailed elaboration, see Teubner, *Constitutional Fragments*. For an interdisciplinary debate on this issue, see the symposium contributions collected in Teubner and Beckers (eds), *Transnational Societal Constitutionalism*. The method of comparative and interdisciplinary enquiries is discussed by Zumbansen, 'Comparative, global and transnational constitutionalism'.
8. Thornhill, 'Niklas Luhmann and the sociology of the constitution', pp. 316 ff.
9. Grimm, 'Achievement of Constitutionalism' p. 13; Loughlin, 'What Is Constitutionalisation?'
10. Oliver and Fedtke (eds), *Human Rights and the Private Sphere*; De Schutter (ed.), *Transnational Corporations and Human Rights*; Joseph, *Corporations and Transnational Human Rights Litigation*.
11. Gardbaum, 'Human Rights and International Constitutionalism'.
12. Trachtman, 'Constitutions of the WTO', pp. 640 ff.
13. Renner, *Zwingendes transnationales Recht*.
14. Fischer-Lescano, *Globalverfassung*.
15. Schneiderman, *Constitutionalizing Economic Globalization*, pp. 328 ff.
16. Behrens, 'Weltwirtschaftsverfassung'.
17. Klabbers, 'Setting the Scene'.
18. See Walker, 'Post-Constituent Constitutionalism'; Weiler and Wind (eds), *European Constitutionalism*.
19. For a critical analysis, see Stiglitz, *Globalization and its Discontents*, pp. 53 ff.
20. Cass, *Constitutionalization of the World Trade Organization*; Gill, *Power and Resistance*.
21. Kjaer, *Constitutionalism in the Global Realm*.
22. Schneiderman, 'Legitimacy and reflexivity in international investment arbitration'.
23. See Renner, *Zwingendes transnationales Recht*, p. 92 ff.; Dalhuisen, 'Legal orders and their manifestations'.
24. Backer, 'Autonomous global enterprise'.
25. Anderson, 'Corporate Constitutionalism'; Zumbansen, '"New governance"'.
26. Kingsbury *et al.*, 'Emergence of global administrative law'.

27 Cassese, 'Administrative law without the state', p. 671.
28 Backer, 'Multinational corporations, transnational law', p. 307.
29 See Dunoff and Trachtman (eds), *Ruling the World?*; Frowein, 'Konstitutionalisierung des Völkerrechts'.
30 See Gardbaum, 'Human Rights and International Constitutionalism'; Peters, 'Compensatory constitutionalism', pp. 585 ff.
31 Nowrot, 'Transnationale Verantwortungsgemeinschaft', pp. 59 ff.
32 For first steps in this direction, see Teubner, *Constitutional Fragments*, chs 3–5.
33 Viellechner, 'Constitutionalism as a cipher'.
34 Crouch, *Strange Non-Death of Neoliberalism*, ch. 6.
35 Koselleck, *Begriffsgeschichten*, pp. 369 ff.
36 Ibid., p. 369.
37 Durkheim, *Division of Labor*, pp. 111 ff.
38 The *locus classicus* is Selznick, *Law, Society and Industrial Justice*, pp. 75 ff., 259 ff.
39 Sinzheimer, 'Wesen des Arbeitsrechts', pp. 108 ff.
40 Preuss, 'La garantie des droits';Ridder, *Zur Verfassungsrechtlichen Stellung der Gewerkschaften*, p. 18; Ridder, *Soziale Ordnung des Grundgesetzes*, pp. 47 ff.
41 Polanyi, *Great Transformation*.
42 Mestmäcker, *Wirtschaft und Verfassung*.
43 Wiethölter, 'Just-ifications'; Wiethölter, 'Zur Regelbildung in der Dogmatik', p. 238.
44 Streeck and Schmitter, *Private Interest Government*.
45 Hall and Soskice (eds), *Varieties of Capitalism*.
46 Sciulli, *Theory of Societal Constitutionalism*.
47 Kumm, 'Beyond golf clubs', p. 508.
48 Searle, 'Social ontology'.
49 Prandini, 'Morphogenesis of Constitutionalism'.
50 See Sciulli, *Theory of Societal Constitutionalism*.
51 Thornhill, 'Towards a historical sociology', pp. 169 ff.
52 Binswanger, *Vorwärts zur Mäßigung*.
53 Rosa and Scheuerman (eds), *High-Speed Society*.
54 Stichweh, 'Towards a General Theory of Function System Crisis'.
55 Stäheli, 'Political Epidemiology'.
56 Habermas, 'New obscurity'.

13

Exogenous self-binding: how social subsystems externalise their foundational paradoxes in the process of constitutionalisation

I Four remarkable phenomena

I aim to establish a link between four remarkable but mutually rather distant phenomena, whose interpretation is subject to considerable uncertainty. The first remarkable phenomenon is the fact that judge-made law is now dramatically expanding in transnational contexts, too. It had already been shocking enough that within the nation state, the courts – which after all are supposed to be no more than *la bouche de la loi* – were producing more and more legal norms themselves even in the presence of a dominant political legislature, in direct contravention of the basic principles of the separation of powers and of democratic legitimacy.[1] Yet now we find that in transnational regimes, this trend is continuing unfettered and even accelerating. In a secondary analysis of empirical data, the sociologist of law Chris Thornhill comes to the conclusion that

> international courts and other appellate actors have assumed a remit that substantially exceeds conventional arbitrational functions. They now increasingly focus on objectives of 'norm-advancement': that is, they invoke rights to shape acts of national legislation and, without clear constitutional mandate, to construct a supra- or transnational normative order.[2]

Critical observers such as Ran Hirschl trace this back to power and interest configurations that favour the illegitimate claims to power of a 'global juristocracy'.[3] Apologist observers such as Josef Esser counter by maintaining that judicial law-making is more rational than its legislative counterpart.[4] Neither interpretation is satisfactory.

Secondly, it has recently been possible to observe a striking return of natural law. While philosophers, historians and legal theorists have been diagnosing the demise of natural law, jurisprudence scholars from both progressive and conservative backgrounds – but also judges in their decision-making practices – have been celebrating the resurrection of arguments grounded in natural law.[5] And this has not been limited to the sustained boom experienced by fundamental and human rights. Here, too, existing explanations are not very satisfactory. They are sought either in hegemonic tendencies in legal culture supported by power and interest groups, as diagnosed by those working in Gramsci's tradition, or, as prominently maintained by Lon Fuller, in powers that work in the arcanum of the law, silently operating an 'inner morality of law' in opposition to the principle of legal positivism that holds sway politically and legally.[6]

A third remarkable phenomenon is a change in direction among protest movements, which some observers interpret as the expression of a new political quality.[7] The conflicts in which these changes appear today are Brent Spar, the World Social Forum, Gorleben, animal rights protests against universities, companynamesucks.com, Stuttgart 21, Wikileaks, the *indegnados* and Occupy Wall Street. The common denominator is that these civil society protests are addressed not (only) against the state, but also, selectively and purposefully, against the organised professional institutions of the economy and of other functional systems that they hold responsible for seriously distorted developments.

The last remarkable phenomenon is the great disparity in status between different types of constitution: the state constitution, the economic constitution and the constitution of science. The dominance, if not exactly the monopoly, of state constitutions is obvious, both in practice and in theory. The status of economic constitutions is already more precarious. Nobody would now deny the actual existence of different economic constitutions and their foundational role for the economy, politics and law. And radical changes to the existing global economic constitution, as laid down in the Washington Consensus, are being advanced with normative bravura at this very moment.[8] But whether these are actually constitutions in the strict sense of the term, and who acts as the constituent power – the economy? politics? the law? society? – are extremely controversial issues. The existence of a constitution of science, in its turn, is really only asserted in a metaphorical sense.[9] Why are there such differences in the constitutional status of social subsystems?

How a constitution deals with its foundational paradox – that is the point that links these four reciprocally separate phenomena. This question is pertinent not only to the state constitution, but also and especially to the constitutions of other social systems.[10] The starting point is Luhmann's argument (discussed in section II below) that the law, with the aid of the state constitution, externalises its foundational paradox by transposing it into politics, while politics externalises its own paradox by transposing it into the law. Over and above this, the question needs to be raised (in section III) whether – and if so, how – the law also pursues a comparable de-paradoxification vis-à-vis other social subsystems. The same question, but now in the opposite direction, is posed (in section IV) when one asks whether other social systems also behave like politics in externalising their paradoxes and transposing them into the law with the aid of a constitution, or whether they employ alternative de-paradoxifications. Both of these lead to the concluding question (in section V), asking what problems follow on from different externalisations. The differences between various approaches to de-paradoxification may shed light on the four initial questions, to wit: Why is judge-made law gaining new prominence transnationally? Under what conditions will a particular kind of natural law make headway against positivism once more even today? Why do protest movements change the targets of their protests? And for what reasons does the constitutionalisation of social subsystems proceed not in accordance with a standard pattern, but with clear differences of intensity?

II Reciprocal paradox externalisation in law and politics

The starting point here is Niklas Luhmann's theory of the state constitution, which gives a central role to how law and politics deal with their foundational paradox.[11] As the law is founded on the binary code of right and wrong, it gets into a tangle with the paradoxes of self-reference when the code is inevitably applied to itself. This foundational paradox exposes law to the suspicion of arbitrariness, undermines its quest for legitimacy and paralyses decisions. The escape routes only lead to the familiar Münchhausen trilemma of the law: infinite regress (religious natural law), arbitrary interruption (Hans Kelsen) or the circularity of the foundation of norms (Herbert Hart). As none of these three offers a satisfactory way out, in the end only one strategy of de-paradoxification has been found to be successful in the past. Law externalises its paradox by transposing it into politics with the aid of the state constitution. In this way, the law seeks its ultimate legitimation in democratic politics, is thus disburdened of its own paradox problem and no longer needs to concern itself with how politics comes to terms with this externalisation.

Politics, on the other hand, has to struggle with an internally insoluble paradox – 'the paradox of the binding of necessarily unbound authority'.[12] How could one bind the sovereign to rational rules and above all to its own promises? A remedy was found only when this paradox was externalised and transposed into the law, something that once again was accomplished by the state constitution. The constitution commits politically unconstrained sovereignty to the process of the law. The state constitution, as a structural coupling between the law and politics, is thus characterised by the fact that *there is a reciprocal externalisation of the foundational paradoxes of politics and law*. Law and politics develop complex forms of an exogenous self-constraint that are – not coincidentally – reminiscent of freedom through self-constraint and of the artful conjunction between self-constraint and externally imposed constraint found in the myth of Odysseus.

Is it possible to generalise this theory of the political constitution? Do other social systems externalise their paradoxes by transposition into the law and vice versa, such that, alongside the state constitution, other subsystem constitutions – an economic constitution, a media constitution, an organisational constitution – also act as instruments of practical paradox management? Luhmann did not pursue this question explicitly. Luhmann, like many state-centred constitutional lawyers, is rather sceptical about an economic constitution, third-party effects of fundamental rights and societal constitutionalism, and also about transnational constitutional phenomena.[13] And yet the inner logic of systems theory virtually requires one to pursue the question of whether a generalisation of the constitutional issues that have become visible in politics and their re-specification for other social systems is indicated.[14] This is because not only politics and law, but every, absolutely every functional system that is based on binary coding gets caught up in paradoxes of self-reference which, if there is no way to circumvent them, lead to paralysis.[15] There is no possibility of avoiding the generalisation. The unanswered question only concerns how de-paradoxification is re-specified in other contexts. Do other social systems also successfully externalise the relevant foundational paradox by transposing it into the legal system with the aid of the constitution – and vice versa? Or are other methods of de-paradoxification applied in non-political subsystems?

III De-paradoxifications of law

1 *The state constitution*

The externalisation of legal paradoxes by transposing them into the political system of the nation state was such a runaway success story in the past that, until the end of the twentieth century, it was implemented not only in constitutional law, but across the board in all fields of law. In the state constitution, in the procedural guarantees of the state governed by the rule of law, in the division of power between legislation and the administration of justice and in constitutional jurisdiction, law-making was ascribed coherently to the political-parliamentary process. Customary law – an evident exception to this – was increasingly marginalised in the nation state. Finally, private law, always unruly in its relation to politics, was constitutionalised when the foundational paradoxes of contract and of private organisations, which are based on private autonomy, were 'rerouted' into the state constitution.[16] Technically speaking, this was achieved by means of more or less plausible fictions: by means of the comprehensive hierarchy of legal norms, which, despite the veneration of private autonomy within private law, also incorporated contracts and associations, by means of the delegation of law-making power to private individuals, by means of the reception and control of social norms by the state and/or their relegation into the purely factual domain.[17]

It had already become obvious within the nation state that the total externalisation of legal paradoxes towards the political system would end up overburdening both the law and politics. The (over-)politicisation of law unleashed by this demonstrated its disintegrating effects at their most extreme in the regimes of national socialism and real socialism, but was also painfully perceptible in the post-war welfare state. This was described as 'legislation failure' by jurists, in a criticism directed both at the instrumentalisation of the production of legal norms by the party-political system and at the unwillingness of politics to react to the externalisation of the legal paradox by engaging in legislative activities that were responsive to the needs of the legal system.[18] But it is only when transnational regimes began to create their own law that externalisation proved to be clearly non-functional. This is because there is no transnational counterpart to the nation-state constitution as the structural link between law and politics within which externalisation could take place. The global rule-making processes taking place on a large scale outside the framework of international law reopen all the problems of the legal paradox which had been encountered in the nation state before they had been successfully transferred to politics.[19] The disorientation of legal doctrine which this entails is so severe that leading jurists describe a *'contrat sans loi'*, i.e. a contract without a basis in the law of a nation state, as logically impossible and pernicious for the law.[20]

2 Social constitutions

In the quest for alternative ways to cope with the legal paradox, the law seems to react by forcing an internal differentiation into subsectors, not in line with criteria internal to the law, but instead by delineating them in such a way that their norm production can bypass the political system and be based on other social systems. This is already apparent in the nation state, with the increasing development of semi-autonomous subsectors of the law, such as economic law, labour law, social law, medical law, media law and science law, undermining the traditional separation of public law and private law.[21] These special legal fields may officially preserve the externalisation towards politics, but behind the scenes they progressively reduce it, shifting the paradox of norm production into the regulated social system itself.[22]

The law's internal differentiation is advancing even more radically at the transnational level. Here, one sees the development of highly specialised legal regimes specific to particular social fields. These regimes are largely detached from public international law and instead closely coupled with the inner rationality of the fields they regulate.[23] 'Public' regimes such as the World Trade Organization, which have come into being as treaties in international law, marginalise the initially present paradox externalisation into politics by successfully asserting far-reaching autonomy vis-à-vis the nation states and by establishing themselves as self-contained regimes, and proceed to generate new forms of structural coupling with the regulated social fields. In 'private' regimes such as the *lex mercatoria*, the *lex sportiva* or the *lex digitalis*, which develop independently of national law and state treaties from the outset, the externalisation of the legal paradox into politics does not even arise. Instead, the foundational paradoxes of these transnational legal orders are displaced directly into the social fields with which they have entered into a close symbiosis.

If the law no longer externalises its paradox by transposing it into politics, but diverts it to other social systems, this means much more than a simple change of law's self-description. This is because the application of the legal code to itself does not just pose the abstract question of the law's legitimation, which is now likely to be answered by reference to the inner rationality of the social subsystems involved rather than by reference to the 'will of the legislator'. The law does not merely change the founding myth within which it conceals its paradoxes, but seeks to place its norm production on a different constitutional foundation. If it is now no longer the state constitution that is used to externalise paradoxes, but the constitutions of social subsectors, that is, the constitution of the economy, of the media, of science and of healthcare, then there are immediate, tangible consequences. To speak with Robert Cover, who considers the jurisgenerative force of a plurality of legal orders to lie in the interaction between nomos and narrative,[24] it is not only the narrative that changes when the way in which paradoxes are tackled is altered: the nomos itself is converted. As the legal paradox is transformed, other processes of norm production take centre stage and substantive legal norms of a different kind come into force.

In transnational regimes, the once dominant law-making process which translates collective political decisions into legal norms is largely replaced by a social norm production that is transformed into applicable law.[25] The contractual mechanism, formal organisation and standardisation are the three great jurisgenerative processes of the new legal pluralism whereby the self-made rules of the economy, but also of science, education, the media and healthcare, become valid law. The role played by the political law-maker or the legislative authorities at work in international politics is thus increasingly restricted to merely reformulating the law created within society.

3 *Protest movements*

This, then, explains why protest movements are changing their addressees, as described above. Protest movements react to the change in the way the paradoxes of law are externalised. They no longer address state authorities as the targets of their protests, but transnational corporations or other social institutions. Protest movements change the direction of their attacks whenever the legal system solves its problems of paradox by turning to contract, formal organisation and standardisation, and looks to political legislation only for its formal legitimation. Protest movements exert social pressure at the points where they believe they detect the causes of distorted social development and, more significantly, real chances to bring about change. This explains why within protest movements, there is a growing potential for a repoliticisation, a re-regionalisation and a re-individualisation of processes of law-making that are no longer concentrated in the political system, but can be found in various different social subsectors.[26] Some authors see these direct contacts by protest movements as evidence of a qualitatively new kind of political struggle, even of a potential societal democracy beyond institutionalised politics.[27]

'Constitutionalism from below' – this is the headline under which the specific contribution made to constitutionalism by protest movements is discussed today. A series of authors – James Tully, Antonio Negri, Gavin Anderson – have observed that the transnational *pouvoir constituant* is moving out of the political institutions and is now manifested in social movements, in the multitude, in a variety of protest movements, in NGOs and in a segmented transnational public sphere.[28] Anderson identifies such a 'transnational constitutionalism from below' in the new 'constituent powers found both within and outside the structures of representative democracy, the latter comprising decolonisation and internationalist movements, alternative NGOs and bodies which escape traditional categorisation, such as the World Social Forum'.[29]

As exaggerated as it may sound to equate protest movements entirely with the *pouvoir constituant*, serious consideration must be given to one suggestion by these authors. By *pouvoir constituant* they no longer mean the all-embracing demos, but only fragmented, partial processes, particularly different social movements. In transnational contexts, it is crystal clear that there is no such thing as a constitutional dynamic that embraces world society as whole, but that what we are seeing instead is a series of extremely heterogeneous constitutionalisation processes. This means abandoning the traditional notion according to which the political constitution gives the collective energy of a society as a whole the form that encapsulates it – as a nation in the past and now as the international community. Instead, modern society's collective potential is no longer available as a unity, but is increasingly compartmentalised in a multiplicity of social potentials, energies and strengths. And if the law alters the way it externalises its paradoxes, targeting social subsectors instead of politics, then the quality of the *pouvoir constituant* necessarily also changes. Law will then no longer seek its legitimation primarily through the political constitution, but through sectorial constitutions. They in turn will need to legitimise their norms directly by reference to a general, societal *ordre public transnational* – without mediation via a political constitution. These sectorial constitutions emerge on the basis of the communicative potentials clustered around the different specialised communication media in society.[30]

4 *Judge-made law*

This also illustrates how the expansion of judge-made law – as indicated above – relates to the externalisation of paradoxes. Judge-made law is beginning to play an unprecedented role, foisted on it by a changed externalisation process. It is no longer merely self-referential in its origins, having been forced to invent concrete rules of 'case law' in the course of litigation so as to solve individual conflicts;[31] it now also takes on board the social norms produced by contract, organisation and standardisation, deriving from this a different form of legitimation that is no longer either legal or political, but social. This elevates the status of judge-made law vis-à-vis legislation, and not only in quantitative terms. Its new quality comes from the fact that case law takes over a genuine constitutional function; however, it does not derive its norms from the state constitution, but from the constitutions of various social subsystems.[32] It needs to be stressed that these constitutions cannot just mirror their subsystemic rationality, but need to find their legitimation in a society-wide *ordre public transnational*.[33]

This can be seen most clearly in one of the most important twentieth-century institutions of private law, in the legal control of standard contracts.[34] Under the guise of contracting, markets have developed authoritative private regulations that no longer govern an individual contractual relationship, but have practically all the characteristics of general legislation. There is no genuine contractual consensus any more: instead, enterprises and business associations establish norms unilaterally, on the basis of asymmetric power relations, comparable to those between state and citizens. Judge-made law has reacted to these privately imposed norms by taking on a dual constitutional role. On the one hand, it legitimates this form of one-sided norm production backed by economic power, downplaying its legitimacy problems by labelling it as 'contractual', and subjects it to specific procedural requirements, thus using secondary rules to regulate private norm production. The political legislature then does nothing more than to incorporate the norms drawn up by judge-made law into the civil code. On the other hand, the courts intervene wholesale in the self-made law of the economy by subjecting it to judicial review of an intensity that is on a par with the constitutional review of political legislation. Shielded by such traditional formulas as good faith and *boni mores*, judge-made law has pieced together a new constitutional control hierarchy, in which the lower-ranking norms of the standard contracts are controlled by higher-ranking constitutional norms. Yet these higher-ranking norms are produced by the principles, not of the political constitution, but of the economic constitution.

Judge-made law plays a comparable role in other social areas, when it subjects the norm production of all sorts of social organisations based on private law – hospitals, universities, trade unions, professional associations, media concerns and, more recently, Internet intermediaries – to a comprehensive legal review. Here, too, it fulfils the above-mentioned dual constitutional function when carrying out the reflexive regulation of private rule-making, on the one hand by a procedural regulation of social rule-making, on the other by checking the substantive norms of internal organisational law for unconstitutionality.

Similarly, judge-made law legitimates and controls social standardisations that are either laid down by private standardisation organisations or that establish themselves naturally in so-called spontaneous communication processes. Here, too, it is not the state constitution, but the sectorial constitution – in healthcare, the system of education, the information media or the Internet – that furnishes the review criteria.

On the global scale, emerging transnational regimes deal with the problems of their foundational legal paradoxes in a similar way. Here, it is even more obvious that the externalisation into politics is possible only within extremely narrow confines. Instead, it is the particular constitutions of the different transnational regimes that make their foundational legal paradoxes disappear by transposing them into their respective social systems. The paradigm here is the *lex mercatoria*, which gives force to *contrats sans loi*, i.e. to free-floating contracts without any extra-contractual foundations. This evident paradox can no longer be accommodated within the law of nation states. In a curious circularity, it relies on the courts of arbitration it has itself created to produce higher-ranking norms, which in turn find the narrative and nomos of the *lex mercatoria* in economic contractual practice.[35]

5 Natural law

There is a clear connection between alternative ways of externalising paradoxes, on the one hand, and natural law, long believed to be moribund and now celebrating its resurrection in specialised fields of law and in transnational legal regimes, on the other. When judge-made law gives force to higher-ranking constitutional norms, it derives its criteria from the internal rationality of social subsystems. Efficiency as a legal principle, the functionality of social organisations, the self-definition of art, the neutrality and objectivity of science, the educational mission of schools and universities and the network adequacy of Internet norms – under legal positivism, social rationality formulas such as these could only become valid legal principles if the legislature made explicit provision for this. Yet such formulas are constantly passing into legal practice from the various different social systems and are transformed into legal principles by judge-made law, then given force as concrete legal norms.[36]

This inflow of substantive principles has long been familiar from state constitutions. The state constitution is construed as a material constitution, because it contains not only formal procedural norms, but also substantive norms and principles. There is only one way to explain their highly problematic 'natural-law' character today. It is not the legal system, but the political system that decides, in the course of lengthy conflicts, about certain fundamental principles of politics, which constitutional law juridically reconstructs, but at the same time drastically alters for legal purposes. The rule of law, the separation of powers, democracy, the welfare state and nowadays environmental protection are examples of such juridically solidified reflexive decisions of the political system that pass into the law via the state constitution. Similarly, in their own reflection processes, other social subsystems develop fundamental principles that are legally reconstructed in the economic constitution, in the constitution of science, etc., and used as criteria for the judicial review of norms. The legal principles of the economic constitution, for example, include the classical liberal principles of property, freedom of contract and competition, but also restrictions on contractual freedom, social obligations of property, fundamental rights vis-à-vis economic power and nowadays ecological sustainability and corporate social responsibility.[37]

The continuity of natural-law thinking is noticeable here. Natural law has always been used to make the paradoxes of self-reference in the legal code disappear.[38] And this formula has always provided a smooth path for substantive principles to make their way into legal practice: from religion in the Middle Ages, from moral philosophy in the Age of Reason, from the political constitution in the nation state and from multiple societal constitutions in the postmodern era. Unlike the old natural law whose origins were religious, rationalist or political, it is now feasible to speak of a sociological natural law, because it uses societal constitutions to reconstruct the rationalities of diverse subsystems within the legal system and transform them into binding principles. And the law does not care whether this has been mandated by the democratically legitimated legislature or not.

IV De-paradoxification in other social systems

If the law, in the course of its development, has broken the political monopoly on externalisation and become internally differentiated in such a way that particular legal regimes shift the legal paradox into the social areas under their care, what do things look like in the opposite direction? Do these other social areas experience reciprocal externalisation, too, so that they in turn cede their foundational paradoxes to the law?

1 *The state constitution*

As discussed above, the foundational paradox of politics becomes visible when the ruler's power becomes reflexive. When power is subjected to the force of power, when hierarchies of power are constructed, then politics, too – much like the law in the Münchhausen trilemma – is exposed to an infinite regress: the regress of overpowering power. And much as in the law, within the unitary cosmology of the medieval period, religious solutions to the problem of *ultima potestas* are convincing. But when, from the Renaissance onwards, politics starts to become independent, when it breaks free of religious bonds, and when it ultimately becomes sovereign and declares itself to be *legibus absoluta*, then the sovereignty paradox, the paradox of the binding of necessarily unbound authority, comes sharply into focus. Within politics, it is insoluble.[39]

It is the state constitution that enables politics to master this paradox, by displacing it outwards. Politics transfers to the law the task of constraining unconstrained sovereignty by means of legal procedures – by organisation as an internal constraint and by fundamental rights as a means of constraining the outward exercise of arbitrary power. This defuses the paradox of politics. Admittedly, it implies a loss of sovereignty, as politics is henceforth entangled in lasting, legally binding relationships. But this is compensated by the fact that the constraint of acts of power by means of their transformation into acts of law puts political decisions on a permanent footing and thus intensifies their efficacy. In this respect, the secret affinity between the communication of power and the normativity of the law shows itself to be more than productive. But being bound to the law becomes truly tolerable for politics only when the machinery of legislation in turn guarantees politics a decisive influence on the law. Only then can the structural coupling of law and politics by the state constitution be advanced to the point of a comprehensive secondary codification of politics by the law. The rule of law is extended to cover all political events and treats every act of power also as an act of law. It is this externalisation of paradoxes executed in complete symmetry – from politics into the law and from the law into politics – that gives state constitutions their unique aura. This aura induced Dieter Grimm to speak about the 'completeness' of state constitutions and Neil Walker to define their 'holistic' character. It is here that we can find the more profound reason why they deny the honorary title of a constitution to the fundamental orders of other functional systems.[40]

2 *The economic constitution*

What role does the law play when the economy is having to cope with its own fundamental paradox – the paradox of scarcity? This paradox paralyses economic action in that the acquisition of finite goods removes scarcity while generating scarcity at the same time. In the past, this blockage could be overcome only when the scarcity paradox was replaced by the clear-cut binary code of property/non-property. But that presumes that every act of economic acquisition 'condenses' vaguely understood positions of having/not-having into durable positions of property/non-property with the necessary firmness. According to Luhmann, this condensation has played a key role in rendering the economy autonomous:

> Condensation means that structures of meaning are available for repetition from situation to situation; and that this happens despite their paradoxical origins and despite being subjected to the opposition of the counter-value. Repetition is condensation of the same, ... in that it enables expectations of the future to be formed, to be acquired as certainties about the fulfilment of needs or about want.[41]

The condensation of social positions into binding certainties cannot be achieved by acts of economic acquisition alone, however. At most, such acts can generate diffuse social expectations in this direction, but they cannot shape them firmly enough to achieve a precarious de-paradoxification that must proceed along three dimensions. In the temporal dimension, property expectations must establish solid bonds that will last for a long time; in the social dimension, they must establish the unambiguous inclusion/exclusion within the group of affected persons, which causes considerable difficulties, especially in the case of collective ownership; and in the substantive dimension, they must generate clearly defined clusters of expectations with regard to rights of use, rights of exclusivity, rights of exploitation and rights of acquisition and their respective boundaries. This can only be achieved by a highly developed legal system. Thus it is the constitution of property that generates a close structural coupling between the economy and the law and in practice externalises the scarcity paradox by transposing it into the law of property.

The property constitution is only the first phase of an economic constitution. As soon as a highly developed monetary economy takes shape, and especially as soon as banks specialise in credit activities, the economic constitution enters a second phase, in which the scarcity paradox takes on a completely different form. De-paradoxification accordingly takes a different path at that point. And the economy again externalises the different paradox which threatens to paralyse monetary transactions by transposing it into the law. In the banking sector, both the ability and the inability to pay are generated simultaneously.

The banking system is based on the paradox of self-reference, on the unity of the ability and the inability to pay. 'The banks have the crucial privilege of being able to sell their debts at a profit.'[42] This paradox can be partially defused if the payment operations take on a reflexive mode, i.e. if money supply operations are applied to money operations in daily transactions. However, these reflexive economic operations remain unstable until an internal hierarchy is created within the banking sector, the hierarchy of central banks in their relation to commercial banks.

Yet the banking hierarchy cannot be institutionalised exclusively via self-regulation, and this applies in particular to the institutionalisation of the central bank. It needs to be supported from outside by hard legal rules that establish a binding framework for the special status of the central bank. The parallels with the hierarchies in the political system and the role of the state constitution are evident. The economy, too, only copes with its monetary paradox with the help of the law, which uses the financial constitution, i.e. norms of procedure, of competence and of organisation, to regulate the establishment and operating methods of the central banks vis-à-vis the commercial banks. As an economic corollary to the different branches of government – the executive, the legislature and the judiciary – the economic constitution establishes what one might call the 'monetative' of the central banks.[43]

The way that the economic constitution de-paradoxifies money circulation is always precarious, however: it is always threatened by the danger of a return of the paradox. The hierarchy in the relationship between the central banks and the commercial banks which the economic constitution underpins has not eliminated the paralysis of the financial system for good:

> The logical and empirical possibility that the entire system will collapse, a return of the paradox and a complete blockage of all operations by the original equivalence capable of payment = incapable of payment cannot be ruled out in this way, but it is made sufficiently improbable.[44]

The recent financial crisis demonstrated that it is anything but 'sufficiently improbable'. The excessive growth compulsion in global financial transactions gave us all a glimpse of a possible default of the banking sector. And it is exactly this point which recent initiatives to reform the financial constitution seek to address in setting out to readjust the hierarchy of the banks all over again. Without these reforms, the central banks have difficulties in exercising sufficient control over the money markets: they are only able to stimulate or de-stimulate them indirectly by way of individual interventions. They can manage the money supply only indirectly via the prime rate, which either facilitates credit or makes it more difficult to obtain. With reforms that strengthen the role played by the central banks vis-à-vis the commercial banks, the law performs the limitative function of the economic constitution, prevents the return of paradoxes and total blockage and at the same time stabilises the self-reflexive relations in payment operations, which would disintegrate if they were not fixed on a legal basis.

The parallels in the way that politics externalises the sovereignty paradox and the way that the economy externalises the scarcity paradox, in each case by transposition into the law, and the fact that the state constitution and the economic constitution thus fulfil the same function are quite astonishing. And yet, major differences are conspicuous. Where the monetary operations of the economy are concerned, there is no sign of the complete secondary coding that forces the political system to apply the binary code legal/illegal to all political operations. Essentially, there are three reasons for this. Firstly, while it is certainly true that economic transactions are regulated by legal norms and subject to judicial controls, it is notable that the equation of a political and a legal operation which takes place in an administrative act has no counterpart in the relation between monetary and legal operations. An administrative act can easily be construed as the implementation of existing legal norms, in many cases even as an application of norms within a strictly conditional programme. This is not the case in economic transactions. To be sure, economic transactions are valid only if certain contractual conditions are met, but they go far beyond these legal conditions and in substance represent just the opposite of a mere implementation of pre-existing norms. Secondly, while the juridification of political decisions further strengthens their collectively binding character, it would be simply counterproductive if individual economic transactions were collectively binding or had a compulsory legal effect for the economy as a whole. The transactions can be allowed to develop their binding effect, economic in intention and guaranteed legally, only at the micro-level of contractual relations and of economic organisations structured in accordance with company law. Only at the micro-level is it possible to talk in terms of a secondary legal coding of economic transactions in the form of contractual acts or corporate acts. In contrast to the political system, where the collective is bound by political decisions, the macro-level remains unconstrained in the economy. The privity principle in common law forbids the extension of binding effects to third parties, to say nothing of extending them to the economic order as a whole. Thirdly, the ongoing concatenation of political operations differs fundamentally from that of economic operations. Political decisions have precedential effects on subsequent decisions: if it intends to deviate from them, politics has to go through the entire legal procedure once again and the deviating decision must be rendered positive by an explicit *actus contrarius*. Future monetary transactions, in contrast, are by no means normatively bound by previous transactions. Instead, the only expectations generated by an individual act of payment in regard to subsequent acts of payment are of a cognitive nature.

These three reasons explain why, despite the parallels in the way in which the economy and politics externalise their paradoxes by transposing them into the law, there are significant differences in the intensity of their constitutionalisation. The decentralisation of decision-making that is prevalent in the economy, the intended restriction of contractual commitments to the contracting partners and the exclusively cognitive style of expectation that binds economic transactions to one another in practice rule out the possibility of completing, in relation to the economy and law, the symmetry of reciprocal externalisations that exists between politics and law. Unlike the state constitution, the economic constitution exhibits a remarkable degree of asymmetry. As illustrated above, it is certainly true that economic law externalises the legal paradox to a very significant degree by transposing it into economic norm production: contract, organisation and standardisation. The economy, however, can only pursue its own legal constitutionalisation to a limited extent if it is to avoid damaging its structural integrity.

3 *The constitution of science*

This asymmetry of externalisations is even more marked in the constitution of science. To be sure, science also has its paradox of self-foundation: only scientific operations can determine reflexively what actually constitutes science. The Cretan paradox, which derives from applying cognitive operations to cognitive operations, is probably the best-known case of a self-referential paradox. But unlike politics and the economy, science finds it mostly impossible to externalise its paradox by shifting it into the law. Normative stipulations which are legally or constitutionally binding and which can be changed only with difficulty are self-destructive for science. It would actually be absurd to interpret cognitive acts as the implementation of rules. Admittedly, even though it portrays itself as undogmatic, science too is no stranger to extensive norm production. Methods are binding; theories are immunised normatively against a change of paradigm; neutrality, objectivity and immunity to interest are accepted professional norms.[45] And yet the juridification of such social norms would generate a paralysis incompatible with the cognitive style. It is no coincidence that the state constitution allows science to keep the right to self-definition, limiting itself to second-order observation.[46] Nor is it any coincidence that the constantly repeated proposals for scientific courts, whose remit would be to issue binding decisions about the validity of the results of new research, have had no success whatsoever. Only a normative style that is always open to being reversed, of a flexibility which is quite unknown to the law, is permissible in science.[47]

Unlike politics and the economy, science cannot pass its paradox on to the law, but has to seek out other ways to achieve de-paradoxification.[48] It finds them mainly in processes internal to science itself. Temporalising the paradox, creating a hierarchy of different levels of analysis, enduring contradictions, antinomies and incommensurabilities, tolerating uncertainty, waiving the requirement of having to decide one way or another, creating a constructivist worldview: these are some of the tools used by science in the attempt to make its paradoxes more bearable.

That does not mean, however, that there can be no such thing as a constitution of science, in which scientific and legal reflections are coupled together structurally. It is just that the internal asymmetry of their coupling is extremely pronounced. As illustrated above, when the law regulates scientific activities, it externalises its paradox by simply shifting it into scientific processes, and it uses the underlying principles of scientific cognition to legitimate legal norms that impact on science. Science in its turn keeps the integrity of its cognitive operations largely free of legal constraints. Only its external borders are to be protected by legal norms. Freedom of science as a guarantee that the cognitive process remains open thus becomes the sole norm of the scientific constitution. The law provides a binding guarantee that science may not be bound by anything but its own freedom. This entails also and in particular its legal protection against corruption by politics, by the economy and by the law itself. The most important task of the constitution of science is 'to stabilise the epistemological difference between the knowledge of science, of politics and of the law itself'.[49] It guarantees this with the aid of 'mechanisms that ... help to prevent science from being colonised by other, alien system rationalities – in particular by the economy and by politics, but also by the law itself. What is to be averted are dedifferentiation tendencies whose aim it is to "replace relevances internal to science with values and norms external to science."'[50] But the law must also guarantee a sufficient plurality of processes within science, so that it is always possible to break down developmental barriers by adopting a fundamental change of perspective. Pluralism and the protection of scientific minorities thus become binding principles of the scientific constitution. But not only that, the external organisational framework of universities, research institutes and professional organisations is also guaranteed in a legally binding manner.[51]

4 Differences in the intensity of constitutionalisation

Taken as a whole, societal constitutionalism – as exemplified here by politics, the economy and science – presents a picture of constitutional pluralism, albeit one that is not at all uniform, but shows differences in the intensity of constitutionalisation. The model of the state constitution therefore cannot be transferred wholesale to other social constitutions. It is true that the issues raised by the state constitution need to be generalised, since all functional systems are exposed to their own paradoxes of self-reference, which they have to neutralise one way or another. But how they do this depends on the affinity between their own structures and the specific normativity developed within the legal system: they can externalise the paradox by shifting it fully into the law, as politics chose to do with the legal secondary codification of its operations; or opt, like the economy, for only a partial externalisation into the law; or, like science, rule out a juridification of their operations and instead adopt other possible methods of de-paradoxification.

This clearly shows why the state constitution occupies a unique position among social constitutions. This position certainly does not derive from the state's constitutional monopoly, as state-centric constitutional lawyers would have us believe, since other disciplines – historiography, economics, sociology and international relations – have long demonstrated the existence of non-state constitutions.[52] Nor is this unique position derived from a hierarchical superiority of the state constitution over the so-called sub-constitutions, as many authors maintain who certainly admit the existence of constitutional pluralism, but are not prepared to renounce the idea that modernity possesses a normative centre, in form of the dominant position of the state constitution.[53] Nor, lastly, does it derive from state constitutions being the only ones of a legal character, while other social constitutions – including transnational regimes – are only 'constituted' *de facto*, or contain only social fundamental values, or are constitutions only in a metaphorical sense. Rather, the reciprocal externalisation of politics into the law and of law into politics is totally symmetrical – this is the reason for the unique position of state constitutions. While the law, in its diverse legal fields, pursues a manifold externalisation of its paradoxes into all sorts of different social systems and so derives its normative contents from the various constitutions of different social areas, in the opposite direction there are dramatic differences in the degree to which the foundational paradoxes of social systems are juridified. To claim that structural couplings only exist in the form of reciprocal relations is to misunderstand structural couplings in general and social constitutions in particular. Indeed, it is quite possible for one social system to be closely coupled to another while that other system, in its operations, is only partly coupled or does largely without structural coupling. It is like love: frequently experienced only on one side, and just in a handful of lucky cases truly reciprocated by the person who is loved.

V Resulting problems

In conclusion, let us take a brief look at the consequences of externalisation. What happens after the constitutional paradox has been externalised? As we have seen, externalisation brings major advantages for the system in question. In some cases, it even is what makes autopoiesis possible in the first place. However, at the same time, it entails some serious costs. The system that outsources its paradox is now subject to an extraneous structural logic. As illustrated above, the differences between the constitutionalisation of politics, of the economy and of science can be explained by the incompatibilities that a complete juridification of their paradoxes can generate. Constitutions drive social systems systematically into a wrong, juridical direction when the high degree of externalisation into the law is incompatible with the systems' own particular structures. The requirement that their own operations be simultaneously subjected to the demands made of legal operations explains why some social systems prefer other routes to de-paradoxification than by shifting their paradoxes into the law.

Another aspect is even more problematic: externalisation exposes the system to the extraneous paradox itself. The law is exposed to the political paradox, politics to the legal paradox. Formulated in general terms, the law is exposed to the paradox of the constituted social system, while the social system is exposed to the legal paradox. There is a danger that the constitution, as a structural coupling of the law with another social system, does not differentiate sufficiently between including and excluding that which is extraneous, as would be necessary for a successful structural coupling.[54] At the latest, this becomes fatal at the point when the externalisation also embraces the system's contingency formula, for example when the principle of legal justice is thoroughly politicised or economised. A fair number of authors argue in favour of politicising the contingency formula of justice, whose operative nucleus lies in the equal treatment of similar cases and the unequal treatment of dissimilar cases, by shifting it towards democracy and the common weal, or of economising it by shifting it towards scarcity reduction and efficiency.

Yet the desired gain in precision fails to materialise, as one contingency formula is merely replaced by another, thus replacing a high degree of uncertainty by another uncertainty of a similarly high degree. What is worse is that the process of determination, which in every case ends in self-transcendence and calls for creative solutions under the dominance of the contingency formula in question, is managing to manoeuvre itself into a position which leaves it facing in the wrong direction. The parties to a legal conflict are offered solutions oriented towards achieving efficiency or policy effectiveness, rather than a fair decision of their conflict: they are offered a stone when they want bread. Maybe it is necessary to draw a clear distinction here between the foundational paradox and the paradox of decision. The unavoidable externalisation of the foundational paradoxes of the law must not lead to the subjection of the legal process to the political or economic decision-making paradox. And the same applies in reverse.

Notes

This chapter was previously published as 'Exogenous self-binding: how social subsystems externalise their foundational paradoxes in the process of constitutionalisation', in Alberto Febbrajo and Giancarlo Corsi (eds), *Sociology of Constitutions: A Paradoxical Perspective* (London: Routledge, 2016), pp. 30–48.

1. The formulas ('legal cognition', judge-made law as 'customary law') offered by contemporary legal theory to describe the issue of judge-made law are typically awkward: cf. Röhl and Röhl, *Allgemeine Rechtslehre*, pp. 571 ff.
2. Thornhill, 'Sociology of constituent power'; Shany, 'No longer a weak department'.
3. Hirschl, *Towards Juristocracy*.
4. *Locus classicus*: Esser, *Grundsatz und Norm*.
5. For an overview of recent natural law theories, see Himma, 'Natural Law'. For transnational human rights as natural law, see Mahlmann, 'Varieties of transnational law'.
6. On the contemporary discussion about Gramsci, see Buckel and Fischer-Lescano (eds), *Hegemonie gepanzert mit Zwang*. For Fuller's concept of natural law, see Fuller, *Morality of Law*.
7. O'Brien *et al.*, *Contesting Global Governance*, p. 2.
8. E.g. Schneiderman, *Constitutionalizing Economic Globalization*.
9. More extensively, although with due caution: Augsberg, 'Wissenschaftsverfassungsrecht', p. 223.
10. On the debate about societal constitutions, particularly in the transnational realm, see Thompson, 'Constitutionalisation of Everyday Life?'; Kjaer, *Constitutionalism in the Global Realm*; Teubner and Beckers (eds), *Transnational Societal Constitutionalism*.
11. Luhmann, 'Verfassung als evolutionäre Errungenschaft'; Luhmann, 'Zwei Seiten des Rechtsstaates'; Luhmann, 'Politische Verfassungen im Kontext'.
12. Luhmann, *Law as a Social System*, p. 408.

13 Luhmann, *Grundrechte als Institution*, pp. 115–16, 205, n. 9; Luhmann, *Law as a Social System*, pp. 487–8.
14 On the method of generalising and respecifying, see Parsons and Ackerman, 'Concept of "Social System"'.
15 Luhmann, *Theory of Society*, vol. 1, p. 219.
16 On the constitutionalisation of the legal order as a whole, see Röhl, 'Verfassungsrecht als wissenschaftliche Strategie?'
17 For the current discussion about the status of customary law and private law, see Röhl and Röhl, *Allgemeine Rechtslehre*, pp. 541 ff., 554 ff.
18 For example, Ruffert, *Vorrang der Verfassung*, p. 223.
19 In detail, see Teubner, 'King's many bodies'.
20 Mann, 'Internationale Schiedsgerichte', p. 127.
21 The significance of this internal differentiation of the law is acknowledged, albeit in connection with a scarcely plausible polemic, as a loss of unity of private law by Zöllner, 'Regelungsspielräume'. On the discussion, see Domej et al. (eds), *Einheit des Privatrechts*.
22 This comes close to the 'constitutional law of law' of Wiethölter, 'Just-ifications', pp. 71 ff.
23 On this, see Koskenniemi, 'Hegemonic Regimes'; Chapter 10 in this volume.
24 Cover, 'Supreme Court, 1982 term'.
25 See for example Nobles and Schiff, 'Using systems theory to study legal pluralism'; Trakman, 'Plural account'; Harrison, 'Regime pluralism'.
26 See Anderson, 'Corporate Constitutionalism'.
27 Crouch, *Strange Non-Death of Neoliberalism*; O'Brien et al., *Contesting Global Governance*, p. 2.
28 Tully, 'Imperialism of Modern Constitutional Democracy', pp. 319, 323 ff.; Hardt and Negri, *Commonwealth*; Anderson, 'Societal constitutionalism'.
29 Anderson, 'Societal constitutionalism', p. 902.
30 Teubner, *Constitutional Fragments*, pp. 61 ff.
31 Fikentscher, *Methoden des Rechts*, pp. 199 ff., 201.
32 For details, see Teubner, 'Societal Constitutionalism'.
33 For an elaboration, see Teubner, *Constitutional Fragments*, pp. 87–8, 157–8. See also Holmes, 'Politics of law', pp. 569 ff.
34 A recent excellent analysis is Femia, 'Desire for text'. For the transnational situation, see Braithwaite, 'Standard form contracts', p. 785.
35 About this, see Teubner, 'Breaking frames'.
36 On the law's recourse to social standards, see Vesting, *Rechtstheorie*, pp. 95 ff.
37 For greater detail about this, see Teubner, *Constitutional Fragments*, pp. 172 ff.
38 Luhmann, 'Third question'.
39 Luhmann, 'Verfassung als evolutionäre Errungenschaft'; Luhmann, 'Zwei Seiten des Rechtsstaates'; Luhmann, 'Politische Verfassungen im Kontext'.
40 Grimm, 'Achievement of Constitutionalism'; Walker, 'Beyond the Holistic Constitution?'
41 Luhmann, *Wirtschaft der Gesellschaft*, p. 188.
42 Ibid., p. 145.
43 More specifically about this, see Chapter 8 in this volume, pp. 175 ff.
44 Luhmann, *Wirtschaft der Gesellschaft*, p. 146.
45 Ziman, *Real Science*.
46 Epistemological insights enter into the legal determination of scientific freedom: see Schmidt-Assmann, 'Wissenschaftsrecht', p. 207.
47 Luhmann, *Wissenschaft der Gesellschaft*, pp. 93 ff.

48 Ibid., pp. 172 ff.
49 Augsberg, 'Wissenschaftsverfassungsrecht', p. 217.
50 Augsberg, 'Subjektive und objektive Dimensionen', p. 82.
51 Hensel, 'Grundrechtskollisionen in der Stiftungsuniversität'.
52 For political science, Thompson, 'Constitutionalisation of Everyday Life'; for social history, Koselleck, 'Begriffsgeschichtliche Probleme'; for economics, Buchanan, *Constitutional Economics*; Thornhill, 'Sociology of constituent power'; for international relations, Trachtman, 'Constitutions of the WTO'.
53 Joerges and Rödl, 'Zum Funktionswandel des Kollisionsrechts II'.
54 Neves identifies transversal paradoxes here, which in themselves come about as a result of the constitutional procedure and can be controlled only insufficiently by constitutional courts: Neves, *Transconstitutionalism*, pp. 51 ff.

Afterword: the milestones of Teubner's neo-pluralism

Alberto Febbrajo

Professor of Sociology of Law, University of Macerata, Italy

Since his first works Gunther Teubner has tried to combine two complementary ways of representing law in our societies: one oriented towards legal operators who are looking with increasing dissatisfaction at the traditional conceptions of law, the other towards sociologists who are searching for a theoretical key capable of identifying the role of different normative orders in a social context.

With the aim of expanding this double perspective Teubner has redefined the scope of legal positivism on the one hand by critically reconsidering its hierarchical structure and, on the other, by stressing the normative functions of social organisations in a pluralistic vision of society. This multi-level construction focuses on a basic question: how can we continue believing in the unity and consistency of the law in an era characterised by the increasing significance of social norms external to the state?

The result is a complex socio-legal theory that Teubner has gradually developed through mutually connected models of law able to represent different kinds of pluralism in different cultural situations.

Five models of law

1 *Autonomous law*

In his very first writings, Teubner set out to contribute to a pluralistic sociological theory of law. An interesting attempt in this sense can be found in his doctoral thesis[1] and more clearly in his *Habilitationsschrift*.[2] In this latter work the author focuses on the internal democracy of associations, such as trade unions, that give themselves an autonomous organisationand use their internal constitutions to select and coordinate widespread external interests.

To tackle this issue, which hovers on the borderline between law, politics and economics, Teubner starts out from the fundamental premise that it is not possible to maintain the unity of a legal order by relying solely on the formal regulations produced by the state. Drawing on different strands of research – such as the sociology of organisations, the theory of democracy and neocorporatism[3] – Teubner sets out to identify some social tasks of the autonomous associaations of organisations that are politically and economically capable of making a relevant impact in an arena dominated – at least formally – by the state.

Autonomous law faces two complementary requirements: the need to limit itself in its selection of specific social purposes and the need to make the best possible use of its potential connections with social regulations and expectations not yet recognised by the state. In this double role autonomous law leaves extensive room for a gradual development of the internal constitutions of social associations that, especially in the non-profit sector, have the ability to replace or complete the work of public institutions.

In the pursuit of these objectives, Teubner's pluralism adopts a perspective that starts out from society rather than from the state, and presupposes that positive norms at every hierarchical level, right up to the state constitution, cannot be the result of a top-down method. It is thus necessary to give due consideration, in particular at the periphery of the legal order, to the choices made by the social sectors in question and to the different levels of approval (or disapproval) obtained by their autonomous norms.

2 *Reflexive law*

During the 1980s, in connection with the general discussion about the crisis of the welfare state,[4] Teubner developed a general definition of law, trying to underline the ability of every legal norm to observe itself and to learn from its effects on social reality.

The resulting model of 'reflexive law' elaborated by Teubner[5] describes a normative control capable of regulating specific sectors of society through a regulatory capacity of the second level.[6] Here Teubner underlines the need to combine a cognitive approach with a normative approach, so as to take into consideration the possibility of self-critical 'regulations of regulations'. This procedure requires an increased demand for social knowledge about variables that have the potential to influence how the state's norms are applied. In other words, reflexive law is, paradoxically enough, a learning law that observes society empirically in so far as it considers any possible appropriate and compatible adjustment of legal norms to social norms.

Since reflexive law is capable of self-variation, it is also able to achieve equilibria that are not excessively burdensome in terms of social costs.[7] Knowing the empirical requirements of its own application, reflexive law can control both its own efficiency and its own effectiveness, so as to keep its legality within socially acceptable limits.

Reflexive law thus seems to make a flexible and primarily 'ecological' use of norms. Much like the therapeutic strategies adopted by homeopathic medicine, it sets out to cure society using norms suggested by society itself.[8]

Following this approach, Teubner considers three pathologies that could occur in the regulatory relationship between law and society: (a) the law's incongruence with social reality, which comes about when the state's regulatory strategies are not suitable for being put into practice; (b) the hyper-legalisation of society, which comes about when legal regulation endangers the self-regulation of society; and (c) the hyper-socialisation of law, which comes about whenever it is the law that is 'politicised' or 'economised' without sufficient self-reflection.[9]

3 *Polycontextural law*

A further development of reflexive law is the model of polycontextural law.[10] Polycontextural law is capable not only of ensuring a second-level regulation, as in the previous model, but also of absorbing the potential conflicts between discourses produced in different social areas. Rather than being ready to recognise the 'struggle among the gods' represented by pluralistic criteria of rationality based on the evaluative orientations that prevail from time to time in different areas of social action, polycontextural law mediates and builds relations between specific social sectors by taking into consideration possible intersections of their typical languages and functional requirements.

This involves a reciprocal stabilisation of legal and non-legal cultures. The law can regulate an economy, typically oriented to ensure mechanisms for managing and redistributing risks, by favouring the development of particular legal institutions and bureaucratic structures capable of solving concrete and tangible problems according to specific programmes.

Teubner sees polycontextural law as a model where elements connected to Weber's types of formal and material rationality flow together, so as to translate the discourses of the various sectors of society interested in the possible effects of legal decisions into the legal system's language. Weber's approach, filtered through the contributions of Lyotard, Habermas and Luhmann, re-emerges in polycontextual law as a tool for illustrating the stabilisation of different social sectors characterised by the possibility of their mutual adjustment in spite of their different logics and 'grammars'.[11]

Polycontextual law is articulated on several levels, consisting not merely of the combination of normative and cognitive regulations, but also of the insertion of specific abilities to respond to non-legal (in particular political or economic) discourses. To avoid both an impracticable unitary rationality and a 'nihilistic' relativism, polycontextual law becomes 'a law of the conflicts of discourses', capable of incorporating the reciprocal references of a plurality of systemic points of view and contributing to their constitutionalisation.[12]

4 *Autopoietic law*

The previous models of autonomous, reflexive and polycontextual law describe a non-hierarchical law that provides social order respectively through a decentralised, ecological and dialogic pluralism. The model of autopoietic law combines these three models in a wider perspective: the selective dimension of autonomous law, the stabilising dimension of reflexive law and the innovative dimension of polycontextual law.

Drawing on the apparent paradox of a law that is potentially open because potentially closed, 'autopoietic' law is capable of closure, when the system imposes its own code on other systems, and of opening, when the system translates into its code the external information required by its functioning.

Combining 'opening' and 'closure', autopoietic law is not only able to produce local social norms, correct existing legal structures and stabilise their potential tensions with social regulations, but appears also able to functionally re-stabilise the unity and continuity of the legal system, despite the necessary changes brought about in order to achieve a synthesis between legal and social norms.[13]

In other words, the model of autopoietic law is developed by means of a combined application of the Luhmannian concept of 'border' and of the concept of 'intersections'. It is presented as a social system that on the one hand uses clear-cut dichotomies based on a dual code (legal–illegal, lawful–unlawful) to define its 'borders', and on the other opens them to a series of intermediate filters that manage to allow their reciprocal 'intersections'.

Autopoietic law guarantees in particular a stable contact, at an intersystemic level, with external 'irritations', 'interferences' and 'noises' coming from different systems and absorbs them, despite their different contents.[14]

Table 1 The systemic hypercycle of autopoietic law

Autopoietic moments	Internal legal circuits
Selection	Jurisprudence
Stabilisation	Administration
Variation	Legislation
Self-representation	Doctrine

Starting from this multi-level process, we can say that, for an autopoietic model, selection is typically taken on by administrative structures: variation by legislation and stabilisation by jurisprudential proceedings. Lastly, the task of re-stabilising the self-representation of dogmatic-conceptual structures can be attributed to the doctrine, which is able to imprint the entire system with unity and consistency.

Taken as a whole, these components constitute an 'internal hypercycle' capable of regulating autopoietic law (see Table 1).[15]

5 Fragmented law

The models of law just described are, in Teubner's work, not only the concluding stage of a process of gradual absorption of potential tensions between positive law and social norms, but also the starting point of an evolution characterised by the fragmentation of the law outside the area of direct control of the state.

These centrifugal forces, in the age of globalisation, are destined to prevail upon the limits of the legal order and allow legally relevant actors to manage problems of constitutional significance without being restricted by the borders of single states. Legal orders are no longer related to the main pillars of the state, i.e. to the physical location of individuals (territory), to their cultural legacy (people) and to the definition of a common weal (sovereignty). The process of 'societal' constitutionalisation is rather supported by a gradual weakening of the spatial, social and material perception of the borders of the state.

Consequently the constitution, which was formally considered the identity card of a legal order, the most comprehensive point from which a legal system can be recognised from outside, and the fundamental tool that guarantees the greatest level of unity in the legal order, is redesigned by 'societal constitutions'.

Teubner underlines the profound differences between traditional 'state constitutions' and 'societal constitutions' that cross state borders and are extensively influenced by the interests of private transnational actors. For the constitutionalism of the eighteenth and nineteenth centuries the main 'concern was to release the energies of political power in nation states and at the same time to limit that power effectively', while now the concern 'is to release quite different social energies – particularly visible in the economy, but also in science and technology, medicine and the new media – and to effectively limit their destructive effects'.[16]

Since it is so heterogeneous and broad in scope, 'constitutionalism beyond the nation state means two different things: constitutional problems arising outside the borders of the nation state in transnational political processes, and at the same time outside the institutionalised political sector in the "private" sectors of global society'.[17]

In this model of law the symbiosis between public and private elements appears to be not only possible, but constitutionally necessary. 'In complete contrast to the usual hierarchical relation between state and private norms, the state codes ... attain their validity from an independent combination of primary and secondary norms in the world of private ordering.' They form 'a closed, non-state system of normative validity that is hierarchically structured within itself. At the top are the principles of corporate constitution, followed by provisions on implementation and monitoring in the middle, while the lower level contains specific behavioural instructions. They thus produce their basis for validity in the form of their own constitutional norms.'[18]

On this basis, Teubner successfully focuses attention on the 'new constitutional question', which maintains the duality of the legal–illegal code, while playing a relevant role, for both public and private law, in a vast range of problems that are perceived to be global.[19]

Legal theory is incapable of tackling these problems if it continues to have the one-to-one link between the constitution and the state and fails to acknowledge the existence of emerging social constructions that tend to produce law independently of the state.[20]

As a matter of fact, each 'sectorial constitution' based on power, money, law or knowledge 'makes use of "constitutive rules" to regulate the abstraction of a homogeneous communicative medium', and in so doing ensures 'that the society-wide impact of their communicative media is guaranteed under different historical conditions'. Therefore sectorial constitutions 'develop organizational rules, procedures, competences, and subjective rights for both these orientations, codifying the separation between the social spheres and thus supporting the functional differentiation of society'.[21]

In this deconstructive perspective we have to adapt a transnational constitutionalism to the conditions of a double fragmentation of world society. While the first fragmentation insists on the constitutions of autonomous global social sectors that are 'in competition with the constitutions of nation states' the second fragmentation renders 'utterly illusory' the 'unitary standards' of a global constitution that in a world society, and insists on 'various regional cultures, each based upon social principles that differ from those of the western world'. This means that 'transnational sub-constitutions do not strive towards a stable balance, but rather follow the chaotic pattern of a "dynamic disequilibrium" between contradictory developments'.[22]

In a nutshell, Teubner's neo-constitutionalism takes the form of a quasi-order where the new social subjects of globalisation can co-exist with the old legal subjects on the basis of reciprocal self-limitations that are guaranteed constitutionally at transnational level, but not immune to conflict.

The only way to conceive a 'global constitution' that will act in order to unify world society is to create a set of 'global fragments – nations, transnational regimes, regional cultures – connected to each other in a constitutional conflict of laws'.[23]

On the one hand, a law fragmented not only at internal and external, but also at national and transnational level does not necessarily imply accepting the optimistic thesis that a real globalisation of traditional legal orders can be achieved in a modern society. In fact, there is no coercive apparatus in place whose breadth of scope and legitimacy are suitable for imposing universally applicable norms and avoiding the constant possibility of conflicts between different constitutional fragments. On the other hand, it is also not plausible to propose the pessimistic thesis that considers emerging transnational subjects to be governed by norms produced exclusively for incompatible interests.

Societal constitutionalism could in various ways be transformed and adapted to the different conditions of globality.[24]

Here a problem becomes central: what role could a constitution oriented to transnational law reserve for politics?[25] In other words, 'how is the role of politics for transnational sub-constitutions then to be formulated in the magic triangle of politics, law and autonomous social spheres? 'Resignation? Guidance? Supervision? Complementarity? Replacement of *la politique* by *le politique*?'[26]

With the theoretical eclipse of a fully state-centred rationality, which as such probably never existed, today's fragmented law seems to contribute to the constitutionalisation not only of political but also of economic systems, multiplying its transnational channels and expanding its areas of influence.

Furthermore an 'unsolved question' remains, especially after the events connected to the recent crisis of financial systems: 'What limits do global financial markets have in their expansion towards the real economy and other areas of society?' Societal constitutions seem to stand apart in this context, generating a veritable exchange of positions between 'hard law' and 'soft law'.[27]

The focus of Teubner's attention is not so much on specific societal constitutions as on the general 'processes' of constitutionalisation to which they belong. This calls for terminological proposals that are more articulated than traditional semantics, and could be sourced by developing the lexicon of the Internet, to which Teubner attributes major importance, especially in his latest works.[28]

Concluding remarks

Teubner's definitions of law identify various sources of constitutional conflicts that are still at the centre of a wide discussion.[29] The approach he suggested in his first works, analysing the constitutional recognition of social actors from a neo-corporativistic perspective, was developed with the definition of increasingly complex models of law (reflexive, polycontextural, autopoietic) that are respectively capable of absorbing, expanding and managing, in a pluralistic framework, problems raised by the crisis of welfare state, the differentiation of legal cultures and the identity of legal systems.[30] Teubner finally enlarges the scope of his theory based on the circular relations between social and legal norms and, focusing on the fragmentation of the law through a plurality of constitutions external to the state, adopts a trans-constitutional perspective (see Table 2).

When we look at this rich catalogue of models of law, inspired by the legal and social problems that have emerged in different situations over the last decades, Teubner's theoretical work seems to be still open to further developments. For dealing with a law set free of its traditional reference to the state and fragmented into societal constitutions, the 'functionalism of distinctions', which allows a specific reflection on the legal order in its social context, seems destined to be gradually overshadowed in favour of a 'functionalism of connections' that is better suited, in the perspective of the general systems theory, to capturing the various functional combinations and superimpositions that are suggested by the fragmented legal orders which actually regulate

Table 2 Teubner's models of law

Model of law	Type of pluralism	Systematic juxtaposition	Prevailing dimension
Autonomous	Local	Centre–periphery	Selection
Reflexive	Ecological	Cognitive–normative	Variation
Polycontextural	Dialogic	Formal–material	Stabilisation
Autopoietic	Functional	Open–closed	Re-stabilisation
Fragmented	Global	External–internal	Deconstruction

our life. This perspective would pave the way for further shifting the accent of Teubner's models of law from systemic differentiations to intersystemic communications.

Notes

1 Teubner, *Standards und Direktiven in Generalklauseln*.
2 Teubner, *Organisationsdemokratie und Verbandsverfassung*.
3 A lively debate about neocorporatism took place in the European University Institute of Florence during the period in which Teubner was there. See Schmitter, 'Democratic theory and neo-corporatist practice'.
4 See in particular Teubner, *Dilemmas of Law in the Welfare State*.
5 Teubner is here making explicit reference to the concept of 'responsive law'. About this concept, see Nonet and Selznick, *Law and Society in Transition*.
6 See Teubner, 'Substantive and reflexive elements', p. 242.
7 As Teubner states, the reflexive model of law 'requires the legal system to view itself as a system-in-an-environment and to take account of the limits of its own capacity as it attempts to regulate the functions and performances of other social subsystems. Thus, its relation to social science knowledge is characterised neither by "reception" nor by "separation" ... Reflexive law needs to utilise and develop only that knowledge necessary to the control of self-regulatory processes in different contexts.' Ibid., pp. 280–1.
8 'A reflexive orientation does not ask whether there are social problems to which the law must be responsive. Instead it seeks to identify opportunity structures that allow legal regulations to cope with social problems without, at the same time, irreversibly destroying valued patterns of social life.' Ibid., p. 274.
9 See Teubner, 'After Legal Instrumentalism?'
10 See Teubner, 'Constitutionalising polycontexturality'.
11 About the Luhmannian source of this transverse perspective, see in general Febbrajo and Harste (eds), *Law and Intersystemic Communication*.
12 Teubner observes that Wittgenstein's linguistic games propose a different kind of pluralism between rules that cannot be traced back to rational principles and to abstract values, but are related to the practice of real 'forms of life' internal to society itself. See the collection of Teubner's essays edited by Annamaria Rufino, *Diritto policontesturale*, p. 35.
13 Teubner condenses the task of combining law's identity and variety, entrusted from a juridical point of view to doctrine, in a formula like 'unitas multiplex' that stress the possibility not only of maintaining but also of enriching the identity of law in situations where a pluralistic approach is relevant. See Teubner, 'Unitas multiplex'.
14 See Teubner, *Law as an Autopoietic System*.
15 The scheme proposed here is simplified in comparison to the one espoused by Teubner. See also Teubner, 'Social Order from Legislative Noise' pp. 609–50.
16 See Teubner, *Constitutional Fragments*, p. 1. Teubner points out that globalisation is not the cause of the crisis of traditional constitutionalisation, but merely a factor that underlines the emergence of a societal constitutionalism more extended and visible than the constitutionalisation of function-systems that already existed in the days of the nation state. This requires a constitutional sociology that 'projects

the constitutional question not only onto the relationship between politics and law, but also onto all areas of society'. Ibid., p. 3.
17 Ibid., pp. 1–2.
18 Ibid., pp. 48–9.
19 The list of problems is long. 'Multinational corporations have violated human rights, the World Trade Organisation has made decisions that have endangered the environment or human health in the name of global free trade; there has been doping in sport and corruption in medicine and science; private intermediaries have threatened freedom of conscience on the Internet; there have been massive invasions of privacy through data collection by private organizations; and recently with particular impact, global capital markets have unleashed catastrophic risks. Each of these scandals poses not just regulatory questions, but also constitutional problems in the strict sense.' Ibid., p. 1.
20 For a wide-ranging discussion of this point, cf. Teubner (ed.), *Global Law without a State*.
21 Teubner, *Constitutional Fragments*, pp. 75–6.
22 Ibid., p. 10.
23 Ibid., p. 14.
24 See Teubner and Fischer-Lescano, *Regime-Kollisionen*.
25 On the importance of the political dimension, also for social constitutions without a state, see Lindahl, 'Societal constitutionalism as political constitutionalism'; Přibáň, 'Constitutionalism as fear of the political?'
26 Teubner, *Constitutional Fragments*, p. 7.
27 Ibid., pp. 47–8.
28 See Teubner, *Networks as Connected Contracts*. The scope of pan-constitutionalism may come across as unreal, surreal or hyper-real, as constitutions are sometimes destined to make merely symbolic utterance of desires, aspirations, projects and interests that may not in fact be put into practice in full or may even be ignored in the courts.
29 See Neves, *Transconstitutionalism*.
30 See Chapter 13 in this volume.

Bibliography

Abbott, Kenneth W., Robert O. Keohane, Andrew Moravcsik et al., 'The concept of legalization', International Organisation, 54 (2000), 401–19.
Abegg, Andreas, Die zwingenden Inhaltsnormen des Schuldvertragsrechts: Ein Beitrag zu Geschichte und Funktion der Vertragsfreiheit (Zurich: Schulthess, 2004).
Abi-Saab, Georges, 'Fragmentation or unification: some concluding remarks', New York University Journal of International Law and Politics, 31:4 (1999), 919–34.
Ackerman, Bruce A., We the People: Transformations (Cambridge, Mass.: Harvard University Press, 2000).
Adorno, Theodor, Minima Moralia: Reflections from a Damaged Life, trans. E. F. N. Jephcott (London: New Left Books, 1974).
Adorno, Theodor W., Negative Dialectics, trans. E. B. Ashton (London: Routledge, 1990).
—, Problems of Moral Philosophy, trans. Rodney Livingstone, ed. Thomas Schröder (Stanford: Stanford University Press, 2000).
Agamben, Giorgio, Homo Sacer: Sovereign Power and Bare Life, trans. Daniel Heller-Roazen (Stanford, Calif.: Stanford University Press, 1998).
—, 'K', in Justin Clemens, Nicholas Heron and Alex Murray (eds), The Work of Giorgio Agamben (Edinburgh: Edinburgh University Press, 2008), pp. 13–27.
—, State of Exception, trans. Kevin Attell (Chicago: University of Chicago Press, 2005).
Ahmed, Ikhlaaq, Alexander Sutton and Richard Riley, 'Assessment of publication bias, selection bias, and unavailable data in meta-analyses using individual participant data: a database survey', British Medical Journal, 344 (2012), d7762.
Albert, Hans, 'Das Problem der Begründung', in Hans Albert, Traktat über kritische Vernunft (Tübingen: Mohr Siebeck, 1968), pp. 9–34.
Albert, Matthias, and Lena Hilkermeier (eds), Observing International Relations: Niklas Luhmann and World Politics (London: Routledge & Kegan, 2004).
Aleinikoff, T. Alexander, 'Sovereignty studies in constitutional law: a comment', Constitutional Commentary, 17 (2000), 197–204.
Alexy, Robert, 'On balancing and subsumption: a structural comparison', Ratio Juris, 16:4 (2003), 433–49.
—, A Theory of Constitutional Rights, trans. Julian Rivers (Oxford: Oxford University Press, 2002).
—, 'Verfassungsrecht und einfaches Recht – Verfassungsgerichtsbarkeit und Fachgerichtsbarkeit', Veröffentlichungen der Vereinigung der deutschen Staatsrechtslehrer, 61 (2002), 7–33.
Alford, Roger P., 'Federal courts, international tribunals, and the continuum of deference', Virginia Journal of International Law, 43 (2003), 675–796.
Allert, Tilman, Die Familie: Fallstudien zur Unverwüstlichkeit einer Lebensform (Berlin: de Gruyter, 1998).
Allott, Philip, 'The emerging universal legal system', International Law FORUM du droit international, 3:1 (2001), 12–17.

Alston, Philip, 'Resisting the merger and acquisition of human rights by trade law: a reply to Petersmann', *European Journal of International Law*, 13 (2002), 815–44.

Amstutz, Marc, 'Contract collisions: an evolutionary perspective on contractual networks', *Law and Contemporary Problems*, 76 (2013), 169–89.

—, *Evolutorisches Wirtschaftsrecht: Vorstudien zum Recht und seiner Methode in den Diskurskollisionen der Marktgesellschaft* (Baden-Baden: Nomos, 2001).

—, 'Die Verfassung von Vertragsverbindungen', in Marc Amstutz (ed.), *Die vernetzte Wirtschaft* (Zurich: Schulthess, 2004), pp. 45–86.

Anderson, Gavin W., 'Corporate Constitutionalism: From Above and Below (but mostly below)', paper presented to International Workshop on 'The Constitutionalization of the Global Corporate Sphere?', Copenhagen Business School, 2009.

—, 'Social democracy and the limits of rights constitutionalism', *Canadian Journal of Law & Jurisprudence*, 17 (2004), 31–59.

—, 'Societal constitutionalism, social movements and constitutionalism from below', *Indiana Journal of Global Legal Studies*, 20 (2013), 881–906.

Appadurai, Arjun, *Modernity at Large: Cultural Dimensions of Globalization*, Public Worlds, 1 (Minneapolis: University of Minnesota Press, 1996).

Applegate, William B., Curt D. Furberg and Robert P. Byungton, 'The Multicenter Isradipine Diuretic Atherosclerosis Study (Midas)', *Journal of the American Medical Association*, 277:4 (1997), 297.

Arnaud, André-Jean, 'Legal interpretation and sociology of law at the beginning of the post-modern era', *Onati-Proceedings*, 2 (1990), 173–92.

Ashagrie, Kebebew, 'Statistics on Working Children and Hazardous Child Labour in Brief' (Geneva, International Labour Office Bureau of Statistics, 2nd edn, 1998), available at www.ilo.org/public/english/standards/ipec/simpoc/stats/child/stats.htm.

Atiyah, Patrick S., *The Rise and Fall of Freedom of Contract* (Oxford: Clarendon Press, 1979).

Atlan, Henri, *Enlightenment to Enlightenment: Intercritique of Science and Myth* (New York: State University of New York Press, 1993).

Augsberg, Ino, 'Subjektive und objektive Dimensionen der Wissenschaftsfreiheit', in Friedemann Voigt (ed.), *Freiheit der Wissenschaft: Beiträge zu ihrer Bedeutung, Normativität und Funktion* (Berlin: de Gruyter, 2012), pp. 65–89.

—, 'Wissenschaftsverfassungsrecht', in Thomas Vesting and Stefan Korioth (eds), *Der Eigenwert des Verfassungsrechts: Was bleibt von der Verfassung nach der Globalisierung?* (Tübingen: Mohr Siebeck, 2011), pp. 203–23.

Austin, John, *The Province of Jurisprudence Determined, and The Uses of the Study of Jurisprudence. With an Introduction by H. L. A. Hart* (London: Weidenfeld & Nicolson, 1954).

Ayres, Ian, and John Braithwaite, *Responsive Regulation: Transcending the Deregulation Debate* (New York: Oxford University Press, 1992).

Backer, Larry Catá, 'The autonomous global enterprise: on the role of organizational law beyond asset partitioning and legal personality', *Tulane Law Journal*, 41 (2006), 541–72.

—, 'Governance without Government OR Government without a State? Gunther Teubner on Complications of Unmooring Corporate Governance From Corporate Law' (Internet blog post, 25 June 2009), available at http://lcbackerblog.blogspot.com/2009/06/gunther-teubner-on-complications-of.html.

—, 'Multinational corporations, transnational law: the United Nations' norms on the responsibilities of transnational corporations as a harbinger of corporate responsibility in international Law', *Columbia Human Rights Law Review*, 37:2 (2006), 287–390.

Baecker, Dirk, *Die Form des Unternehmens* (Frankfurt: Suhrkamp, 1993).
—, *Organisation und Gesellschaft* (Witten-Herdecke: Universität, 2002).
Baker, J. H., 'The law merchant and the common law before 1700', *Cambridge Law Journal*, 38 (1979), 295–322.
Baker, Mark B., 'Tightening the toothless vise: codes of conduct and the American multinational enterprise', *Wisconsin International Law Journal*, 20 (2001), 89–142.
Banakar, Reza, 'In search of Heimat: a note on Franz Kafka's concept of law', *Law & Literature*, 22 (2010), 463–90.
Bar, Christian von, *Internationales Privatrecht*, vol. 1 (Munich: Beck, 1987).
Barak, Aharon, 'Constitutional human rights and private law', *Review on Constitutional Studies*, 3 (1996), 218–81.
Barjiji-Kastner, Fatima, *Ohnmachtssemantiken: Systemtheorie und Dekonstruktion* (Weilerswist: Velbrück, 2007).
Bass, Naomi, 'Implications of the TRIPS Agreement for developing countries: pharmaceutical patent laws in Brazil and South Africa in the 21st century', *George Washington International Law Review*, 34 (2002), 191–223.
Bauman, Zygmunt, *Postmodern Ethics* (London: Blackwells, 1993).
Beck, Ulrich, *Risk Society* (London: Sage Publications, 1992).
—, 'Umweltpolitik in der Risikogesellschaft', *Zeitschrift für angewandte Umweltforschung*, 4 (1991), 117–22.
Becker, Annette, Fatma Dörter, Kirsten Eckhardt et al., 'The association between a journal's source of revenue and the drug recommendations made in the articles it publishes', *Canadian Medical Association Journal*, 183 (2011), 544–8.
Béguin, Jacques, 'Le développement de la *lex mercatoria* menace-t-il l'ordre juridique international?', *McGill Law Journal*, 30 (1985), 478–538.
Behrens, Peter, 'Weltwirtschaftsverfassung', *Jahrbuch für Neue Politische Ökonomie*, 19 (2000), 5–27.
Bendel, Klaus, 'Funktionale Differenzierung und gesellschaftliche Rationalität', *Zeitschrift für Soziologie*, 22 (1993), 261–78.
Benjamin, Walter, 'Critique of Violence', in Walter Benjamin, *Reflections: Essays, Aphorisms, Autobiographical Writings* (New York: Schocken, 1986), pp. 277–300.
—, 'Critique of Violence', in Walter Benjamin, *Selected Writings*, vol. 1: *1913–1926*, ed. Marcus Bullock and Michael W. Jennings (Cambridge, Mass.: Belknap Press, 1997).
—, *Gesammelte Schriften*, vol. 2 (Frankfurt: Suhrkamp, 1977).
Bercusson, Brian, 'Globalizing Labour Law: Transnational Private Regulation and Countervailing Actors', in Gunther Teubner (ed.), *Global Law without a State* (Aldershot: Dartmouth, 1997), pp. 133–78.
Berg, Henk de, and Matthias Prangel, *Kommunikation und Differenz: Systemtheoretische Ansätze in der Literatur- und Kunstwissenschaft* (Opladen: Westdeutscher Verlag, 1993).
Berger, Klaus-Peter, 'The international arbitrator's applications of precedents', *Journal of International Arbitration*, 9 (1992), 4–22.
Berman, Harold, 'The Law of International Commercial Transactions (Lex Mercatoria)', in W.S. Surrey and D. Wallace (eds), *Lawyer's Guide to International Business Transactions: The Law of International Commercial Transactions (Lex Mercatoria)* (Philadelphia: American Law Institute – American Bar Association, 1983), pp. 1–65.
Berman, Harold, 'World law', *Fordham International Law Journal*, 18 (1994), 1617–23.
Berman, Paul Schiff, 'The globalization of jurisdiction', *University of Pennsylvania Law Review*, 151:2 (2002), 311–545.

Bernstein, Edward A., 'Law & Economics and the structure of value adding contracts: a contract lawyer's view of the Law & Economics literature', *Oregon Law Review*, 74:1 (1995), 189–238.
Betlem, Gerrit, and André Nollkaemper, 'Giving effect to public international law before domestic courts: a comparative analysis of the practice of consistent interpretation', *European Journal of International Law*, 14 (2003), 569–89.
Bianchi, Andrea, 'Globalization of Human Rights: The Role of Non State Actors', in G. Teubner (ed.), *Global Law without a State* (Aldershot: Dartmouth, 1997), pp. 179–212.
Binswanger, Hans Christoph, *Vorwärts zur Mäßigung: Perspektiven einer nachhaltigen Wirtschaft* (Hamburg: Murmann, 2009).
—, *Die Wachstumsspirale: Geld, Energie und Imagination in der Dynamik des Marktprozesses* (Marburg: Metropolis, 2006).
Bitbol, Michel, 'En quoi consiste la 'Révolution Quantique'?', *Revue Internationale de Systémique*, 11 (1997), 215–39.
Black, Julia, 'Constitutionalising self-regulation', *Modern Law Review*, 59 (1996), 24–55.
—, 'Reviewing Regulatory Rules: Responsibility to Hybridisation', in J. Black, P. Muchlinski and P. Walker (eds), *Commercial Regulation and Judicial Review* (Oxford: Hart, 1998), pp. 123–58.
Blecher, Michael, *Zu einer Ethik der Selbstreferenz, oder, Theorie als Compassion: Möglichkeiten einer kritischen Theorie der Selbstreferenz von Gesellschaft und Recht* (Berlin: Duncker & Humblot, 1991).
Böckenförde, Ernst-Wolfgang, *Staat, Nation, Europa: Studien zur Staatslehre, Verfassungstheorie und Rechtsphilosophie* (Frankfurt: Suhrkamp, 1999).
Böckenförde, Markus, 'Zwischen Sein und Wollen: Über den Einfluss umweltvölkerrechtlicher Verträge im Rahmen eines WTO-Streitbeilegungsverfahrens', *Zeitschrift für ausländisches und öffentliches Recht und Völkerrecht*, 63 (2003), 971–1005.
Bodeker, Gerard, 'Traditional medical knowledge, intellectual property rights, and benefit sharing', *Cardozo Journal of International and Comparative Law*, 11 (2003), 785–812.
Böll, Heinrich, *The Lost Honor of Katharina Blum, or, How Violence Develops and Where it can Lead*, trans. Leila Vennewitz (New York: Penguin Books, 1994).
Bombardier, Claire, Loren Laine, Alise Reicin et al., 'Comparison of upper gastrointestinal toxicity of Rofecoxib and Naproxen in patients with rheumatoid arthritis: VIGOR Study Group', *New England Journal of Medicine*, 343:21 (2000), 1520–8.
Bonell, Michael Joachim, 'Das autonome Recht des Welthandels: Rechtsdogmatische und rechtspolitische Aspekte', *Rabels Zeitschrift*, 42 (1978), 485–506.
Bothe, Michael, 'The Historical Evolution of International Humanitarian Law, International Human Rights Law, Refugee Law and International Criminal Law', in Horst Fischer et al. (eds), *Krisensicherung und Humanitärer Schutz – Crisis Management and Humanitarian Protection: Festschrift für Dieter Fleck* (Berlin: Berliner Wissenschaftsverlag, 2004), pp. 37–47.
Boudon, Raymond, *Effets pervers et ordre social* (Paris: Presse Universitaire Française, 1977).
Braeckmans, Herman, 'Paralegale normen en Lex Mercatoria', *Tijdschrift voor Privatrecht*, 23 (1986), 1–70.
Braithwaite, Joanne P., 'Standard form contracts as transnational law: evidence from the derivatives markets', *Modern Law Review*, 75:5 (2012), 779–805.
Braithwaite, John, 'Enforced self-regulation: a new strategy for corporate crime control', *Michigan Law Review*, 80:7 (1982), 1466–507.

Braune, Fernando, and Naira Menezes, 'The patentability of chemical, biochemical, pharmaceutical and biotechnological inventions in Brazil', *Patent World*, 108 (1999), 46–8.
Bredt, Stephan, *Die demokratische Legitimation unabhängiger Institutionen: Vom funktionalen zum politikfeldbezogenen Demokratieprinzip* (Tübingen: Mohr Siebeck, 2006).
Breyer, Stephen G., *Regulation and its Reform* (Cambridge, Mass.: Harvard University Press, 1982).
Brilmayer, Lea, 'The role of substantive and choice of law policies in the formation and application of choice of law rules', *Hague Recueil des Cours*, 252 (1995), 9–112.
Brodocz, André, 'Strukturelle Kopplung durch Verbände', *Soziale Systeme*, 2 (1996), 361–87.
Brüggemeier, Gert, 'Constitutionalisation of Private Law: The German Perspective', in Tom Barkhuysen and Siewert Lindenbergh (eds), *Constitutionalisation of Private Law* (Leiden: Brill, 2008), pp. 59–82.
Brunkhorst, Hauke, 'Ist die Solidarität der Bürgergesellschaft globalisierbar?', in Hauke Brunkhorst, *Globalisierung und Demokratie: Wirtschaft, Recht, Medien* (Frankfurt: Suhrkamp, 2000), pp. 274–86.
—, 'Die Legitimationskrise der Weltgesellschaft: Global Rule of Law, Global Constitutionalism und Weltstaatlichkeit', in Mathias Albert and Rudolf Stichweh (eds), *Weltstaat und Weltstaatlichkeit* (Wiesbaden: VS, 2007), pp. 63–108.
—, *Solidarity: From Civic Friendship to a Global Legal Community* (Cambridge, Mass.: MIT Press, 2005).
Buchanan, James M., *Constitutional Economics* (Oxford: Blackwell, 1991).
Bucher, Andreas, and Pierre-Yves Tschanz, *International Arbitration in Switzerland* (Basle: Helbig & Lichtenhahn, 1989).
Buckel, Sonja, *Subjektivierung und Kohäsion: Zur Rekonstruktion einer materialistischen Theorie des Rechts* (Weilerswist: Velbrück, 2007).
— and Andreas Fischer-Lescano (eds), *Hegemonie gepanzert mit Zwang: Zivilgesellschaft und Politik im Staatsverständnis Antonio Gramscis* (Baden-Baden: Nomos, 2007).
Buergenthal, Thomas, 'Proliferation of international courts and tribunals: is it good or bad?', *Leiden Journal of International Law*, 14:2 (2001), 267–75.
Bumke, Christian, 'Universitäten im Wettbewerb', *Veröffentlichungen der Vereinigung der Deutschen Staatsrechtslehrer*, 69 (2009), 407–61.
Burke-White, William W., 'A community of courts: toward a system of international criminal law enforcement', *Michigan Journal of International Law*, 24 (2002), 1–101.
Calliess, Gralf-Peter, *Prozedurales Recht* (Baden-Baden: Nomos, 1999).
—, 'Reflexive transnational law: the privatisation of civil law and the civilisation of private law', *Zeitschrift für Rechtssoziologie*, 24:2 (2002), 185–217.
Calliess, Gralf-Peter, and Peer Zumbansen, *Rough Consensus and Running Code: A Theory of Transnational Private Law* (Oxford: Hart, 2010).
Campbell, David, 'The limits of concept formation in legal science', *Social & Legal Studies*, 9 (2000), 439–47.
Canaris, Claus-Wilhelm, *Grundrechte und Privatrecht: Eine Zwischenbilanz* (Berlin: de Gruyter, 1999).
Carbonneau, Thomas E., 'Rendering arbitral awards with reasons: the elaboration of a common law of international transactions', *Columbia Journal of Transnational Law*, 23 (1985), 579–614.

Cass, Deborah Z., *The Constitutionalization of the World Trade Organization: Legitimacy, Democracy and Community in the International Trading System* (Oxford: Oxford University Press, 2005).

Cassese, Antonio, 'Ex iniuria ius oritur: are we moving towards international legitimation of forcible humanitarian countermeasures in the world community?', *European Journal of International Law*, 10 (1999), 23–31.

—, 'When may senior state officials be tried for international crimes? Some comments on the Congo v. Belgium case', *European Journal of International Law*, 13 (2002), 853–77.

Cassese, Sabino, 'Administrative law without the state: the challenge of global regulation', *New York University Journal of International Law and Politics*, 37 (2005), 663–94.

Castells, Manuel, *The Rise of the Network Society*, The Information Age, 1 (Oxford: Blackwell, 1st edn, 1996).

Chan, An-Wen, Asbjorn Hróbjartsson, Mette T. Haahr et al., 'Empirical evidence for selective reporting of outcomes in randomized trials: comparison of protocols to published articles', *Journal of the American Medical Association*, 291:20 (2004), 2457–65.

Charney, Jonathan, 'The impact on the international legal system of the growth of international courts and tribunals', *New York University Journal of International Law and Politics*, 31:4 (1999), 697–708.

—, 'Is international law threatened by multiple international tribunals?', *Hague Recueil des Cours*, 271 (1998), 101–382.

Cheadle, Halton, and Dennis Davis, 'The application of the 1996 constitution in the private sphere', *South African Journal of Human Rights*, 13 (1997), 44–66.

Christensen, Ralph, and Andreas Fischer-Lescano, *Das Ganze des Rechts: Vom hierarchischen zum reflexiven Verständnis deutscher und europäischer Grundrechte* (Berlin: Duncker & Humblot, 2007).

Christodoulidis, Emilios, 'Against Substitution: The Constitutional Thinking of Dissensus', in Martin Loughlin and Neil Walker (eds), *The Paradox of Constitutionalism: Constituent Power and Constitutional Form* (Oxford, New York: Oxford University Press, 2007), pp. 189–208.

Cicero, Marcus Tullius, *De natura deorum* (London: Methuen, 1896).

Clam, Jean, 'Die Grundparadoxie des Rechts und ihre Ausfaltung: Beitrag zu einer Analytik des Paradoxen', in Gunther Teubner (ed.), *Die Rückgabe des zwölften Kamels: Niklas Luhmann in der Diskussion über Gerechtigkeit* (Stuttgart: Lucius & Lucius, 2000), pp. 109–43.

—, 'Wie dicht sind Opfer? Zur Entscheidung der Frage nach dem Ort der Transzendenz in heutiger Gesellschaft', *Zeitschrift für Rechtssoziologie*, 29 (2008), 37–52.

Clapham, Andrew, *Human Rights in the Private Sphere* (Oxford: Oxford University Press, 1996).

—, *Human Rights Obligations of Non-State Actors* (Oxford: Oxford University Press, 2006).

Cleveland, Sarah, 'Global labor rights and the Alien Tort Claims Act', *Texas Law Review*, 76 (1998), 1533–79.

Cohen, Jean, and A. Arato, *Civil Society and Political Theory* (Cambridge, Mass.: Harvard University Press, 1992).

Cohen, Joshua, 'Procedure and Substance in Deliberative Democracy', in S. Benhabib (ed.), *Democracy and Difference: Contesting the Boundaries of the Political* (Princeton: Princeton University Press, 1996), pp. 95–119.

Cohen, Stanley, 'Social-Control Talk: Telling Stories about Correctional Change', in David Garland and Peter Young (eds), *The Power to Punish: Contemporary Penality and Social Analysis* (London: Heinemann, 1983), pp. 101–29.

Collins, Hugh, *Justice in Dismissal: The Law of Termination of Employment* (Oxford: Oxford University Press, 1992).

—, 'The Sanctimony of Contract', in Richard Rawlings (ed.), *Law, Society and Economy: Centenary Essays for the London School of Economics and Political Science 1895–1995* (Oxford: Clarendon Press, 1997), pp. 63–89.

Conrad, Dieter, *Freiheitsrechte und Arbeitsverfassung*, Schriften zum öffentlichen Recht, 22 (Berlin: Duncker & Humblot, 1965).

Cornell, Drucilla, 'The relevance of time to the relationship between the philosophy of the limit and systems theory', *Cardozo Law Review*, 13 (1992), 1579–603.

Corngold, Stanley, Jack, Greenberg, and Benno Wagner (eds), *Franz Kafka: The Office Writings* (Princeton: Princeton University Press, 2009).

Correa, Carlos, and Sisule Musungu, 'The WIPO Patent Agenda: The Risk for Developing Countries', South Center, Trade-Related Agenda, Development and Equity Working Paper 12 (November 2002), available at www.southcentre.org/publications/wipopatent/toc.htm.

Cotterrell, Roger, *Law's Community: Legal Theory in Sociological Perspective* (Oxford: Clarendon Press, 2006).

Cottier, Thomas, and Maya Hertig, 'The prospects of 21st century constitutionalism', *Max Planck Yearbook of United Nations Law*, 7 (2003), 261–328.

Cover, Robert M., 'The Supreme Court, 1982 term – foreword: nomos and narrative', *Harvard Law Review*, 97:1 (1983), 4–68.

Craswell, Richard, 'Contract Law: General Theories', in Boudewijn Bouckaert and Gerit de Geest (eds), *Encyclopedia of Law and Economics*, vol. I3: *The Regulation of Contract* (Cheltenham: Edward Elgar, 2000), pp. 1–24.

Cremades, Bernardo M., 'The impact of international arbitration on the development of business law', *Boston University International Law Journal*, 31 (1983), 526–34.

—, and Steven L. Plehn, 'The new lex mercatoria and the harmonization of the laws of international commercial transactions', *Boston University International Law Journal*, 2 (1984), 317–48.

Creutz, Helmut, 'Vollgeld und Grundeinkommen', *Zeitschrift für Sozialökonomie*, 133 (2002), 14–19.

Crone, Hans Caspar von der, *Rahmenverträge: Vertragsrecht – Systemtheorie – Ökonomie* (Zurich: Schulthess, 1993).

Crouch, Colin, *The Strange Non-Death of Neoliberalism* (Cambridge: Polity Press, 2011).

D'Amato, Anthony, 'International Law as an Autopoietic System', in Rüdiger Wolfrum and Volker Roeben (eds), *Developments of International Law in Treaty Making* (Vienna: Springer, 2005), pp. 335–400, available at http://anthonydamato.law.northwestern.edu.

Dahrendorf, Ralf, 'Anmerkungen zur Globalisierung', in Ulrich Beck (ed.), *Contract and Organisation: Legal Analysis in the Light of Economic and Social Theory* (Frankfurt: Suhrkamp, 1998), pp. 31–54.

Dalhuisen, Jan H., 'Legal orders and their manifestations: the operation of the international commercial and financial legal order and its lex mercatoria', *Berkeley Journal of International Law*, 24 (2006), 129–91.

Darcy de Oliveira, Miguel, and Rajesh Tandon, 'An Emerging Global Civil Society', in Miguel Darcy de Oliveira and Rajesh Tandon (eds), *Citizens: Strengthening Global Civil Society* (Washington, DC: Civicus, 1994), pp. 1–17.

David, René, 'Le droit du commerce international: une nouvelle tâche pour les législateurs nationaux ou une nouvelle 'lex mercatoria'?', in Unidroit (ed.), *New Directions in International Trade Law* (New York: Oceana, 1977), pp. 5–20.

Davis, Dennis, Patrick Macklem and Guy Mundlak, 'Social Rights, Social Citizenship, and Transformative Constitutionalism: A Comparative Assessment', in Joanne Conaghan, Richard M. Fischl and Karl Klare (eds), *Labour Law in an Era of Globalization* (Oxford: Oxford University Press, 2002), pp. 511–34.

De Angelis, Catherine, Jeffrey M. Drazen, Frank A. Frizelle *et al.*, 'Clinical trial registration: a statement from the International Committee of Medical Journal Editors', *New England Journal of Medicine*, 351 (2004), 1250–1.

De George, Richard T., 'The status of business ethics: past and future', *Journal of Business Ethics*, 6:3 (1987), 201–11.

De Schutter, Olivier (ed.), *Transnational Corporations and Human Rights* (Oxford: Hart, 2006).

Delaume, Georges R., 'Comparative analysis as a basis of law in state contracts: the myth of the lex mercatoria', *Tulane Law Review*, 63 (1989), 575–611.

Deleuze, Gilles, and Félix Guattari, *On the Line*, trans. John Johnson (New York: Semiotext(e), 1983).

Derrida, Jacques, 'Before the Law', in Jacques Derrida, *Acts of Literature*, ed. Derek Attridge (London: Routledge, 1992), pp. 181–220.

—, 'Des tours de Babel', in Jacques Derrida, *Psyche: l'invention de l'autre*, vol. 1 (Paris: Galilée, 1987), pp. 203–35.

—, 'Force of law: the mystical foundation of authority', *Cardozo Law Review*, 11 (1990), 919–1046.

—, *Given Time, vol. 1: Counterfeit Money*, trans. Peggy Kamuf (Chicago: University of Chicago Press, 1992).

—, *Margins of Philosophy*, trans. Alan Bass (Chicago: University of Chicago Press, 1982).

—, *Of Grammatology*, trans. Gayatri Chakravorty Spivak (Baltimore: Johns Hopkins University Press, corrected edn, 1998).

—, *On Cosmopolitanism and Forgiveness*, trans. Mark Dooley and Michael Hughes (London: Routledge, 2001).

—, *The Other Heading: Reflections on Today's Europe*, trans. Pascale-Anne Brault and Michael B. Naas (Bloomington: Indiana University Press, 1992).

—, *Politics of Friendship*, trans. George Collins (London: Verso, 1997).

—, 'Le siècle et le pardon', *Le monde des débats*, 9 (December 1999).

—, *Specters of Marx*, trans. Peggy Kamuf (New York: Routledge, 1994).

—, *Writing and Difference*, trans. Alan Bass (Chicago: University of Chicago Press, 1978).

—, 'Préjugés: devant la loi', in Jacques Derrida, *La faculté de juger* (Paris: Minuit, 1985), pp. 87–139.

Dickersin, Kay, 'The existence of publication bias and risk factors for its occurrence', *Journal of the American Medical Association*, 263:10 (1990), 1385–9.

—, Yuan-I Min and Curtis L. Meinert, 'Factors influencing publication of research results: follow-up of applications submitted to two institutional review boards', *Journal of the American Medical Association*, 267:3 (1992), 374–8.

Dickinson, Laura, 'The promise of hybrid courts', *American Journal of International Law*, 97 (2003), 295–310.

Diederichsen, Uwe, 'Das Bundesverfassungsgericht als oberstes Zivilgericht', *Archiv für die civilistische Praxis*, 198 (1998), 171–260.

—, 'Die Selbstbehauptung des Privatrechts gegenüber dem Grundgesetz', *Archiv für die civilistische Praxis*, 197 (1997), 57–64.

Dinwoodie, Graeme B., 'The development and incorporation of international norms in the formation of copyright law', *Ohio State Law Journal*, 63 (2001), 733–82.
—, 'A new copyright order: why national courts should create global norms', *University of Pennsylvania Law Review*, 149 (2000), 469–581.
Dirnagl, Ulrich, and Martin Lauritzen, 'Fighting publication bias: introducing the negative results sections', *Journal of Cerebral Blood Flow and Metabolism*, 30:7 (2010), 1263–4.
Domej, Tanja, Bianka S. Dörr, Urs H. Hoffmann-Nowotny et al. (eds), *Einheit des Privatrechts, komplexe Welt: Herausforderungen durch fortschreitende Spezialisierung und Interdisziplinarität*, Jahrbuch Junger Zivilrechtswissenschaftler (Stuttgart: Boorberg, 2008).
Douzinas, Costas, and Ronnie Warrington, *Justice Miscarried: Ethics and Aesthetics in Law* (New York: Harvester Wheatsheaf, 1994).
Dreier, Horst, *Dimensionen der Grundrechte: Von der Wertordnungsjudikatur zu den objektiv-rechtlichen Grundrechtsgehalten* (Hanover: Hennies & Zinkeisen, 1993).
Dreier, Ralf, 'Niklas Luhmanns Rechtsbegriff', *Archiv für Rechts- und Sozialphilosophie*, 88:3 (2002), 305–22.
Dunoff, Jeffrey L., and Joel Trachtman (eds), *Ruling the World? Constitutionalism, International Law and Global Government* (Cambridge: Cambridge University Press, 2008).
Dupuy, Jean-Pierre, 'Deconstructing deconstruction: supplement and hierarchy', *Evolution, Order and Complexity*, 7 (1990), 101–21.
—, and Gunther Teubner (eds), *Paradoxes of Self-Reference in the Humanities, Law and the Social Sciences*, Stanford Literature Review (Saratoga, California: Anma Libri, 1990).
Dupuy, Pierre-Marie, 'The danger of fragmentation or unification of the international legal system and the International Court of Justice', *New York University Journal of International Law and Politics*, 31:4 (1999), 791–808.
Dürig, Günter, 'Art. 1 GG', in Günter Dürig and Theodor Maunz (eds), *Grundgesetz. Kommentar* (Munich: C. H. Beck, 1957), art. 1, para. 5 ff.
—, 'Grundrechte und Zivilrechtsprechung', in Theodor Maunz (ed.), *Vom Bonner Grundgesetz zur gesamtdeutschen Verfassung: Festschrift Hans Nawiasky* (Munich: Isar, 1956), pp. 157–210.
Durkheim, Emile, *The Division of Labor in Society*, trans. George Simpson (New York: Free Press, 1933 [1883]).
Easterbrook, Philippa J., Jesse A. Berlin, Ramana Gopalan et al., 'Publication bias in clinical research', *The Lancet*, 337 (1991), 867–72.
Ehrlich, Eugen, *Fundamental Principles of the Sociology of Law*, trans. Walter L. Moll (Cambridge, Mass.: Harvard University Press, 1936).
Eisenberg, Melvin A., 'Relational Contracts', in J. Beatson and D. Friedmann (eds), *Good Faith and Fault in Contract Law* (Oxford: Clarendon Press, 1995), pp. 291–304.
Ellickson, Robert C., 'Bringing culture and human frailty to rational actors: a critique of classical law and economics', *Chicago Kent Law Review*, 65:1 (1989), 23–56.
Engle, Karen, 'After the Collapse of the Public/Private Distinction: Strategizing Women's Rights', in Dorinda G. Dallmeyer (ed.), *Reconceiving Reality: Women and International Law* (Washington: American Society of International Law, 1993), pp. 143–55.
Esser, Josef, *Grundsatz und Norm in der richterlichen Fortbildung des Privatrechts: Rechtsvergleichende Beiträge zur Rechtsquellen- und Interpretationslehre* (Tübingen: Mohr Siebeck, 1956).
—, 'Richterrecht, Gerichtsgebrauch und Gewohnheitsrecht', in Josef Esser and Hans Thieme (eds), *Festschrift für Fritz von Hippel* (Tübingen: Mohr & Siebeck, 1967), pp. 95–130.

—, *Vorverständnis und Methodenwahl in der Rechtsfindung: Rationalitätsgrundlagen richterlicher Entscheidungspraxis* (Frankfurt: Athenäum, revised and expanded edn, 1972).

Ewald, Francois, *L'État providence* (Paris: Grasset & Fasquelle, 1986).

Eyding, Dirk, Monika Lelgemann, Ulrich Grouven *et al.*, 'Reboxetine for acute treatment of major depression: systematic review and meta-analysis of published and unpublished placebo and selective serotonin reuptake inhibitor controlled trials', *British Medical Journal*, 341:7777 (2010), c4737.

Fanelli, Daniele, 'Do pressures to publish increase scientists' bias? An empirical support from US States data', *PLOS ONE*, 5:4 (2010), 1–7.

Fassbender, Bardo, 'The United Nations Charter as constitution of the international community', *Columbia Journal of Transnational Law*, 37 (1998), 529–619.

Febbrajo, Alberto, and Gorm Harste (eds), *Law and Intersystemic Communication: Understanding Structural Coupling* (Farnham: Ashgate, 2013).

Felici, Lucio, and Maurizio Trifone, *Il grande dizionario Garzanti della lingua italiana* (Milan: Garzanti, 1st edn, 1987).

Femia, Pasquale, 'Desire for text: bridling the divisional strategy of Contract', *Law and Contemporary Problems*, 76 (2013), 150–68.

Feyerabend, Paul, *Against Method: Outline of an Anarchist Theory of Knowledge* (London: Verso, 4th edn, 2010).

Fidler, David P., 'Global outbreak of avian influenza A (H5N1) and international law', *ASIL Insights*, 2004/01 (2004), available at www.asil.org/insights.

Fikentscher, Wolfgang, *Methoden des Rechts in vergleichender Darstellung*, vol. 4 (Tübingen: Mohr Siebeck, 1977).

Fischer-Lescano, Andreas, 'Die Emergenz der Globalverfassung', *Zeitschrift für ausländisches und öffentliches Recht und Völkerrecht*, 63:3 (2003), 717–60.

—, *Globalverfassung: Die Geltungsbegründung der Menschenrechte* (Weilerswist: Velbrück, 2005).

—, 'Globalverfassung: Verfassung der Weltgesellschaft', *Archiv für Rechts- und Sozialphilosophie*, 88 (2002), 349–78.

—, 'Kritik der praktischen Konkordanz', *Kritische Justiz*, 2 (2008), 166–77.

—, 'Luhmanns Staat und der transnationale Konstitutionalismus', in Marcelo Neves and Rüdiger Voigt (eds), *Die Staaten der Weltgesellschaft: Luhmanns Staatstheorie* (Baden-Baden: Nomos, 2007), pp. 99–113.

—, 'Odious Debts und das Weltrecht', *Kritische Justiz*, 36:2 (2003), 225–39.

Fischer-Lescano, Andreas and Moritz Renner, 'Europäisches Verwaltungsrecht und Völkerrecht', in Jörg P. Terhechte (ed.), *Verwaltungsrecht in der Europäischen Union* (Baden-Baden: Nomos, 2011), pp. 359–71.

Fish, Stanley, *Doing What Comes Naturally: Change, Rhetoric, and the Practice of Theory in Literary and Legal Studies* (Oxford: Oxford University Press, 1989).

Fisher, Irving, *100% Money* (London: Pickering & Chatto, 1997 [1935]).

Fitzpatrick, Peter, 'The impossibility of popular justice', *Social & Legal Studies*, 1 (1992), 199–215.

—, 'Law and societies', *Osgoode Hall Law Journal*, 22 (1984), 115–38.

Fletcher, George P., 'Paradoxes in legal thought', *Columbia Law Review*, 85 (1985), 1263–92.

Flood, John, 'The Cultures of Globalization: Professional Restructuring for the International Market', in Yves Dezalay and David Sugarman (eds), *Professional Competition and Professional Power: Lawyers, Accountants and the Social Construction of Markets* (London: Routledge, 1995), pp. 139–69.

Foerster, Heinz von, 'Das Gleichnis vom blinden Fleck: Über das Sehen im allgemeinen', in Gerhard Johann Lischka (ed.), *Der entfesselte Blick: Symposion, Workshops, Ausstellung* (Berne: Benteli, 1993), pp. 14–47.
—, *Observing Systems* (Seaside, Calif.: Intersystems Publications, 1981).
—, 'Through the Eyes of the Other', in Frederick Steyer (ed.), *Research and Reflexivity* (London: Sage, 1991), pp. 21–8.
Folkers, Horst, 'Johannes mit Aristoteles ins Gespräch über die Gerechtigkeit vertieft: Epilegomena zum 12. Kamel des Niklas Luhmann', *Zeitschrift für Rechtssoziologie*, 21 (2000), 61–107.
Forst, Rainer, 'Die Rechtfertigung der Gerechtigkeit: Rawls' Politischer Liberalismus und Habermas' Diskurstheorie in der Diskussion', in Hauke Brunkhorst and Peter Niesen (eds), *Das Recht der Republik: Festschrift für Ingeborg Maus* (Frankfurt: Suhrkamp, 1999), pp. 105–68.
Foucault, Michel, *Discipline and Punish*, trans. Alan Sheridan (New York: Vintage/ Random House, 1979).
—, *The Order of Things: An Archaeology of the Human Sciences* (London: Tavistock, 1974).
—, 'Prison Talk', in Michel Foucault, *Power / Knowledge: Selected Interviews and Other Writings, 1972–1977*, ed.Colin Gordon (Brighton: Harvester, 1980), pp. 37–54.
Fouchard, Philippe, *L'arbitrage commercial international* (Paris: Dalloz, 1965).
—, 'La loi régissant les obligations contractuelles en droit international privé français', in Frédéric-Edouard Klein and Frank Vischer (eds), *Colloque de Bâle sur la loi régissant les obligations contractuelles, 30 et 31 octobre, 1980: Rapports et procès-verbaux des débats*, Schriftenreihe des Instituts für Internationales Recht und Internationale Beziehungen, 33 (Basle: Helbing & Lichtenhahn, 1983), pp. 81–114.
Franck, Thomas, 'The 'powers of appreciation': who is the ultimate guardian of UN legality', *American Journal of International Law*, 86 (1992), 519–23.
Frankenberg, Günter, 'Down by Law: Irony, Seriousness, and Reason', in C. Joerges and D. Trubek (eds), *Critical Legal Thought: An American-German Debate* (Baden-Baden: Nomos, 1989), pp. 315–52.
Franzen, Martina, *Breaking News: Wissenschaftliche Zeitschriften im Kampf um Aufmerksamkeit* (Baden-Baden: Nomos, 2011).
Freedland, Mark, 'Government by contract and public law', *Public Law*, 76 (1994), 86–104.
Freitag, Hans Otto, *Gewohnheitsrecht und Rechtssystem* (Berlin: Duncker und Humblot, 1976).
Freyberger, Harald J., Wolfgang Schneider and Rolf-Dieter Stieglitz, *Kompendium: Psychiatrie, Psychotherapie, Psychosomatische Medizin* (Basle: Karger, 11th edn, 2002).
Friedland, Roger, and Robert Alford, 'Bringing Society Back In: Symbols, Practices, and Institutional Contradictions', in Paul DiMaggio and Walter Powell (eds), *The New Institutionalism* (Chicago: University of Chicago Press, 1992), pp. 232–63.
Friedman, Daniel, and Daphne Barak-Erez, 'Introduction', in Daniel Friedman and Daphne Barak-Erez (eds), *Human Rights in Private Law* (Oxford: Hart, 2001).
Friedman, Lawrence M., *Contract Law in America: A Social and Economic Case Study* (Madison: University of Wisconsin Press, 1965).
—, 'Erewhon: the coming global legal order', *Stanford Journal of International Law*, 37 (2001), 347–64.
Frowein, Jochen A., 'Konstitutionalisierung des Völkerrechts', in Klaus Dicke *et al.* (eds), *Völkerrecht und internationales Privatrecht in einem sich globalisierenden*

internationalen System: Auswirkungen der Entstaatlichung transnationaler Rechtsbeziehungen (Heidelberg: Müller, 2000), pp. 427–47.

Fuchs, Peter, *Der Eigen-Sinn des Bewußtseins: Die Person – die Psyche – die Signatur* (Bielefeld: transcript, 2003).

Fugh-Berman, Adriane J., 'The haunting of medical journals: how ghostwriting sold 'HRT'', *PLOS Medicine*, 7:9 (2010), e1000335.

Fuller, Lon, *The Morality of Law* (New Haven: Yale University Press, 1969).

Fung, Archon, Dara O'Rourke and Charles Sabel, *Can We Put an End to Sweatshops?* (Ann Arbor, Mich.: Beacon, 2004).

Gallie, Walter B., 'Essentially contested concepts', *Proceedings of the Aristotelian Society*, 56 (1956), 167–98.

Galtung, Johan, 'Institutionalized conflict resolution: a theoretical paradigm', *Journal of Peace Research*, 2 (1965), 348–97.

Gamillscheg, Franz, 'Die Grundrechte im Arbeitsrecht', *Archiv für die civilistische Praxis*, 164 (1964), 385–445.

Gardbaum, Stephen, 'The 'horizontal effect' of constitutional rights', *Michigan Law Review*, 102 (2003), 387–459.

—, 'Human Rights and International Constitutionalism', in Jeffrey L. Dunoff and Joel Trachtman (eds), *Ruling the World? Constitutionalism, International Law and Global Government* (Cambridge: Cambridge University Press, 2008), pp. 233–57, available at http://ssrn.com/paper=1088039.

Geiger, Theodor, *Vorstudien zu einer Soziologie des Rechts* (Berlin: Duncker & Humblot, 1964).

Gelling, Leslie, 'Negative results have a value', *Nurse Researcher*, 20:6 (2013), 3.

Gerstenberg, Oliver, *Bürgerrecht und deliberative Demokratie: Elemente einer pluralistischen Verfassungstheorie* (Frankfurt: Suhrkamp, 1997).

—, 'Justification (and justifiability) of private law in a polycontextural world', *Social & Legal Studies*, 9 (2000), 419–30.

—, 'Private Law, Constitutionalism and the Limits of the Judicial Role', in Craig Scott (ed.), *Torture as Tort: Comparative Perspectives on the Development of Transnational Human Rights Litigation* (Oxford: Hart Publishing, 2001), pp. 687–703.

Giddens, Anthony, *The Consequences of Modernity* (Stanford: Stanford University Press, 1990).

Gierke, Otto von, *Das Wesen der menschlichen Verbände* (Leipzig: Duncker & Humblot, 1902).

Gill, Stephen, *Power and Resistance in the New World Order* (Basingstoke, Hampshire: Macmillan, 2003).

Glendon, Ann, 'Rights Talk: The Impoverishment of Political Discourse', in Don E. Eberly (ed.), *The Essential Civil Society Reader* (Oxford: Rowman & Littlefield, 2000), pp. 305–16.

Goldman, Berthold, 'The Applicable Law: General Principles of Law – the Lex Mercatoria', in J. D. M. Lew (ed.), *Contemporary Problems in International Arbitration* (London: The Eastern Press, 1986), pp. 113–25.

—, 'Frontières du droit et 'lex mercatoria', *Archives de Philosophie du Droit*, 9 (1964), 177–92.

—, 'La lex mercatoria dans les contrats et l'arbitrage international: réalite et perspectives', *Journal du Droit International (Clunet)*, 106 (1979), 475–505.

—, 'Nouvelles réflexions sur la Lex Mercatoria', in Christian Dominicé, Robert Patry and Claude Reymond (eds), *Festschrift Pierre Lalive: Études de droit international en l'honneur de Pierre Lalive* (Basle: Helbing & Lichtenhahn, 1993), pp. 241–55.

Gómez-Jara Díez, Carlos, *La culpabilidad penal de la empresa* (Madrid: Marcial Pons, 2005).
Goodman, Nelson, *Ways of Worldmaking* (Indianapolis: Hackett, 1978).
Gordon, Robert, 'Unfreezing legal reality: critical approaches to law', *Florida State University Law Review*, 15 (1987), 195–220.
Graber, Christoph, *Zwischen Geist und Geld: Interferenzen von Kunst und Wirtschaft aus rechtlicher Sicht* (Baden-Baden: Nomos, 1994).
—, and Gunther Teubner, 'Art and money: constitutional rights in the private sphere', *Oxford Journal of Legal Studies*, 18:1 (1998), 61–73.
Graziani, Augusto, *The Monetary Theory of Production* (Cambridge: Cambridge University Press, 2003).
Griffiths, John, 'What is legal pluralism?', *Journal of Legal Pluralism and Unofficial Law*, 24 (1986), 1–55.
Grigera Naon, Horacio A., *Choice-of-Law Problems in International Commercial Arbitration* (Tübingen: J. C. B. Mohr, 1992).
Grimm, Dieter, 'The Achievement of Constitutionalism and its Prospects in a Changed World', in Petra Dobner and Martin Loughlin (eds), *The Twilight of Constitutionalism?* (Oxford: Oxford University Press, 2010), pp. 3–22.
—, 'Gesellschaftlicher Konstitutionalismus: Eine Kompensation für den Bedeutungsschwund der Staatsverfassung?', in Matthias Herdegen *et al.* (eds), *Staatsrecht und Politik: Festschrift für Roman Herzog zum 75. Geburtstag* (Munich: C. H. Beck, 2009), pp. 67–81.
—, *Soziale, wirtschaftliche und politische Voraussetzungen der Vertragsfreiheit: Eine vergleichende Skizze* (Frankfurt: Suhrkamp, 1987).
Guillaume, Gilbert, 'The future of international judicial institutions', *International and Comparative Law Quarterly*, 44:4 (1995), 848–62.
Gumbrecht, Hans Ulrich, and Ludwig K. Pfeiffer (eds), *Paradoxien, Dissonanzen, Zusammenbrüche: Situationen offener Epistemologie* (Frankfurt: Suhrkamp, 1991).
Gunningham, Neil, and Joseph Rees, 'Industry self-regulation: an institutional perspective', *Law and Policy*, 19 (1997), 363–414.
Günther, Gotthard, 'Cybernetic Ontology and Transjunctional Operations', in Gotthard Günther, *Beiträge zur Grundlegung einer operationsfähigen Dialektik*, vol. 1 (Hamburg: Meiner, 1976), pp. 249–83.
—, 'Life as Poly-Contexturality', in Gotthard Günther, *Beiträge zur Grundlegung einer operationsfähigen Dialektik*, vol. 1 (Hamburg: Meiner, 1976), pp. 283–306.
Günther, Klaus, and Shalini Randeria, *Recht, Kultur und Gesellschaft im Prozeß der Globalisierung* (Bad Homburg: Reimers, 2001).
Guzman, Andrew T., 'Arbitrator liability: reconciling arbitration and mandatory rules', *Duke Law Journal*, 49 (2000), 1279–334.
Haar, Charles Monroe, and Daniel William Fessler, *The Wrong Side of the Tracks: A Revolutionary Rediscovery of the Common Law Tradition of Fairness in the Struggle against Inequality* (New York: Simon and Schuster, 1986).
Habermas, Jürgen, *Between Facts and Norms: Contributions to a Discourse Theory of Law and Democracy*, trans. William Rehg (Cambridge, Mass.: MIT Press, 1996).
—, *Legitimation Crisis*, trans. Thomas McCarthy (Boston: Beacon Press, 1975).
—, 'The new obscurity: the crisis of the welfare state and the exhaustion of utopian energies', *Philosophy and Social Criticism*, 11 (1986), 1–18.
—, *The Philosophical Discourse of Modernity* (Cambridge, Mass.: MIT Press, 1987).
—, *The Structural Transformation of the Public Sphere: An Inquiry into a Category of Bourgeois Society*, trans. Thomas Burger with the assistance of Frederick Lawrence (Cambridge: Polity Press, 1st paperback edn, 1992 [1962]).

—, 'Vorbereitende Bemerkungen zu einer Theorie der kommunikativen Kompetenz', in Jürgen Habermas and Niklas Luhmann (eds), *Theorie der Gesellschaft oder Sozialtechnologie: Was leistet die Systemforschung?* (Frankfurt: Suhrkamp, 1971), pp. 101–41.

—, 'Wahrheitstheorien', in Helmut Fahrenbach (ed.), *Wirklichkeit und Reflexion: Walter Schulz zum 60. Geburtstag* (Pfullingen: Neske, 1973), pp. 211–65.

Hadfield, Gillian K., 'Bias in the evolution of legal rules', *Georgetown Law Journal*, 80 (1992), 583–616.

Hahn, Marcus, 'Vom Kopfstand des Phonozentrismus auf den Brettern der Systemtheorie, oder, Luhmann und/oder Derrida – einfach eine Entscheidung? Anmerkungen zu 'Die Form der Schrift' von Niklas Luhmann', *Soziale Systeme*, 2 (1996), 283–306.

Hall, Peter A., and David Soskice (eds), *Varieties of Capitalism: The Institutional Foundations of Comparative Advantage* (Oxford: Oxford University Press, 2005).

Hanschel, Dirk, *Environment and Human Rights: Cooperative Means of Regime Implementation*, MZES Arbeitspapiere, 29 (Mannheim: Mannheimer Zentrum für Europäische Sozialforschung, 2000).

Hardt, Michael, and Antonio Negri, *Commonwealth* (Cambridge, Mass.: Harvard University Press, 2009).

—, *Multitude: War and Democracy in the Age of Empire* (New York: Penguin, 2004).

Harrison, James, 'Regime pluralism and the global regulation of oil pollution liability and compensation', *International Journal of Law in Context*, 5 (2009), 379–91.

Hart, Herbert L. A., *The Concept of Law* (Oxford: Clarendon Press, 1961).

—, 'Self-Referring Laws', in H. L. A. Hart, *Essays in Jurisprudence and Philosophy* (Oxford: Clarendon Press, 1983), pp. 170–8.

Hasenclever, Andreas, Peter Mayer and Volker Rittberger, 'Integrating theories of international regimes', *Review of International Studies*, 26 (2000), 3–33.

—, *Theories of International Regimes* (Cambridge: Cambridge University Press, 1997).

Hauriou, Maurice E., *Aux sources du droit: Le pouvoir, l'ordre et la liberté* (Paris: Bloud & Gay, 1933).

Hayek, Friedrich A., *Denationalization of Money: An Analysis of the Theory and Practice of Concurrent Currencies* (London: Institute of Economic Affairs, 1978).

Held, David, *Democracy and the Global Order: From the Modern State to Cosmopolitan Governance* (Cambridge: Polity Press, 1995).

Helfer, Laurence, 'Constitutional analogies in the international legal system', *Loyola of Los Angeles Law Review*, 37 (2003–2004), 193–238.

Helfer, Laurence, 'Regime shifting: the TRIPS Agreement and new dynamics of international intellectual property lawmaking', *Yale Journal of International Law*, 29 (2004), 1–83.

Heller, Thomas C., 'Legal Discourse in the Positive State: A Post-Structuralist Account', in G. Teubner (ed.), *Dilemmas of Law in the Welfare State* (Berlin: de Gruyter, 1985), pp. 173–99.

Henry, Stuart, 'The Construction and Deconstruction of Social Control: Thoughts on the Discursive Production of State Law and Private Justice', in J. Lowmann, R. Menzies and T. Palys (eds), *Transcarceration: Essays in the Sociology of Social Control* (Aldershot: Gower, 1987), pp. 89–108.

—, *Private Justice* (Boston: Routledge and Kegan Paul, 1983).

Hensel, Isabell, 'Grundrechtskollisionen in der Stiftungsuniversität: Überwältigte Einheit oder organisierte Vielfalt', in Gralf-Peter Callies *et al.* (eds), *Soziologische Jurisprudenz: Festschrift für Gunther Teubner zum 65. Geburtstag* (Berlin: de Gruyter, 2009), pp. 509–30.

Herdegen, Matthias, 'The "constitutionalization" of the UN security system', *Vanderbilt Journal of Transnational Law*, 27:1 (1994), 135–60.
Hesse, Konrad, *Grundzüge des Verfassungsrechts der Bundesrepublik Deutschland* (Heidelberg: C. F. Müller, 4th edn, 1999).
Hestermeyer, Holger, 'Access to medication as a human right', *Max Planck Yearbook of United Nations Law*, 8 (2004), 101–80.
Higgins, Rosalynn, *Problems & Process: International Law and How We Use It* (Oxford: Clarendon Press, 1994).
Highet, Keith, 'The enigma of the lex mercatoria', *Tulane Law Review*, 63:3 (1988–89), 613–28.
Himma, Kenneth Einar, 'Natural Law', *Internet Encyclopaedia of Philosophy*, available at www.iep.utm.edu/natlaw/.
Hirsch, Alfred (ed.), *Übersetzung und Dekonstruktion* (Frankfurt: Suhrkamp, 1997).
Hirschl, Ran, *Towards Juristocracy: The Origins and Consequences of the New Constitutionalism* (Cambridge, Mass.: Harvard University Press, 2004).
Hoering, Uwe, 'Bhopal und kein Ende oder: Der Secondhand-Kapitalismus und die Ökologie', *Peripherie: Zeitschrift for Politik und Ökonomie in der Dritten Welt*, 21 (1985), 53–9.
Hoffmann, Bernd von, 'Grundsätzliches zur Anwendung der "lex mercatoria" durch internationale Schiedsgerichte', in K. Schurig and H.-J. Musielak (eds), *Festschrift für Gerhard Kegel* (Stuttgart: Kohlhammer, 1987), pp. 215–33.
Hoffmann-Riem, Wolfgang (ed.), *Regulierte Selbstregulierung als Steuerungskonzept des Gewährleistungsstaates* (Berlin: Duncker & Humblot, 2001).
Hofstadter, Douglas R., *Gödel, Escher, Bach: An Eternal Golden Braid* (New York: Basic Books, 1979).
—, 'Nomic: A Self-Modifying Game Based on Reflexivity in Law', in Douglas R. Hofstadter ed, *Metamagical Themas: Questing for the Essence of Mind and Pattern* (New York: Bantam, 1985), pp. 70–86.
Hogan, James, 'Publish and Be Damned! Independent Producers and Democratic Accountability', LSE Department of Sociology Working Paper 14/97 (London, 1997).
Holmes, Pablo, 'The politics of law and the law of politics: the political paradoxes of transnational constitutionalism', *Indiana Journal of Global Legal Studies*, 21 (2014), 553–83.
Holmes, Stephen, 'Poesie der Indifferenz', in D. Baecker *et al.* (eds), *Theorie als Passion* (Frankfurt: Suhrkamp, 1987), pp. 15–45.
Holtbrügge, Dirk, and Nicola Berg, 'Menschenrechte und Verhaltenskodizes in multinationalen Unternehmungen', in Petra Bendel and Thomas Fischer (eds), *Menschen- und Bürgerrechte: Ideengeschichte und Internationale Beziehungen* (Erlangen: Zentralinstitut für Regionalforschung an der Universität Erlangen-Nürnberg, 2004), pp. 181–211.
Honneth, Axel, *Das Andere der Gerechtigkeit: Aufsätze zur praktischen Philosophie* (Frankfurt: Suhrkamp, 2000).
Horton, Richard, 'Medical editors trial amnesty', *The Lancet*, 350:9080 (1997), 756.
Horwitz, Morton J., 'The history of the public/private distinction', *University of Pennsylvania Law Review*, 130 (1982), 1423–8.
Huber, Joseph, 'Geldordnung II: Reform der Geldschöpfung. Vollgeld-Konzept und Seigniorage Reform', 2009, available at www.soziologie.uni-halle.de/huber/docs/geldordnung-ii-reform-der-geldschoepfung-durch-vollgeld-mai-09.pdf.
Huber, Joseph, and James Robertson, *Creating New Money: A Monetary Reform for the Information Age* (London: New Economics Foundation, 2000).

Husserl, Edmund, *Cartesian Meditations: An Introduction to Phenomenology* (The Hague: Nijhoff, 1960).
Hutter, Michael, and Gunther Teubner, 'Homo Oeconomicus and Homo Juridicus: Communicative Fictions?', in Theodor Baums, Klaus Hopt and Norbert Horn (eds), *Corporations, Capital Markets and Business in the Law: Liber Amicorum Richard M. Buxbaum* (The Hague: Kluwer, 2000), pp. 569–84.
—, 'The parasitic role of hybrids', *Journal of Institutional and Theoretical Economics*, 149 (1993), 706–15.
Institut für Qualität und Wirtschaftlichkeit im Gesundheitswesen, 'Bupropion, Mirtazapin und Reboxetin zur Behandlung der Depression – A05–20C-Abschlussbericht', IQWiG-Berichte, 68 (2011).
International Institute for the Unification of Private Law, *Principles of International Commercial Contracts* (Rome: Unidroit, 1994).
Jackson, Bernard J., *Law, Fact and Normative Coherence* (Liverpool: Deborah Charles, 1988).
Jäger, Herbert, *Makrokriminalität: Studien zur Kriminologie kollektiver Gewalt* (Frankfurt: Suhrkamp, 1989).
Jefferson, Thomas, 'Thomas Jefferson to John Wayles Eppes, June 24, 1813', in Paul L. Ford (ed.), *The Works of Thomas Jefferson: Federal Edition*, vol. 11 (New York: G. P. Putnam's Sons, 1904–05 [1813]), pp. 297–306, available at http://oll.libertyfund.org/titles/807.
Jefferson, Tom, Mark Jones, P. Doshi et al., 'Neuraminidase inhibitors for preventing and treating influenza in healthy adults and children', *Cochrane Database of Systematic Reviews* (2012), issue 1, art. No. CD008625, 10.1002/14651858.CD008965.pub3.
Jessop, Bob, 'The Economy, the State and the Law: Theories of Relative Autonomy and Autopoietic Closure', in A. Febbrajo and G. Teubner (eds), *State, Law, and Economy as Autopoietic Systems: Regulation and Autonomy in a New Perspective* (Milan: Giuffrè, 1992), pp. 187–263.
Jessup, Philip C., *Modernes Völkerrecht* (Vienna: Humboldt Verlag, 1950).
Joerges, Christian, 'The impact of European integration on private law: reductionist perceptions, true conflicts and a new constitutional perspective', *European Law Journal*, 3 (1997), 378–406.
—, 'Das Rechtssystem der transnationalen Handelsschiedsgerichtsbarkeit', *Zeitschrift für das gesamte Handels- und Wirtschaftsrecht*, 138 (1974), 549–68.
—, *Verbraucherschutz als Rechtsproblem: Eine Untersuchung zum Stand der Theorie und zu den Entwicklungsperspektiven des Verbraucherrechts* (Heidelberg: Recht und Wirtschaft, 1981).
—, 'Zur Legitimität der Europäisierung des Privatrechts: Überlegungen zu einem Recht-Fertigungs-Recht für das Mehrebenensystem der EU', in Christian Joerges and Gunther Teubner (eds), *Rechtsverfassungsrecht* (Baden-Baden: Nomos, 2003), pp. 183–213.
—, and Florian Rödl, 'Zum Funktionswandel des Kollisionsrechts II: Die kollisionsrechtliche Form einer legitimen Verfassung der postnationalen Konstellation', in Gralf-Peter Calliess et al. (eds), *Soziologische Jurisprudenz: Festschrift für Gunther Teubner zum 65. Geburtstag* (Berlin: de Gruyter, 2009), pp. 765–78.
Joseph, Sarah, *Corporations and Transnational Human Rights Litigation* (Oxford: Hart, 2004).
Jull, Andrew, Iain Chalmers and Anthony Rodgers, 'Clinical trials in NZ: does anybody know what's going on?', *New Zealand Medical Journal*, 115:1167 (2002), U269.
Kafka, Franz, *The Complete Stories* (New York: Random, 1972).

—, *The Penguin Complete Short Stories of Franz Kafka*, ed. Nahum N. Glatzer (London: Allen Lane, 1983).
—, *The Trial*, trans. Breon Mitchell (New York: Schocken, 1998).
Kahn, Paul W., 'On Pinochet', *Boston Review*, 24:1 (1999), available att www.bostonreview.net.
Kahn, Philippe, 'Droit international économique, droit du développement, lex mercatoria: concept unique ou pluralisme des ordres juridiques?', in Berthold Goldman (ed.), *Le droit des relations économiques internationales* (Paris: Librairies Techniques, 1982), pp. 97–107.
—, 'La lex mercatoria: point de vue français après quarante ans de controverses', *McGill Law Journal*, 37 (1992), 413–27.
Kälin, Walter, 'Menschenrechtsverträge als Gewährleistung einer objektiven Ordnung', *Berichte der deutschen Gesellschaft für Völkerrecht, 33: Aktuelle Probleme des Menschenrechtsschutzes* (1994), 9–48.
Kämper, Eckard, and Johannes F. K. Schmidt, 'Netzwerke als strukturelle Kopplung: Systemtheoretische Überlegungen zum Netzwerkbegriff', in Johannes Weyer (ed.), *Soziale Netzwerke: Konzepte und Methoden der sozialwissenschaftlichen Netzwerkforschung* (Munich: Oldenbourg, 1999), pp. 211–35.
Kant, Immanuel, *Critique of Judgment: Including the First Introduction*, trans. Werner S. Pluhar (Indianapolis and Cambridge: Hackett, 1987).
—, *Perpetual Peace*, trans. Helen O'Brien (London: Sweet & Maxwell, 1927).
Karavas, Vagios, *Digitale Grundrechte: Zur Drittwirkung der Grundrechte im Internet* (Baden-Baden: Nomos, 2006).
—, and Gunther Teubner, 'www.companynamesucks.com: the horizontal effect of fundamental rights on "private parties" within autonomous Internet law', *Constellations*, 12 (2005), 262–82.
Karnell, Gunnar, 'Will the consumer law field be the Waterloo of the new lex mercatoria?', *Svensk Juristtidning* (1981), 427–37.
Kassis, Antoine, *Théorie générale des usages du commerce* (Paris: Librairie générale de droit et de jurisprudence, 1984).
Kegel, Gerhard, and Klaus Schurig, *Internationales Privatrecht* (Munich: Beck, 8th edn, 2000).
Kelsen, Hans, 'Das Problem der Gerechtigkeit', in Hans Kelsen, *Reine Rechtslehre* (Vienna: Deuticke, 2nd edn, 1960).
—, *Pure Theory of Law* (Berkeley: University of California Press, 1978 [1934]).
Kennedy, Duncan, 'Comment on Rudolf Wiethölter's "Materialization and Proceduralization in Modern Law" and "Proceduralization of the Category of Law"', in Christian Joerges and David M. Trubek (eds), *Critical Legal Thought: An American–German Debate* (Baden-Baden: Nomos, 1989).
Kerchove, Michel van de, and François Ost, *Le droit ou les paradoxes du jeu* (Paris: Presses Universitaires de France, 1992).
—, *Le système juridique entre ordre et désordre* (Paris: Presses Universitaires de France, 1988).
Kesselheim, Aaron, 'Covert pharmaceutical promotion in free medical journals', *Canadian Medical Association Journal*, 183:5 (2011), 534–5.
Kiesow, Rainer Maria, *Das Alphabet des Rechts* (Frankfurt: Fischer, 2004).
Kingsbury, Benedict, Nico Krisch and Richard B. Stewart, 'The emergence of global administrative law', *Law and Contemporary Problems*, 68:3 (2005), 15–61.
Kissinger, Henry, 'The pitfalls of universal jurisdiction', *Foreign Affairs*, 80:4 (2001), 86–96.

Kjaer, Poul F., *Constitutionalism in the Global Realm: A Sociological Approach* (London: Routledge, 2014).
—, 'The metamorphosis of the functional synthesis: a continental European perspective on governance, law and the political in the transnational space', *Wisconsin Law Review*, 2010:2 (2010), 489–534.
Klabbers, Jan, 'Setting the Scene', in Jan Klabbers, Anne Peters and Geir Ulfstein (eds), *The Constitutionalization of International Law* (Oxford: Oxford University Press, 2009), pp. 1–44.
Klecatsky, Hans, René Marcic and Herbert Schambeck (eds), *Die Wiener rechtstheoretische Schule: Ausgewählte Schriften von Hans Kelsen, Adolf Julius Merkl und Alfred Verdross*, 2 vols (Vienna: Europa-Verlag, 1968).
Kleist, Heinrich von, *Michael Kohlhaas: A Tale from an Old Chronicle* (New York: Melville, 2005).
Koh, Harald Hongju, 'Transnational legal process', *Nebraska Law Review*, 75 (1996), 181–207.
Koschorke, Albrecht, 'Die Grenzen des Systems und die Rhetorik der Systemtheorie', in Albrecht Koschorke and Cornelia Vismann (eds), *Widerstände der Systemtheorie: Kulturtheoretische Analysen zum Werk von Niklas Luhmann* (Berlin: Akademie Verlag, 1999), pp. 49–60.
—, and Cornelia Vismann (eds), *Widerstände der Systemtheorie: Kulturtheoretische Analysen zum Werk von Niklas Luhmann* (Berlin: Akademie Verlag, 1999).
Koselleck, Reinhart, *Begriffsgeschichten: Studien zur Semantik und Pragmatik der politischen und sozialen Sprache* (Frankfurt: Suhrkamp, 2006).
—, 'Begriffsgeschichtliche Probleme der Verfassungsgeschichtsschreibung', in Reinhart Koselleck, *Begriffsgeschichten: Studien zur Semantik und Pragmatik der politischen und sozialen Sprache* (Frankfurt: Suhrkamp, 2006), pp. 365–401.
Koskenniemi, Martti, *The Gentle Civilizer of Nations: The Rise and Fall of International Law 1870–1960* (Cambridge: Cambridge University Press, 2002).
—, 'Global Legal Pluralism: Multiple Regimes and Multiple Modes of Thought' (5 March 2005), available at www.helsinki.fi/eci/Publications/Koskenniemi/MKPluralism-Harvard-05d%5B1%5D.pdf.
—, 'Hegemonic Regimes', in Margaret Young (ed.), *Regime Interaction in International Law: Facing Fragmentation* (Cambridge: Cambridge University Press, 2012), pp. 305–24.
—, 'The police in the temple: order, justice and the UN: a dialectical view', *European Journal of International Law*, 6 (1995), 325–48.
—, and Päivi Leino, 'Fragmentation of international law? Postmodern anxieties', *Leiden Journal of International Law*, 15 (2002), 553–79.
Krajewska, Atina, 'Bioethics and human rights in the constitutional formation of global health', *Laws* (2015), 771–802.
—, 'In Search of the Holy Grail of Transparent and Coherent Global Health Law', paper presented to Third Global Conference on Transparency Research, JMC HEC, Paris, 2013.
Krasner, Stephen D., 'Structural causes and regime consequences: regimes as intervening variables', *International Organization*, 36:2 (1982), 185–205.
— (ed.), *International Regimes* (Ithaca and London: Cornell University Press, 1983).
Kratochwil, Friedrich, and John Gerard Ruggie, 'International organization: a state of the art on an art of the state', *International Organization*, 40 (1986), 753–75.
Krebs, Michael, and Reinhard Rock, 'Unternehmungsnetzwerke – eine intermediäre oder eigenständige Organisationsform?', in Jörg Sydow and Arnold Windeler

(eds), *Management interorganisationaler Beziehungen: Vertrauen, Kontrolle und Informationstechnik* (Opladen: Westdeutscher Verlag, 1994), pp. 322–45.

Krimsky, Sheldon, *Science in the Public Interest: Has the Lure of Profits Corrupted Biomedical Research?* (New York: Rowman & Littlefield Publishers, 2003).

Krippendorff, Klaus, 'Paradox and Information', in Brenda Dervin and Melvin Voigt (eds), *Progress in Communication Sciences*, vol. 5 (Norwood: Ablex, 1984), pp. 45–71.

Kumm, Mattias, 'The Best of Times and the Worst of Times: Between Constitutional Triumphalism and Nostalgia', in Petra Dobner and Martin Loughlin (eds), *The Twilight of Constitutionalism?* (Oxford: Oxford University Press, 2010), pp. 201–19.

—, 'Beyond golf clubs and the judicialization of politics: why Europe has a constitution properly so called', *American Journal of Comparative Law*, 54 (2006), 505–30.

Kuo, Ming-Sung, 'Between fragmentation and unity: the uneasy relationship between global administrative law and global constitutionalism', *San Diego International Law Journal*, 10 (2009), 439–67.

Ladeur, Karl-Heinz, *'Abwägung' – ein neues Paradigma des Verwaltungsrechts: Von der Einheit der Rechtsordnung zum Rechtspluralismus* (Frankfurt: Campus, 1984).

—, 'Die Autonomie der Bundesbank: Ein Beispiel für die institutionelle Verarbeitung von Ungewißheitsentscheidungen', *Staatswissenschaften und Staatspraxis*, 3 (1992), 486–508.

—, 'Helmut Ridders Konzeption der Meinungs- und Pressefreiheit in der Demokratie', *Kritische Justiz*, 32 (1999), 281–300.

—, *Kritik der Abwägung in der Grundrechtsdogmatik* (Tübingen: Mohr Siebeck, 2004).

—, *Das Medienrecht und die Ökonomie der Aufmerksamkeit: In Sachen Dieter Bohlen, Maxim Biller, Caroline von Monaco u.a.* (Cologne: Halem, 2007).

—, 'Methodische Überlegungen zur gesetzlichen "Ausgestaltung" der Koalitionsfreiheit', *Archiv des öffentlichen Rechts*, 131:4 (2006), 643–67.

—, *Postmoderne Rechtstheorie: Selbstreferenz – Selbstorganisation – Prozeduralisierung* (Berlin: Duncker & Humblot, 1992).

—, 'Das subjektive Recht als Medium der Selbsttransformation der Gesellschaft und Gerechtigkeit als deren Parasit', *Zeitschrift für Rechtssoziologie*, 29 (2008), 109–24.

—, 'Towards a legal theory of supranationality: the viability of the network concept', *European Law Journal*, 3 (1997), 33–54.

—, and Lars Viellechner, 'Die transnationale Expansion staatlicher Grundrechte: Zur Konstitutionalisierung globaler Privatrechtsregimes', *Archiv des Völkerrechts*, 46 (2008), 42–73.

Langen, Eugen, *Transnational Commercial Law* (Leiden: A. W. Sijthoff, 1973).

Latour, Bruno, *Politics of Nature: How to Bring the Sciences into Democracy*, trans. Catherine Porter (Cambridge, Mass., and London: Harvard University Press, 2004).

—, *We Have Never Been Modern*, trans. Catherine Porter (Hemel Hempstead: Harvester Wheatsheaf, 1993).

Lauterpacht, Hersch, 'Restrictive interpretation and the principle of effectiveness in the interpretation of treaties', *British Yearbook of International Law*, 26 (1949), 48–85.

Law and Treatment Access Unit of the AIDS Law Project & Treatment Action Campaign, *The Price of Life. Hazel Tau and Others vs GlaxoSmithKline and Boehringer Ingelheim: A Report on the Excessive Pricing Complaint to South Africa's Competition Commission* (2003), available at /www.alp.org.za/view.php?file=/resctr / pubs/20030813_PriceCover.xml.

Legendre, Pierre, *Le crime du caporal Lortie*, Leçons, 8 (Paris: Fayard, 1994).

Lehmkuhl, Dirk, 'The resolution of domain names vs. trademark conflicts: a case study on regulation beyond the nation state, and related problems', *Zeitschrift für Rechtssoziologie*, 23 (2002), 61–78.

Lenoble, Jacques, and André Berten, *Dire la norme: Droit, politique et énonciation* (Brussels: Story-Scientia, 1990).

Lenski, Sophie-Charlotte, *Personenbezogene Massenkommunikation als verfassungsrechtliches Problem: Das allgemeine Persönlichkeitsrecht in Konflikt mit Medien, Kunst und Wissenschaft* (Berlin: Duncker & Humblot, 2007).

Lessard, Hester, 'The idea of the "private": a discussion of state action doctrine and separate sphere ideology', *Dalhousie Law Review*, 10 (1986), 107–38.

Lessig, Lawrence, *Code and Other Laws of Cyberspace* (New York: Basic Books, 1999).

Levinas, Emmanuel, *Otherwise than Being, or, Beyond Essence*, trans. Alphonso Lingis (Pittsburgh: Duquesne University Press, 1998).

—, *Totality and Infinity: An Essay on Exteriority*, trans. Alphonso Lingis (The Hague: Nijhoff, 1979).

Lewis, Theresa Beeby, 'Patent protection for the pharmaceutical industry: a survey of patent laws of various countries', *International Lawyer*, 30:4 (1996), 835–65.

Lexchin, Joel, Lisa Bero, Benjamin Djulbegovic et al., 'Pharmaceutical industry sponsorship and research outcome and quality: systematic review', *British Medical Journal*, 326:7400 (2003), 1167–70.

Lindahl, Hans, 'Constituent Power and Reflexive Identity: Towards an Ontology of Collective Selfhood', in Martin Loughlin and Neil Walker (eds), *The Paradox of Constitutionalism: Constituent Power and Constitutional Form* (Oxford: Oxford University Press, 2007), pp. 9–24.

—, 'Societal constitutionalism as political constitutionalism: reconsidering the relation between politics and global legal orders', *Social and Legal Studies*, 20:2 (2011), 230–47.

Littlechild, Stephen C., *Economic Regulation of Privatised Water Authorities* (London: Department of Environment, 1986).

—, *Regulation of British Telecommunications' Profitability* (London: Department of Trade and Industry, 1984).

Locke, Richard, Fei Quin and Alberto Brause, 'Does Monitoring Improve Labour Standards? Lessons from Nike', Corporate Social Responsibility Initiative Working Paper No. 24 (Cambridge, Mass.: John F. Kennedy School of Government, Harvard University, 2006), pp. 1–47, available at www.hks.harvard.edu/m-rcbg/CSRI/publications/workingpaper_24_locke.pdf.

Loquin, Eric, 'L'application des règles anationales dans l'arbitrage commercial international', in Chambre de Commerce International (ed.), *L'apport de la jurisprudence arbitrale* (Paris: CCI 440/1, 1986), pp. 67–122.

Loughlin, Martin, 'What Is Constitutionalisation?', in Petra Dobner and Martin Loughlin (eds), *The Twilight of Constitutionalism?* (Oxford: Oxford University Press, 2010), pp. 47–72.

Luhmann, Niklas, *Art as a Social System*, trans. Eva M. Knodt (Stanford: Stanford University Press, 2000).

—, *Ausdifferenzierung des Rechts: Beiträge zur Rechtssoziologie und Rechtstheorie* (Frankfurt: Suhrkamp, 1981).

—, 'Closure and Openness: On Reality in the World of Law', in G. Teubner (ed.), *Autopoietic Law: A New Approach to Law and Society* (Berlin: de Gruyter, 1987), pp. 335–48.

—, 'The Coding of the Legal System', in A. Febbrajo and G. Teubner (eds), *State, Law, and Economy as Autopoietic Systems: Regulation and Autonomy in a New Perspective* (Milan: Giuffrè, 1992), pp. 145–85.

—, 'Deconstruction as second-order-observing', *New Literary History*, 24 (1993), 763–82.

—, 'The Differentiation of Society', trans. Stephen Holmes and Charles Larmore, in Niklas Luhmann, *The Differentiation of Society* (New York: Columbia University Press, 1982), pp. 229–54.
—, 'Die Form "Person"', *Soziale Welt*, 42 (1991), 166–75.
—, 'Gerechtigkeit in den Rechtssystemen der modernen Gesellschaft', in Niklas Luhmann, *Ausdifferenzierung des Rechts: Beiträge zur Rechtssoziologie und Rechtstheorie* (Frankfurt: Suhrkamp, 1981), pp. 374–418.
—, *Grundrechte als Institution: Ein Beitrag zur politischen Soziologie* (Berlin: Duncker & Humblot, 1965).
—, 'The Individuality of the Individual: Historical Meanings and Contemporary Problems', in Niklas Luhmann, *Essays on Self-Reference* (New York: Columbia University Press, 1990), pp. 107–22.
—, 'Individuum und Gesellschaft', *Universitas*, 39 (1983), 1–11.
—, 'Interaction, Organization, and Society', trans. Stephen Holmes and Charles Larmore, in Niklas Luhmann, *The Differentiation of Society* (New York: Columbia University Press, 1982), pp. 69–89.
—, *Introduction to Systems Theory* (Cambridge: Polity Press, 2013).
—, *Law as a Social System*, trans. Klaus A. Ziegert (Oxford: Oxford University Press, 2004).
—, 'Legal argumentation: an analysis of its form', *Modern Law Review*, 58 (1995), 285–98.
—, 'Limits of steering', *Theory, Culture & Society*, 14 (1997), 41–57.
—, 'Observing re-entries', *Graduate Faculty Philosophy Journal*, 16 (1993), 485–98.
—, *Organization and Decision* (Cambridge: Cambridge University Press, 2018).
—, 'Das Paradox der Menschenrechte und drei Formen seiner Entfaltung', in Niklas Luhmann, *Soziologische Aufklärung 6: Die Soziologie und der Mensch* (Opladen: Westdeutscher Verlag, 1995), pp. 218–25.
—, 'The Paradox of System Differentiation', in Jeffrey C. Alexander and Paul Colomy (eds), *Differentiation Theory and Social Change* (New York: Columbia University Press, 1990), pp. 409–40.
—, 'Die Paradoxie des Entscheidens', *Verwaltungsarchiv*, 84 (1993), 287–310.
—, 'The paradoxy of observing systems', *Cultural Critique*, 31 (1995), 37–55.
—, *Political Theory in the Welfare State* (Berlin: de Gruyter, 1990).
—, *Die Politik der Gesellschaft* (Frankfurt: Suhrkamp, 2000).
—, 'Politische Verfassungen im Kontext des Gesellschaftssystems', *Der Staat*, 12 (1973), 1–22, 165–82.
—, *Rechtssystem und Rechtsdogmatik* (Stuttgart: Kohlhammer, 1974).
—, 'Religion and ultimate paradox: a symposium on aspects of the sociology of Niklas Luhmann', *Sociological Analysis*, 46 (1985), 1–36.
—, *Religious Dogmatics and the Evolution of Societies*, trans. and with an introduction by Peter Beyer, Studies in Religion and Society, 9 (New York: Edwin Mellen, 1984).
—, 'Die Sinnform Religion', *Soziale Systeme*, 2 (1996), 3–33.
—, *Social Systems*, trans. John Bednarz, Jr. with Dirk Baecker (Stanford: Stanford University Press, 1995).
—, 'Society, Meaning, Religion – Based on Self Reference', in P. Colomy (ed.), *Neofunctionalist Sociological Theory* (Aldershot, Hampshire: Brookfield, 1990), pp. 208–33.
—, *A Sociological Theory of Law*, trans. Elisabeth King-Utz and Martin Albrow, ed. Martin Albrow (London: Routledge, 1985).
—, *Soziologische Aufklärung 2: Aufsätze zur Theorie der Gesellschaft* (Opladen: Westdeutscher Verlag, 1975).

—, 'Der Staat als historischer Begriff', in Marcel Storme (ed.), *Mijmeringen van een Jurist* (Antwerp: Kluwer, 1984), pp. 139–54.

—, 'Der Staat des politischen Systems: Geschichte und Stellung in der Weltgesellschaft', in Ulrich Beck (ed.), *Perspektiven der Weltgesellschaft* (Frankfurt: Suhrkamp, 1998), pp. 345–80.

—, 'Steuerung durch Recht? Einige klarstellende Bemerkungen', *Zeitschrift für Rechtssoziologie*, 11 (1990), 137–60.

—, 'Sthenography', *Stanford Literature Review*, 7 (1990), 133–9.

—, 'Subjektive Rechte: Zum Umbau des Rechtsbewußtseins für die moderne Gesellschaft', in Niklas Luhmann, *Gesellschaftsstruktur und Semantik: Studien zur Wissenssoziologie der modernen Gesellschaft*, vol. 2 (Frankfurt: Suhrkamp, 1981), pp. 45–104.

—, *A Systems Theory of Religion* (Stanford: Stanford University Press, 2013).

—, *Theory of Society*, vol. 1 (Stanford: Stanford University Press, 2012).

—, *Theory of Society*, vol. 2 (Stanford: Stanford University Press, 2013).

—, 'The third question: the creative use of paradoxes in law and legal history', *Journal of Law and Society*, 15 (1988), 153–65.

—, 'Verfassung als evolutionäre Errungenschaft', *Rechtshistorisches Journal*, 9 (1990), 176–220.

—, 'Why does society describe itself as postmodern?', *Cultural Critique*, 30 (1995), 171–86.

—, 'Wie lassen sich latente Strukturen beobachten?', in P. Watzlawick and P. Krieg (eds), *Das Auge des Betrachters – Beiträge zum Konstruktivismus: Festschrift für Heinz von Foerster* (1991), pp. 61–74.

—, *Die Wirtschaft der Gesellschaft* (Frankfurt: Suhrkamp, 1988).

—, *Die Wissenschaft der Gesellschaft* (Frankfurt: Suhrkamp, 1990).

—, 'The World Society as a Social System', in Niklas Luhmann, *Essays on Self-Reference* (New York: Columbia University Press, 1990), pp. 175–90.

—, 'The world society as a social system', *International Journal of General Systems*, 8 (1982), 131–8.

—, 'Zeit und Gedächtnis', *Soziale Systeme*, 2 (1996), 307–30.

—, 'Zwei Seiten des Rechtsstaates', in The Institute of Comparative Law in Japan (ed.), *Conflict and Integration: Comparative Law in the World Today* (Tokyo: Chuo University Press, 1989), pp. 493–506.

Lyotard, Jean-François, *The Differend: Phrases in Dispute*, trans. George Van Den Abbeele (Manchester: Manchester University Press, 1987).

—, *Lessons on the Analytic of the Sublime*, trans. Elisabeth Rottenberg (Stanford: Stanford University Press, 1994).

Macaulay, Stewart, 'Private Government', in L. Lipson and S. Wheeler (eds), *Law and the Social Sciences* (New York: Russell Sage, 1986), pp. 445–518.

MacCormick, Neil, and Ota Weinberger, *An Institutional Theory of Law* (Dordrecht: Kluwer, 1986).

Macneil, Ian R., 'Relational contract theory: challenges and queries', *Northwestern University Law Review*, 94:3 (2000), 877–908.

—, 'Relational contract: what we do know and do not know', *Wisconsin Law Review*, 1985 (1985), 483–525.

Mahlmann, Matthias, 'Varieties of transnational law and the universalistic stance', *German Law Journal*, 10 (2009), 1325–36.

Maniruzzaman, Abul, 'The lex mercatoria and international contracts: a challenge for international commercial arbitration?', *American University International Law Review*, 14:3 (1999), 657–734.

Mann, Frederick A., 'England rejects 'delocalised' contracts and arbitration', *The International and Comparative Law Quarterly*, 33:1 (1984), 193–8.
—, 'Internationale Schiedsgerichte und nationale Rechtsordnung', *Zeitschrift für das Gesamte Handelsrecht*, 130 (1968), 97–129.
Manne, Geoffrey, and Joshua Wright, 'Google and the limits of antitrust: the case against the case against Google', *Harvard Journal of Law and Public Policy*, 34:1 (2011), 171–244.
Marschik, Axel, *Subsysteme im Völkerrecht: Ist die Europäische Union ein 'Self-Contained Regime'?* (Berlin: Duncker & Humblot, 1997).
Martenczuk, Bernd, *Rechtsbindung und Rechtskontrolle des Weltsicherheitsrats: Die Überprüfung nichtmilitärischer Zwangsmaßnahmen durch den Internationalen Gerichtshof* (Berlin: Duncker & Humblot, 1996).
Martinez, Jenny S., 'Towards an international judicial system', *Stanford Law Review*, 56 (2003), 429–529.
Marx, Karl, *Capital: A Critique of Political Economy*, vol. 1 (London: Penguin Books, 1982).
Mathews, Jud, and Alec Stone Sweet, 'All things in proportion? American rights review and the problem of balancing', *Emory Law Journal*, 4 (2011), 102–79.
Mayer, Pierre, 'Mandatory rules of law in international arbitration', *Arbitration International*, 2:4 (1986), 274–93.
McConnaughay, Philip J., 'Rethinking the role of law and contracts in East-West commercial relationships', *Virginia Journal of International Law*, 41:2 (2001), 427–80.
Mead, George Herbert, *Mind, Self and Society from the Standpoint of a Social Behaviourist* (Chicago: University of Chicago Press, 1967).
Medicus, Dieter, 'Der Grundsatz der Verhältnismäßigkeit im Privatrecht', *Archiv für die civilistische Praxis*, 192 (1992), 35–70.
Medicus, Dieter, and Jens Petersen, *Bürgerliches Recht* (Munich: Vahlen, 26th edn, 2017).
Medwedjew, Shores A., *Der Fall Lyssenko: Eine Wissenschaft kapituliert* (Hamburg: Hoffmann & Campe, 1971).
Menke, Christoph, *Reflections of Equality* (Stanford: Stanford University Press, 2006).
Merry, Sally Engle, 'Legal pluralism', *Law & Society Review*, 22:5 (1988), 869–96.
Mertens, Joachim, 'Lex Mercatoria: A Self-Applying System Beyond National Law?', in Gunther Teubner (ed.), *Global Law without a State* (Aldershot: Dartmouth, 1997), pp. 31–44.
Mestmäcker, Ernst Joachim, *Wirtschaft und Verfassung in der Europäischen Union* (Baden-Baden: Nomos, 2006).
Meyer, John W., John Boli, George M. Thomas *et al.*, 'World society and the nation-state', *American Journal of Sociology*, 103 (1997), 144–81.
Meyer, Rudolf, *Bona fides und lex mercatoria in der europäischen Rechtstradition*, Quellen und Forschungen zum Recht und seiner Geschichte, 5 (Göttingen: Wallstein-Verlag, 1994).
Micklitz, Hans-W., and Norbert Reich (eds), *Public Interest Litigation before European Courts* (Baden-Baden: Nomos Verlagsgesellschaft, 1996).
Miegel, Meinhard, *Exit: Wohlstand ohne Wachstum* (Berlin: Propyläen, 2010).
Mitchell, Ronald B., 'Sources of transparency: information systems in international regimes', *International Studies Quarterly*, 42 (1998), 109–30.
Mitnick, Barry M., *The Political Economy of Regulation: Creating, Designing, and Removing Regulatory Forms* (New York and Guildford: Columbia University Press, 1980).
Muchlinski, Peter T., '"Global Bukowina' Examined: Viewing the Multinational Enterprise as a Transnational Law-Making Community', in Gunther Teubner (ed.), *Global Law without a State* (Aldershot: Dartmouth, 1997), pp. 79–108.

Mueller, Milton, *Ruling the Root: Internet Governance and the Taming of Cyberspace* (Cambridge: Mass.: MIT Press, 2002).
—, 'Universal service in telephone history: a reconstruction', *Telecommunications Policy*, 17:5 (1993), 352–69.
Müller, Thomas, *Verwaltungsverträge im Spannungsfeld von Recht, Politik und Wirtschaft* (Basle: Helbing & Lichtenhahn, 1997).
Mustill, Lord Justice, 'The New Lex Mercatoria', in Maarten Bos and Ian Brownlie (eds), *Liber Amicorum Lord Wilberforce* (Oxford: Clarendon Press, 1987), pp. 149–83.
Nadelman, Ethan, 'Global prohibition regimes: the evolution of norms in international society', *International Organisation*, 44 (1990), 479–526.
National Economic Development Office, *A Study of UK Nationalised Industries: Their Role in the Economy and Control in the Future: A Report to the Government from the National Economic Development Office* (London: HMSO, 1976).
Nelken, David, 'Law in action or living law? Back to the beginning in sociology of law', *Legal Studies*, 4 (1984), 157–74.
Neves, Marcelo, *Transconstitutionalism* (London: Hart, 2013).
Nimmer, Raymond, and Patricia Krauthaus, 'Globalization of law in intellectual property and related commercial contexts', *Law in Context: Socio-Legal Journal*, 10 (1992), 80–103.
Nobles, Richard, and David Schiff, 'Using systems theory to study legal pluralism: What could be gained?', *Law & Society Review*, 46 (2012), 265–95.
Nonet, Philippe, 'Time and law', *Theoretical Inquiries in Law* (2007), 311–32.
—, and Philip Selznick, *Law and Society in Transition* (New York: Harper Row, 1978).
Nowotny, Helga, 'The Changing Nature of Public Science', in Helga Nowotny (ed.), *The Public Nature of Science under Assault: Politics, Markets, Science and the Law* (Berlin and Heidelberg: Springer, 2005), pp. 1–28.
Nowrot, Karsten, 'Den "Kinderschuhen" entwachsen: Die (Wieder-)Entdeckung der rechtssoziologischen Perspektive in der Dogmatik der Völkerrechtssubjektivität', *Zeitschrift für Rechtssoziologie*, 28 (2007), 21–48.
—, 'Die transnationale Verantwortungsgemeinschaft im internationalen Wirtschaftsrecht', in Christian Tietje and Karsten Nowrot (eds), *Verfassungsrechtliche Dimensionen des internationalen Wirtschaftsrechts* (Stuttgart: Boorberg, 2007), pp. 55–101.
O'Brien, Robert, Anne Marie Goetz, Jan A. Scholte et al., *Contesting Global Governance: Multilateral Economic Institutions and Global Social Movements* (Cambridge: Cambridge University Press, 2002).
Oellers-Frahm, Karin, 'Multiplication of international courts and tribunals and conflicting jurisdiction: problems and possible solutions', *Max Planck Yearbook of United Nations Law*, 5 (2001), 67–104.
Ogorek, Regina, 'Adam Müllers Gegensatzphilosophie und die Rechtsausschweifungen des Michael Kohlhaas', in Hans-Joachim Kreutzer (ed.), *Kleistjahrbuch 1988/89* (Berlin: Erich Schmidt Verlag, 1988), pp. 96–131.
Ogus, Anthony L., 'Rethinking self-regulation', *Oxford Journal of Legal Studies*, 15:1 (1995), 97–108.
Oliver, Dawn, and Jorg Fedtke (eds), *Human Rights and the Private Sphere: A Comparative Study* (New York: Routledge, 2007).
Olsen, Frances, 'Constitutional law: feminist critiques of the public/private distinction', *Constitutional Commentary*, 10:2 (1993), 319–28.
Osman, Filali, *Les principes généraux de la lex mercatoria* (Paris: Librairie générale de droit et de jurisprudence, 1992).
Parsons, Talcott, *The System of Modern Societies* (Englewood Cliffs: Prentice Hall, 1971).

—, and Charles Ackerman, 'The Concept of "Social System" as a Theoretical Device', in Gordon J. DiRenzo (ed.), *Concepts, Theory and Explanation in the Behavioral Sciences* (New York: Random House, 1966), pp. 19–40.
Pauer-Studer, Herlinde, *Autonom leben: Reflexionen über Freiheit und Gleichheit* (Frankfurt: Suhrkamp, 2000).
Paulsson, Jan, 'La lex mercatoria dans l'arbitrage C.C.I.', *Revue de l'Arbitrage* (1990), No. 1, 55–100.
Paulus, Andreas L., *Die internationale Gemeinschaft im Völkerrecht: Eine Untersuchung zur Entwicklung des Völkerrechts im Zeitalter der Globalisierung* (Munich: Beck, 2001).
Pauwelyn, Joost, 'The role of public international law in the WTO: how far can we go?', *American Journal of International Law*, 95 (2001), 535–78.
Perez, Oren, *Ecological Sensitivity and Global Legal Pluralism: Rethinking the Trade and Environment Conflict* (Oxford: Hart, 2004).
Perritt, Henry H., 'Dispute resolution in cyberspace: demand for new forms of ADR', *Ohio State Journal on Dispute Resolution*, 15:3 (2000), 675–704.
—, 'Economic and other barriers to electronic commerce', *University of Pennsylvania Journal of International Economic Law*, 21 (2000), 563–84.
Perrow, Charles, *Normal Accidents: Living with High-Risk Technologies* (New York: Basic Books, 1984).
Peters, Anne, 'Compensatory constitutionalism: the function and potential of fundamental international norms and structures', *Leiden Journal of International Law*, 19 (2006), 579–610.
Petersen, Hanne, and Henrik Zahle (eds), *Legal Polycentricity: Consequences of Pluralism in Law* (Aldershot: Dartmouth, 1995).
Petersmann, Ernst-Ulrich, 'Constitutionalism and international adjudication: how to constitutionalize the U.N. dispute settlement system?', *New York University Journal of International Law and Politics*, 31:4 (1999), 753–90.
—, 'Time for a United Nations "global compact" for integrating human rights into the law of worldwide organizations: lessons from European integration', *European Journal of International Law*, 13 (2002), 621–50.
Petryna, Adriana, *When Experiments Travel: Clinical Trials and the Global Search for Human Subjects* (Princeton: Princeton University Press, 2009).
Pfeffer, Christian, and Bjorn R. Olsen, 'Editorial: Journal of Negative Results in Biomedicine', *Journal of Negative Results in BioMedicine*, 1 (2002), 2.
Placentinus, 'Quaestiones de iuris subtilitatibus', in Hermann Fitting (ed.), *Quaestiones de iuris subtilitatibus des Irnerius* (Berlin: J. Guttentag, 1894 [1192]).
PLoS Medicine Editors, 'Ghostwriting revisited: new perspectives but few solutions in sight', *PLOS Medicine*, 8:8 (2011), e1001084.
Polanyi, Karl, *The Great Transformation: The Political and Economic Origins of Our Time* (Boston: Beacon, 1944 [1957]).
Pollock, Rufus, 'Is Google the next Microsoft? Competition, welfare and regulation in Internet search', *Review of Network Economics*, 9:4 (2010), art. 4.
Posner, Eric A., 'Arbitration and harmonization of international commercial law: a defense of Mitsubishi', *Virginia Journal of International Law*, 39 (1999), 647–70.
Posner, Richard A., 'The decline of law as an autonomous discipline: 1962–1987', *Harvard Law Review*, 100 (1987), 761–80.
Post, David, 'Anarchy, state, and the Internet: an essay on law-making in cyberspace', *Journal of Online Law*, art. 3 (1995).
Post, David G., 'The "unsettled paradox": the Internet, the state, and the consent of the governed', *Indiana Journal of Global Legal Studies*, 5 (1998), 521–43.

Post, David N., 'Of black holes and decentralized law-making', *Vanderbilt Journal of Entertainment Law and Practice*, 2:1 (2000), 70–8.
Powell, Walter W., 'Neither market nor hierarchy: network forms of organization', *Research in Organizational Behavior*, 12 (1990), 295–336.
—, and Paul J. DiMaggio (eds), *The New Institutionalism in Organizational Analysis* (Chicago and London: University of Chicago Press, 1991).
Power, Michael, *The Audit Society: Rituals of Verification* (Oxford: Oxford University Press, 1997).
Prandini, Riccardo, 'The Morphogenesis of Constitutionalism', in Petra Dobner and Martin Loughlin (eds), *The Twilight of Constitutionalism?* (Oxford: Oxford University Press, 2010), pp. 309–26.
Preuss, Ulrich K., 'Disconnecting Constitutions from Statehood: Is Global Constitutionalism a Promising Concept?', in Petra Dobner and Martin Loughlin (eds), *The Twilight of Constitutionalism?* (Oxford: Oxford University Press, 2010), pp. 23–46.
—, 'La garantie des droits: "les droits horizontaux"', in Michel Troper and Dominique Chagnollaud (eds), *Traité international de droit constitutionnel*, vol. 3 (Paris: Dalloz, 2012), pp. 233–70.
—, 'Rationality Potentials of Law: Allocative, Distributive and Communicative Rationality', in C. Joerges and D. Trubek (eds), *Critical Legal Thought: An American-German Debate* (Baden-Baden: Nomos, 1989), pp. 525–55.
Přibáň, Jiří, 'Constitutionalism as fear of the political? A comparative analysis of Teubner's *Constitutional Fragments* and Thornhill's *A Sociology of Constitution*', *Journal of Law and Society*, 39:3 (2012), 441–71.
Princen, Thomas, and Matthias Finger, *Environmental NGOs in World Politics: Linking the Local and the Global* (London: Routledge, 1994).
Probst, Peter, and Franz von Kutschera, 'Paradox', in Joachim Ritter and Karlfried Gründer (eds), *Historisches Wörterbuch der Philosophie*, vol. 7 (Basle: Schwabe, 1989), pp. 81–97.
Prosser, Tony, *Law and the Regulatory Process* (Oxford: Clarendon Press, 1997).
Quack, Christian, and Alix Wackerbeck, 'Die Verpflichtung zur Registrierung und Veröffentlichung klinischer Studien: Darstellung der europäischen Rechtslage im Vergleich zur US-Regelung nach dem FDA Amendment Act', *GesundheitsRecht*, 1 (2010), 6–12.
Raiser, Ludwig, 'Rechtsschutz und Institutionenschutz im Privatrecht', in Rechtswissenschaftliche Abteilung der Rechts- und Wirtschaftswissenschaftlichen Fakultät der Universität Tübingen (ed.), *Summum ius summa iniuria* (Tübingen: Mohr Siebeck, 1963), pp. 145–67.
Raiser, Thomas, *Grundlagen der Rechtssoziologie* (Tübingen: Mohr Siebeck, 4th edn, 2007).
Rawls, John, *A Theory of Justice* (Cambridge, Mass.: Harvard University Press, 1971).
Renner, Moritz, *Zwingendes transnationales Recht: Zur Struktur der Wirtschaftsverfassung jenseits des Staates* (Baden-Baden: Nomos, 2011).
Resta, Eligio, *L'ambiguo diritto* (Milan: Franco Angeli, 1984).
—, 'La struttura autopoietica del diritto moderno', *Democrazia e diritto*, 25(5) (1985), 59–74.
Ridder, Helmut, *Die Freiheit der Kunst nach dem Grundgesetz* (Berlin: Vahlen, 1963).
—, *Die soziale Ordnung des Grundgesetzes* (Opladen: Westdeutscher Verlag, 1975).
—, *Zur verfassungsrechtlichen Stellung der Gewerkschaften im Sozialstaat* (Stuttgart: Fischer, 1960).
Riedel, Manfred, 'Gesellschaft, bürgerliche', *Geschichtliche Grundbegriffe*, 2 (1975), 719–800.

Rieth, Lothar, 'Deutsche Unternehmen, soziale Verantwortung und der Global Compact', *Zeitschrift für Wirtschafts- und Unternehmensethik*, 4 (2003), 372–91.

Rinken, Alfred, 'Geschichte und heutige Valenz des Öffentlichen', in Gerd Winter (ed.), *Das Öffentliche heute: Kolloquium zu Ehren von Alfred Rinken* (Baden-Baden: Nomos, 2002), pp. 7–74.

Robé, Jean-Philippe, 'Multinational Enterprises: The Constitution of a Pluralistic Legal Order', in Gunther Teubner (ed.), *Global Law without a State* (Aldershot: Dartmouth, 1997), pp. 45–77.

Robertson, James, 'National and International Financial Architecture: Two Proposals, Inquiry into the Banking Crisis. Evidence Submitted to the House of Commons Select Committee on the Treasury' (2009), available at www.parliament.uk/parliamentary_committees/treasury_committee/tc0708pn85.cfm.

Röhl, Hans C., 'Verfassungsrecht als wissenschaftliche Strategie?', in Hans-Heinrich Trute *et al.* (eds), *Allgemeines Verwaltungsrecht – zur Tragfähigkeit eines Konzepts* (Tübingen: Mohr Siebeck, 2008), pp. 821–36.

Röhl, Klaus F., *Allgemeine Rechtslehre*, Academia iuris (Cologne: Heymann, 1995).

—, *Allgemeine Rechtslehre: Ein Lehrbuch*, Academia iuris (Cologne and Munich: Heymann, 2nd edn, 2001).

Röhl, Klaus F., and Hans Christian Röhl, *Allgemeine Rechtslehre: Ein Lehrbuch*, Academia iuris (Cologne and Munich: Heymann, 3rd revised edn, 2008).

Romano, Cesare P., 'The proliferation of international judicial bodies: the pieces of the puzzle', *New York University Journal of International Law and Politics*, 31:4 (1999), 709–52.

Romano, Frank, 'International Conventions and Treaties', in Siegrun D. Kane and Mark A. Steiner (eds), *Global Trademark and Copyright 1998: Protecting intellectual property rights in the International Marketplace*, Intellectual Property Course Handbook Series, G-536 (New York: Practising Law Institute, 1998), pp. 545–624, available at http://plus.pli.edu/Browse/Title?fq=title_id:(195336).

Romano, Santi, *L'ordinamento giuridico* (Florence: Sansoni, 2nd edn, 1918).

Rosa, Hartmut, *Beschleunigung: Die Veränderung der Temporalstrukturen in der Moderne* (Frankfurt: Suhrkamp, 2005).

—, 'The speed of global flows and the pace of democratic polics', *New Political Science*, 27 (2005), 445–59.

—, and William E. Scheuerman (eds), *High-Speed Society: Social Acceleration, Power and Modernity* (University Park: Penn State Press, 2009).

Rosen, Lawrence, *The Anthropology of Justice: Law as Culture in Islamic Society* (Cambridge: Cambridge University Press, 1989).

Ross, Alf, 'On self-reference and a puzzle in constitutional law', *Mind*, 78 (1969), 1–24.

Rothstein, Bo, *Just Institutions Matter: The Moral and Political Logic of the Universal Welfare State* (Cambridge: Cambridge University Press, 1998).

Rottleuthner, Hubert, 'Biological Metaphors in Legal Thought', in G. Teubner (ed.), *Autopoietic Law: A New Approach to Law and Society* (Berlin: de Gruyter, 1987), pp. 97–127.

Rousseau, Charles, 'De la compatibilité des normes juridiques contradictoires dans l'ordre international', *Revue Général de Droit International Public*, 39 (1932), 133–92.

Ruffert, Matthias, *Vorrang der Verfassung und Eigenständigkeit des Privatrechts: Eine verfassungsrechtliche Untersuchung zur Privatrechtswirkung des Grundgesetzes* (Tübingen: Mohr Siebeck, 2001).

Rüfner, Wolfgang, 'Grundrechtsadressaten', in Josef Isensee and Paul Kirchhof (eds), *Handbuch des Staatsrechts der Bundesrepublik Deutschland*, vol. 9 (Heidelberg: C. F. Müller, 3rd edn, 2011), para. 83–125.

Ruggie, John, 'Protect, Respect, and Remedy: A Framework for Business and Human Rights. Report of the Special Representative of the Secretary-General on Human Rights and Transnational Corporations and Other Business Enterprises, A/HRC/8/5' (2008), 6–13.

Rühl, Giesela, 'Party Autonomy in the Private International Law of Contracts: Transatlantic Convergence and Economic Efficiency', in Eckart Gottschalk et al. (eds), *Conflict of Laws in a Globalized World* (Cambridge: Cambridge University Press, 2007), pp. 153–83.

Sandrock, Otto, 'Die Fortbildung des materiellen Rechts durch die Internationale Schiedsgerichtsbarkeit', in Karl-Heinz Böckstiegel (ed.), *Rechtsfortbildung durch Internationale Schiedsgerichtsbarkeit* (Cologne: Heymann, 1989), pp. 21–81.

Santos, Boaventura de Sousa, 'Law: a map of misreading: toward a postmodern conception of law', *Journal of Law and Society*, 14 (1987), 279–99.

—, 'Modes of production of law and social power', *International Journal of the Sociology of Law*, 13 (1984), 299–336.

—, 'State transformation, legal pluralism and community justice: an introduction', *Social and Legal Studies*, 1:2 (1992), 131–42.

—, *Toward a New Common Sense: Law, Science and Politics in the Paradigmatic Transition* (New York: Routledge, 1995).

—, *Toward a New Legal Common Sense: Law, Globalization and Emancipation* (Evanston: Northwestern University Press, 2003).

Saro-Wiwa, Ken, *Flammen der Hölle. Nigeria und Shell: Der schmutzige Krieg gegen die Ogoni* (Reinbek: Rowohlt, 1996).

Sauter, Wolf, 'Universal service obligations and the emergence of citizens' rights in European telecommunications liberalisation', *Utilities Law Review*, 7 (1996), 104–10.

Savigny, Friedrich Karl von, *System of the Modern Roman Law*, trans. William Holloway, vol. 1 (Madras: Higginbotham, 1867).

Schaaber, Jörg, Michael Kochen, Bruno Müller-Oerlinghausen et al., 'Warum unabhängige Arzneimittelzeitschriften und Fortbildungsveranstaltungen wichtig sind', in Klaus Lieb et al. (eds), *Interessenkonflikte in der Medizin: Hintergründe und Lösungsmöglichkeiten* (Berlin and Heidelberg: Springer, 2011), pp. 237–52.

Schäfer, Hans-Bernd, and Katrin Lantermann, 'Choice of Law from an Economic Perspective', in Jürgen Basedow and Toshiyuko Kono (eds), *An Economic Analysis of Private International Law*, Materialien zum ausländischen und internationalen Privatrecht (Tübingen: Mohr Siebeck, 2006), pp. 87–120.

Schanze, Erich, 'Potential and Limits of Economic Analysis: The Constitution of the Firm', in T. Daintith and G. Teubner (eds), *Contract and Organisation: Legal Analysis in the Light of Economic and Social Theory* (Berlin: de Gruyter, 1986), pp. 204–18.

Schepel, Harm, *The Constitution of Private Governance: Product Standards in the Regulation of Integrating Markets* (Oxford: Hart, 2005).

Schierbeck, Jens, 'Operational Measures for Identifying and Implementing Human Rights Issues in Corporate Operations', in Asbjorn Eide, Ole Bergesen and Pia Goyer (eds), *Human Rights and the Oil Industry* (Antwerp: Intersentia, 2000), pp. 161–77.

Schlosser, Peter, *Das Recht der internationalen privaten Schiedsgerichtsbarkeit* (Tübingen: Mohr, 2nd edn, 1989).

Schluchter, Wolfgang, *Religion und Lebensführung*, vol. 1 (Frankfurt: Suhrkamp, 1988).

Schmidt-Assmann, Eberhard, 'Wissenschaft – Öffentlichkeit – Recht', in Horst Dreier (ed.), *Rechts- und staatstheoretische Schlüsselbegriffe: Legitimität – Repräsentation – Freiheit: Symposion für Hasso Hofmann zum 70. Geburtstag* (Berlin: Duncker & Humblot, 2005), pp. 67–98.

—, 'Wissenschaftsplanung im Wandel', in Wilfried Erbguth, Janbernd Oebbecke and Hans-Werner Rengeling (eds), Planung. Festschrift für Werner Hoppe zum 70. Geburtstag (Munich: C.H. Beck, 2000), pp. 649–65.
—, 'Wissenschaftsrecht im Ordnungsrahmen des öffentlichen Rechts', JuristenZeitung, 45 (1989), 205–11.
Schmitt, Carl, The Concept of the Political, trans. George Schwab (Chicago: University of Chicago Press, 1996).
—, 'Freiheitsrechte und institutionelle Garantien der Reichsverfassung', in Carl Schmitt, Verfassungsrechtliche Aufsätze aus den Jahren 1924–1954 (Berlin, 1985 [1931]), pp. 140–78.
—, Political Theology: Four Chapters on the Concept of Sovereignty, trans. George Schwab (Cambridge, Mass.: MIT Press, 1985).
Schmitter, Philippe C., 'Democratic Theory and Neo-Corporatist Practice', Social Research, 50:4 (Winter 1983), 885–928.
Schmitthoff, Clive M., 'Nature and Evolution of the Transnational Law of Commercial Transactions', in N. Horn and C. M. Schmitthoff (eds), The Transnational Law of International Commercial Transactions (Deventer: Kluwer, 1982), pp. 19–31.
—, 'Das neue Recht des Welthandels', Rabels Zeitschrift (1964), 47–77.
—, Schmitthoff's Export Trade: The Law and Practice of International Trade (London: Stevens & Sons, 9th edn, 1990).
Schmuhl, Hans-Walter, Grenzüberschreitungen: Das Kaiser-Wilhelm-Institut für Anthropologie, menschliche Erblehre und Eugenik 1927 bis 1945 (Göttingen: Wallstein, 2005).
Schneiderman, David, Constitutionalizing Economic Globalization: Investment Rules and Democracy's Promise (Cambridge: Cambridge University Press, 2008).
—, 'Legitimacy and reflexivity in international investment arbitration: a new self-restraint?', Journal of International Dispute Settlement, 2 (2011), 1–25.
Schott, Gisela, Henry Pachl, Ulrich Limbach et al., 'Finanzierung von Arzneimittelstudien durch pharmazeutische Unternehmen und die Folgen, Teil 1: Qualitative systematische Literaturübersicht zum Einfluss auf Studienergebnisse, -protokoll und -qualität', Deutsches Ärzteblatt international, 107:16 (2010), 279–85.
—, —, — et al., 'Finanzierung von Arzneimittelstudien durch pharmazeutische Unternehmen und die Folgen, Teil 2: Qualitative systematische Literaturübersicht zum Einfluss auf Autorschaft, Zugang zu Studiendaten sowie auf Studienregistrierung und Publikation', Deutsches Ärzteblatt international, 107:17 (2010), 295–301.
Schulz, Andrea, 'The Relationship between the Judgments Project and Other International Instruments', Preliminary Document No. 24, Hague Conference on Private International Law, The Hague, 2003, available at www.hcch.net/doc/jdgm_pd24e.pdf.
Schumpeter, Joseph A., The Theory of Economic Development (Cambridge, Mass.: Harvard University Press, 1934).
Schütz, Anton, 'Desiring society: autopoiesis beyond the paradigm of mastership', Law and Critique, 2 (1994), 149–64.
—, 'Sons of the Writ, Sons of Wrath: Pierre Legendre's Critique of Law-Giving', in Peter Goodrich (ed.), Law and the Postmodern Mind (Ann Arbor, Mich.: University of Michigan Press, 1998), pp. 193–222.
—, 'Thinking the law with and against Luhmann, Legendre, Agamben', Law and Critique, 11 (2000), 107–36.
—, 'The Twilight of the Global Polis: On Losing Paradigms, Environing Systems, and Observing World Society', in Gunther Teubner (ed.), Global Law without a State (Aldershot: Dartmouth, 1997), pp. 257–93.

—, 'Von einem neuerdings erhobenen gerechten Ton in der autopoietischen Jurisprudenz', *Zeitschrift für Rechtssoziologie*, 29 (2008), 53–80.

Schwabe, Jürgen, *Die sogenannte Drittwirkung der Grundrechte: Zur Einwirkung der Grundrechte auf den Privatrechtsverkehr* (Munich: Goldmann, 1971).

Sciulli, David, *Corporate Power in Civil Society: An Application of Societal Constitutionalism* (New York: New York University Press, 2001).

—, *Theory of Societal Constitutionalism: Foundations of a Non-Marxist Critical Theory* (Cambridge: Cambridge University Press, 1992).

Scott, Colin, 'The Juridification of Regulatory Relations in the UK Utilities Sectors', in J. Black, P. Muchlinski and P. Walker (eds), *Commercial Regulation and Judicial Review* (Oxford: Hart, 1998), pp. 19–62.

Scott, Craig, Abid Qureshi, Paul Michell et al., 'A memorial for Bosnia: framework of legal arguments concerning the lawfulness of the maintenance of the United Nations Security Council's arms embargo on Bosnia and Herzegovina', *Michigan Journal of International Law*, 16:1 (1994), 1–140.

Scott, W. Richard, *Institutions and Organizations* (Thousand Oaks: Sage, 1995).

Searle, John R., 'Social ontology: some basic principles', *Anthropological Theory*, 6 (2006), 12–29.

Selznick, Philip, *Law, Society and Industrial Justice* (New York: Russell Sage, 1969).

—, *The Moral Commonwealth: Social Theory and the Promise of Community* (Berkeley: University of California Press, 1992).

Senf, Bernd, 'Bankgeheimnis Geldschöpfung' (2009), available at www.goldseiten.de/content/kolumnen/artikel.php?storyid=12360.

Shahabuddeen, Mohamed, 'Consistency in Holdings by International Tribunals', in N. Ando, E. McWhinney and R. Wolfrum (eds), *Liber Amicorum Judge Shigeru Oda* (The Hague: Kluwer Law International, 2002), pp. 633–50.

Shany, Yuval, 'No longer a weak department of power? Reflections on the emergence of a new international judiciary', *European Journal of International Law*, 20 (2009), 81–91.

Shaw, Martin, *Global Society and International Relations: Sociological Concepts and Political Perspectives* (Cambridge: Polity Press, 1995).

Shelton, Dinah, *Remedies in International Human Rights Law* (Oxford: Oxford Universitiy Press, 1999).

Siehr, Kurt, 'Sachrecht im IPR, transnationales Recht und lex mercatoria', in W. Holl and U. Klinke (eds), *Internationales Privatrecht, internationales Wirtschaftsrecht* (Cologne: Heymann, 1985), pp. 103–26.

Simma, Bruno, 'NATO, the UN and the use of force: legal aspects', *European Journal of International Law*, 10:1 (1999), 1–22.

—, 'Self-contained regimes', *Netherlands Yearbook of International Law*, 16 (1985), 111–36.

Simon, Gérald, *Puissance sportive et ordre juridique étatique* (Paris: Librairie générale de droit et de jurisprudence, 1990).

Sinclair, Ian, *The Vienna Convention on the Law of Treaties* (Manchester: Manchester University Press, 2nd edn, 1994).

Sinzheimer, Hugo, 'Das Wesen des Arbeitsrechts', in Otto Kahn-Freund and Thilo Ramm (eds), *Arbeitsrecht und Rechtssoziologie* (Frankfurt: Europäische Verlagsanstalt, 1976 [1927]), pp. 108–14.

Slaughter, Anne-Marie, 'A global community of courts', *Harvard International Law Journal*, 44 (2003), 191–219.

Smith, Mary Lee, 'Publication bias and meta-analysis', *Evaluation in Education*, 4 (1980), 22–4.

Spahn, Peter, 'Oikos und Polis: Beobachtungen zum Prozeß der Polisbildung bei Hesiod, Solon und Aischylos', *Historische Zeitschrift*, 231 (1980), 529–64.
Spencer Brown, George, *Laws of Form* (New York: Julian Press, 1972).
Spickhoff, Andreas, 'Internationales Handelsrecht vor Schiedsgerichten und staatlichen Gerichten', *Rabels Zeitschrift für ausländisches und internationales Privatrecht*, 56 (1992), 116–41.
Stäheli, Urs, 'Latent Places of the Political in Luhmann's Systems Theory: Towards a Politics of Deparadoxification', Working Paper No. 5, Centre for Theoretical Studies, University of Essex, Colchester, 1995.
—, 'Political Epidemiology and the Financial Crisis', in Poul F. Kjaer, Gunther Teubner and Alberto Febbrajo (eds), *The Financial Crisis in Constitutional Perspective: The Dark Side of Functional Differentiation* (Oxford: Hart, 2011), pp. 123–42.
—, *Sinnzusammenbrüche: Eine dekonstruktive Lektüre von Niklas Luhmanns Systemtheorie* (Weilerswist: Velbrück Wissenschaft, 2000).
Stark, Agneta, 'Privatisation in a Gender and Economic Perspective', paper presented to From Dissonance to Sense Conference, Department of Private Law, University of Helsinki, Porvoo, Finland, 1997.
Stein, Ursula, *Lex mercatoria: Realität und Theorie* (Frankfurt: Klostermann, 1995).
Steindorff, Ernst, *Sachnormen im internationalen Privatrecht* (Frankfurt: Klostermann, 1958).
Steinhauer, Fabian, 'Derrida, Luhmann, Steinhauer: Über Dekonstruktion, System und Rhetorik', *Zeitschrift für Rechtssoziologie*, 29 (2008), 167–90.
—, 'Das Grundrecht der Kunstfreiheit: Kommentar zu einem Grundlagentext von Helmut Ridder', in Thomas Vesting, Stefan Korioth and Ino Augsberg (eds), *Grundrechte als Phänomene kollektiver Ordnung: Zur Wiedergewinnung des Gesellschaftlichen in der Grundrechtstheorie und Grundrechtsdogmatik* (Tübingen: Mohr Siebeck, 2013), pp. 247–81.
Stenner, Paul, 'Is autopoietic systems theory alexithymic? Luhmann and the sociopsychology of emotions', *Soziale Systeme*, 10:1 (2004), 159–85.
Stern, Jerome, and R. John Simes, 'Publication bias: evidence of delayed publication in a cohort study of clinical research projects', *British Medical Journal*, 315:7109 (1997), 640–5.
Stewart, Richard B., 'Regulation and the Crisis of Legalization in the United States', in T. Daintith (ed.), *Law as Instrument of Economic Policy: Comparative and Critical Perspectives* (Berlin: de Gruyter, 1988), pp. 97–136.
—, 'Regulation in a liberal state: the role of non-commodity values', *Yale Law Journal*, 92 (1983), 1537–612.
Stichweh, Rudolf, 'Einheit und Differenz im Wissenschaftssystem der Moderne', in Jost Halfmann and Johannes Rohbeck (eds), *Zwei Kulturen der Wissenschaft – Revisited* (Weilerswist: Velbrück, 2007), pp. 213–28.
—, 'Towards a General Theory of Function System Crisis', in Poul F. Kjaer, Gunther Teubner and Alberto Febbrajo (eds), *The Financial Crisis in Constitutional Perspective: The Dark Side of Functional Differentiation* (Oxford: Hart, 2011), pp. 53–72.
—, *Die Weltgesellschaft: Soziologische Analysen* (Frankfurt: Suhrkamp, 2000).
—, *Wissenschaft, Universität, Professionen* (Frankfurt: Suhrkamp, 1994).
—, 'Zur Theorie der Weltgesellschaft', *Soziale Systeme*, 1 (1995), 29–45.
Stiglitz, Joseph, *Globalization and its Discontents* (London: Penguin, 2002).
Stoll, Peter-Tobias, 'Biotechnologische Innovationen: Konflikte und rechtliche Ordnung', in Adrienne Héritier, Michael Stolleis and Fritz Scharpf (eds), *European and International Regulation after the Nation State: Different Scopes and Multiple Levels* (Baden-Baden: Nomos, 2004), pp. 261–77.

Stolleis, Michael, *Geschichte des öffentlichen Rechts in Deutschland*, vol. 4 (Munich: C. H. Beck, 2012).
Streeck, Wolfgang, *Re-Forming Capitalism: Institutional Change in the German Political Economy* (Oxford: Oxford University Press, 2009).
—, and Philippe C. Schmitter, *Private Interest Government: Beyond Market and State* (London: Sage, 1985).
Suber, Peter, *The Paradox of Self-Amendment: A Study of Logic, Law, Omnipotence and Change* (New York. Peter Lang, 1990), out of print, available at www.earlham.edu/~peters/writing/psa/index.htm.
Summerer, Thomas, *Internationales Sportrecht vor dem staatlichen Richter in der Bundesrepublik Deutschland, Schweiz, USA und England* (Munich: Florentz, 1990).
Sun, Haochen, 'The road to Doha and beyond: some reflections on the TRIPS Agreement and public health', *European Journal of International Law*, 15 (2004), 123–50.
Sunstein, Cass R., 'Paradoxes of the regulatory state', *University of Chicago Law Review*, 57 (1990), 407–41.
Sutton, Alexander, Sue J. Duval, R. L. Tweedie *et al.*, 'Empirical assessment of effect of publication bias on meta-analysis', *British Medical Journal*, 320:7249 (2000), 1574–7.
Swann, Stephen, 'Private into Public Law: Fiduciary Power and Judicial Review', paper presented to From Dissonance to Sense Conference, Department of Private Law, University of Helsinki, Porvoo, Finland, 1997.
Taggart, Michael, 'Public Utilities and Public Law', in P. Joseph (ed.), *Essays on the Constitution* (Wellington: Brooker's, 1995), pp. 214–64.
Terhechte, Jörg Philipp, *Konstitutionalisierung und Normativität der europäischen Grundrechte* (Tübingen: Mohr Siebeck, 2011).
Teubner, Gunther, 'After Legal Instrumentalism? Strategic Models of Post-Regulatory Law', *International Journal of Sociology of Law*, 12 (1984), 375–400.
—, 'Alienating Justice: On the Social Surplus Value of the Twelfth Camel', in David Nelken and Jirí Pribán (eds), *Law's New Boundaries: Consequences of Legal Autopoiesis* (Aldershot: Ashgate, 2001), pp. 21–44.
—, 'Altera pars audiatur: Law in the Collision of Discourses', in Richard Rawlings (ed.), *Law, Society and Economy* (Oxford: Clarendon Press, 1997), pp. 149–76.
—, 'Autopoiesis and Steering: How Politics Profits from the Normative Surplus of Capital', in Roland J. in t' Veld et al. (eds), *Autopoiesis and Configuration Theory: New Approaches to Societal Steering* (Dordrecht: Kluwer, 1991), pp. 127–41.
—, 'Breaking frames: the global interplay of legal and social systems', *American Journal of Comparative Law*, 45 (1997), 149–69.
—, *Constitutional Fragments: Societal Constitutionalism and Globalization* (Oxford: Oxford University Press, 2012).
—, 'Constitutionalising polycontexturality', *Social and Legal Studies*, 19 (2011), 17–38.
—, 'Contracting worlds: invoking discourse rights in private governance regimes', *Social and Legal Studies*, 9 (2000), 399–417.
—, 'The Corporate Codes of Multinationals: Company Constitutions Beyond Corporate Governance and Co-Determination', in Rainer Nickel (ed.), *Conflict of Laws and Laws of Conflict in Europe and Beyond: Patterns of Supranational and Transnational Juridification* (Oxford: Hart, 2009), pp. 261–76.
—, 'De collisione discursuum: communicative rationalities in law, morality and politics', *Cardozo Law Review*, 17 (1996), 901–18.
—, 'Dealing with Paradoxes of Law: Derrida, Luhmann, Wiethölter', trans. Iain L. Fraser, in Oren Perez and Gunther Teubner (eds), *On Paradoxes and Inconsistencies in Law* (Oxford: Hart, 2006), pp. 41–64.

—, *Dilemmas of Law in the Welfare State* (Berlin: de Gruyter, 1986).
—, *Diritto policontesturale: Prospettive giuridiche della pluralizzazione dei mondi sociali*, ed. Annamaria Rufino (Naples: La città del sole, 1999).
—, 'Dreiers Luhmann', in Robert Alexy (ed.), *Integratives Verstehen. Zur Rechtsphilosophie Ralf Dreiers* (Tübingen: Mohr Siebeck, 2005), pp. 199–211.
—, 'Episodenverknüpfung: Zur Steigerung von Selbstreferenz im Recht', in D. Baecker et al. (eds), *Theorie als Passion* (Frankfurt: Suhrkamp, 1987), pp. 423–46.
—, 'Expertise as Social Institution: Internalising Third Parties into the Contract', in David Campbell, Hugh Collins and John Wightman (eds), *Implicit Dimensions of Contract: Discrete, Relational and Network Contracts* (Oxford: Hart, 2003), pp. 333–64.
—, 'Ein Fall von struktureller Korruption? Die Familienbürgschaft in der Kollision unverträglicher Handlungslogiken', *Kritische Vierteljahresschrift für Gesetzgebung und Rechtswissenschaften*, 83 (2000), 388–404.
— (ed.), *Global Law without a State* (Aldershot: Dartmouth, 1997).
—, 'Global Private Regimes: Neo-Spontaneous Law and Dual Constitution of Autonomous Sectors?', in Karl-Heinz Ladeur (ed.), *Globalization and Public Governance* (Oxford: Oxford University Press, 2003), pp. 71–87.
—, 'Hybrid Laws: Constitutionalizing Private Governance Networks', in Robert A. Kagan, Martin Krygier and Kenneth Winston (eds), *Legality and Community: On the Intellectual Legacy of Philip Selznick* (Berkeley: Berkeley Public Policy Press, 2002), pp. 311–31.
—, 'Idiosyncratic Production Regimes: Co-evolution of Economic and Legal Institutions in the Varieties of Capitalism', in John Ziman (ed.), *The Evolution of Cultural Entities: Proceedings of the British Academy* (Oxford: Oxford University Press, 2002), pp. 161–81.
—, 'Ist das Recht auf Konsens angewiesen?', in H.-J. Giegel (ed.), *Kommunikation und Konsens* (Frankfurt: Suhrkamp, 1992), pp. 197–201.
—, 'The king's many bodies: the self-deconstruction of law's hierarchy', *Law and Society Review*, 33 (1998), 763–87.
—, *Law as an Autopoietic System*, trans. Anne Bankowska and Ruth Adler, ed. Zenon Bankowski (London: Blackwell, 1993).
—, 'Legal irritants: good faith in British law or how unifying law ends up in new divergencies', *Modern Law Review*, 61 (1998), 11–32.
—, *Networks as Connected Contracts*, ed. Hugh Collins (Oxford: Hart, 2011).
—, *Organisationsdemokratie und Verbandsverfassung: Rechtsmodelle für politisch relevante Verbände* (Tübingen: Mohr, 1978).
—, 'Social Order from Legislative Noise: Autopoietic Closure as a Problem for Legal Regulation', in Gunther Teubner and Alberto Febbrajo (eds), *State, Law and Economy as Autopoietic Systems: Regulation and Autonomy in a New Perspective*, European Yearbook in the Sociology of Law, double issue 1991–92 (Milan: Giuffré, 1992), pp. 609–50.
—, 'Societal Constitutionalism: Alternatives to State-Centred Constitutional Theory?', in Christian Joerges, Inger-Johanne Sand and Gunther Teubner (eds), *Transnational Governance and Constitutionalism* (Oxford: Hart, 2004), pp. 3–28.
—, *Standards und Direktiven in Generalklauseln: Möglichkeiten und Grenzen der empirischen Sozialforschung bei der Präzisierung der Gute-Sitten-Klauseln im Privatrecht* (dissertation, Tübingen, 1970), Studien und Texte zur Theorie und Methodologie, 8 (Frankfurt: Athenäum Verlag, 1971).
—, 'State policies in private law? Comment on Hanoch Dagan', *American Journal of Comparative Law*, 56 (2008), 835–44.

—, 'Substantive and reflexive elements in modern law', *Law and Society Review*, 17:2 (1983), 239–86.
—, 'The two faces of janus: rethinking legal pluralism', *Cardozo Law Review*, 13 (1992), 1443–62.
—, 'Unitas multiplex: corporate governance in group enterprises', in Gunther Teubner and David Sugarman (eds), *Regulating Corporate Groups in Europe* (Baden-Baden: Nomos, 1990), pp. 67–104.
—, and Anna Beckers (eds), Transnational Societal Constitutionalism, special issue of *Indiana Journal of Global Legal Studies*, 20:2 (2013), 523–1060.
—, and Andreas Fischer-Lescano, *Regime- Kollisionen: Zur Fragmentierung des Weltrechts* (Frankfurt: Suhrkamp, 2006).
Thompson, Grahame F., 'The Constitutionalisation of Everyday Life?', in Poul Kjaer and Eva Hartmann (eds), *The Evolution of Intermediary Institutions in Europe: From Corporatism to Governance* (London: Palgrave, 2015), pp. 177–97.
Thornhill, Chris, 'Niklas Luhmann and the sociology of the constitution', *Journal of Classical Sociology*, 10:4 (2010), 315–37.
—, 'A sociology of constituent power: the political code of transnational societal constitutions', *Indiana Journal of Global Legal Studies*, 20 (2013), 551–603.
—, 'Towards a historical sociology of constitutional legitimacy', *Theory and Society*, 37 (2008), 161–97.
Tomkins, Adam, 'On Being Sceptical about Human Rights', in Tom Campbell, Keith D. Ewing and Adam Tomkins (eds), *Sceptical Essays on Human Rights* (Oxford: Oxford University, 2001), pp. 1–11.
Tomuschat, Christian, 'International Law as the Constitution of Mankind', in United Nations (ed.), *International Law on the Eve of the Twenty-First Century* (New York: United Nations Publications, 1997), pp. 37–51.
Tonks, Alison, 'A clinical trials register for Europe', *British Medical Journal*, 325:7376 (2002), 1314–15.
Trachtman, Joel P., 'The constitutions of the WTO', *European Journal of International Law*, 17:3 (2006), 623–46.
Trakman, Leon E., 'A plural account of the transnational law merchant', *Transnational Legal Theory*, 2 (2011), 309–45.
Tramèr, Martin R., D. John Reynolds, Andrew Moore *et al.*, 'Impact of covert duplicate publication on meta-analysis: a case study', *British Medical Journal*, 315:7109 (1997), 635–40.
Treves, Tullio, 'Conflicts between the International Tribunal for the Law of the Sea and the International Court of Justice', *New York University Journal of International Law and Politics*, 31:4 (1999), 809–21.
Tully, James, 'The Imperialism of Modern Constitutional Democracy', in Neil Walker and Martin Loughlin (eds), *The Paradox of Constitutionalism: Constituent Power and Constitutional Form* (Oxford: Oxford University Press, 2007), pp. 315–38.
United Nations General Assembly, *A More Secure World: Our Shared Responsibility. Report of the High-Level Panel on Threats, Challenges and Change*, United Nations, A/59/565 (New York: United Nations, 2004).
Varela, Francisco J., 'Whence Perceptual Meaning? A Cartography of Current Ideas', in Francisco J. Varela and Jean-Pierre Dupuy (eds), *Understanding Origins: Contemporary Views on the Origin of Life, Mind and Society* (Dordrecht: Kluwer, 1992), pp. 235–63.
Verschraegen, Gert, 'Differentiation and Inclusion: A Neglected Sociological Approach to Fundamental Rights', in Mikael Rask Madsen and Gert Verschraegen (eds),

Making Human Rights Intelligible: Towards a Sociology of Human Rights (Oxford: Hart, 2013), pp. 61–80.

Vesting, Thomas, 'Politische Verfassung? Der moderne (liberale) Verfassungsbegriff und seine systemtheoretische Rekonstruktion', in Gralf-Peter Calliess et al. (eds), *Soziologische Jurisprudenz: Festschrift für Gunther Teubner zum 65. Geburtstag* (Berlin: de Gruyter, 2009), pp. 609–26.

—, *Rechtstheorie: Ein Studienbuch* (Munich: Beck, 2007).

—, *Die Tagesschau-App und die Notwendigkeit der Schaffung eines 'Intermedienkollisionsrechts'*, Karlsruher Dialog zum Informationsrecht, 4 (Karlsruhe: KIT Scientific Publishing, 2013).

Viellechner, Lars, 'Constitutionalism as a cipher: on the convergence of constitutionalist and pluralist approaches to the globalization of Law', *Goettingen Journal of International Law*, 4 (2012), 599–623.

—, *Transnationalisierung des Rechts* (Weilerswist: Velbrück, 2013).

Viens, A. M., and Julian Savulescu, 'Introduction to the Olivieri Symposium', *Journal of Medical Ethics*, 30:1 (2004), 1–7.

Villey, Michel, *Leçons d'histoire de la philosophie du droit* (Paris: Dalloz, 1957).

Virally, Michel, 'Un tiers droit? Réflexions théoriques', in B. Goldman (ed.), *Le droit des relations économiques internationales* (Paris: Librairies Techniques, 1982), pp. 373–85.

Vismann, Cornelia, 'Das Gesetz 'DER Dekonstruktion'', *Rechtshistorisches Journal*, 11 (1992), 250–64.

Vöneky, Silja, *Die Fortgeltung des Umweltvölkerrechts in internationalen bewaffneten Konflikten*, Beiträge zum ausländischen öffentlichen Recht und Völkerrecht, 145 (Vienna and New York: Springer-Verlag, 2001).

Voser, Nathalie, 'Mandatory rules of law as a limitation on the law applicable in international commercial arbitration', *American Review of International Arbitration*, 7 (1996), 319–58.

Wagner, Elke, *Der Arzt und seine Kritiker: zum Strukturwandel medizinkritischer Öffentlichkeiten am Beispiel klinischer Ethik-Kommissionen* (Stuttgart: Lucius & Lucius, 2011).

Wahl, Rainer, 'In Defence of "Constitution"', in Petra Dobner and Martin Loughlin (eds), *The Twilight of Constitutionalism?* (Oxford: Oxford University Press, 2010), pp. 220–44.

Walker, Neil, 'Beyond the Holistic Constitution?', in Petra Dobner and Martin Loughlin (eds), *The Twilight of Constitutionalism?* (Oxford: Oxford University Press, 2010), pp. 291–308.

—, 'The EU and the WTO: Constitutionalism in a New Key', in Grainne de Burca and Joanne Scott (eds), *The EU and the WTO: Legal and Constitutional Issues* (London: Hart Publishing, 2001), pp. 31–58.

—, 'The idea of constitutional pluralism', *Modern Law Review*, 65 (2002), 317–59.

—, 'Post-Constituent Constitutionalism: The Case of the European Union', in Martin Loughlin and Neil Walker (eds), *The Paradox of Constitutionalism: Constituent Power and Constitutional Form* (Oxford: Oxford University Press, 2008), pp. 247–68.

Wallerstein, Immanuel, *The Capitalist World Economy* (Cambridge: Cambridge University Press, 1979).

Walter, Christian, 'Constitutionalizing (inter)national governance: possibilities for and limits to the development of an international constitutional law', *German Yearbook of International Law*, 44 (2001), 170–201.

Walz, Rainer, *Steuergerechtigkeit und Rechtsanwendung: Grundlinien einer relativ autonomen Steuerrechtsdogmatik* (Heidelberg: Decker, 1980).
Walzer, Michael, *Spheres of Justice: A Defence of Pluralism and Equality* (New York: Basic Books, 1984).
Wapner, Paul, 'Politics beyond the state: environmental activism and world civic politics', *World Politics*, 47 (1995), 311–40.
Wasser, Harald, 'Psychoanalyse als Theorie autopoietischer Systeme', *Soziale Systeme*, 1 (1995), 329–50.
Watson, Geoffrey R., 'Constitutionalism, judicial review, and the world court', *Harvard International Law Journal*, 34:1 (1993), 1–45.
Watzlawick, Paul, Janet Beavin Bavelas and Don D. Jackson, *Pragmatics of Human Communication: A Study of Interactional Patterns, Pathologies, and Paradoxes* (New York and London: W. W. Norton, 1967).
Weber, Gaby, *Die Verschwundenen von Mercedes-Benz* (Hamburg: Libertäre Assoziation, 2001).
Weber, Max, *Economy and Society*, trans. Ephraim Fischoff et al., ed. *Guenther Roth and Claus Wittich* (Berkeley: University of California Press, 1978).
—, *Gesammelte Aufsätze zur Wissenschaftslehre* (Tübingen: Mohr Siebeck, 3rd edn, 1968).
Weick, Karl E., 'Educational organizations as loosely coupled systems', *Administrative Science Quarterly*, 21 (1976), 1–19.
—, *The Social Psychology of Organizing* (Reading: Addison-Wesley, 1979).
Weil, Prosper, 'Towards relative normativity in international law?', *American Journal of International Law*, 77:3 (1983), 413–42.
Weiler, Joseph H., *The Constitution of Europe: 'Do the New Clothes Have an Emperor?' and Other Essays on European Integration* (Cambridge: Cambridge University Press, 1999).
—, and Marlene Wind (eds), *European Constitutionalism beyond the State* (Cambridge: Cambridge University Press, 2003).
Weinrib, Ernest J., *The Idea of Private Law* (Cambridge, Mass.: Harvard University Press, 1995).
Weisbrod, Carol, *Emblems of Pluralism: Cultural Differences and the State* (Princeton: Princeton University Press, 2002).
Wheatley, Steven, 'Deliberating Cosmopolitan Ideas: Does a Democratic Conception of Human Rights Make Sense?', in Olivier de Frouville (ed.), *Le cosmopolitisme juridique* (Paris: Pedone, 2015), available at http://ssrn.com/abstract=2485068.
Wieacker, Franz, *A History of Private Law in Europe: With Particular Reference to Germany* (Cambridge: Cambridge University Press, 1996).
Wielsch, Dan, 'Die epistemische Analyse des Rechts: Von der ökonomischen zur ökologischen Rationalität in der Rechtswissenschaft', *JuristenZeitung*, 64:2 (2009), 67–76.
Wiethölter, 'Rudolf, Begriffs- oder Interessenjurisprudenz – falsche Fronten im IPR und Wirtschaftsverfassungsrecht: Bemerkungen zur selbstgerechten Kollisionsnorm', in Alexander Lüderitz (ed.), *Festschrift für Gerhard Kegel* (Frankfurt: Metzner, 1977), pp. 213–63.
—,'Ist unserem Recht der Prozeß zu machen?', in Axel Honneth et al. (eds), *Zwischenbetrachtungen: Im Prozeß der Aufklärung. Jürgen Habermas zum 60. Geburtstag* (Frankfurt: Suhrkamp, 1989), pp. 794–812.
—, 'Just-ifications of a Law of Society', in Oren Perez and Gunther Teubner (eds), *Paradoxes and Inconsistencies in the Law* (Oxford: Hart, 2005), pp. 65–77.

—, 'Materialization and Proceduralization in Modern Law', in G. Teubner (ed.), *Dilemmas of Law in the Welfare State* (Berlin: de Gruyter, 1985), pp. 221–49.
—, 'Proceduralization of the Category of Law', in C. Joerges and D. Trubek (eds), *Critical Legal Thought: An American-German Debate* (Baden-Baden: Nomos, 1989), pp. 501–10.
—, 'Recht und Politik: Bemerkungen zu Peter Schwerdtners Kritik', *Zeitschrift für Rechtspolitik* (1969), 155–8.
—, *Rechtswissenschaft* (Frankfurt: Fischer, 1968).
—, 'Social Science Models in Economic Law', in T. Daintith and G. Teubner (eds), *Contract and Organization: Legal Analysis in the Light of Economic and Social Theory* (Berlin: de Gruyter, 1986), pp. 52–67.
—, 'Verrechtlichung', unpublished manuscript, Frankfurt, 1995, on file with the author.
—, 'Zum Fortbildungsrecht der (richterlichen) Rechtsfortbildung: Fragen eines lesenden Recht-Fertigungslehrers', *Kritische Vierteljahreszeitschrift für Gesetzgebung und Rechtswissenschaft*, 3 (1988), 1–28.
—, 'Zur Argumentation im Recht: Entscheidungsfolgen als Rechtsgründe?', in Gunther Teubner (ed.), *Entscheidungsfolgen als Rechtsgründe: Folgenorientiertes Argumentieren in rechtsvergleichender Sicht* (Baden-Baden: Nomos, 1994), pp. 89–120.
—, 'Zur Regelbildung in der Dogmatik des Zivilrechts', *Archiv für Rechts- und Sozialphilosophie*, 78, Beiheft 45 (1992), 222–40.
Wightman, John, 'Private Law and Public Interests', in Thomas Wilhelmsson and Samuli Hurri (eds), *From Dissonance to Sense: Welfare State Expectations, Privatisation and Private Law* (Aldershot: Ashgate, 1999), pp. 253–76.
Wilder, Lisa, 'Local Futures? From Denunciation to Revalorization of the Indigenous Order', in Gunther Teubner (ed.), *Global Law without a State* (Aldershot: Darmouth, 1997), pp. 215–94.
Wilhelmsson, Thomas, 'Private Law 2000: Small Stories on Morality Through Liability', in T. Wilhelmsson and S. Hurri (eds), *From Dissonance to Sense: Welfare State Expectations, Privatisation and Private Law* (Aldershot: Ashgate, 1999), pp. 221–51.
Williamson, Oliver, 'Comparative economic organization: the analysis of discrete structural alternatives', *Administrative Science Quarterly*, 36 (1991), 269–96.
Williamson, Oliver, *The Economic Institutions of Capitalism: Firms, Markets, Relational Contracting* (New York: Free Press, 1985).
—, *The Mechanisms of Governance* (Oxford: Oxford University Press, 1996).
Willke, Helmut, *Heterotopia: Studien zur Krisis der Ordnung moderner Gesellschaften* (Frankfurt: Suhrkamp, 2003).
—, *Ironie des Staates: Grundlinien einer Staatstheorie polyzentrischer Gesellschaft* (Frankfurt: Suhrkamp, 1992).
—, 'Societal Guidance through Law', in A. Febbrajo and G. Teubner (eds), *State, Law, and Economy as Autopoietic Systems: Regulation and Autonomy in a New Perspective* (Milan: Giuffrè, 1992), pp. 353–87.
—, *Stand und Kritik der neueren Grundrechtstheorie: Schritte zu einer normativen Systemtheorie* (Berlin: Duncker & Humblot, 1975).
Wilson, J. Q., *The Politics of Regulation* (New York: Basic Books, 1980).
Winston, Kenneth, 'Self-incrimination in context: establishing procedural protections in juvenile and college disciplinary proceedings', *Southern California Law Review*, 48:4 (1975), 813–51.
Wittgenstein, Ludwig, *Philosophical Investigations* (Oxford: Blackwell, 1989).

Wood, Stephen G., and Brett G. Scharffs, 'Applicability of human rights standards to private corporations: an American perspective', *American Journal of Comparative Law*, 50 (2002), 531–66.

World Health Organization, *Treat 3 Million by 2005 Initiative: WC 503.2* (Geneva: WHO, 2003).

Yamin, Alicia Ely, 'Not just a tragedy: access to medications as right under international law', *Boston University International Law Journal*, 21 (2003), 101–45.

Young, Oran, *International Governance: Protecting the Environment in a Stateless Society* (Ithaca: Cornell University Press, 1994).

—, 'International regimes: toward a new theory of institutions', *World Politics*, 39 (1986), 104–22.

Yozell, Emily, 'The Castro Alfaro Case: Convenience and Justice – Lessons for Lawyers in Transcultural Litigation', in Lance Compa and Stephen Diamond (eds), *Human Rights, Labor Rights, and International Trade* (Philadelphia: University of Pennsylvania Press, 1996), pp. 273–92.

Zamora, Stephen, 'Is there customary international economic law?', *German Yearbook of International Law*, 32 (1989), 9–42.

Zarlenga, Stephen A., *The Lost Science of Money* (Valatie and New York: American Monetary Institute, 2002).

Ziman, John, *Real Science: What It Is, and What It Means* (Cambridge: Cambridge University Press, 2000).

Zizek, Slavoj, *Enjoy Your Symptom!* (New York: Routledge, 1992).

Zöllner, Wolfgang, *Die Privatrechtsgesellschaft im Gesetzes- und Richterstaat* (Cologne: Schmidt, 1996).

—, 'Regelungsspielräume im Schuldvertragsrecht: Bemerkungen zur Grundrechtsanwendung im Privatrecht und zu den sogenannten Ungleichgewichtslagen', *Archiv für die civilistische Praxis*, 196 (1996), 1–36.

Zumbansen, Peer, 'Comparative, global and transnational constitutionalism: the emergence of a transnational legal-pluralist order', *Global Constitutionalism*, 1:1 (2012), 16–52.

—, '"New governance" in European corporate law regulation as transnational legal pluralism', *European Law Journal*, 15:2 (2009), 246–76.

Index

Note: 'n.' after a page reference indicates the number of a note on that page

Abbott, K. W. 270 n.36
Ackerman, B. A. 208n.17
Ackermann, J. 175
addiction
  collective 175–82
  individual 175, 179–80
  law 33, 181
  social 3, 7, 175–82, 193, 207
Adorno, T. W. 16, 27, 34, 37n.12, 38n.47, 39n.69, 73
Agamben, G. 35, 86, 88–90, 92–4, 101n.2, 101n.12, 102n.14, 110, 116, 126n.34, 126n.50
Albert, M. 269n.19, 271n.61
Alexy, R. 38n.44, 98, 297n.14
Alford, R. 79, 151n.10, 152n.16, 152n.35, 268
Allott, P. 315n.6
Alston, P. 256, 274n.127
ambivalence 72
  contract 6, 156, 162
  legal 63, 88–9, 97–9
  paradox and 65, 68
Amstutz, M. 81n.5, 211n.77, 270n.34
analytical jurisprudence 26
Anderson, G. W. 125nn.18–19, 125nn.21–2, 126n.49, 172n.41, 324, 337n.26, 337.n8, 337n.29
aporias
  justice 25, 28, 33
  law 28, 63, 64, 68, 74, 77
Appadurai, A. 271n.46

argumentation, legal *see* legal argumentation
Augsberg, I. 297n.21, 298n.47, 299n.62–3, 300n.83, 336n.9, 338n.49–50
Austin, J. 223
auto-constitutionalisation *see* self-constitutionalisation
autonomisation 77, 80, 110, 114–19, 192–6, 241
autonomy
  discourses 119, 133, 156–60, 166
  economy 131, 134, 194, 205–7, 305–6, 310
  global law 217–19
  institutional 79, 114–16, 119, 153n.60, 186, 282–3
  law 51, 80, 92, 95, 181, 222
  legal regimes 77, 146–7, 243–67, 322
  norm-setting 91, 145, 156
  personal 79, 111, 114–16, 119, 160, 169, 186
  politics 114, 191, 194, 196
  private 129–45, 156, 160, 169, 228, 321
  rights and 114–20, 282–95
  science 194, 197, 283–7, 292–5, 300n.83
  social 51–3, 76–80, 114–16, 119, 132–40, 183–4, 216, 284, 311
  Wiethölter on 76, 134, 301n.89

autopoiesis 133, 151n.9, 180, 335, 342–3
  deconstruction and 14, 40–56

Backer, L. C. 210n.67, 315n.24, 316n.28
Baecker, D. 170n.11, 171n.31, 272n.65
Barak, A. 125n.18, 172n.41
Barjiji-Kastner, F. 82n.45
Beck, U. 269n.28
Beckers, A. 315n.7, 336n.10
Bendel, K. 170n.12
Benjamin, W. 30, 35, 42–3, 73, 165, 171n.27
Berman, P. S. 234n.27, 244, 251, 269.n18, 270nn.38–9, 270n.43, 272n.78
Binswanger, H. C. 208n.5, 208n.8–9, 208n.37, 209n.37, 210n.55, 212n.102
Bitbol, M. 171n.20
Black, J. 151, 152n.38, 153n.60
Blecher, M. 58n.51
blind spot 6, 8, 14, 30, 46–8, 52–4, 159–64 *passim*, 171n.15–16
Borges, J. L. 99
Bredt, S. 211n.91
Brüggemeier, G. 125n.20, 125n.31
Brunkhorst, H. 210n.67, 211n.81, 212n.99, 269n.19, 271n.56,
Buckel, S. 37, 37n.15, 336n.6

Calliess, G.-P. 209n.32, 210n.67, 269n.33, 271n.56
Campbell, D. 170n.6
Canaris, C.-W. 125n.20
capillary constitution 176, 183–91 *passim*, 201, 207, 314
central banks 51, 177–8, 189–93, 197–207 *passim*, 212n.100, 330–1

Christensen, R. 297n.15, 301n.89
civil society pressures on constitutionalisation 308
  see also protest movements
Clam, J. 38n.46, 66, 82n.25
Clapham, A. 172n.41, 297n.12, 298n.32
Clinton, B. 213, 215
code(s)
  binary, of economy 44–5, 176, 199, 287, 329
  binary, of law 5, 22, 31–6, 43, 50, 67–8, 86–9, 176, 199–200, 223–5, 313, 342–4
  binary, of science 194, 287–9, 298n.41
  constitutional 5, 176, 198–201, 312–13
  digital 303
    see also digital constitution
  externalisation of paradox and 319–31
  meta- 5, 198–201, 312
    see also constitutional codes
  plurality of 140, 166
co-evolution 157, 159, 195, 200, 211n.77, 243
Cohen, J. 152n.35
colère public 32
collective actor(s) 105–18, 176–9, 196, 239, 307–8
  addiction 176, 179
  rights and 105–6, 118, 284, 297n.24, 303–5
collective institution(s) 282–5, 288–91, 295
Collins, H. 142, 151, 171n.35, 172n.41
collision
  directrice 76
  norm 155, 167–8, 182, 238–40, 253, 259

INDEX

rationality *see* rationality conflicts
regime 237–77
see also conflict of laws
commercialisation *see* economisation
compulsion to grow 208n.9, 313–14
  economy 175–85, 330
  law 36
  politics 186, 193, 330
  see also self-destructive growth
conflict *see* collision
conflict of laws 345
  constitutional rights as rules of 119, 280, 284, 294–6
  inter-regime 249–59
  intersystemic 218, 238–40
  Wiethölter on 59–64, 68–9, 74–8, 81n.5
conflicts, rationality *see* rationality conflicts
constitution
  corporate 306, 344
  digital 196, 303
  economic *see* economic constitution
  financial 188–93, 197–8, 204–7, 330
    see also economic constitution
  formal versus material 311, 326, 346
  global *see* global constitution
  Labour Constitution 309
  nation-state *see* state constitution
  political *see* state constitution
  societal *see* societal constitutionalism
  state *see* state constitution
  transnational *see* global constitution
  WTO 189, 258–60, 305–6
constitutional arenas 311–12
constitutional code 5, 176, 198–201, 312–13
constitutional functions 190–2, 194, 198, 201, 311

constitutionalisation
  global *see* global constitution; global constitutionalism
  societal *see* societal constitutionalism
  transnational *see* global constitution; global constitutionalism
constitutionalism
  global *see* global constitutionalism
  new 189, 305
  societal *see* societal constitutionalism
  transnational *see* global constitutionalism
constitutional moment 176, 182–3, 207
constitutional norms 193–6, 209n.46, 247, 303, 312
  economy 187, 205, 325
  judge-made law and 325–7
  transnational 304–7, 311, 325–6
constitutional paradox 190, 202, 318–35
constitutional pluralism 247, 334
constitutional question, new 183, 302–4, 315n.6, 344
constitutional rights *see* human rights
constitutional sociology 191, 210n.57, 302–16, 347n.16
constitutional subjects 192, 304, 307
constitutive function 191–2, 311
constitutive rules 191, 311, 344
contextual adequacy 282, 285, 290–2
contingency formula 20–4, 29, 33, 35–6, 54–6, 71–3, 335–6
  justice as 20–2, 24, 33, 54, 71
contract
  bilateralisation 142–3, 155, 167–9
  as constitution 61–2, 79, 166–70
  as *différance* 164
  expert 155, 167–9
  fragmentation of 154–72

hybridisation 79, 147–50, 154–72
liability 155, 168–9, 264
non-economic 131–2
obligation to conclude 142
privity 142–3, 155, 168–9, 331
relational 156, 158, 168, 170n.6, 171n.18
self-validating 220–2, 225–9, 323, 326
  see also lex mercatoria
standard 142, 220, 226–8, 230, 232, 245–6, 261–2, 325
as 'the task of the translator' 165–7, 169–70
transaction, versus 131, 171n.15, 201
unity of 156–60, 171n.13
universal service duties 140–2
as wave and particle 161–3
corporate actor see collective actor
corporate codes of conduct 187, 220, 270n.43, 306
corporate constitution 306, 344
corporations, transnational see transnational corporations
corporatism 220, 228, 310, 340, 347n.3
corruption 139–40, 218–19, 280, 286, 333
Cotterrell, R. 37n.2, 38n.33
Cottier, T. 271n.56
Cover, R. M. 323, 337n.24
Cremades, B. M. 235n.63, 235n.81
critical theory 69, 74, 133, 216, 234n.45
cyberlaw 209n.35, 250, 302–3
  see also digital constitution; lex digitalis

Davis, D. 125n.18, 125n.21
deconstruction 72–5, 96, 102n.17, 171n.28
  systems theory and 14–15, 30–1, 40–58, 67–8, 70, 161
  Wiethölter and 63–5, 67, 70, 74–8, 80
De George, R. T. 153n.40
Deleuze, G. 4, 260, 275n.132
de Man, P. 64
democracy
  globalisation and 214, 221, 304, 306–7, 324
  human rights and 124, 127n.72
  privatisation and 128–9
  societal constitutionalism and 187, 202–5, 207, 209n.34, 211n.90, 302, 309, 311–12, 323
Derrida, J. 14–15, 25, 166, 176, 185, 315n.4
  on contract 164, 171n.26
  on justice and law 29–32, 35, 40, 43–4, 55–7, 72–5, 91, 96, 126n.36, 127n.71, 234n.45
  on Kafka 85, 91, 93, 96, 101n.1, 101n.10, 101n.13, 102n.17–18
  Luhmann and 40–58, 63, 68, 72, 82n.45
  Wiethölter and 63, 73–5, 82n.45
Diagoras of Melos 296n.1
différance 40–1, 45–6, 52–3, 72, 164
digital constitution 196, 303
Dinwoodie, G. B. 250–1, 272nn.77–8
distinction directrice 30, 46–8, 199, 201, 225
Dong, B. 278–9
double movement 45, 58n.26, 192
double reflexivity 194–8, 201, 210n.63, 312
Dupuy, J.-P. 57n.13, 58n.26
Dürig, G. 299n.58, 299n.61
Durkheim, E. 16, 32, 79, 226, 309

ecologisation 188, 206
economic constitution 77, 177, 187–210, 309–10, 318, 320, 325, 328–32
  global 191, 209n.41, 302, 305, 318
  transnational 189, 210n.63
economisation 131, 136, 143–4, 147, 151, 309
effets pervers 35, 150
Ehrlich, E. 113, 213, 215–18, 221, 223
epistemology 45, 194–5, 197, 247, 333, 337n.46
equality
  justice and 15, 22, 37n.20, 133
  legal 19–22, 24, 29, 36, 335
  political 19, 37n.22
  social 15, 108–12
Esser, J. 38n.29, 234n.30, 318
evolution 51–2, 64, 144, 164
  legal 144, 219, 230–1, 236n.82, 242
  science 287–8, 291–3, 298n.44
  see also co-evolution
Ewald, F. 79
expansionary tendencies 36, 285–6, 293, 296
expert contract *see* contract, expert
externalisation
  in contract 143, 167, 227, 261
  of paradox 4–5, 51, 58n.38, 226–7, 319–36
  Wiethölter on 134

Femia, P. 337n.34
Fessler, D. W. 153n.45
financial constitution 188–93, 197–8, 204–7, 330
  see also economic constitution
financial crisis 176–80, 190, 198, 207, 330
Fischer-Lescano, A. 37, 211n.92, 269n.33, 271n.56, 297n.15, 336n.6, 348n.24

Fisher, I. 208n.5, 209n.39, 210n.56
Fitzpatrick, P. 235n.57, 269n.17, 233n.22
Foerster, H. v. 19, 38n.34, 171n.16, 194
Folkers, H. 39n.58, 39n.61–2, 39n.66
formal versus material constitution 311, 326, 346
Forst, R. 37, 37n.9
Foucault, M. 17, 110, 116–17, 119, 127n.59, 185, 235n.57, 298n.36
foundational paradox *see* constitutional paradox
founding myth 205, 322
fragmentation 3, 6, 343–6
  contract 154–5, 165, 168
  global law 237–49, 262, 266, 267, 268n.8, 269n.17, 306
  private law 129, 144–7
  social 16–18, 31, 108, 110, 115–19, 130, 132, 183, 216, 222
Freedland, M. 143, 151n.2, 153n.48
Friedland, R. 37, 79, 151n.10, 152n.16, 152n.35
Friedman, L. M. 170n.2, 270n.42
Fuchs, P. 126n.39, 126n.41, 126n.43, 127n.52
Fuller, L. 79, 318, 336n.6
functional differentiation 36, 54, 69
  constitutions and 191–2, 311, 344
  contract and 159, 163–4
  dark side of 182–3
  globalisation and 233n.12, 242
fundamental rights *see* human rights

Gallie, W. B. 210n.76
Galtung, J. 297n.22
Gamillscheg, F. 126n.49
Gardbaum, S. 297n.12, 298n.33
Geiger, T. 223

generalisation and re-specification 122, 311, 320, 337n.14
Gerstenberg, O. 151, 151n.10, 152n.35, 153n.56, 170n.6
Giddens, A. 214, 233n.12, 233n.14
global administrative law 306–7
Global Bukowina 8, 213–21
global constitution 183–211 *passim*, 209n.41, 247–8, 302–16
  UN constitution as 259
global constitutionalism 5, 189–198 *passim*, 209n.41, 210n.65, 210n.67, 304–12, 315n.7, 344–5
  from below 324
globalisation 50–1, 58n.32, 213–36 *passim*, 304, 306–7, 324
  financial 177, 191
  legal 214–18, 229, 240, 345
  polycentric 240–1
  social sectors 216–18, 222, 240–2, 244, 345
  see also Luhmann, globalisation
global law 213–36, 237–77, 345
global society *see* world society
Goodman, N. 17
Gordon, R. 170n.6
governance, transnational 253, 259
Graber, C. 127n.61, 153n.53, 153n.61, 172n.41, 300n.75
Gramsci, A. 318, 336n.6
Graziani, A. 208n.6
Greenspan, A. 175–6, 208n.1
Griffiths, J. 235n.52, 235n.54, 235n.60
Grigera Naon, H. A. 275n.131
Grimm, D. 170n.2, 210n.65, 211n.93, 328
Guattari, F. 260
Guillaume, G. 268n.9, 269n.13
guilt 56, 87, 89–90, 92
Günther, G. 17, 37n.10, 58n.35, 151n.9

Haar, C. M. 153n.45
Habermas, J. 69, 151n.5, 151n.11, 211n.90, 234n.45, 314
  Derrida and 63, 74
  justice 16–19, 38n.42, 52
  systems theory and 52–3, 74
Hafner, G. 268n.11, 269n.13–15
Hall, P. A. 316n.45
Hardt, M. 125n.21, 337n.28
Hart, H. L. A. 58n.36, 210n.66, 226, 234n.38, 319
Hasenclever, A. 270n.35, 270n.44
Hayek, F. A. v. 144, 205, 260
Hegel, G. W. F. 60, 65, 82n.26
Held, D. 269n.19, 269n.22
Henry, S. 233n.22, 235n.55
Hertig, M. 271n.56
Hesse, K. 297n.14
Hestermeyer, H. 124n.3
Hilkermeier, L. 269n.19, 271n.61
Hirschl, R. 318, 336n.3
hitting the bottom 176, 181–2, 207
Hofstadter, D. R. 235n.65
Holmes, S. 81n.4
Horwitz, M. J. 151n.4
Huber, J. 178, 190, 208n.5, 209n.38, 209n.44, 212n.96
human rights 36, 64, 172n.41
  as collective institutions 282–3, 295, 297n.19, 297n.24
  horizontal effect of 105–27, 188, 209n.35, 278–301, 304
  impersonal 127n.63, 148, 153n.61, 170
  institutional 114–15, 119, 126n.46, 126n.48, 172n.40
  mental and bodily integrity 112–22
  participation 78, 109, 203, 309
  transnational 214, 246, 253, 268n.5, 271n.53, 274n.123, 304–8, 336n.5
  see also contextual adequacy

Husserl, E. 45–8, 52, 179
hybridity 5–6, 153n.60, 212n.100
  constitutional 184, 199–201, 312–13
  contract 154–6, 162–5
  courts 238, 268n.5
  private law 129, 144, 147–9

ICANN 251, 253, 270n.37, 270n.43, 305
inter-legality 242–3
international community 203, 266, 324
international organisations
  collisions between 238, 253, 256–8
  constitutionalisation 189, 305–8
  juridification 189, 243, 270n.36, 306
  see also non-governmental organisations
intersubjectivity 16, 49, 52

Jäger, H. 127n.55, 297n.22
Jefferson, T. 202, 211n.84
Jessop, B. 170n.12
Jessup, P. C. 273n.85
Joerges, C. 81n.5, 210n.67, 211n.87, 235n.76, 236n.89, 272n.68, 272n.83, 338n.53
John, St. (evangelist) 32
judge-made law 26, 77, 229, 317, 324–6, 336n.1
juridification
  constitutionalisation and 196, 198, 248, 303
  economy 131, 232, 331
  excessive 5, 7, 86–8, 180–3
  foundational paradox 334–5
  human rights 123
  private law and 131–2, 145, 149
  science 332–4

transnational regimes 189, 243, 245, 253, 263–4, 270n.36, 306
  see also international organisations, juridification
justice
  self-subversive 13–39
  theories 14, 24, 27, 29, 54
justicialisation 36

Kafka, F. 1, 84–102
Kahn, P. W. 276n.160
Kälin, W. 275n.129
Kant, I. 82n.22, 102n.16, 215–16, 218
Karavas, V. 37, 209n.35, 210n.67, 300n.72
Kegel, G. 59–61, 64, 272n.82
Kelsen, H. 18, 37n.19, 98, 234n.37, 245, 319
Kennedy, D. 59
Kerchove, M. v. d. 38n.33, 234n.45
Kiesow, R. M. 101n.4
Kjaer, P. F. 210n.58, 210n.63, 210n.67, 211n.83, 211n.87, 315n.21, 336n.10
Kleist, H. v. 13–15, 24, 31–2, 36, 99, 208n.15
Koschorke, A. 57n.7, 82n.21
Koselleck, R. 37n.5, 309, 338n.52
Koskenniemi, M. 127n.60, 268n.8, 269n.17, 271n.50, 276n.150, 277n.180
Krajewska, A. 297n.21, 299n.63, 300n.83
Krasner, S. D. 270n.44
Kratochwil, F. 270n.35, 270n.44
Kumm, M. 211n.78, 316n.47
Kuo, M.-S. 210n.63, 210n.67

Labour Constitution 309
labour unions 184, 188, 214, 308, 325, 340

Ladeur, K.-H. 38n.46, 81n.5, 83n.61, 125n.31, 126n.46, 126n.48, 127n.57, 208n.25, 209n.26, 209n.35, 212n.101, 234n.45, 267
land grabbing 304
Latour, B. 1, 162–4
Lauterpacht, H. 263, 274n.116, 276n.152
law, judge-made *see* judge-made law
law and literature 31, 85, 97–100
law and society 13–14, 54, 68, 76, 81, 223, 341
Learned Hand, B. 149
legal/illegal 5, 22, 30, 50, 62, 67–8, 87–8, 199–200, 223–7, 313, 331
legal/non-legal 23, 223–5, 341
legal argumentation 23, 25, 27–8, 51, 73
legal pluralism 17, 213–36, 239–40, 244, 269n.19, 270n.38, 323
legal sociology 3, 14, 18–19, 97–9, 304, 308
Legendre, P. 116, 127n.70
Lessard, H. 125n.30
Lessig, L. 315n.5
Levinas, E. 32, 35–6, 46, 48, 75
lex constructionis 246, 253, 261–3, 275n.139
lex digitalis 244, 259, 262, 270n.42, 322
lex mercatoria 219–36, 246, 253, 263–4, 270n.42, 306, 322, 326
lex sportiva 214, 262, 322
limitative function 186–7, 191–2, 198, 201, 311, 331
limitative rule 193–4, 305, 311, 313
Lindahl, H. 209n.46, 348n.25
literature *see* law and literature
Littlechild, S. C. 152n.32
Locke, R. 208n.22
Loughlin, M. 37, 315n.9

Luhmann, N. 152n.36, 153n.39, 209n.29, 234n.45, 296n.8
communication 45–53, 68–70, 83n.59, 102n.20, 123, 126n.39, 171n.13, 179
compulsion to grow 182, 208n.16, 208n.19, 209n.49
constitution 171n.40, 195, 208n.23, 209n.51, 319–20
Derrida and 29–30, 35, 40–58, 63, 72–3
economic system 210nn.71–3, 329–30
globalisation 233n.12, 233n.16, 234n.43, 237, 241–2, 269n.19, 269nn.32–3, 271n.63, 301n.88
justice 20–4, 29–30, 33, 35, 40–58, 123
Latour and 162–3
law 20–4, 92–3, 98–9, 233n.7, 237, 269nn.32–3, 301n.88
polycontexturality 20, 49–51, 54, 151n.9
reflexivity 210n.62, 210n.68
rights 125n.23, 126n.38, 171n.40, 295, 297n.26, 299n.60, 300n.82
science 298n.42, 298n.44, 300n.70
Teubner and 5–6, 8, 342
Wiethölter and 63, 68–73, 79–80, 83n.59
Luther, M. 143
Lyotard, J.-F. 17, 46–7, 110, 120, 123, 152n.15, 234n.45, 342
Lysenko, T. D. 287

Macauley, S. 233n.22, 235n.56
Macneil, I. R. 170n.6
Magritte, R. 23, 111
Mann, F. A. 234n.34–5, 337n.20
Mannheim, K. 216
Marschik, A. 274n.114, 276n.150

Martenczuk, B. 276n.148
Marx, K. 58n.32, 65, 114, 116, 182, 241
Marxism 131
matrix, anonymous 116–22, 127n.54, 284, 300n.69
Mauss, M. 55
Medicus, D. 170n.8
Mengele, J. 116
Menke, C. 37n.21
Merkl, J. 245, 271n.47
Mestmäcker, E. J. 310, 316n.42
meta-code *see* code(s), meta-
motivation–competence dilemma 314
Münchhausen trilemma 26, 61, 68, 319, 328

narrative 157, 323, 326
nation-state constitution *see* state constitution
natural law 24–5, 32, 50, 71, 200, 318–9, 326–7, 336n.5–6
Negri, A. 125n.21, 324
Nelken, D. 38n.30
network
 actor–network theory 162
 communicative 110, 118, 188, 218
 contracts and 142–3, 163, 169, 227
 global 218, 231, 306–7
 inter-regime 240, 248–50, 260, 264–7, 273n.102
 intersystem 79, 83n.61, 142–3, 163, 169
 legal operations 19, 51
 pharmaceutical 288–93
'network society' 77, 271n.64
Neves, M. 338n.54, 348n.29
new constitutionalism 189, 305
new constitutional question 183, 302–4, 315n.6, 344

NGOs *see* non-governmental organisations
Nietzsche, F. 32
Nobles, R. 37, 337n.25
Nonet, P. 35, 347n.5
non-governmental organisations 137, 246
 constitutionalisation and 184, 188, 270n.42, 294, 300n.71, 305, 308, 324
 see also international organisations

Olivieri, N. 296n.7
ordre public 20, 60, 263, 306, 308, 324–5
ordre public transnational 260, 307, 324–5
Ost, F. 38n.33, 234n.45

parable 31, 35, 84–100 *passim*
paradox 4–5
 alterity 49–50
 conflict and 4–5, 59–83
 constitutional *see* constitutional paradox
 creativity of 35, 43–4, 52, 65
 de-paradoxification 2, 4, 29, 43–56 *passim*, 58n.18, 65–78 *passim*, 93, 211n.78, 225–7, 319–38 *passim*
 double-contingency 49–50
 economy 41–2, 44–5, 50–1, 56, 197
 externalisation 5, 227, 317–38
 foundational 1–2, 5, 42–6, 48–51, 90, 92, 228, 317–38
 human rights 64, 123, 295
 law 14–5, 21–39 *passim*, 41–5, 50–1, 54–6, 57n.13, 59–83, 86–99 *passim*, 225
 paradoxification 44, 51, 67–9
 political 186, 197

re-paradoxification 46, 50, 65, 70, 75
self-reference 57n.13, 64, 86, 197, 225–7
Pauwelyn, J. 271n.51, 274n.118, 275n.142
Perez, O. 125n.16, 261, 275n.139
Perritt, H. H. 270n.37, 270n.42
Petersen, J. 170n.8
Petersmann, E.-U. 256, 274n.127
pharmaceutical companies 105–6, 122, 254–7 *passim,* 278–301 *passim*
pharmaceutical concerns, enterprises, groups *see* pharmaceutical companies
plain money 176–7, 188–207
Plehn, S. L. 234n.33, 235n.63, 235n.71
pluralism, legal *see* legal pluralism
Polanyi, K. 192, 269n.25, 309
political constitution *see* state constitution
politicisation
  case law 78
  consumer 150, 187, 206
  economy 51, 202, 206–7, 212n.100
  excessive 180, 183, 186, 299n.60, 321, 335, 341
  law 51, 61–2, 215, 232, 239, 321, 323
  privatisation and 150
  society 129, 135, 202
politics 19, 30–1, 201–6, 208n.21, 211n.93, 212n.99
  constitutionalisation 186–7, 191–2, 195–6, 199, 311–12, 319–22, 327–8, 334
  economy and 134–40, 201–8, 212n.100
  expansion 113–15, 135, 181, 183, 297n.26

international 214–17, 219, 232, 253, 260–1, 303, 307, 323
law and 70, 79, 135–7, 195, 199, 217, 263, 319–22, 327–8, 334
structural coupling 135–7, 147, 195, 217
see also state constitution
Pollock, R. 315n.1–3
polycontexturality 16–18, 37n.10, 50–1, 130–70 *passim,* 341–2
polytheism 7, 30, 71, 109, 241
positive law
  critique of 74, 88
  justice and 25–7, 33–5, 43, 54–6, 57n.6, 96
  lex mercatoria as 219–20, 222, 228
pouvoir constituant 307, 316n.49, 324
Prandini, R. 209n.52, 210n.57, 210n.67
Preuss, U. K. 170n.12, 209n.46, 210n.67, 316n.40
private government 141, 224–5, 285, 309
private regulation 224–5, 241, 244, 307, 325
privatisation 128–53
professional associations 137, 226, 231, 245, 312, 325
programme(s) 50, 185
  economy 45, 200–1
  law 21, 33, 67, 124, 200–1, 331, 341
  science 287–8, 291
Prosser, T. 151n.3, 153n.65, 153n.67
protest movements 5, 150–1, 184, 188, 305–22 *passim,* 323–4
public/private 129–34, 137–8, 151n.4, 202, 266
publication bias 278–301
public interest 128–9
  litigation 151, 153n.68, 187, 294, 304
public opinion 260–2, 304

Raiser, L. 61, 75
rationality conflicts 133, 139, 241–2, 246, 252–9, 296n.8
see also collision
Rawls, J. 16–19, 25, 37n.17
reciprocity 15–18, 37n.11, 42, 75–9, 108, 166, 169, 171n.30
re-entry 2–3, 15, 37n.7, 156–7, 163, 211n.79
  human rights 114–15, 123
  law 23, 29–30, 35, 68–9, 258
  law and economy 200–1
reflexivity
  legal system 28, 70, 195–8, 201, 228, 247–9, 312
  medial 195, 312
  social system 18, 194–8, 201, 203, 210n.63, 247–8, 312
regime 133
  conflict 248–67, 295, 322
  constitutionalisation 247–8, 304–15
  constitutions 190, 247–8, 304–15, 322–3
  economic 136–8, 141, 144, 149, 150
  networking *see* network, inter-regime
  public versus private 129–51 *passim*, 203, 243–6
  structural coupling 134–5, 144, 147, 149
  transnational 107, 123, 129, 183, 189–90, 203, 214, 230–1, 237–77, 295, 304–15, 317, 321–3, 326
regulation 138, 340–4
  economic versus social 138, 152n.34
  financial and economic system 177–208, 330
  legal 131, 137, 181, 185, 197, 341
  political 132, 141, 145, 183–90 *passim*, 208n.20, 243, 287, 292, 305

  private 224–5, 241, 244, 307, 325
  self- 132–3, 135, 145, 148, 150, 208n.21, 214, 293, 295, 310, 330, 341
Renner, M. 204, 210n.67, 211n.92, 211n.94, 315n.13, 315n.23
respecification *see* generalisation
Resta, E. 235n.73
Ridder, H. 127n.63, 211n.85, 283, 297n.19
Robertson, J. 208n.5, 209n.43, 212n.96
Rödl, F. 210n.67, 211n.87, 338n.53
Röhl, H. C. 152n.12, 336n.1, 337n.16–17
Röhl, K. F. 152n.12, 336n.1, 337n.17
Romano, F. 273n.99
Rosa, H. 181, 314
Rosen, L. 24
Rottleuthner, H. 37, 38n.48
Rousseau, C. 273n.84
Ruffert, M. 337n.18
Ruggie, J. 270n.35, 270n.44, 297n.12

Santos, B. d. S. 151n.10, 269n.17, 269n.19
Savigny, F. K. v. 221
Schanze, E. 234n.41, 235n.78
Schelling, F. W. J. 166
Schepel, H. 210n.67
Scheuerman, W. E. 314
Schiff, D. 37, 337n.25
Schmidt-Assmann, E. 297n.12, 298n.37, 298n.45, 337n.46
Schmitt, C. 26, 28, 41, 283, 297n.19
Schmitthoff, C. M. 235n.67, 235n.71–2, 235n.79
Schneiderman, D. 209n.41, 315n.15, 315n.22, 336n.8
Schumpeter, J. A. 208n.6

Schütz, A. 37, 38n.46, 126n.35, 233n.9, 233n.12, 234n.45, 269n.19
Schwebel, S. M. 268n.9, 269n.13
science 171n.38
　autonomy, threats to 140, 284–300
　constitution of 194, 196–7, 332–4
　expansion of 116, 119, 181–3, 303
Sciulli, D. 83n.58, 171n.37, 171n.39, 209n.33, 209n.54, 271n.56, 310, 316n.50
Scott, C. 151
secondary versus primary norms/rules 195–6, 198, 210n.66, 226–7, 247–8, 344
Seed, R. G. 143
self-binding 317–38
self-constitutionalisation 194–7, 203, 312
self-destructive growth 7, 175–212 *passim*
　see also compulsion to grow
self-foundation of social systems 312, 332
self-limitation 7, 18, 124, 182–7, 313–15, 345
　economy 187, 190, 192–3, 207
　political 114, 120, 183, 186–7, 311
self-slander 86–8
self-subversive justice 13–39
self-transcendence 4, 15, 25–6, 29–33, 35, 94–5, 336
self-validation 225–8
　see also contract, self-validating
Selznick, P. 79, 146, 152n.35, 153n.57–8, 171n.40, 299n.59, 301n.87, 316n.38, 347n.5
Senf, B. 208n.5, 210n.56, 212n.102
shadow of politics 204–6, 211n.93
Shahabuddeen, M. 268n.10, 277n.172
Shelton, D. 268n.5

Simmel, G. 60
Sinzheimer, H. 316n.39
Smith, M. L. 296n.9
social movements *see* protest movements
societal constitutionalism 125n.21, 183–212, 248, 271n.56, 310, 334
　transnational 304, 310–12, 315n.7, 336n.10, 345, 347n.16
society *see* law and society
soft law/hard law 231–2, 345
Soros, G. 128
Soskice, D. 152n.31, 316n.45
Spencer Brown, G. 37n.7, 38n.37, 211n.79
spontaneous sphere 187, 209n.34, 211n.92, 312, 314
Stäheli, U. 57n.7, 82n.36, 316n.55
state action 106, 116, 285
state constitution 194–5, 199, 318–22, 326–8, 334
Stein, U. 227, 235n.69, n.79–80, 236n.83, n.89
Steinhauer, F. 37, 38n.46, 297n.19, 297n.24, 298n.46
Stewart, R. B. 152n.34
Stichweh, R. 210n.70, 233n.12, 269n.19, 298n.35, 298n.43, 316n.54
Stiglitz, J. 315n.19
Stirton, L. 151
Streeck, W. 208n.4, 316n.44
structural coupling, constitution 176, 195–204, 217, 247–8, 320–36
Suber, P. 58n.36, 81n.13, 235n.65
subjective right(s) 61–2, 75–6, 90–1, 94
　constitutional rights and 201, 281–4
　human rights and 108–9, 117–18, 125n.31, 127n.57

INDEX

supplement 47–8, 53, 158
sustainability 187–8, 200, 327

Taggart, M. 151n.3
third-party effects of fundamental rights *see* human rights, horizontal effects
Thom, R. 67
Thompson, G. F. 336n.10, 338n.52
Thornhill, C. 208n.18, 209n.47, 210n.57, 211n.88, 303, 315n.8, 316n.51, 317, 338n.52
totalitarian tendencies 36, 119, 166, 169
Trachtman, J. P. 315n.12, 316n.29, 338n.52
trade union *see* labour union
transcendence formula 29, 31, 56–7, 71
transnational constitution *see* global constitution
transnational constitutionalism *see* global constitutionalism
transnational corporations 105–7, 122, 304, 323
transnationalisation *see* globalisation
transnational law *see* global law
transnational private sector 106–7
Tully, J. 209n.41, 210n.67, 324

Vesting, T. 37, 211n.95, 297n.28, 299n.63, 337n.36
Viellechner, L. 209n.35, 297n.24, 316n.33
Vismann, C. 57n.7, 102n.17
Voser, N. 275n.130, 276n.153, 276n.155

Wahl, R. 211n.81, 212n.99
Walker, N. 271nn.56–7, 328, 337n.40
Wallerstein, I. 216–17
Walter, C. 210n.67, 270n.37, 271n.56
Walz, R. 81n.5
Walzer, M. 17–18, 138, 152n.35
Watzlawick, P. 81n.13, 81n.15, 82n.20
Weber, M. 16, 24, 30, 71, 87, 98, 125n.29, 182, 241, 296n.8, 341–2
Weick, K. E. 38n.36, 153n.54
Weil, P. 268n.6, 269n.31
Wieacker, F. 39n.63, 170n.2
Wielsch, D. 210n.67
Wiethölter, R. 37, 37n.11, 38n.47, 39n.68, 59–83, 127n.70, 134, 152n.23, 171n.30, 234n.45, 299n.64, 310, 316n.43, 337n.22
Wilhelmsson, T. 151n.10, 152n.14, 152n.35, 153n.66
Willke, H. 153n.61, 171n.13, 272n.66
Winston, K. 153n.57
Wittgenstein, L. 16, 53, 347n.12
world society 182, 213–17, 269n.19, 301n.88
  constitutionalisation 247–8, 303–8, 324–5
  fragmentation 237–48, 253, 267, 324
WTO constitution 189, 258–60, 305–6

Young, O. 270n.40, 270n.44

Ziman, J. 171n.38, 337n.45
Zizek, S. 171n.17
Zöllner, W. 337n.21
Zumbansen, P. 210n.67, 315n.7, 315n.25

EU authorised representative for GPSR:
Easy Access System Europe, Mustamäe tee 50,
10621 Tallinn, Estonia
gpsr.requests@easproject.com

www.ingramcontent.com/pod-product-compliance
Lightning Source LLC
Chambersburg PA
CBHW070817250426
43672CB00031B/2762